Walking with a Bible and a Gun:
The Rise, Fall, and Return of American Identity

Walking with a Bible and a Gun
The Rise, Fall, and Return of American Identity

By
E. Michael Jones

FIDELITY PRESS

South Bend, Indiana
2025

Published by FIDELITY PRESS in South Bend, Indiana
www.fidelitypress.org
(574) 289-9786
Copyright © 2025 by E. Michael Jones
First Edition, First Printing 2025

All rights reserved. No part of this book may be reproduced, stored in a retrieval system, or transmitted in any form or by any means, electronic, mechanical, photocopying, recording or otherwise, without the prior permission of Fidelity Press.

Printed and bound in the United States of America by Sheridan Press

1 2 3 4 5 6 10 09 08 07 06 05 04

Library of Congress Cataloguing in Publication Data

Jones, E. Michael
  Walking with a Bible and a Gun: The Rise, Fall, and Return of American Identity
  ISBN 978-0-929891-34-7
  Hardback, 9 x 6 inches, 553 pages

Part I: Errand Into the Satanic Wilderness. Part II: The Romantic Rehabilitation of Nature. Part III: The Return of the Satanic Wilderness.

In his classic book on the meaning of the frontier, Frederick Jackson Turner cited a statute from Virginia which described an American as a Warlike Christian Man:

"Provided alwayes," ran the quaint statute, "and it is the true intent and meaning of this act that for every five hundred acres of land to be granted in pursuance of this act there shall be and shall be continually kept upon the said land one christian man between sixteen and sixty years of age perfect of limb, able and fitt for service who shall alsoe be continually provided with a well fixed musquett or fuzee, a good pistoll, sharp simeter, tomahawk and five pounds of good clean pistoll powder and twenty pounds of sizable leaden bullets or swan or goose shott to be kept within the fort directed by this act besides the powder and shott for his necessary or useful shooting at game. Provided also that the said warlike christian man shall have his plot of land to be laid out in a geometricall square or as near that figure as conveniency will admit," etc. Within two years the society was required to cause a half acre in the middle of the "co-habitation" to be palisaded "with good sound pallisadoes at least thirteen foot long and six inches diameter in the middle of the length thereof, and set double and at least three foot within the ground."

"Such in 1701," Jackson continues:

was the idea of the Virginia tidewater assembly of a frontiersman, and of the frontier towns by which the Old Dominion should spread her population into the upland South. But the "warlike Christian man" who actually came to furnish the firing line for Virginia, was destined to be the Scotch-Irishman and the German with long rifle in place of "fuzee" and "simeter," and altogether too restless to have his continual abode within the space of two hundred acres.

Table of Contents

Introduction p. 13

Part I: Errand Into the Satanic Wilderness

Chapter One: Danforth's Errand, p. 29

Chapter Two: The Salem Witch Trial, p. 45

Chapter Three: The Racial Vector of American Identity, p. 59

Chapter Four: The Reformation as Looting Operation, p. 67

Chapter Five: Bacon's Rebellion and the Invention of Whiteness, p. 81

Chapter Six: The "False Bottom" of Puritan Theology, p. 87

Chapter Seven: Solomon Stoddard and the Half-Way Covenant, p. 103

Chapter Eight: Benjamin Franklin and the Rationalist Reaction, p. 113

Chapter Nine: Jonathan Edwards and the Great Awakening, p. 119

Chapter Ten: George Whitefield and John Wesley, p. 127

Chapter Eleven: The Great Awakening Leads to the American Revolution, p. 131

Part II: The Romantic Rehabilitation of Nature

Chapter Twelve: Daniel Boone: Essence Meets Existence, p. 141

Chapter Thirteen: Natty Bumppo and the "Core Myth" of American Identity, p. 147

Chapter Fourteen: James Fenimore Cooper Goes to Rome, p. 159

Chapter Fifteen: Ralph Waldo Emerson: Bourgeois Satanism p. 163

Chapter Sixteen: Nathaniel Hawthorne goes to Rome, p. 169

CHAPTER SEVENTEEN: HENRY DAVID THOREAU AND MORAL NATURE, P. 175

CHAPTER EIGHTEEN: ORESTES BROWNSON: THE FIRST AMERICAN CATHOLIC, P. 185

CHAPTER NINETEEN: "DAGGER JOHN" HUGHES AND ETHNIC CATHOLICISM, P. 199

CHAPTER TWENTY: THE RACIAL DOUBLE STANDARD, P. 209

CHAPTER TWENTY-ONE: HOW THE IRISH BECAME WHITE, P. 213

CHAPTER TWENTY-TWO: THE BEECHER FAMILY: NATIVISM AND MORAL COLLAPSE, P. 221

CHAPTER TWENTY-THREE: HAWTHORNE IN ROME, P. 225

CHAPTER TWENTY-FOUR: WHY HAWTHORNE WAS MELANCHOLY, P. 255

CHAPTER TWENTY-FIVE: ANTHONY COMSTOCK'S REFORM
    OF WAR-RAVAGED SEXUAL MORALITY, P. 265

CHAPTER TWENTY-SIX: HENRY WARD BEECHER DIMMESDALE REDIVIVUS, P. 269

CHAPTER TWENTY-SEVEN: SAMUEL CLEMENS: BEECHER'S INNOCENT, P. 277

CHAPTER TWENTY-EIGHT: ROSE HAWTHORNE AND "THE SILENT MINISTRY OF PAIN," P. 289

CHAPTER TWENTY-NINE: VICTORIA WOODHULL AND FREE LOVE, P. 293

CHAPTER THIRTY: CHRISTOPHER NEWMAN, MAN OF THE WEST, P. 297

CHAPTER THIRTY-ONE: HENRY ADAMS, THE OLD MAN OF THE EAST, P. 309

CHAPTER THIRTY-TWO: GEORGE LATHROP CONVERTS TO CATHOLICISM, P. 317

C CHAPTER THIRTY-THREE: CLOVER ADAMS COMMITS SUICIDE, P. 325

CHAPTER THIRTY-FOUR: ROSE HAWTHORNE BECOMES A NUN, P. 329

CHAPTER THIRTY-FIVE: THEODORE ROOSEVELT AND MUSCULAR CHRISTIANITY, P. 331

CHAPTER THIRTY-SIX: JOHN IRELAND AND AMERICANISM, P. 339

CHAPTER THIRTY-SEVEN: THE GREENE BROTHERS CREATE THE AMERICAN HOUSE, P. 355

CHAPTER THIRTY-EIGHT: FREDERICK JACKSON TURNER AND THE CLOSING OF THE FRONTIER, P. 369

Part III: The Return of the Satanic Wilderness

Chapter Thirty-Nine: Jack London and the Urbanization of America, p. 377

Chapter Forty: Ernest Hemingway: Modernity in the Woods, p. 387

Chapter Forty-One: William Faulkner and The Bear, p. 403

Chapter Forty-Two: Walter Lippman and the
   Repudiation of Jeffersonian Democracy, p. 409

Chapter Forty-Three: Gary Cooper and The Virginian, p. 417

Chapter Forty-Four: Owen Wister Creates the Cowboy, p. 421

Chapter Forty-Five: Ayn Rand and the Jewish Take on American Identity, p. 435

Chapter Forty-Six: Clint Eastwood: Dirty Harry and the Race Issue, p. 451

Chapter Forty-Seven: The Moynihan Report, p. 461

Chapter Forty-Eight: Critical Race Theory and the
   Destruction of American Identity, p. 473

Chapter Forty-Nine: The Unforgiven: America Goes to Hell, p. 483

Chapter Fifty: Joe Ritchey: A Preacher without a Gun, p. 497

Chapter Fifty-One: Joe Ritchey and Abdul Haq, p. 503

Chapter Fifty-Two: Joe Ritchey Converts to Catholicism, p. 507

Chapter Fifty-Three: Et in Arcadia Ego, p. 513

Epilogue, p. 519.

Index, p. 525.

Introduction

Sue: You're an American.
Walt: What does that mean?
Sue: Clint Eastwood, Gran Torino

Not too long ago I received an e-mail from a subscriber to *Culture Wars* who claimed that he could trace his family's roots in this country back to 1683. That man became a Catholic because of reading my books and listening to my podcasts. His new Catholic identity, however, created an unexpected problem. He no longer knew what it meant to be an American.

This man is not alone. According to Samuel Huntington, America has been going through an identity crisis. Under President Clinton "the ideologies of multiculturalism and diversity eroded the legitimacy of the remaining central elements of American identity, the cultural core and the American Creed."[1] The rise of identity politics and Critical Race Theory began in the 1990s when:

> Americans engaged in intense debates over immigration and assimilation, multiculturalism and diversity, race relations and affirmative action, religion in the public sphere, bilingual education, school and college curricula, school prayer and abortion, the meaning of citizenship and nationality, foreign involvement in American elections, the extraterritorial application of American law, and the increasing political role of diasporas here and abroad. Underlying all these issues is the question of national identity. Virtually any position on any one of these issues implies certain assumptions about that identity.[2]

The Clintons made it clear that to be a true American one had to be a member of one of the special interest groups which constituted the Democratic Party. In doing this, the Clintons launched their own "great revolution" which based itself on the civil rights revolution, while nullifying *the* American Revolution of 1776 as their way of proving "that we literally can live without having a dominant European culture."[3] That identity shift began during the last year of the Reagan administration. On January 15, 1987, Jesse Jackson, scion of the Civil Rights Movement, turned that premise into a slogan when he marched down Palm Drive, Stanford University's grand entrance, chanting, "Hey,

---

[1] Samuel P. Huntington, *Who Are We?* (New York, NY: Simon & Schuster, 2004), p. 9.
[2] Huntington, *Who Are We?*, p. 18.
[3] Huntington, *Who Are We?*, p. 18.

hey, ho, ho, Western Civ has got to go."[4] During the 1990s, multiculturalists fought a winning battle over the curriculum at the university which eventually routed the idea that there was one coherent understanding of what it meant to be an American.

The high point of American identity found expression in 1961 when Robert Frost invoked the "heroic deeds" of America's founding at President John F. Kennedy's inauguration. God's "approval" of America's founding, Frost continued, introduced "a new order of the ages" into human history which was about to enter a "golden age of poetry and power."[5] In spite of the crimes committed in America's name:

> Our venture in revolution and outlawry
>
> Has justified itself in freedom's story
>
> Right down to now in glory upon glory.[6]

That golden age came to an abrupt end less than three years later when John F. Kennedy was murdered in a *coup d'etat* which has had tragic consequences to this day. One of the tragic consequences of the Kennedy assassination was loss of American identity.

Thirty-two years later, Maya Angelou, America's new poet laureate, denounced the same America that Robert Frost had praised in 1961 as now "wedded forever to fear, yoked eternally to brutishness" and a threat to the ethnic, racial, and religious identities of those who had suffered as a result of America's "armed struggles for profit" and its "bloody sear" of "cynicism."[7] Within 30 years the political pendulum had swung from chauvinism to collective self-abasement, and any understanding that Americans shared a common identity got lost in the process.

Samuel Huntington wrote *Who Are We?* in the wake of the attack on the World Trade Center in Manhattan on September 11, 2001, expecting a revitalization and reaffirmation of American identity. But the short-lived wave of patriotism which was orchestrated in the wake of 9/11 failed to stem the erosion of American identity, which has accelerated dramatically over the quarter century since the publication of *Who Are We?* Over the last quarter century, in fact, the exact opposite of what Huntington predicted has happened, and we have witnessed a deliberate attempt to destroy what is left of national identity through the weaponization of race and gender.

The George Floyd riots and the emergence of Black Lives Matter epitomized the rise of identity politics and the racial balkanization of America. During

---

4 Robert Curry, "'Hey, Hey, Ho, Ho, Western Civ Has to Go,'" Intellectual Takeout, June 11, 2019, https://intellectualtakeout.org/2019/06/hey-hey-ho-ho-western-civ-has-got-to-go/

5 Huntington, *Who Are We?*, pp. 5-6.

6 Huntington, *Who Are We?*, p. 5.

7 Huntington, *Who Are We?*, p. 9.

Introduction

those riots, blacks could engage in mayhem with impunity. If the riots in the wake of George Floyd showed that groups like Black Lives Matter had privileges that put them above the law, the Unite the Right rally in Charlottesville in August 2017 showed that anyone who identified as white had lost the right to free speech and the right to assemble, both of which were guaranteed by the Constitution. The white organizers of that rally were blamed for the violence which the local police orchestrated in collaboration with Antifa. They were then subjected to law suits orchestrated by Roberta Kaplan, a self-described "chubby lesbian kike"[8] with Jewish privilege, allowing her to weaponize the American legal system against those who proclaimed themselves loyal Americans. The unexpected sequel to the George Floyd riots took place in Washington, D.C., on January 6, 2021, when the FBI, the media and the Democrat-controlled Congress turned a protest by patriotic Americans who thought that the Constitution guaranteed their rights to free speech and assembly into an "insurrection" which landed many of them in prison.

During the twenty years period following the 9/11 attacks, a dramatic shift had taken place in the American political landscape. Instead of reaffirming American identity in a time of crisis, feminist politicians like Michigan's Governor Gretchen Whitmer and her Jewish lesbian Attorney General Dana Nessel portrayed the people they were elected to represent as enemies of the state and then went on to collaborate with the FBI by orchestrating entrapment schemes that would land naïve believers in the American system in prison. American identity had not only not been affirmed, it had been weaponized against the very people who most believed in it. Being a patriotic American had become a criminal offense. As a result, the issue which Huntington posed in the wake of the 9/11 attacks led not to a surge of patriotism and unity but rather to a series of questions which remain unanswered:

> "We Americans" face a substantive problem of national identity epitomized by the subject of this sentence. Are we a "we," one people or several? If we are a "we," what distinguishes us from the "thems" who are not us? Race, religion, ethnicity, values, culture, wealth, politics, or what? Is the United States, as some have argued, a "universal nation," based on values common to all humanity and in principle embracing all peoples? Or are we a Western nation with our identity defined by our European heritage and institutions? Or are we unique with a distinctive civilization of our own, as the proponents of "American exceptionalism" have argued throughout our history? Are we basically a political community whose identity exists only in a social contract embodied in the Declaration of Independence and other founding documents? Are we multicultural, bicultural, or unicultural, a mosaic or a melting pot? Do we have any meaningful identity as a nation that transcends our subnational ethnic, religious, racial identities? These questions remain for Americans in their

---

8 See E-Book *Jewish Privilege* at Fidelitypress.org

post-September 11 era. They are in part rhetorical questions, but they are also questions that have profound implications for American society and American policy at home and abroad.[9]

Huntington resolved those questions as quickly as he raised them by declaring in one bold stroke that in spite of the perturbations caused by the rise of multiculturalism and identity politics, America remains an Anglo-Protestant country. "The principal theme of this book is the continuing centrality of Anglo-Protestant culture to American national identity."[10] America is "the child of the Reformation."[11] By the Reformation, Huntington means specifically "the English Puritan Revolution," which he describes as "the single most important formative event of American political history."[12] More specifically, the iteration of the Reformation which the Puritans founded on Massachusetts Bay involves:

> the English language; Christianity; religious commitment; English concepts of the rule of law, the responsibility of rulers, and the rights of individuals; and dissenting Protestant values of individualism, the work ethic, and the belief that humans have the ability and the duty to try to create a heaven on earth, a "city on a hill." Historically, millions of immigrants were attracted to America because of this culture and the economic opportunities it helped to make possible.[13]

This Anglo-Protestant culture has been "central to American identity for three centuries,"[14] and Huntington sees no reason why it should not serve as the template for another three centuries, as long as Americans "recommit themselves to the Anglo-Protestant culture, traditions, and values that for three and a half centuries have been embraced by Americans of all races, ethnicities, and religions and that have been the source of their liberty, unity, power, prosperity, and moral leadership as a force for good in the world."[15]

If America is Anglo-Protestant, then its antithesis is Hispano-Catholic. Shortly after writing *Who Are We?* Huntington wrote *The Hispanic Challenge* at a time when:

> A massive Hispanic influx raised questions concerning America's linguistic and cultural unity. Corporate executives, professionals, and Information Age technocrats espoused cosmopolitan over national identities. The

---

9 Huntington, *Who Are We?*, p. 9.
10 Huntington, *Who Are We?*, p. 30.
11 Huntington, *Who Are We?*, p. 63.
12 Huntington, *Who Are We?*, p. 63.
13 Huntington, *Who Are We?*, p. xv.
14 Huntington, *Who Are We?*, p. xvi.
15 Helen Chernikoff, "Why Haven't White Supremacists Held A New Charlottesville? Meet Roberta Kaplan.," Forward, July 1, 2018, https://forward.com/news/418633/white-supremacist-richard-spencer-gay-marriage/

Introduction

teaching of national history gave way to the teaching of ethnic and racial histories. The celebration of diversity replaced emphasis on what Americans had in common. The national unity and sense of national identity created by work and war in the eighteenth and nineteenth centuries and consolidated in the world wars of the twentieth century seemed to be eroding. By 2000, America was, in many respects, less a nation than it had been for a century. The Stars and Stripes were at half-mast and other flags flew higher on the flagpole of American identities.[16]

The inescapable corollary to Huntington's claim that America is Anglo-Protestant is that Catholics pose a threat to American identity. The main issue, however, is not that Huntington perceives Catholics as the enemy; the main issue is that he doesn't understand Protestantism. Like most Whig historians, he gets his definition of Protestantism from Weber. Huntington calls Weber's Protestant work ethic "the religion of work," which misses the point. Like the melting pot, the Protestant work ethic is a myth which obscures the fact that by the 20th century assimilation took place according to religion, which meant that an immigrant became an American by becoming first, not an Anglo-Protestant but rather a Protestant, a Catholic, or a Jew. The sociological theory explaining that transformation is known as the triple melting pot, which explains not only the real matrix of assimilation but also the conflict between those three groups which destroyed any coherent understanding of American identity.

The Weber thesis has been an integral part of that obfuscation because Protestant identity, especially one based on Puritanism, has always been crypto-Jewish. In his 1907 book *Jews and Modern Capitalism*, Werner Sombart points out that everything Weber said about Puritans was *a fortiori* true of Jews. If Sombart's earlier book on capitalism caused Weber to write his articles on the Puritan spirit, those articles led Sombart to write his book on the Jews and modern capitalism. "In fact," Sombart writes, "Max Weber's researches are responsible for this book. I have already mentioned that Max Weber's study of the importance of Puritanism for the capitalistic system was the impetus that sent me to consider the importance of the Jew, especially as I felt that the dominating ideas of Puritanism which were so powerful in capitalism were more perfectly developed in Judaism and were also of a much earlier date."[17] Having read Weber's thesis, Sombart wonders:

> whether all that Weber ascribes to Puritanism might not with equal justice be referred to Judaism, and probably in a greater degree; nay, it

---

16 Huntington, *Who Are We?*, pp. 4-5.

17 Werner Sombart, *The Jews and Modern Capitalism* (New Brunswick, NJ: Transaction Books, 1982), p. 248.

might well be suggested that that which is called Puritanism is really Judaism.[18]

According to Sombart, Puritanism is nothing more than an aberrant form of Judaism because both are based on "the preponderance of religious interests, the idea of divine rewards and punishments, asceticism within the world, the close relationship between religion and business, the arithmetical conception of sin, and, above all, the rationalization of life."[19]

No matter how often establishment thinkers like Huntington invoke Weber's thesis on the Protestant work ethic, it has become an a-historical fantasy which distracts from a fundamental fact of Protestantism. Work had nothing to do with the Reformation, which began as a looting operation which despoiled the monasteries of 900 years of accumulated labor. The Reformation was based on theft of Church property. The Reformation sought to consolidate those ill-gotten gains through theological contortions of the sort Tawney characterized accurately when he wrote that "the upstart aristocracy of the future had their teeth in the carcass, and, having tasted blood, they were not to be whipped off by a sermon."[20] Weber, and Huntington misunderstood the theological trajectory of Protestantism, which was basically a theological justification of looting after the fact.

A more recent version of the same misunderstanding of Protestantism can be found in *La Defaite de l'Occidante*, a book in which Emmanuel Todd claims that the current collapse of the American empire has been caused by the evaporation of Protestantism, which he describes as its hidden grammar. America is now facing defeat in the Ukraine because of the complete disappearance of the Christian foundation of its culture, "*un phénomène historique crucial qui, justement, explique la pulvérisation des classes dirigeantes américaines.*"[21] Protestantism, which "to a large extent, has been the economic strength of the West, is dead."[22] The United States and England have been caught up in a "centripetal, narcissistic then nihilistic drift," which has led both the present empire and its predecessor to the "Zero State," which he defines as a nation state which is "no longer structured by its original values," because the Protestant work ethic and the feeling of responsibility which previously animated its population have evaporated.[23]

---

18 Sombart, *Modern Capitalism*, p. 192.
19 Sombart, *Modern Capitalism*, p. 192.
20 R. H. Tawney, *Religion and the Rise of Capitalism: A History and Study* (London: Hazell, Watson & Viney, Ltd., 1948, first edition 1926), http://pombo.free.fr/tawney1922simil.pdf.
21 Emmanuel Todd, *La Defaite de l'Occidante* (The Defeat of the West), (Gallimard, 2024), Kindle edition p. 30. a crucial historical phenomenon which, precisely, explains the dispersal of the American ruling classes.
22 Todd, p. 30.
23 Todd, p. 337

Introduction

Trump and Biden epitomize the apotheosis of the Zero State because Washington's decisions in both administrations are no longer moral or rational. The Zero State was preceded by the Zombie State, which retained the form of religion emptied of its content. Todd sees Benjamin Franklin as the classic example of a Zombie Protestant, who no longer practices his religion but retains its ethics, attached to the values of honesty, work, seriousness, and always aware that man only has a limited amount of time.[24] Zombie Protestant society emerged in Europe when Germany and Great Britain created a world:

> in which religious practice withers but where the social values of religion persist, as well as the rites of passage prescribed by the various Churches. Neither baptism, nor marriage, nor burial are called into question. But, as a sign that the West no longer respects the biblical commandment to "grow and multiply," – fertility is falling in the middle classes. Deprived of its supervision, the Protestant work ethic in Britain devolved into pure nationalism.[25] Literacy is a fundamental Protestant value because *sola scriptura* requires the masses to be literate in order to have access to the Scriptures, which makes every man his own priest, thus promoting democracy and egalitarianism.

Like Samuel Huntington, Todd derives his understanding of Protestantism from Max Weber's famous book *The Protestant Ethic and the Spirit of Capitalism*. In his attempt to answer the question "*Qu'est-ce quel'Occident?*" Todd specifically identifies himself as a pupil of Weber. Todd is "*en bon élève de Max Weber, qui plaça la religion de Luther et de Calvin à la source de ce qui apparaissait à son époque comme la supériorité de l'Occident.*"[26]

Conspicuous by its absence from Todd's list of foundational revolutions which created the Anglo-American empire was the revolutionary decade of the 1640s in England, which preceded the Glorious Revolution by 40 years. Todd, for some reason, omitted the prime example of the Revolutionary spirit in both England and New England, namely, the Puritans, who are doubly significant because of their overt and obvious link to the Jewish revolutionary spirit, but also because one of the most famous Puritans was John Milton, the man who wrote the Protestant epic *Paradise Lost*, which portrayed Satan as the patron saint of Protestantism. Both William Blake and Percy Bysshe Shelley believed that Satan was the hero of *Paradise Lost*:

> They both critiqued Milton's Satan by finding several imperfections in *Paradise Lost*. Both tried to surpass Milton by creating their own

---

24 Todd, p. 214; un protestant zombie typique, qui ne pratique plus sa religion mais en conserve l'éthique, attaché aux valeurs d'honnêteté, de travail, de sérieux, et toujours conscient que l'homme ne dispose que d'un temps limité.

25 Todd, p. 216.

26 Todd, p. 139. a good student of Max Weber, who placed the religion of Luther and Calvin at the source of what appeared in his time as the superiority of the West.

perfect version of Milton's Satan. Shelley goes a step beyond Blake when designing his Satan by producing a new tragic hero that does not have a hamartia.[27]

Protestantism may be the hidden grammar of the American Empire, but Satanism is the hidden grammar of Protestantism. Herman Melville understood this, as did virtually every other writer of the American Renaissance, the literary movement in the mid-19th century which gave birth to American identity. In *Moby Dick*, First Mate Starbuck rebuked Captain Ahab for the "madness" involved in taking "vengeance on a dumb brute . . . that simply smote thee from blindest instinct" by describing it as "blasphemy." Ahab, who seems predestined for destruction at his own hand, doubles down, like a good Emersonian, and says, "Talk not to me of blasphemy, man; I'd strike the sun if it insulted me."[28]

As they are getting ready to sail on the *Pequod*, Ishmael and Queequeg are confronted by a strange figure who "levelled his massive forefinger at the vessel in question" and asked them: "Shipmates, have ye shipped in that ship?" The name of the "ragged old sailor" is Elijah. When Ismael admits that he and Queequeg have signed a contract binding them to sail on a whaling expedition with Captain Ahab, Elijah asks "Anything there about your souls?"

It's a question Americans have been asking about the ship of state for a long time. The question became especially relevant when Stockton Rush's aptly named submarine the *Titan* imploded with all hands-on board near the wreck of the *Titanic*, which each passenger paid $250,000 to view. Rush has been described as "a cowboy who cut too many corners," but he is clearly an avatar of Captain Ahab. Docile to the conventional narrative, Ishmael thinks that Ahab is "a good whale hunter and a good captain to his crew," but the stranger Elijah knows that he is more than that. Ishmael and Queequeg have made a pact with the devil, but like most Americans they don't understand how. After signing the contract, everything is "all fixed and arranged" in a way that mirrored covenant theology and Calvinist predestination. Like his namesake, Elijah is a prophet without honor in his native place. The *Pequod* is the ship of state; Ahab is the psychopath who sits at the helm as it sails to its doom. Stockton Rush is Captain Ahab. All CEOs are psychopaths and narcissists, and before you raise any objections, it is always the exception which proves the rule. A psychopath is now captain of the ship of state, which is America, which is the world's fourth great religion, as Yale Professor David Gelernter has pointed out. But like Emmanuel Todd, David Gelernter did not point out that Satanism is the hidden grammar of the religion known as America. America was a Protestant colony, and so it should come as no surprise that

---

27 "Blake's and Shelley's Reader Responses to Milton's Satan in *Paradise Lost*," FSU Digital Repository University Libraries, https://diginole.lib.fsu.edu/islandora/object/fsu:204641
28 Herman Melville, *Moby Dick*, chapter 38.

Introduction

Satanism became the hidden grammar of the English Reformation before it could be exported to America. Shakespeare pointed this out in Ulysses' speech in *Troilus and Cressida*, when he described the aftermath of the Reformation and its inexorable trajectory:

> Take but degree away untune that string
> and hark what discord follows. Each thing meets
> In mere oppugnacy. The bounded waters
> Should lift their bosoms higher than the shores
> And make a sop of all this solid globe;
> Strength should be the lord of imbecility,
> And the rude son should strike his father dead;
> Force should be right, or, rather, right and wrong,
> Between whose endless jar justice resided,
> Should lose their names, and so should justice too.
> Then everything includes itself in power,
> Power into will, will into appetite,
> And appetite, an universal wolf,
> So doubly seconded with will and power,
> Must make perforce an universal prey
> And last eat up himself.[29]

Shakespeare's play is set in ancient Greece, but he is really talking about the situation in Elizabethan England in the aftermath of the Reformation, when the crown had lost all legitimacy but retained its hold on power by transforming Catholic England into the world's first police state. Shakespeare's genius lay in his ability to describe accurately if poetically, the novel form of government which the Reformation introduced to England.

Todd calls it nihilism, which is closely related to Satanism. Because nature abhors a vacuum, the void created by the disappearance of Protestantism was filled by "nihilism," which Todd defines as "an amoralism stemming from an absence of values."[30] Nihilism, he tells us, "denies reality and truth; it is a cult of lies."[31] Nihilism leads to narcissism, both of which are based on a denial of reality that has become pandemic in societies which claim that "a man can become a woman, and a woman can become a man," an affirmation which Todd describes as false and "close to the theoretical heart of Western nihilism."[32] Because "right and wrong . . . have lost their names," a man can become a woman if the powerful decree it possible. That has political ramifications because it also means that a nuclear treaty with Iran under

---

29 *Troilus and Cressida*, Act 1, Scene 3, Folger Shakespeare Library, https://www.folger.edu/explore/shakespeares-works/troilus-and-cressida/read/1/3/
30 Todd, p. 33. un amoralisme découlant d'une absence de valeurs.
31 Todd, p. 346.
32 Todd, p. 334.

Obama can transform, overnight, into an aggravated sanctions regime under Trump.[33]

Todd indicates obliquely that Satanism is the hidden grammar of the Zero State when he claims that a "satanic ritual" ("*une sorte de rituel économico-philosophico-satanique*") served as the demarcation point between the era of the WASP elite and the moment it was succeeded by the Synagogue of Satan as America's ruling class. Blinded by the superficial categories he has appropriated from Max Weber, Todd fails to see not only that the hidden grammar of Protestantism is Satanic, but more importantly, that America became the Great Satan when the Jews took over its culture. Todd insists that the disappearance of Protestantism is "the decisive explanatory key" to understanding "the current global turbulence"[34] without telling us who succeeded the WASPs as America's new ruling class. Todd claims that "religious extinction," (*l'extinction religieuse*) led to "the disappearance of social morality and collective feeling; to a process of centrifugal geographic expansion combining with a disintegration of the original heart of the system"[35] as if it were an impersonal act of nature without human actors at the helm.

Satanism has been the trajectory of the Anglo-American empire ever since Satan gave his famous speech at the beginning of *Paradise Lost*. When Percy Bysshe Shelley wanted to light the fire of rebellion in Ireland, he could find no better phrase than the one Satan used to rouse the demons in hell: "Awake, arise, or be forever fallen." Milton's heroic Satanism first becomes apparent at the beginning of the speech when Satan, who has been expelled from heaven, wakes up in the sea of flame which is now not only his eternal home but his kingdom as well. Satan begins by saying farewell to heaven, but soon gets to the point:

> Farewell happy Fields
> Where Joy forever dwells: Hail horrours, hail
> Infernal world, and thou profoundest Hell
> Receive thy new Possessor: One who brings
> A mind not to be chang'd by Place or Time.
> The mind is its own place, and in itself
> Can make a Heav'n of Hell, a Hell of Heav'n.
> What matter where, if I be still the same,
> And what I should be, all but less then he
> Whom Thunder hath made greater? Here at least
> We shall be free; th'Almighty hath not built
> Here for his envy, will not drive us hence:
> Here we may reign secure, and in my choyce

---

33 Todd, p. 334.
34 Todd, p. 30.
35 Todd, p. 31.

Introduction

> To reign is worth ambition though in Hell:
> Better to reign in Hell, than serve in Heav'n.

"Here at least," the Puritans said when they arrived in America, "we may reign secure." After the Puritan dictator Oliver Cromwell died in 1660, a wave of revulsion at the excesses of Puritanism swept through England, best symbolized by the mob which exhumed Cromwell's body and hanged it. Cromwell's head popped off during this act of desecration, and its whereabouts remain unknown to this day, but his revolutionary spirit had departed from England while his head was still on his shoulders, migrating across the Atlantic to Massachusetts, where it became the *spiritus movens* behind the American Revolution a century later.

The Methodist divine William Fletcher understood this best. In a letter denouncing the "seditious sophism" which Rev. Richard Price, the nonconformist supporter of both the American and French revolutions, espoused in his sermons, Fletcher compared Price to Satan with specific reference to Milton's epic. Price's wicked speech could have been made by:

> Satan to the Son of God, when, according to Milton's fancy, they encountered each other in the heavenly plains. I meet thee in the field to defend my freedom and assert the liberty of these heavenly legions. Before I pierce thy side with my spear, let me pierce thy conscience with my arguments. "In a free state in heaven, where liberty is perfect, everyone is his own legislator. To be free, is to be guided by one's own will; and to be guided by the will of another, is the character of servitude." They call the Messiah The Prince ; but for as much as thou sayest, I do nothing of myself, and art not ashamed to add, Father, Not My will, but thine be done; and to teach the mean Spirits who follow thee to pray, Thy Will be done in heaven and on earth; it is plain, that thou restrainest the power of self-government, and introducest slavery."[36]

Satanic liberty is another word for slavery. Fletcher echoes Satan's speech directly when he ascribes to Price and other supporters of the American Revolution, the notion that "self-government and supremacy in hell, are preferable to servile obedience and subordinate grandeur in heaven." Fletcher concludes his argument by claiming that the "speech of the patriotic Seraph," otherwise known as Satan, "is formed upon the [same] principles laid down in Dr. Price's pamphlet." It is that Satanic spirit "which deluges America and threatens to overflow Great Britain itself."[37]

In 1776 Thomas Paine quoted Milton's Satan in *Common Sense*, the pamphlet he wrote urging the colonies to rebel against the mother country

---

36 John William Fletcher, *American patriotism farther confronted with reason, Scripture, and the constitution: observations on the dangerous politicks taught by mr. Evans, and dr. ... a Scriptural plea for the revolted colonies*, Kindle edition. Loc 1754.

37 Fletcher, Location 1836

England. "Reconciliation," Paine told the colonists, "is *now* a fallacious dream. Nature hath deserted the connection, and art cannot supply her place. For, as Milton wisely expresses, 'never can true reconcilement grow where wounds of deadly hate have pierced so deep.'"[38] In order not to offend the religious sensibilities of his American audience, Paine did not cite the rest of Satan's speech, which concludes by carrying the Satanic logic of rebellion to its inevitable conclusion:

> So farewell hope, and, with hope, farewell fear,
> Farewell remorse! All good to me is lost;
> Evil, be thou my Good: by thee at least
> Divided empire with Heaven's King I hold,
> By thee, and more than half perhaps will reign;
> As Man ere long, and this new World, shall know.

On January 10, 1776, Thomas Paine invoked Satan as the presiding spirit of the American Revolution with the publication of his pamphlet *Common Sense*, which "became an immediate sensation" after being "sold and distributed widely and read aloud at taverns and meeting places." If we consider its distribution in "proportion to the population of the colonies at that time," *Common Sense* "had the largest sale and circulation of any book published in American history."[39] Seven months after the publication of *Common Sense*, Satan's speech became the basis for America's Declaration of Independence. Even though all of the signers of that declaration were in full rebellion against the Calvinism which inspired Milton, the signers of the Declaration of Independence expressed the gist of Satan's speech when they wrote: "when a long train of abuses and usurpations, pursuing invariably the same Object evinces a design to reduce them under absolute Despotism, it is their right, it is their duty, to throw off such Government, and to provide new Guards for their future security."[40]

America was destined to become what the Ayatollah Khomeini referred to as "the Great Satan," the moment Milton's co-religionists stepped onto the shores of Massachusetts Bay. Consequently, the sons of those Puritans were the best interpreters of that spirit as it morphed into Unitarianism and then apostasy over the course of the 19th century. Ralph Waldo Emerson most certainly read *Paradise Lost*. His most famous essay, "Self-Reliance," resonates with the same Satanic spirit and cadence. Having learned from Milton that

---

38 "1776: Paine, Common Sense (Pamphlet)," OLL, https://oll.libertyfund.org/pages/1776-paine-common-sense-pamphlet

39 Moncure Daniel Conway (1893), *The Life of Thomas Paine*, taken from Project Gutenberg, https://www.gutenberg.org/browse/authors/c#a1283; "Common Sense," *Wikipedia: The Free Encyclopedia*, https://en.wikipedia.org/wiki/Common_Sense

40 "United States Declaration of Independence," *Wikipedia: The Free Encyclopedia*, https://en.wikipedia.org/wiki/United_States_Declaration_of_Independence

Introduction

The mind is its own place, and in itself
Can make a Heav'n of Hell, a Hell of Heav'n.

Emerson concluded that "Nothing is at last sacred but the integrity of your own mind." When a generation raised on a different understanding of the Bible demurred, saying "But these impulses may be from below, not from above," Emerson countered by invoking Satan: "They do not seem to be to be such, but if I am the Devil's child, I will live then from the Devil." Emerson got the idea that he was "the Devil's child" from the Calvinist principle of total depravity, which he rejected while retaining the Satanic gist of the Protestant revolutionary spirit.

Emerson's neighbor Nathaniel Hawthorne inherited the same Calvinist legacy, and like Emerson, he rejected it, but he could never accept Emerson's naïve optimism and remained a prisoner of the dark forest which he described in "Young Goodman Brown" after Brown left his wife Faith to meet up with the Devil. Confronted with the devil's impatience, all Young Goodman Brown could say is that "Faith kept me back a while" before being welcomed into "the communion of your race," which is that "Evil is the nature of mankind." As Young Goodman Brown noted when he saw Goody Cloyse, "that woman taught me my catechism." Faith kept the American Republic back a while, but the emergence of the American Empire after World War II has been one long plunge into Satanism. Like Satan, the dark figure who welcomed Young Goodman Brown into the forest, the Puritan minister explains that "evil must be your only happiness." America, if by that we mean the world's fourth great religion, has been a centuries-long pact with the devil. America is more than its hidden grammar. American identity is also based on the lived identities of people who came here looking for a better life. How these two vectors produced something new is the subject of this book.

PART I

ERRAND INTO THE SATANIC WILDERNESS

Part 1

Engaging Into the Satanic Wilderness

Chapter 1

Danforth's Errand

In 1670 Samuel Danforth delivered a sermon entitled "A Brief Recognition of New-Englands Errand into the Wilderness." Danforth was pastor of the Puritan church in Roxbury, Massachusetts, a graduate of Harvard College, an astronomer and an associate of Rev. John Eliot, the Apostle to the Indians. Despite his education, he found himself at a loss to explain the novelty of the Puritans' position in the New World, and so he ransacked the Bible until he found the word "Wilderness" in Matthew 11, where John the Baptist was described in the *Vulgate* as "*vox clamans in deserto.*"

Danforth's "Errand into the Wilderness" was a "classic example of the New England jeremiad," a genre which attempted to answer the question "What is it that distinguisheth New-England from other Colonies and Plantations in America?"[41] The answer was the Reformed Faith, grounded in Calvinist principles, which had rendered the Puritans odious in the eyes of their fellow Englishmen and had prompted them, "before God, Angels, and Men," into "leaving your Country, Kindred and Fathers houses, and transporting your selves with your Wives, Little Ones and Substance over the vast Ocean into this waste and howling Wilderness."[42]

Danforth got the term "Wilderness" from the English translation of the Bible. He imposed it on the terrain which the Puritans discovered when they founded the Massachusetts Bay Colony in 1630. When the Jews came to John the Baptist and asked him to identify himself, John said, "I am as Isaiah prophesied, 'a voice that cries in the wilderness/Make a straight way for the Lord'" (John 1:23). The term for wilderness in the Latin Vulgate was "*deserto.*" Desert is a much closer approximation of the terrain east of the Jordan River where John baptized than the seemingly interminable forest which was the main characteristic of life in the Massachusetts Bay Colony, which Massachusetts took its name from the tribe of indigenous people, who lived in the Great Blue Hill region south of Boston. The term roughly translates as "at or about the Great Hill."

---

[41] Samuel Danforth, *A Brief Recognition of New-Englands Errand into the Wilderness: an Online Electronic Text Edition*, editor Paul Royster, 1670, University of Lincoln Nebraska, Digital Commons, https://digitalcommons.unl.edu/libraryscience/35/

[42] Danforth, *A Brief Recognition.*

When the separatist Pilgrims had arrived ten years earlier, they called their settlement Plymouth, after a town in England. In both instances, the English Protestants imposed names on an unexplored continent to make sense of their lives in an alien environment where the customs of the country they left behind no longer applied. Together those two names bespoke the essence of the American founding as an "Anglo-Protestant nation," an identification which Samuel Huntington still found persuasive at the beginning of the 21st century. Settlers, as Huntington pointed out, create the form. Immigrants conform to it.

Massachusetts differed from Virginia, a colony which was created as a plantation for commercial purposes. The desire for wealth didn't motivate the Puritans. A desire for "Liberty to walk in the Faith of the Gospel with all good Conscience according to the Order of the Gospel, and your enjoyment of the pure Worship of God according to his Institution, without humane Mixtures and Impositions" moved the Puritans to uproot themselves and settle in an alien environment that was nothing like the arid country east of the Jordan River, where John baptized the Hebrews and Jesus.

Something similar happened in Virginia 100 years later. The paradigms were radically different in a way that bespoke the transition from the Reformation to the Enlightenment in America, or the difference between the climate of Virginia and the climate of Massachusetts, but neither paradigm had anything to do with the New World.

The paradigm imposed on Virginia in the 18th century was Arcadia, the Greek vision of pastoralism and harmony with nature. Over the course of the 18th century, the Virginia colony was portrayed as a real-life Arcadia in the New World by people like Thomas Jefferson, Robert Beverley, and J. Hector St. John de Crèvecœur. Virginia, wrote Robert Beverley in *The History and Present State of Virginia*, was "so agreeable, that Paradice itself seem'd to be there, in its first Native Lustre."[43]

If the paradigm which explained the hidden grammar of New England Puritanism was Satan in *Paradise Lost* explaining to his fellow demons "here we shall be free," Virginia a century later had become "paradise regained." America was no longer a "howling wilderness" because Virginia had become Arcadia. Thomas Jefferson, who grew up Virginia when it was frontier territory, was the antithesis of the Puritan divine. Jefferson's redaction of the Bible was intended as a corrective to those who succumbed to Calvinism's denigration of human nature. According to the Enlightenment, man's ability to live in "the state of nature" in places like Virginia abolished Calvin's understanding of original sin. Crèvecœur doesn't mention Arcadia in his *Letters from an American Farmer* because Arcadia had become an unnecessary fiction. America had taken its place as a category of reality. "With the appearance

---

43 Marx, *The Machine in the Garden*, p. 76.

Part I: Errand Into the Satanic Wilderness

of Crèvecœur's Letters in 1782," Leo Marx tells us, "the assimilation of the ancient European fantasy to conditions in the New World was virtually complete."[44] "America," he says, "was neither Eden nor a howling desert."[45] Marx claimed that America was "a symbolic middle landscape created by mediation between art and nature,"[46] but he could make that claim only with the benefit of hindsight. As of the 18th century, America was both Eden and a howling desert, depending on where you lived. The conflict implicit in those metaphors would get resolved by force of arms in the Civil War, when the victors imposed their understanding of the world on the vanquished, but by then the Puritanism which was the essence of American identity had been modified beyond recognition by the exigencies of the frontier, where essence met existence, as the English settlers moved inexorably westward.

Unlike the poets who praised it, the inhabitants of Arcadia lived during a golden age, which Christians referred to as prelapsarian because Genesis had explained that their ultimate forebears, Adam and Eve, had lived in harmony with nature before the Fall in the Garden of Eden. So, Arcadia was more a garden than untamed nature. It was a landscape that had been tamed by the human mind but not destroyed. Every Christian attempt to return to that prelapsarian harmony with nature, however, has been haunted by its impossibility, symbolized in the Book of Genesis by the angel with the flaming sword, who prevented return to the garden.

The attempt was made nonetheless, but always with a premonition that it was bound to fail. That ambivalence is best symbolized in Nicolas Poussin's painting *Les bergers d'Arcadie* (The Arcadian Shepherds), which depicts three idealized shepherds and (presumably) a shepherdess contemplating an austere tomb on which is written the Latin inscription "*Et in Arcadia ego*," Even in Arcadia I am present. The "I" in the phrase refers to death.

The desire to impose either Greek or Biblical paradigms on America was Platonic; it assumed the Platonic cosmos of eternal forms and temporal flux that corresponded to the Greek understanding of nature. Europe broke with Greek models in the Middle Ages because in his treatise on Being and Essence St. Thomas Aquinas showed that "Existence is the form which calls essence into being. . . . In a true sense then, the most normal, that is, most perfective element of substance is existence and not substantial form."[47] The wilderness of Trans-Jordan and the pastoral garden known as Arcadia are Platonic forms which have nothing to do with America but which were imposed nonetheless

---

44 Marx, *Machine in the Garden*, p. 116.
45 Marx, *Machine in the Garden*, p. 43.
46 Marx, *Machine in the Garden*, p. 71.
47 Thomas Aquinas, *Thomas Aquinas: On Being and Essence* (*de Ente et Essentia*), trans. Robert T. Miller, Medieval Sourcebook, Fordham University, 1997, https://origin-rh.web.fordham.edu/halsall/basis/aquinas-esse.asp

as the Europeans' way of making sense of what Miranda described in *The Tempest* as the "brave new world."

Limited by paradigms purloined from the Bible, but also faced with the necessity of establishing the social order *ab ovo*, the Puritans chose the covenant God made with Moses as their model for the New England theocracy. The Puritan ideal of the covenant "bound each individual to obey God first and foremost and at the same time bound him to submit himself to the will of the group for the common good."[48] All of the seminal documents of the English colonies—from "the Mayflower Compact of the Pilgrims in 1620, the first code of laws adopted in Virginia in 1610, the famous sermon of John Winthrop on board the *Arabella* in 1630, and the Cambridge Platform of Massachusetts of 1648"—were based on the Anglo-Protestant understanding of the Hebrew covenant.[49] John Winthrop's famous sermon referring to the Massachusetts Bay Colony as "a utopian city upon a hill," is based on his understanding that the Puritans had:

> entered into a Covenant with him for this worke. . . . Now if the Lord shall please to heare vs, and bring vs in peace to the place wee desire, then hath hee ratified this Covenant and sealed our Commission [and] will expect a strickt performance of the Articles contained in it, but if wee shall neglect the observation of these Articles . . . seekeing greate things for our selues and our posterity, the Lord will surely breake out in wrathe against vs [and] be revenged. . . . For this end wee must be knit together as one man, wee must entertaine each other in brotherly Affection, wee must be willing to abridge our selues of our superfluities for the supply of others necessities.[50]

Because one of the pillars of the Reformed faith was *sola scriptura*, the Bible became the main source of paradigms or templates or forms or categories of the mind which helped the Puritans understand their situation in the New World. When it came to naming places, the only other options were English place names like Cambridge or incomprehensible Indian names like Massachusetts, which means "great-hill-small-space" in the Algonquin tongue. But even that term got refracted through the lens of the Bible when John Winthrop referred to the new colony as "a city on a hill."

> For we must consider that we shall be as a city upon a hill. The eyes of all people are upon us. So that if we shall deal falsely with our God in this work we have undertaken, and so cause him to withdraw his present help from us, we shall be made a story and a by-word through the world.[51]

---

48 McLoughlin, *Revivals, Awakenings, and Reform*, p. 35.
49 McLoughlin, *Revivals, Awakenings, and Reform*, p. 35.
50 McLoughlin, *Revivals, Awakenings, and Reform*, pp. 36-7.
51 "A City on a Hill": Reflections on John Winthrop's Vision for Christian Living, Posted by web@rhb.org on April 5, 2024, Reformation Heritage Books, https://www.heritagebooks.

Part I: Errand Into the Satanic Wilderness

Ronald Reagan invoked Winthrop's powerful image in his January 1989 farewell address as the best summary of his eight years in office. Reagan had restored America's messianic mission of bringing freedom to the world. God must have been listening because 11 months later the Berlin Wall came down. The collapse of the Soviet Union two years later confirmed Americans' understanding of themselves as chosen by God to spread American values and inaugurate the "end of history," as Francis Fukuyama put it in a famous essay which celebrated the golden age of unipolar dominance which could be described as the *Pax Americana*, were it not for all of the wars America started during that period. The failing war in the Ukraine not only put an end to that delusion, it inaugurated an identity crisis of biblical proportions.

The Puritans also favored biblical names for their children and their settlements because it confirmed them in their belief that they were God's chosen people. They were more than just English freebooters who had internalized the real lesson of the Reformation, which is that crime pays as long as what is stolen is the property of the Catholic Church or gold from Spanish galleons. The English would hang fellow citizens for stealing a spoon, but they knighted Francis Drake for plundering the Spanish Main. Piracy was a uniquely English institution in the New World, and like the Reformation which inspired it, piracy needed to be sanctioned by some sort of divine command. That never happened and eventually the British Navy turned on the pirates to whom they had granted Letters of Marque, and that uniquely English institution had to wait to be immortalized in the words and music of Gilbert and Sullivan in their operetta *The Pirates of Penzance*. The "pirate king" sinks "a few more ships, it's true/Than a well-bred monarch ought to do," but they still manage to "get through" because terrorists like Francis Drake do the "dirty work" of looting for them.

Although the Puritans did not come to the New World to plunder Spanish galleons loaded with gold, they weren't going to let the natives stand in the way of their expanding empire either. "You have solemnly professed before God, Angels and Men," Samuel Danforth declaimed to the congregation at Roxbury, Massachusetts in 1670 on the occasion of the election of officers for the Massachusetts General Court, "that the Cause of your leaving your Country, Kindred and Fathers houses, and transporting your selves with your Wives, Little Ones and Substance over the vast Ocean into this waste and howling Wilderness, was your Liberty to walk in the Faith of the Gospel with all good Conscience according to the Order of the Gospel, and your enjoyment of the pure Worship of God according to his Institution, without humane Mixtures and Impositions."[52]

---

org/blog/a-city-on-a-hill-reflections-on-john-winthrops-vision-for-christian-living/
52 Danforth, *A Brief Recognition*.

Or as Satan put it in the Puritan epic *Paradise Lost*: "Here we shall be free." But free to do what? Were there any limits on this new-found freedom? And if so, who imposed them and by what right? The English aristocracy which stole the property of the Catholic Church during the Reformation handed religious authority over to clerics who were willing to justify the theft. The Puritans chafed under the hegemony of the Anglican Church because they rightly understood that it had no authority to tell them what to do other than the authority which arose out of force, which Shakespeare made clear in Ulysses' speech in *Troilus and Cressida*.

In mentioning freedom, Satan was, of course, referring to Hell, which is what America became for its native inhabitants in the wake of English migration. In this the English colonists differed from their French and Spanish counterparts, who were guided by the Catholic Church, which recognized that Indians were human beings on June 2, 1537 when Pope Paul III issued the Encyclical *Sublimis Deus*, which forbade the enslavement of the indigenous peoples of the Americas and all other indigenous peoples who could be discovered later or were previously known. *Sublimis Deus* stated that the Indians were "fully rational human beings who have rights to freedom and property, even if they are heathen."[53] So intermarriage became the rule in New France and New Spain. Because of the intermarriage between Spaniards and the native peoples of Mexico, Jose Vasconcelos Calderon referred to Mexicans as "the cosmic race."[54]

Because the founders of the English colonies were in rebellion against the Catholic faith, they had to ransack the Bible for the categories of the mind which would justify their enterprise, and they found them chiefly in the Old Testament, more specifically in the stories of the Exodus and even more importantly in the story of how the Hebrews invaded Canaan and perpetrated genocide on its native peoples. The term "genocide" is, of course, an anachronism, but the behavior of the Puritans was modeled, nonetheless, on their interpretation of themselves as Hebrews and the Indians as Amalek, a designation which lent divine sanction to genocide, no matter what term we use to describe it.

The Puritan general Oliver Cromwell got the idea of treating the Irish like Amalek from the Puritans in New England. During the siege of Drogheda, which took place from September 3 to September 11, 1649, Cromwell "personally ordered all the inhabitants to be killed." As a result, 1,000 Irish attending Sunday Services at the Church of St. Peter were "put to the sword" along with "all of their friars . . . except two who were taken prisoner and killed." Cromwell described these war crimes as "a great thing" done "not by

---

53 "*Sublimis Deus*," *Wikipedia: The Free Encyclopedia*, https://en.wikipedia.org/wiki/Sublimis_Deus

54 "La raza cósmica (The Cosmic Race)," *Wikipedia: The Free Encyclopedia*, https://en.wikipedia.org/wiki/La_raza_c%C3%B3smica

Part I: Errand Into the Satanic Wilderness

power or might but by the Spirit of God," and it was to "God alone"[55] that Cromwell gave the glory in a way that conveniently absolved him of any moral responsibility for his actions, echoing Luther's attempt to absolve himself of adultery and broken vows in *De Servo Arbitrio*, his treatise on free will.

During the same Irish campaign, the Oxford historian Anthony Wood, who chronicled Cromwell's atrocities firsthand, reported that 3,000 unarmed civilians, including women and children hiding in "vaults underneath the church" in Tredagh, were "put to the sword."[56]

Cromwell seemed to delight in killing the Irish in their churches, probably because it expressed hatred for the Catholic faith as well as hatred for the Catholic Irish even though English law for centuries recognized the church as a sacred place and sanctuary where fugitives could not be arrested, much less murdered. Churches were considered sanctuaries by law in England from the fourth to—not coincidentally—the seventeenth century, when Cromwell invoked Amalek to overturn that principle.

In declaring the Irish Amalek, Cromwell was only repeating what the Puritans had done to the Indians in Massachusetts. On May 26, 1637, a Puritan war party attacked Mystic Fort in a pre-dawn raid which left 500 adults and children of the Pequot tribe dead. The Pequot Massacre, which was "the first defeat of the Pequot people by the English in the Pequot war, a three-year war instigated by the Puritans to seize the tribe's traditional land."[57] The Pequot Massacre is considered:

> the first genocide to take place in New England. The Puritan justification for killing men, women and children was ironically expressed by the Puritan leader, John Underhill who declared that because "sometimes the Scripture declareth women and children must perish with their parents.... We had sufficient light from the Word of God for our proceedings."[58]

Just as Ronald Reagan invoked John Winthrop's "city on a hill" to give moral justification to the final phase of the anti-Communist crusade, Binyamin Netanyahu, who attended high school in Cheltenham Township outside Philadelphia, invoked Amalek to justify genocide in Gaza. Rabbis told IDF soldiers to kill Palestinian women and children just as the Israelites were "commanded to destroy the Amalekites by killing man, woman, infant and suckling."[59]

---

55 Hugh J. Curran, "Israel's Netanyahu: an Oliver Cromwell for our Times," Informed Comment, January 20, 2024, https://www.juancole.com/2024/01/israels-netanyahu-cromwell.html

56 Curran, "Israel's Netanyahu."

57 "May 26, 1637: Pequot Massacre," Zinn Education Project, https://www.zinnedproject.org/news/tdih/pequot-massacre/

58 "May 26, 1637: Pequot Massacre," Zinn Education Project.

59 Curran, "Israel's Netanyahu."

Walking with a Bible and a Gun

Latter day Marcionites blame Yahweh for the excesses of Zionists like Netanyahu, but the problem started with the Reformation when the Bible was taken out of the Catholic Church which created it. Judaizing English revolutionaries then used it as a justification for their crimes in exactly the same way that the Israelis are using it today.

Puritanism wasn't limited to New England. Even Anglicans and Quakers in Virginia held Puritan views, which "in sectarian form were widely diffused in Maryland and Rhode Island, which tolerated all sects."[60] Puritanism, as Huntington has pointed out, was the essence of Protestantism, a term which Protestants have been unable to define, as Max Weber's futile efforts have shown. The only thing we know for certain is that Protestantism began with the looting of Church property.

The Reformation in England was, as William Cobbett pointed out in detail, a looting operation which "privatized" 900 years of accumulated wealth which the Catholic Church had put in service to all Englishmen, but especially the poor. Cobbett mentions the fact that at the end of the 15th century an Englishman need walk no further than six miles in any direction before he came across an institution of the Catholic Church which was willing to show him hospitality for a night or to nurse him to health if he were sick. There was no theological justification for the English Reformation. It was a looting operation run by the aristocracy who looked greedily at Church property. "The upstart aristocracy of the future," to cite R. H. Tawney's memorable phrase in *Religion and the Rise of Capitalism*, "had their teeth in the carcass, and having tasted blood, they were not to be whipped off by a sermon."[61]

The theological justification for the Reformation came from Germany, where it was rooted in lust among the clergy and greed among the aristocrats who protected the clergy, who obligingly handed Church property over to the aristocrats, who then obligingly made the Reformed clergy head of the newly created state church. Lust and rebellion against legitimate authority united the first generation of reformed clergy.

Unable to control his passions, Martin Luther turned his moral failures into one of the pillars of Reformed thought when he wrote *De Servo Arbitrio* in the wake of his marriage to Katerina von Bora. After becoming a slave to his passions, Luther decided to abolish free will and blame his sins on God. As some indication that he had become passion's slave, Luther called his wife Katerina, whose nickname was Kaethe, *Kette*, which is the German word for chain. Sometimes he would use the Latin word *Catena* as when he wrote to another priest who had also broken the vow of celibacy, when he said *"Meine Catena gruesst deine Catena."* My chain greets your chain. Luther

---

60 McLoughlin, *Revivals, Awakenings, and Reform*, p. 38.

61 R. H. Tawney, *Religion and the Rise of Capitalism: A History and Study* (London: Hazell, Watson & Viney, Ltd., 1948, first edition 1926), http://pombo.free.fr/tawney1922simil.pdf

Part I: Errand Into the Satanic Wilderness

described himself as a *famosus amator* because he was notorious for his sexual indulgence. Because he could not control his tendency to gluttony, anger, and lust, Luther decided that he lacked free will and then rationalized his failure by creating the principle of the enslaved will.[62]

All of the first-generation Reformers had similar problems. Zwingli was a notorious sexual reprobate who nevertheless insisted that he had never slept with a married woman, a virgin or a nun. He was drawn to Reformed doctrines like innate depravity and the enslaved will for the same reasons as Luther.

Three hundred years after Luther nailed his 97 theses to the Church door in Wittenberg, Nathaniel Hawthorne melded the Reformers into one literary paradigm which stood for all of them when he created Dimmesdale, the tortured Puritan minister who was both a visible saint and an adulterer, as the main character in *The Scarlet Letter*. Like Dimmesdale and Luther, Zwingli had a conversion experience which put him above the moral law, when he learned in 1505 that "for the first time that the death of Christ was once offered for our sins, by which we have been saved."[63]

Because Zwingli's "conversion" antedated his ordination to the priesthood, it comes as no surprise that he denigrated the invalid sacraments he confected. His conversion to the theology of the Reformation preceded his entire career as a priest. Living a double life causes psychological distress, as Dimmesdale discovered, and so it must have been with a sense of relief that Zwingli married his concubine in Zurich after finally throwing of the last vestiges of the Catholic priesthood to which he had bound himself by vows of celibacy. The Reformed doctrine of *Sola Scriptura* allowed the sexually liberated Protestant clergy to ransack the Bible for rationalizations of their infidelity, but it also led to constant warring with other Reformers who had different opinions on issues like the Eucharist. It also led to actual warfare. Zwingli died at the Battle of Kappell on October 11, 1531.

Thomas Muentzer, who also quarreled with Luther, led the German peasants into a disastrous military confrontation with Philip of Hesse's troops in the battle of Frankenhausen. Six thousand peasants died but Muentzer escaped only to be captured, tortured, and executed a few days after the battle, demonstrating again the link between sexual deviance, bad theology, insurrection, and bloodshed that would repeat itself in the New World under the aegis of the Puritan strain of English Calvinism after the execution of the king of England.

Calvin, the spiritual father of Puritanism was no exception. His biography, however, is more deeply encrypted than that of the overtly sexual Luther

---

62 Cf. E. Michael Jones, *Degenerate Modern*s, p. 235ff for more on the sexual roots of Luther's theology.

63 Bullinger, quoted in Gordon, F. Bruce. Zwingli (p. 18). Yale University Press. Kindle Edition.

or Zwingli because of the nature of his sins. Calvin and Michael Servetus, the Spanish reformer and polymath who discovered the circulation of blood before Harvey, were students of the Latinist priest and pedophile Mathurin Cordier.

Bruce Gordon reports that Calvin, after his abrupt departure from Noyon, went back to Paris under dangerous circumstances to meet Servetus in 1534. He also points out that Calvin's first theological book, *Psychopannychia*, was essentially a long letter to Servetus.[64] He also notes that Servetus was part of the "Italian circle in Paris."[65] Servetus was Spanish, not Italian, but the word "Italian" meant homosexual.[66] But Calvin was spurned by his boyhood friend, who did not show up for the arranged meeting, which Calvin brought up when they met in Geneva in 1553.[67]

Between 1534 and 1553, Calvin turned on his erstwhile friend and made it clear that if Servetus ever darkened his doorstep, he would not leave the city alive.[68] Calvin made good on his promise when Servetus was burned at the stake in Geneva on October 27, 1553. By then, Servetus's homosexuality was internationally known, and as Jeffrey Matsen has demonstrated, the English literary spy and agent of Walsingham, Christopher Marlowe, viewed Calvin's killing of Servetus as a case of one homosexual murdering another.[69]

Calvin's handpicked successor in Geneva Theodore Beza had similar problems. Beza said that by 1544, he "had already completely renounced the Catholic Mass,"[70] which seems clear enough from his clandestine marriage, together with the book of poems he was working on at the time, a pseudonymously published collection of Latin verses titled *Poemata Juvenilia*, which contained erotic poetry. As Laurie Langbauer pointed out, "Beza's *juvenailia* were notorious for their lewdness. [Beza] had to live down this early indiscretion during his later life as a Calvinist (when Catholic critics censured his poems as simply about adultery and sodomy)."[71] As Anne Prescott records, "even some of his friends… [referred] to the love poems

---

64 Gordon, *Calvin*, p. 43.

65 Gordon, *Calvin*, p. 43.

66 Puff, *Sodomy*, pp. 117–18, 125–28. The phrase "Italian wedding" meant anal sex (127). Luther noted that every county has its vice: Greeks are "whorers," Italians are sodomites (127). As we have already seen, he regarded Czechs as gluttons, Germans as drunkards, and Wends (Slavs who lived in today's NE Germany) as thieves.

67 Puff, *Sodomy*, p. 43.

68 Puff, *Sodomy*, p. 217.

69 Jeffrey Masten, "Bound for Germany: Heresy, Sodomy, and a New Copy of Marlowe's Edward II." TLS. Times Literary Supplement, no. 5725–5726 (December 21, 2012): pp. 17–20.

70 Scott M. Manetsch, *Theodore Beza and the Quest for Peace in France, 1572-1598* (Leiden: Brill Academic, 2021), p. 422

71 Laurie Langbauer, *The Juvenile Tradition: Young Writers and Prolepsis, 1750-1835* (Oxford: OUP, 2016), p. 67.

with real or pretended shock."[72] The most scandalous poem was about a youth named "Beza" struggling to decide whether to love Candida or a man named Audebert.[73] This singular use of his own real name allowed his enemies to identify the book's author as the by-then-famously austere Reformer, Beza. In the poem, Beza finds himself caught between Candida who "desires to have the whole Beza," and "Audebert [who] is so desirous of his Beza/ That he burns to enjoy Beza entirely." Beza chooses Audebert: "But if it must be one,/ I give preference to you, Audebert."[74]

Once publicly exposed, Beza immediately repudiated the poems, a ritual he was forced to repeat till his dying day. As he wrote in the dedication to his *Confessio Fidei*:

> As respects those poems, who is there that either has condemned them more than I, their unhappy author, or that detests them more than I do today? Would, therefore, that they might at length be buried in perpetual oblivion![75]

The two founding principles of the Reformation are lust and avarice. Lust characterized the first generation of Catholic priests who avidly joined in with Luther because they were already involved in concubinage. Greed was the prime motivation of the princes, who spirited Luther off to the Wartburg, where he was held hostage to write justifications for their theft of Church property.

The Puritans in New England inherited a tendency to both vices. Lust darkened the New England mind leading to an ontological insecurity. That insecurity was a salient characteristic of Puritan thought, and the main reason they needed covenant theology was to cover the nakedness of their religion which lost the protective covering of custom and its association with the apostolic succession through the Catholic Church. New England theology was based on an ontological and theological insecurity which the Puritans inherited from John Calvin. In countless sermons, that insecurity expression in the metaphor of the "bottom" or "foundation."

Settlers had to prioritize existence over essence if they wanted to survive. Debates about the relationship between Custom and Nature, or *nomos* and *phusis*, or existence and essence were meaningless in the New World because custom simply did not exist there. Deprived of *theologia naturalis* by Luther's hatred of the whore reason, the Puritans had to create their essence as a society

---

72 Anne Lake Prescott, "English Writers and Beza's Latin Epigrams: The Uses and Abuses of Poetry." Studies in the Renaissance 21 (1974): 83–117, p. 85.

73 Winfried Schleiner, "That Matter Which Ought Not To Be Heard Of," *Journal of Homosexuality* 26:4 (1994): 41–75, p. 44. See also, Diarmaid MacCullogh, "Reformation Time and Sexual Revolution." New England Review 24:4 (2003): 6–31, esp. p. 24.

74 Schleiner, p. 44.

75 Quoted in Henry Baird's favorable biography by Theodore Beza: *The Counsellor of the French Reformation, 1519-1605* (New York: Putnam, 1899), p. 28.

by a pure act of the will. The covenant was the biblical template the Puritans chose as foundation of their society and the crucial metaphor which linked existence and essence during the crucial formative years of the Massachusetts Bay Colony. The covenant was a metaphysical concept because it served as a foundational principle. Even though the thought of Aristotle was repugnant to the Reformers, the Puritan divines had to turn the covenant into the biblical equivalent of Aristotle's uncaused cause and unmoved mover, because the only other alternative was the abyss or what Aristotle called the infinite regress. As a result, Puritan divines had to become metaphysicians in spite of themselves if they wanted to provide a secure foundation for a political philosophy which grew out of their tenuous situation on the frontier. In his tract, *The New Covenant*, John Preston described the covenant in distinctly metaphysical terms as:

> the ground of all you hope for; it is that that every man is built upon, *you have no other ground but this*, God hath made a covenant with you and you are in covenant with him (my emphasis).[76]

In "New Englands True Interest," another election sermon delivered in Boston on April 9, 1668, William Stoughton delivered what might be termed a metaphysical jeremiad by preaching on the necessity of the covenant as the foundational project of the Puritan state:

> The solemn work of this day is Foundation-work; not to lay a new Foundation, but to continue and strengthen, and beautifie and build upon that which hath been laid. Give me leave, therefore, Honoured and Beloved, to awaken, and call upon you, in the name of him who sends me, with reference into those Foundations that are held forth to us in the Text for if these should be out of course, what could the Righteous do? If we should frustrate and deceive the Lords expectations, that his Covenant-interest in us, and the workings of his Salvation be made to cease, then All were lost indeed; Ruine upon Ruine, Destruction upon Destruction would come, until one stone were not left upon another.[77]

The covenant served as a stop gap; it calmed the anxiety Puritan divines like Stoughton felt about the metaphysical foundations of the Puritan state. That

---

[76] "The New Covenant, or, The Saints Portion: a Treatise Unfolding the All-sufficiencie of God, Mans Uprightness, and the Covenant of Grace, Delivered in Fourteen Sermons Upon Gen. 17. 1.2.; Whereunto are Adioyned Foure Sermons upon Eccles. 9. 1.2, 11.12," Digitalpuritan.net, http://www.digitalpuritan.net/Digital%20Puritan%20Resources/Preston,%20John/The%20New%20Covenant.txt.html

[77] William Stoughton, "New-Englands true interest not to lie, or, A treatise declaring from the word of truth the terms on which we stand, and the tenure by which we hold our hitherto-continued precious and pleasant things shewing what the blessing God expecteth from his people, and what they may rationally look for from him / delivered in a sermon preached in Boston in New-England, April 29, 1668, being the day of election there, by Mr. W. Stoughton ..." (Cambridge: S.G. and M.J., 1670), https://quod.lib.umich.edu/e/eebo2/A61699.0001.001?view=toc

Part I: Errand Into the Satanic Wilderness

anxiety is quite palpable in "New Englands True Interest," and rightly so because the social order in New England was based on two contradictory impulses that can be reduced to faith and reason. Reason gives certitude, but faith is in things unseen. Faith, by definition, therefore, cannot provide metaphysical certitude. Aquinas began his *Summa Contra Gentiles*, by claiming that the "necessary foundation" of every branch of science, including the science of government, begins with proofs by reason alone of the existence of God. All of Aquinas's *a posteriori* proofs of God's existence are based on the impossibility of an infinite regress, which Aristotle demonstrated in his *Metaphysics*. If the certainty which derives from these metaphysical principles is "not had," according to Aquinas, "every consideration about divine things necessarily fails."[78]

The Scholastics could invoke Aristotelian metaphysics as a preamble to the faith, but that approach was barred to followers of Luther and Calvin, whose fundamental principles were *sola fide*, *sola scriptura*, and *sola gratia*, all of which were based on faith and not on reason, which Luther had called a whore. Protestantism could survive on custom in Europe, but not in the "howling Wilderness," where custom did not exist. Metaphysical certainty was a non-negotiable requirement for anyone who wanted to found a lasting and viable colony in the New World, but that certainty could not be found in the realm of faith. The result was an insecurity which the Puritan divines tried mightily to hide behind more and more devout professions of faith.

From John Calvin, the Puritans inherited both the insecurity and the piety which tried to disguise it. The crucial issues of whether a preamble to faith was possible, whether man by unaided reason could ascend to knowledge about God, whether God's existence was an article of faith or of reason, in short, the heart of the metaphysical tradition and natural theology was swept away by the force of the Protestant doctrines, *sola fide*, *sola gratia*, *sola scriptura*. This outburst of faith had far-reaching consequences for the very beliefs which gave Protestantism its force as it critically undermined the basis of its own certainty. One could not reason to the existence of God because reason in divine things was totally incapacitated and depraved. The fervor of Protestant piety was based not on the firm foundation of reason but upon immediate intuitions over which they had no power.

Thus, Calvin bequeaths a heritage in which faith and the quest for certainty are mutually antagonistic. We achieve piety at the expense of reason and certainty at the expense of belief. One could be reasonable only by rejecting piety and pious only by rejecting reason. Calvin brought about a revolution

---

78 The specter of Protestant insecurity about the foundation of their religion is not unique to English Puritans. It has haunted Protestant thinkers well into the 20th century, as Emil Brunner points out in *Natur und Gnade*, when he writes: "Over the long haul, the Church can't tolerate the rejection of *theologia naturalis* any more than its misuse. The main task of our generation is to find our way back to a correct understanding of theologia naturalis" (my trnslation).

in consciousness based upon an inversion of the relationship between faith and reason, and the magnitude of the change can be measured by comparing Aquinas's use of the same terms. "Among those things that must be considered concerning God," he writes in the first book of the *Summa Contra Gentiles*,

> there comes first, as the necessary foundation of the whole science, the consideration by which we demonstrate that God exists. For if this is not had, every consideration about divine things necessarily fails.

Natural theology, which was for Aquinas the culmination of metaphysics and the foundation of all knowledge of God, becomes for Calvin an abyss, upon which everything is based but supports nothing.

Because American thought is at its deepest level Calvinistic, the motion of American intellectual life tends to follow these two mutually contradictory impulses. The fact that the Puritans needed to create a social order *ab ovo* necessitated a "self-grounded reason," as well as a need to attain certainty which would get to the bottom and provide a foundation for the newly created city on a hill. Yet because Calvin sees the mind as a "forge of idols," the desire for certainty is subverted into idolatry, which must be repressed. The natural desire for certainty creates idols which piety must destroy. Idolatry in other words, leads to iconoclasm, and then the vacuum created by iconoclasm leads back to idolatry because nature abhors a vacuum. Once begun, this vicious circle follows a downward spiral toward complete skepticism and the destruction of faith and discourse. Calvin's break with the metaphysical tradition and the notion of arché or first principle which it presupposed created a vacuum that had to be filled. Yet as a result of the break with being, anti-metaphysical man is condemned to posit a first principle, which is inadequate to the task it must fulfill. By his very rejection of the science of being qua being, the Calvinist must create idols which other Calvinists are just as inevitably forced to destroy. As soon as X (for X read covenant, the law, nature, the self, grammar, the abyss) becomes the arché or bottom (and something must fill this position) it becomes simultaneously an idol which iconoclasm will ultimately destroy, which will in turn lead to the vacuum which will create another more "basic" idol. Man's misuse of reason constructs idols; his piety deconstructs them.

Calvin was aware of this dialectic and of the break with being which caused it, but he associated both with the consequences of original sin. "This inversion of the order of things," he says in his *Commentary* on I Corinthians 1:21, "the ingratitude of men deserved." But once the break was made, nothing but the annihilation of discourse could bring a final stop to it. Protestantism begets nothing but more Protestantism. The break with metaphysics caused the erosion of anything put in its place because nothing can be the arché but the arché. No idol is adequate because nothing is more basic than being. Calvin's fideism leads paradoxically yet inevitably to the destruction of faith — first in reason, then in God, and then any idol substituted for God, and finally

Part I: Errand Into the Satanic Wilderness

in the self which created the idols. By destroying the foundation in the name of piety, Calvin plunged faith and reason and man himself into the abyss, as Shakespeare saw. Once existence as the arbiter of essence is abandoned, will takes over:

> Then everything includes itself in power,
> Power into will, will into appetite,
> And appetite, an universal wolf,
> So doubly seconded with will and power,
> Must make perforce an universal prey
> And last eat up himself.[79]

---

[79] *Troilus and Cressida*, Act 1, Scene 3, Folger Shakespeare Library, https://www.folger.edu/explore/shakespeares-works/troilus-and-cressida/read/1/3/

Chapter 2

The Salem Witch Trial

Calvin's theology put the Puritans in an intolerable psychological situation that was intensified by their isolation in the New World. After the Reformation was codified as three principles: *sola scriptura*, *sola fide*, and *sola gratia*, Jean Calvin, the French jurist, incorporated these terms into his *Institutes*, where he tried to integrate them into a legal framework. Calvin, not Luther became the guiding spirit behind Puritanism as it tried to make sense of life in the New World. *Sola gratia* created bind for New England Puritans that would have far-reaching psychological consequences for nascent America. It placed the Puritan settlers in an impossible situation. According to Calvinist theology, salvation depended on "grace alone." That claim simultaneously cut the nerve of human effort while denying souls the source of grace Christ provided in the sacraments of the Catholic Church. Deprived of the Eucharist, the Puritans became spiritually malnourished and more likely to fall into sin. Deprived of the psychological relief which sacramental confession provided, guilt distorted the body politic until Puritan culture finally exploded in the homicidal moral panic known as the Salem witch trials.

In the winter of 1692, a number of adolescent girls started to manifest strange behavior in Salem, Massachusetts. Although the town fathers didn't know it at the time, Betty Parris and Abigail Williams had been consorting with the minister's black slave Tituba, who had been brought from Barbados and in all likelihood had picked up a passing knowledge of voodoo there, which the Puritan girls found fascinating. Whatever else it was, voodoo was also an interesting way to pass time during New England's long, dull winters.

Soon the girls started showing signs of what may very well have been demonic possession. The girls "screamed, threw things about the room, uttered strange sounds, crawled under furniture, and contorted themselves into peculiar positions." They also "complained of being pinched and pricked with pins."[80]

---

[80] "Salem Witch Trials," *Wikipedia: The Free Encyclopedia*, https://en.wikipedia.org/wiki/Salem_witch_trials#:~:text=The%20Salem%20witch%20trials%20were,fourteen%20women%20and%20five%20omen).

A doctor was called in, but he quickly found himself out of his depth. What was going on was beyond the medical expertise of his day. As a result, there was only one possible conclusion: "The evil hand is on them," the doctor said, and from then on, the girls' strange behavior was a matter for the clergy.

As Marion Starkey relates in his account of the affair in *The Devil in Massachusetts*, the town minister, Reverend Parris:

> proclaimed a state of emergency and appealed for help to the ministers of the North Shore. When Dr. Griggs had relegated the affliction from the physical world to the spiritual, he had thrust the responsibility for its treatment upon the ministry. It was now plain that the devil was at work in Salem Village, and since even the devil cannot produce results on this scale without human accomplices, it was equally plain that he had commissioned witches here.[81]

The girls were asked to reveal the names of the witches who were tormenting them, and the famous Salem Witch Trials came about as a result. Once the ministers got involved in the case and once the affair became public, the girls were put in a very uncomfortable position. They could either admit that they had been doing voodoo with Tituba, which would almost certainly warrant severe punishment for them and death for Tituba, or they could start naming other people as witches. Human nature being what it is, they chose the latter course, and 20 innocent people, mostly Salem's marginalized, were put to death.

Once the minister and the judges accepted the girls' testimony as true, their prestige was on the line. They had to go along. According to Starkey, the significant thing about the Salem witch trials was not that it was initiated by crazed adolescent girls but that that behavior was confirmed by the community:

> In the long run what was remarkable here was less the antics of the girls than the way the community received them. It was the community—extended in time to include the whole Bay Colony—that would in the end suffer the most devastating attack of possession, and not only the ignorant, but the best minds.

Eventually one girl and two judges recanted. Starkey traces the hysteria to the baleful effects of Calvinism combined with a general sense of isolation in the colony and a feeling that with the impending turn of the century the millennium was at hand. "Similar examples of mass hysteria," he writes,

> and on a far more enormous scale had occurred repeatedly in the Middle Ages, and always like this one in the wake of stress and social disorganization, after wars or after an epidemic of the Black Death. There

---

[81] Marion L. Starkey, *The Devil in Massachusetts: A Modern Enquiry into the Salem Witch Trials* (Knopf Doubleday Publishing Group, 1989 reprint).

Part I: Errand Into the Satanic Wilderness

had been the Children's Crusades, the Flagellantes, the St. Vitus' Dance, and again and again there had been outbreaks of witchcraft. Sweden had recently had one, and on such a scale as to make what was going on in Salem Village look trivial.

But Starkey confuses our understanding of the situation in Salem by lumping witchcraft with other unrelated instances of mass hysteria, obscuring the fact that witch hunts were one of the main *sequelae* of the Reformation in Europe.

The *Malleus Maleficarum*, the *locus classicus* of witch hunting, was first published in the German city of Speyer in 1486 with the clergyman Heinrich Kramer as its author. Kramer had been expelled from Innsbruck two years earlier by the local bishop, who denounced him as "senile and crazy."[82] Given its poor initial reception, the book would have been forgotten, but in 1519, two years after Luther posted his 95 theses, a new edition appeared with the Dominican Jacob Sprenger as its co-author, 33 years after the book's initial printing and 24 years after Sprenger's death.

The Reformation had given Kramer's sex-obsessed diatribe a new lease on life as "the most severe prosecutions [of witchcraft] took place between the years 1560 and 1630, largely ending in Europe around 1780."

Witch-hunts were irrevocably bound up with the social dislocation created by the Reformation. Public concern about witchcraft increased dramatically during the second half of the 16th century, the pivotal period when the new faith was actively contested by the Church. James Sharpe claims that witchcraft operated "within the context of the Reformation and Counter-reformation," but that it did not become a major factor in people's lives until the Reformation, and it died out as the religious situation across Europe settled down and stabilized.[83] In England, for example, the last person executed for witchcraft was Jane Wenham in 1712, when England was settled and unified with Scotland. It was probably the most peaceful time to be English.[84]

The main judge at the Salem Witch Trials was John Hathorne, born in Salem on August 4, 1641 the eldest son of Major William Hathorne. John, having imbibed the Jewish revolutionary spirit which was the hidden grammar

---

82 "Malleus Maleficarum," *Wikipedia: The Free Encyclopedia*, https://en.wikipedia.org/wiki/Malleus_Maleficarum

83 According to Merry Wiesner, the Spanish killed only a handful of witches, the Portuguese just one, and the Italians none. Many of the Catholic countries were in southern Europe, and the witch craze seemed to take hold more in the northern part, like Germany, France and Scotland. Others argue that witchcraft was merely an alternative way of accusing heretics, without calling it "heresy," but even if that were the case prosecutions in Scotland of witches did not really begin until 1590. Sociologist Nachman Ben-Yehuda, on the other hand, argues that: Only the most rapidly developing countries, where the Catholic church was weakest, experienced a virulent witch craze (i.e., Germany, France, and Switzerland). Where the Catholic Church was strong (Spain, Italy, Portugal) hardly any witch craze occurred … .

84 Helene Harrison, "Witchcraft and the Reformation," Tudor Blogger, May 2, 2013, https://tudorblogger.com/2013/05/02/witchcraft-and-the-reformation-2/

of Puritanism, deposed the king's governor in Massachusetts in the aftermath of the Glorious Revolution of 1688. A new charter was imposed on the colony in 1691 which did little to calm the sense of insecurity the revolutionaries had created. The witchcraft trials came one year later.[85] From January until September 1692, "twenty persons and two dogs were accused, tried, found guilty of witchcraft, and executed," and "150 persons were in jail awaiting trial on that charge; and 200 more had been accused of the same crime."[86]

Puritan theology contributed to these deaths. In 1689, Cotton Mather, who would later witness those hangings with his father Increase, wrote a treatise entitled *Memorable Providences Relation to Witchcraft and Possessions* in which he claimed that:

> The New Englanders are a people of God settled in those, which were once the devil's territories. ... I believe that never were more satanical devices used for the unsettling of any people under the sun than what have been employed for the extirpation of the vine which God has here planted. . . . Wherefore, the devil is now making one attempt more upon us; an attempt more difficult, more surprising, more snarled with unintelligible circumstances than any that we have hitherto encountered ... a horrible plot against the country by witchcraft, and a foundation of witchcraft then laid, which if it were not seasonably discovered would probably blow up and pull down all the churches in the country.[87]

On June 19, five women were hanged as witches after being interrogated by Judge Hathorne. Before she died, Sarah Good, one of the condemned women:

> uttered a curse long remembered in the Hawthorne family. Just before her hanging, the Rev. Nicholas Noyes screamed at her: "You're a witch, and you know you are." To which Goody Good cried back: "You're a liar! I'm no more a witch than you're a wizard! And if you take my life God will give you blood to drink!" Later historians attributed this curse to Rebecca Nurse, also hanged this day, and addressed not to Noyes but to Hathorne. The curse made a lasting impression on Nathaniel Hawthorne, John Hathorne's great-great-grandson, who wove it into the plot of his second novel *The House of Seven Gables*.[88]

In the preface to *The Scarlet Letter* known as "The Customs House," Nathaniel Hawthorne apologized for John Hathorn's behavior and begged to have the curse removed from his family. "I know not, Hawthorne wrote:

> whether those ancestors of mine bethought themselves to repent and ask pardon of Heaven for their cruelties; or whether they are now groaning

---

85 Bird, *From Witchery to Sanctity*, p. 21.
86 Bird, *From Witchery to Sanctity*, p. 22.
87 Bird, *From Witchery to Sanctity*, p. 23.
88 Bird, *From Witchery to Sanctity*, p. 29.

under the heavy consequences of them, in another state of being. At all events, I, the present writer, as their representative, hereby take shame upon myself for their sakes, and pray that any curse incurred by them—as I have heard, and as the drearly and unprosperous condition of the race, for many a long year back, would argue to exist—may be now and henceforth removed.[89]

Unlike modern commentators, Cotton Mather and Nathaniel Hawthorne felt that the New England forest was the realm of the devil and that the visible saints went there to worship him. Hawthorne states his case in his brilliant allegorical tale "Young Goodman Brown." The link between ostentatious Puritan piety in the town and devil worship in the forest is Calvinism. As the inhabitants of the town stream toward the devil's sabbath, Brown is shocked to see Goody Cloyse and exclaims "That woman taught me my catechism," prompting Hawthorne to say that "there was a world of meaning in that comment."[90]

The "grave and dark clad company" Young Goodman Brown encountered in the forest included "faces that would be seen next day at the council board of the province, and others which Sabbath after Sabbath looked devoutly heavenward and benignantly over the crowded pews, from the holiest pulpits in the land."[91] This was no mere hypocrisy, as the sermon of the minister demon makes clear when he welcomes Brown to "the communion of your race"[92] because "evil is the nature of mankind. Evil must be your only happiness. Welcome again, my children, to the communion of your race."[93]

If innate and total depravity is the lesson Brown learned from Goody Cloyse's catechism lessons, why is it surprising that witches come to the forest to worship the devil? In his Custom House preface to *The Scarlet Letter* Hawthorne tells us that his tale is situated in "a neutral territory, somewhere between the real world and fairy-land, where the Actual and the Imaginary may meet, and each imbue itself with the nature of the other."[94]

Three hundred years after Luther nailed his 97 theses to the Church door in Wittenberg, Nathaniel Hawthorne melded the Reformers into one literary paradigm when he created Arthur Dimmesdale, the tortured Puritan minister who was both a visible saint and an adulterer, as the main character in *The Scarlet Letter*. Indeed, most of the characters in Hawthorne's romance are historical figures, which he emphasizes in his preface. Mistress Hibbins,

---

89 Bird, *From Witchery to Sanctity*, p. 31.
90 Nathaniel Hawthorne, *Hawthorne: Selected Tales and Sketches* (New York: Holt, Reinhardt, and Winston, 1950), p. 154.
91 Tales, p. 155.
92 Tales, p. 160.
93 Tales, p. 161.
94 Nathaniel Hawthorne, *The Scarlet Letter*, Amazon Kindle, Location 506.

the witch, is one of those historical figures. She is "Governor Bellingham's bitter-tempered sister," who was executed a few years later in spite of her prominence. In *The Scarlet Letter*, she attempts to lure the adulteress Hester Prynne into joining the "merry company in the forest," but Hester, unlike Young Goodman Brown, whose Faith held him back only a while, refuses to join because of her daughter Pearl. Had the magistrates taken Pearl from her, however, Hester "would willingly have gone with thee into the forest and signed my name in the Black Man's book too, and that with mine own blood!"[95]

The torment Dimmesdale feels is every bit as real as the witch who hears Dimmesdale's anguished cry from the scaffold and interprets is as "the clamour of the fiends and night-hags, with whom she was well known to make excursions in the forest,"[96] which is equally real even if Dimmesdale had trouble distinguishing them from cries "uttered only within his imagination."[97]

The Scarlet Letter describes the psychological plight of a minister who is simultaneously one of the visible elect on earth and an adulterer, a plight not uncommon among those "saved" by grace alone. Its plot unfolds around three scaffold scenes. The most important for our purposes is the second, during which a guilt-ridden Dimmesdale is driven at midnight to the same scaffold upon which Hester Pyrnne previously had to don the scarlet letter in front of the assembled populace of Boston. This public acknowledgement of guilt was denied to Dimmesdale who had stood by silently, knowing full well that he was Hester's partner in sin. In this second scaffold scene, he bares his chest to an empty public square in an ambiguous gesture which both proclaims and camouflages his guilt.

Dimmesdale finds partial release on the midnight scaffold when he joins hands with Hester and Pearl, but the "tumultuous rush of new life, other life than his own pouring like a torrent into his heart, and hurrying through all his veins, as if the mother and the child were communicating their vital warmth to his half-torpid system,"[98] eventually dissipates because Dimmesdale refuses Pearl's request the he also stand on the scaffold "to-morrow noontide."

Dimmesdale finally acknowledges his guilt in the third scaffold scene. When the letter A appears in the sky no one can tell whether it is real or imagined. Hawthorne attributes the celestial appearance "solely to the disease in his own eye and heart,"[99] even though someone from the town saw the same thing as a sign that Governor Winthrop became an angel when he died. The "dull red light" Dimmesdale saw in the sky had no shape other than

---

95 Hawthorne, *The Scarlet Letter*, p. 55.
96 Hawthorne, *The Scarlet Letter*, p. 81.
97 Hawthorne, *The Scarlet Letter*, p. 83.
98 Hawthorne, *The Scarlet Letter*, p. 85.
99 Hawthorne, *The Scarlet Letter*, p. 87.

Part I: Errand Into the Satanic Wilderness

the one conferred on it by his "guilty imagination," which is a reality which determines his thoughts and his perceptions.

The second scaffold scene depicts the return of the repressed sin of adultery, but more importantly the Puritan repression of sacramental confession, which was seen as one of the impositions on the pure faith which led the Puritans to leave England. Because sacramental confession was the prime example of the "humane Mixtures and Impositions" which necessitated the Puritans' "Errand into the Wilderness," Nathaniel Hawthorne was obsessed with it and its psychological necessity for his entire adult life, confiding to James Russell Lowell that the original plan for *The Scarlet Letter* had Dimmesdale confess his sin to a Catholic priest. The inherent implausibility of a *deus ex machina* which would have ruined the plot did not lead him to abandon the idea of confession. Instead, it intensified his determination to understand its psychological necessity in a world created *ab ovo* by its theological rejection.

The Scarlet Letter is the chronicle of a "hidden sin," which according to Puritan theology should not exist. According to Calvinist theology and the tenets of the Puritan faith, Dimmesdale was a "visible saint" who had been saved by grace alone and had, as a result, no need of the sacraments. The claim was theologically preposterous but widely accepted among the Puritans, and it would take two centuries before Hawthorne could explain how "the outward guise of purity was but a lie, and that, if truth were everywhere to be shown, a scarlet letter would blaze forth on many a bosom besides Hester Prynne's."[100] Hester Prynne's public admission of guilt allowed her to gain insight into the disconnect between essence and existence in the moral life of the Massachusetts Bay Colony. The "form of this earthly saint," which the people of Boston saw as "a venerable minister or magistrate," who was "the model of piety and justice, to whom that age of antique reverence looked up, as to a mortal man in fellowship with angels"[101] turned out to be "the Devil" as Goody Cloyse cried out when she encountered him in the forest with Young Goodman Brown.[102]

If the minister in the forest is the devil, then Roger Chillingworth is the diabolical parody of the father confessor that the Puritans never had. In Chillingworth, Hawthorne created a character halfway between Adam Weishaupt, who transformed the Jesuit examination of conscience into *Seelenanalyse* as a form of social control, and Sigmund Freud, who perfected that technique by transforming it into psychoanalysis. Chillingworth probes Dimmesdale's soul under the guise of administering a "medicine" which only aggravates the disease. Chillingworth thus became "Satan's emissary,"[103] a

---

100 Hawthorne, *The Scarlet Letter*, p. 31, location 1170.
101 Hawthorne, *The Scarlet Letter*, p. 32.
102 Nathaniel Hawthorne, "Young Goodman Brown," In *Hawthorne: Selected Tales and Sketches* (New York: Holt, Reinhardt, and Winston, 1950), p. 153.
103 Hawthorne, *The Scarlet Letter*, p. 63.

Walking with a Bible and a Gun

diabolical agent" who had been granted "the Divine permission, for a season, to burrow into the clergyman's intimacy, and plot against his soul."[104]

Newly arrived in Puritan Boston from England after delays at sea and captivity by Indians, Chillingworth had stood in the crowd near the scaffold when Hester, his wife, who had preceded him to Boston, was forced to don the scarlet letter as the emblem of her adultery. When her eyes met his, he put his finger to his lips imposing on her a vow of silence that would prevent her from revealing he was her husband and allow him access to Dimmesdale as his physician and spiritual advisor. The link between body and soul quickly becomes apparent as Dimmesdale's health declines. His illness "grew out of his heart" and typified, like his long-buried corpse that later blasted plant life above his grave because "some hideous secret that was buried with him" that "he had done better to confess during his lifetime."[105]

"The saint on earth" was in reality "the vilest, the worst of sinners, an abomination."[106] Guilt leads Dimmesdale toward "bloody scourge" and other "practices more in accordance with the old, corrupted faith of Rome than with the better light of the church in which he had been born and bred," [107] but not to the confessional. What ensues is a debate on the psychological and physiological merits of sacramental confession. Because he found no psychic release in the scourge, Dimmesdale is driven "to the verge of a disclosure," which is precisely what Chillingworth was hoping for when he claimed that "all the powers of nature call so earnestly for the confession of sin."

> "That, good sir, is but a phantasy of yours," replied the minister. "There can be, if I forbode aright, no power, short of the Divine mercy, to disclose, whether by uttered words, or by type or emblem, the secrets that may be buried in the human heart. The heart, making itself guilty of such secrets, must perforce hold them, until the day when all hidden things shall be revealed. Nor have I so read or interpreted Holy Writ, as to understand that the disclosure of human thoughts and deeds, then to be made, is intended as a part of the retribution. That, surely, were a shallow view of it. No, these revelations, unless I greatly err, are meant merely to promote the intellectual satisfaction of all intelligent beings, who will stand waiting, on that day, to see the dark problem of this life made plain. A knowledge of men's hearts will be needful to the completest solution of that problem. And I conceive, moreover, that the hearts holding such miserable secrets as you speak of, will yield them up, at that last day, not with reluctance, but with a joy unutterable."

---

104 Hawthorne, *The Scarlet Letter*, p. 63.
105 Hawthorne, *The Scarlet Letter*, p. 67.
106 Hawthorne, *The Scarlet Letter*, pp. 77-8.
107 Hawthorne, *The Scarlet Letter*, p. 78.

Part I: Errand Into the Satanic Wilderness

"Then why not reveal it here?" asked Roger Chillingworth, glancing quietly aside at the minister. "Why should not the guilty ones sooner avail themselves of this unutterable solace?"

"They mostly do," said the clergyman, griping hard at his breast as if affected with an importunate throb of pain. "Many, many a poor soul hath given its confidence to me, not only on the death-bed, but while strong in life, and fair in reputation. And ever, after such an outpouring, oh, what a relief have I witnessed in those sinful brethren! even as in one who at last draws free air, after a long stifling with his own polluted breath. How can it be otherwise? Why should a wretched man—guilty, we will say, of murder—prefer to keep the dead corpse buried in his own heart, rather than fling it forth at once, and let the universe take care of it!"

"Yet some men bury their secrets thus," observed the calm physician.

"True; there are such men," answered Mr. Dimmesdale. "But not to suggest more obvious reasons, it may be that they are kept silent by the very constitution of their nature. Or—can we not suppose it?—guilty as they may be, retaining, nevertheless, a zeal for God's glory and man's welfare, they shrink from displaying themselves black and filthy in the view of men; because, thenceforward, no good can be achieved by them; no evil of the past be redeemed by better service. So, to their own unutterable torment, they go about among their fellow-creatures, looking pure as new-fallen snow, while their hearts are all speckled and spotted with iniquity of which they cannot rid themselves."

"These men deceive themselves," said Roger Chillingworth, with somewhat more emphasis than usual, and making a slight gesture with his forefinger. "They fear to take up the shame that rightfully belongs to them. Their love for man, their zeal for God's service—these holy impulses may or may not co-exist in their hearts with the evil inmates to which their guilt has unbarred the door, and which must needs propagate a hellish breed within them. But, if they seek to glorify God, let them not lift heavenward their unclean hands! If they would serve their fellow-man, let them do it by making manifest the power and reality of conscience, in constraining them to penitential self-abasement! Would thou have me to believe, O wise and pious friend, that a false show can be better—can be more for God's glory, or man's welfare—than God's own truth? Trust me, such men deceive themselves!"

"It may be so," said the young clergyman, indifferently, as waiving a discussion that he considered irrelevant or unseasonable. He had a ready faculty, indeed, of escaping from any topic that agitated his too sensitive and nervous temperament.—"But, now, I would ask of my well-skilled physician, whether, in good sooth, he deems me to have profited by his kindly care of this weak frame of mine?"[108]

"You would tell me, then, that I know all?" said Roger Chillingworth, deliberately, and fixing an eye, bright with intense and concentrated intelligence, on the minister's face. "Be it so! But again! He to whom only the outward and physical evil is laid open, knoweth, oftentimes, but half the evil which he is called upon to cure. A bodily disease, which we look upon as whole and entire within itself, may, after all, be but a symptom of some ailment in the spiritual part. Your pardon once again, good sir, if my speech give the shadow of offence. You, sir, of all men whom I have known, are he whose body is the closest conjoined, and imbued, and identified, so to speak, with the spirit whereof it is the instrument."

"Then I need ask no further," said the clergyman, somewhat hastily rising from his chair. "You deal not, I take it, in medicine for the soul!"

Dimmesdale's rational psychology is based on a radical disjunction between body and soul typical of Hawthorne's age, which claimed that the soul was an angel inhabiting a bodily machine.[109] Chillingworth's rational psychology is more incarnational and, therefore, more acute in understanding that "a sickness, a sore place, if we may so call it, in your spirit hath immediately its appropriate manifestation in your bodily frame."[110]

The consequences of Chillingworth's more sophisticated understanding of the body's relationship to a troubled soul leads him to propose a corresponding treatment:

"Would you, therefore, that your physician heal the bodily evil? How may this be unless you first lay open to him the wound or trouble in your soul?"[111]

"No, not to thee! not to an earthly physician!" cried Mr. Dimmesdale, passionately, turning his eyes, full and bright, and with a kind of fierceness, on old Roger Chillingworth. "Not to thee! But, if it be the soul's disease, then do I commit myself to the one Physician of the soul! He, if it stand with His good pleasure, can cure, or he can kill. Let Him do with me as, in His justice and wisdom, He shall see good. But who art thou, that meddlest in this matter? that dares thrust himself between the sufferer and his God?"

---

108 Hawthorne, *The Scarlet Letter*, p. 67-70
109 See E. Michael Jones, *The Angel and the Machine*.
110 Hawthorne, *The Scarlet Letter*, p. 71.
111 Hawthorne, *The Scarlet Letter*, p. 71.

Part I: Errand Into the Satanic Wilderness

Dimmesdale is, of course, correct in suspecting the ulterior motives behind Chillingworth's Illuminist weaponization of the examination of conscience, but he is wrong in denying the need for sacramental confession which lay behind Illuminist distortions. Confessing to God alone is confessing to no one. It is a gesture that compounds the sin and sets up neurotic psychological reactions to guilt that manifest themselves repeatedly in Protestant cultures which are aware that Christ died for sinners but prohibits them from joining the Church he created for their salvation.

Chillingworth, the Calvinist, blames his behavior on "the old faith." He is both totally depraved and predestined. Chillingworth's behavior is determined by a "dark necessity,"[112] but there is "no substance"[113] in Dimmesdale's penance because he will not acknowledge it in public. "A rare case," Chillingworth muttered after Dimmesdale rushed out of the room "with a frantic gesture."[114]

"I must needs look deeper into it. A strange sympathy betwixt soul and body! Were it only for the art's sake, I must search this matter to the bottom."[115]

Two hundred years after his great, great grandfather hanged witches, Hawthorne gave psychological meaning to the Puritans' metaphysical quest for "the bottom" by creating the archetypal American as a guilt-ridden minister. Existence and essence meet at the frontier. *The Scarlet Letter* is a romance that occupies the neutral ground between essence and existence known as the frontier.

In the false spring which Dimmesdale encounters in the forest when Hester lets her hair down and casts off the scarlet letter, both sinners resolve to escape from their collective past by heading west. After telling Dimmesdale that "What we did had a consecration of its own,"[116] Hester suggests leaving Boston and heading off to "the wilderness . . . until some few miles hence the yellow leaves will show no vestige of the white man's tread," or the guilt which flows from his religion. Citing Satan in *Paradise Lost*, she tells Dimmesdale "there thou art free."[117]

But is the moral law something invented by the white man? The debate would continue until Hawthorne's day; indeed, his neighbor Ralph Waldo Emerson wrote "Nature" to refute the Calvinist understanding of the forest as the abode of the devil. But Dimmesdale retained the skepticism about human nature that he had inherited from his Puritan forbears, realizing that by proposing the frontier as an escape from guilt, Hester wants him to realize a dream:

---

112 Hawthorne, *The Scarlet Letter*, p. 102.
113 Hawthorne, *The Scarlet Letter*, p. 117.
114 Hawthorne, *The Scarlet Letter*, p. 71.
115 Hawthorne, *The Scarlet Letter*, pp. 70-72.
116 Hawthorne, *The Scarlet Letter*, p. 120.
117 Hawthorne, *The Scarlet Letter*, p. 121.

> "It cannot be!" answered the minister, listening as if he were called upon to realize a dream. "I am powerless to go."[118]

But Hester has apparently imbibed from the forest the same spirit which prompted Emerson to write not only "Nature," but also "Self-Reliance." Dimmesdale could follow the example of John Eliot, the apostle to the Indians, and become "the teacher and apostle of the red men. Or, as is more thy nature, be a scholar and a sage among the wisest and the most renowned of the cultivated world. Preach! Write! Act!"[119]

Hester is an Emersonian *avant la lettre* swept up into 19th century illusions about man being born free in the state of nature and capable of returning to that state by a sheer act of the will and a compass that points westward. Hester claims that by removing the scarlet letter "the past is gone." This defiant gesture has an:

> exhilarating effect—upon a prisoner just escaped from the dungeon of his own heart—of breathing the wild, free atmosphere of an unredeemed, unchristianized, lawless region. "Let us not look back," answered Hester Prynne. "The past is gone! Wherefore should we linger upon it now? See! With this symbol I undo it all and make it as if it had never been!"[120]

Hester takes off her cap and lets her luxurious hair down. Emboldened by Hester's gesture, Dimmesdale kisses Pearl, "hoping that a kiss might prove a talisman to admit him into the child's kindlier regards,"[121] only to discover that the minister's kiss is not only meaningless in the forest but that it evokes disgust in Pearl, who "broke away from her mother, and, running to the brook, stooped over it, and bathed her forehead, until the unwelcome kiss was quite washed off and diffused through a long lapse of the gliding water."[122]

As Pearl points out, Dimmesdale can only acknowledge his sin in the dark forest, where confession is meaningless:

> In the dark night-time he calls us to him, and holds thy hand and mine, as when we stood with him on the scaffold yonder! And in the deep forest, where only the old trees can hear, and the strip of sky see it, he talks with thee, sitting on a heap of moss! And he kisses my forehead, too, so that the little brook would hardly wash it off! But, here, in the sunny day, and among all the people, he knows us not; nor must we know him! A strange, sad man is he with his hands always over his heart.[123]

---

[118] Hawthorne, *The Scarlet Letter*, p. 121.
[119] Hawthorne, *The Scarlet Letter*, p. 122.
[120] Hawthorne, *The Scarlet Letter*, p. 125.
[121] Hawthorne, *The Scarlet Letter*, p. 135.
[122] Hawthorne, *The Scarlet Letter*, p. 135.
[123] Hawthorne, *The Scarlet Letter*, p. 146.

Part I: Errand Into the Satanic Wilderness

Intoxicated by the prospect of freedom in the wilderness, Dimmesdale forgot that no man "can wear one face to himself and another to the multitude, without finally getting bewildered as to which may be the true."[124] Dimmesdale and Hester are brought back to reality when Pearl in disgust attempts to wash off Dimmesdale's kiss in the brook which divides them. "I have a strange fancy," observed the sensitive minister, "that this brook is the boundary between two worlds. . . ."[125]

The brook separates reality from illusion. It is synonymous with the frontier, which in nascent America defines the meeting point between Calvinist essence and wilderness existence. After the Puritans failed to impose Calvinism on the wilderness, Emerson, in the person of Hester, tried to impose Rousseau's rejection of original sin on it by way of reaction. Hawthorne, imbued with a wisdom which transcended the narrow confines of New England thought, saw that that project was doomed to fail. America would learn in the expensive school of experience that only existence calls essence into being. The frontier would transform Calvinism, but Dimmesdale is no frontiersman. He is too well versed in lessons of the soul to believe that there can be a geographical cure for guilt. Hester is brought back to reality by Pearl, who stands on the other side of a mysterious dividing line in the middle of the forest. "Wilt thou come across the brook, and own thy mother, now that she has her shame upon her—now that she is sad?" "Yes; now I will!" answered the child, bounding across the brook"[126] which divides existence from essence. Hester puts the letter back on because "the forest cannot hide it."[127] At this point, the evil deed they committed "invests itself with the character of doom" as Hester "gathered up the heavy tresses of her hair and confined them beneath her cap."[128]

The forest is still the realm of the devil. Returning from the forest, Dimmesdale is beset with "impulses . . . to do some strange, wild, wicked thing or other, with a sense that it would be at once involuntary and intentional, in spite of himself, yet growing out of a profounder self than that which opposed the impulse."[129] One of those temptations was to utter "certain blasphemous suggestions that rose into his mind respecting the communion supper."[130] But what were those suggestions? That the "communion supper" was an invalid parody of the Catholic Mass and incapable of dispensing grace? Once again, the repressed returned in the words of the devil, as it had when the minister

---

124 Hawthorne, *The Scarlet Letter*, p. 136.
125 Hawthorne, *The Scarlet Letter*, p. 131.
126 Hawthorne, *The Scarlet Letter*, p. 133.
127 Hawthorne, *The Scarlet Letter*, p. 133.
128 Hawthorne, *The Scarlet Letter*, p. 133.
129 Hawthorne, *The Scarlet Letter*, p. 137.
130 Hawthorne, *The Scarlet Letter*, p. 138.

told the truth about Calvinism in the forest, claiming "evil is the nature of mankind."

Because she has been granted the Satanic power to "penetrate in every bosom, the deep mystery of sin, the fountain of all wicked arts,"[131] Mistress Hibbins knows that the minister has "made a visit into the forest,"[132] and recognizing him as a kindred evil spirit asks for permission to accompany him the next time he goes there because she recognizes their "secret intimacy of connexion."[133]

Unlike Young Goodman Brown, whose "dying hour was gloom," Dimmesdale achieves a redemption of sorts when he acknowledges his sin in public. The sign of that redemption is Pearl's kiss, now freely given because both are standing on the reality side of the brook. In spite of that redemption, Hawthorne can't overcome the pessimism about human nature which he inherited from his Puritan forebears which he depicts in the image of "the ruined wall":

> As a man who had once sinned, but who kept his conscience all alive and painfully sensitive by the fretting of an unhealed wound, he might have been supposed safer within the line of virtue than if he had never sinned at all. And be the stern and sad truth spoken, that the breach which guilt has once made into the human soul is never, in this mortal state, repaired. It may be watched and guarded, so that the enemy shall not force his way again into the citadel, and might even in his subsequent assaults, select some other avenue, in preference to that where he had formerly succeeded. But there is still the ruined wall, and near it the stealthy tread of the foe that would win over again his unforgotten triumph.[134]

The "individual stress and cultural distortion" which the lack of sacramental confession created would recur with monotonous regularity among American Protestants well into the 20th century, as phenomena as diverse as praying in tongues and Promise Keepers showed. William G. McLoughlin argues that one of the *sequelae* of the Salem Witch Trials was the Great Awakening, another example of mass hysteria which occurred roughly forty years later when "the synthesis that had emerged following the Puritan Awakening began to disintegrate."[135]

---

131 Tales, p. 161.
132 Hawthorne, *The Scarlet Letter*, p. 140.
133 Hawthorne, *The Scarlet Letter*, p. 141.
134 Hawthorne, *The Scarlet Letter*, p. 125.
135 McLoughlin, *Revivals, Awakenings, and Reform*, p. 44.

Chapter 3

The Racial Vector of American Identity

There are two vectors for American Identity. The dominant vector is east/west, and its classic presentation is Frederick Jackson Turner's frontier thesis. "The Significance of the Frontier in American History" was delivered as a speech in 1893 at the time of the Columbian exhibition in Chicago, commemorating the 400th anniversary of the discovery of America. It was later published as an article and still later delivered as a series of lectures that led to a professorship at Harvard University.

The east/west vector is ethnic and religious, and it came into being when the first English settlers arrived in the new world at the beginning of the 17th century and began a trek westward that would define American identity. That trek continued throughout the 19th century when large numbers of Irish and German Catholics arrived in the wake of the Potato Famine in Ireland and the Revolution of 1848 in Germany. The high tide of 19th century ethnic immigration from Europe led to the Nativist riots, the founding of the second Ku Klux Klan, and the Immigration Act of 1924 because of the threat it posed to Anglo-Protestant hegemony over American culture.

After World War II, the Anglo-Protestants, now known as White Anglo-Saxon Protestants or WASPs, allied themselves with Jews in liberal groups like Americans for Democratic Action, and created a counter narrative based on a north/south trajectory which was racial and marginalized ethnic or religious considerations. The historical event which overturned the east/west trajectory and installed the racial north/south trajectory of "racial oppression and white-supremacism" as "the dominant feature" and "parametric constant, of United States history"[136] was the Civil Rights Movement of the 1960s. American identity, according to this new, essentially Marxist reading of American history, "as represented in the Declaration of Independence and the Constitution of 1789," saw all of American history as a manifestation of "racial oppression."[137] Theodore W. Allen, who made these claims, stated explicitly that his north/south Marxist racial narrative contradicted Turner's "frontier" thesis, which posited western migration and not slavery as the fundamental

---

136 Theodore W. Allen, *The Invention of the White Race: The Origin of Racial Oppression*, Kindle Edition, p. 1054.
137 Allen, p. 1051.

form of American identity.[138] Allen challenged Turner's frontier hypothesis by claiming that slavery and white privilege, "more than any other factor, has shaped the 'contours of American history'–from the Constitutional Convention of 1787 to the Civil War, to the overthrow of Reconstruction, to the Populist Revolt of the 1890s, to the Great Depression, to the civil rights struggle and 'white backlash' of our own day."[139] Allen knows this because:

> the present-day United States bears the indelible stamp of the African-American civil rights struggle of the 1960s and after, a seal that the "white backlash" has by no means been able to expunge from the nation's consciousness.[140]

Allen based his study on "the records of the seventeenth and early eighteenth centuries,"[141] when the social construct known as whiteness came into being and replaced Marxist categories like "the class struggle dimension of colonial history." The "light of a consciousness raised by the modern civil rights movement,"[142] derived from the Black-Jewish alliance, which began in earnest when the Spingarn brothers created the National Association of Colored People on February 12, 1909. First published in 1994, Allen's book "presents a full-scale challenge to what the author refers to as 'The Great White Assumption,'" namely, "the unquestioning, indeed unthinking acceptance of the 'white' identity of European-Americans of all classes as a natural attribute rather than a social construct."[143] In doing this he turns a social construct into a moral imperative. This decision is problematic because of the challenge it poses to the role of religion, the usual source of moral imperatives in American history.

In his *magnum opus The Invention of the White Race: The Origin of Racial Oppression*, Allen projects these categories onto American history in a way that renders religion and ethnicity epiphenomenal at best and ultimately irrelevant. This transformation becomes almost immediately problematic when he attempts to deal with the Reformation, which is the source of every subsequent social problem in America from the capitalist exploitation of labor, to the policy of genocide which the Puritans inaugurated against the Indians, to the religious discrimination against the Irish in Ireland which was the basis of the penal laws, which drove so many Irishmen to emigrate to America. Every single category upon which Allen bases his argument came into being in the aftermath of the Reformation and contradicts his racial hypothesis,

---

138 Allen, p. 1057.
139 Allen, p. 1058.
140 Allen, p. 1060.
141 Allen, p. 969,
142 Allen, p. 969.
143 Allen, p. 19.

Part I: Errand Into the Satanic Wilderness

which imposed racial categories created three centuries later onto the events he claimed to explain.

The racial, north/south vector of American identity rose to prominence after World War II when the United States government became involved in the social engineering of the American people. Its classic expression is Gunnar Myrdal's book *The American Dilemma*, which referred to America's race problem and was written during World War II, by America's psychological warfare establishment, which was made up of Jews like Louis Wirth and WASPs like Princeton demographer Frank Notestein who were eager to weaponize racial discrimination as a stalking horse for the ethnic cleansing of Catholic ethnics from the big cities of the North.

That plan was codified into law when the Supreme Court handed down its *Brown v. School Board* decision in 1954. In his book on the collapse of the Black-Jewish Alliance, Murray Friedman said that *Brown* was based on the "Jewish science" of disciples of anthropologist Franz Boas. In *Brown vs. School Board*, the United States Supreme Court sided with the Boasian environmentalists against the racial biological determinists in a way that assumed that human nature could be changed by making changes in the environment like urban renewal (*Berman v. Parker* was handed down in the same year) and education. *Brown* led immediately to the Civil Rights Movement, which became the inspiration for the scholars who claimed that race was a social construct which had little or nothing to do with biology, an idea which had fallen into disfavor after the defeat of the Nazi regime in Germany.

Prominent among those scholars was Theodore W. Allen, who also popularized the concept of "white privilege." By the end of the 20th century, Allen's north/south racial trajectory replaced Turner's east/west frontier thesis as the explanation of the basis of American identity. The east/west trajectory corresponded to a confrontation between existence and essence as the crucible out of which American identity emerged. Allen's Marxist racial hypothesis nullified the role of religion, ethnicity, and—even more ironically—environment as essential categories of American identity.

Theodore William Allen was born in Indiana on August 23, 1919. After his family moved to West Virginia, Allen became a coal miner and a union activist with the United Mine Workers. Allen became a member of the Communist Party at the age of 17, and his adoption of Marxist categories informed all of his later writings on race, which he saw as thwarting any united front the proletariat could mount against capitalist oppression.

In the 1940s Allen moved to New York City, where he combined labor activism and intellectual work, doing industrial economic research at the Labor Research Association while teaching economics at the Jefferson School of Social Science, a school founded in New York by the Communist Party in 1944. After that school closed its doors because of pressure from the House Un-American Activities Committee, Allen taught mathematics at the Crown

Heights Yeshiva in Brooklyn, where he held "a variety of jobs, from factory worker to retail clerk, mechanical design draftsman, postal mail handler (and member of the Local of the National Postal Mail Handlers Union), and librarian at the Brooklyn Public Library."[144]

Allen began his career as an independent scholar in 1965, when he along with Noel Ignatiev published "White Blindspot," which popularized the concept of "white skin privilege." In 1967, when the Black-Jewish Alliance collapsed in the wake of the Ocean Hill-Brownsville teacher strike, which pitted Blacks against Jews, and the publication of Harold Cruse's book *The Crisis of the Negro Intellectual*, which complained about Jewish control of the Harlem branch of the Communist Party, Allen co-authored a book entitled *Can White Workers/Radicals Be Radicalized?* with Ignatiev, who would later become the founder of Critical Race Theory at Harvard University. According to historian Jeffrey B. Perry, Allen dedicated "his entire adult life" to "the emancipation of the working class and for socialism."[145] His understanding of the "invention of the white race" was inspired by opposition to the Civil Rights Movement which relied on biology, and it eventually routed the last vestiges of biological determinism in academe, replacing them with "the proposition that race is 'a social and cultural construction,'" which had become so widely accepted by the end of the 20th century that it had become "an academic cliché."[146]

Allen's adoption of racial categories had serious consequences for his attempt to understand the roots of slavery. He either does not understand or falsifies the role religion played in the upheavals of the 16th and 17th centuries, Allen describes the effect of the English Protestant Reformation on "racial oppression in Ireland" as "adventitious"[147] but admits that peasant uprisings, "at intervals between 1530 and 1560 set half the counties of England in a blaze."[148] He also admits that peasant uprisings lasted until 1650. The Nine Years' War[149] in Ireland, sometimes known as the Tyrone Rebellion, didn't end until 1603 and led to the notorious Penal Laws. Add to that the various Jacobite Risings of the 18th century, and we are talking about centuries of religious wars spawned by the Reformation, but Allen imposes Marxist categories on them all to disguise their real cause, which was the Protestant break with the Catholic Church.

---

144 "Theodore W. Allen," *Wikipedia: The Free Encyclopedia*, https://en.wikipedia.org/wiki/Theodore_W._Allen

145 "Theodore W. Allen," *Wikipedia*.

146 "Theodore W. Allen," *Wikipedia*.

147 Allen, p. 666.

148 Allen, p. 668.

149 "Nine Years' War (Ireland)," *Wikipedia: The Free Encyclopedia*, https://en.wikipedia.org/wiki/Nine_Years%27_War_(Ireland)

Part I: Errand Into the Satanic Wilderness

The central thesis of Allen's *magnum opus* is that "there were no 'white' people" in Virginia when the first Africans arrived there in 1619.[150] The work force in the Virginia plantation at that time was English: "they had been English when they left England, and naturally they and their Virginia-born children were English, they were not 'white.'"[151]

Allen is right correct that only "contradictions and howling absurdities . . . result from attempts to splice genetics and sociology."[152] Expositions of "phenotype" explain nothing when it comes to the causality of action in human history. Both the plantation owners and their indentured slaves were English. They were not American, because that identity did not exist then; "they had been English when they left England, and naturally they and their Virginia-born children were English, they were not 'white.'"[153]

As in England, the economic oppression and dislocation which flowed from the Reformation led to revolution. But by proposing race as the fundamental category which explains life in the Virginia plantation, Allen ignores the significance of religion in restructuring life in England and the role it played in the creation of England's colonies abroad. Blinded by the materialist categories he derived from Marxism, Allen refers to the unemployment which the enclosure laws created as "the capitalist overthrow of the English peasantry in the first half of the sixteenth century"[154] as if it had nothing to do with the looting of Church property and other confiscations known as the Reformation. Instead of linking that unrest with its obvious cause in religious strife, Allen associates the religious wars of the 16th, 17th, and 18th centuries with the bread riot of 1381 known as Wat Tyler's Rebellion, which Allen claims "wrought the end of the feudal order in England."[155] To say the feudal order did not exist in England in the 15th century is just one of many preposterous claims which flow from the naïve projection of Marxist categories on an age which was deeply religious. Allen then describes the Pilgrimage of Grace as somehow connected with Wat Tyler's rebellion but disconnected from Catholic concerns. After admitting that "Henry VIII's suppression of monasteries" and unnamed "ecclesiastical issues"[156] played a role in the northern rebellion known as the Pilgrimage of Grace, Allen assures us that "the first demands of the peasants were social and not religious,"

---

150 Allen, p. 14.
151 Allen, p. 14.
152 Allen, p. 13.
153 Allen, p. 14.
154 Allen, p. 666.
155 Allen, p. 668.
156 Allen, p. 669.

because for them it was a class struggle "of the poor against the rich," based on their demands "against raised rents and enclosures."[157]

The Pilgrimage of Grace became a serious threat to the hegemony of the Reformed party in England when Robert Aske, a country gentleman and lawyer took York with an armed force of around 30,000 armed men on October 24, 1536.[158] If the first demands weren't religious, why was one of the rebel demands "a return of England to papal obedience."[159]

Because that return would have serious economic consequences for the Duke of Norfolk and other members of the nobility who had enriched themselves with the theft of Church property, those demands were never taken seriously by them, and negotiations became simply a ruse which played for time "until adequate forces could be assembled" at which point all of the concessions were forgotten and Norfolk went on the offensive. Aske paid dearly for placing his trust in a representative of perfidious Albion. He was executed for treason, and the Pilgrimage of Grace "achieved nothing."[160] When Allen tells us that "The peasants fought," but in the end they could not stop the "rich ... stealing the property of the poor,"[161] he should have instead said "stealing the property of the Church" because the poor by definition did not own property, if by property we mean land. The poor, however, were the beneficiaries of Church sponsored Purgatory societies, which allowed them to graze their sheep on the lands put to that use by deceased benefactors in exchange for prayers for their souls. The violent uprooting of this and similar religious regulations of economic exchange led to the Pilgrimage of Grace in England and Bacon's Rebellion in Virginia.

The terrifying possibility that African slaves and Irish slaves might unite as proletarians became a reality during Bacon's Rebellion of 1676-77. In order to prevent further collaboration, the "ruling elite," according to Allen "deliberately instituted a system of racial privileges in order to define and establish the 'white race.'"[162] Allen says that the English oligarchs suppressed rebellion by deliberately creating a middle class which would ride herd on the newly created class of beggars and wage slaves, but he fails to link the creation of that class of beggars to the looting of the monasteries and the subsequent enclosure of arable land during the Reformation, which brought them into being. Allen cites Eric Williams who asserts that "white servitude was the

---

[157] Allen, p. 669.
[158] "Pilgrimage of Grace," *Britannica*, https://www.britannica.com/event/Pilgrimage-of-Grace
[159] "Pilgrimage of Grace," *Britannica*.
[160] "Pilgrimage of Grace," *Britannica*.
[161] Allen, p. 670.
[162] Allen, p. 642.

historic base upon which slavery was constructed."[163] He also cites Lerone Bennett, Jr's claim that "white servitude was the proving ground" for black chattel slavery:

> The plantation pass system, the slave trade, the sexual exploitation of servant women, the whipping-post and slave chain and branding iron, the overseer, the house servant, the Uncle Tom: all these mechanisms were tried out and perfected on white men and women.... [I]t is plain that nothing substantial can be said about the mechanisms of black bondage in America except against the background and within the perspective of white bondage in America.[164]

Allen, however, fails to see that "white servitude" was a product of the Reformation, which paved the way for slavery in the new world by first creating a state church which served the interest of the looters at the expense of the general population, which was reduced to penury, and later, at the time of the Puritans, by giving looters religious sanction by identifying them as latter day Hebrews, whose enemies were *ipso facto* Amalek, who were to be exterminated in the name of God. The economic system which was based on slavery in the Virginia plantation and came to be known as capitalism flowed from these perverse religious principles, which came into being because of the Reformation. William Cobbett understood this connection.

---

163 Allen, p. 723.
164 Allen, p. 723.

Chapter 4

The Reformation as Looting Operation

Karl Marx was a fervent admirer of William Cobbett's understanding of the Reformation, probably because Cobbett was so acute in pointing out that capitalism as well as Protestantism were based on theft. Marx's followers, however, have become so intoxicated with the idea that religion is a form of opium, that they have ignored its significance in world history, especially in the period when capitalism came into being.

When Parliament passed the Act of Supremacy in 1534, making the king the head of the Church in England, the result, according to Cobbett, was widespread misery:

> As this church, "by law established" advanced, all the remains of Christian charity vanished before it. The indigent, whom the Catholic Church had so tenderly gathered under her wings were now, merely for asking alms, branded with red-hot irons and made slaves, though no provision was made to prevent them from perishing from hunger and cold; and England, so long famed as the land of hospitality, generosity, ease and plenty, and security to person and property, became under a Protestant church, a scene of repulsive selfishness, of pack-horse toil, of pinching want, or rapacity and plunder and tyranny that made the very names of law and justice a mockery.[165]

Parliament then passed the Act of Succession, which "legalized Henry's marriage with Anne Boleyn, as well as decreeing that any children of theirs would be legitimate heirs of the crown."[166] Cobbett claims that "The couple jogged on apparently without quarreling for about three years" because Henry had "begun the grand work of confiscation, plunder and devastation" and therefore did not "have a great deal of time for family squabbles."[167]

In January 1536 Queen Catherine died, and five months later the king's new wife died too after being charged with treason, adultery and incest with her brother Lord Rockford. Between those two deaths, in March of 1536,

---

165 William Cobbett, *A History of the Protestant Reformation in England and Ireland* (New York: P. J. Kenedy, 1895), p. 115.
166 Bella Wyborn d'Abrera, *The King with a Pope in his Belly* (Melbourne and London: Hill House Publishers, 2008), p. 81.
167 Cobbett, *Reformation*, p. 31.

Parliament decreed the looting of 376 monasteries. The main executor of that plan was Thomas Cromwell, Thomas More's successor, who had arranged a "visitation" of the monasteries the year before to ascertain where the loot might be found. Another purpose of that visitation was to find evidence of moral dereliction that could used as a pretext to seize the property of the monks and nuns.

Like Jakob Fugger, the Catholic banker from Augsburg who opposed Luther, Cromwell had spent his youth in Venice, where he learned the usury trade. Unlike Jakob Fugger, Cromwell served the Venetians as a mercenary. Like Jakob Fugger, Cromwell returned to his native land to put what he had learned in Italy into practice, but unlike Jakob Fugger, Cromwell put his understanding of finance in the service of the new gospel which Luther and Calvin were preaching on the continent, and which the Fugger family abhorred. Luther hated the Fuggers and the economic system they helped create in the Germanies, but according to the cunning of reason, the Protestants in England were the first to declare that usury was no sin. England made the system of state-sponsored usury which came to be known as capitalism the law of the land and the economic system of the modern world. The first step was to pass acts taking from the pope all authority and power over the Church in England and giving to the King all authority in ecclesiastical matters.

Once the Parliament had been cowed into making a king into a pope and a bastard into an heir, it could hardly object to turning the Church's property into the king's personal treasure chest. With the vision of what had happened to John Fisher and Thomas More still fresh in their minds, the Parliament was in no mood to resistance the theft of church property. It was either share the loot or share the fate of Fisher and More. Or as the king put it, "I hear . . . that my bill will not pass, but I will have it pass or I will have some of your heads." At that point, "the bill passed, and all was given him as he desired."[168]

What followed was without precedent in the history of Christian England, both in the ferocity of the looters and the defenseless surprise and horror of the victims. Cobbett captures the gist of what happened in his compelling account:

> Think of a respectable peaceful, harmless and pious family broken in upon all of a sudden, by a brace of burglars, with murder written on their scowling brows, demanding an instant production of their title-deed, money and jewels; imagine such a scene as this and you have then some idea of the visitations of these monsters who came with the grimace of the tyrant on their lips, who menaced the victims with charges of high treason, whose recluse and peaceful lives rendered them wholly unfit to cope with at once crafty and desperate villainy.[169]

---

168 Cobbett, *Reformation*, p. 80.
169 Cobbett, *Reformation*, pp. 78-9.

Part I: Errand Into the Satanic Wilderness

The wealth the monasteries had accumulated over 900 years disappeared forever in a matter of weeks. It included the gold which had been passed on from antiquity and found service in adorning the altars of the kingdom, where it served not only as a store of value but a reminder that the purpose of all earthly possessions was in service to the world to come. The gold which had adorned sacred books was ripped off those books and then trodden into the mud in the looters' haste for more plunder:

> Never, in all probability, since the world began, was there so rich a harvest of plunder. The ruffians of Cromwell entered the convents; they tore down the altars to get away this gold and silver; ransacked the chests and drawers of the monks and nuns; tore off the covers of books that were ornamented with the precious metals. These books were all in manuscript. Single books had taken, in many cases, half a lifetime to compose and to copy out fair. Whole libraries, the getting of which together had taken ages upon ages and had cost immense sums of money, were scattered abroad by these hellish ruffians, when they had robbed the covers of the rich ornaments. The ready money, in the convents, down to the last shilling was seized.[170]

Cowed by the king's threats, the leadership class in England turned on their own people. This looting of 645 monasteries, 90 colleges, 110 hospitals and 2374 chanteries and free chapels did more than deprive the people of England of a wealth of property put to social use; it brought about the redefinition of property itself. A century and a half after the looting, the Whig placeman John Locke redefined the notion of private property as absolute in both right and use in a way congenial to the descendants of the looters who reasserted their hegemony in the wake of the consolidation of Protestant power during the Glorious Revolution. The change in the conception of property in England began in practice—not in theory—when Parliament, reacting to the carrot of shared loot and the stick of ignominious death, agreed to condone the king's theft. "To obtain that concurrence of the parliament, he held out to those who composed it, a participation in the spoils of the monasteries."[171] Theory followed praxis; praxis did not follow theory, as Tawney indicated in *Religion and the Rise of Capitalism*. Capitalism did not flow from Protestant theology; Protestant theology flowed from the need to justify Capitalism and the looting upon which it was based. Tawney claims that the epitaph of property was written by Locke when he wrote that "The supreme power cannot take from any man any part of his property without his own consent."[172]

---

170 Cobbett, *Reformation*, pp. 78-9.
171 Cobbett, *Reformation*, p. 77.
172 R. H. Tawney, *Religion and the Rise of Capitalism: a Historical Study* (Holland Memorial Lectures, 1922) (Gloucester, Mass: Peter Smith, 1962), p. 258.

Since Capitalism was born out of theft, in particular the theft of Church property which the Whig magnates still held tightly in their grasp, Locke's definition is rich in irony, an irony not lost on Tawney who claims that Locke's platitudinous redefinition of property was "forgotten as soon as it was written. For to the upper classes in the 18th century, the possession of landed property by a poor man seems in itself a surprising impertinence which it was the duty of Parliament to correct, and Parliament responded to the call of its relatives outside the House with the pious zeal of family affection."[173]

Unlike the religious leaders of the Reformation, who all sounded like Scholastics when they wrote about economic matters, Locke granted property unheard of rights. In fact, there is something bordering on the sacred in Locke's redefinition of property rights.

The key to understanding the origin of capitalism, however, is praxis not theory, and the praxis which theory needed to justify in subsequent generations was the theft of Church property. The looting was the fait accompli around which all theory needed to be arranged. The looting was the original sin of English capitalism that all subsequent theory was created to justify. Theology was nothing more than a pretext to distract the populace from the looting of its spiritual and material patrimony. Tawney catches the gist of the transaction nicely "The upstart aristocracy of the future had their teeth in the carcass, and, having tasted blood, they were not to be whipped off by a sermon."[174]

Only with the gradual acceptance of the looting did ideas, financed largely by the looters, began to change. Even David Hume, no stranger to the Whig financing of ideas, claimed that Church property, having social use, influenced the definition of property when he described monks as, "Not having equal motives to avarice with other men, they were the best and most indulgent landlords."[175] Cobbett seconded this thought when he wrote: "When the church's lands became private property, the rents were raised, the money spent at a distance from the estates, and the tenants exposed to the rapacity of stewards."[176] Concretely, the social use of property as inaugurated by the Catholic Church in England meant that even in Surrey, a section of England with "very little natural wealth in it":

> It would have been a work of some difficulty for a man so to place himself, even in this poor heathy county, at six miles distance from a place where the door of hospitality was always open to the poor, to the aged, the orphan, the widow and the stranger. Can any man now place himself in that whole county within any number of miles of any such door?[177]

---

173 Tawney, *Religion and the Rise of Capitalism*, p. 400.
174 Tawney, *Religion and the Rise of Capitalism*, p. 143.
175 Cobbett, *Reformation*, p. 108.
176 Cobbett, *Reformation*, p. 108.
177 Cobbett, *Reformation*, p. 90.

Part I: Errand Into the Satanic Wilderness

The Reformation was a looting operation in both England and Germany, but it was carried out more effectively and more ruthlessly in England, where power was more centralized. Heinrich Pesch, S.J., the Aquinas of Catholic economic thought, claims that economic progress ended with the Reformation:

> The era of humanism and of the Reformation constitutes a deep incursion into the continuing economic, and especially into the agricultural conditions in Germany. With it begins a new period. The continuity of prior development is interrupted, and the peasant middle class is destroyed and the farmer himself reduced to most degrading serfdom.[178]

To cow the Catholic populace into accepting the new order of things and to safeguard their newly acquired loot, the representatives of the new capitalist regime had to devise what Pesch calls "the absolute police state of the early modern era." This police state "represented a relapse back toward the ancient state of the Roman imperial era," and it "brought with it an intolerable excess of state sovereignty." That meant that "there was virtually no recognition of any legal limits to state dominion over its citizens."[179]

The economic theory which accompanied this police state was the proto-Capitalist theory known as mercantilism. The goal of mercantilism was the accumulation of gold by the state and by the powerful actors who controlled the affairs of state. After the Reformers broke with the Catholic Church, the modern state, and in particular Holland, France, and England in this period, was to conduct its affairs divorced from moral considerations. "The moral law, integrity, justice and humanity for all practical purposes no longer had any bearing on regulating international relations. Impassioned selfishness, brutal supremacy, malice and cunning decided all issues."[180] The entire period from 1600 to 1800, during which chattel slavery came into being in America, was "one marked by warfare lasting for years and decades."[181]

Any economic system this brutal and wasteful was bound to cause a reaction, and mercantilism gave birth by way of reaction to laissez faire economics which became the dominant economic theory in England and France by the late 18th century and early 19th centuries. "The excess of regulation gave rise to the desire for greater freedom, and it eventually put an end to the police state...."[182]

Both mercantilism (or nascent capitalism) and the laissez-faire capitalism which succeeded it shared a contempt for the moral law, which would have

---

178 Heinrich Pesch, *Liberalism, Socialism and Christian Social Order Book II* (Lewiston, ME: The Edwin Mellen Press, 2000), p. 188.
179 Heinrich Pesch, *Lehrbuch der Nationalökonomie*, translated and edited by Rupert J. Ederer, (Lewiston, NY: Edwin Mullen Press, 2002), I, 1, p. 211.
180 Pesch, *Lehrbuch*, II, 1, p. 64.
181 Pesch, *Lehrbuch*, II, 1, p. 64.
182 Pesch, *Lehrbuch*, I, 1, p. 211.

increasingly disastrous consequences because "If there is no recognition of a natural law, the state is left to its own resources; its only underlying basis then is force and violence which have to bow before superior power and greater force of a successful revolution."[183] The dialectic which began in the 16th century with the looting of Church property and eventuated in capitalism reached fruition in the 19th century, when it was confronted by its nemesis revolution.

Shakespeare, writing when the great looting of Church property was still a memory fresh in the mind of every Englishman, encapsulated the essence or unwritten constitution of the new regime in Ulysses' famous speech in *Troilus and Cressida*, when he predicted that removing statecraft and economic life from the purview of the moral law would bring about the reign of the "universal wolf," appetite.[184]

The creation of "private property" in the modern sense of the term, which is to say, property over which the owner had absolute rights, was a consequence of the looting and a reaction to the insecurity which it engendered, lest another thief come along and steal the stolen goods from the thief who stole them in the first place. Both private property and capitalism found their origin in a looting operation which was sanctified under the name of religious reform:

> Like all the other wild schemes and cruel projects relative to the poor, we trace it at once back to the "Reformation," that great source of the poverty and misery and degradation of the main body of the people of this kingdom. The "Reformation" despoiled the working classes of their patrimony; it tore from them that which nature and reason had assigned them; it robbed them of that relief for the necessitous, . . . which had been confirmed to them by the law of God and the law of the land. It brought a compulsory, a grudging, an unnatural mode of relief, calculated to make the poor and the rich hate each other, instead of binding them together as the Catholic mode did, by the bonds of Christian charity. But of all of its consequences that of introducing a married clergy has, perhaps, been the most prolific in mischief. This has absolutely created an order for the procreation of dependents on the state: for the procreation of thousands of persons annually, who have no fortunes of their own and who must be somehow maintained by burdens imposed upon the people.[185]

For 900 years, human labor had been stored in England's monasteries, where it was put to social use. That stream of labor was diverted by the looting of Church property, and from then onward the wealth of England flowed into the pockets of a few influential looters and the rest of the population was left to its own devices, which meant more often than not, pauperism, poverty and

---

183 Pesch, *Lehrbuch*, I, 1, p. 213.
184 Shakespeare, *Troilus*, 119-124.
185 Cobbett, *Reformation*, p. 62.

Part I: Errand Into the Satanic Wilderness

proletarianism. Cobbett traces "the immediate cause" of "the poverty and degradation of the main body of the people . . . back to the Reformation, one of the effects of which was to destroy those Monastic institutions, which . . . retain the produce of labor in the proper places and distributed it in a way naturally tending to make the lives of the people easy and happy."[186]

As in Florence during the 15th century, the cleverest thieves became bankers. Thomas Cromwell, who learned Italian financial techniques in Venice, soon started lending out the wealth he acquired from looting at usurious interest rates. The clever looters could acquire the property of the less clever looters by lending them money and then foreclosing their mortgages when they could no longer meet their payments. As the property of the Church migrated from the hands of the looters into the hands of the usurers, the new economic regime which had grown up in violent reaction to the Catholicism of the Middle Ages and which we call Capitalism took on its final form and became a regime of state-sponsored usury. Capitalism began with the theft of labor. In this instance, it began with the confiscation of the labor that had been accumulated in monasteries, which was then transferred into the hands of absentee landlords, who, if they mortgaged their property, ended up handing it over to the usurers. The revenues which once accrued from the application of labor to the soil and were held in trust by the monasteries were now "carried away to a great distance, and expended amongst those from whose labor bore no part of them."[187]

"Plunder," Cobbett says by way of summation, "was the mainspring of the Reformation. . . . The 'reformation' was not the work of virtue, of fanaticism, of error, of ambition, but of a love of plunder. This was its great animating principle; this it began in; in this it proceeded till there was nothing left for it to work on."[188]

By May 1536, the king had tired of looting for the nonce. With his greed satiated for the moment, he returned to his primary vice, lust, newly awakened by Jane Seymour, whom Anne unluckily discovered sitting on the king's knee. Jane Seymour finally provided the king with a male heir. The future King Edward was a sickly child who never knew his mother because her life had been sacrificed at his birth by a king avid for a male heir.

On May 19, 1536 Anne Boleyn was beheaded in the tower after having been accused of incest with her brother, who was also executed for the same crime. Cobbett describes the legislation of March 1536 as "an act of sheer tyranny."[189] The act enabling the confiscation of Church property:

---

186 Cobbett, *Reformation*, p. 70.
187 Cobbett, *Reformation*, p. 73.
188 Cobbett, *Reformation*, p. 44.
189 Cobbett, *Reformation*, p. 73.

began the ruin and degradation of the main body of the people of England and Ireland; as it was the first step taken, in legal form, for robbing the people under the pretense of reforming their religion, as it was the precedent on which the future plunderers proceeded, until they had completely impoverished the country; as it was the first of a series of deeds of rapine by which this formerly well-fed and well-clothed people have in the end been reduced to rags and to worse than jail allowance for food.[190]

The looting of Church property in England took place on an unprecedented scale. The princes in Germany, no less rapacious than the King of England and no less avid in their greed to seize Church property, simply could not loot on such a grand scale because of the limited size of their domains. The monasteries which the Benedictine monks had founded almost a millennium ago represented a store of value which enriched the country by putting that stored wealth at the service of the common good. A monastery, according to Cobbett:

> was the center of a circle in the country, naturally drawing to it all that were in want of relief, advice, and protection, and containing a body of men or of women, having no cares of their own and having wisdom to guide the inexperienced and wealth to relieve the distressed.[191]

What preceded that theft was 900 years of labor in the form of Christian culture which had decreed that property was to be put to social use. By the time Cobbett wrote his jeremiad, that idea had disappeared from the mind of the Englishman who by then had convinced himself that the wretched poverty which the workingman suffered in the 19th century had always existed. As Cobbett put it, "Englishmen in general suppose that there were always poor-laws and paupers in England. They ought to remember that for 900 years under the Catholic religion there were neither."[192]

Capitalism would never grow beyond its origins in looting. The looting of Libyan assets by Hilary Clinton, the American Secretary of State, in the spring of 2011 could be traced backward in a direct line to the looting of Church property in 1536 as two different expressions of capitalism's formal causality. Religious reform was used as the theoretical justification for the looting in England in 1536 every bit as much as humanitarian concern was used in 2011 to justify the looting of $30 billion in Libyan assets. Then as now, "Religion, conscience was always the pretext, but in one way or another, robbery, plunder was always the end."[193]

---

190 Cobbett, *Reformation*, p. 81.
191 Cobbett, *Reformation*, p. 74.
192 Cobbett, *Reformation*, p. 81.
193 Cobbett, *Reformation*, p. 101.

Part I: Errand Into the Satanic Wilderness

Shakespeare agreed with Cobbett but was unwilling to lose his head for the privilege of saying so explicitly, and so he set the dramas which couched his critique in safely distant ancient lands. Ulysses' speech in *Troilus and Cressida* is a damning description of the trajectory of revolutionary capitalism. The same holds true of Timon of Athens. When Timon is informed by Flavius his steward that his extravagance has led to insolvency, Timon, like one of the looting lords in England, tells him, "Let all my lands be sold,"[194] apparently unaware that they are already mortgaged to the hilt.

> Flavius: 'Tis all engaged, some forfeited and gone
> And what remains will hardly stop the mouth
> Of present dues. The future comes apace.
> What shall defend the interim? And at length
> How goes our reckoning?

Timon, the great landowner, is stunned by the revelation that he is out of money and can only exclaim, "To Lacedaemon did my land extend." Like the less clever looters in England, Timon failed to understand that the looting didn't stop when the last monastery fell into private hands. Usury followed the first wave of looting. Shakespeare was too young to have been an eyewitness, but the experience was so universal that it was fresh in everyone's memory. The Reformation brought about the rise of usury by suppressing the Church, which had been the only bulwark against it:

> The Catholic church held the lending of money for interest, or gain, to be directly in the face of the gospel. It considered all such gain as usurious and of course criminal. It taught the making of loans without interest, and thus it prevented the greedy minded from amassing wealth in that way in which wealth is most easily amassed. Usury amongst Christians was wholly unknown until the wife-killing tyrant had laid his hands on the property of the church and the poor.[195]

Once the influence of the Catholic Church was destroyed, usury made a rapid return and England became "a den of thieves and of thieves too, of the lowest and most despicable character."[196] Shakespeare based the plot of Timon of Athens on the historical fact that usury followed hard on the heels of looting. "Before two lifetimes had passed, very nearly the whole of the loot had left the hands of the impoverished crown, and was in the power of the new millionaires, and their landed class had already begun to govern England and to destroy the old popular monarchy of the English."[197]

---

[194] William Shakespeare, "Timon of Athens," in *Shakespeare: The Complete Works*, edited by G. B. Harrison, 1315-1348, (New York: Harcourt, Brace & World, Inc., 1952), Act II, scene ii.
[195] Cobbett, *Reformation*, p. 104.
[196] Cobbett, *Reformation*, p. 107.
[197] Belloc, p. 114.

England was now ruled by a clique of usurers, as Alcibiades, the soldier who shed his blood defending Athens, learns to his shock and chagrin when he is banished. "Banish me?" Alcibiades exclaims. No, he declaims, rather "Banish usury" instead, because it is usury "that makes the Senate ugly."

> I have kept back their foes
> While they have told their money and let out
> Their coin upon large interest—I myself
> Rich only in large hurts. All those for this?
> Is this the balsam that the usuring Senate
> Pours into captains' wounds? Banishment?[198]

Usury had rendered life in England "nasty, brutish, and short," to use Hobbes' phrase:

> In London, groups of tradesmen . . . formed actual syndicates to exploit the market. Rack-renting, evictions, and the conversions of arable land to pasture were the natural result, for the surveyors wrote up values at each transfer, and unless the purchaser squeezed his tenants, the transaction would not pay.[199]

Once the looters realized that they could mortgage their stolen properties they had stolen in exchange for ready cash, cash began to chase property, and an orgy of land speculation followed. The "furor of land speculation" between 1540 and 1550 began when the guilds and chantries which came onto the market in 1547 were added to the Abbey lands which had come onto the market a decade earlier. These lands were "bought for the rise." The land was now owned not to bring forth food but rather to be held for a time and sold for a profit so that the speculator could profit off of the on-going real estate bubble, a practice which would have serious consequences for labor:

> The lands of the Abbey of Whitby, for example, pass first to the Crown, and are then sold by it to the Duke of Northumberland, who in turn sells them to Sir John Yorke. . . . When property changed hands three times in the course of ten days, it could hardly fail to be rack-rented or the transaction would not pay. What happened to the tenants? Here and there, as at Whitby and Washerne, a bitter outburst against their new masters shows that the result has been what we should expect. But for the rest, a cloud descends, and we cannot say. It is only in such occasional glimpses that we catch the solid earth shifting beneath the feet of those who till it.[200]

---

198 Shakespeare, *Timon*, Act III, scene vi.
199 R. H. Tawney, *The Agrarian Problem in the 16th Century* (New York: Longmans, Green, and Co, 1912), p. 140.
200 Tawney, *Agrarian*, pp. 381-2.

Part I: Errand Into the Satanic Wilderness

Speculation led to rack-renting and enclosure, and enclosure led to expulsion from the land, vagabondage and poverty:

> Observers were agreed that the increase in pauperism had one capital cause in the vagrancy produced by the new agrarian regime; and the English Poor Law system, or the peculiar part of it providing for relief of the able-bodied, which England was the first of European countries to adopt, came into existence partly as a form of social insurance against the effect of the rack rents and evictions, which England was the first European country to experience.[201]

By 1548, the seizure of Church property had led to the enclosure crisis. For centuries England's main export had been wool, first raw wool to the weavers of Florence and then as finished cloth to the markets in Antwerp. Once the lords of manors had acquired large tracts of Church land by theft, they had no compunction about "the cutting adrift of a piece of land from the common course of cultivation in use, by placing a hedge or paling round it, and utilizing it according to the discretion of the individual encloser, usually with the object of pasturing sheep."[202]

The issue of enclosure had begun at least as early as 1460 when Medici agents were buying up wool for their textile factories in Florence. At that time, a chantry priest in Warwickshire wrote a detailed account of its effects. If, however, the problem existed before the confiscation of the monastic estates, its aggravation by the fury of spoilation let loose by Henry and Cromwell is not open to serious question. "The greatest popular outcry against enclosing occurred about the middle of the 16th century, in the years 1548 to 1550."[203] "Agrarian plunder," Tawney tells us, "stirred the cupidity of the age," and "for ten years a sinister hum, as of the floating of an immense land syndicate, with favorable terms for all sufficiently rich, or influential or mean to get in on the ground floor"[204] provided the background noise of an immense looting operation. The movement began with the greed of the landlords, but it was:

> accompanied by land speculation and rack-renting, which is intensified by the land hunger which causes successful capitalists who have money in trade, to buy up land as a profitable investment for their savings, and by the sale of corporate property which took place on the dissolution of the monasteries and the confiscation of part of the gild estates.[205]

The first consequence was a rise in prices; the second was a drop in employment as small holdings were thrown together and the laborer "is driven off the

---

201 Tawney, *Agrarian*, p. 4.
202 Tawney, *Agrarian*, p. 6.
203 Tawney, *Agrarian*, p. 11.
204 Tawney, *Religion*, p. 138.
205 Tawney, *Agrarian*, pp. 6-7.

land, either by direct eviction, or by a rise in rents and fines or by mere intimidation."[206]

A pall settled over England in the wake of the Reformation. The enclosures led to "a drift into the towns and a general lowering in the standard of rural life, due to the decay of the class which formerly sent recruits to the learned professions, which was an important counterpoise to the power of the great landed proprietors, and which was the backbone of the military forces of the country."[207] This pall coincided with capitalism, and it has never been dispelled. The looting of the monasteries caused a disruption of the social order that drove men into bankruptcy and then turned them into revolutionaries.

After Timon discovers that he is bankrupt, he urges those who find themselves in a similar situation to turn on their new masters:

> Timon: Bankrupts, hold fast.
> Rather than render back, out with your knives,
> And cut your trusters' throats! Bound servants
> Steal!
> Large-handed robbers your grave masters are,[208]

Timon, now living in a cave by the seashore, discovers gold while looking for a root to eat. He then gives a speech indicating that gold has brought about the transvaluation of all traditional values:

> What is here?
> Gold? Yellow, glittering, precious gold? No gods,
> I am no idle votaries. Roots, you clear Heavens!
> Thus much of this will make black white, foul fair,
> Wrong right, base noble, old young, coward valiant.
> This yellow slave
> Will knit and break religions, bless the accursed,
> Make the hoar leprosy adored, place thieves,
> And give them title, knew and approbation
> With Senators on the bench. This is it
> That makes the wappened widow wed again—
> She, whom the spital house and ulcerous sores
> Would cast the gorge at—this embalms and spices
> To the April day again. Come, damned earth,
> Thou common whore of mankind, that put'st at odds.
> Among the rout of nation, I will make thee
> Do thy right nature.

---

206 Tawney, *Agrarian*, p. 7.
207 Tawney, *Agrarian*, p. 8.
208 William Shakespeare, *Timon of Athens*, Act IV, scene I, Without the Walls of Athens.

Part I: Errand Into the Satanic Wilderness

Timon addresses his speech to two whores, who accompany Alcibiades as camp followers of his army. Whoring becomes a metaphor for commerce corrupted by usury because, as Timon puts it, "They love thee not that use thee." Since usury is universal, the revolutionaries will have to kill everyone:

> Let not thy sword skip one
> Pity not honored age for his white beard.
> He is an usurer.

The prospect of wide-spread slaughter hardly concerns Timandra the whore. She represents the universal corruption which has descended on England in the wake of the looting of Church property. Like Cranmer, the representative of the first estate, and Cromwell, the representative of the second, Timandra wants "more gold." She tells Timon: "Believe't that we'll do anything for gold."[209]

As in Athens so in England, usury brought about insurrection. Speculation led to rack-renting and enclosure. Rack-renting and enclosure led to insurrection.

---

209 Shakespeare, *Timon of Athens*, Act IV, scene I.

Chapter 5

Bacon's Rebellion and the Invention of Whiteness

The insurrection in Virginia was known as Bacon's Rebellion. As in Protestant England, so in its colony in Virginia: "The people heartily detested these Protestant tyrants and their acts. General discontent prevailed, and this in some areas, broke out into open insurrection."55 The Virginia plantation aristocracy, in collaboration with the same group of people who enslaved the Irish on the Ulster plantation, which came into being two years after the founding of Virginia, "invented the 'white race' as a social-control mechanism in response to the labor solidarity manifested in the later, civil-war stages of Bacon's Rebellion (1676–77)" when "foure hundred English and Negroes in Arms"[210] united in a gesture of proletarian solidarity which galvanized the owners of Virginia plantation's large tobacco plantations into inventing the "white race" as "a ruling-class social-control formation."[211] Allen's Marxist preference for proletarian revolution as a paradigm of world history moved him to cite revolution and not the religious dislocation which caused it as the mainstream of world history:

> the Haitian Revolution ushered in an era of emancipation that in eighty-five years broke forever the chains of chattel bondage in the Western Hemisphere–from the British West Indies (1833–48), to the United States (1865), to Cuba (1868–78), to Brazil (1871–78). It was in Haiti that the Great Liberator, Simon Bolivar, twice found refuge and assistance when he had been driven from Venezuela. Pledging to the Haitian president, Pétion, that he would fight to abolish slavery, Bolivar sailed from Haiti at the end of 1816 to break the colonial rule of Spain in Latin America.[212]

Allen's concentration on revolution and class conflict blinded him to the significance of the Reformation in creating England's enclosure laws, which began in 1604 and stayed in effect for the next three centuries, eventually appropriating 6.8 million acres of farmland. Blinded by his Marxist categories,

---

210 Allen, p. 644.
211 Allen, p. 642.
212 Allen, p. 659.

Allen fails to mention the Reformation as the cause of increased enclosure laws and the subsequent fall into unprecedented poverty:

> The price of wool rose faster than the price of grain, and the rent on pasture rose to several times the rent on crop land. The owners increased the proportion of pasture at the expense of arable land. One shepherd and flock occupied as much land as a dozen or score of peasants could cultivate with the plough. Ploughmen were therefore replaced by sheep and hired shepherds; peasants were deprived of their copyhold and common-land rights, while laborers on the lords' demesne lands found their services in reduced demand. Rack-rents and impoverishing leasehold entry fees were imposed with increasing severity on laboring peasants competing with sheep for land. At the beginning of the sixteenth century, somewhere between one sixth and one third of all the land in England belonged to abbeys, monasteries, nunneries and other church enterprises. In the process of the dissolution the monasteries, most of the estimated 44,000 religious and lay persons attached to these institutions were cast adrift among the growing unemployed, homeless population. As these lands were expropriated, under Henry VIII the process of conversion to pasture was promoted more vigorously than it had been by their former owners. . . . the proportion of the people receiving poor relief was greater in the 1631–40 period than at any other time before or since.[213]

The Reformation was also one of the main causes of English colonization in the New World. Unlike Spain, Portugal, and France, where the Reformation failed to take root and as a result could not cause massive social dislocation, England was beset with a wave of looting which displaced millions of people from the land depriving them of traditional ways of earning a livelihood. Because of the "surplus population" which that looting created, England's new Protestant oligarchy needed a means of "'venting' the nation's surplus of 'necessitous people' into New World plantations."[214] England got rid of the surplus population which the enclosure laws created by shipping them off to Virginia:

> Richard Johnson, in his promotional pamphlet Nova Britannia, noted that England abounded "with swarmes of idle persons ... having no meanes of labour to releeve their misery." He went on to prescribe that there be provided "some waies for their forreine employment" as English colonists in America. Commenting on the peasant uprising in the English Midlands in 1607, the House of Lords expressed the belief that unless war or colonization "vent" the daily increase of the population, "there must break out yearly tumours and impostures as did of late."[215]

---

213 Allen, pp. 661-2.
214 Allen, p. 662.
215 Allen, p. 663.

Part I: Errand Into the Satanic Wilderness

The discovery of tobacco as a cash crop was "by far the most momentous fact in the history of Virginia in the seventeenth century."[216] It saved the Virginia plantation from extinction, but it soon caused problems of its own. Tobacco production was labor intensive. The "servants" in Virginia who had been forced into exile by the Reformation's theft of the land that had sustained them were now starving in America because of the effects of tobacco monoculture. The collapse of the price of tobacco caused Bacon's rebellion because:

> chattel bond-servitude in Virginia in the 1620s was indeed a negation of previously existing laws and customs, but it was imposed by one set of colonists on another set of colonists. It was not, therefore, an act of racial oppression (no more than was the 1547 slave law in England), but merely an extremely reactionary sort of class oppression.[217]

What Allen refers to as "class oppression" was actually based in reality on the dehumanization of fellow Englishmen which followed inexorably from the Reformation. The alienation of Church property and the subsequent demotion of English citizens to unemployed beggars, vagabonds, and highway men that marked the beginning of the Reformation was followed by its intensification at the hands of Judaizing Puritans, who viewed the non-elect as Amalek and felt free to exterminate them, as Cromwell would do at Drogheda, when Irish Catholics gathered for protection in their churches thinking they were sanctuaries. The Puritans had already wrought this change in Ireland without any attempt to render the Irish "white," because the Reformation had already destroyed any idea of what Allen called "Christian fellowship,"[218] which was an essential concept of the universal, Catholic Church.

Allen accomplishes this shift in identity through his peculiar use of the term "race," which straddles the world in which it meant ethnic group and a post-World War II world which adopted a new meaning that was identical to phenotype. That change was occasioned by the government's involvement in social engineering. Allen rightly claims that "Irish history afford[s] insights into American racial oppression and white supremacy" because it "presents a case of racial oppression without reference to alleged skin color or, as the jargon goes, 'phenotype.'"[219] Oppression in Ireland was exclusively religious in nature. Both the oppressor and the oppressed were phenotypically identical. Allen uses race in an ambiguous fashion which obscures the role religion played in the formation of the Ulster and Virginian plantations, because religion is not a valid category for Marxists, even though it was the primary justification Cromwell used in perpetrating genocide on the phenotypically identical Irish. For Marxists, "racial oppression" is the fundamental category,

---

216 Allen, p. 732.
217 Allen, p. 929.
218 Allen, p. 954.
219 Allen, p. 60.

not religion. Allen invokes Karl Marx, who posited the "unity of working people in all countries" as a fundamental category while at the same time explaining how that fundamental category was subverted by the creation of "white privilege." Edmund Burke is closer to the mark because he bases his argument on religious categories which were categories of reality which were clearly recognized by the people at that time when he "observed that the English Protestant Ascendancy regarded the Irish 'as enemies to God and Man, and indeed, as a race of savages who were a disgrace to human nature.'"[220]

What Allen refers to as "the assault upon the tribal affinities, customs, laws and institutions of the Africans, the American Indians and the Irish by English/ British and Anglo-American colonialism,"[221] was inextricably bound up with religion because it began in Ireland, where the Catholic Irish were phenotypically indistinguishable from their Protestant oppressors.

Allen is forced to admit that the Reformation played a role in the subjugation of Ireland. The Irish had been oppressed for centuries before 1613, but the most ruthless and successful attempt "to reduce Ireland to its control in the latter part of the sixteenth century coincided with the full and final commitment of England to the Reformation."[222] Allen claims that:

> In this historical context the Protestant Reformation worked its purpose out by recasting anti-Irish racism in a deeper and more enduring mold. What had fed primarily on simple xenophobia now, as religio-racism, drank at eternal springs of private feelings about "man and God." The historian and member of the British House of Commons Thomas Babington Macaulay would say that the Reformation "brought new divisions to embitter the old ... a new line of demarcation was drawn; theological antipathies were added to the previous differences and revived the dying animosities of race."[223]

Allen is trading on the historical ambiguity associated with the term race, which in Macauley's day referred to ethnicity and not phenotype, which is how Allen uses the term. Allen is consistent in this ambiguity. In trying to explain the situation in Ireland, Allen is forced to refer to religious categories as the cause of "racial" oppression:

> The failure of the surrender-and-regrant policy became apparent at the very time the split with Rome resulting from the English Protestant Reformation was bringing new complications and greater urgency to the "Irish problem." Here began the redefinition of the struggle between England and Ireland as one of Protestant against Catholic, a process which

---

220 Allen, p. 72.
221 Allen, p. 73.
222 Allen, p. 98.
223 Allen, p. 99.

Part I: Errand Into the Satanic Wilderness

took more than a century to reach its fullest development. Encouraged by Rome and Spain, Irish Catholics, Anglo and Gaelic, began to show occasional readiness to unite not just for a change of English government, but for the end of English rule in Ireland.[224]

Slavery began in Ireland, where it was color blind and based on hatred of Catholicism at a time when "England was poised at the threshold of its career as a world colonial power, with Ireland as its first objective."[225] The laborers on the Ulster plantation that was founded following the defeat of the Irish-Jacobite cause in the war of 1689–91 were punished because they were Catholics, not because they were Irish, certainly not because they were "white," and yet Allen refers to the Penal Laws which subjected the Catholic Irish to *de facto* slavery as "the hallmark of racial oppression characteristic of Protestant Ascendancy,"[226] with no understanding that the conjunction of Protestant Ascendancy and White Supremacy is an oxymoron.

The Puritan revolution inaugurated an era of unprecedented economic exploitation. Slavery, as we now understand the term, was a Protestant invention according to which the Puritans first identified the Irish of the Ulster plantation and then the Indians of the Virginia plantation as Amalek. The deprivation of rights which eventuated in the enslavement of Africans stemmed from Puritan Judaizing theology first applied to the phenotypically indistinguishable Irish because of their religion. Oppression in Ireland was based on religion, not race, as Allen confusingly claims:

> An Englishman who traveled in Ireland in 1764 observed that their condition was "little better than slavery." That same year Lord Chesterfield, who had served as Lord Lieutenant of Ireland twenty years before, declared: "The poor people of Ireland are used worse than the negroes."[227] The precedent which got established in Ireland was theological, not biological. When [Irish historian] Maureen Wall claimed that: "The religious bar operated to exclude the Catholic majority from all positions of importance ... in the same way as the colour bar has operated to ensure white ascendancy in African countries,"[228] she was pointing out the fundamental difference between the two colonies not their common denominator in race.

Allen claims that at the beginning of the 18th century, Virginia led the way among Anglo-American continental colonies in codifying the concept that, "race, not class ... [is] the great distinction in society."[229] But even in Virginia,

---

224 Allen, p. 117.
225 Allen, p. 122.
226 Allen, p. 137.
227 Allen, p. 154.
228 Allen, p. 150.
229 Allen, p. 154.

racial laws were elastic enough to exclude "popish recusants, convicts, negroes, mulattoes and Indian servants, and others not being Christians," and that they "shall be deemed and taken to be persons incapable in law, to be witnesses in any case whatsoever."[230]

Allen repeatedly tells us that the Protestant Ascendancy in Ulster was "a system of racial oppression,"[231] consistently confusing the issue by his equivocal use of the term race, which means alternatively ethnic group and phenotype. He uses confusing phrases like "the great all-pervasive effect of the racial oppression wrought in the name of Protestant Ascendancy"[232] turning religious discrimination into something which fits his Marxist racial paradigm, as when he describes the emergence of Belfast as a major industrial center "based on the Protestants' heritage of two centuries of racial privileges."[233] Allen continues to confuse the reader when he claims that the founding of the Ulster plantation in 1609 was marked by "the system of racial oppression that would come to be called Protestant Ascendancy."[234] When Allen claims, the situation in America was "Ulster writ large," he undermines his own racial thesis. Virginia and Ulster shared no racial common denominator. Religion and religion alone was the basis for economic exploitation in Ireland. In discussing the United States' Indian Removal policy in 1832, Allen points out that "White Stick Creeks and Cherokees fought on the victorious 'American' side under the command of General Andrew Jackson,"[235] once again undermining his racial thesis.

Racial laws were Talmudic, which is to say, based on DNA, which is what established Jewish identity but only in the absence of baptism, which negated any biological right to call oneself a Jew. The same rule applied to "whites" in the South, where quota laws stressed the importance of measures "for the importation of white Servants," but added as a codicil "the Irish Papist excepted."[236] American Irish Papist was a dual identity that was contradictory because even if the Irish could be considered "white," their newfound American identity did not spare them from being attacked because they were Catholic during the Nativist riots in Philadelphia and Boston during the 1840s.

---

230 Allen, p. 158.
231 Allen, p. 161.
232 Allen, p. 228.
233 Allen, p. 227.
234 Allen, p. 219.
235 Allen, p. 240.
236 Allen, p. 242.

Chapter 6

The "False Bottom" of Puritan Theology

Samuel Willard epitomized that Puritan synthesis. His solution to the ontological insecurity Calvin bequeathed to the Puritans was the Covenant, which was based on revelation. But his *summa*, *A Compleat Body of Divinity*, which appeared in 1727, seven years before the beginning of the Great Awakening, was based on reason. Basically, he tried to square the circle. Perry Miller refers to *A Compleat Body of Divinity* as "a systematic review of the colony's theology" which could be called "New England's summa." Ernest Benson Lowrie second's Miller's view by calling it "the closest thing to being a *Summa Theologiae* that Puritan New England ever produced."[237] Unfortunately, it was only viewed as such by scholars writing 300 years after it appeared in print. In Miller's *The New England Mind: The Seventeenth Century*, one out of every ten references is to Willard, and in one chapter the ratio goes as high as one in every four. Despite the scholarly encomia, when *A Compleat Body of Divinity* lumbered off the press in 1727 it provided answers to questions which New England was no longer asking. Part of the problem lies with a proper definition of the term *summa*.

In spite of their repeated assertion that Willard wrote a *summa*, neither Miller nor Lowrie is very precise about how Willard's *summa* fits into the tradition he is supposed to have emulated. Miller uses the word repeatedly without explanation. Lowrie gives some indication of what he means but not much. "Broadly speaking," he writes, "the exposition moves from Willard's metaphysical beliefs to his ethical theory, to his Christian reflections on the human situation in the light of the cardinal mysteries of the Puritan Creed." Lowrie loses Willard's full significance by constricting his presentation, avoiding a dive into the origin of Willard's ideas. "No attempt is made," Lowrie continues, describing his intentions, "to trace the various ideas to their origins. Neither is it the intent to seize upon one or two organizing motifs to differentiate Willard's theology from other positions."[238]

By the mid-seventeenth century, Calvinist orthodoxy had a number of competing paradigms for the organization of reformed dogmatics. Protestant

---

[237] Ernest Benson Lowrie, *The Shape of the Puritan Mind: The Thought of Samuel Willard* (New Haven: Yale University Press, 1974), p. 3.
[238] Lowrie, p. 6.

scholasticism, and I am taking Willard as one of its prime representatives, had at its disposal the whole tradition of Christian dogmatics, including the great syntheses of the Middle Ages, as well as the *summa* of the founder of the reformed tradition, Calvin's *Institutes*. The differences between the two paradigms are many, but one major one – and here we raise an issue central to the nature of what a *summa* is – is where to begin. Does one begin within faith or with some necessary prolegomenon to faith such as proofs for the existence of God, as Aquinas did? Or does one begin with a discussion of the nature of our knowledge of God as Calvin did? Does the advent of grace bring with it its own starting point, or is there something outside of faith, which faith itself must rest upon?

In simply deciding where to begin, Willard had to make a number of significant theological decisions. Their desire for method drew the Puritans toward the comprehensive form and minute organization that the *summa* as a theological genre provided, but it must have been apparent to Puritan scholastics that the form and the content of the *summa* were not totally independent of each other. The *summa* is comprehensive not only because it organizes the doctrines of faith but also because it gives faith its proper position in the orders of knowing and being. Thus, to assume, as Reformed Theology did, that there is a radical discontinuity between faith and reason has implications for the form in which one casts any comprehensive description of the faith, and, more importantly, for the beginning or foundation of that description. In the history of dogmatic theology form and content interacted with each other in a dialectical and oftentimes only partially conscious way, innovations in theology producing slightly different forms and vice versa. But there was no unanimity among even reformed theologians of the seventeenth century as to either the form or the starting point of reformed dogmatics. As James Jones writes in *The Shattered Synthesis*:

> Although it was customary in Puritan circles to begin a systematic discussion of theology with a discussion of man's knowledge of God, as Calvin did in the *Institutes*, Willard bases his summa, *A Compleat Body of Divinity*, on the *Shorter Catechism of the Westminster Assembly* thus placing its foundation wholly within the realm of faith. Willard's *summa* presupposes faith and because of this it rested upon faith as its foundation. By choosing the catechism as his organizational framework, Willard makes a significant theological decision before he puts a word on paper. Because its foundation lies completely within faith, Willard's *Compleat Body* qualifies as a *summa* in only a very truncated form. Even Calvin with all his suspicion of unaided reason saw knowledge of God as lying partially outside of the realm of faith. Man has a *sensus divinitatis* within himself and can recognize *signae Deitatis* in nature. Because its first principles belong to the supernatural order, catechetics – and therefore any *summa* based on a catechism – begins with faith. In

its starting point and organizational principle, *A Compleat Body* is more fideist than Calvin's *Institutes*, yet fideist with an eye to getting results. *A Compleat Body*'s emphasis lay, "upon the summons to action, let theology define capability as it may."[239] Perhaps because of the spiritual needs of his flock, a congregation in which "declension" was rampant, Willard trimmed theory to augment practice. But at the time of the publication of *A Compleat Body* Puritanism was rapidly changing from confession to an ethic, and one of the main causes of this change was the dubious intellectual status of its foundational principles, most especially the principle of all Puritan principles, the covenant.

Even though Willard's pragmatic choice of a starting point makes him more of a fideist than Calvin in his choice of a starting point, his desire for method renders the Protestant principles *sola fide, sola gratia, sola scriptura* inadequate.

Willard was simultaneously a Calvinist and a scholastic. His attempt to reconcile these two views pulled him in two different directions at once. Willard as a scholastic and a proponent of method is confronted with the natural desire for certainty, or the noetic imperative, which is best expressed in the first sentence of Aristotle's *Metaphysics*, "All men naturally have an impulse to get knowledge." But Willard the Calvinist is confronted with man as a rational creature whose reason is completely deranged because of the Fall. The noetic imperative is necessary to any *summa*, but it is not necessarily congruent with every theology. Aquinas uses it as the basis for his theology, but Aquinas had a different understanding of the relationship between faith and reason than Willard or Calvin. "The natural desire to know," Aquinas writes in a deliberate attempt to echo Aristotle:

> cannot be stilled until we know the first cause, not in any sort of way but in its essence. Now the first cause is God. Therefore, the final end of the rational creature is the vision of the divine essence.[240]

In contrast, Willard's theological tradition questioned the ability of man's unaided intellect to reach the first cause, it also rejected the notion of the first cause as an idolatrous falsification of the true nature of the transcendent God. As a result, Willard's method is at odds with his theology. His tradition not only questioned the power of the intellect, thereby throwing the noetic imperative in doubt, it also used the abasement of the intellect as the *sina qua non* of piety. In his *Commentary* on John 16:9, Calvin tells us that "every attempt to reach the truth is essentially a perverted attempt, and only alienates him all the more from God the Father."[241] In his *Sermon on Deuteronomy* 4:19,

---

239 Perry Miller, *The New England Mind: From Colony to Province* (Cambridge, Mass.: Harvard University Press, 1955), p. p. 213.
240 Frederick Copleston, S.J., *Thomas Aquinas* (London: Search Press, 1976), p. 60.
241 T.F. Torrance, *Calvin's Doctrine of Man* (London: Lutterworth Press, 1949), p. 150.

Calvin goes even farther in separating reason and faith and nullifying the noetic imperative:

> It is a very hard thing to forsake our own reason, so as not to *be wise* in our own conceits or to behave ourselves after our own liking, but to admit that there is nothing but vanity and un-truth in us and to learn to humble ourselves. *That is contrary to our nature*, for we have a fond belief that we are wise of ourselves. God, on the contrary, will have us bereft of in-turned understanding and self-grounded reason and to give ourselves over to be governed by his spirit (my emphasis).[242]

Man's rational nature has entered into a state of total depravity because of original sin that is so profound that reason can no longer apprehend anything spiritual, not even, presumably, the existence of God because "To try to rise by ourselves and from ourselves," Calvin writes in his *Commentary on Isaiah* 40:22, "would be as ridiculous as to elevate ourselves by leaping for we immediately fall back upon the earth." "The only preparation a man can make," Calvin says in the *Institutes* describing man's role in his own salvation, "is to deny himself and empty himself." One of the major consequences of the Fall, according to Calvin, is that reason alone can in no way lead man to God. Again, Calvin is brutally unambiguous about the intellectual powers that remain with fallen man:

> The reason and wisdom which the first man had were not in himself but rather in that he was fashioned after the image of God. . . and therefore as soon as he was separated from his Creator, who is the fountain of all Good, he could not but be deprived of all graces which God had bestowed on man. . . . Therefore, the natural man is not able to understand the things which belong to the Spirit; they cannot understand at all: the power or ability is not in us. . . so that God must enlighten us by a special grace or else we shall never judge of His Word or Works as becomes us.

Willard stands at the crossroads of two mutually antagonistic traditions. As a scholastic he must rely on reason and method to seek a foundation for his faith, implying of course the efficacy of reason in achieving spiritual truths. But as a Calvinist and believer in innate depravity and its consequent derangement of reason, he must deny that reason perverted by original sin can ever achieve any truth about divine things. According to Aristotle, man can create a method of knowing – indeed according to Aristotle he is condemned to do so – yet according to Calvin he must ultimately reject the structures he is condemned to create as not only false but a danger to his salvation as well. Indeed, any knowledge of spiritual things which does not come from Scripture is a chimera, mere illusion and a source of idolatry. Any knowledge

---

242 Torrance, p. 145.

of God that does not come from the Scriptures is ultimately an idol that must be smashed in the name of piety.

A Compleat Body soon manifests a type of vacillation that makes it a very different type of book than either of Aquinas's two *summas* or Calvin's *Institutes*. In spite of its fideist beginning, *A Compleat Body* does not engage in diatribes against reason, making it more medieval in tone than the *Institutes*. It contains many passages that could have come right out of Aquinas although they are not arranged as Aquinas would arrange them. Willard devotes much time and energy to problems associated with natural theology and foundational principles, but for him natural theology and the foundation of belief are no longer synonymous as they were for Aquinas. The closer we examine the relationship between faith and reason in Willard's theology, the more we find, not fusion, but vacillation. Willard legitimates both the Aristotelean and the Calvinist options and chooses between them as he sees fit. In doing so, he is the paradigmatic Puritan, which is to say, a practical Calvinist, with all of the contradictions that implies.

Theologians in the reformed tradition have difficulty reaching agreement on Calvin's natural theology and questions on the foundations of faith. In his introduction to Heinrich Heppe's *Reformed Dogmatics*, Ernst Bizer faults Heppe, a representative of what Karl Barth calls the "old orthodoxy" for betraying "a definite uncertainty in the treatment of the natural knowledge of God. . . This lack of clarity, then as now, was not confined to one locus." Bizer faults Heppe for failing to realize that "in dogmatics we are dealing only with the revealed God."[243] Yet in stating his case this way Bizer fails to see that much of the confusion in the "old orthodoxy" simply recapitulates the vacillation in Calvin's own natural theology. Calvin's descendants – and Willard, in America at least, is one of the most ambitious – attempt to rehabilitate reason but fail to reconcile it with faith. "Knowledge of God," writes Peter Martyr, "is naturally innate."[244] It is a given, a certain and distinct idea in every man. There is consequently a *religio naturalis*. Yet once Heppe establishes the existence of natural theology from his sources, he immediately begins to vitiate its worth. *Religio naturalis* is not *religio salutaris*. It is insufficient to lead us to salvation, and, as Calvin points out, does little more than render us inexcusable in God's eyes. Knowledge outside of revelation is, in Calvin's words, "empty speculation," or, in an even more telling phrase, "the frigid dogma of Aristotle."[245] True knowledge of divine things is not imparted by flesh and it leads nowhere. Heppe simultaneously affirms the existence and

---

[243] Ernst Bizer, Intro., *Reformed Dogmatics*, by Heinrich Heppe, trans., G.T. Thomson (Grand Rapids, Mich.: Baker Books, 1978), p. xii.

[244] Heinrich Heppe, *Reformed Dogmatics*, trans., G.T. Thomson (Grand Rapids, Mich.: Baker Books, 1978), p. 1.

[245] John Calvin, *Institutes of the Christian Religion*, trans., John Allen (Philadelphia: Presbyterian Board of Christian Education, 1956), p. 67. All subsequent references in text.

denies the value of *religio naturalis*. The sole principle of religious knowledge remains for Heppe and the "old orthodoxy" what it was for Calvin, namely revelation alone. "With these provisos, we say that no human reason is the principle by which or through which or in consequence of which we believe, or the foundation or law or norm of what is to be believed by the prescriptions of which we judge."[246] After admitting that "reason is the instrument or the means by which we may be led to faith," Heppe disqualifies it for something it never claimed it could do:

> it is not the principle on which the dogmas of faith are derived or the foundation on which they rest.... Reason cannot be the norm of religion, either as corrupt (*because it is not only beneath faith but against it*) or as sound (because such reason is not found in any corrupt man). Thus the solid and sure archetectonic principle of theology is "divine & revelation" (my emphasis).[247]

In the preceding passages we have a restatement of the goals of natural theology and simultaneously a rejection of its ability to reach these goals. Heppe rejects the possibility that natural theology can be a prolegomenon to faith, yet he does not deny that man needs a foundation in reason which is certain in order to do theology, which is based on logical deductions from premises provided by faith. The word Trinity is not found in the Bible. It came into being after a centuries long discussion in Greek based on premises which can be found in the Bible but only understood properly after they have been subjected to rational discourse, implying of course that reason is sound enough to arrive at the truth that is implicit in revelation.

The reformed tradition rejected natural theology as a source of answers, but it did not reject the quest that prompted natural theology in the first place, i.e., the need for certainty. If there were no need for certainty, there would be no dogmatics. Yet if theology is exclusively revealed theology, then everything a believer holds as true is based on faith and therefore *ipso facto* uncertain. If faith were certain, it would not be faith. Once faith is defined as in opposition to reason, theology is in the problematic position of having to choose between belief and certainty. This antithetical relationship between faith and reason in reformed theology created a unique situation in which the solutions of natural theology were rejected in the name of piety. But the rejection of these answers paradoxically made the project of natural theology and its goal – namely certainty about divine things – all the more urgent. Calvin destroyed certainty in the name of piety, and his followers, finding the uncertainty unbearable, looked for some new compromise that would provide the certainty of the metaphysical tradition without sacrificing the fideism of Calvin's fierce iconoclasm.

---

246 Heppe, p. 7-8.
247 Heppe, p. 8.

Part I: Errand Into the Satanic Wilderness

The solution to this dilemma was the covenant. Many scholars, most notably Perry Miller in "The Marrow of Puritan Divinity" have noted the central role the covenant has played in the Puritan accommodation of human needs to Calvinist imperatives, but no one so far as I know has noticed how closely the covenant coincides with the role and imagery traditionally associated with metaphysics and natural theology. Calvinism had placed the Puritans in a bind; they could be either certain or pious, when as theologians they had to be both simultaneously. "Some kind of revision of Calvinism," Miller writes describing this dilemma, "seemed absolutely inevitable if the doctrine of justification by faith were not to eventuate in a complete disregard of moral performance."[248] As a result, covenant theology, according to Miller, became the "theoretical foundation for metaphysics and state and church."[249] With all respect to Miller, metaphysics by definition can have no foundation outside of itself. To say that the covenant was the foundation of Puritan metaphysics means that the covenant was Puritan metaphysics, created to satisfy the demands of a mutually irreconcilable reason and faith in an unprecedented and ultimately impossible way. Covenant theology could not become the basis for metaphysics without itself becoming a metaphysical principle. If revealed and natural theology were compatible for Aquinas, it was only by remaining distinct forms of knowing. The first truths of pure and practical reason were completely certain and completely distinct from the tenets of faith. Beyond that, the tenets of faith could only exist based on metaphysical ideas like the principle of non-contradiction. The Puritan synthesis, however, attempted to strengthen reason by basing it on faith (faith in the covenant) and succeeded in merely weakening both.

Ernest Lowrie describes the structure of *A Compleat Body* as moving "from Willard's metaphysical beliefs to his ethical theory, to his Christian reflections on the human situation in the light of the cardinal mysteries of the Puritan Creed."[250] Lowrie passes over the fact that *A Compleat Body*, based as it is on the *Shorter Catechism*, locates its metaphysical beliefs completely within the realm of faith, Willard's beginning sermons have an undeniably metaphysical ring to them, but they participate only obliquely and by analogy in the metaphysical project of ascertaining first truths because all metaphysical discussion in *A Compleat Body* is based on a tacit acceptance of the tenets of faith. Willard's discussion would be incomprehensible outside of the catechism which provides its organizational structure and as a consequence the certainty it attempts to provide is merely an illusion.

Unlike Calvin and Aquinas, Willard, following the *Shorter Catechism*, begins with the end of man as his first consideration. He begins neither with

---

248 Perry Miller, *Errand Into the Wilderness* (Cambridge, Mass.: The Belknap Press of Harvard University Press, 1964), p. 89.
249 Miller, *Errand*, p. 489.
250 Lowrie, p. 6.

the proofs of God's existence as Aquinas does nor with man's knowledge of God as Calvin does, but rather with God as man's chief end and supreme happiness. He begins, in other words, by presupposing that God exists but also that we can know his intentions for us clearly and unambiguously. Willard's first discussion is a curious amalgam of faith and reason. By combining "Why did God make me?" with the first principle of the practical reason, "Good is to be pursued and evil avoided," he uses metaphysical sounding arguments to demonstrate truths of the catechism which must be based on revelation. Willard draws again and again on the metaphysical tradition to establish the fundamental nature of God as our chief end. "Such an End there must be," he tells us, "or man can never be blessed, because he could never come to his resting place, but must be left in a Labyrinth and carried on in an endless pursuit of happiness."[251] The existence of a final goal is certain because if there were no goal there could be no action. Yet even in the act of paraphrasing Aristotle and the scholastic tradition, Willard introduces in terms like the "labyrinth," the vocabulary of modern skepticism. Unregenerate man, Willard tells us, "hath no Chief, and therefore is on a false bottom."[252]

In the image of the "false bottom," Samuel Willard bequeaths to American intellectual life a paradigm which represents the insecurity of fideism when faced with metaphysical tasks. That paradigm retained its force for generation after generation of American writers from Jonathan Edwards to Henry David Thoreau to Henry Adams to Eugene O'Neill. The rightness of our position depends upon the certitude of first principles, the metaphysical "bottom." Yet if we stand on a "false bottom" our certitude threatens to give way beneath us. Thus the "false bottom" expresses the necessity of indemonstrable first principles and simultaneously doubts about the adequacy of the metaphysical method. How can the man of faith find certainty? What, if anything, is beneath him to sustain him? The difficulty in answering these questions comes from Willard's unfortunate tendency to mix his philosophical metaphors. Reason can alone provide certainty, and Willard, by his use of metaphysical argument, seems to acquiesce in this belief. Without an end or *telos*, he tells us, echoing Aristotle's understanding of the infinite regress, man is confronted with an "infinite subordination. . . no resting place and an endless quest." And herein resides the paradox because according to Willard the only way we can know that end is through faith, which cannot be certain. As a consequence, the false bottom becomes the symbol which simultaneously explains and subverts Willard's theology. Willard can never reach certainty because his arguments are ultimately based on a catechism, which presupposes faith. As a result, the "false bottom" becomes the paradigm of the metaphysician who bases his arguments on the assumptions of faith. Although it uses metaphysical

---

251 Samuel Willard, *A Compleat Body of Divinity* (New York: Johnson Reprint Corp., 1969), p. 3.
252 Willard, *Compleat Body*, p. 3.

arguments, *A Compleat Body* is not within the metaphysical tradition because it does not begin with the bottom, which can only be found in the certainty of first principles. Unlike natural theology which rests on the proofs of the existence of God, which in turn rest on first principles of being like the self-evident principle of non-contradiction, Willard posits a being who functions as the chief end of all things without first proving that that being exists.

Willard's most radical departure from the metaphysical tradition, however, takes place in his discussion of how man is to attain this ultimate end. Willard answers Question II, "What rule hath God given to direct us how we may glorify and enjoy him?" with characteristically reformed emphasis. "The Word of God (which is contained in the Scripture of the Old and New Testament) is the *ONLY* Rule to direct us how we may glorify and enjoy him."[253]

Unlike Calvin, who mocks it outright, Willard respected the metaphysical tradition enough to use its imagery and vocabulary in his *summa*. "What the sun is to the world," Willard tells us echoing Aristotle, "that the Scripture is to the church."[254] This analogy is just one example of the sleight of hand Willard performs in his attempt to align the certainty of philosophical method with the intensity of faith. Here as elsewhere Willard retains the arguments and the images, but they had lost their meaning. The difficulty we have in comprehending divine things lies not in the comprehensibility of the things themselves but in the capacity of our understanding, Aristotle tells us in the *Metaphysics*, "for as owl's eyes are at noonday, so is our mental vision blind to what in its own nature is the most evident of all."[255] This sun image is a touchstone of the metaphysical tradition. The sun is the humanly incomprehensible being which creates comprehensibility by the light it casts on everything else. And it is incomprehensible not because of what it is in itself but because of the finite capacity of the human mind which tries to grasp it. As Aquinas writes in the *Summa Contra Gentiles*:

> For assuredly that God exists is, absolutely speaking, self-evident, since what God is is His own being. Yet because we are not able to conceive in our minds that which God is, that God exists remains unknown in relation to us. So, too, that every whole is greater than its part is, absolutely speaking, self-evident, but it would perforce be unknown to one who could not conceive the nature of a whole. Hence it comes about, as it is said in *Metaphysics II* that "our intellect is related to the most knowable things in reality as the eye of an owl is related to the sun."[256]

---

253 Willard, *Compleat Body*, p. 10.
254 Willard, *Compleat Body*, p. 51.
255 Aristotle, *Metaphysics*, trans. Richard Hope (Ann Arbor, Mich.: Ann Arbor Paperbacks, 1978), p. 55.
256 St. Thomas Aquinas, *Summa Contra Gentiles*, trans. Anton C. Pegis, F.R.S.C. (Notre Dame, Indiana: University of Notre Dame Press, 1975), p. 81.

In the *Summa Theologiae*, Aquinas comes to the same conclusion and uses the same image:

> Since everything is knowable according as it is actual, God, Who is pure act without any admixture of potentiality, is in Himself supremely knowable. But what is supremely knowable in itself, may not be knowable to a particular intellect, on account of the excess of the intelligible object above the intellect; as, for example, the sun, which is supremely visible, cannot be seen by the bat by reason of its excess of light.[257]

Willard, as we have already seen, retains the imagery of metaphysics but under conditions which vitiate its meaning and consequently the meaning and certainty of the entire metaphysical tradition. Willard's piety is comfortable with neither the certainty of unaided reason nor Calvin's skepticism, and the contortions in Willard's metaphors reflect his attempt to create a consistent theology. "Natural men," he writes in *A Compleat Body* "are not competent to judge in this case, as well may a blind man's word be taken that the sun hath no light in it. . . . Natural men are fools and blind in spiritual things."[258]

Willard modified the metaphysical image, and in modifying it, he destroyed it. If men are blind in spiritual matters, and not as Aristotle and Aquinas maintain, merely dim-sighted, then theology, which is the rational arrangement of divine things, is a dangerous illusion. Since anything the believer may say is necessarily outside of Scripture and therefore subject to the noetic effects of the fall, all theology may be a falsification and an idol of deranged reason and therefore a danger to his soul. By modifying the metaphysical image Willard in the name of piety destroys not only reason but theology as well and consequently the basis for the very work he is writing. "As plain as the Scriptures are," he writes in a variation of the metaphysical tradition that is simultaneously the annihilation of that tradition, "there is need of the illumination of the Spirit to help us to understand them aright." Willard writes:

> This is not to supply any defect in the Scripture, but to help our infirmity: It is to restore eyesight to us. The sun shone before as brightly as afterwards, but the blind man saw it not 'till his eyes were opened.[259]

Willard's theology demands that man be totally blind, yet in espousing total blindness Willard simultaneously destroys any possible theology, or at least the certainty that goes with it as a rational structure. If we are totally blind, knowledge of any and all divine things must wait on the arbitrary decision of

---

257   St. Thomas Aquinas, *Summa Theologica*, trans. Fathers of the English Dominican Province (New York: Benziger Brothers, Inc., 1947), p. 49.

258   Willard, *Compleat Body*, p, 31.

259   Willard, *Compleat Body*, p. 31.

Part I: Errand Into the Satanic Wilderness

God. Yet if this is the case, we are back once again in the terrible uncertainty that led us to theologize in the first place.

If, as Willard implies, the covenant presupposes faith, then it cannot provide certainty and therefore can be no foundation for the faith. If, on the other hand, as Willard equally implies, the covenant gives the believer certainty or something to stand on, then it cannot be simultaneously an article of faith. The failure of the covenant theology lay in the fact that it tried to have it both ways.

Thus, the Puritan synthesis was illusory from the start because the covenant could not provide a meeting ground between faith and reason. It attempted to satisfy both piety and the desire for certainty and did neither because Willard did not understand the metaphysical language and imagery that he tried to appropriate as a basis for the covenant. "There are some Principles," he tells us, which:

> belong to the Rule which as they have diverse others depending upon, and resting from them, so they are not deducible from others, being themselves prime truths, and so except they had been declared in terms would never have been discovered to us, or inferred from others; such in special the mysteries of Redemption, and the Doctrine of faith in Christ; of these the scripture gives us a distinct and full account.[260]

Like other passages from *A Compleat Body*, we have here an assertion that starts off in the realm of reason using the explicit vocabulary of the metaphysical tradition but which ends up in the realm of belief discussing truths that can only be known by revelation and accepted through faith. Willard gives no explanation of how he crossed from one realm to the other. He also gives no indication that he is aware that the meaning of his metaphors has changed. First principles, the basis of metaphysical knowledge, are, according to that tradition, those principles which are known immediately and with absolute certainty as soon as the meaning of each term is understood. "The principles of eternal things," Aristotle explains:

> are necessarily most true; for they are true always and not merely sometimes; and there is nothing which explains their being what they are, for it is they that explain the being of all other things.[261]

These principles are the most certain, although not the easiest to grasp because if they were not true nothing would be either true or false. Willard, however, unwittingly equates first principles, the most certain knowledge, with the tenets of faith which are not only not immediately certain and which will never be certain this side of heaven, simply because they are tenets of faith. Willard's attempt to put Puritanism on a solid foundation fails because he has

---

[260] Willard, *Compleat Body*, p. 29.
[261] Aristotle, *Metaphysics*, p. 36.

no idea of what a foundation is. *A Compleat Body* fails as a *summa* because of Willard's inability to first separate and then bring together faith and reason. Willard inherited the metaphysical project of finding certainty or of getting to the bottom – indeed, according to Aristotle, all men are condemned to this project – yet he espoused a theology which thwarted the metaphysical project from the moment of its inception. Just as unfortunately, Willard's knowledge of the metaphysical tradition was neither strong enough to make him realize the inadequacy of his method nor acute enough to make him questions the assumptions of his theology. Willard was aware enough of the metaphysical tradition to make the attempt at writing a *summa*, but not aware enough to see that his *summa* was doomed from the start. The certainty that comes from considering being as being and which is expressed in first principles which have no prior explanation but which are themselves the basis for all explanation is the foundation of all certainty. If there is to be any certainty this must be its source. Yet through his misunderstanding of first principles, Willard makes all knowledge depend upon faith, and if all knowledge depends upon faith, then no knowledge is certain, and Puritanism becomes an inadvertent prolegomenon to skepticism. If first principles are within the realm of faith, they are *ipso facto* uncertain. And if there is no certainty and faith hangs over the abyss, then men, to use the phrase of Jonathan Edwards, who drew just this conclusion, have "nothing to stand on" in "Sinners in the Hand of an Angry God." If in reality, men have nothing to stand on, then the covenant is a dangerous illusion, which should be swept away in the name of God's absolute and terrible sovereignty.

When Willard emphasizes method too much, he destroys faith, when he emphasizes faith too much, he negates man's ability to reach certainty and leaves him prey to antinomian irrationality. Man has a natural desire for happiness, yet the light of nature is both insufficient and deceptive in its ability to guide him to happiness. Indeed, the light of nature is so deficient that it can't lead him to the faith which he needs to complete his journey. How then is conversion, possible? When the only rule for attaining happiness is to be found in the Word of God, which is of course based on faith, then we can have no certainty; we cannot even be sure that the object of our faith exists. If natural reason is totally inadequate as a guide in spiritual matters, there can be no certainty. The only security is in faith, but faith is unfortunately by definition uncertain. Yet if we have no certainty, then we have no foundation for our theology. "If man would attain certain knowledge of God that satisfies him," Heppe tells us, "he must not limit himself to this *cognitio Dei naturalis*" because:

> The knowledge of the divine nature gained from God's revelation in the works of nature is but inadequate and uncertain, after the fall has utterly

defaced the divine images in man. It leads only to the definitions of Plato and Aristotle, quite useless for the heart and sinful consciousness of man.

If reason is "utterly defaced," how can man recognize the good? And if he can't recognize what is good, why should he want to be saved? The implication of these passages is quite unprecedented. Natural knowledge is no longer difficult to achieve and limited in scope; it is now "useless." Calvin destroyed certainty in the name of piety and Willard is in a similar bind. The only foundation or bottom is what we can be sure of, namely a firm belief based on the truths of reason, the first principles of metaphysics, or, as Calvin pejoratively calls them, "the frigid dogma of Aristotle." But because the things we can be sure of are worthless with regard to salvation, the only knowledge efficacious for salvation is found in the Scriptures, which means that this knowledge must be accepted on faith. This in turn means that we can possess no certainty about it, and that therefore it cannot serve as a foundation or bottom. It cannot fulfill the desire for certainty that led us to systematize in the first place. Willard's vacillation between the order of faith and the order of reason, between revealed and natural theology, shows his desires to be methodic and pious simultaneously, yet it shows at the same time his inability to reconcile these increasingly antithetical desires. Because he is a Calvinist, Willard feels with Heppe that "living knowledge comes only through the spirit," and that "whosoever feign other opinions and attempt to obtain knowledge of God in a different way, deceive themselves and worship the idols of their own heart." Yet because he is writing a *summa*, Willard must find some foundational certainty for all he writes, which will, in effect, guarantee that theology as a human structure is possible.

The keystone that holds the natural and super-natural demands of Willard's theological arch together is the covenant. In it, Willard thought that his dilemma was resolved and that faith and reason found a meeting ground. In the covenant man is given certainty because God freely binds his terrifying and incomprehensible power to a legal contract, yet man is saved from the danger of simply worshipping idols created by a fallen and depraved intellect because the idea of the covenant springs from the Old Testament. The covenant became a way of restoring the certainty of the metaphysical tradition to the intolerable insecurity of Calvinist theology. After Reformed theology posits a *cognitio Dei naturalis*, it denies the efficacy of that knowledge. Willard smuggles the rational foundation which his summa lacks back into his theology surreptitiously in the form of the covenant. Natural theology is useless, but the covenant fulfills its primary function, namely that of reaching the bottom and giving us something to stand on, by returning to us the certainty that Calvin denied. "Happiness," Willard tells us:

> was proposed to man at first in a covenant way.... Hence there was a fixed or stated way to which Man's being made happy was restrained. For

if Happiness were not promised to man absolutely but hypothetically, it must needs depend upon that hypothesis. . . .

The covenant is the hypothesis that is not hypothetical. The covenant is "the foundation of our own hope to enjoy life eternal." It is "the first link of the chain and that which fastens all." "The covenant," Willard tells us, "is here made the foundation of all consolation to the people of God." The covenant is not like the frigid dogmas of Plato and Aristotle, "a meer notion of man's invention, but that which hath clear and firm footing in the word of God," which means that it is not certain because faith, as St. Paul tells us in Hebrews 11:1 "is the assurance of things hoped for," and "the conviction of things not seen."

Willard's mixed metaphors and his attempt to have it both ways attempt to give him the best of both worlds. To give us certainty Willard describes the covenant as the "first link," the absolute bottom and foundation to which absolutely nothing is prior, mimicking Aristotle's unmoved mover. Yet to allay our fears about self-grounded reason and the idols of Plato and Aristotle, Willard tells us that the covenant is not "a meer notion of man's invention, but that which hath clear and firm footing in the word of God." Unfortunately, this undoes the certainty he previously established by locating the covenant in Scripture and thereby denying its efficacy as a "first link." "Clear and firm footing in the Word of God" becomes the inadvertent oxymoron which simultaneously defines and unravels covenant theology. The truths of Scripture are above man's capacity; firm footing is something he needs beneath him to reach up. But the one cannot serve as a substitute for the other. The covenant attempts to do both and ends by making revelation too simple and reason too precarious. To satisfy the demands of faith and reason, Willard invented a "hypothesis" which subverts both. In the *Doctrine of the Covenant of Redemption*, Willard writes:

> Now the putting of this into a covenant adds emphasis to it; that it should not only be thought of, but indentured for and firmly ratified in an Everlasting and unchangeable compact. . . and therefore when God would call us to the contemplation of his great love to us, *he leads us up thus far*. . . [my emphasis].[262]

The covenant leads Willard up in the same way that unaided reason could lead Aquinas to the conclusion that God existed and that He possessed certain necessary characteristics. Consequently, the covenant provided Willard and his followers with the best of both worlds; it gave them the hope of salvation and the certainty of natural reason. Described in language reserved for the first principles of being, the covenant provided certainty. It was a foundation, an arché, and a bottom upon which man could base all

---

262 Samuel Willard, *The Doctrine of the Covenant of Redemption* (Boston: 1695), Evans No. 684, p. 55.

Part I: Errand Into the Satanic Wilderness

of his intellectual structures, including the structures of theology. At the same time, Willard could deny that the covenant was a product of heathen philosophy by reminding his congregation that it was based on the arbitrary decision of God and found in scripture. Because the covenant came from God and not man, Willard could use it to save Puritanism from degenerating into Arminian complacency. Yet because the covenant provided a foundation, a basis, a method, and a legalized *quid pro quo*, Willard could also use it as a bulwark against antinomian enthusiasm.

The covenant provided a neat solution to every problem. It had, however, one flaw; it didn't work. By the time covenant theology was fully codified in Willard's compendious and exhaustive *Compleat Body*, no one believed in it anymore.

Forced to play the role of a metaphysics and a natural theology, the covenant becomes exactly what Willard and his contemporaries feared the most, a "false bottom," one which threatens to give way without warning and plunge the believer into the abyss. Created to allow both piety and certainty, it becomes a false bottom which supports neither.

Willard's covenant began as a compromise and ended by satisfying no one. It could provide neither certainty nor transcendence; it could satisfy neither the demands of reason nor the longing of faith. A few years after the publication of *A Compleat Body of Divinity*, iconoclastic piety would leave believers dangling over the abyss, suspended from the thin thread of God's pleasure while rationalism would offer man a secure position as a human cog in a cosmic machine.

Chapter 7

Solomon Stoddard and the Half-Way Covenant

Samuel Willard's Puritan *summa*, *A Compleat Body of Divinity* was dead on arrival when it rolled off the presses in 1727. Willard is a magnificent anachronism. He has the distinction of codifying a tradition that died before it could be described, a tradition that was obsolete before it was completely formulated. Willard's posthumous gift to New England was a set of answers to obsolete questions, or, in the words of Sydney Ahlstrom, "a legacy to posterity which posterity ignored." Indeed, his editors apologized for the very work they were bringing out, indicating that *A Compleat Body of Divinity* might disappoint its readers because Willard was "less exact in his Philosophical Schemes and Principles" than an age that was "just emerging out of those obscurities might demand."

The Puritan synthesis was mission impossible because of its inherent contradictions. But Puritanism expired in New England for a simpler, more banal, reason: no one could explain whether the election which was necessary for church membership could be transmitted biologically to the next generation. Was it like original sin, transmitted by the act of sexual intercourse? Or was election a conscious choice that had to be renewed personally by each subsequent generation? The Jews, who were the model the Judaizing Puritans followed on their errand into the wilderness, solved the problem by making election (the Puritan term for "chosenness") inheritable via the mother. No Puritan was daring (or crazy) enough to propose this solution, but absent the biological basis for Jewish identity which became the norm after the destruction of the Temple, none of the Puritan divines could come up with a plausible explanation of how election got passed from one generation to the next.

The solution to this theological dilemma came to be known as the Half-Way Covenant, and its most famous exponent was Solomon Stoddard. Born on September 27, 1643 and baptized as an infant, Stoddard succeeded Rev. Eleazer Mather as pastor of the Congregationalist Church in Northampton,

Massachusetts Bay Colony at some time around 1670,[263] when it was then on the frontier.

At this point existence – the frontier – intervened to resolve the contradictions in Puritan essence which the divines could not untangle on their own. Exposure to the natural man, i.e., the Indian created theological problems which Solomon Stoddard could only solve with a gun. Frederick Jackson Turner tells us that "One of the most striking phases of frontier adjustment, was the proposal of the Rev. Solomon Stoddard of Northampton in the fall of 1703, urging the use of dogs "to hunt Indians as they do Bears."[264] Stoddard's proposal was based on his experience of Puritans returning from Indian captivity after they had gone completely native and returned "painted and garbed as Indians and speaking the Indian tongue, and the half-breed children of captive Puritan mothers," but worst of all they returned "Catholic in religion," because the Indians had been instructed in the Catholic faith by French Jesuits.[265]

There were other more alarming instances of "the transforming influence of the Indian frontier upon the Puritan type of English colonist."[266] When Timothy Dwight, President of Yale University, toured the western frontier around the time of the war of 1812, he discovered that the "foresters" who had been transformed by the frontier were worse off than the women who had returned from Indian captivity because they:

> cannot live in regular society. They are too idle, too talkative, too passionate, too prodigal, and too shiftless to acquire either property or character. They are impatient of the restraints of law, religion, and morality, and grumble about the taxes by which the Rulers, Ministers, and Schoolmasters are supported. . . . After exposing the injustice of the community in neglecting to invest persons of such superior merit in public offices, in many an eloquent harangue uttered by many a kitchen fire, in every blacksmith shop, in every corner of the streets, and finding all their efforts vain, they become at length discouraged, and under the pressure of poverty, the fear of the gaol, and consciousness of public contempt, leave their native places and betake themselves to the wilderness.[267]

In 1794 the Governor of Louisiana had similar things to say about the "roving spirit" of the frontiersman:

> A rifle and a little corn meal in a bag are enough for an American wandering alone in the woods for a month. . . . With logs crossed upon

---

263 "Solomon Stoddard," *Wikipedia: The Free Encyclopedia*, https://en.wikipedia.org/wiki/Solomon_Stoddard

264 Frederick Jackson Turner, *The Frontier Thesis*, Kindle, p. 17.

265 Turner, *The Frontier Thesis*, Kindle, p. 17.

266 Turner, *The Frontier Thesis*, Kindle, p. 17.

267 Turner, *The Frontier Thesis*, Kindle, p. 87.

one another he makes a house, and even an impregnable fort against the Indians. . . . Cold does not terrify him, and when a family wearies of one place, it moves to another and settles there with the same ease.[268]

Confronted by the degeneracy the frontier created, Solomon Stoddard allowed existence to modify essence. Stoddard tried to save the Puritan synthesis through a series of compromises which allowed partial membership rights to persons not yet converted to the Puritan church by lessening the different between "elect" members of the church and regular members. In a move which cast doubt on the efficacy of sacramental baptism, membership was now based, in part, on an "experience" which the half-way covenanters described as conversion. How this fit into the traditional understanding of membership in the Church based on baptism was not clear, and these contradictory criteria for membership continued side by side with no theological foundation or justification. The *Encyclopedia Brittanica* tries to explain that contradiction by claiming that the Half-Way Covenant:

> allowed the children of baptized but unconverted church members to be baptized and thus become church members and have political rights. Early Congregationalists had become members of the church after they could report an experience of conversion. Their children were baptized as infants, but, before these children were admitted to full membership in the church and permitted to partake of the Lord's Supper, they were expected to also give evidence of a conversion experience. Many never reported a conversion experience but, as adults, were considered church members because they had been baptized, although they were not admitted to the Lord's Supper and were not allowed to vote or hold office.[269]

Once again, existence trumped essence. Stoddard's theology "was not widely accepted in Boston but was popular on the frontier."[270] Second generation Puritans flocked to Stoddard's church because he liberalized church policy concerning church membership, denouncing "drinking and extravagance"[271] in a way that emphasized moral effort, thereby subtly undermining the Calvinist understanding of predestination, total depravity, and, most importantly, the doctrine of *sola gratia*. The Calvinist understanding of predestination had denigrated moral effort in a way that was now life-threatening because of the dangers the frontier posed to simple survival.

The covenant was especially important to the Puritans because it granted political legitimacy to regicides by identifying them as God's chosen people. Moses leading God's chosen people out of bondage in the land of Egypt fit

---

268 Turner, *The Frontier Thesis*, Kindle, p. 65.
269 "Half-Way Covenant," *Britannica*, https://www.britannica.com/event/Half-Way-Covenant
270 "Solomon Stoddard," *Wikipedia*.
271 "Solomon Stoddard," *Wikipedia*.

exactly into the Errand into the Wilderness narrative, according to which the Puritan divines, like Moses, led the Elect out of bondage in England into a place where the Puritans could say "Here we are free," as John Milton's Satan claimed in the Protestant epic *Paradise Lost*. Needless to say, some modifications in the narrative were necessary. Massachusetts was hardly the land of milk and honey that Joshua and his 12 Hebrew spies described to Moses, and so the story of the Hebrew conquest of Canaan in Numbers 13:1 had to be conflated with Matthew's account of John baptizing in Trans-Jordan simply because the crucial word "wilderness" in Matthew's gospel was a necessary concession to the reality of existence on the edge of what seemed to be an endless forest. It was the first of many concessions that the Protestant essence would make during the settlers' confrontation with existence in the New World. Eventually the concessions which existence in the "howling Wilderness" forced on the Puritans would transform Protestantism into a secular ethos for the Republic which emerged at the time of the American Revolution, until it ultimately became Americanism, "the Fourth Great Western Religion,"[272] in time for the emergence of the American empire, which resolved a contradiction between experiential religion and sacramental religion which had become too large to ignore. The decision to allow the baptized but "unconverted" to join led to a dramatic increase in attendance at Stoddard's church, but like Willard's Puritan *summa*, the Half-Way Covenant lacked a sound foundation in either faith or reason.

Stoddard's theology was a classic example of how existence on the frontier modified the essence of Puritan theology. The exigencies of survival on the frontier forced Stoddard to abandon *a priori* concepts like total depravity and Calvinist predestination and replace them with moral virtues like temperance and chastity, which rehabilitated the moral effort that made survival on the frontier more likely. In an attempt to save Puritanism from its fate as a "dying religion," the "pope" of the Connecticut River Valley, as Increase Mather called him, "insisted that the sacrament of the Lord's Supper should be available to all who lived outwardly pious lives and had a good reputation in the community, even if they weren't full members of the church."[273] As a result of the exigencies of the frontier, which prioritized existence over essence as a priority in the ongoing fight to survive in the wilderness, a practical solution was hammered out which allowed Stoddard's church to flourish over the short haul, but ultimately provided intellectual satisfaction to no one, not even his grandson.

In 1726, one year before Willard's Puritan "*summa*" *A Compleat Divinity* rolled off the press, twenty-three year old Jonathan Edwards became his grandfather's assistant at the congregationalist church Stoddard had inherited

---

272 David Gelernter, *Americanism: The Fourth Great Western Religion* (Doubleday, 2007).
273 "Solomon Stoddard," *Wikipedia*.

in Northampton, Massachusetts. Sensing that Stoddard had not resolved the contradictions in Willard's *Compleat Divinity*, Edwards decided to create a more secure foundation for Puritanism by going back to its source in Calvin and looking at it through the lens of Lockean psychology and Newtonian physics. Edwards had read Locke's *Essay concerning Human Understanding* as an undergraduate and "greedily devoured"[274] its contents, deriving more pleasure from its pages "than the most greedy miser finds, when gathering handfuls of silver and gold, from some newly discovered treasure."[275]

In his *Essay Concerning Human Understanding*, Locke defined knowledge as "the perception of the connexion of and agreement, or disagreement and repugnancy of any of our ideas."[276] By accepting Locke's understanding that ideas are "the first element in knowledge,"[277] Edwards' cut himself off from being, thus dooming his metaphysical quest for a foundation from its inception. If all the mind can know are ideas, Edwards had no way of knowing if those categories of the mind corresponded to categories of reality. Since truth is "*adequatio rei et intellectus*,"[278] the correspondence of the mind and the thing, Edwards could not say if his ideas were true, and if they were not true, he could not explain why his congregation should believe them. Once again, the Puritan who started out on the metaphysical quest of discovering the bottom or something to stand on was thwarted by the philosophical provincialism that was a necessary consequence of the Reformation. Unlike Aquinas, who claimed that existence called essence into being, Locke dismissed essence by denigrating it as based on "innate ideas," making being thereby totally a function of the human mind, whose "furniture" was ideas, and turning ontology into epistemology or, more radically, psychology. By destroying the mind's connection with being, Locke turned Edwards into an idealist, thereby confounding the foundation seeking metaphysical project at the heart of Puritanism. Aquinas believed that our cognitions came from the senses, "*principium nostrae cognitionis est a sensu*,"[279] but that those principles once established allowed us to make contact with being, from which we derived knowledge of essence. Empiricism, unfortunately, never allowed the mind to emerge from the realm of ideas, subjectivizing all knowledge, and in doing that Locke and Edwards fell into the error of the sophist Protagoras, who made man the measure of all things. There is a sense in which the world is an idea, but only insofar as that idea can be found in the mind of God. Idea in that instance is another word for essence. In the mind of man, ideas or

---

274 Faust & Johnson, *Jonathan Edwards*, p. xxiv.

275 Faust & Johnson, *Jonathan Edwards*, p. xxv.

276 "John Locke," *Britannica*, https://www.britannica.com/topic/epistemology/John-Locke

277 John Locke, *An Essay Concerning Human Understanding*, Volume I (New York: Dover Publications, 1959), p. lviii.

278 Thomas de Aquino, *Summa Theologiae*, Ques. xvi, Art. 1, 3.

279 Thomas de Aquino, *Summa Theologiae*, I^a q. 84-89

categories of the mind, do not necessarily correspond to categories of reality. When they do, they take on the transcendental character of the truth. In the mind of God, however, categories of the mind and categories of reality are one and the same because in God existence and essence coalesce in one self-subsistent being. Because in God existence and essence are identical, God's speech is performative. Existence follows from God's word, as described in the book of Genesis (1:4): "God said 'Let there be light,' and there was light."

Deprived of an adequate understanding of the metaphysical tradition because of his Protestantism, Edwards became an idealist. Reading Locke, Edwards concluded that, "the world is therefore an ideal one."[280] Edwards then recapitulates the errors of modern philosophy *avant la lettre* by conflating idealism and pantheism. "Space," Edwards tells us after claiming that the world is ideal, "is God."[281] The origin of Edwards' idealism has stumped scholars to this day. It is, according to I. Woodbridge Riley, "the most difficult in the history of American philosophy." "Was it the product of precocious genius, or an adaptation of the Berkeleian system, or a blending of the idealistic hints and suggestions then in the air?"[282]

Even more perplexing is Edwards' simultaneous conversion to pantheism. Sounding as if he has just read Spinoza rather than Bishop Berkeley, Edwards tells us that:

> Space is this Necessary eternal infinite and Omnipresent being, we find that we can with ease Concieve how all other beings should not be, we Can remove them out of our Minds and Place some Other in the Room of them, but Space is the very-thing that we Can never Remove, and Concieve of its not being, If a man would imagine space any where to be Divided So as there should be Nothing between the Divided parts, there Remains Space between notwithstanding and so "the man-Contradicts himself and it is self-evident I believe to every man that space is necessary, eternal, infinite, & Omnipresent, but I had as Good speak Plain, I have already said as much as that Space is God.[283]

---

280 Faust & Johnson, *Jonathan Edwards*, p. xxvii.

281 Faust & Johnson, *Jonathan Edwards*, p. 19.

282 Faust & Johnson, *Jonathan Edwards*, p. xxviii.

283 Faust & Johnson, *Jonathan Edwards*, p. 19. The most famous proponent of the notion that Space is God is Baruch Spinoza, whose *Tractatus* appeared in 1670 at around the time Danforth was describing the Puritan errand into the wilderness. Roughly 40 years after Edwards wrote his *magnum opus*, *Freedom of the Will*, Fichte published the first iteration of his *Wissenschaftslehre*, which turned Spinoza on its head by claiming that infinite substance was an idea. Pantheism and Idealism, in other words, shared the same error. Spinoza collapsed everything into what Descartes called the *res extensa*, and Fichte collapsed everything into the *res cogitans*, rendering truth, which is the correspondence of the two, impossible for both philosophers. Edwards has the distinction of making both philosophical mistakes at the same time by conflating the mind of God with the substance of the universe, which Edwards describes as "the infinitely exact, and precise, and perfectly stable idea, in God's mind, together with his stable Will, that the same shall gradually be communicated

Part I: Errand Into the Satanic Wilderness

According to the standard version of his intellectual odyssey, Edwards:

> played a very prominent part in many of the major philosophical and theological controversies of the time. . . . In the middle of the century, he fought staunchly for the Calvinistic theory of the freedom of the will. A little later, he was the recognized champion of the Calvinistic forces in the bitter conflict over the doctrine of the total depravity of man. Finally, he plunged into the controversy over the nature of virtue and put on the Calvinistic armor in defense of the doctrine of election. . . . In the midst of these controversies, Edwards erected a stately and well buttressed theological and philosophical system, a system built both of materials inherited from his Calvinistic forebears.[284]

Whig history of this sort ignores the fact that Edwards' project was doomed from the start. Edwards was a metaphysical autodidact who inherited from Puritan forebears like Samuel Willard the compulsion to write a *summa* which would put the *Errand into the Wilderness* on a firm ontological basis. Like Nathaniel Hawthorne, New England's psychiatrist, Edwards was a provincial with no way of breaking out of the Anglo-Centric view of the world forged by the Reformation and confirmed by the Glorious Revolution. He simply accepted the fundamental tenets of Calvinism as a category of reality when instead they were based on categories of the mind—like total depravity and the enslaved will—which emanated from Luther's guilty conscience and resonated with the sexual guilt which the horny, vow breaking priests and nuns who made up the first generation of the reformed party in Germany all shared. The same was true *mutatis mutandis* of Calvin and Beza. As a result, Edwards could provide neither an historical nor a philosophical context for the main pillars of his theology. Edward's defense of the enslaved will is unreadable and riddled with philosophical errors. Far from being "a stately and well buttressed theological and philosophical system," Edwards' attempt to unite Calvin and Locke was futile from the start and based on his misunderstanding of important philosophical principles.

Edwards began his philosophical quest in 1734 by writing "A Divine and Supernatural Light," a treatise on the Reformed principle of *sola gratia*. This "light" was "immediately imparted to the soul by God, of a different nature from any that is obtained by natural means,"[285] which appears to restate the traditional understanding of grace, which was seen as perfecting nature. Grace collaborated with nature to strengthen the will. But for the Reformers, grace obliterated nature by turning the will into a slave of passion. Following Luther and Calvin, Edwards divorced grace from moral effort, claiming

---

to us, and to other minds, according to certain fixed and exact established Methods and Laws."

284 Faust & Johnson, *Jonathan Edwards*, p. xv.
285 Faust & Johnson, *Jonathan Edwards*, p. 102.

that "virtue cannot be cultivated. It cannot be developed by repeated good choices."[286] Edwards thus undermined the basis of the half-way covenant, which emphasized moral effort, and in doing so he paved the way for his expulsion from the Northampton congregation 16 years later.

In 1755, five years after he had been kicked out of his grandfather's congregation in Northampton and three years before he would die of a smallpox inoculation in Princeton, New Jersey, Edwards wrote his treatise on "The Nature of True Virtue," in a vain attempt to square the circle made up of the Calvinist doctrines of innate depravity and predestination, on the one hand, and what Immanuel Kant would call "practical reason" on the other.

In "The Nature of True Virtue," Edwards confounded any coherent understanding or practical reason by basing his argument on a misunderstanding of the principle of synderesis, which "turns human nature to good and objects to evil" by forming the human conscience according to the principles of morality. Synderesis is the mind's assent to the first principle of practical reason, which is that good is to be pursued and evil avoided. Conscience derives from synderesis:

> A mistaken conscience does not stop a person's orientation to the truth, and error can be fixed. Conscience and God's law both bind for Aquinas, not because conscience is perfect or reason is independent of the law, but because conscience mediates God's norms to humans doing a particular action. This is done through the application of synderesis, which is always ordered to moral truth, meaning to God.[287]

Conscience is another example of existence calling essence into being but now in the realm of practical reason. Synderesis properly understood means that man is constrained to choose the good. Because the mind and, therefore, conscience is fallible and influenced by passion, man often chooses an apparent good over the true good. Because of the powerful influence of Calvinism over both his education and his culture, Edwards interpreted synderesis in light of Calvin's understanding of predestination, thereby coming up with a new and quasi-philosophical understanding of the enslaved will by conflating synderesis with the infinite regress, which Aristotle had disproved in his *Metaphysics*. By claiming that each "motive," the term Edwards uses to describe each decision of the will, is determined by a previous motive, which must of necessity end in the unmotivated motive, which all men call God, Edwards, like Luther, makes God the author of evil. Edwards begins this philosophical trek by invoking beauty. Beauty, along with the good and the true, is a transcendental, which means that it is an attribute of being and,

---

286 Faust & Johnson, *Jonathan Edwards*, p. xciv.

287 Cajetan Cuddy, OP., "6 – St. Thomas Aquinas on Conscience," Cambridge Core (Cambridge University Press, 2021), https://www.cambridge.org/core/books/abs/christianity-and-the-laws-of-conscience/st-thomas-aquinas-on-conscience/EF72F23BE0741D93C4A4B54C5980DD63

therefore, of God, but the notion of transcendentals is immediately muddied by association with terms like "benevolence," a term taken eclectically from the Scottish Enlightenment.

According to Edwards, virtue cannot be cultivated. It cannot be developed by repeated good choices. Here again he falls back upon his favorite argument in the *Freedom of the Will*. Each virtuous volition of an agent must proceed either from a preceding virtuous choice or be immediately imparted to the agent. Now every good choice cannot have its origin in an antecedent act of the will, for there must somewhere be a first act from which all others spring. This first act, which by definition cannot spring from a previous choice, must result from impulses external to the agent's will. Edwards concluded, then, that virtue could not be cultivated by repeated acts of choice. It must "take its rise from creation or infusion by God." No truly virtuous acts are begotten, said Edwards, before the marriage of God and the soul. "Seeming virtues and good works before, are not so indeed. They are a spurious brood, being bastards, and not children." "All moral good is from God."[288]

The result was a mish-mash of bad theology and bad philosophy which satisfied no one and eventually got Edwards expelled from the congregation in Northampton in 1750. At that point, Edwards joined the great migration westward and accepted an assignment in Stockbridge, Massachusetts, which had succeeded Northampton as the frontier line which separated existence from essence. Edward's new assignment allowed Edwards to minister to the Indians and carry his own theology to the insane conclusions which its equally insane premises required:

> What is commonly called love of complacence, presupposes beauty. For it is no other than delight in beauty; or complacence in the person or Being beloved for his beauty. If virtue be the beauty of an intelligent Being, and virtue consists in love, then it is a plain inconsistence, to suppose that virtue primarily consists in any love to its object for its beauty; either in a love of complacence, which is delight in a Being for his beauty, or in a love of benevolence, that has the beauty of its object for its foundation. For that would be to suppose that the beauty of intelligent beings primarily consists in love to beauty; or, that their virtue first of all consists in their love to virtue. Which is an inconsistence and going in a circle. Because it makes virtue, or beauty of mind, the foundation or first motive of that love wherein virtue originally consists, or wherein the very first virtue consists; or, it suppose the first virtue to be the consequence and effect of virtue. So that virtue is originally the foundation and exiting cause of the very beginning or first Being of Virtue. Which makes the first virtue, both the ground, and the consequence, both cause and effect of itself. Doubtless virtue primarily consists in something else besides any effect or consequence of virtue. If virtue consists primarily in love to virtue, then

---

288 Faust & Johnson, *Jonathan Edwards* p. xciv.

virtue, the thing loved, is the love of virtue: so that virtue must consist in the love of the love of virtue. And if it be the love of, it must be answered, it is the love of virtue. So that there must be the love of the love of the love of virtue, and so on *in infinitum*. For there is no end of going back in a circle. We never come to any beginning, or foundation. For it is without beginning and hangs on nothing.[289]

Once again Edwards, true to his Calvinist heritage, hijacks the vocabulary of the metaphysical tradition but only to tell his bewildered congregation that everything "hangs on nothing."

---

[289] Faust & Johnson, *Jonathan Edwards*, p. 353.

Chapter 8

Benjamin Franklin and the Rationalist Reaction

The repressed always returns. If man is a rational creature, he cannot live without practical reason, which is another word for morality. By returning to Calvin, Edwards cut the nerve of moral effort once again, thereby paving the way for Ben Franklin. Franklin, who had been baptized by Samuel Willard and raised as a Presbyterian when Cotton Mather was still alive, decided that he could achieve "moral perfection" on his own.

In 1734, in the same year that Jonathan Edwards proclaimed that "All moral good is from God,"[290] Benjamin Franklin was chosen Grand Master of the Masonic lodge of Pennsylvania. Franklin had arrived all but penniless as a 12-year-old in Philadelphia. He had enough money in his pocket to buy a loaf of bread, but his economic prospects were bright because Philadelphia was the most thriving metropolis in the 13 English colonies and opportunities for bright young men abounded. The lack of custom which crippled New England theology favored those who could pluck opportunity from the fecund womb of existence, and Franklin knew how to seize those opportunities, rising from an apprentice printer to the man who epitomized the American Enlightenment.

In 1736, Franklin became clerk of the General Assembly of Pennsylvania and organized the Union Fire Company in Philadelphia.[291] In 1737, Franklin became deputy postmaster of Philadelphia, an office which allowed him to send out copies of *Poor Richard's Almanac* at a reduced price, the sale of which eventually made him independently wealthy and able to represent the United States as ambassador to France at the crucial moment of independence. In addition to being a printer, entrepreneur and diplomat, Franklin was also a scientist and inventor. In 1742 he set to work on his famous stove. In 1743, he brought the men together who eventually established the American Philosophical Society. In 1746, he embarked upon a series of experiments in electricity which led to a scientific theory as well as something as practical as the lightning rod. In 1753, Franklin became deputy postmaster general of

---

290 Faust & Johnson, *Jonathan Edwards*, p. xciv.
291 Goodman, *Benjamin Franklin Reader*, p. 5.

North America, a post which increased the reach of his publications. In 1757, Franklin organized the first fire insurance company in America as well as founding the University of Pennsylvania, and the hospital associated with it before leaving for London to serve as colonial agent of the province of Pennsylvania.[292]

Franklin was also a homespun moral philosopher. Franklin, who was three years younger than Edwards, created a system of moral self-improvement which provided an alternative to the latter's claim that all moral good came from God. Franklin was moved to embark on this project because he had been "religiously educated as a Presbyterian,"[293] according to Calvinist principles which negated moral effort. Because he was constantly bombarded by "dogmas of that persuasion" like "election" and "reprobation," which "appeared to me unintelligible,"[294] Franklin stopped going to church and spent his Sunday mornings reading books of a more practical bent.

At this point in his life, Ben Franklin was not an American. When he arrived in England in July 1757, one year before Jonathan Edwards died, he was "an ardent British imperialist."[295] Samuel Huntington concurs:

> In January 1760 Benjamin Franklin hailed Wolfe's defeat of the French on the Plains of Abraham and proudly proclaimed, "I am a Briton." In July 1776, Franklin signed the Declaration renouncing his British identity. In a few years Franklin transformed himself from a Briton into an American. He was not alone. Between the 1740s and the 1770s a large proportion of the settlers in North America also changed their identity from British to American while maintaining even more intense loyalties to their states and localities. This was a quick and dramatic shift in collective identities. The causes of this rapid emergence of an American identity are complex.[296]

It could instead be argued that Franklin became an American only after he arrived in France on December 21, 1776 as the colonies' ambassador seeking financial support for the revolution against England. Franklin's diplomatic efforts proved wildly successful largely because Franklin symbolized America, and as such the idea that America was the embodiment of the Enlightenment:

> The homely philosophy of Poor Richard, published in French, was the guide and comfort of an untold number of Louis XVI's subjects. Franklin's scientific papers and inventions attracted an ever-increasing audience. Distinguished persons from every country in Europe were eager to visit him, especially now that the Americans had triumphed. His

---

292 Goodman, *Benjamin Franklin Reader*, p. 5.
293 Goodman, *Benjamin Franklin Reader*, p. 117.
294 Goodman, *Benjamin Franklin Reader*, p. 117.
295 Goodman, *Benjamin Franklin Reader*, p. 7.
296 Huntington, *Who Are We?*, p. 109; Thomas de Aquino, *Summa Theologiae*, I^a q. 84-89.

name was at the heads of scores of programs, societies, publications, and entertainments.[297]

"The great Dr. Franklin represented America, and, for his hosts, this America deserved the support of France."[298] America came into being on March 20, 1778 when King Louis XVI recognized America as a nation. Franklin went on to borrow 20 million francs from the French, which allowed the Americans to field the army which defeated the British at Yorktown in October 1781. On November 20, 1781, shouts of exultation rang in the streets of Paris at the news of the signal victory of American and French arms in October. "Peace now appeared inevitable,"[299] prompting Franklin to opine: "I have been apt to think that there has never been, nor ever will be, any such thing as a *good* war, or a *bad* peace."[300]

As another example of how existence modified essence, Franklin abandoned vegetarianism after observing nature and finding that it corresponded with what he wanted to do.

> I believe I have omitted mentioning that, in my first voyage from Boston, being becalm'd off Block Island, our people set bout catching cod, and hauled up a great many. Hitherto I ad stuck to my resolution of not eating animal food, and on this occasion I consider'd, with my master Tryon, the taking, every fish as a kind of unprovoked murder, since none of them had, or ever could do us any injury that might justify the slaughter. All this seemed very reasonable. But I had formerly been a great lover of fish, and, when this came hot out of the frying-pan, it smelt admirably well. I balanc'd some time between principle and inclination, till I recollected that, when the fish were opened, I saw smaller fish taken out of their stomachs; then-thought I, "If you eat one another, I don't see why we mayn't eat you." So I din'd upon cod very heartily; and continued to eat with other people, returning only now and then occasionally to a vegetable diet.[301]

Like Luther and Nietzche, Franklin discovered that religion was ultimately a ratification of the will: "So convenient a thing is it to be a *reasonable creature*, since it enables one to find or make a reason for every thing one has a mind to do." Franklin had been raised as a Presbyterian but soon gave up that faith. He then discovered that he was "under no religious restraint,"[302] which allowed him to give free rein to his sexual passions. As a result:

---

297 Goodman, *Benjamin Franklin Reader*, p. 26.
298 Goodman, *Benjamin Franklin Reader*, p. 21.
299 Goodman, *Benjamin Franklin Reader*, p. 24.
300 Goodman, *Benjamin Franklin Reader*, p. 25.
301 Goodman, *Benjamin Franklin Reader*, p. 76.
302 Goodman, *Benjamin Franklin Reader*, p. 85.

that hard-to-be-governed passion of youth hurried me frequently into intrigues with low women that fell in my way, which were attended with some expense and great inconvenience, besides a continual risque to my health by a distemper which of all things I dreaded, though by great good luck I escaped it.[303]

Bewildered by the proliferation of sects, their emotional excess, and their constant feuding with each other, Ben Franklin decided to create his own religion. After Franklin stopped going to church, he "conceiv'd the bold and arduous project of arriving at moral perfection"[304] via the following method. Franklin created a list of 13 virtues, which included temperance, chastity, and humility, and devoted one week to the study of each in a program which allowed him to go through all 13 virtues four times a year. In dealing with temperance, he exhorted himself "Eat not to dullness; drink not to elevation." To achieve humility, Franklin strove to "imitate Jesus and Socrates." To become chaste, Franklin resolved to "use venery" but "rarely" and only "for health or offspring, never to dullness, weakness, or the injury of your own or another's peace or reputation."[305]

The results of Franklin's attempt to achieve moral perfection were disappointing. After a year, Franklin found himself fuller of moral faults than when he embarked on his project. Struck by "the difficulty of obtaining good and breaking bad habits,"[306] Franklin concluded that the whole project might be "a kind of foppery in morals," that would make him look "ridiculous" and worse "envied and hated" by his friends.[307] Abandoning his goal of "moral perfection," Franklin settled for the consolation prize, which was that he was better for the effort. His attempt to acquire temperance granted him "long-continued health." Frugality made him rich, and sincerity and justice made him agreeable to everyone, even the young.[308] Considering his attempt to become humble, Franklin discovered that he had more success in acquiring the appearance of that virtue than in acquiring the reality,[309] because, as he put it, "no one of our natural passions is so hard to subdue as *pride* for, even if I could conceive that I had completely overcome it, I should probably be proud of my humility."[310]

---

303 Goodman, *Benjamin Franklin Reader*, p. 107.
304 Goodman, *Benjamin Franklin Reader*, p. 119.
305 Goodman, *Benjamin Franklin Reader*, p. 120.
306 Goodman , *Benjamin Franklin Reader*, p. 125.
307 Goodman, *Benjamin Franklin Reader*, p. 126.
308 Goodman, *Benjamin Franklin Reader*, p. 126.
309 Goodman, *Benjamin Franklin Reader*, p. 128.
310 Goodman, *Benjamin Franklin Reader*, p. 129.

Part I: Errand Into the Satanic Wilderness

Eventually, Franklin like his Puritan forebears tried to come up with a creed of his own, but without "any of the distinguishing tenets of any particular sect." The tenets of his creed were:

"That there is one God, who made all things.

"That he governs the world by his providence.

"That he ought to be worshiped by adoration, prayer, and thanksgiving.

"But that the most acceptable service of God is doing good to man.

"That the soul is immortal.

"And that God will certainly reward virtue and punish vice, either here or hereafter."[311]

Franklin died on April 17, 1790 at the age of 84, universally celebrated as "the genius of eighteenth-century America."[312] One year later, "a poor French translation of his autobiography down to the year 1731 appeared under the title: *Memoir de la vie privee de Benjamin Franklin.*"[313]

In the eyes of the French, Benjamin Franklin became the man who epitomized America. Like Prometheus, Franklin stole fire from the skies with his kite and key and used that fire to liberate man from religious prejudice, inspiring the French to march into the abyss of revolution in a way that was more Satanic than the American paradigm which inspired them.

If Edwards erred on the side of favoring essence at the expense of existence, Franklin erred in the opposite direction by favoring existence in a way that denied that there was any essential, i.e., God-given elements which determined the parameters of man's behavior. If man was a creature and God his creator, man operated according to a plan which should at least consult revelation, but this is precisely what Franklin avoided because religion had degenerated into a proliferation of sects whose common denominator was a desire to quarrel with each other over tenets Franklin found irrelevant.

Edwards' failure to understand the psychological roots of the Reformation in sexual sin led him off on a theological wild goose chase which contributed to the total collapse of Calvinism. Like Edwards' theology which was an incoherent and unstable mish-mash of Calvinist principle justified by Enlightenment thinkers like Locke and Newton, the New England synthesis known as Puritanism split along the lines of faith and reason, with Benjamin Franklin epitomizing the Enlightenment reaction to Protestant irrationality. In the end, Franklin's attempt to achieve moral perfection based on his own efforts proved as futile as Edwards' negation of moral effort and total reliance on grace. Both were swept away by the Great Awakening.

---

311 Goodman, *Benjamin Franklin Reader*, p. 130.
312 Goodman, *Benjamin Franklin Reader*, p. 35.
313 Goodman, *Benjamin Franklin Reader*, p. 40.

CHAPTER 9

JONATHAN EDWARDS AND THE GREAT AWAKENING

Existence vetoed essence once again in the outburst of religious hysteria that has come to be known as the Great Awakening, a movement which swept everything—covenant theology, Edwards' neo-Calvinism, and Franklin's rationalism—before it. Perry Miller stressed the role which "the leveling forces of frontier life" played in the Great Awakening, which began in 1734, the year in which Daniel Boone, the paradigmatic frontiersman, was born. The Great Awakening amplified the frontier:

> As the seventeenth century ended, Perry Miller noted, the character of the people underwent a change; they moved further into the frontier, they became more absorbed in business and profits than in religion and salvation, their memories of English social stratification grew dim ... the frontier conspired with the popular disposition to lessen the prestige of the cultured classes and to enhance the social power of those who wanted their religion in a more simple, downright, and "democratic" form. . . . [However,] not until the decade of the Great Awakening [1735-45] did the popular tendency receive distinct articulation through leaders who openly renounced the older conception.[314]

Because of the twin doctrines of innate depravity and predestination, Puritanism was unable to come up with a "common set of moral understandings about good and bad, right and wrong, in the realm of individual and social action" that "any coherent and viable society" needed. When the last ditch lucubrations of Jonathan Edwards made this failure painfully apparent, the visible Elect on earth left their churches and headed off to the woods, where they chose emotional catharsis over rational arguments.

In America, reason confounded led to the emotionalism of the Great Awakening via antinomianism, which had plagued the Puritan Utopia of the Massachusetts Bay Colony as early as 1638 when Anne Hutchinson was expelled from Boston. Once the Reformation broke with the Catholic Church and its adoption of the Aristotelian metaphysical tradition as its

---

314 McLoughlin, *Revivals, Awakenings, and Reform*, p. 44.

philosophical grammar, Puritanism led to antinomianism. In his book on the Great Awakening, McLoughlin describes that philosophical tradition as the "delicate but firm balance of the idealism of Platonic thought (or the mysticism of the saints) and the realism of Aristotelian thought (or the skepticism of the humanist)." This is a debatable proposition, but the slide into antinomianism from Protestant premises is not:

> When Anne Hutchinson claimed that she governed her thought and actions by direct revelations from God and that the Holy Spirit dwelt in her heart, so that she did not need learning or the Bible to understand God's will, the Puritans of Massachusetts banished her for losing her balance. They treated even more harshly than the Quakers, who claimed to receive "leadings" from the Holy Spirit and to be guided by the "inner light" of God's divinity that dwells in all men. Yet the Antinomians and the Quakers were part of that same rebellion against Anglican formalism and sacerdotalism.[315]

Without a metaphysical foundation based on essence as derived from the mind of the Creator, the political understanding of man as the measure of all things quickly devolved into the rule of the strong over the weak. Skepticism flourishes only in academic settings or in the rarefied atmosphere of scholarly discourse of the sort that Hume was rich enough to indulge in with impunity. It could not flourish on the frontier, any more than concepts like predestination and innate depravity. When the Puritan synthesis collapsed, suppressed antinomianism resurfaced as the Great Awakening. Edwards' idealism had serious philosophical consequences, especially in the political realm.

In 1734, Edwards described the outbreak of revivalistic fervor in his parish as "a surprising work of God."[316] Edwards' career as a philosopher/theologian was interrupted by an outburst of mass hysteria which fit in well with the irrationalism of Edwards' doctrine of grace. Both were symptomatic of the collapse of the Puritan synthesis which became too obvious to ignore with the appearance of Willard's *summa* in 1726.

The Great Awakening began in Edwards's own Connecticut River village, Northampton, Massachusetts, in 1734, and spread "over the whole eastern seacoast from Maine to Georgia"[317] until it finally sputtered out from emotional exhaustion in 1749. Faced with the incoherence of the Half-Way covenant, Stoddard's grandson Jonathan Edwards tried to rescue New England Puritanism by returning to its Calvinist sources, with help from Enlightenment thinkers like John Locke and Isaac Newton. The result was even more incoherent than Willard's *summa*. By the time Edwards got

---

315 McLoughlin, *Revivals, Awakenings, and Reform*, p. 42.
316 McLoughlin, *Revivals, Awakenings, and Reform*, p. 45.
317 Faust & Johnson, *Jonathan Edwards*, p. xvii.

Part I: Errand Into the Satanic Wilderness

around to formulating his metaphysics, no one was listening because the Connecticut River Valley had become swept up into a religious movement which McLoughlin describes as "the most extensive intercolonial event," which "reached in virtually every kind of community and crossroads," whose effects were "profoundly unsettling to the established order and then became creative elements in establishing a new order," which included the War of Independence and subsequent nation-building endeavors.[318] McLoughlin cites Perry Miller and Alan Heimert, who:

> argue with considerable effect that the awakening began "a new era, not merely of American Protestantism, but in the evolution of the American mind," that it was a watershed, a break with the Middle Ages, a turning point, a "crisis."[319]

The Great Awakening prepared the way for the American Revolution and the birth of the American nation because it "made the thirteen colonies into a cohesive unit" which shared " a sense of unique nationality, and had inspired them with the belief that they were, 'and of right ought to be,' a free and independent people."[320] McLoughlin lists no fewer than four great awakenings, which take place at "critical disjunctions of our self-understanding,"[321] making the antinomian irrationalism that constituted their essence an essential constituent of American identity. The second great awakening occurred "shortly after the Constitution had launched the American republic," and it "created the definitions of what it meant to be 'an American.'"[322]

McLoughlin compared the Great Awakening to "a string of firecrackers," that:

> began with private explosions of the personality in emotional conversion experiences; these occurred in scattered local revivals in the 1720s and 1730s throughout the colonies. Then, after 1739, when the experience had taken common shape and been given general articulation, the whole of British North America, from Georgia to Nova Scotia, seemed to explode like a string of firecrackers. Massive and continuous revival meetings were kept in motion by traveling preachers from 1740 to 1745. In some places the established authorities tried to quench the riotous behavior of the awakened. In others the local authorities were themselves caught up in it and supported it. There were also examples of nativist reaction among old-light opponents of the awakening, who saw it as the work of

---

318 McLoughlin, *Revivals, Awakenings, and Reform*, p. viii.
319 McLoughlin, *Revivals, Awakenings, and Reform*, p. viii.
320 McLoughlin, *Revivals, Awakenings, and Reform*, p. 1.
321 McLoughlin, *Revivals, Awakenings, and Reform*, p. 2.
322 McLoughlin, *Revivals, Awakenings, and Reform*, p. 1.

the devil or of popular demagogues intent on arousing the rabble against their rulers.[323]

Bushman called the Great Awakening "a psychological earthquake."[324] McLoughlin claims that the Great Awakening came about because of a "growing incongruence between prescriptive norms and prevailing circumstances," which is the conflict between essence and existence.[325] "Friction," he continues, "increased everywhere."[326] The collapse of the Puritan synthesis combined with the exigencies of existence on the Frontier created friction as the two tectonic plates of existence and essence ground against each other until they finally slipped into a new alignment, with existence, as epitomized by the frontier, taking precedence over essence. Like the earthquakes which are the source of this metaphor, the new alignment was accompanied by destructive violence which rearranged life in the colonies.

The Great Awakening was also a reaction to the Enlightenment. Hoping that the Enlightenment could tame the irrational elements which were sweeping away the last vestiges of Puritanism, Charles Chauncy tried to keep religion within the bounds of reason, as defined by Enlightenment thinkers like Locke, Hume, Smith and other Scottish Enlightenment thinkers:

> Chauncy's objection to the preaching of terror was part of a more sweeping condemnation of the Revival. He felt that the religious enthusiasts of the Awakening appealed merely to men's passions. He was disgusted by the irrational extravagance of the movement. It was, he charged, "a *plain stubborn Fact*, that the *Passions* have, *generally*, in *these Times*, been apply'd to, as though the main Thing in Religion was to throw them into Disturbance." Violently he attacked the whole movement as a vain and dangerous explosion of emotion. "Nor unless some Persons are made sensible" of this fact, he wrote, "and take Care to keep their Passions within the Restraints of Reason, may it be expected that Things should be reduced to a State of Order." The phrase "Passions within die Restraints of Reason" indicates the fundamental principle upon which Chauncy based his condemnation of the Awakening. He believed that in all things reason should govern. "The plain Truth," he insisted, is that "an *enlightened Mind*, and not *raised Affections*, ought always to be the Guide of those who call themselves Men; and this, in the Affairs of Religion, as well as other Things." "*Reasonable Beings*," he declared, "are not to be guided by *Passion* or *Affection*, though the Object of it should be GOD, and the Things of another World."[327]

---

323 McLoughlin, *Revivals, Awakenings, and Reform*, p. 59.
324 McLoughlin, *Revivals, Awakenings, and Reform*, p. 57.
325 McLoughlin, *Revivals, Awakenings, and Reform*, p. 52.
326 McLoughlin, *Revivals, Awakenings, and Reform*, p. 52.
327 Faust & Johnson, *Jonathan Edwards*, pp. xx-xxi.

Part I: Errand Into the Satanic Wilderness

Chauncy's main opponent in the battle for the Puritan mind was Jonathan Edwards. Chauncy "did not hesitate in analyzing Edwards's position to cast some slurs upon the man himself, suggesting in one place that Edwards might 'not be suppos'd to be in a proper Temper of Mind to receive the Truth.'"[328]

The preachers who sided with the emotionalism of the Great Awakening were known as the "New Lights." With Edwards as their intellectual leader, they:

> stood at all major points in the controversy squarely with them and squarely in opposition to Chauncy and to the group of which Chauncy was the acknowledged spokesman. Chauncy bewailed the overemphasis upon the affections and the passions in the Revival. Edwards complained that they were not played upon enough. "Our people, he wrote, "do not so much need to have their heads stored, as to have their hearts touched." Chauncy declared that religion ought to be primarily a matter of reason, that "an *enlightened Mind*, and not *raised Affections*" ought to be the guide in religion as in all other things. Edwards asserted that religion is primarily a matter of the affections, and devoted *A Treatise Concerning Religious Affections (1746)* to proving the point.[329]

Chauncy accused Edwards of the "preaching of terror,"[330] as part of a broader critique which claimed that "the religious enthusiasts of the Awakening appealed merely to men's passions."[331] Chauncy went on to attack the Great Awakening as "a vain and dangerous explosion of emotion."[332] Edwards responded to Chauncy's attack by claiming that terror was necessary to keep men from falling into hell.[333] And to prove his point, Edwards gave what is arguably the most famous sermon in American history. Edwards delivered "Sinners in the Hands of an Angry God," in Northampton in 1741 in a deliberated dispassionate manner focusing his eyes on the bell rope at the back of the church while at the same time trying to ignore as best he could the shriekings his sermon evoked when he told them:

> Unregenerate man is a loathsome insect dangling in mid-air over the flames of hell with nothing supporting him but a gossamer thread that threatens to snap at any moment. Worse still, God hates you. "The God that holds you over the pit of hell, much as one holds a spider or some loathsome insect, over the fire, abhors you and is dreadfully provoked."

---

328 Faust & Johnson, *Jonathan Edwards*, pp. xx-xxi.
329 Faust & Johnson, *Jonathan Edwards*, p. xxiii.
330 Faust & Johnson, *Jonathan Edwards*, p. xix.
331 Faust & Johnson, *Jonathan Edwards*, p. xx.
332 Faust & Johnson, *Jonathan Edwards*, p. xx.
333 Faust & Johnson, *Jonathan Edwards*, p. xxii.

God hates you and there's not a damn thing you can do about it: "God has laid himself under no obligation, by any promise to keep any natural man out of hell one moment."[334] You're damned if you do and damned if you don't because human effort is meaningless because when it comes to salvation, man is a totally passive "loathsome insect":

> So that, thus it is that natural men are held in the hand of God, over the pit of hell; they have deserved the fiery pit, and are already sentenced to it; and God is dreadfully provoked, his anger is as great towards them as to those that are actually suffering the executions of the fierceness of his wrath in hell, and they have done nothing in the least to appease or abate that anger, neither is God in the least bound by any promise to hold them up one moment; the devil is waiting for them, hell is gaping for them, the flames gather and flash about them, and would fain lay hold on them, and swallow them up; the fire pent up in their own hearts is struggling to break out: and they have no interest in any Mediator, there are no means within reach that can be any security to them. In short, they have no refuge, nothing to take hold of; all that preserves them every moment is the mere arbitrary will, and uncovenanted, unobliged forbearance of an incensed God.[335]

The real terrors Edwards evokes, however, are metaphysical because creation fades away into insignificance compared to the wrath of God, who dangles man by a slender thread over the flames of eternal punishment:

> That world of misery, that lake of burning brimstone, is extended abroad under you. There is the dreadful pit of the glowing flames of the wrath of God; there is hell's wide gaping mouth open; and you have nothing to stand upon, nor any thing to take hold of; there is nothing between you and hell but the air; it is only the power and mere pleasure of God that holds you up.[336]

Edwards brought the metaphysical doubt which Stoddard described as the "false bottom," to an end by telling his congregation "you have nothing to stand upon." The metaphysical terror which ensued provoked "outcries, faintings, and fits" which were "often welcomed as gracious signs of divine favor."[337] After Edwards told his congregation that "Their foot shall slide in due time. . . the assembly appeared deeply impressed and bowed down with an awful conviction of their sin and danger. There was such a breathing of

---

334 Edwards, *Sinners in the Hands*.
335 Edwards, *Sinners in the Hands*.
336 Edwards, *Sinners in the Hands*.
337 Faust & Johnson, *Jonathan Edwards*, p. xvii.

distress and weeping, that the preacher was obliged to speak to the people and desire silence, that he might be heard."[338]

Edwards was restrained compared to the excesses of James Davenport, who:

> turn'd his Discourse to others, and with the *utmost Strength* of his Lungs address himself to the Congregation, under these and such-like Expressions; viz. You poor unconverted Creatures, in the Seats, in the Pews, in the Galleries, I wonder you don't drop into Hell! It would not surprise me, I should not wonder at it, if I should see you drop down *now, this Minute* into Hell. You Pharisees, Hypocrites, *now, now, now*, you are going right into the Bottom of Hell. I wonder you don't drop into Hell by Scores, and *Hundreds*, etc. . . . [339]

Davenport then

> came out of the Pulpit, and stripped off his upper Garments, and got into the Seats, and leapt up and down some time, and clapt his Hands, and *cried out* in those Words, the War goes on, the Fight goes on, the Devil goes down, the Devil goes down; and then betook himself to *stamping* and *screaming* most dreadfully.[340]

Deprived for generations of the grace which flows from sacramental confession, Englishmen showed up at rallies in both England and America convinced that they were damned. Ronald Knox provides a colorful description of the uproar Methodist rallies were creating in England and Ireland.[341]

---

338 Faust & Johnson, *Jonathan Edwards*, p. xvii.
339 Faust & Johnson, *Jonathan Edwards*, p. xviii.
340 Faust & Johnson, *Jonathan Edwards*, p. xviii.
341 Knox, Enthusiasm, p. 531. At Cardiff ('58) 'two or three were cut to the heart and cried to God with strong cries and tears'. At Norwich ('60) 'a young woman, who had contained herself as long as she could, sunk down and cried aloud. I found this was a new thing at Norwich.' At Otley, near Leeds ('60) 'the Holy Ghost made intercession in all that were present'—this was at a meeting of devout persons. 'At length the travail of their souls burst out into loud and ardent cries... . One cried out, in exceeding great agony, Lord, deliver me from my sinful nature ... a second, with loud and dismal shrieks, I am in hell; O, save me, save me! . . . Thus they continued for the space of two hours.' At Barley, Herts. ('62), 'a middle-aged woman dropped down at my side, and cried aloud for' mercy'. At Limerick ('62) 'many more were brought to the birth. All were in floods of tears, cried, prayed, roared aloud, all of them lying on the ground.' At Macclesfield ('62) 'a man fell down and cried aloud for mercy. In a short time, so did several others. At Grimsby ('64) 'all the gentry of the town were present; and so was our Lord in an uncommon manner. Some dropped down as dead. . . One was carried away in violent fits. I went to her after the service. She was strongly convulsed from head to foot, and shrieked out in a dreadful manner. The unclean spirit did tear her indeed, but his reign was not long.' At Stroud ('65) 'a young man cried out, *I am damned!* and fell to the ground. A second did so quickly after, and was much convulsed, and yet quite sensible.' At Montrath, Ireland ('69), 'in a few minutes her strength failed, and she sunk to the ground. I was sorry they carried her away.' At Enniscorthy ('69) 'one dropped down like a stone; many trembled and wept exceedingly'. At Newcastle ('72) 'an eminent backslider came into my mind, and I broke off abruptly. . . . Is *James Watson here? If he be, shew thy power.* Down

McLoughlin claims that guilt was the driving force behind the Great Awakening, but he can't explain the source of the guilt, claiming that "The guilt is not specific but unconscious, repressed. It is felt as an inexplicable burden, bearing down, which none of the ordinary stress-release mechanisms can relieve."[342] McLoughin also notes that "these periods of cultural readjustment have been associated almost wholly with the Protestant churches,"[343] but he fails to explain why. He gets close to the heart of the matter when he says that the Great Awakening provided an "ecstatic release from the burden of guilt and fear,"[344] but he fails to trace this need for "ecstatic release" to its roots in Protestant theology particularly the paradoxical attitude toward grace. After proclaiming *sola gratia* as one of the pillars of the Reformation, the Protestant Reformers then deprived their flocks of the sources of grace which Christ provided. They did this by abolishing all sacraments but baptism. Especially grave was the abolition of sacramental confession, which left the Elect with no way to deal with the guilt which flowed from their sins.

The lasting effect of "Sinners in the Hands of an Angry God" and its ilk was not what Edwards intended. "Unconverted men," Edwards had told the men who had created the farms of the Connecticut River Valley, "walk over the pit of hell on a rotten covering, and there are innumerable places in this covering so weak that they will not bear their weight, and these places are not seen."[345] Swept up in the emotionalism of the Great Awakening, those men believed him even though their plows had not broken through this thin crust. But after the emotional high wore off, the same men who had rolled shrieking on the floor of the Church in Northampton, stood up, dusted off their clothes, shrugged their shoulders, and headed west, to clear new forests and break new ground. With them they took anger at being manipulated by an inhuman religion that had no authority from either God or man and a resolve not to be pushed around by preachers anymore. Religious essence would have to conform henceforth to the categories of existence which the frontier evoked.

---

dropped James Watson like a stone. In Wales ('74) 'it was a good time. The power of the Lord was unusually present both to wound and to heal.' At Coleford (84) when I began to pray, the flame broke out. Many cried aloud, many sunk / to the ground, many trembled exceedingly.' In London (86) the I power of God came mightily upon us, and there was a general cry. But the voice of two persons prevailed over the rest, one praying, and the other shrieking as in the agonies of death.

342 McLoughlin, *Revivals, Awakenings, and Reform*, p. 65.

343 McLoughlin, *Revivals, Awakenings, and Reform*, p. 2.

344 McLoughlin, *Revivals, Awakenings, and Reform*, p. 21.

345 Jonathan Edwards, *Sinners in the Hands of an Angry God*, Sermon, July 8, 1741, Blue Letter Bible, https://www.blueletterbible.org/Comm/edwards_jonathan/Sermons/Sinners.cfm

Chapter 10

George Whitefield and John Wesley

John Wesley arrived in Georgia along with his brother Charles on February 2, 1736, two years after the Great Awakening broke out in the Connecticut River Valley. According to McLoughlin:

> The Methodist movement began within the Church of England in the 1730s, when John Wesley and George Whitefield were both members of "The Holy Club" at Oxford. Wesley, like Whitefield, went to the colony of Georgia in 1736 to strengthen Anglicanism, but Whitefield proved a far more successful revivalist in the American colonies. Wesley, on the other hand, was far more successful in England. For a time, the two worked closely together, but in 1739 they split after a bitter theological dispute over Calvinism. Wesley attacked the doctrines of predestination and irresistible grace, while Whitefield defended them. Whitefield could never have played so important a part in the First Great Awakening in the colonies had he not been a Calvinist. Wesley took the view that Christ died for the salvation of all men (not just for the predestined elect) and that men have an important role to play in obtaining their own salvation.[346]

Methodism would rescue sexual morality from the sins of its Protestant forebears in America and England, but as the Great Awakening raged on both sides of the Atlantic, it became clear that guilt was its *spiritus movens*. Unlike Whitefield, who clung tenaciously to the tenets of Calvinism, John Wesley was able to succeed where Edwards failed because he claimed that the emotions which the Great Awakening evoked displayed "free, full and present salvation from all guilt, all the power and all the in-being of sin."[347]

Hearing about the "narrative of surprising conversions" while in far off England, George Whitefield arrived in the colonies in 1736 and drove the fervor to new heights. According to McLoughlin:

> Whitefield allowed full range to his flair for histrionics. He would sing hymns, wave his arms, tell stories in colloquial language, employ vivid imagery, weep profusely over his own melo dramatic appeals, and pray

---

346 McLoughlin, *Revivals, Awakenings, and Reform*, p. 94.

347 Ronald Knox, *Enthusiasm: A Chapter in the History of Religion* (Oxford: Clarendon Press, 1950), p. 541.

extemporaneously and directly to God, as though he were talking to him. One provincial American who had never seen anything like it claimed the effect was electric. No one supposed that preachers were to appeal so directly and powerfully to the emotions of their audience (it had not been done since the 1630s). Moralizing and doctrinal sermons had for several generations become the accepted formula for colonial preaching. Whitefield deemphasized the institutional side of religion and emphasized the personal responsibility of the individual.[348]

Whitefield's preaching "set a new style" which impressed people as diverse as Jonathan Edwards and Benjamin Franklin:

> Edwards' wife marveled at his "deep-toned, yet clear and melodious voice" and declared it "wonderful to see what a spell he casts over an audience. ... I have seen upwards of a thousand people hang on his words with breathless silence, broken only by an occasional half-suppressed sob." One ordinary farmer, who saddled his horse, hoisted his wife behind him, and rode madly into town when he heard Whitefield had arrived, said that when Whitefield mounted the scaffold erected for him on the village green, "he looked almost angellical, a young slim, slender youth before some thousands of people & with a bold undainted [undaunted] countenance & my hearing how god was with him every where as he came along it solumnized my mind & put me in a trembling fear before he began to preach, for he looked as if he was Cloathed with authority from ye great god."[349]

Ben Franklin was equally impressed by Whitefield's voice, but instead of taking his words to heart, Franklin calculated how many people could hear what he was saying:

> He had a loud and clear voice, and articulated his words and sentences so perfectly, that he might be heard and understood at a great distance, especially as his auditories, however numerous, observ'd the most exact silence. He preach'd one evening from the top of the Court-house steps, which are in the middle of Market-street, and on the west side of Second-street, which crosses it at right angles. Both streets were fill'd with his hearers to a considerable distance. Being among the hindmost in Market-street, I had the curiosity to learn how far he could be heard, by retiring backwards down the street towards the river; and I found his voice distinct till I came near Front-street, when some noise in that street obscur'd it. Imagining then a semi-circle, of which my distance should be the radius, and that it were fill'd with auditors, to each of whom I allow'd two square feet, I computed that he might well be heard by more than thirty thousand. This reconcil'd me to the newspaper accounts of

---

348 McLoughlin, *Revivals, Awakenings, and Reform*, p. 61.
349 McLoughlin, *Revivals, Awakenings, and Reform*, p. 62.

Part I: Errand Into the Satanic Wilderness

his having preach'd to twenty-five thousand people in the fields, and to the antient histories of generals haranguing whole armies, of which I had sometimes doubted.[350]

Franklin felt that Whitefield abused the people who came to hear him preach, "by assuring them they were naturally *half beasts and half devils.*"[351]

As early as 1739, even its most ardent supporters had to admit that the Great Awakening was getting out of hand. Grace that produced "*swooning away* and *falling to the Ground* . . . bitter *Shriek'tngs* and *Screamings*; *Convulsion-like Tremblings* and *Agitations, Stragglings* and *Tumblings,*"[352] destroyed nature; it did not perfect it, as Aquinas said it should. Edwards noticed that people who were "brought off from Inordinate Engagedness after the world . . . have been ready to Run into the other Extreme of too much neglecting their worldly Business & to mind nothing but religion."[353] Edwards concluded that "if God had manifested a little more of himself to her she would Immediately have sunk & her frame dissolved under it."[354] Amazing grace was destroying nature instead of perfecting it. Edwards' preaching was inspiring such "great longings to die" that his Uncle Hawley, "the last Sabbath day morning, Laid violent Hands on himself & Put an End to his Life by Cutting his own throat."[355] Under Edwards' supervision, Calvinism had become a suicide cult.

Puritanism collapsed in America because "adjustment to the frontier broke down the traditions they brought with them."[356] Ultimately, Calvinism had to cede primacy of place to "common sense," McLoughlin's term for existence, so that New Englanders could "face the Indians and the wilderness in organized townships."[357] McLoughlin claims that the Great Awakening exposed "a long conflict between the demands of authority and the permissiveness of freedom" which eventually gave birth to "the American pattern of constitutional and responsible liberty," which contributed to "the dynamism of the American cultural core."[358]

As Emmanuel Todd could have predicted, the collapse of the form led to violence:

> more often than not this reunited sense of national millenarian purpose has led Americans into war in the effort to speed up the fulfillment of their manifest destiny. It might be more accurately said that our periods

---

350 Goodman, *Benjamin Franklin Reader*, p. 143.
351 Goodman, *Benjamin Franklin Reader*, p. 140.
352 Faust & Johnson, *Jonathan Edwards*, p. xviii.
353 Faust & Johnson, *Jonathan Edwards*, p. 77.
354 Faust & Johnson, *Jonathan Edwards*, p. 80.
355 Faust & Johnson, *Jonathan Edwards*, p. 83.
356 McLoughlin, *Revivals, Awakenings, and Reform*, p. 32.
357 McLoughlin, *Revivals, Awakenings, and Reform*, p. 35.
358 McLoughlin, *Revivals, Awakenings, and Reform*, p. 35.

of great awakening have produced wars rather than resulted from them. All our wars, like Cromwell's against Charles I, have been understood as holy crusades against error within and evil without. Cromwell first destroyed the monarchy and its Cavaliers and then tried to eradicate the Celtic Catholics in Ireland. The colonists, after the First Awakening, first defeated the French and Indians and then threw off the corrupt king and Parliament. The Americans, after the Second Awakening, first eliminated the Indians and Mexicans and British from the West and then attacked those who would secede from the covenant in order to uphold black slavery. At the height of their Third Awakening, Americans stopped attacking big business and turned against "the Hun" to save the world for democracy; the war against Naziism was simply a continuation of that effort.[359]

Existence trumped essence in religion, and the Methodist Jesus, liberated from the strait jacket of Calvinism, was "asking the people to judge and act in terms of their own experiential needs and satisfactions."[360] When *Vox populi* became *Vox Dei*, "itinerant evangelism" contributed to "the emergence of intercolonial unity and the forming of a single American identity."[361] The Great Awakening not only paved the way for the emergence of the American republic, it paved the way for the American Empire because "If God spoke through the common man, the voice of the people was the voice of God. If he spoke everywhere in the same way, then mobility to the West was part of God's plan for perfecting the world."[362] By the time George Washington died in 1799, the Englishmen who had separated from the land of their forebears were asking "What did it mean to be an American?"[363]

---

359 McLoughlin, *Revivals, Awakenings, and Reform*, p. 23.
360 McLoughlin, *Revivals, Awakenings, and Reform*, p. 85.
361 McLoughlin, *Revivals, Awakenings, and Reform*, p. 86.
362 McLoughlin, *Revivals, Awakenings, and Reform*, p. 87.
363 McLoughlin, *Revivals, Awakenings, and Reform*, p. 98.

Chapter 11

The Great Awakening Leads to the American Revolution

Like Samuel Willard before him, Edwards released his *magnum opus*, *The Nature of True Virtue*, into a world which considered it irrelevant to the lives they were leading on the frontier. Even in England, an island with no frontier, Edwards' justification of the enslaved will was met with polite dismissal no matter how many times he cited John Locke. When Boswell reported that Edwards "puzzled" him "so much as to freedom of the human will, by stating with wonderful acute ingenuity, our being actuated by a series of motives which we cannot resist, that the only relief I got was to forget it," Dr. Johnson dismissed the matter with the remark "All theory is against the freedom of the will, all experience for it."[364]

Every successful revolution leads to a civil war. American history is no exception, even though the Civil War occurred some 85 years after the American Revolution. The seeds of that split can be seen in attitudes of two of the most influential founding fathers, Thomas Jefferson and John Adams. If Jefferson represented existence in the person of the frontiersman who rewrote the Bible in light of existence on the frontier, John Adams represented the eastern mercantile class who claimed that there were limits that essence imposed on existence. In a letter to the Massachusetts militia written on October 11, 1798, Adams wrote:

> But should the People of America, once become capable of that deep . . . simulation towards one another and towards foreign nations, which assumes the Language of Justice and moderation while it is practicing Iniquity and Extravagance; and displays in the most captivating manner the charming Pictures of Candour, frankness & sincerity while it is rioting in rapine and Insolence: this Country will be the most miserable Habitation in the World. Because We have no Government armed with Power capable of contending with human Passions unbridled by . . . morality and Religion. Avarice, Ambition . . . Revenge or Galantry, would break the strongest Cords of our Constitution as a Whale goes

---

[364] Jonathan Edwards, *Representative Selections* (New York: Hill and Wang, 1935), p. lvi.

through a Net. Our Constitution was made only for a moral and religious People. It is wholly inadequate to the government of any other."[365]

Nothing dramatized Adams' claim better than the two differing perceptions of the same cultural icon, Ben Franklin. For Americans he is the kindly balding and bespectacled old man in the Disney film *Ben and Me*, the same persona who gets trotted out for parades and advertising campaigns. But for the French, Franklin is the "Electrical Ambassador" who exploited the French thirst for scientific learning and then mobilized it politically. "It is universally believed in France," wrote John Adams, "that his electric wand has accomplished all this revolution." The "French" Franklin was very similar to the French Revolution, and in this an antithesis to the American event which inspired its name if not its outcome and philosophy. The Promethean tamer of celestial fire was a creation of the French imagination and needs. Franklin as the "harbinger of liberty" meant that liberty would be defined according to those needs, and not necessarily as it had been defined in America under the auspices of a very different revolution.

But as the terms of the argument proliferate, so do the equivocations. As with revolution, so with liberty, the Americans had one idea and the French had another, each expressed by the same word. John Adams, unlike Thomas Jefferson – with whom, however, he reached a surprising degree of consensus in later life – could hardly be considered part of the Jacobin party even though he was, in the American sense of the term, a *bona fide* "revolutionary." The dichotomy between the French and American revolutions becomes apparent in his works. In reading the Marquis de Condorcet's *Progress of the Human Mind*, Adams became so exercised at Condorcet's views that he felt compelled to express himself in the margins of his copy of the book. Condorcet felt that "no bounds have been fixed to the improvement of the human faculties, that the perfectibility of man is absolutely infinite," and as a result priests had become dupes of religious "fables" that enslaved man, but Adams was of another, equally forceful opinion. "Just as you and yours," he wrote in the margin of Condorcet's book, "have become the dupes of your own atheism and profligacy, your nonsensical notions of liberty, equality, and fraternity. . . . Your philosophy, Condorcet, has waged a more cruel war on truth than was ever attempted by king or priest." When Condorcet proposed the natural equality of mankind as the foundation of morality, Adams affirmed, again in the margins, that "there is no such thing [as morality] without the supposition of a God. There is no right or wrong in the universe without the supposition of a moral government and an intellectual and moral governor."[366]

---

365 *From John Adams to Massachusetts Militia*, October 11, 1798. https://founders.archives.gov/documents/Adams/99-02-02-3102
366 Krason, pp. 87–88.

Part I: Errand Into the Satanic Wilderness

America, in other words, was different from France, certainly when it came to terms like *revolution* and *liberty*. Indeed, the prime difference between the American and Jacobin "revolutionary" regimes revolved around the moral law, a fact noticed by Alexis de Tocqueville, one of the most perceptive observers of American mores in the nineteenth century. Tocqueville had the sequelae of the French Revolution fresh in his mind when he came to America to see if democracy was salvageable as a principle of social order. After touring the country and taking into account the peculiarities of government, geography, and mores, Tocqueville concluded that the United States was unique as a successful democracy because it differed from the classical examples where democracy had inevitably led to tyranny because the customs in the United States were congruent with the moral law. Like Adams and unlike his countryman Condorcet, Tocqueville saw religion and morals not only as compatible with democratic liberty, he saw them as its essential *conditio sine qua non*. Unlike the Jacobins, who saw religion as the enemy of "science" and progress, Tocqueville saw it as the guardian of morals, which in turn became the guarantor of social order. The dichotomy Tocqueville draws between "revolutionary" America and revolutionary France was a striking instantiation of the same classical tradition in politics which Barruel drew on in his *History of Jacobinism*. Ethics, economics (from the *oikos* or family), and politics are in effect three concentric circles radiating out from the good; they are the way man achieves the good as an individual, as a member of the family, and as a member of society respectively. Tocqueville is at first struck by the absence of religion in public life as effected by the separation of church and state, but concludes that appearances can be deceiving:

> In the United States religion exercises but little influence upon the laws and upon the details of public opinion; but it directs the customs of the community, and, by regulating domestic life, it regulates the state.[367]

In this regard, America was the antithesis of revolutionary France where the revolutionary "tries to forget his domestic troubles by agitating society." In America, on the other hand, the average citizen "derives from his own home that love of order which he afterwards carries with him into public affairs."

> I do not question that the great austerity of manners that is observable in the United States arises, in the first instance, from religious faith. Religion is often unable to restrain man from the numberless temptations which chance offers; nor can it check that passion for gain which everything contributes to arouse, but its influence over the mind of woman is supreme, and women are the protectors of morals. There is certainly no country in the world where the tie of marriage is more respected than in America or where conjugal happiness is more highly or worthily appreciated. In Europe almost all the disturbances of society arise from the irregularities

---

367 Tocqueville, *Democracy in America*, p. 304.

of domestic life. To despise the natural bonds and legitimate pleasures of home is to contract a taste for excesses, a restlessness of heart and fluctuating desires. Agitated by the tumultuous passions that frequently disturb his dwelling, the European is galled by the obedience which the legislative powers of the state exact. But when the American retires from the turmoil of public life to the bosom of his family, he finds in it the image of order and peace. There his pleasures are simple and natural, his joys are innocent and calm; and as he finds that an orderly life is the surest path to happiness, he accustoms himself easily to moderate his opinions as well as his tastes. While the European endeavors to forget his domestic troubles by agitating society, the American derives from his own home that love of order which he afterwards carries with him into public affairs.[368]

The reason that Tocqueville believed that American was unique is simple: "There is no country in the world where the Christian religion retains a greater influence over the souls of men than in America." Liberty, as defined by the Enlightenment in France, became a consequence of and an excuse for immoral behavior, and social chaos and terror were the results. In America, democracy succeeded because there "every principle of the moral world is fixed and determinate." Social innovation and political adventurism find a natural brake in America because the tenets of the moral order are so deeply engrained in the mores of its citizens. A certain stability in the social order, therefore, necessarily follows:

> Thus, the human mind is never left to wander over a boundless field; and whatever may be its pretensions, it is checked from time to time by barriers that it cannot surmount. Before it can innovate, certain primary principles are laid down, and the boldest conceptions are subjected to certain forms which retard and stop their completion.[369]

In America, existence provided a check on utopian schemes that did not happen in France. "The revolutionists of America," Tocqueville continues:

> are obliged to profess an ostensible respect for Christian morality and equity, which does not permit them to violate wantonly the laws that oppose their desires; nor would they find it easy to surmount the scruples of their partisans even if they were able to get over their own. Hitherto none in the United States has dared to advance the maxim that everything is permissible for the interests of society, an impious adage which seems to have been invented in an age of freedom to shelter all future tyrants. Thus, while the law permits the Americans to do what they please, religion prevents them from conceiving and forbids them to commit what is rash or unjust.

---

368 Tocqueville, *Democracy in America*, p. 304.
369 Tocqueville, *Democracy in America*, p. 305.

Part I: Errand Into the Satanic Wilderness

By the time Tocqueville wrote those lines, religion, or essence, had been modified by the wilderness, or existence, in ways that brought crazy Protestant sects like Puritanism and Quakerism into greater alignment with practical reason, creating the idea that American democracy was different. That idea became the crux of just about all of Henry James's novels, where brash and innocent American morals confronted decadent but nonetheless still-appealing European mores. The world of Daisy Miller and Christopher Newman is more than Victorian; it is American and, therefore, innocent, bespeaking a new Adam in a new world, where the constraints and dichotomies of the past no longer applied. The prime dichotomy which America had proven wrong existed between the poles of freedom and license. Democracy, according to classical political theory, was always the lowest form of government and the last because the unrestrained passions of "free" men invariably created so much social chaos that tyranny was the inevitable consequence. Because men could not impose order on themselves, as was invariably the case with democracy, order had to be imposed from without. Hence, tyranny, according to the ancients, was always the natural consequence of democracy. If America proved this ancient maxim wrong, it was by regulating freedom at its source in personal morality. Self-government, if that is what democracy is, was saved from its own excesses by government of the self – in other words, as Tocqueville demonstrated, that America's citizens adhered to the moral law and therefore made dictatorship unnecessary.

Writing roughly 130 years after Tocqueville, John Courtney Murray made the same point in *We Hold These Truths*. Like Adams and Tocqueville, Murray saw a "radical distinction between the American and the Jacobin traditions" because America, although it has "its share of agnostics and unbelievers . . . has never known organized militant atheism on the Jacobin, doctrinaire socialist or communist model; it has rejected parties and theories which erect atheism into a political principle."[370] Religion, as Adams said, is the guarantor of morals, and moral restraint is the guarantor of freedom because it retards the spread of social disorder, which invariably brings a tyrant in its wake. "Freedom" without morals is a contradiction in terms, one which got lived out to its horrific end in the French Revolution, the Weimar Republic, the Soviet Union, and in the weird versions of French culture that flourished in Indo-China after World War II. According to Murray, the American experience is not only different, it is the antithesis of the French Revolution because:

> Part of the inner architecture of the American ideal of freedom has been the profound conviction that only a virtuous people can be free. It is not an American belief that free government is inevitable, only that it is possible, and that its possibility can be realized only when the people

---
370 Murray, *We Hold These Truths*, p. 29.

as a whole are inwardly governed by the recognized imperatives of the universal moral law.

Murray wrote those words in 1960 and died before the decade was out. He did not, as a result, live to see the American experiment come crashing down around him when the culture he loved took his prediction as if it were a dare. Murray makes clear that the American "exception" has one cause: the fact that the moral order has been incorporated into American mores and allowed to flourish there unimpeded by the American constitution's concept of limited government. Adherence to the moral law is, in this view, the *sine qua non* of freedom:

> The American experiment reposes on Acton's postulate, that freedom is the highest phase of civil society. But it also reposes on Acton's further postulate, that the elevation of a people to this higher phase of social life supposes, as its condition, that they understand the ethical nature of political freedom. They must understand, in Acton's phrase, that freedom is "not the power of doing what we like, but the right of being able to do what we ought." The people claim this right, in all its articulated forms, in the face of government; in the name of this right, multiple limitations are put upon the power of government. But the claim can be made with the full resonance of moral authority only to the extent that it issues from an inner sense of responsibility to a higher law. In any phase civil society demands order. In its highest phase of freedom, it demands that order should not be imposed from the top down, as it were, but should spontaneously flower outward from the free obedience to the restraints and imperatives that stem from inwardly possessed moral principle. In this sense democracy is more than a political experiment; it is a spiritual and moral enterprise. And its success depends upon the virtue of the people who undertake it. Men who would be politically free must discipline themselves. Likewise institutions which would pretend to be free with a human freedom in their workings must be governed from within and made to serve the ends of virtue. Political freedom is endangered in its foundations as soon as the universal moral values, upon whose shared possession the self-discipline of a free society depends, are no longer vigorous enough to restrain the passions and shatter the selfish inertia of men. The American ideal of freedom as ordered freedom, and therefore an ethical ideal, has traditionally reckoned with these truths, these truisms.[371]

When Murray claimed that "Men who would be politically free must discipline themselves," he expressed "the profound conviction that only a virtuous people can be free." In doing so, he defined the essence of the American experiment which emerged from the American Revolution after

---

371 Murray, *We Hold These Truths*, pp. 36–37.

Part I: Errand Into the Satanic Wilderness

Calvinist essence got modified by the American frontier. America had become a political experiment based on a moral foundation, and as such it was the antithesis of the Illuminist tradition of Adam Weishaupt, which proposed, in the same year that Americans declared their independence, a way of governing men covertly by first ascertaining and then gratifying their illicit passions. Weishaupt's Illuminist option took on force after World War I when the technology to implement it became available.

Part II
The Romantic Rehabilitation of Nature

Chapter 12

Daniel Boone: Essence meets Existence

"I have never in my life seen a Kentuckian who didn't have a gun, a pack of cards, and a jug of whiskey."   — Andrew Jackson[372]

The Adamses, Henry James favorably observed, "have a very pretty little life."[373]

On July 14, 1776, ten days after the 13 colonies declared independence from England in Philadelphia, Jemima Boone, daughter of the famous frontiersman Daniel, along with Elizabeth and Frances Callaway, were captured by a Cherokee-Shawnee raiding party as the girls' canoe floated down the Kentucky River. After learning that they had been spirited across the Ohio River into Shawnee territory, Boone immediately organized a rescue party and caught up with the Indian kidnappers three days later as they were building a fire for breakfast. After Boone shot one of the kidnappers, the Indians retreated allowing him to rescue the girls and take them home. The incident not only made Boone famous, but it also made the rifle the symbol of American identity. Daniel Boone became an American legend because the rifle allowed him to take the law, which did not exist on the frontier, into his own hands. That idea lodged permanently in the American psyche and would recur over and over again throughout the 20th century, most notably in Clint Eastwood movies, where the gun became the magic wand which solved American's race problem.

Daniel Boone was born two years before the beginning of the Great Awakening. When Jonathan Edwards died in Princeton, New Jersey, on March 22, 1758, at the age of fifty-four, Daniel Boone was 24 years old. Boone is most frequently portrayed with a rifle in his hands. This may seem odd because Boone started off in life as a Quaker from Pennsylvania and went on to achieve fame as the man who guided settlers through the Cumberland

---

372 "Andrew Jackson," goodreads, https://www.goodreads.com/quotes/871276-i-have-never-in-my-life-seen-a-kentuckian-who
373 Brown, *The Last American Aristocrat*, p. 179.

Walking with a Bible and a Gun

Gap into Kentucky. He was the first Englishman to breach the wall which the Appalachian Mountains posed to western migration. To do that, Boone needed a musket. As soon as Boone picked up the musket which was the indispensable instrument which allowed him to survive on the frontier, he had to abandon his pacifist religion. He thus became the archetypal American, who allowed existence to determine essence.

Ben Franklin's experiences provide another striking example of Quakerism as a religion which could not survive the test of existence. As a true son of Boston, where two members of the Society of Friends were hanged in 1659 because of religious beliefs which allowed them to run around naked,[374] Franklin hated Quakers, largely because of their hypocrisy, which revolved around the idea of self-defense. Franklin concluded that "the defense of the country was not disagreeable to any of them, provided they were not requir'd to assist in it."[375] That hypocrisy became apparent to him as a young man, while sailing from Boston to Philadelphia, when Franklin and the rest of the crew descried a sail on the horizon which bespoke an imminent attack from pirates:

> Their captain prepar'd for defense; but told William Penn, and his company of Quakers, that he did not expect their assistance, and they might retire into the cabin, which they did, except James Logan, who chose to stay upon deck, and was quarter'd to a gun. The suppos'd enemy prov'd a friend, so there was no fighting; but when the secretary went down to communicate the intelligence, William Penn rebuk'd him severely for staying upon deck, and undertaking to assist in defending the vessel, contrary to the principles of Friends, especially as it had not been required by the captain. This reproof, being before all the company, piqu'd the secretary who answer'd, *"I being thy servant, why did thee not order me to come down? But thee was willing enough that I should stay and help to fight the ship when thee thought there was danger."*[376]

Quakers were avid to retain their property but were unwilling to defend it themselves, a situation which required them to pay others to do it for them while at the same time disguising that fact from themselves and everyone else. This required:

> a variety of evasions to avoid complying, and modes of disguising the compliance when it became unavoidable. The common mode at last was, to grant money under the phrase of its being "*for the kings use,*" and never to inquire how it was applied. . . . they could not grant money to buy powder, because that was an ingredient of war; but they voted an aid to

---

374 "The Boston martyrs –four Quakers hanged," My Four Legged Stool, July 26, 2018, https://www.myfourleggedstool.com/blog/the-boston-martyrs-four-quakers-hanged

375 Goodman, *Benjamin Franklin Reader*, p. 147.

376 Goodman, *Benjamin Franklin Reader*, pp. 148-9.

Part II: The Romantic Rehabilitation of Nature

New England of three thousand pounds, to be put into the hands of the governor, and appropriated it for the purchasing of bread, flour, wheat, or other grain. Some of the council, desirous of giving the House still further embarrassment, advis'd the governor not to accept provision, as not being the thing he had demanded; but he reply'd, "I shall take the money, for I understand very well their meaning; *other grain* is gunpowder," which he accordingly bought, and they never objected to it.[377]

Quakers had no qualms about purchasing a cannon as long as it was denominated "a fire engine."[378] Because their religion had been made up by human beings at one time, Quakers felt that its tenets could be modified at another, leaving them nothing but expediency as a guide:

> "When we were first drawn together as a society," says he, "it had pleased God to enlighten our minds so far as to see that some doctrines, which we once esteemed truths, were errors; and that others, which we had esteemed errors, were real truths. From time to time, He has been pleased to afford us farther light, and our principles have been improving, and our errors diminishing. Now we are not sure that we are arrived at the end of this progression, and at the perfection of spiritual or theological knowledge; and we fear that, if we should once print our confession of faith, we should feel ourselves as if bound and confin'd by it, and perhaps be unwilling to receive further improvement, and our successors still more so, as conceiving what we their elders and founders had done, to be something sacred, never to be departed from."[379]

Like Jonathan Edwards, the Quakers were flummoxed by the impossibility of the infinite regress. Once again it was turtles all the way down. The Quakers were confirmed, however, in their ignorance of basic metaphysical principles by the "inner light" which made the entire sect infallible and impossible to talk to.

Franklin may have hated Quakers, but he was no Voltaire. He did not sign every letter "*Ecrasez l'infame*," largely because there was no Catholic Church of any significance to crush in America, and crushing Quakerism was hardly worth the effort. Instead, he concluded that the sects which proliferated in America were like men travelling in foggy weather and that all of them should be treated with benign neglect:

> This modesty in a sect is perhaps a singular instance in the history of mankind, every other sect supposing itself in possession of all truth, and that those who differ are so far in the wrong; like a man traveling in foggy weather, those at some distance before him on the road he sees wrapped up in the fog, as well as those behind him, and also the people in the

---

377 Goodman, *Benjamin Franklin Reader*, p. 149.
378 Goodman, *Benjamin Franklin Reader*, p. 150.
379 Goodman, *Benjamin Franklin Reader*, p. 150.

fields on each side, but near him all appears clear, tho' in truth he is as much in the fog as any of them. To avoid this kind of embarrassment, the Quakers have of late years been gradually declining the public service in the Assembly and in the magistracy, choosing rather to quit their power than their principle.[380]

In 1742, Daniel Boone's family ran afoul of their local Quaker community when Boone's parents were forced to make a public apology because their eldest daughter Sarah married a non-Quaker while visibly pregnant. When his eldest son Israel also married outside of the Quaker community in 1747, Squire Boone refused to apologize and was expelled from the Quaker meeting house in Pennsylvania.

Three years later, Squire Boone set the pattern for his son Daniel's life when he sold his property in Pennsylvania and moved to a frontier settlement in North Carolina. Daniel Boone never went to church again. "Although he always considered himself a Christian and had all of his children baptized,"[381] existence on the frontier modified the essence of religion in a way which would bring the archetypal American into being. The Puritans of Massachusetts were by nature bellicose, as Cromwell had shown in England and Ireland, but a Pennsylvanian was a Quaker who picked up a gun as he headed west. Over the course of the following centuries, the Puritans and Quakers would merge into generic Americans because their existence on the frontier called forth a new essence, known as American identity, as common experience of existence molded the 13 colonies into one nascent nation.

After using his gun to rescue his daughter from Indian captivity, Daniel Boone became the paradigmatic frontiersman pioneering the way that allowed farmers to enter the rich pastures of Kentucky and then move on to Missouri, "where this settlement was long a trademark on the frontier."[382] Boone opened the way for civilization by "finding salt licks, and trails, and land."[383] Boone, according to Turner, epitomized the "militant expansive movement in American life." His passage through the Cumberland Gap foretold the expansion of:

> settlement across the Alleghanies in Kentucky and Tennessee; the Louisiana Purchase, and Lewis and Clark's transcontinental exploration; the conquest of the Gulf Plains in the War of 1812-15; the annexation of Texas; the acquisition of California and the Spanish Southwest. They represent, too, frontier democracy in its two aspects personified in Andrew Jackson and Abraham Lincoln. It was a democracy responsive

---

380 Goodman, *Benjamin Franklin Reader*, p. 150-1.
381 "Daniel Boone," *Wikipedia: The Free Encyclopedia*, https://en.wikipedia.org/wiki/Daniel_Boone
382 Turner, p. 7.
383 Turner, p. 7.

Part II: The Romantic Rehabilitation of Nature

to leadership, susceptible to waves of emotion, of a "high religeous voltage"—quick and direct in action. . . . A new society had been established, differing in essentials from the colonial society of the coast. It was a democratic self-sufficing, primitive agricultural society, in which individualism was more pronounced than the community life of the lowlands. . . . It was a region of hard work and poverty, not of wealth and leisure. Schools and churches were secured under serious difficulty, if at all; but in spite of the natural tendencies of a frontier life, a large portion of the interior showed a distinctly religious atmosphere.[384]

The Cumberland Gap provided the same "gate of escape from the bondage of the past"[385] which Dimmesdale rejected in his reverie in the forest with Hester and Pearl. Daniel Boone was Dimmesdale's opposite because he led "hundreds of North Carolina backwoodsmen"[386] into Tennessee and Kentucky, where the "bonds of custom" were broken and "unrestraint" was "triumphant."[387] Protestantism was no match for "the stubborn American environment" and "its imperious summons to accept its conditions."[388] The American environment caused a total reversal of the relationship between nature and grace. In Europe, grace perfected nature. In America, nature perfected grace.

---

[384] Turner, p. 36.
[385] Turner, p. 13.
[386] Turner, p. 40.
[387] Turner, p. 13.
[388] Turner, p. 13.

Chapter 13

Natty Bumppo and the "Core Myth" of American Identity

Fifty years after Boone rescued his daughter, James Fenimore Cooper took his story and reworked it into the plot of his most famous novel *The Last of the Mohicans*. Cooper created the first pan-American paradigm because he was the first American writer. Thanks to Cooper's skill as a novelist, the real Daniel Boone became the mythic Natty Bumppo. Cooper:

> Almost single-handedly in the 1820s . . . invented the key forms of American fiction—the Western, the sea tale, the Revolutionary romance—forms that set a suggestive agenda for subsequent writers, even for Hollywood and television. Furthermore, in producing and shrewdly marketing fully 10 percent of all American novels in the 1820s, most of them best sellers, Cooper made it possible for other aspiring authors to earn a living by their writings. That was a rare prospect at a time when "American literature" still seemed like a contradiction in terms and when, even in England, many writers received little income from their work. Owing to this combination of literary innovation and business acumen, Cooper can be said to have invented not just an assortment of literary types but the very career of the American writer. So deep and enduring has been his effect that it is impossible to map the country's cultural landscape without him. As much as the political "Founding Fathers," Cooper left a documentary imprint on the national mind.[389]

In writing *The Leatherstocking Tales*, Cooper created the first example of the archetypal American.[390] Cooper wrote *The Pioneers*, the first installment of his *Leatherstocking Tales* in 1823, three years after Boone's death, when Boone had already become the archetypal frontiersman in the eyes of the English colonists. Cooper cemented Boone's status by turning him into Natty Bumppo, who grew younger and more mythic with each installment of *The Leatherstocking Tales*. Like Daniel Boone, Cooper was raised as a Quaker.

---

389 Franklin, *James Fenimore Cooper*, p. xi.
390 "Capture and rescue of Jemima Boone," *Wikipedia: The Free Encyclopedia*, https://en.wikipedia.org/wiki/Capture_and_rescue_of_Jemima_Boone

Walking with a Bible and a Gun

Cooper's family came from a settlement just north of Philadelphia known as Byberry, which fittingly became home to the largest insane asylum in the area. Cooper's Quaker roots prompted his biographer Wayne Franklin to say that:

> The alliance between Cooper and the Yankee settlers was an odd one. Cooper came from a Quaker background in the Delaware valley above Philadelphia. Although no active Friend himself, he had followed the sect's pacifist principles in shunning a direct role in the Revolution. By contrast, the Yankee emigrants sprang from militant Puritan ancestors who had persecuted New England's Quakers and other dissenters. And, although there were Loyalists enough in New England during the Revolution, the Yankee states had sent out hordes of fighters to wage war against Britain. Militarism was as ingrained among Puritans as pacifism was among Quakers. But in this new campaign against the American continent, the sometime Quaker William Cooper and these Puritan offspring would meet and join forces.[391]

Like the role which the Glorious Revolution played in England by giving Cavaliers and Roundheads a common Protestant identity, Cooper united Puritans and Quakers by placing them on the frontier and giving them guns, at which point they became Americans. By the time Natty Bumppo emerged as the hero of *The Last of the Mohicans*, he was no longer the toothless old man of *The Pioneers*, long bypassed by the westward march of the frontier. He was a vibrant man of action in the prime of life who epitomized the energetic decisiveness of the new nation. Natty was the quintessential American because he could act in unprecedented contexts without recourse to custom or law. The instrument which enabled that ability was the rifle, which, according to Cooper, was an integral part of Natty's motley costume:

> The frame of the white man, judging by such parts as were not concealed by his clothes, was like that of one who had known hardships and exertion from his earliest youth. His person, though muscular, was rather attenuated than full; but every nerve and muscle appeared strung and indurated by unremitted exposure and toil. He wore a hunting shirt of forest-green, fringed with faded yellow, and a summer cap of skins which had been shorn of their fur. He also bore a knife in a girdle of wampum, like that which confined the scanty garments of the Indian, but no tomahawk. His moccasins were ornamented after the gay fashion of the natives, while the only part of his under dress which appeared below the hunting-frock was a pair of buckskin leggings, that laced at the sides, and which were gartered above the knees, with the sinews of a deer. A pouch and horn completed his personal accouterments, though a rifle of great length, which the theory of the more ingenious whites had

---

391 Franklin, *James Fenimore Cooper*, p. 2.

Part II: The Romantic Rehabilitation of Nature

taught them was the most dangerous of all firearms, leaned against a neighboring sapling."[392]

After the publication of *The Leatherstocking Tales*, American identity involved the ability to fire a rifle, a skill which made religion unnecessary. Cooper portrays this transformation in *The Last of the Mohicans* in the debate between Natty and David, the hapless choir director who wanders in the wilderness armed with nothing but a pitchpipe. Natty quickly cuts to the heart of the matter when he asks David: "Can you use the smoothbore, or handle the rifle?"

"Praised be God," David the hapless psalmist replies, "I have never had occasion to meddle with murderous implements! I practice no such employment. . . . I follow no other than my own high vocation, which is instruction in sacred music!"[393]

Natty, who is also known as Hawkeye, is dismissive of David's psalmody:

> "'Tis a strange calling!" muttered Hawkeye, with an inward laugh, "to go through life, like a catbird, mocking all the ups and downs that may happen to come out of other men's throats. Well, friend, I suppose it is your gift, and mustn't be denied any more than if 'twas shooting, or some other better inclination."[394]

Cooper is too sophisticated a writer to turn Natty Bumppo into the 19th century version of Dirty Harry. In referring to David's pitchpipe as "the tooting we'pon of the singer,"[395] Natty ridicules the "strange calling" of the frontier psalmist, but he gets carried away by David's music in spite of himself. After hearing David's music fill the "confined cavern" with the "thrilling notes of the flexible voices,"[396] Natty:

> who had placed his chin on his hand with an expression of cold indifference, gradually suffered his rigid features to relax, until, as verse succeeded verse, he felt his iron nature subdued, while his recollection was carried back to boyhood, when his ears had been accustomed to listen to similar sounds of praise, in the settlements of the colony.[397] . . . His roving eyes began to moisten, and before the hymn was ended scalding tears rolled out of fountains that had long seemed dry, and followed each other down those cheeks, that had oftener felt the storms of heaven than any testimonials of weakness.[398]

---

392 Mohicans, loc. 413.
393 Mohicans, loc. 928.
394 Mohicans, loc. 930.
395 Mohicans, loc. 3167.
396 Mohicans, loc. 943.
397 Mohicans, loc. 945.
398 Mohicans, loc. 948-9.

Cooper's psychological sophistication in showing Natty's nostalgia for the religion of his childhood, however, should not blind us to the fact that he saw Calvinism as the enemy of all decent Americans. In spite of his ability to move Natty's soul with his music, David the choirmaster is a Calvinist who claims that "the true spirit of Christianity" means "that he who is to be saved will be saved, and he that is predestined to be damned will be damned. This is the doctrine of truth, and most consoling and refreshing it is to the true believer."[399]

After, tellingly, "examining into the state of his rifle with a species of parental assiduity" before he speaks, Natty rejects David's Calvinism, as "the belief of knaves, and the curse of an honest man. I can credit that yonder Huron was to fall by my hand, for with my own eyes I have seen it; but nothing short of being a witness will cause me to think he has met with any reward, or that Chingachgook there will be condemned at the final day."[400]

David, however, is determined to defend the old religion:

"You have no warranty for such an audacious doctrine, nor any covenant to support it," cried David who was deeply tinctured with the subtle distinctions which, in his time, and more especially in his province, had been drawn around the beautiful simplicity of revelation, by endeavoring to penetrate the awful mystery of the divine nature, supplying faith by self-sufficiency, and by consequence, involving those who reasoned from such human dogmas in absurdities and doubt; "your temple is reared on the sands, and the first tempest will wash away its foundation. I demand your authorities for such an uncharitable assertion (like other advocates of a system, David was not always accurate in his use of terms). Name chapter and verse; in which of the holy books do you find language to support you?"[401]

Cooper was acute enough to know that the temple known as the American religion of Nature, which Emerson would articulate at Harvard ten years later was "reared on the sands" every bit as much as the foundationless Calvinism it replaced. Natty, however, is not intimidated by what David has learned in books because he has access to a higher authority:

"Book!" repeated Hawkeye, with singular and ill-concealed disdain; "do you take me for a whimpering boy at the apron string of one of your old gals; and this good rifle on my knee for the feather of a goose's wing, my ox's horn for a bottle of ink, and my leathern pouch for a cross-barred handkercher to carry my dinner? Book! what have such as I, who am a warrior of the wilderness, though a man without a cross, to do with books? I never read but in one, and the words that are written there are

---

399 Mohicans, loc. 1948-9.
400 Mohicans, loc. 1949.
401 Mohicans, loc. 1954-9.

too simple and too plain to need much schooling; though I may boast that of forty long and hard-working years."

"What call you the volume?" said David, misconceiving the other's meaning.

"'Tis open before your eyes," returned the scout; "and he who owns it is not a niggard of its use. I have heard it said that there are men who read in books to convince themselves there is a God. I know not but man may so deform his works in the settlement, as to leave that which is so clear in the wilderness a matter of doubt among traders and priests. If any such there be, and he will follow me from sun to sun, through the windings of the forest, he shall see enough to teach him that he is a fool, and that the greatest of his folly lies in striving to rise to the level of One he can never equal, be it in goodness, or be it in power."[402]

By the time Cooper wrote *The Last of the Mohicans*, Calvinism had been defeated by the religion of Nature. As soon as he "discovered that he battled with a disputant who imbibed his faith from the lights of nature, eschewing all subtleties of doctrine," David, like the Calvinists of Boston who were on their way to becoming Unitarians, "willingly abandoned a controversy from which he believed neither profit nor credit was to be derived."[403] Natty doesn't need to read books because he "imbibed his faith from the lights of nature, eschewing all subtleties of doctrine. . . ."[404]

To the frontiersman, metaphysics was a term which denoted something between contempt and derision:

The Old Dominion has long been celebrated for producing great orators; the ablest metaphysicians in policy; men that can split hairs in all abstruse questions of political economy. But at home, or when they return from Congress, they have negroes to fan them asleep. But a Pennsylvania, a New York, an Ohio, or a western Virginia statesman, though far inferior in logic, metaphysics, and rhetoric to an old Virginia statesman, has this advantage, that when he returns home he takes off his coat and takes hold of the plow. This gives him bone and muscle, sir, and preserves his republican principles pure and uncontaminated.[405]

Natty was a metaphysician *malgre lui* because he had access to the existence which calls essence into being. Nature taught him transcendental lessons which no American could have learned from books, not from Locke and Rousseau even. Natty could have learned this lesson by reading Aquinas's treatise on Being, but there is no indication that Cooper knew of its existence.

---

402 Mohicans, loc. 1954-64.
403 Mohicans, loc. 1969-70.
404 Mohicans, loc. 1969.
405 Frederick Jackson Turner, *The Frontier in American History*, Amazon Kindle, e-book, p. 11.

Existence had a power to teach that was so profound that it could modify essence, bypassing the normal channels of intellectual influence. The American word for existence was Nature. Natty derived wisdom from his experience of the Logos which God imparted to creation as *logoi spermatikoi* even if he was not familiar with that term and even if he hadn't read the treatise on Being in which Aquinas stated this profound idea explicitly for the first time in human history.

Cooper's paradigm of the archetypal American possessed a sophistication which subsequent models lacked because he understood in an inchoate way that faith and reason were complementary, even if his characters didn't. Those who were raised to believe, as Luther did, that reason was a whore, came to the opposite conclusion. Those who had an intimate relationship with the wilderness, as Natty did, knew that Logos was present there. When Protestantism disputed that fact, Revelation lost whatever credibility it had, and the Romantic heirs of Puritanism who came to be known as Unitarians threw the Christian baby out with the Calvinist bathwater, by thinking that the religion of Nature, their term for the metaphysical tradition which Calvinism spurned, could supplant Revelation. No matter how powerful the Logos of experience was, it could not supplant Revelation. Cooper is smart enough to understand that the decision to abandon Revelation because of the contaminating effect of Calvinism brought with it serious consequences, which he demonstrates when Natty is forced to admit that there is some power in David's song:

> Hawkeye listened while he coolly adjusted his flint and reloaded his rifle; but the sounds, wanting the extraneous assistance of scene and sympathy, failed to awaken his slumbering emotions. Never minstrel, or by whatever more suitable name David should be known, drew upon his talents in the presence of more insensible auditors; though considering the singleness and sincerity of his motive, it is probable that no bard of profane song ever uttered notes that ascended so near to that throne where all homage and praise is due. The scout shook his head, and muttering some unintelligible words, among which "throat" and "Iroquois" were alone audible, he walked away, to collect and to examine into the state of the captured arsenal of the Hurons.[406]

Because beauty is a transcendental, it brings man into the presence of the good and the true, both of which are attributes of being and therefore characteristic of God. Beauty evokes more than just sentimental nostalgia in Natty, it also is a formidable weapon against the Indians. Caught in the midst of a battle, where according to Natty only the rifle should hold sway, David raises:

> his voice to its highest tone, he poured out a strain so powerful as to be heard even amid the din of that bloody field. More than one savage

---

406 Mohicans, loc. 1981.

rushed toward them, thinking to rifle the unprotected sisters of their attire, and bear away their scalps; but when they found this strange and unmoved figure riveted to his post, they paused to listen. Astonishment soon changed to admiration, and they passed on to other and less courageous victims, openly expressing their satisfaction at the firmness with which the white warrior sang his death song.[407]

From Natty's point of view, David was saved by "the protecting spirit of madness"[408] which left him "utterly disregarded as a subject too worthless even to destroy,"[409] but the simple fact remains that it was his singing and not Natty's rifle which protected Cora at the crucial moment of her impending death. The narrator says that David was "deluded by his success," but the facts speak for themselves, and the effectiveness of "so holy an influence," no matter how ironically intended, is undeniable. In creating David as Natty's foil in *The Last of the Mohicans*, Cooper distanced himself from Natty's effusions about the magical nature of the rifle, an approach that would be picked up by Romantics like Thoreau and Emerson but ignored by Cooper's epigoni in the 20th Century, especially when Hollywood took up the gun narrative in innumerable Westerns.

The "power of psalmody was suspended in the terrible business of that field of blood through which we have passed,"[410] but the suspension was only temporary. After the battle died down, psalmody "recovered its influence even over the souls of the heathen,"[411] providing an alternative to the rifle, a fetish which had no meaning to the first generation of American Cooperians. In spite of being moved, no less than the Indians, by the beauty of the psalms put to music, Natty remains obdurate in his anti-intellectualism: "Put up the tooting we'pon, and teach your throat modesty. Five words of plain and comprehendible English are worth just now an hour of squalling."[412] Ultimately Calvinism and the religion of Nature which replaced it are both wrong, in addition to being incompatible. In response to Calvinist David's question, "What art thou," Natty responds, "A man like yourself; and one whose blood is as little tainted by the cross of a bear, or an Indian, as your own. Have you so soon forgotten from whom you received the foolish instrument you hold in your hand?"

After failing to convince David, Natty improbably breaks into song, or his approximation thereof, which "would, probably, in a more refined state

---

407 Mohicans, loc. 3000.
408 Mohicans, loc. 3017.
409 Mohicans, loc. 3026.
410 Mohicans, loc. 3803.
411 Mohicans, loc. 3803.
412 Mohicans, loc. 4583.

of society have been termed 'a grand crash'"[413] or more probably "Among his actual auditors" as a sign of "mental alienation."[414] The reality of armed conflict with the native Indians eventually interrupts Natty's nostalgic reverie and subverts psalmody's power. At this point, the "tooting we'pon of the singer"[415] must be put aside because of more pressing issues:

> "Yes," said Hawkeye, dropping his rifle, and leaning on it with an air of visible contempt, "he will do their singing. Can he slay a buck for their dinner; journey by the moss on the beeches, or cut the throat of a Huron? If not, the first catbird he meets is the cleverer of the two. Well, boy, any signs of such a foundation?... Do you think the bullet of that varlet's rifle would have turned aside, though his sacred majesty the king had stood in its path?" returned the stubborn scout.[416] Natty concludes, "we come to fight, not to musikate. Until the general whoop is given, nothing speaks but the rifle."[417]

If Calvinism were right about total depravity and the fallen world which man inhabits on this earth—the realm which Natty calls Nature—then how is it possible that David's music has power over the Indian soul? The two men have reached the impasse which has plagued America since its inception. America had to settle for grace without nature or nature without grace, because no Puritan understood that grace perfects nature. James Fenimore Cooper's understanding of nature was at odds with the understanding of nature his father derived from ultimately Calvinist sources. This had serious ecological consequences. Unlike his son, William Cooper:

> proclaiming settlement an unmitigated good, was profoundly attached to the social values that dominated views of the frontier in his age. Settlers gave order to the disorder of mere nature, thereby justifying their usurpation of Native American rights as well as their destruction of native plants and animals. Looking back on a career spent settling 750,000 acres, William Cooper cast his activities in precisely these terms: "I laid me down to sleep in my watch-coat," he wrote of his first night alone in Otsego, "nothing but the melancholy Wilderness around me." Soon he was taking pride in helping reclaim "such large and fruitful tracts from the waste of the creation." Thoreau, although he earned his keep in part by surveying nature into woodlot, field, and pasture, could not have naively uttered such a phrase as *the waste of the creation*. But neither could William Cooper's youngest son. In *The Pioneers*, as Natty Bumppo reminds the reader, it is the settlers who bring their "wasty ways"

---

413 Mohicans, loc. 4699.
414 Mohicans, loc. 4699.
415 Mohicans, loc. 3167.
416 Mohicans, loc. 3167-3442.
417 Mohicans, loc. 5597.

Part II: The Romantic Rehabilitation of Nature

into nature with them, rending the fabric of the forest and deracinating the order previously established there by God and the children of God, meaning primarily the Indians but also Natty himself.[418]

Unlike his father William, James Fenimore Cooper was "infected with his own generation's more romantic attitudes, he knew nature as a source of order—and humanity as too often the cause of disharmony or worse."[419] This consciousness turned Natty Bumppo into "a force whose entry into human action brings the power of nature to bear on the artifice of social constructions. His invention was a tour de force that demonstrated the author's genuine talent. There was nothing like Natty Bumppo in all American literature—or other literatures—to date."[420]

Virtually every American writer in the 19th century was influenced by *The Leatherstocking Tales*. In the middle of the 20th century, I remember walking with my mother to the local library and taking home copies of *The Deerslayer* and *The Last of the Mohicans*, the latter illustrated by N. C. Wyeth's dramatic paintings. In this I was like Francis Parkman "who in 1852 was poised to become the great historian of the frontier."[421] When Parkman:

> looked back at a youth spent ranging the woods at his grandfather's farm outside Boston, he like Emerson recalled Cooper's books as "the chosen favorites" of his boyhood reading. Parkman's own first ventures into literature were stories he wrote of frontier warfare and forest wandering, and once he turned to history with the publication of *The Conspiracy of Pontiacin* in 1851, his purpose was to ballast Cooper's vision with the weight of historical truth. Parkman's project—writing a "history of the American forest"—was itself a tribute to Cooper's profound influence on shaping the imagination of the country.[422]

Natty Bumppo exerted this "profound influence" because he was both mythic and undeniably "real," or as Parkman put it: "The tall, gaunt form of Leather-Stocking, the weather-beaten face, the bony hand, the cap of fox-skin, and the old hunting frock, polished with long service, seem so palpable and real, that, in some moods of mind, one may easily confound them with the memories of his own experience."[423]

Parkman was not alone in idolizing Cooper and his archetypal American hero. D. H. Lawrence wrote enthusiastically about the "marvelously beautiful" scenes in *The Pioneers*: "Pictures!" he exclaimed. "Some of the loveliest, most

---

418 Franklin, *James Fenimore Cooper*, p. 3-4.
419 Franklin, *James Fenimore Cooper*, p. 4.
420 Franklin, *James Fenimore Cooper*, p. 457.
421 Franklin, *James Fenimore Cooper*, p. xxvii.
422 Franklin, *James Fenimore Cooper*, p. xxvii.
423 Franklin, *James Fenimore Cooper*, p. xxvii.

glamorous pictures in all literature."[424] Henry David Thoreau got the idea for *Walden* from "Natty's fictional home by the shores of Lake Otsego. At Walden, Thoreau was seeking what Cooper had urged Americans to imagine or discover—a relation to nature that did not destroy the wild but rather cherished and internalized it. In Natty, Cooper had shown the way."[425]

This tribute was echoed a century later by poet and critic Yvor Winters: Natty Bumppo, he wrote, has "a life over and above the life of the books in which he appears, a reality surpassing that even of an historical figure such as Daniel Boone." Winters claims that the seventh chapter of *The Deerslayer*, in which Natty confronts, peacefully parts from, and then is forced to kill an Indian warrior out of self-defense, was "probably as great an achievement of its length as one will find in American fiction outside of Melville."[426]

Before Franklin wrote his book, Cooper was "the last major figure in early American culture lacking a full biography"[427] in spite of the "revolutionary role" he played in the establishment of American literature."[428] Melville had "quite literally" grown up reading Cooper's books.[429] Mark Twain's attempt to ruin Cooper's literary reputation belies the fact that he couldn't have written *The Adventures of Huckleberry Finn* without relying on paradigms and concepts which Cooper had established in *The Leatherstocking Tales*:

> The spiritual father of Huck Finn was none other than Natty Bumppo—a demotic Euro-American hero who resists the confines of "sivilization" and, with a member of another race as his companion, finds his freedom in nature. No wonder that Mark Twain felt a need to hunt down and kill Natty's own progenitor.[430]

In reworking Daniel Boone into Natty Bumppo, James Fenimore Cooper created the "core myth"[431] of America:

> Reflecting back over his career a year before his death, Cooper himself concluded that the center of his achievement lay in the five Leather-Stocking Tales. That immense collective monument, a mythic chronicle stretching from the 1740s to the time of Lewis and Clark, captured the key epochs and themes of American life: it was, as historian Francis Parkman would put it in 1852, "an epitome of American history." True to his position as the first writer to work with the frontier, Cooper did not envision the whole series from the outset. He wrote *The Pioneers* (1823) as

---

424 Franklin, *James Fenimore Cooper*, p. xxvii.
425 Franklin, *James Fenimore Cooper*, p. xxix.
426 Franklin, *James Fenimore Cooper*, p. xxvii.
427 Franklin, *James Fenimore Cooper*, p. xi.
428 Franklin, *James Fenimore Cooper*, p. xv.
429 Franklin, *James Fenimore Cooper*, p. xxi.
430 Franklin, *James Fenimore Cooper*, p. xxii.
431 Franklin, *James Fenimore Cooper*, p. xxvii.

a fictional exploration of his now-lost boyhood home, Cooperstown, and introduced the figure of Natty Bumppo into it almost inadvertently—not as the intended hero but as a "low" character probably meant to provide little more than a bit of local color. Yet Leather-Stocking soon took over a good deal of the book's meaning, winning the author's regard as well as that of his readers. Ralph Waldo Emerson, barely out of Harvard, read "that national novel" with such enthusiasm that, many years later, he would write of the debt that ("in common with almost all who speak English") he owed Cooper for the "happy days" spent with that and other books. Emerson was notorious for his low opinion of fiction, but even he had been swept along during those first days of Cooper's fame.[432]

Cooper's contemporaries were struck by his portrayals of Nature. Francis Parkman was "haunted" by:

> the images in Cooper's books—by "the dark gleaming hill-embosomed lakes," the "tracery of forest against the red evening sky," even the "dark and rugged scenery" of the bloodiest of Cooper's books, *The Last of the Mohicans*. In Cooper, landscape is not a series of pretty pictures; it takes on moral value in itself. Like the sea, it is no backdrop but a fundamental fact of life, a contingent force in human experience.[433]

Natty Bumppo was, in Parkman's terms "so palpable and real, that, in some moods of mind, one may easily confound them with the memories of his own experience."[434] By the time Natty Bumppo emerged as the hero of *The Last of the Mohicans,* he was no longer a toothless old man long bypassed by the westward march of the frontier. He was a vibrant man of action in the prime of life who epitomized the energetic decisiveness of the new nation. He was the quintessential American because he could act in unprecedented contexts without recourse to custom or law. Natty embodied the self-reliance which Emerson celebrated in his famous essay. In creating Natty Bumppo, Cooper "invented the core myth of the expansive new nation,"[435] but the first generation of his American disciples ignored what Natty said about the rifle and concentrated on what Cooper said about Nature. Ignoring what Natty had to say about the musket, Ralph Waldo Emerson derived instead the term "self-reliance" from his reading of Cooper, "two years after Cooper's first use of the term."[436]

At this point a darker element enters the mythography. Natty, the American version of the noble savage, used his gun to kill other men. By the time the frontier closed in 1890, the American Empire became a metaphysical, if not

---

432 Franklin, *James Fenimore Cooper,* p. xxvi.
433 Franklin, *James Fenimore Cooper,* p. xxviii.
434 Franklin, *James Fenimore Cooper,* p. xxvii.
435 Franklin, *James Fenimore Cooper,* p. xxvii.
436 Franklin, *James Fenimore Cooper,* p. 167.

religious construct that lost its innocence as the preachers started using their guns to kill those who failed to accept the empire's imperatives.

Chapter 14

James Fenimore Cooper Goes to Rome

On June 2, 1826, James Fenimore Cooper and his family set sail for Europe on the *Hudson*, a fast packet boat of the Black X line.[437] After the initial success of *The Last of the Mohicans*, Cooper wrote *The Prairie* while living in Paris. Parisian Booksellers, he wrote to Luther Bradish, his literary agent in New York, "are now nibbling at my book, and profess a readiness to purchase—Mohicans has done very well, they tell me, and it will give the Prairie, a better chance."[438] In doing this, Cooper embodied the paradoxical nature of American identity. Just as wilderness existence had modified Calvinist essence and called forth a new being known as the American, Western "existence" only had meaning in light of the eastern essence known as Europe. Cooper's first experience of Europe occurred when he shipped off as a teenage merchant seaman after dropping out of Yale. The idea that *The Prairie*, along with *The Pioneers* and *The Last of the Mohicans*, would "form a complete series of tales, descriptive of American life"[439] occurred to Cooper in Paris, not Cooperstown, and was a complete reversal of the American experience of deriving essence from existence by heading west. If Daniel Boone became an American *an sich* when he picked up a rifle and passed through the Cumberland Gap into Kentucky, Cooper, like so many writers after him (Henry James, Henry Adams, Mark Twain, and Ernest Hemingway spring immediately to mind) became an American *fuer sich* when he arrived in Paris. The terms stem from Hegel's understanding of the dialectic, indicating that America needed European cultural forms, the novel being a prime example, to become fully conscious of its identity. The novel was a form of literature which arose from European antecedents all of which were traceable to Christianity, and more importantly for Protestant Americans, to Catholicism. If Protestantism was the essence which got modified in light of existence in the "howling wilderness," literary Pilgrims

---

437 Franklin, *James Fenimore Cooper*, p. 1.
438 Franklin, *James Fenimore Cooper*, p. 7.
439 Franklin, *James Fenimore Cooper*, p. 10.

from Washington Irving to Jack Kerouac learned that something more aesthetically powerful preceded the religion of their Puritan forebears when they arrived on the continent. England didn't count because both shared a common Anglo-Protestant identity which was based on centuries of reaction to happenings on the Catholic continent. The connection between the mother country and her former colonies was still too close for comfort. Like a newly emancipated adolescent, Cooper went out of his way to antagonize his British hosts:

> Writing to Jane Welsh Carlyle on July 12, 1828, the socialite Anna D. B. Montagu thus reported snippily of Cooper, whom she must have encountered in London some months earlier, that he was "one of [her] disappointments." She had read and very much liked *The Last of the Mohicans* but found its author "rude, irritable, a very Yankee, with all the little pride of a little mind."[440]

When Cooper crossed the English Channel to the continent and made his first contact with Catholic culture, wonder replaced Yankee truculence as his characteristic emotion. Antwerp provided "a sort of double epiphany" because it offered "important instruction on two unrelated issues—Roman Catholic practice and the deeper background of New York history."[441] As with later American pilgrims, Cooper discovered that beauty, in particular "the spectacular Onze-Lieve-Vrouwekathedraal" (Cathedral of Notre Dame) in the marketplace a few blocks from his hotel and "one of the noblest Gothic structures on the continent," transported him to realms that could hardly be imagined by Americans who grew up in crude frontier settlements like Cooperstown, New York. Antwerp introduced Cooper to a transcendental realm which did not exist in North America.[442] The Catholic religion could survive in the catacombs, but it flowered as the established religion of Europe in the 1,200 years which followed Constantine's Edict of Milan in ways that were now beautifully palpable in its art and architecture, and "Cooper was certainly moved."[443] Three years later on a visit to equally Catholic Liege, Cooper expressed what Franklin called "the Protestant sense of regret or foreclosure" when he wrote: "I sometimes wish I had been educated [as] a Catholic in order to unite the poetry of religion with its higher principles."[444] Like his fellow Americans, Cooper's mind had been colonized by the categories of Whig history, making it difficult to understand how the most Catholic Swiss cantons were also the most Republican:

---

440 Franklin, *James Fenimore Cooper*, p. 39.
441 Franklin, *James Fenimore Cooper*, p. 42.
442 Franklin, *James Fenimore Cooper*, p. 42.
443 Franklin, *James Fenimore Cooper*, p. 42.
444 Franklin, *James Fenimore Cooper*, p. 42.

Part II: The Romantic Rehabilitation of Nature

This fact was far more challenging to American prejudices than the dissonant "neatness" of a Catholic town. Cooper was to spend goodly amounts of time in dominantly Catholic cantons such as Unterwalden and especially Schwyz, whose symbolic importance for the history of Swiss political independence called forth his admiration.[445]

Cooper found the Benedictine monastery at Einsiedeln in the canton of Schwyz particularly perplexing:

> because with its throngs of believing pilgrims, many of the poorest classes, it was so evidently a throwback, as a Protestant modernist understood the matter, to earlier modes. And yet it stood in a canton whose original resistance to the Hapsburgs made it a potent emblem of modern political values. Clearly, again, not all things an American saw in Europe could be sifted using American screens.[446]

Cooper was deeply conflicted, caught between a "dogged protestant" guide who was determined to impose Whiggish categories of the mind like the Black Legend on the Swiss categories of reality he encountered when he saw "masses of impoverished Catholic pilgrims converging to worship before the Lady of the Hermits,"[447] Cooper tried to make sense of a "great air of faith in something," on the one hand and "every appearance of excessive ignorance," on the other.[448] Cooper, according to his biographer:

> was confronting a kind of Catholic peasant culture he had not met before, and it took him time to adjust to it, a process made much harder by the fact that Einsiedeln stood in the heart of one of the most republican of the Swiss cantons. His own background had taught him nothing of such knotted attitudes and practices.[449]

When Cooper arrived at the Vatican, the beauty of St. Peter's Basilica overwhelmed his Protestant American prejudices. When Cooper entered the Piazza San Pietro, the spectacular open air vestibule to entering the basilica, he found himself "standing at the foot of a vast square, with colonnades, on a gigantic scale, sweeping in half circles on each side of me, two of the most beautiful fountains I had ever seen throwing their waters in sheets down their sides between them, and the facade of St. Peter's forming the background."[450] Yet, it was nothing compared to what followed. After entering the basilica:

> Cooper began to weep. He had brought his young son Paul with him, and Paul, not yet five years old but raised on an incessant diet of

---

445 Franklin, *James Fenimore Cooper*, p. 52.
446 Franklin, *James Fenimore Cooper*, p. 52.
447 Franklin, *James Fenimore Cooper*, p. 54.
448 Franklin, *James Fenimore Cooper*, p. 54.
449 Franklin, *James Fenimore Cooper*, p. 54.
450 Franklin, *James Fenimore Cooper*, vol. II, p. 70.

European wonders, clung tightly to the novelist's leg as if he, too, had been "oppressed with the sense of the vastness of the place." Paul "kept murmuring, '*Qu'est-ce que c'est?—qu'est-ce que c'est?—Est-ce une église?*'" That was the right way to begin a Roman residence. Through his time there, Cooper liked attending vespers at Peter's and took the whole family on Christmas, an experience that even [his wife] Susan, usually on her guard where Catholicism was concerned, found delightful.[451]

If he had stayed in Rome longer without the notorious anti-Catholic Samuel F. B. Morse, who "urinated on a public wall near a figure of the Madonna,"[452] causing a tense encounter with the locals, who were "full of feeling, and grace, and poetry, and a vast number are filled with a piety that their maligners would do well to imitate,"[453] Cooper might have become a Catholic. But the tourist eventually supplanted the pilgrim and Cooper succumbed to the sensory overload that is the tourist's occupational hazard in places like Italy. By the time he arrived in Lombardy, Cooper grew weary of viewing "pictures, cathedrals, and ruins"[454] situated in "towns of ten and twenty thousand souls."[455] Cooper tired of his visit to Venice after eight days, even after conceding that he had never been "so much struck with any other place on entering it."[456]

By the time he arrived in Dresden, Cooper's ability to absorb the beauty which surrounded him succumbed to cultural indigestion. Confronted by a celebration of Martin Luther and Philip Melanchthon's *Augsburg Confession* to Emperor Charles V in 1530, Cooper found himself overwhelmed by the "contrasts and conflicts" which were the legacy of the Reformation in Germany and too culturally exhausted to adjudicate their claims. Instead, he returned to France, where he immersed himself in the political conflicts which culminated in the Revolution of 1830.

---

451 Franklin, *James Fenimore Cooper*, vol. II, p. 70.
452 Franklin, *James Fenimore Cooper*, vol. II, p. 73.
453 Franklin, *James Fenimore Cooper*, vol. II, p. 72.
454 Franklin, *James Fenimore Cooper*, vol. II, p. 83.
455 Franklin, *James Fenimore Cooper*, vol. II, p. 83.
456 Franklin, *James Fenimore Cooper*, vol. II, p. 86.

Chapter 15

Ralph Waldo Emerson Bourgeois Satanism

If, as Paul Johnson claims, Emerson was "the archetypal American intellectual of the nineteenth century,"[457] and in some sense the first American, he was a creation of James Fenimore Cooper, the first American novelist. Paul Johnson makes invidious comparisons between Emerson and the "cringing" spirit of Washington Irving, but the similarities between the two become more striking as both become fully conscious of their American identity:

> Early American intellectuals, like Washington Irving, took their tone and manners, their style and content, from Europe, where they spent much of their time; they were a living legacy of cultural colonialism. The emergence of a native and independent American intellectual spirit was itself a reaction to the cringing of Irving and his kind. The first and most representative exponent of this spirit and the man who was the archetypal American intellectual of the nineteenth century was Ralph Waldo Emerson (1803— 82), who proclaimed that his object was to extract "the tapeworm of Europe from America's body and brain, to cast out the passion for Europe by the passion for America."[458]

In order to do that, however, Emerson, like his mentor Cooper, had to travel to Europe. Emerson's essay "Nature" is based on descriptions he derived from Cooper's *Leatherstocking Tales*, refracted through the lens of German Idealism, which he learned firsthand from Thomas Carlyle during his *Wanderjahr* in Europe, which began in December 1832, two months after Emerson resigned as pastor of the Second Church in Boston, and one year after the death of his first wife, Ellen Tucker Emerson. By the time Emerson left for Europe, he had concluded that "the profession," by which he meant the Congregationalist ministry, which demanded that "he act always like a saint," was "antiquated"[459] and ready to be replaced by the traveling lecturer

---

457 Johnson, *Intellectuals*, p. 139.
458 Johnson, *Intellectuals*, p. 139.
459 Porte, *Emerson in His Journals*, p. 53.

on the Lyceum circuit who espoused a "Socratic paganism" instead of "an effete superannuated Christianity," which he saw as "the dead forms of our forefathers."[460]

Like Cooper, when Emerson traveled to Europe, he discovered the roots of a Catholicism which he had only experienced in the attenuated branches of the immigrant Irish community in Boston. On February 25, 1827, Emerson noted in his diary that he had "attended Mass in the Catholic Church" presumably in Boston. The service left him underwhelmed because even though the Mass was in Latin and the sermon in English, "the audience, who are Spaniards understand neither."[461]

Emerson's attitude changed when he experienced the beauty of Catholic churches in their native, which is to say, European context. Beauty was the transcendental which allowed Emerson to "shuck off . . . the 'corpse-cold' Unitarianism of Cambridge and Boston" and hope that the Congregationalists would "carve & paint & inscribe the walls of our churches in New England" according to the aesthetic principles he discovered after "his first taste of European shrines."[462] The beauty he imbibed from Catholic art led Emerson to ask "How could anybody who had been in a catholic church devise such a deformity as a pew?"[463] Inspired by his trips to Europe and the beauty he imbibed from his visits to Catholic churches there, Emerson encouraged a young girl, "in the midst of rich decorous Unitarian friends in Boston" to convert to Catholicism:

> Her friends, who are also my friends, lamented to me the growth of this inclination. But I told them that I think she is to be greatly congratulated on the event. . . . She has lived in great poverty of events. In form & years a woman, she is still a child, having had no experiences, and although of a fine liberal susceptible expanding nature, has never yet found any worthy object of attention; has not been in love, nor been called out by any taste except lately by music, and sadly wants adequate objects. In this church perhaps she shall find what she needs, in a power to call out the slumbering religious sentiment. It is unfortunate that the guide who has led her into this path is a young girl of a lively forcible but quite external character who teaches her the historical argument for the Catholic faith. I told A. that I hoped she would not be misled by attaching any importance to that. If the offices of the Church attract her, if its beautiful forms & humane spirit draw her, if St Augustine & St Bernard, Jesu & Madonna, Cathedral, Music & Masses, then go, for thy dear heart's sake, but do not go out of this icehouse of Unitarianism all external, into an

---

460 Porte, *Emerson in His Journals*, p. 53.
461 Porte, *Emerson in His Journals*, p. 63.
462 Porte, *Emerson in His Journals*, p. 88.
463 Porte, *Emerson in His Journals*, p. 88.

icehouse again of externals. At all events I charged her to pay no regard to dissenters but to suck that orange thoroughly.[464]

Emerson, however, was incapable of taking the same step he urged the nameless "young lady" to take. Porte feels that "Emerson's prickly Americanism" trumped the favorable aesthetic impressions which the beauty of Naples had made on him, prompting Porte to describe that beauty as "a gaudiness he considered merely external" even "though his aesthetically starved senses reached out eagerly for nourishment."[465] Caught half-way between what Porte calls "the superstitious trappings of the Roman Catholic Church" and "the worn-out forms of Unitarianism,"[466] Emerson resolved both that dialectic and his own dilemma by claiming "I am thankful that I am an American as I am thankful that I am a man,"[467] implying that America was now a religion.

Like most American writers in the period which began in the 1820s and ended a little over a century later, Emerson felt more American in Europe than he did at home. As he awaited his return to America from his first trip to Europe, Emerson wrote "I thank the Great God who has led me through this European scene, this last schoolroom in which he has pleased to instruct me." One of the great benefits of traveling to the schoolroom known as Europe was the opportunity which it afforded of "meeting men of genius" who "talk sincerely."[468] These men are "above the meanness of pretending to knowledge which they have not, and they frankly tell you what puzzles them." And Thomas Carlyle was one of the greatest among them. Carlyle was, in fact, "so amiable that I love him"[469] in spite of differing on sexual morality.

When he met Carlyle in August 1833 at his farm in Craigenputtock, Emerson was shocked at the Carlyles' views on sexuality. He felt compelled to "defend American standards of morals at a dinner party in John Foster's house attended by Dickens, Carlyle and others."[470] When Carlyle and Dickens "replied that chastity in the male sex was as good as gone in our times, and in England was so rare that they could name all the exceptions. Carlyle evidently believed that the same things were true in America." Emerson felt called to disabuse them of their mistaken notions. Emerson refused to concede the

---

464 Porte, *Emerson in His Journals*, p. 286.
465 Porte, *Emerson in His Journals*, p. 89.
466 Porte, *Emerson in His Journals*, p. 89.
467 Porte, *Emerson in His Journals*, p. 116.
468 "The Home of Ralph Waldo Emerson," https://www.ralphwaldoemersonhouse.org/blog-travel
469 "The Home of Ralph Waldo Emerson," https://www.ralphwaldoemersonhouse.org/blog-travel
470 Johnson, *Intellectuals*, p. 140.

field of sexual morality to his cynical English counterparts and urged them to follow the American example of "wise chastity."[471]

"I assured him," Emerson replied, that "it was not so with us; that, for the most part, young men of good standing and good education with us, go virgins to their nuptial bed, as truly as their brides."[472]

When Emerson returned to Europe in 1847, he was "shocked by the revolution in sexual values that he found characteristic of modern cities."[473] Spending a month in Paris during the spring of 1848, Emerson noticed ubiquitous advertisements for medicines which promised a cure for "secret," (i.e., venereal) diseases and concluded that "extremes of vice" and "animal indulgence" were inextricably linked to life in Paris.[474] When Carlyle and Dickens claimed that the same thing was true of New York, Emerson felt called to correct their understanding of American morals.

In 1838, years after his encounter with Mr. and Mrs. Carlyle, Emerson published his essay "Nature," which proclaimed that "visible nature must have a spiritual and moral side. . . . The laws of moral nature answer to those of matter as face to face in a glass."[475] When Emerson entered "nature," he learned that "every natural process is but a version of a moral sentence. The moral law lies at the centre of nature and radiates to the circumference. It is the pith and marrow of every substance, every relation, and every process."[476]

Emerson's response to the dead Newtonian universe he had inherited from his English forbears got modified both by German Idealism, which saw nature as a manifestation of Spirit, and by New England sexual mores, which corresponded more closely to the Logos of practical reason than anything he could find on the continent or even in England, which was basking under the bright light of moral clarity which Methodism had bequeathed to the Victorian era.

Morality is another term for practical reason, which is the means whereby man achieves the good through action. Like Fichte, Emerson saw action guided by practical reason as the instrument which made thought real in the world and rescued it from the solipsism which came about when man did not act on what he knew, the predicament which ran through all of Hawthorne's fiction. Existence could call essence into being "so long as the active powers predominate over the reflective." In saying this Emerson liberated New England from materialism. The opposite of materialism was idealism, which is "a hypothesis to account for nature by other principles that those of carpentry

---

471 Porte, *Emerson in His Journals*, p. 438.
472 Johnson, *Intellectuals*, p. 140; Porte, *Emerson in His Journals*, p. 362.
473 Porte, *Emerson in His Journals*, p. 362.
474 Porte, *Emerson in His Journals*, p. 362.
475 Emerson, *Nature*, in *The American Tradition in Literature*, p. 1055, 1053."
476 Emerson, p. 1058.

Part II: The Romantic Rehabilitation of Nature

and chemistry" which he had learned from the German Idealists by way of Carlyle. If, however, idealism did nothing more than "deny the existence of matter, it does not satisfy the demands of the spirit. It leaves God out of me. It leaves me in the splendid labyrinth of my perceptions to wander without end."[477] By resisting "with indignation any hint that nature is more short-lived or mutable than spirit," Emerson promoted human activity every bit as much as New England Calvinism had denied it.

But what happened when the reflective powers predominated over the active? Hawthorne explored that situation in his own life and in his fiction, especially in *The Blithedale Romance*, where man was bifurcated into one character who could act without understanding anything and another whose understanding of the complexity of life prohibited action. Emerson escaped this dilemma because he was not a sensual man who "conforms thoughts to things. Chastity endowed the mind with what Samuel Taylor Coleridge called an 'esemplastic' power, which allowed it to unify multiplicity in works of art. When that esemplastic power succeeded, morality became the mark of a poet, who 'conforms things to his thoughts.'" Emerson was a poet who "conforms things to his thoughts."

Emerson was a respected citizen of Concord, Massachusetts, whose inhabitants were the church-going, socially conservative heirs of the revolutionary movement known as Puritanism. The name of that paradox was Unitarianism, which Perry Miller described as "'liberal' in theology" but "conservative" in its "social thinking and its metaphysics."[478] In creating a false dichotomy, Miller revealed himself as captive to the same dialectic he sought to explain. Emerson was instead conservative in his sexual morality but Satanic in his politics. The contrast is both striking and undeniable.

In "From Edwards to Emerson," Perry Miller claimed that Ralph Waldo Emerson derived Transcendentalism from native Calvinist sources. Like John Milton who made Satan the hero of *Paradise Lost*, Emerson espoused a Satanic form of rebellion in "Self-Reliance" which endeared him to New England Unitarians, who were determined to preserve social propriety in spite of their revolutionary ideas, and Friedrich Nietzsche, who deliberately infected himself with syphilis after hearing *Tristan und Isolde* and had nothing but contempt for "flatheads" like George Eliot, who were determined to preserve Victorian sexual morality while espousing philosophical nihilism. Hawthorne and Emerson shared an allegiance to the "dual heritage"[479] of New England, which, according to Miller:

---

477 Emerson, p. 1068.
478 Perry Miller, "Jonathan Edwards to Emerson," *The New England Quarterly*, December 1940, p. 606.
479 Miller, p. 600.

commenced with a clear understanding that both mysticism and pantheism were heretical, and also with a frank admission that such ideas were dangerous to society, that men who imbibed noxious errors from an inner voice or from the presence of God in the natural landscape would reel and stagger through the streets of Boston and disturb the civil peace.[480]

Conflating the naked Quakers with the Puritans who hanged them, Miller continues: "the emergence of Unitarianism out of Calvinism was a very gradual, almost an imperceptible, process."[481] Gradual or not, the main thing that changed in New England during the period which stretched from "Sinners in the Hands of an Angry God" to "Self-Reliance" was the Calvinist understanding of Original Sin. In their multi-generational history of the Hawthorne family, Otto and Katherine Bird claimed that "The denial of original sin and the inheritance of it was a hard blow against orthodox Puritan belief. But the killing blow came with the denial of the divinity of Jesus Christ and the turn to Unitarianism."[482]

---

480 Miller, p. 599.
481 Miller, p. 612.
482 Bird, *From Witchery to Sanctity*, p. 36

Chapter 16

Nathaniel Hawthorne Goes to Rome

Nathaniel Hawthorne kept the New England Puritan legacy alive in his tales and novels. His farewell to Calvinism was as tentative as his acceptance of the regnant Unitarian orthodoxy of his day, symbolized best by Emerson. Judging from the standards of the late 20th century, Marion Montgomery concludes that: "Hawthorne's Roger Chillingworth stands forth to our experience as a more convincing figure of man than Emerson's 'Man Thinking.' The fictional character is firmly anchored in the realities of the human heart, while Emerson's dream image has about it the vagueness of wishful thinking."[483]

Hawthorne hated Calvinism, but he was reluctant to abandon the idea of Original Sin as completely as Emerson had done. Bereft of sound theological principles because of his cultural background, Hawthorne was incapable of correcting either Edwards's exaggeration of the effects of Original Sin or Emerson's dismissal of it, but, forced to choose sides, Hawthorne chose Puritanism over Transcendentalism as the more realistic alternative. Rather than refute Calvinism theologically, Hawthorne chose to portray the psychological consequences which flowed from its premises. Nothing makes this more evident than the great speech at the end of "Young Goodman Brown," when the Puritan minister in the forest explains the full consequence of the Calvinist understanding of Original Sin understood as total depravity:

> "Welcome, my children," said the dark figure, "to the communion of your race. Ye have found thus young your nature and your destiny. My children, look behind you!"
>
> They turned and flashing forth, as it were, in a sheet of flame, the fiend worshippers were seen; the smile of welcome gleamed darkly on every visage.
>
> "Lo," the Puritan minister continued:
>
> "there ye stand my children," said the figure in a deep and solemn tone, almost sad with its despairing awfulness, as if his once angelic nature would yet mourn for our miserable race. "Depending on one another's

---

483 Montgomery, *Why Hawthorne Was Melancholy*, p. 56.

hearts, ye had still hoped that virtue were not all a dream. Now are ye undeceived. Evil is the nature of mankind. Evil must be your only happiness. Welcome again, my children to the communion of your race."

"Young Goodman Brown" was Hawthorne's attempt to deal with the psychological distortions that the Calvinist principle of total depravity had imposed on his ancestors. The classic American expression of this belief can be found in Jonathan Edwards' famous sermon "Sinners in the Hands of an Angry God," in which unregenerate man is compared to a spider dangling from a thin gossamer link over a fire. God is the only thing that keeps him from perdition. Because grace destroys nature without perfecting it, substance disappears beneath unregenerate man's feet leaving him "nothing to stand on," and "nothing between you and hell but the air" and "a great furnace of wrath, a wide and bottomless pit, full of the fire of wrath, that you are held over in the hand of God," hanging "by a slender thread."

Hawthorne was 21 years old when the American Unitarian Association was founded in 1825 as New England's antidote to Calvinist pessimism.[484] Hawthorne was 34 years old when Emerson gave his address to the Harvard Divinity School on July 15, 1838, and it is as a total repudiation of everything that Hawthorne said in "Young Goodman Brown," three years earlier, except the fundamentally Satanic premise that both works shared. What conclusions do we draw if "evil is the nature of mankind"? Emerson sided with the devil and gave expression to the Satanic strain of American thought in "Self-Reliance" when he wrote "If I am the devil's child, I will live then from the devil," because "No law can be sacred to me but the law of my own nature. Good and bad are but names very readily transferable to that or this; the only right is what is after my constitution, the only wrong what is against it."

That is the central point of departure in "Self-Reliance," as it is the central assurance made to budding intellectuals in "The American Scholar." Of that scholar, Emerson confidently asserts that "He and he alone knows the world."[485]

Emerson took Fichte and Schelling's abolition of Kant's *Ding an sich* to heart and transposed its consequences to post-Calvinist America by speculating that "perhaps there are no objects," an assertion which leads him to claim that God is an idea:

> We have learned that we do not see directly, but mediately, and that we have no means of correcting these colored and distorting lenses which we are.... Perhaps these subject lenses have a creative power; perhaps there are no objects. Once we lived in what we saw; now, the capaciousness of this new power, which threatens to absorb all things, engages us. Nature, art, persons, letters, religions, objects, successively tumble in, and God

---

484 Bird, *From Witchery to Sanctity*, p. 39.
485 Montgomery, *Why Hawthorne Was Melancholy*, p. 30.

Part II: The Romantic Rehabilitation of Nature

is but one of its ideas. Nature and literature are subjective phenomena; every evil and every good thing is a shadow which we cast.[486]

Like Friedrich Nietzsche, who was an admirer of Emerson and the son of a Lutheran minister, Emerson took the Reformation to its logical conclusion by making it an expression of Satanic will. Emerson was endorsing the very thing which Shakespeare and Plato feared. After justice became the opinion of the powerful, power transformed itself into will, and then into appetite, which then became the universal wolf which ended up devouring itself. Emerson reframed this trajectory in American terms in "Self-Reliance" when he wrote:

> Nature is thoroughly mediate. It offers all its kingdom to man as the raw material which he may mould into what is useful. . . . One after another [man's] victorious thought comes up with and reduces all things, until the world becomes at last a realized will—the double of man.[487]

Actually, Nature became the double of powerful men, who used this subjective departure from the objective order of the universe, symbolized by the music of the spheres, to establish the reign of the universal wolf, whose god is Satan, which is precisely what Hawthorne said in "Young Goodman Brown" and Emerson said in "Self-Reliance," even if they differed on whether to condemn what happened or to praise it.

One of the fundamental paradoxes of Hawthorne's life can be found in his radical ambivalence toward the culture of Concord, Massachusetts, a place which merged Satanic will with bourgeois respectability and made him one of its most respected members. Both Hawthorne and Emerson were sons of the Puritans. Both were in rebellion against that legacy, but Hawthorne could never accept the rejection of Calvinist tradition on Emerson's terms. When Emerson transferred "Calvinistic election from the province of God to that of Nature, a step toward that pallid paganism he champions as Unitarianism, in which man only is divine,"[488] Hawthorne demurred and parted ways with Emerson intellectually even though they would remain friends until Hawthorne's death. Montgomery tells us that:

> Emerson's neighbor, Nathaniel Hawthorne, sees in the Sage of Concord an image of the rising new man who has come at last to dominate our world; he reacts sharply to his neighbor Emerson, spokesman for a modernist thought Hawthorne discovers rising all about him and which Hawthorne, as prophetic poet, opposes.[489]

---

486 Montgomery, *Why Hawthorne Was Melancholy*, p. 42.
487 Montgomery, *Why Hawthorne Was Melancholy*, p. 63.
488 Montgomery, *Why Hawthorne Was Melancholy*, p. 25.
489 Marion Montgomery, *Why Hawthorne Was Melancholy*, (La Salle, Illinois: Sherwood Sugden & Company Publishers, 1984), p. 24.

But, Montgomery continues, Hawthorne "did not attempt to oppose it at the level of philosophical discourse."[490] Indeed, he lacked the philosophical principles that would make its refutation possible. Hawthorne attempted instead to portray in art what Emerson could not demonstrate in philosophy. Confronted with Calvin's exaggeration of Original Sin as total depravity, Hawthorne could not follow Emerson's endorsement of the Reformation as a Satanic exaltation of the will to power to its logical conclusion in Transcendentalism. Confronted with Emerson's dismissal of Original Sin, Hawthorne found himself incapable of accepting either alternative but incapable of refuting them philosophically, and so he descended into gloom. He became, like Young Goodman Brown, "darkly meditative." At the end of his life, Hawthorne became, like Young Goodman Brown, "A stern, a sad, a darkly meditative, a distrustful, if not desperate man" whose "dying hour was gloom."

But before that happened Hawthorne was given a reprieve from New England gloom when he arrived in Rome in 1858 fresh from the stint as consul in Liverpool which earned him enough money to bring him and his family to the seat of the religion his ancestors abhorred but whose art he admired.

Hawthorne's most fruitful literary period corresponded with the birth of his daughter Rose on May 20, 1851. Rose felt that her father "could see through me as easily as if I were in one of his own books."[491] Two years after her father's death, Rose "made it a point to read all of her father's writings at fifteen except *The Scarlet Letter*. She put this romance off until eighteen, writing that she had been told its subject matter was too sophisticated for a younger girl."[492] *The Scarlet Letter*, Hawthorne's most famous work, was published in the same year that Rose was conceived. Hawthorne's second novel *The House of the Seven Gables* was published in the same year Rose was born, the year which also saw the publication of *A Wonder Book for Girls and Boys*. Hawthorne wrote *The Blithedale Romance* between December 1851 and April 1852, followed by *The Life of Franklin Pierce*, the "presidential campaign biography for his college chum. . . who was elected the fourteenth President of the United States."[493] That book earned Hawthorne an appointment as U.S. consul in Liverpool, so he moved to England in 1853, the same year in which *The Tanglewood Tales for Girls and Boys* rolled off the press in America.

With one major exception, 1853 marked the end of Hawthorne's career as a writer. For the next 11 years, Hawthorne would write copious journal entries about his experiences in England, France, and Italy. The former ended up in

---

490 Montgomery, *Why Hawthorne Was Melancholy*, p. 24.
491 Bird, *From Witchery to Sanctity*, p. 115.
492 Bird, *From Witchery to Sanctity*, p. 120.
493 Bird, *From Witchery to Sanctity*, p. 115.

Part II: The Romantic Rehabilitation of Nature

Our Old Home, and the latter in *The Marble Faun*, which was the last novel he completed.

The novelist Henry James was one of Hawthorne's most perceptive readers. His father knew Hawthorne personally. James's novella "Daisy Miller" is set in Rome and deals with the theme of American innocence in a way that bespoke Henry James's appropriation of *The Marble Faun*. Like William Dean Howells, who wrote his own novel about American innocents in Rome, James could not have written "Daisy Miller" without having first read *The Marble Faun*. James felt that Hawthorne's early work based on his New England roots "combined in a singular degree the spontaneity of the imagination with a haunting care for moral problems."[494] When it came to writing about Italy, however, Hawthorne was "exquisitely and consistently provincial."[495] Hawthorne was 50 years old before he first ventured forth from the New England villages whose history and culture were the source of his art. As a result, his experience was too "narrow" to encompass something as monumental as Rome:

> Hawthorne's experience had been narrow. His fifty years had been spent, for much the larger part, in small American towns—Salem, the Boston of forty years ago, Concord, Lenox, West Newton—and he had led exclusively what one may call a village life. This is evident, not at all directly and superficially, but by implication and between the lines, in his desultory history of his foreign years. In other words, and to call things by their names, he was exquisitely and consistently provincial. I suggest this fact not in the least in condemnation, but, on the contrary, in support of an appreciative view of him. I know nothing more remarkable, more touching, than the sight of this odd, youthful-elderly mind, contending so late in the day with new opportunities for learning old things, and, on the whole, profiting by them so freely and gracefully. The Note-Books are provincial, and so, in a greatly modified degree, are the sketches of England, in *Our Old Home*; but the beauty and delicacy of this latter work are so interwoven with the author's air of being remotely outside of everything he describes, that they count for more, seem more themselves, and finally give the whole thing the appearance of a triumph, not of initiation, but of the provincial point of view itself.[496]

James claims that Hawthorne's contact with Italy was "extremely superficial." "His contact with the life of the country, its people and its manners, was simply that of the ordinary tourist," but a "tourist" who combined a:

---

494 James, *Hawthorne*, p. 145.

495 Henry James, *Hawthorne* (Vail-Ballou Press, Inc.: Binghamton, NY, 1879 – Reprinted in 1956), p. 117.

496 James, *Hawthorne*, pp. 116-7.

mixture of subtlety and simplicity, his interfusion of genius with what I have ventured to call the provincial quality, is most apparent. To an American reader this latter quality, which is never grossly manifested, but pervades the Journals like a vague natural perfume, an odour of purity and kindness and integrity, must always, for a reason that I will touch upon, have a considerable charm; and such a reader will accordingly take an even greater satisfaction in the Diaries kept during the two years Hawthorne spent in Italy; for in these volumes the element I speak of is especially striking.[497]

---

[497] James, *Hawthorne*, p. 125.

Chapter 17

Henry David Thoreau and Moral Nature

In his essay "From Edwards to Emerson," Perry Miller explained the paradox of Emerson's generation, which was revolutionary when it came to government but "puritanical and etiolated" when it came to sex.[498] The term comes from Paul Johnson, who was neither puritanical nor etiolated when it came to sex. After his death, Johnson's mistress Gloria Stewart claimed that "Sex has always been a very important part of his life. Paul loved to be spanked and it was a big feature of our relationship. I had to tell him he was a very naughty boy."[499] Interviewed by *The Observer*, Johnson admitted that he'd "been having an affair," but claimed nonetheless that he was a firm believer in "family values."[500]

Like his mentor Emerson, Thoreau felt that "Nature" was "startingly moral."[501] There was "never an instant's truce between virtue and vice. Goodness is the only investment that never fails."[502] Like Natty Bumppo, Thoreau learned that "the laws of the universe" were never morally indifferent in the school of nature. Living in nature demanded the "command over our passions, and over the external senses of the body" because "good acts are declared by the *Veda* to be indispensable in the mind's approximation to God."[503] If, as Aquinas said, lust darkened the mind, Thoreau felt that chastity was the necessary condition for its enlightenment. Chastity enabled "the flowering of man; and what are called Genius, Heroism, Holiness, and the like, are but various fruits which succeed it."[504]

---

498 Johnson, *Intellectuals*, p.140.
499 Al Kamen, "Fan Males," *The Washington Post*, May 21, 1998, https://www.washingtonpost.com/archive/politics/1998/05/22/fan-males/0d3528a0-53e2-4271-9213-aac6ad24b8a5/
500 Al Kamen, "Fan Males," *The Washington Post*, May 21, 1998, https://www.washingtonpost.com/archive/politics/1998/05/22/fan-males/0d3528a0-53e2-4271-9213-aac6ad24b8a5/
501 Henry David Thoreau, *Walden*, p. 108.
502 Thoreau, *Walden*, p. 108.
503 Thoreau, *Walden*, p. 108.
504 Thoreau, *Walden*, p. 108, loc. 2778.

Walking with a Bible and a Gun

Henry David Thoreau became a member of Emerson's household in the spring of 1841, three years after the publication of "Nature."[505] Emerson could not have written Nature without first reading Cooper's *Leatherstocking Tales*, and both exerted an even greater effect on the mind of Emerson's protégé Thoreau:

> who read Cooper while at Harvard in the 1830s [and] imbibed the core myth from his frontier novels. When Thoreau went to live at Walden Pond in 1845, his hut by the water literalized Natty's fictional home by the shores of Lake Otsego. At Walden, Thoreau was seeking what Cooper had urged Americans to imagine or discover—a relation to nature that did not destroy the wild but rather cherished and internalized it. In Natty, Cooper had shown the way.[506]

Walden Pond was the philosophical sequel to Lake Otsego:

> Cooper, anticipating Henry David Thoreau, expressed his reverence for nature by treating this one microcosm of the American continent with extraordinary affection. Moreover, in going to his pond to live in his cabin, Thoreau was reenacting in ritual form the solitary life Cooper had imagined for his forest hero in the Leather-Stocking saga. The light shining upward from the heavenly water of Walden was in that sense but the refracted glow of Cooper's Glimmerglass. In speaking of the Ganges, Thoreau might also have mentioned the Susquehanna.[507]

After reading Cooper as a child, Thoreau decided to put what he learned into practice near the end of March 1845, when he "borrowed an axe and went down to the woods by Walden Pond, nearest to where I intended to build my house, and began to cut down some tall, arrowy white pines, still in their youth, for timber."[508]

Thoreau began his sojourn at Walden on Independence Day. On July 4, 1845, Thoreau accepted "a cheerful invitation to make my life of equal simplicity, and I may say innocence, with Nature herself."[509] Thoreau is certainly aware of Natty Bumppo's attachment to his rifle. Thoreau tells us that "We cannot but pity the boy who has never fired a gun; he is no more humane, while his education has been sadly neglected."[510] After admitting that "almost every New England boy among my contemporaries shouldered a fowling-piece between the ages of ten and fourteen,"[511] Thoreau, nonetheless,

---

505 Porte, *Emerson in His Journals*, p. 214
506 Franklin, *James Fenimore Cooper*, p. xxix
507 Franklin, *James Fenimore Cooper*, p. 3
508 Thoreau, *Walden*, Kindle, p. 19.
509 Thoreau, *Walden*, p. 43.
510 Thoreau, *Walden*, p. 105.
511 Thoreau, *Walden*, p. 104.

says that "I . . . sold my gun before I went into the woods,"[512] because "the only true America" is a spiritual enterprise that has little or nothing to do with guns. When Thoreau first entered the woods, his "excuse" for carrying a gun was based on his belief that it might aid him in his study of ornithology. After learning from existence, however, Thoreau found that his fowling piece had become a hindrance to "closer attention to the habits of the birds," and so he decided to "omit the gun."[513]

Thoreau "went to the woods" because, as he put it:

> I wished to live deliberately, to front only the essential facts of life, and see if I could not learn what it had to teach, and not, when I came to die, discover that I had not lived. I did not wish to live what was not life, living is so dear; nor did I wish to practise resignation, unless it was quite necessary. I wanted to live deep and suck out all the marrow of life, to live so sturdily and Spartan-like as to put to rout all that was not life, to cut a broad swath and shave close, to drive life into a corner, and reduce it to its lowest terms, and, if it proved to be mean, why then to get the whole and genuine meanness of it, and publish its meanness to the world; or if it were sublime, to know it by experience, and be able to give a true account of it in my next excursion. For most men, it appears to me, are in a strange uncertainty about it, whether it is of the devil or of God, and have somewhat hastily concluded that it is the chief end of man here to "glorify God and enjoy him forever."[514]

The collapse of Calvinism allowed Thoreau to mock that religion from the point of view of the newly discovered religion of nature, which casts a "halo of light around my shadow" that allowed him to "fancy myself one of the elect."[515] Thoreau chose to live in the woods to escape from Calvinism because "our manners have been corrupted by communication with the saints."[516]

During his sojourn at the pond, Thoreau discovered a congruity between what Kant called pure and practical reason, or as Thoreau put it "What I have observed of the pond is no less true in ethics" because logos is common to both.[517] The fact that God is the author of nature allows Thoreau to draw certain conclusions:

> When I see on the one side the inert bank—for the sun acts on one side first—and on the other this luxuriant foliage, the creation of an hour, I am affected as if in a peculiar sense I stood in the laboratory of the Artist who made the world and me—had come to where he was still at

---

[512] Thoreau, *Walden*, p. 104.
[513] Thoreau, *Walden*, p. 104.
[514] Thoreau, *Walden*, p. 44.
[515] Thoreau, *Walden*, p. 99.
[516] Thoreau, *Walden*, p. 38.
[517] Thoreau, *Walden*, p. 143, Location 3617.

work, sporting on this bank, and with excess of energy strewing his fresh designs about. . . . The atoms have already learned this law. . . . The very globe continually transcends and translates itself, and becomes winged in its orbit. The whole tree itself is but one leaf, and rivers are still vaster leaves whose pulp is intervening earth, and towns and cities are the ova of insects in their axils. . . . You here see perchance how blood-vessels are formed. . . . What is man but a mass of thawing clay?[518]

The mind is not an angel hovering over a dead universe. "The earth is not a mere fragment of dead history."[519] Nature is "hieroglyphic,"[520] which is to say at once cryptic but also bursting with a meaning that is decipherable if we have the right frame of mind. Missing from the conventional accounts of Thoreau's sojourn next to Walden Pond was the role chastity played in clearing the mind so that it could apprehend nature's lessons. Purity, by which Thoreau meant chastity or sexual morality was essential to understanding nature's relationship to God, or as Thoreau put it:

> Man flows at once to God when the channel of purity is open. By turns our purity inspires and our impurity casts us down. He is blessed who is assured that the animal is dying out in him day by day, and the divine being established.[521]

The term "animal" refers to the sensual part of man's composite nature. Thoreau's education at Harvard saddled him with a dualistic understanding of human nature which saw the soul as inhabiting a machine which turned man into "fauns and satyrs," in which "the divine" was "allied to beasts," making us "creatures of appetite," turning "our very life" into "our disgrace."[522] Living in the woods taught Thoreau that "all purity is one."[523] Temperance leads to chastity, and chastity leads to clarity of mind. Clarity of mind allows man to see nature as it really is, which liberates him from irrational conventions. Man can achieve the exalted state which was the goal of union with nature by practicing temperance because "all sensuality is one"[524]:

> All sensuality is one, though it takes many forms; all purity is one. It is the same whether a man eat, or drink, or cohabit, or sleep sensually. They are but one appetite, and we only need to see a person do any one of these things to know how great a sensualist he is. The impure can neither stand nor sit with purity. When the reptile is attacked at one mouth of his

---

518 Thoreau, *Walden*, pp. 151-2.
519 Thoreau, *Walden*, p. 152.
520 Thoreau, *Walden*, p. 152.
521 Thoreau, *Walden*, p. 108.
522 Thoreau, *Walden*, p. 108.
523 Thoreau, *Walden*, p. 109.
524 Thoreau, *Walden*, p. 109.

Part II: The Romantic Rehabilitation of Nature

burrow, he shows himself at another. If you would be chaste, you must be temperate.[525]

If you are not temperate, you cannot be chaste. If you are not chaste, you will not be able to learn the lessons Nature is willing to teach:

> From exertion come wisdom and purity; from sloth ignorance and sensuality. In the student sensuality is a sluggish habit of mind. An unclean person is universally a slothful one, one who sits by a stove, whom the sun shines on prostrate, who reposes without being fatigued. If you would avoid uncleanness, and all the sins, work earnestly, though it be at cleaning a stable. Nature is hard to be overcome, but she must be overcome. What avails it that you are Christian, if you are not purer than the heathen, if you deny yourself no more, if you are not more religious?[526]

In his more pessimistic moods, Emerson felt there was no "bottom" to existence because "the universe is like an infinite series of planes, each of which is a false bottom, and when we think our feet are planted now at last on the Adamant, the slide is drawn out from under us."[527] Emerson is referring to the Calvinist denigration of nature which found its culmination in "Sinners in the Hands of an Angry God," when Edwards told unregenerate man that he had "nothing to stand on." Nature was a rotten covering over an "abyss" which threatened to give way at any moment. But Emerson and Thoreau rejected the skepticism which resulted from an understanding of nature as an infinite regress of one abyss under another. Emerson claimed that "they are all contained & bottomed at last, & I have only to endure." The main lesson Thoreau learned by being chaste was that "Heaven is under our feet is well as over our heads."[528] The climax of Thoreau's sojourn in "nature" arrives when Thoreau plumbs its depths and recovers "the long-lost bottom of Walden Pond."[529]

> As I was desirous to recover the long-lost bottom of Walden Pond, I surveyed it carefully, before the ice broke up, early in '46, with compass and chain and sounding line. There have been many stories told about the bottom, or rather no bottom, of this pond, which certainly had no foundation for themselves. It is remarkable how long men will believe in the bottomlessness of a pond without taking the trouble to sound it. I have visited two such Bottomless Ponds in one walk in this neighborhood.

---

525 Thoreau, *Walden*, p. 109.
526 Thoreau, *Walden*, p. 109.
527 Porte, *Emerson in His Journals*, p. 275.
528 Thoreau, *Walden*, p. 140.
529 Thoreau, *Walden*, p. 141, Location 3556.

Many have believed that Walden reached quite through to the other side of the globe.[530]

Like Jonathan Edwards, some New Englanders claimed that the bottomless pond was "the undoubted source of the Styx and entrance to the Infernal Regions from these parts."[531] Others failed to find the bottom of Walden Pond because they attempted to plumb its depths with "a wagon load of inch rope" which measured nothing but "the vain attempt to fathom their truly immeasurable capacity for marvellousness."[532] Because chastity allowed contact with reality, Thoreau was able to assure his readers that:

> Walden has a reasonably tight bottom at a not unreasonable, though at an unusual, depth. I fathomed it easily with a cod-line and a stone weighing about a pound and a half and could tell accurately when the stone left the bottom, by having to pull so much harder before the water got underneath to help me. The greatest depth was exactly one hundred and two feet, to which may be added the five feet which it has risen since, making one hundred and seven. This is a remarkable depth for so small an area; yet not an inch of it can be spared by the imagination. What if all ponds were shallow? Would it not react on the minds of men? I am thankful that this pond was made deep and pure for a symbol. While men believe in the infinite some ponds will be thought to be bottomless.[533]

Bottom is another word for reality. "Be it life or death, we crave only reality."[534] Thoreau was "determined to know beans," because all creation has metaphysical significance because it was created by God. Creation may or may not be derivable from faith alone, but the existence of God is an article of reason not faith which remained hidden from the New England mind because of Calvin's exaggeration of the effects of the Fall. This is what Thoreau discovered by spending two years in "Nature." Since God is the author of nature, nature reflects his being. Existence calls forth essence:

> God himself culminates in the present moment and will never be more divine in the lapse of all the ages. And we are enabled to apprehend at all what is sublime and noble only by the perpetual instilling and drenching of the reality that surrounds us. The universe constantly and obediently answers to our conceptions; whether we travel fast or slow, the track is laid for us. Let us spend our lives in conceiving then. The poet or the artist never yet had so fair and noble a design but some of his posterity at least could accomplish it. Let us spend one day as deliberately as Nature,

---

530 Thoreau, *Walden*, p. 141.
531 Thoreau, *Walden*, p. 141.
532 Thoreau, *Walden*, p. 141.
533 Thoreau, *Walden*, p. 141.
534 Thoreau, *Walden*, loc. 1277.

and not be thrown off the track by every nutshell and mosquito's wing that falls on the rails. Let us rise early and fast, or break fast, gently and without perturbation. . . . Let us settle ourselves, and work and wedge our feet downward through the mud and slush of opinion, and prejudice, and tradition, and delusion, and appearance, that alluvion which covers the globe, through Paris and London, through New York and Boston and Concord, through Church and State, through poetry and philosophy and religion, till we come to a hard bottom and rocks in place, which we can call reality, and say, This is, and no mistake; not a Nilometer, but a Realometer, that future ages might know how deep a freshet of shams and appearances had gathered from time to time.[535]

By plumbing the depths of *Walden Pond*, Thoreau learned "there is a solid bottom everywhere," a discovery which put an end to the metaphysical uncertainty which was the legacy of Calvinism and found its culmination when Jonathan Edwards announced that unregenerate men had "nothing to stand on" shortly before it expired in the enthusiastic excess of the Great Awakening.

The lesson Thoreau derived from his years in the woods was "universal innocence."[536] Unfortunately, the euphoria Thoreau experienced when he made contact with the metaphysical certainty he described as "reality" led him to draw unwarranted conclusions. In claiming that "In a pleasant spring morning all men's sins are forgiven,"[537] Thoreau attributed to nature powers which she did not have. Nature, as Hawthorne demonstrated in the forest scene in *The Scarlet Letter*, cannot forgive sins. Thoreau derived the notion that it could from the attenuated understanding of Revelation which he derived from his childhood and youth, when he was forced to attend mandatory Bible readings as a student at Harvard.

Unlike Emerson and Hawthorne, who were exposed to Catholic culture when they toured the continent, Thoreau had no direct experience of the sacramental nature of the Catholic Church. But by attributing the power to forgive sins to nature alone, he showed how Catholic categories formed the minds of even those who thought Catholicism was darkest superstition. How else would he know such forgiveness was possible? Certainly not by watching the sun come up, as he claimed when he wrote

> We loiter in winter while it is already spring. In a pleasant spring morning, all men's sins are forgiven. Such a day is a truce to vice. While such a sun holds out to burn, the vilest sinner may return.[538]

---

535 Thoreau, *Walden*, pp. 47-8.
536 Thoreau, *Walden*, p. 157, Location 3952.
537 Thoreau, *Walden*, p. 155, Location 3903.
538 Thoreau, *Walden*, p. 155.

The extrapolation of the religion of nature to include the forgiveness of sin would have brought a wry smile to the lips of the man who wrote *The Scarlet Letter*, but even seeing the confessional in St. Peter's Basilica could not bring Hawthorne into the Church.

Similarly, Emerson's favorable impressions of Catholicism faded when he returned to Concord. In late 1862, when the famous convert to Catholicism Father Isaac Hecker visited Emerson and expressed a desire "to read lectures on the Catholic Church, in Concord," Emerson told him that:

> nobody would come to hear him, such was the aversion of people, at present, to theological questions; & not only so, but the drifting of the human mind was now quite in another direction than to any churches. Nor could I possibly affect the smallest interest in anything that regarded his church. We are used to this whim of a man's choosing to put on & wear a painted petticoat, as we are to whims of artists who wear a mediaeval cap or beard, & attach importance to it; but, of course, they must say nothing about it to us, & we will never notice it to them, but will carry on general conversation, with utter reticence as to each other's whimsies: but if once they speak of it, they are not the men we took them for, & we do not talk with them twice. But I doubt if any impression can be made on Father Isaac. He converted Mrs. Ward, &, like the lion that has eaten a man, he wants to be at it again, & convert somebody.[539]

In Concord, the practice of "religious rites" had disappeared 40 years earlier, and Emerson had no desire to resurrect them under Catholic auspices:

> We used, forty years ago, religious rites in every house, which have disappeared. There is no longer, in the houses of my acquaintants, morning or evening family prayer, or grace said at table, or any exact observance of the Sunday, except in the houses of clergymen. I have long ceased to regret this disuse. It is quite impossible to put the dial-hand back. The religion is now where it should be. Persons are discriminated as honest, as veracious, as generous & helpful, as conscientious, or having public & universal regards; are discriminated according to their aims, & not by these ritualities.[540]

But the younger generation didn't share Emerson's lack of regret for the desuetude of religious observance. Many of them were "running into the Catholic Church," something Emerson found "disgusting,"[541] even though he and his generation had "nothing . . . to offer them instead."[542] As an alternative to Catholicism, Emerson proposed "stoicism," which was "always attractive to the intellectual," but unfortunately, it had "no temples, no Academy, no

---

539 Porte, *Emerson in His Journals*, p. 508.
540 Porte, *Emerson in His Journals*, p. 508.
541 Porte, *Emerson in His Journals*, p. 509.
542 Porte, *Emerson in His Journals*, p. 509.

Part II: The Romantic Rehabilitation of Nature

commanding Zeno or Antoninus." Emerson was a devotee of "pure Ethics," but the religion he had confected around it had no "cultus," by which he meant "a fraternity with assemblings & holy days, with song & book, with brick & stone."[543] In the absence of those traditions, Emerson had to content himself with the lecture circuit which the Lyceum, which he called "the University of the People,"[544] and the railroad made possible. Through Lyceum, he could proselytize the young with "words out of heaven" which "are imparted to happy uncontrollable Pindars, Hafizes, Shakspeares, & not to Westminster Assemblies of divines."[545] John Henry Cardinal Newman expressed the futility of similar forms of "natural supernaturalism" in England when he wrote in *The Idea of a University*: "Quarry the granite rock with razors, or moor the vessel with a thread of silk; then may you hope with such keen and delicate instruments as human knowledge and human reason to contend against those giants, the passion and the pride of man."[546]

---

543 Porte, *Emerson in His Journals*, p. 509.
544 Porte, *Emerson in His Journals*, p. 472.
545 Porte, *Emerson in His Journals*, p. 509.
546 "John Henry Newman," goodreads, https://www.goodreads.com/quotes/9412292-quarry-the-granite-rock-with-razors-or-moor-the-vessel

Chapter 18

Orestes Brownson: The First American Catholic

In December 1835, an impecunious Harvard junior by the name of Henry Thoreau wrote to the then famous Orestes Brownson and asked for his assistance in finding a job.[547] Thoreau had written to Brownson on seeing the first number of the *Boston Quarterly*, "I like the spirit of independence which distinguishes it. It is high time that we knew where to look for the expression of *American* thoughts."

After learning that Thoreau knew German, Brownson "sat up until midnight talking with him," after which they "struck heartily to studying German, and getting all they could of the time together, like old friends."[548] Thoreau never got the job he hoped to obtain with Brownson's assistance, but two years later, on December 30, 1837, he wrote back to Brownson thanking him for the "six short weeks" he spent in the Brownson household as a tutor to Orestes's sons, which he referred to as "the morning of a new *Lebenstag*. They are to me a dream that is dreamt, but which returns from time to time in all its original freshness. Such a one I would dream a second and third time, and then tell it before breakfast."[549]

Orestes Brownson was born in the town of Stockbridge, Vermont on September 16, 1803.[550] As a child, Brownson "had the manners, the tone, and tastes of an old man" whose "reading was confined principally to the Scriptures, all of which I had read through before I was eight, and a great part of which I knew by heart before I was fourteen years old."[551] The lens through which Brownson viewed the Scriptures was Calvinism. Jumping into the debate over free will and election, Brownson "stoutly" defended free will "against [Jonathan] Edwards, who confounds volition with judgment, and

---

547 Theodore Maynard, Orestes Brownson Yankee, Radical, Catholic (The Macmillan Company, New York, 1943), p. 54.
548 Maynard, *Orestes Brownson Yankee, Radical, Catholic* p. 54.
549 Maynard, *Orestes Brownson Yankee, Radical, Catholic* p. 55.
550 Orestes Brownson, *The Convert*, Kindle edition, loc. 78.
551 Brownson, *The Convert*, loc. 100.

maintains that the will is necessarily determined by the state of the affections and the motives presented to the understanding."[552] Brownson decided as a child that he wanted to be "a minister of religion, and to devote myself to the work of bringing people to the knowledge and the love of God."[553] Once he made that decision, Brownson had to decide which denomination he intended to join, which immediately precipitated him into theological questions which he could not answer. Nobody told Brownson "that baptism was necessary" for salvation, nor was he told anything about the nature of the church into which one had to be baptized. Instead, Brownson was told that he must "get religion" by having certain experiences like having "a change of heart" or being "born again" even though he did not understand how they could be brought about.[554] Confronted with myriad sects, Brownson found that "the Methodist preachers appeared to have the stronger lungs."[555] Because they "preached in a louder tone," the congregation "shouted more," convincing Brownson that they were the best sect. "I thought them the best," he related in his autobiography, "because they made the most noise, and gave the most vivid pictures, of hell-fire, and the tortures of the damned."[556]

The one thing all Protestant sects had in common was distrust of reason. Luther claimed reason was a whore. The Calvinists said that it could not be trusted because of man's innate depravity. Appalled by that idea, the Methodists eschewed reason in favor of emotion. All chose faith—*sola fide*—as the alternative to reason without recognizing that faith was impossible without reason as its preamble. Without reason, revelation was incomprehensible. Convinced that he needed a community to "lead a religious life,"[557] Brownson gritted his teeth and became a member of the Presbyterian Church in Ballston, New York in October 1822.[558] He later wrote:

> I did not believe what these people said, and yet were they not right? They were. They told me to submit my reason to revelation. I will do so. I am incapable of directing myself. I must have a guide. I will hear the Church. I will surrender, abnegate my own reason, which hitherto has only led me astray, and make myself a member of the Church, and do what she commands me.[559]

It was on these terms which Brownson was baptized and received into the Presbyterian communion:

---

552 Brownson, *The Convert*, loc. 107-109.
553 Brownson, *The Convert*, loc. 120.
554 Brownson, *The Convert*, loc. 144.
555 Brownson, *The Convert*, loc. 154.
556 Brownson, *The Convert*, loc. 155.
557 Brownson, *The Convert*, loc. 203.
558 Brownson, *The Convert*, loc. 222.
559 Brownson, *The Convert*, loc. 219.

Part II: The Romantic Rehabilitation of Nature

> I did not ask whether the Presbyterian church was the true Church or not, for the Church question had not yet been fairly raised in my mind, and as it did not differ essentially from the Standing Order, and claimed to be the true Church, and was counted respectable, I was satisfied. What it believed was of little consequence, since I had resolved to abnegate my own reason, and take the Church for my guide.[560]

Unsurprisingly, difficulties followed almost immediately. After he became a Presbyterian minister, Brownson discovered that the tenets of Calvinism were self-contradictory. He was told that because reason was depraved, he had to follow God's word. "But how am I to know that it is God's word, or that there is any God at all, if my reason is totally depraved, and to be discarded as a false light?"[561]

Because Americans received their first notions of Christianity through Calvinism, they were "never able to reconcile faith and reason, or to harmonize nature and grace."[562]

Before long, it became clear to him that Presbyterianism was logically incoherent. Worse, it created an intolerable bind in the minds of its followers, because "in proportion as we discredit reason, we must discredit revelation. Reason must at least be the preamble to faith, and nature must precede and be presupposed by grace."[563] Brownson was now convinced that he had made a mistake because:

> I had no sympathy with the Presbyterian spirit, and should need a long and severe training to sour and elongate my visage sufficiently to enjoy the full confidence of my new brethren. Every day's experience proved it. In our covenant we had bound ourselves to watch over one another with fraternal affection. I was not long in discovering that this meant that we were each to be a spy upon the others, and to rebuke, admonish, or report them to the Session. My whole life became constrained. I dared not trust myself, in the presence of a church member, to a single spontaneous emotion; I dared not speak in my natural voice. We were allowed no liberty and dared enjoy ourselves only by stealth. The most rigid Catholic ascetic never imagined a discipline a thousandth part as rigid as the discipline to which I was subjected. The slightest deviation was a mortal sin, the slightest forgetfulness was enough to send me to hell. I tried for a year or two to stifle my discontent, to silence my reason, to repress my natural emotions, to extinguish my natural affections, and to submit patiently to the Calvinistic discipline.[564]

---

560 Brownson, *The Convert*, loc. 213-9.
561 Brownson, *The Convert*, loc. 366.
562 Brownson, *The Convert*, loc. 340.
563 Brownson, *The Convert*, loc. 367.
564 Brownson, *The Convert*, loc. 253-66.

That discipline involved an intolerable double standard:

> What you are to believe is the Bible. You must take the Bible as your creed, and read it with a prayerful mind, begging the Holy Ghost to aid you to understand it aright. But while the church refused to take the responsibility of telling me what doctrines I must believe, while she sent me to the Bible and private judgment, she yet claimed authority to condemn and excommunicate me as a heretic, if I departed from the standard of doctrine contained in her Confession. This I regarded as unfair treatment. It subjected me to all the disadvantages of authority without any of its advantages. Be one thing or another, said I; either assume the authority and the responsibility of teaching and directing me, or leave me with the responsibility of my freedom. Either bind me or loose me. Do not mock me with a freedom which is no freedom, or with an authority which is illusory. If you claim authority over my faith, tell me what I must believe, and do not throw upon me the labor and responsibility of forming a creed for myself.[565]

The Presbyterians claimed the right to break away from the Catholic Church, but Brownson had no right to break away from the Presbyterians. Brownson had "given up the free exercise of my own reason for the sake of an authoritative teacher" who told him that he needed to interpret the Bible according to his own lights but was a heretic if that interpretation didn't coincide with Presbyterianism. "Am I not a man," he wondered, "and as a man have I not as much right to follow my private opinion as they had to follow theirs?"[566]

"If they had a right to break from her and set up their private understanding of Scripture, why have I not the right to break from them, and from the Presbyterian church, follow my private understanding, and set up a church of my own?"[567]

The answer was inescapable: "It was clear to me that the Presbyterian church, though the church of one class of the Reformers, was not and could not be the Church of Christ, and therefore it could have no legitimate authority over me."[568] What was true of Presbyterianism was *a fortiori* true of sects based on emotion, like the Methodists. Brownson concluded that "If Christ had a church on earth which he had founded, and which had authority to teach in his name, it was evidently the Roman Catholic Church."

At that point, Brownson's identity as an American, who was *ipso facto* a Protestant, took over and informed him that conversion to Catholicism was "out of the question," because Catholicism, according to the prejudices of the day, was "everything that was vile, base, odious, and demoralizing. It had

---

[565] Brownson, *The Convert*, loc. 273-282.
[566] Brownson, *The Convert*, loc. 298.
[567] Brownson, *The Convert*, loc. 303.
[568] Brownson, *The Convert*, loc. 306.

been condemned by the judgment of mankind, and the thought of becoming a Catholic found and could find at that time no entrance into my mind. I should sooner have thought of turning Jew, Gentoo, or Buddhist."

Confronted with the choice between "the Catholic Church or no Church," Brownson abandoned faith in favor of reason and became a rationalist. Brownson was only following the premises established by his culture to their logical conclusion, which made clear that "since I cannot be a Catholic, I must be a no church man, and deny all churches, make war upon every sect claiming the slightest authority in matters of faith or conscience."[569] He realized that the "natural result of Calvinism" was "a perpetual struggle . . . between faith and reason."[570] As a result, Brownson's Protestant countrymen

> either denied reason to make way for revelation, or revelation to make way for reason. The one class declaimed against reason, used reason against reason, and sometimes assigned, apparently, a very good reason why reason ought not to be used. The other class, either openly denied all supernatural revelation, or admitting it in words, explained away all its supernaturalness, and brought it within the sphere of the natural order, and subjected it to the dominion of natural reason.[571]

The contradictions in Calvinism turned Brownson into a rationalist. Accepting reason allowed Brownson to transform himself from "an intellectual desperado" into someone who could "reclaim my reason, I reclaim my manhood, and henceforth I will, let come what may, be true to my reason, and preserve the rights and dignity of my human nature."[572]

In 1824, at the tender age of 21, Brownson changed from "a Supernaturalist to a Rationalist" and became a preacher of "Universalism," because before becoming a Presbyterian, he been initiated into the mysteries of that religion by a sister of his mother, "who had in her youth listened to the preaching of Dr. Winchester, one of the earliest Universalist preachers in America."[573] Winchester was "the patriarch of American Universalism, and at the time when I became a Universalist minister was its oracle, very nearly its Pope."[574]

With reason alone as his guide, Dr. Winchester confected his religion out of "the Bible, Ethan Allen's *Oracles of Reason*, a deistical work, and his own reflections."[575] Following his example, Brownson "necessarily excluded from revelation the revelation of anything supernatural or above reason,"[576]

---

569 Brownson, *The Convert*, loc. 315.
570 Brownson, *The Convert*, loc. 329.
571 Brownson, *The Convert*, loc. 331-2.
572 Brownson, *The Convert*, loc. 372-3.
573 Brownson, *The Convert*, loc. 405.
574 Brownson, *The Convert*, loc. 490.
575 Brownson, *The Convert*, loc 522.
576 Brownson, *The Convert*, loc. 577.

and "reduced Christianity to a system of natural religion, or, of moral and intellectual philosophy."[577] As a result, "natural reason" became "the measure of revealed truth."[578]

After freeing himself from the irrationality of Calvinism, Brownson discovered that "our natural reason is weak," depriving us of an "infallible means of knowing the truth, of knowing what it is that God requires of us, the belief and worship that will be acceptable to him."[579] Man's weakness in knowing the truth is mild compared to his weakness in putting the truth into action:

> None of us do as well as we know. The spirit is willing, but the flesh is weak. I see the right, I approve it, and yet pursue the wrong. My will is weak, and my appetites and passions are strong.[580]

Ignoring his misgivings about his new religion, Brownson became a Universalist minister in the summer of 1826 at the age of 22. His new religion made him an anti-Christian who was now at war with morality as well. Universalism's denial of the authority of Scripture led inexorably to denying any "objective distinction between virtue and vice, between good and evil." In following reason, Brownson had "lost the Bible, lost my Saviour, lost Providence, lost reason itself, and had left me only my five senses, and what could fall under their observation,—that is, reduced myself to a mere animal."[581] After the fear of hell and the hope of heaven had disappeared, Brownson was left with "nothing but this world,"[582] which he decided to turn into a "paradise on earth," under the tutelage of the Scottish utopian socialist Robert Owen and the English political philosopher William Godwin, whose *Enquiry Concerning Political Justice*, had influenced him more "than any other book except the Scriptures."[583] Godwin also introduced him to "every error the human mind is capable of inventing."[584] From reading Godwin, Brownson learned that marriage, which Godwin described as "the most odious of all monopolies," is "repugnant to justice."[585]

After his conversion, Brownson discovered a logic to Godwin's error because "Marriage in the Christian sense is really practicable with the majority of the non-laboring classes only by the grace of the sacrament."[586] Christian marriage

---

577 Brownson, *The Convert*, loc. 582.
578 Brownson, *The Convert*, p. 583.
579 Brownson, *The Convert*, loc. 548.
580 Brownson, *The Convert*, loc. 553-9.
581 Brownson, *The Convert*, loc. 770.
582 Brownson, *The Convert*, loc. 812.
583 Brownson, *The Convert*, loc. 1025.
584 Brownson, *The Convert*, loc. 1027.
585 Brownson, *The Convert*, loc. 1034.
586 Brownson, *The Convert*, loc. 1096.

Part II: The Romantic Rehabilitation of Nature

is "above the strength of human nature in our present fallen state, and needs Christian grace."[587] If "love is necessary, fatal, independent of free will," as both the Calvinists and the rationalist infidels claim, then "the doctrine of Mary and William Godwin, the poet Shelley, Robert Owen, Frances Wright, and the advocates of Free Love, is reasonable and just."[588] Calvinism, in other words, led inevitably to free love. Fidelity in marriage is impossible without the grace provided by the sacrament. Christian marriage is, in fact, immoral "because no one has a right to promise to do what it does not depend on his free will to perform."[589] Because it denies free will, Calvinism leads inexorably to free love. After Brownson made the prediction, he lived to see it fulfilled in the famous Beecher family, which descended from the lofty Calvinism of Lyman Beecher to the serial adulteries of his son Henry within one generation.

In 1832 Brownson became a Unitarian minister, which allowed him to "put humanity in the place of God"[590] and by following the example of "the carnal Jews" give "an earthly sense to all the promises and prophesies of the Messiah,"[591] so that he and his congregation could look for their reward in this world. By the time he had become its minister, Unitarianism had "demolished Calvinism" and had "made an end in all thinking minds of everything like dogmatic Protestantism," but it had put in its place a "negative, cold, and lifeless" religion which satisfied nobody.[592] By the 1840s, a cry was heard from the newly released captives:

> Not only in Boston was this cry heard. It came to us on every wind from all quarters,—from France, from Germany, from England even, and Carlyle in his Sartor seemed to lay his finger on the plague-spot of the age. Men had reached the centre of indifference, under a broiling sun in the Rue had pronounced the everlasting "No." Were they never to be able to pronounce the everlasting "Yes?"[593]

As an example of what Hegel would call the cunning of reason, the lectures of Theodore Parker got Brownson thinking about the Catholic Church. After writing a review of Parker's published lectures, Brownson "began to discover that the doctrine of the Church in the Catholic sense was far profounder and truer than the doctrine of No-Church asserted by Dr. Channing and my Unitarian friends."[594] After reviewing Parker's essays, Brownson was "led by an invincible logic to assert the Catholic Church as the true Church or living

---

587 Brownson, *The Convert*, loc. 1099.
588 Brownson, *The Convert*, loc. 2015.
589 Brownson, *The Convert*, loc. 1217.
590 Brownson, *The Convert*, loc. 1370.
591 Brownson, *The Convert*, loc. 1385.
592 Brownson, *The Convert*, loc. 1516.
593 Brownson, *The Convert*, loc. 1522.
594 Brownson, *The Convert*, loc. 3192-3193.

body of Christ."⁵⁹⁵ Brownson was, nonetheless, held back from converting on the spot because of the Protestant prejudices he had unconsciously imbibed as an American:

> To the Protestant mind this old Catholic Church is veiled in mystery, and leaves ample room to the imagination to people it with all manner of monsters, chimeras, and hydras dire. We enter it and leave no bridge over which we may return. It is a committal for life, for eternity. To enter it seemed to me, at first, like taking a leap in the dark, and it is not strange that I recoiled, and set my wits to work to find out, if possible, some compromise, some middle ground on which I could be faithful to my Catholic tendencies without uniting myself with the present Roman Catholic Church.⁵⁹⁶

By 1842, Brownson felt that:

> In every Protestant sect there was in 1842 a movement party, at war with the fundamental principle of Protestantism, and demanding Church union and Church authority. It seemed that Protestantism had culminated, that the work of disintegration and destruction had gone so far that it could go no farther, and that a reaction in earnest, and not likely to be suspended, had commenced through the whole Christian world against the Protestant Reformation."⁵⁹⁷

In 1843 Brownson had achieved such "a respectable position in the American literary world,"⁵⁹⁸ that he could talk about a growing Catholic reaction in "the more serious portion of the Protestant sects" that constituted nothing less than "The secret history of my own country for several years prior to 1844."⁵⁹⁹ Sensing that the Catholic moment had arrived in America not only for him personally but for the intellectual elite which subscribed to his magazine, Brownson approached Right Reverend Benedict Joseph Fenwick, "the learned bishop of Boston," in the last week of May 1844 and "avowed my wish to become a Catholic."⁶⁰⁰ Brownson admitted that "it was unpleasant to take such a step," but he consoled himself with the thought that "to be eternally damned would, after all, be a great deal unpleasanter."⁶⁰¹

In late March 1845, Thoreau took up residence at Walden Pond inaugurating his religion of Nature. Before that happened, Isaac Hecker:"did his best to take Thoreau with him, offering to pay his expenses for a trip to Rome, choosing

---

595 Brownson, *The Convert*, loc. 3215-3218.
596 Brownson, *The Convert*, loc. 3264-3270.
597 Brownson, *The Convert*, loc. 3299-3302.
598 Brownson, *The Convert*, loc. 3315-3317.
599 Brownson, *The Convert*, loc. 3304-3305.
600 Brownson, *The Convert*, loc. 3366-3371.
601 Brownson, *The Convert*, loc. 3366-3371.

Part II: The Romantic Rehabilitation of Nature

him because Henry could sleep on the ground and live on bread and water; such a visit would be sure to finish Henry off, he thought." But Thoreau only growled, "What is the use of your joining the Catholic Church? Can't you get along without hanging on to her skirts?"

Stunned by Brownson's conversion, Emerson and Alcott did their best to rescue Hecker from the clutches of the Catholic Church. In order to distract him, they took Hecker to see the Shakers. On this visit, Alcott showed himself positively inquisitorial. So, in a milder way, did Emerson, who asked "Ernest the Seeker" one day while they were out walking, "Mr. Hecker, I suppose it was the art, the architecture, and so on in the Catholic Church which led you to her?" "No," he answered, "but it was what caused all that."

Emerson was right in seeing that beauty was a transcendental, along with the good and the true, and that the experience of beauty at places like St. Peter's Basilica in Rome led American tourists to entertain the proposition that the Catholic faith which inspired this beauty might also be true. This is certainly what happened to Hawthorne. Even James Fenimore Cooper, creator of the American archetype Natty Bumppo and the religion of nature, had burst into tears when he entered St. Peter's. Hecker was sure that the same thing would have happened to Thoreau, but he wasn't willing to go to Rome. Because he wasn't willing to back down, the Transcendentalists had to give up on Hecker as a hopeless case. He claimed afterwards to have been the first to break the Transcendentalist camp.[602]

The synchronicity of these events showed that religion, like nature, abhorred the vacuum which the collapse of Calvinism had created. Within a period of 18 months, the practice of religion was recast in America, creating the form of religious practice to this day.

Thoreau left Walden on September 6, 1847, convinced that his generation of Americans could put foundations under "castles in the air." He died on May 6, 1862. "As we live longer," Emerson noted in his diary after Thoreau died, "we live on in a lessening minority."

Unlike Thoreau, the Transcendentalists found Brownson too argumentative and opinionated.[603] Fearing that Brownson's "expansiveness and truculence would swamp them all," Emerson advised the Transcendentalists to "bring out their own little magazine," the *Dial*, which in spite of (or perhaps because of) its lilac cover, came across as more than slightly effete, and "never succeeded in pushing its circulation beyond three hundred copies." Transcendentalism, according to historian Theodore Maynard, "was too sensitive a plant to entrust to the over-vigorous hands of a Brownson."[604] Bronson Alcott delivered a typically Delphic opinion when he opined that the *Brownson Quarterly*

---

602 Maynard, *Orestes Brownson Yankee, Radical, Catholic*, p. 116.
603 Maynard, *Orestes Brownson Yankee, Radical, Catholic*, p. 83.
604 Maynard, *Orestes Brownson Yankee, Radical, Catholic*, p. 83.

"satisfies me not, nor Emerson. It measures not the meridian but the morning ray; the nations wait for the gnomon that shall mark the broad noon."[605] Theodore Parker was less gnomic when he compared the *Dial* to "a band of men and maidens daintily arrayed in finery" and the *Boston Quarterly* to "a body of stout men in blue frocks, with great arms and hard hands, and legs like the Pillars of Hercules."[606]

Brownson was able to speak to the American intellectual elite because he knew all of them personally. In a rare insight he derived from his reading of "Self-Reliance" and personal contact with Emerson, Brownson felt Emerson's poetry could only find favor with "devil worshippers."[607]

Brownson placed Nathaniel Hawthorne "at the head of American writers" as an artist but faulted him for condoning adultery in *The Scarlet Letter*.[608] Like Hawthorne, Washington Irving had "imagination, though not of the highest order." His friend the historian George Bancroft, on the other hand, had "fancy, a rich and exuberant fancy, but very little imagination." Brownson then accused Bancroft of writing history to make facts fit his theories: "His method … is manifestly a disingenuous method, defensible on the score neither of morals nor of art."[609]

According to Brownson's verdict, all of the artists and writers who made up the American Renaissance were intellectually and spiritually stunted because they had been raised in a Protestant country, where there was "an inherent antagonism" between their religion and what he called "the American order," which was founded not on Protestantism, "but on the natural law, natural justice and equity as explained by the church, long prior to the Protestant movement of Luther and his associates."[610]

With the collapse of Calvinism in the 1840s, Protestantism became obsolete and had "fallen into the past," giving way to "the church of the future," which "already exists in our country" as the Catholic Church.[611] America now needed the Catholic Church more than the Catholic Church needed America because "it is only through Catholicity that the country can "fulfill its mission."[612]

Hawthorne's contemporary Oliver Wendell Holmes claimed that Calvinism died on November 1, 1855, and he wrote a poem celebrating its demise entitled "The Deacon's Masterpiece," which described Calvinism as a

---

605 Maynard, *Orestes Brownson Yankee, Radical, Catholic*, p. 83.
606 Maynard, *Orestes Brownson Yankee, Radical, Catholic*, p. 83.
607 Maynard, *Orestes Brownson Yankee, Radical, Catholic*, p. 216.
608 Maynard, *Orestes Brownson Yankee, Radical, Catholic*, p. 217.
609 Maynard, *Orestes Brownson Yankee, Radical, Catholic*, p. 217.
610 but on the natural law, natural justice and equity as explained by the church, long prior to the Protestant movement of Luther and his associates
611 Maynard, *Orestes Brownson Yankee, Radical, Catholic* p. 251.
612 Maynard, *Orestes Brownson Yankee, Radical, Catholic* p. 251.

Part II: The Romantic Rehabilitation of Nature

"marvlous, all-encompassing theological machine," which was "built in such a logical way/ It ran a hundred years to the day," until "it went to pieces all at once./ All at once, and nothing first/Just as bubbles do when they burst."[613]

The collapse of Calvinism created a proliferation of sects which Emerson and Thoreau's religion of nature, no matter how much it suited the temperament of the etiolated Unitarian sect known as Transcendentalism, could not contain. Most of these movements could be found in what Charles Grandison Finney referred to as the "burnt district" located in western New York state. Mother Lee, foundress of the Shakers, was born in 1736 on the eve of the Great Awakening, when Jonathan Edwards was fighting a rearguard action in defense of Calvinist orthodoxy. By the time the Second Great Awakening ran out of steam in 1840, Calvinism was gone and the vacuum its demise created was filled by a congeries of bizarre sects which characterized American spiritual life in the 1840s, as "a wild excitement" passed through that region which the locals called "a revival of religion, but which turned out to be spurious." When the "extravagant excitement" burned itself out, a reaction set in that was "so extensive and profound" that it left "the impression on many minds that religion was a mere delusion."[614]

William Miller was born on February 15, 1782, in Pittsfield Massachusetts, in what was then still the frontier. During the Battle of Plattsburgh, in the War of 1812, Miller survived a mortar explosion without a scratch. Taking this a sign from God, Miller abandoned his Deism, and the "deistic view of a distant God far removed from human affairs." He later wrote, "It seemed to me that the Supreme Being must have watched over the interests of this country in an especial manner, and delivered us from the hands of our enemies... So surprising a result, against such odds, did seem to me like the work of a mightier power than man."[615]

After meditating on Daniel 8:14, which stated that "Unto two thousand and three hundred days; then shall the sanctuary be cleansed," Miller was brought to the "solemn conclusion" that the world was going to end in 1843. After Jesus Christ failed to show up on October 22, 1844, the revised appointed date, Miller's followers experienced what they called "the Great Disappointment." The reaction of Hiram Edson, one of Miller's followers, to Christ's no show, was typical: "Our fondest hopes and expectations were blasted, and such a spirit of weeping came over us as I never experienced before.... We wept, and wept, till the day dawn." Sensing a moment of opportunity, Ellen White had a vision in December 1844 which rescued Miller's followers from the Great

---

613 Debby Applegate, *The Most Famous Man in America: The Biography of Henry Ward Beecher* (Random House Publishing Group), Kindle Edition, p. 300.

614 "Burned-over district," *Wikipedia: The Free Encyclopedia*, https://en.wikipedia.org/wiki/Burned-over_district

615 "William Miller (preacher)," *Wikipedia: The Free Encyclopedia*, https://en.wikipedia.org/wiki/William_Miller_(preacher)

Disappointment and allowed her to start her own religion, a Judaizing sect which eschews pork and holds its sabbath on Saturday known as the Seventh Day Adventists, whose headquarters can now be found in Berrien Springs, Michigan.

The most notorious fruit of the Second Great Awakening was another Judaizing sect now known as the Church of the Latter-Day Saints, but then known as the Mormons, which Sydney E. Ahlstrom described as a "a sect, a mystery cult, a new religion, a church, a people, a nation, or an American subculture; indeed, at different times and places it is all of these."[616]

During the Second Great Awakening the Mormon Church experienced rapid growth while settling on the Missouri frontier. The Mormons also experienced ten years of conflict with the citizens of Missouri as they were persecuted for their religious beliefs and practices.[617]

Joseph Smith, the founder of Mormonism, claimed that his sect had descended from the ten lost tribes of Israel, a notion which Increase Mather had launched two centuries earlier in his book *Iewes in America*. Because they were Hebrews, the Mormon men were allowed to have multiple wives. In his *magnum opus Enthusiasm*, Monsignor Ronald Knox claimed that when men created religions, polygamy was the rule, but when women created religions, celibacy was the rule. This was born out in the careers of Mother Lee, who imposed sexual abstinence on the Shakers and Joseph Smith or Brigham Young, who allowed polygamy. Polygamy and other Jewish notions like the ability to consider their enemies Amalek antagonized the moral sense of American settlers wherever the Mormons went, forcing them to leave Palmyra, New York and settle in Kirtland, Ohio, and from there to move to Jackson County, Missouri, where they arrived in 1833, only to be expelled five years later, when the governor of Missouri issued an "extermination order" against them. The Mormons then relocated to a small town called Commerce, which they renamed Nauvoo, until violence escalated once again in 1844, when Smith was killed by an angry mob, forcing his successor Brigham Young to re-locate once again this time to what is now Salt Lake City in what was then Utah Territory.[618]

Both Isaac Hecker and Orestes Brownson converted to Catholicism in the *annus mirabilis* of 1844. Brownson received the Sacrament of Confirmation on October 20, 1844, six months after entering the Church and "just 22

---

616 Stefanie M. Vaught, "Religious Intolerance in the Second Great Awakening: The Mormon Experience in Missouri," Thesis, Georgia State University, 2013, https://scholarworks.gsu.edu/cgi/viewcontent.cgi?article=1080&context=history_theses#:~:text=During%20the%20Second%20Great%20Awakening,their%20religious%20beliefs%20and%20practices.

617 Vaught, "Religious Intolerance in the Second Great Awakening."

618 Vaught, "Religious Intolerance in the Second Great Awakening."

Part II: The Romantic Rehabilitation of Nature

years after I had joined the Presbyterians.[619] After Brownson converted to Catholicism, his friends "turned away in disgust"[620] because they were "unable to perceive any logical or intellectual connection between my last utterances before entering the Church and my first utterances afterwards."[621] As a result of their incomprehension, the American intellectual elite who subscribed to his journal "looked upon my conversion, after all, as a sudden caprice, or rash act taken from a momentary impulse, or in a fit of intellectual despair, for which I had in reality no good reason to offer. So they turned away in disgust, and refused to trouble themselves any longer with the seasonings of one on whom so little reliance could be placed, and who could act without any rational motive for his action."[622] Brownson, in other words, had lost his American audience before he could introduce himself to his new Catholic co-religionists, who, even if they could read, had no understanding of and little sympathy for the collapse of Calvinism which united them as Americans.

The collapse of Calvinism and the ensuing cultural vacuum which it created reverberated across the territory which had previously been the arena of the Great Awakening, causing problems even in nominally Quaker areas like Pennsylvania. One month before the death of Joseph Smith on May 6, 1844, Nativist riots broke out in what was then the heavily Irish Catholic Philadelphia suburb of Kensington. Three thousand angry Protestants drawn largely from the city's mechanic class gathered near a Catholic school to listen to a number of speakers who excoriated Kensington's Irish Catholic immigrants as "foreigners who were strangers in the land, people of questionable loyalty and un-American traits."[623] When an Irish constable tried to establish order, he was shot in the face, and the nativist mob attempted to storm the Sisters of Charity convent school to set it on fire, only to be driven off after one nativist was killed. One day later, a mob bent on revenge carrying an American flag bearing the words "This is the flag trampled underfoot by the Irish papists," regrouped at Independence Hall, marched to St. Michael's Church, and burned it to the ground.[624] One day later, the mob returned and burned down St. Augustine's Church, after its library was dragged out into the street and set on fire. According to Loughery's account:

> Gravestones were overturned in Catholic cemeteries. Priests and nuns fled their rectories and convents and were sheltered by their parishioners. The more affluent Catholic families decamped from the city, and Bishop Kenrick himself was ushered out of town by his nervous staff.

---

619 Brownson, *The Convert*, loc. 3443-3445.
620 Brownson, *The Convert*, loc. 3468-3473.
621 Brownson, *The Convert*, loc. 3468-3473.
622 Brownson, *The Convert*, loc. 3468-3473.
623 Loughery, *Dagger John*, p. 157.
624 Loughery, *Dagger John*, p. 157.

The authorities could do little to stop the three-day rampage, and an estimated thirty homes of Irish residents were vandalized or burned to the ground before order was restored.[625]

Eventually, a grand jury issued a report blaming the Irish for the violence. Taking a middle of the road position, a prominent Philadelphia businessman noted in his diary, "Blame attaches to both parties, but I hold the Irish Catholics the most culpable as the original aggressors. Bishop Hughes of N.Y. stirred up the flame in that city by preventing the use of the Bible in public schools & his indiscreet interference with the popular elections."[626]

German Catholic Churches in the Nativists' direct line of march were spared, indicating that a causes of anti-Catholic feeling in Philadelphia was that the Irish were undercutting the wages of the local mechanic class. When Bishop John Hughes of New York addressed "the plight of the working class,"[627] he caught the attention of Isaac Hecker, "a Brook Farm utopian and recent Catholic convert who was planning to enter the priesthood."[628] Hecker promptly relayed the information to Orestes Brownson, who was also contemplating conversion to the Catholic Church. Hecker "thought Hughes and Brownson might have a good deal in common, at least on the topics of labor and economic justice" because Hughes' speech displayed "a fierce social conscience." It was a speech, Hecker continued, that Brownson himself "could have given."[629]

Eventually Hecker would be instrumental in persuading Brownson to move from Boston, where he entered the Church in the last week of May 1844, to New York, where he became her apologist under Archbishop Hughes. Both Hecker and Brownson were convinced that the Church needed to take a new approach to evangelizing American Protestants and bringing them into the Church, and they believed they could assist the essentially foreign clergy and episcopacy in their work.

---

625 Loughery, *Dagger John*, p. 157.
626 Loughery, *Dagger John*, p. 159.
627 Loughery, *Dagger John*, p. 165.
628 Loughery, *Dagger John*, p. 165.
629 Loughery, *Dagger John*, p. 165.

Chapter 19

"Dagger John" Hughes and Ethnic Catholicism

No one epitomized the foreign-born episcopacy better than Archbishop "Dagger John" Hughes, who looked favorably upon Brownson's conversion and, at Hecker's urging was willing to bring him to New York. Hecker and Brownson came from the elite Boston circle of intellectuals known as the Transcendentalists. They believed that their labors in the intellectual vineyards of New England gave them insight into the American identity in the wake of Calvinism's collapse that would bring large numbers of the disaffected into the Church. How this fit into the plans of the Irish episcopacy remained an unanswered question. In early 1855, Brownson wrote to Hecker, claiming that: "I think as you do. The simple truth is our old controversialists have their method, and they will look with distrust on our new method, and fancy it full of danger. Very few of them have any suspicion that times have changed and that old errors are to be refuted under new forms & from a different stand-point."[630]

The arrangement Hecker brokered in bringing Brownson together with Hughes quickly descended into a dispute about American identity and whether Catholics had one or not. If we are talking about the overwhelming majority of Catholics in the United States in the 1840s, then the answer was no. They were primarily Irish and German Catholics living in America at that time for economic purposes as was the case with the English settlers who came over in the 16th and 17th centuries. If Ralph Waldo Emerson was the first English descendant who thought of himself as an American, Orestes Brownson was the first Englishman who thought of himself as an American Catholic. Hecker's and Brownson's controversial works "have been written for a state of things which has passed or is passing away in this country," Brownson wrote, referring to the demise of Calvinism, which had nothing to do with the Catholicism of the Irish peasants now living in cities like Boston, New York, and Philadelphia. Instead of addressing the needs of the immigrant Irish who constituted the majority of Hughes's flock in New York,

---

630 Maynard, *Orestes Brownson Yankee, Radical, Catholic* p. 263.

Brownson and Hecker wanted to convert "those who have outgrown all the forms of dogmatic Protestantism, and are looking, like Emerson and Parker, for something beyond the reformation, and have glimpses of a truth, a beauty, a perfection above it, to which they long to attain. . . . These are the real American people."[631]

Brownson and Hecker, as a result, found themselves in a bind having to choose between "the real American people," who were violently anti-Catholic, and the Irish immigrants who were Catholic but violently anti-English, anti-Protestant, and in no sense American. Complicating the situation was the immigrants' ferocious desire to be accepted by a Protestant majority which held them in contempt even if it were willing to hire them as domestic maids and ditch diggers. Poor Paddy worked on the Railway,[632] and when he got home at night, his thoughts were far from Transcendental. The effete Transcendentalists held him in contempt, and they held Brownson in contempt after his conversion for consorting with Paddy, whose concerns were *infra dig*.

When the lace curtain Irish left the shanty behind, their highest aspiration was to be accepted. By the end of the 19th century, Bishop John Ireland (1838 – 1918) was their champion, and assimilation was their goal. As a result:

> American Catholics were then (as to some extent they still are) somewhat timid people, who asked for little more than to be left alone. The problem that engrossed the ecclesiastical authorities was one of taking care of the flood of Catholic immigrants; it was impossible to make any general apostolic effort, though this was the work to which the Paulists specially addressed themselves. Whatever controversy was engaged in reduced itself to attempts to refute anti-Catholic calumny. Otherwise, it was best for Catholics not to make themselves too conspicuous among a people with whom Nativism had not ceased to be endemic.[633]

Hecker told Brownson to move to New York because Archbishop Hughes takes "a great interest in you." In addition, Hecker continued, "There is no question Bishop H. is the most able bishop we have, and a *Review* started here with his patronage would have much greater advantages than at any other place in the union."[634] Brownson was initially reluctant to leave Boston, the city where he had established his reputation, but eventually his expulsion from the Transcendentalists' synagogue combined with "some philosophical discoveries" he had made, which could help Catholic theologians to convert unbelievers, persuaded him to move to New York, where he hoped to

---

631 Maynard, *Orestes Brownson Yankee, Radical, Catholic* p. 263.

632 Kellyoneill, "Luke Kelly Paddy On The Railway," YouTube, April 2, 2007, https://www.youtube.com/watch?v=lEwWmiW248c

633 Maynard, *Orestes Brownson Yankee, Radical, Catholic*, p. 392.

634 Loughery, *Dagger John*, p. 166.

Part II: The Romantic Rehabilitation of Nature

collaborate with Hughes in bringing America into the Catholic Church. After Brownson arrived, Hughes began to suspect that Brownson wanted to bring the Catholic Church into America, and to give the bishop his due, there was evidence to support that claim.

As a new convert, Brownson "dreaded" to have his philosophical discoveries "rejected by the Catholic bishop," but he soon discovered that that unnamed Catholic bishop was "far more likely, bred as he had been in a different philosophical school from myself, to oppose than to accept it."[635] Brownson was an American philosopher who happened to be Catholic every bit as much as he was a Catholic philosopher who happened to be an American, but he insisted on saying that "philosophy," by which he probably meant Thomism, "did not conduct me into the Church." Brownson was a Thomist *malgre lui*, because he understood intuitively even if he never stated it explicitly that existence calls essence into being. He joined the Church after he had gained what he called "a real philosophy," which he defined as "a philosophy which takes its principles from the order of being, from life, from things as they are or exist, instead of the abstractions of the schools."[636] Grace eventually perfected nature. At that point, "faith flowed in, and I seized with joy and gladness the Christian Church and her dogmas."[637] Because existence provided a sound foundation, Brownson's submission to the Catholic Church was "an intelligent, a reasonable act."[638]

Brownson had, as a result, no regrets after he joined the Church. During the nearly 13 years between May of 1844, when he joined the Church, and the publication of his autobiography in 1857, Brownson "found not the slightest reason to regret the step I took."[639] As a Catholic, he "felt and enjoyed a mental freedom which I never conceived possible while I was a non-Catholic."[640] He joined a Church, however, that was "made up in great part of the humbler classes of the Catholic populations of the Old World, for three hundred years subjected to the bigotry, intolerance, persecutions, and oppressions of Protestant or quasi-Protestant governments. . . ."[641] This persecution led to unfortunate consequences for the Irish immigrants, who, although nominally Catholic:

> are no credit to their religion, to the land of their birth, or to that of their adoption. No Catholic will deny that the children of these are to a great extent shamefully neglected and suffered to grow up without the simplest

---

635 Brownson, *The Convert*, loc. 3395-3400.
636 Brownson, *The Convert*, loc. 3537-3540.
637 Brownson, *The Convert*, loc. 3540.
638 Brownson, *The Convert*, loc. 3608.
639 Brownson, *The Convert*, loc. 3801-3802.
640 Brownson, *The Convert*, loc. 3783-3784.
641 Brownson, *The Convert*, loc. 3809-3813.

elementary moral and religious instruction, and to become recruits to our vicious population, our rowdies, and our criminals. This is certainly to be deplored but can easily be explained without prejudice to the Church, by adverting to the condition to which these individuals were reduced before coming here."[642]

After consorting with the Protestant elite in Boston and Concord at the moment of their greatest cultural influence in America, Brownson joined a church, in which:

> The majority of our Catholic population is made up of the unlettered peasantry, small mechanics, servant girls, and common laborers, from various European countries, and however worthy in themselves, or useful to the country to which they have migrated, cannot, in a worldly and social point of view at least, be taken as a fair average of the Catholic population in their native lands.[643]

Brownson held great hopes for future generations of Catholics, but in the meantime he could not "pretend that the Catholic population of this country are a highly literary people, or that they are in any adequate sense an intellectually cultivated people."[644]

Brownson felt that the newly arrived Catholic immigrants did not understand American democracy because they:

> have migrated for the most part from foreign Catholic populations, that have either been oppressed by non-Catholic governments directing their policy to crush and extinguish Catholicity, or by political despotisms which sprang up in Europe after the disastrous Protestant revolt in the sixteenth century, and which recognized in the common people no rights, and allowed them no equality with the ruling class.[645]

Because they have had no experience in self-government, Catholic immigrants:

> have a tendency in seeking to follow out American democracy to run into extreme radicalism, or when seeking to preserve law and order, to run into extreme conservatism. They do not always hit the exact medium. But this need not surprise us, for no one can hit that medium unless his interior life and habits have been formed to it. Non-Catholic foreigners are less able than Catholic foreigners to do it, if we except the English, who have been trained under a system in many respects analogous to our own; and no small portion of our own countrymen, "to the manner born," make even more fatal mistakes than are made by any portion of our Catholic

---

642 Brownson, *The Convert*, loc. 3813-3818.
643 Brownson, *The Convert*, loc. 3834-3837.
644 Brownson, *The Convert*, loc. 3845-3846.
645 Brownson, *The Convert*, loc. 3608-3611.

population,—chiefly, however, because they adopt a European instead of an American interpretation of our political and social order.[646]

Telling the Irish that they would do well to imitate the English, who had been oppressing them for centuries was never a good idea, but it was especially off-putting in 1844 when "the English" were burning down Catholic convents and churches. Brownson then launched into a whiggish interpretation of European history which excoriated Philip II of Spain by claiming that if he had succeeded in bringing the Spanish Netherlands back under Catholic control, "Europe would most likely have been plunged into a political and social condition as unenviable as that into which old Asia has been plunged for these four hundred years." Heading further down a path that was guaranteed to alienate even non-immigrant Catholics, Brownson claimed that "Providence . . . raised and directed the tempest that scattered the Grand Armada"[647] because "free thought was prohibited" in Catholic countries. As a result, "it is hard to find a literature tamer, less original, and living than that of Catholic Europe all through the eighteenth century, down almost to our own times."[648]

The Catholic clergy came to be regarded as "the chief supporters of the despot," thereby alienating Catholics who "cherished the spirit of resistance" and ultimately bringing about the French Revolution, which "rightly interpreted," was nothing less than "the indignant uprising of a misgoverned people against a civil despotism that affected injuriously all orders, ranks, and conditions of society."[649] During the 18th century, "the Catholic party, yielding to the sovereigns, lost to some extent, for the eighteenth century, the control of the mind of the age, and failed to lead its intelligence."[650] Brownson's conclusion is clear. In order to regain "control of the mind of the age," the Catholic Church needed to learn from America, because Americans understand that:

> This idea of power, whether in Church or State, as a delegated power or trust, is inseparable from the American mind, and hence the American feels always in its presence his native equality as a man, and asserts, even in the most perfect and entire submission, his own personal independence and dignity, knowing that he bows only to the law or to the will of a common Master. His submission he yields because he knows that it is due, but without servility or pusillanimity. But though I entertain these views of what have been for a long time the policy of so-called Catholic

---

646 Brownson, *The Convert*, loc. 3890-3896.
647 Brownson, *The Convert*, loc. 3949-3953.
648 Brownson, *The Convert*, loc. 3958-3963.
649 Brownson, *The Convert*, loc. 3964-3971.
650 Brownson, *The Convert*, loc. 3999-4000.

governments, and so to speak, the politics of European Catholics, I find in them nothing that reflects on the truth or efficiency of the Church.[651]

The Catholic Church would do well to adopt the American understanding of power because she has for too long treated the faithful as if they are "slaves" or "machines."[652] Because at present, the Catholic population in America has "not yet moulded, save in religion, into one homogeneous body," it exhibits features "more or less repulsive to the American wedded to his own peculiar nationality and but recently converted to the Catholic faith."[653] That repulsive character will disappear once "these heterogeneous elements" amalgamate into a common identity which is both Catholic and American. To do this, Catholics must adopt "the tone and features of the country" in which they reside. This will prove "the force of Catholicity, and its vast importance in forming a true and noble national character and in generating a true, generous, and lofty patriotism. In a few years they will be the Americans of the Americans, and on them will rest the performance of the glorious work of sustaining American civilization and realizing the hopes of the founders of our great and growing Republic."[654]

After saying good-bye to the anti-Calvinists who made up the American Renaissance, Brownson said hello to the Irish, who were the dominant force in the Catholic Church in Boston. Brownson eventually moved to New York at Hecker's suggestion, where he came in contact with Archbishop "Dagger John" Hughes. Unfortunately, Brownson was too Catholic for the Yankees, and too American for the Catholics, especially the newly arrived Irish Catholic immigrants. In saying that the Catholic Church in America needed "a new sort of leadership," Brownson ran afoul of the Irish hierarchy, which had been propelled into that role willy nilly because of the sheer numbers of Irish immigrants who arrived in the wake of chronic starvation in Ireland culminating in the potato famine of 1846-7.

Bishop John Hughes, archbishop of New York, affectionately known as Dagger John because of the peculiar way he made the cross when signing his correspondence, epitomized that group of Irish Catholic immigrants.

More than anyone else up to that moment in American history, Brownson created an American Catholic identity, which was distinct from the Catholic identity which groups like the Irish, Germans, Italians, and Poles—to name the ethnic big four—brought over to America with them. Only someone with Brownson's truculent personality could have succeeded in pulling off a task of this magnitude. The Irish bishops, the group which greeted Brownson's Americanism with the most skepticism, were not by nature or education

---

651 Brownson, *The Convert*, loc. 4023-4029.
652 Brownson, *The Convert*, loc. 4032-4033.
653 Brownson, *The Convert*, loc. 4065-4073.
654 Brownson, *The Convert*, loc. 4065-4073.

philosophical, especially not when faced with the survival of its flock in an overwhelmingly anti-Catholic environment, as evidenced by the Nativist riots.

Despite his truculence and the suspicion of his class which was endemic to the Irish, Brownson surprisingly had a marked effect on the mind of the American episcopacy at a crucial moment in American history for both Catholics and anti-Catholic nativist bigots. In 1874, commenting on an article he wrote on Archbishop Spalding, who died two years previously, the *Catholic Advocate* of Louisville, Kentucky, where Spalding had been bishop before being transferred to Baltimore, wrote:

> In lifting the countenances of Catholics from their time-out-of-mind cringingness to brute force, we are disposed to assign, as the chief instrument in God's hands, not his Grace of Baltimore, but Dr. Brownson himself. ... At his feet, more than at those of any other man that taught in America, have the Catholic Bishops sat. . . . Brownson's vocation has been to teach the teachers. . . . Brownson has been an eminently providential man." Of himself he could say with perfect truth: "Born and reared in the bosom of the persecuting class, we did not and could not make a proper allowance for the effect of ages of persecution or oppression on its victims. We came into the church with a bold, determined spirit, which had never been crushed by persecution, and very naturally gained among Catholics the reputation of being haughty, proud, arrogant, harsh, and overbearing, especially of being shockingly imprudent, while we thought we only exercised the firm and independent spirit that became the freeman, and the defender of the rights and dignity of the truth he loves and knows he possesses." He increased Catholic morale even when he was a disturbing force among Catholics. . . . but it is to be feared that they came to hate Catholics all the more because of the aggressive tone he used in order "to put Protestantism on the defensive" as he called it. . . . Infidels they are, he declared, and it is of no little importance to let it be seen that no man can be a Protestant and be at the same time a Christian or follower of our Lord and Saviour Jesus Christ.[655]

During the commencement ceremony at Fordham in July 1856, Hughes criticized Brownson for his Americanism. In response to Brownson's commencement speech, in which he claimed that "United States and Catholicism would, in the end, prove to be uniquely, even providentially, well suited to each other,"[656] thereby creating a national Catholic identity which could not be identified with their separate ethnic groups, Hughes arose and launched into a harangue that was less calculated to refute his ideas and

---

655 Maynard, *Orestes Brownson Yankee, Radical, Catholic*, pp. 392-3.
656 Loughery, *Dagger John*, p. 244.

more calculated to "put the man in his place."[657] Hughes claimed that "it was a mistake to identify an eternal, transhistorical faith with any single nationality."[658] Dagger John wanted Fordham students to know that:

> there was nothing unique about the American character that should make Catholics feel they should more speedily adapt to American culture, forget or downplay their European origins, or try to accommodate themselves in any special way to a society that had been frequently hostile and even violent toward them. He argued that, for all anyone knew, more waves of violence might lie ahead. Catholics should not assume the proverbially open-armed country to which they pledged allegiance would not turn against them at some future time. Then they would have to be prepared to fight all over again. So much for an "American Catholic Church." And so much for a speaker who did not recognize and honor one particular ethnic group—that is, the Irish—for all that it had done to see that Catholicism took root on this side of the Atlantic."[659]

The contretemps at Fordham took place as America stood on the brink of the Civil War, a conflict which replaced the East/West axis of American identity by imposing a black-white, north-south dichotomy as the fundamental polarity in American life. This racial polarity was reaffirmed in 1954 when the Supreme Court handed down *Brown v. School Board*, which along with *Berman v. Parker* became the pillars of post-World War II social engineering. The government's manipulation of race, as derived from an understanding of the Civil War as a battle against slavery, obscured the real polarity of American identity which was religious and took place on an axis which stretched from east to west, corresponding to the metaphysical terms existence and essence. But even the Civil War could be described as a function of *Drang nach Westen* vs. *Drang nach Osten* because the main issue which precipitated the Civil War was the expansion of slavery into western territories and whether they would be admitted to the union as slave or free states.

On May 24, 1856, two months before Dagger John upbraided Orestes Brownson at the Fordham University commencement address, John Brown, a Connecticut Yankee with extreme antislavery views, attacked an isolated farm at Pottawatomie Creek, Kansas territory, dragging five unarmed men and boys from their home and brutally murdering them. He then freed eleven slaves after killing their owner in the hope of setting off a slave rebellion. In 1859, Brown tried to foment a slave rebellion again, this time by marching a 21-man army armed with pikes and rifles to the Federal Armory at Harper's Ferry, West Virginia. Brown failed once again and was executed for his efforts, but his attempt struck terror into the hearts of slave owners throughout the

---

657 Loughery, *Dagger John*, p. 244.
658 Loughery, *Dagger John*, p. 244.
659 Loughery, *Dagger John*, p. 245.

Part II: The Romantic Rehabilitation of Nature

south largely because of the sympathetic treatment Brown found at the hands of abolitionists like Emerson and Thoreau in places like Concord, Massachusetts.[660]

In 1862 Nathaniel Hawthorne wrote an essay entitled "Chiefly About War Matters," in which he offended many New Englanders by attacking Emerson for his support of John Brown. In response to Emerson's claim that Brown "made the Gallows as venerable as the Cross," Hawthorne called Brown a "blood-stained fanatic" and concluded that "nobody was ever more justly hanged."[661]

---

660 "John Brown," American Battlefield Trust, https://www.battlefields.org/learn/biographies/john-brown

661 Chiefly About War Matters, *Wikipedia: The Free Encyclopedia*, https://en.wikipedia.org/wiki/Chiefly_About_War_Matters

Chapter 20

The Racial Double Standard

Allen's treatment of Archbishop "Dagger John" Hughes exposes the double standard implicit in his understanding of the white race. Allen is correct when he claims that "whiteness" was a social construct created to convey moral approval, but he then fails to tell us that the Marxist revolutionary movement of the 1960s known as the Civil Rights Movement simply turned the meaning of this term upside down in a way that was no less absolute by claiming that it conveyed moral disapproval. How did a social construct become a moral imperative? If whiteness should not have conveyed privilege in the period preceding World War II, why did blackness contain moral privilege in the years following it? Abolitionism was based on the understanding that race demanded a moral response, but the Irish Catholic clergy felt no need to adopt standards that were culturally and religiously alien and were imposed on them by Nativists who hated Catholics.

The Irish had mixed feelings when it came to abolitionism. Daniel O'Connell rejected what he called "the filthy aristocracy of skin,"[662] and sided with the American abolitionists in linking their cause with the repeal of the union of England and Ireland. In this he differed from the rank-and-file Irishman in America, who made a clear distinction between the two issues and thought that linking Irish independence with radical abolitionism spelled doom for the Irish cause. Archbishop John Hughes was caught in the crossfire. Allen frames the terms of the conflict differently:

> A choice was to be posed between O'Connell and Hughes; between Pope Gregory XVI's denunciation of slavery and the apologetics for it put forward by Bishop England of Charleston; and, within the "Irish-American heart," between the reverence for O'Connell, Catholic Liberator, embattled leader of the historic struggle for repeal of the Union, and the blandishments of white supremacy.[663]

Allen, as we have come to expect, misstates the case. The choice Irish Americans faced was between two competing moralities: Protestant revolutionary abolitionism, which portrayed the terrorist John Brown

---

662 Allen, p. 333.
663 Allen, p. 298.

as a saint, and Catholic moral teaching which was never absolute in its condemnation of slavery. In his letter to Philemon, Paul "was describing and addressing an interpersonal conflict within the context of slavery, he was neither prescribing the system of slavery nor endorsing it as a good or godly practice."[664] Archbishop Hughes earned the ire of Theodore Allen, who described him as an "organization man," who simultaneously represented the interests of the Catholic Church and the "white race"[665] in a way that was morally repugnant. When it came to the abolitionist cause in America, policy determined morality, as it would when the left adopted the civil rights movement as its sacred cause in the 1960s. When it came to the Catholic Church, the opposite was the case. Morality determined policy. Archbishop Hughes was shepherd to a flock which had no dog in the fight that Protestant radicals were steering toward the bloodiest conflict in the history of a country where the Irish were considered contemptible by the very people who were hectoring them to support the abolitionist cause. Because he was a Catholic from another country which had suffered oppression at the hands of the same Protestant sects that controlled America and as members of the Nativist movements were burning Catholic churches and convents to the ground, Hughes was in no hurry to join the ranks of his oppressors in the name of a solidarity which was purely instrumental on their part. And so he refused to take the side of the abolitionists against what the radical abolitionist William Lloyd Garrison described as "a stupendous conspiracy. . . between the leading Irish demagogues, the leading pseudo-Democrats, and the Southern slaveholders."[666] His decision was made easier by the fact that:

> by the early 1840s there was "fairly unanimous agreement" among the Catholic clergy and press in the United States that "the principles and methods of Garrisonian abolitionism were not only a threat to the safety of the country but also in conflict with Catholic ethics and ideals."[667]

Indeed, visits to Spanish and American sugar plantations in 1853 convinced Hughes that the plight of African slaves was no worse than the plight of the Irish working man in the cities of the North. In May 1854, Hughes preached a sermon at St. Patrick's Cathedral based on his travels to Cuba and the South in light of John 10:11-16 which portrayed the slave owner as commissioned by God to be "a shepherd over his flock of slaves."[668] "Is not the father of the family," Hughes asked in a way Allen found unconvincing, "invested with the power of god that he is a sovereign, commanding and expecting to be

---

664 https://shereadstruth.com/philemon-onesimus/
665 Allen, p. 293.
666 Allen, p. 299.
667 Allen, p. 297.
668 Allen, p. 313.

obeyed, as he should?" All God demanded was that the shepherd exert a good Christian influence on the slaves:

> Hughes was convinced that the lot of the Africans was improved by being kidnapped and enslaved in America. He was reinforced in this opinion by the fact that when he had asked plantation slaves whether they would prefer to stay as they were in America or to go back to Africa, they had unanimously told him that they much preferred being slaves in America. He apparently did not ask them whether they would prefer freedom to bondage. From the beginning of the Civil War, Hughes condemned the very idea that the abolition of slavery might be a war aim, saying Irish-Americans would not fight for such a cause, adding that if Lincoln had such an intention, he ought to resign the presidency. Hughes denounced the Emancipation Proclamation before the ink was dry. And he blamed the New York Draft Riots of the summer of 1863 on the belief that the government intended to make Negroes equal to white men.[669]

Allen believes that the Catholic Church was morally culpable for its refusal to take sides on the slavery question, which he saw as the fundamental moral issue of that time. The Irish, however, sided with Hughes, preferring to "give unto Caesar the things that are Caesar's" rather than be dragooned into a fight which did not concern them. When the Irish fresh off the boat enlisted in the Union Army to fight Catholic Mexico and subsequently decided that they were fighting for the wrong side and created the San Patricio brigade to fight for Catholic Mexico, they were universally vilified as traitors to a country which held them in contempt because they were Catholic. Orestes Brownson understood that contempt because, as a convert to Catholicism, he knew first-hand how:

> The Yankee hod-carrier, or Yankee wood-sawyer, looks down with ineffable contempt upon his brother Irish hod-carrier or Irish wood-sawyer. In his estimation, "Paddy" hardly belongs to the human family. Add to this that the influx of foreign laborers, chiefly Irish, increases the supply of labor, and therefore apparently lessens relatively the demand, and consequently the wages of labor, and you have the elements of a wide, deep, and inveterate hostility on the part of your Yankee laborer against your Irish laborer, which manifests itself naturally in your Native American Party.[670]

Many Irishmen had learned that lesson and refused to be drawn into the abolition battle, recommending instead, as the Catholic *Freeman's Journal* had done, that *Uncle Tom's Cabin* be put on the Index of Forbidden Books "since its abolitionism was just an American version of 'Red Republicanism.'"[671] Allen

---

669 Allen, p. 313.
670 Allen, p. 179.
671 Allen, p. 309.

concludes that Hughes caved into pressure and became "an organization man" who capitulated to the mores of "the predominately Protestant American, slaveholder-dominated society" and an apologist for the "white race,"[672] by urging the Irish to "merge socially and politically with the American people,"[673] when the opposite was the case. Hughes opposed western migration, the main vector of American assimilation, because it would take the Irish into territories where the absence of Catholic clergy would have tempted them to become members of sects like the Methodists, whom even O'Connell saw as "calumniating enemies of Catholicity and the Irish."[674]

Unlike Bishop John Ireland of St. Paul, Minnesota at a later date, Hughes had reservations about the assimilation of the Irish in America. Assimilation was acceptable only if the Irish were able to retain their identity as Catholics, and only if they had the right to judge messianic political movements like abolitionism on their own terms and not the terms dictated to them by Protestants who didn't like them. When Allen claims that the Irish balked at joining the abolitionist crusade because they "accepted their place in the white-race system of social control and claimed the racial privileges entailed by it,"[675] he fails to see that the real issue was loss of Catholic identity, not "white privilege," which, as the Nativist riots showed, was nonexistent for Irish Catholics.

---

672 Allen, p. 311.
673 Allen, p. 312.
674 Allen, p. 315.
675 Allen, p. 317.

Chapter 21

How the Irish Became White

In his book *How the Irish Became White*, the late Harvard professor Noel Ignatiev adopted Allen's thesis about the creation of the white race and applied it not to the South, where slavery began, but to Philadelphia, where Ignatiev grew up during the second half of the 20th century. There were no slaves living in Philadelphia in 1940, the year in which he was born, but Ignatiev claims that the Philadelphia Irish were now the main beneficiaries of white privilege. "In becoming white," Ignatiev contends, "the Irish ceased to be Green."[676] Both Ignatiev and Allen, whose book *The Creation of the White Race* serves as the template for *How The Irish Became White*, were Marxists, which means that religion, which Marx called "the opiate of the Masses," does not provide the fundamental categories of their analysis, which is one of the main reasons that they claim that the Irish, who were overwhelmingly Catholic, became white. Ignatiev construes Archbishop John Hughes's repudiation of Daniel O'Connell's denunciation of slavery, as based on a racial antagonism to abolitionism, ignoring Hughes' religious insight which saw abolitionism as "thronged with bigoted and persecuting religionists; with men who, in their private capacity, desire the extermination of Catholics by fire and sword."[677]

The understanding that abolitionists were anti-Catholic Nativists was widespread in Catholic circles, as was the reluctance of Irish Catholics to fight the battles of their enemies, especially when those battles would "bathe the whole South in blood."[678] Like Allen, Ignatiev ignores the religious dimensions of the Irish position and instead portrays it as a racial struggle. The Penal Laws discriminated against the Irish as Catholics, but Ignatiev describes them as establishing Ireland "as a country in which Irish Catholics formed an oppressed race."[679] As we have already noted, when Msgr. O'Connell used the term race in his letters to Bishop John Ireland in the 1890s, he was referring to the ethnic difference between the Irish and the German factions at Catholic University of America, not phenotype.

---

676 Ignatiev, *How the Irish became White* (Kindle edition), p. 4.
677 Ignatiev, p. 14.
678 Ignatiev, p. 14.
679 Ignatiev, p. 39.

Walking with a Bible and a Gun

Writing in the aftermath of the Civil Rights Movement, when the term clearly meant phenotype, Ignatiev confuses the issue by consistently failing to specify which sense of the term he is using. When he writes, "Eighteenth-century Ireland presents a classic case of racial oppression" is he referring to ethnicity or phenotype? The same term becomes even more confusing when he writes: "Catholics there were known as native Irish, Celts, or Gaels (as well as 'Papists' and other equally derogatory names), and were regarded, and frequently spoke of themselves, as a 'race,' rather than a nation."[680] Nation is based on "natio," the Latin word for ethnicity, which is based primarily on language and religion. In the 19th century, "race" and "*nation*" were synonyms for ethnicity, not opposites, as Ignatiev uses them. In the latter half of the 20th century, when Ignatiev wrote his book, "race" meant phenotype exclusively, and is therefore inapplicable to the situation in Ireland at the time of the Penal Laws. Ignatiev's repeated use of the term race fails to make these distinctions and is consistently confusing, as when he writes:

> The racial and class hierarchy was enforced by the Dissenters, who were mostly Presbyterian farmers, mechanics, and small tradesmen, descendants of soldiers settled by Cromwell and Scots settled later in Ulster.[681]

At another point Ignatiev clearly states that "Under the Protestant Ascendancy the masses of Irish" were "Catholics," who "lived in conditions of misery so severe that they elicited pity and condemnation from Dr. Johnson, Edmund Burke, and a host of others, including the most famous satire in the English language, Jonathan Swift's *A Modest Proposal* (1729)."[682] But instead admitting that religion is the sole criterion establishing their identity under the Protestant Ascendancy in Ireland, he then adds even more confusingly: "Thus, as a portion of the Irish diaspora became known as 'the Irish,' a racial (but not ethnic) line invented in Ireland was recreated as an ethnic (but not racial) line in America."[683]

The Irish were Catholic in Ireland, and that fact constituted the main source of their oppression there. The Irish did not cease to be Catholic when they came to America, where religion also constituted the main source of their oppression, as the Nativist riots and Archbishop Hughes's reaction to them showed. Becoming "white" did not change the lot of the Irish in Philadelphia, where, even according to Ignatiev's testimony, "it was by no means obvious who was "white." In the early years Irish were frequently referred to as "niggers turned inside out"; the Negroes, for their part, were sometimes called "smoked

---

680 Ignatiev, p. 40.
681 Ignatiev, p. 40.
682 Ignatiev, p. 40.
683 Ignatiev, p. 45.

Part II: The Romantic Rehabilitation of Nature

Irish."[684] The Irish derived no benefit from being "white": an anonymous Negro is quoted as saying, "My master is a great tyrant. He treats me as badly as if I was a common Irishman."[685]

Undeterred by his own evidence to the contrary, Ignatiev boldly states his thesis, claiming that the Irish "opted . . . for the privileges and burdens of whiteness"[686] because "white supremacy was not a flaw in American democracy but part of its definition, and the development of democracy in the Jacksonian period cannot be understood without reference to white supremacy."[687]

Ignatiev then blames the victim, claiming "the assimilation of the Irish into the white race made it possible to maintain slavery,"[688] ignoring the fundamental issue of religion, not race when "a largely Irish"[689] mob burned down an abolitionist hall in Philadelphia as retaliation for the anti-Irish nativist rioters who set fire to convents in Philadelphia and Boston. Comparing the systems of slave and free labor in America, Orestes Brownson, the famous convert to Catholicism, felt that the Irish gained nothing from "white privilege" because slavery was "decidedly" less oppressive than the free labor system which exploited the Irish:

> If the slave has never been a free man, we think, as a general rule, his sufferings are less than those of the free laborer at wages. As to actual freedom, one has just about as much as the other. The laborer at wages has all the disadvantages of freedom and none of its blessings, while the slave, if denied the blessings, is freed from the disadvantages.[690]

By claiming that the Irish had white privilege in Philadelphia, Ignatiev shared the same anti-Catholic animus that characterized the WASP-Jewish alliance that formed the basis for the Philadelphia branch of Americans for Democratic Action, which came into being when the Left Liberals expelled the communists from their movement.

The Irish in Philadelphia harbored just as much "racial" animus against the Germans as they did against blacks. Even Ignatiev concedes that: "When Irish workers encountered Afro-Americans, they fought with them, it is true, but they also fought with immigrants of other nationalities, with each other, and with whomever else they were thrown up against in the marketplace. When a new immigrant first entered a factory, he remained suspect until he revealed from what part of Ireland he had come."[691]

---

684 Ignatiev, p. 47.
685 Ignatiev, p. 48.
686 Ignatiev, p. 69.
687 Ignatiev, p. 77.
688 Ignatiev, p. 79.
689 Ignatiev, p. 88.
690 Ignatiev, p. 91.
691 Ignatiev, p. 108.

Walking with a Bible and a Gun

Ignatiev's mentor Allen claims that when the Irish became "white" Americans, they "explicitly rejected their own national heritage to become part of the system of 'white' racial oppression of African-Americans."[692] But the evidence he produces makes a different point altogether. The Irish never gave up the Catholic faith, which according to the theory known as the triple melting pot became their ethnic identity in America after three generations. Allen describes Archbishop Hughes as "an 'organization man' in a double sense: for the Church and for the 'white race,'"[693] but Hughes's main concern was not whether during the inevitable process of assimilation the Irish would become "white," which was a meaningless term in the Catholic lexicon, but that they would become Protestant, especially if they moved out of the ethnic parishes of New York City and headed west. Even someone as fervently anti-slavery as "the Liberator," Daniel O'Connell, understood that there were "doctrinal differences between himself, as a Catholic, and Dissenters,"[694] who made up the backbone of the abolitionist movement and were also at the forefront of the anti-Catholic Nativist movement, Lyman Beecher being a good example of both. Most Irish were interested in repeal of the Penal laws and separation from England, and they did not want that cause linked to abolition. In his attempt to understand why Dagger John Hughes refused to side with the abolitionists, Allen once again down played the importance of religion when he claimed that "Irish-American mistrust of Protestantism" got "translated" into "fervent support of Protestant slaveholders,"[695] when in fact it instead got translated into neutrality on an issue that was ultimately of no concern to the Irish, who had troubles enough of their own. Religious difference trumped any racial sympathy, not the other way around. Allen bloviates that this "apparent inconsistency is seen to be explained by the principle of 'merger' with the 'white' people. By this light, the Protestantism of the abolitionists was the threat to be stressed, rather than the Protestantism of the defenders of slavery." Hughes refused to be drawn into the American Civil War because he felt the Irish had no dog in that fight. As Allen is forced to admit:

> Twenty-five days after the attack on Fort Sumter, and twenty-two days after Lincoln's call for 75,000 volunteers to fight the insurrection, Archbishop Hughes, writing to a Southern bishop, takes a stand of "non-interference" in the war; he neither encourages "Catholics to take part in it," nor advises them "not to do so."[696]

---

692 Allen, p. 320.
693 Allen, p. 293.
694 Allen, p. 296.
695 Allen, p. 315.
696 Allen, p. 326.

Part II: The Romantic Rehabilitation of Nature

Allen nevertheless continues to engage in identity theft by suppressing the Catholic identity of the Irish workers in New York, who "did not express their demands and aims in terms of Irishness, but in the name of 'white workingmen.'"[697] In claiming that "no 'white' orphanages were burned for fear of 'competition' in the labor market,"[698] Allen again ignores the Nativist Riots in Philadelphia and Boston, which did result in the destruction convents and orphanages.

Allen and his disciple Ignatiev are proposing a moral argument based on the moral certainty which both Jews and Protestants derived from their participation in the civil rights movement of the 1960s, a Protestant operation which was also the high water mark of the Black-Jewish alliance. Stated in its simplest terms, Allen's position is that the arbitrary "social construct" known as race is morally binding on the conscience of Irish Catholics, who must become fervent abolitionists if they want to avoid the odium of Marxist disapproval.

Unlike Allen who was raised in largely Protestant environments in both Indiana and West Virginia, Noel Ignatiev, author of *How the Irish became White*, was a Jew from Philadelphia, who like Allen, started off as a Communist labor organizer and came late to academe. Both men viewed American history from a Marxist perspective through which they perceived race as the fundamental determinant of American identity. Both men projected Marxist categories onto the Reformation, turning that quintessentially religious event into an example of class struggle leading to revolution but rendering the reality which informed it invisible. This projection led to a fatal misunderstanding of the religious motivation which inspired 17th century Judaizing English Protestant sects like the Puritans. Judaized Christianity is the only common denominator which can unite Puritan regicide, the religious subjugation of the Irish under Cromwell, migration to America, and the subsequent ethnic cleansing and genocide of the Indians, events which Allen cannot organize in a coherent pattern because of the materialistic Marxist racial categories he imposes *a-priori*. Allen claimed that the invention of the "white" race and the origin of racial oppression in "the pattern setting Virginia colony' could be found in "class struggle"[699] at a time when class struggle did not exist and when the slave owners were racially indistinguishable from the slaves. He did so by ignoring the reality of the religious differences which separated Catholics and Protestants that were the so interwoven into the fabric of their societies that they constituted its formal cause.

The history of racial oppression began with the Reformation, and more particularly the revolutionary weaponization of Reformation principles which

---

697 Allen, p. 337.
698 Allen, p. 338.
699 Allen, p. 12.

the Puritans found in the Old Testament. Cromwell was not motivated by "class struggle," even if he was a revolutionary. He was not motivated by greed or financial gain or wealth through looting, which was the primary cause of the early Reformation in England. Cromwell was motivated by his understanding of himself as the reincarnation of the leader of the Hebrews who subdued Canaan by breaking with all law and custom and acting solely according to their understanding of God's will.

The source of oppression, both racial and religious, in both the Virginia plantation in the New World and the Ulster plantation in Ireland, is the Reformation, and in particular the intensification of Reformation principles which Puritanism effected when it weaponized the Old Testament story of Joshua's conquest of Canaan and turned it into a revolutionary manifesto that justified ethnic cleansing, genocide, and the economic exploitation that was an intrinsic part of what later came to be known as capitalism. If religion is ultimately nothing more than "the opiate of the masses," it is not surprising that Marxists would give it short shrift in terms of causality and quickly shift the discussion to investigations of class and capital as the real causal factors in the race question. In doing this, the Marxists imposed 19th century materialistic categories onto an age when religion was the prime motivation for Protestants and Catholics in the global struggle for power which the Reformation had unleashed. Neither monetary gain nor the revolutionary struggle against capitalist exploitation was powerful enough to justify regicide, but religion was, especially the Judaized Christianity known as Puritanism which allowed Cromwell to see himself as Phineas:

> the High Priest of the time of Moses who saved the Israelites from a great plague by standing out against idolatry and by by-passing due legal process and summarily executing a leading member of the Israelite community caught in an adulterous embrace with a Midianite (heathen) woman. This story was the basis of a sermon preached to Parliament in December 1648 and applied to current politics, and it is referred to by Cromwell both at the time and in a letter to Lord Wharton after the event.[700]

Puritanism was a revolutionary movement made up of nominally Protestant English Judaizers who saw themselves as the spiritual heirs of the Old Testament Hebrews:

> Throughout his life Cromwell had a strong sense of God's providence. It was rooted in his reading of the Old Testament, which at one level is the story of God's personal appearances – in dreams, visions, burning bushes, pillars of fire – to challenge his chosen people and to give them

---

[700] John Morrill, "King killing no murder: Cromwell in 1648," The Cromwell Association, https://www.olivercromwell.org/wordpress/articles/king-killing-no-murder-cromwell-in-1648/

stark choices: obedience and reward, disobedience and punishment; obedience and the rewards of Canaan, disobedience and slavery in Egypt or Babylon.[701]

Cromwell could only justify a crime as heinous as regicide by claiming that God commanded it:

> The sweep of Cromwell's writings throughout 1648 suggests a man who feels guided by God and clear of the end though not quite of the means. The change can be traced back to his histrionics in Parliament on 3 January 1648 when, gripping his sword handle, he asserted that the King had broken his trust and that this represented a fundamental change. The Army had previously committed itself to monarchy "unless necessity enforce an alteration." Note that word "necessity" again.[702]

"Necessity" is a concept the English Puritans derived from their reading of Luther, in particular his treatise on the enslaved will, which justified his marriage to the ex-nun Catherina von Bora after the fact:

> By the time of Pride's Purge, Cromwell's encounter with the bible had caused him to see in the choices God had presented to his chosen people in ancient Israel the same choices he was presenting to his new chosen people. The choices were strictly comparable, but they were false choices: to follow God's preferred route and enter the Promised Land, to ignore it and trek back to Egypt.[703]

As he swept through South Wales in June 1648, Cromwell told Fairfax that his military victories "have been the wonderful works of God breaking the rod of the oppressor, as in the day of Midian, not with garments much rolled in blood but by the terror of the Lord."[704] Cromwell saw himself as a latter-day Gideon, "who had been called from the plough to lead the armies of Israel."[705] Like Gideon, who executed the kings of the Midianites, Cromwell was a regicide. Like Gideon, Cromwell harried the king's fleeing army for 200 miles after the Battle of Preston. His account of that battle "reads less like other accounts of the battle of Preston than it does of the Biblical account of Gideon's defeat of the Midianites at Ain Harod."

The source of "racial" oppression in both England and Ireland can be found in Cromwell's proof texting from the Old Testament. It cannot be found in Marxist concepts like class struggle, and most certainly not in any theory of white privilege, since as Allen admitted, the form white did not exist when the Puritans created the paradigm of American identity.

---

701 Morrill, "King killing no murder."
702 Morrill, "King killing no murder."
703 Morrill, "King killing no murder."
704 Morrill, "King killing no murder."
705 Morrill, "King killing no murder."

WALKING WITH A BIBLE AND A GUN

Puritans imposed racial oppression on America by ransacking the Old Testament for paradigms which would allow genocide, ethnic cleansing, and ruthless economic exploitation in both the Ulster and the Virginia plantations. The indigenous Irish and the indigenous American Indians were declared Amalek by the Puritans who were now the followers of Gideon, who was commissioned by God to exterminate the natives. No other paradigm fits both situations as well as the Judaizing religious concept of the Puritans known as Protestantism, whose era began with the theft of church property, the real cause of the Reformation. That theft necessitated a break with Rome, the universal Church, which meant the rise of national churches led by members of the international Protestant conspiracy, which now viewed natives of their own countries as suspicious because of their allegiance to the forms of the old Catholic faith, necessitating a police state as the primary form of social control. If the English Protestants viewed their own countrymen as suspect, it is not surprising that Puritans like Cromwell, strengthened by his tendentious interpretation of the Old Testament, would view Papists, American Indians, and Negroes as doubly suspect and liable to even more draconian measures. Over the course of the 120 years from the confiscation of Church property to the revolutionary decade of the 1640s, the dissenters who did not receive their share of the loot became resentful of the privileged clergy who had no more legitimacy than the dissenters but were rewarded with government approval as administrators of the state church and a significant portion of the largesse that went with that office. This group of revolutionaries distilled that bitterness into revolutionary action by identifying themselves as heirs of Joshua, who were entitled to kill the king. Cromwell cited the story of Phineas as his justification and went on to remove Amalek from Ulster and Virginia. This paradigm, and not capitalist class conflict, provided the form which justified genocide, ethnic cleansing, and the ruthless exploitation of labor known as slavery in America, and it is completely invisible to those whose minds have succumbed to the numbing effect of dialectical materialism.

CHAPTER 22

THE BEECHER FAMILY: NATIVISM AND MORAL COLLAPSE

In 1837, sensing the danger that the westward heading pioneers might fall into the hands of Catholics or Methodists, Henry Ward Beecher accepted a post as pastor of a small congregation in Lawrenceburg, Indiana. No one was more sympathetic to the abolitionist cause than the Beecher family. Henry's father Lyman Beecher was America's most prominent Calvinist. His daughter Harriet Beecher Stowe would become famous as the author of *Uncle Tom's Cabin*, which became the most popular book in America, second only to the Bible, after it was published in 1852. When Mrs. Stowe met with Abraham Lincoln, he greeted her by saying "so you are the little woman who wrote the book that started this great war."[706]

In 1856, four years after the publication of Harriet's famous book, her brother, Henry Ward Beecher, who would become "the most famous man in America,"[707] felt that something more than words were needed to put an end to slavery. In 1855, Henry Ward Beecher along with a group of around 70 New England emigrants from New Haven, Connecticut had founded the town of Wabaunsee, Kansas. Inspired by one of Beecher's abolitionist sermons, the settlers called their town the Beecher Rifle Colony, based on the fact that Beecher smuggled Sharp rifles into his newly founded congregation in crates labeled "Beecher's Bibles."[708]

In doing this, Henry Ward Beecher became the archetypal American. Like Daniel Boone before him, who started out in life as a Quaker, Beecher became the quintessential American of his age when he allowed the gun to modify his religion after heading West. After shipping Sharp rifles to his congregation in crates marked Bibles, Beecher became a preacher with a gun, a more accurate description of his American identity than Frederick

---

706 "Harriet Beecher Stowe Meets Lincoln," *Civil War on the Western Border*, The Kansas City Public Library, https://civilwaronthewesternborder.org/timeline/harriet-beecher-stowe-meets-lincoln

707 Applegate, *The Most Famous Man in America*.

708 "Beecher Bible and Rifle Church," *Wikipedia: The Free Encyclopedia*, https://en.wikipedia.org/wiki/Beecher_Bible_and_Rifle_Church

Law Olmstead's description of him as "a rare combination of philosopher and fighter."[709] The Calvinism which Beecher inherited from his father morphed into armed insurrection after Beecher moved to Indiana and got caught up in the final violent phase of the abolitionist movement which began with John Brown's murderous attack on an isolated farm house in Pottawatomie, Kansas on May 25, 1856.

After the Civil War, the Calvinism which Henry had learned from his father Lyman morphed once again from militant abolitionism into the prosperity Gospel, which made him famous as pastor of the Plymouth Church in Brooklyn. The West had changed his religion to something quintessentially American. Eventually, the gun would turn the ever-malleable sects which dominated religious life after the Civil War into Americanism, "the fourth great Western Religion."[710]

The trajectory of the American republic took a westerly direction which allowed existence, or the wilderness, to modify essence, which invariably meant the Protestant understanding of Christianity. The lower classes, epitomized by Daniel Boone, headed west, picked up a gun, and dropped or changed their religious denomination from impractical imports like Quakerism or Puritanism to emotionally satisfying sects like Methodism, or as in the case of Thoreau, they adopted the religion of Nature.

The upper or literary classes, epitomized by Cooper and Emerson (who invented the religion of Nature) as well as Hawthorne and Henry Adams, headed east, which meant that they sailed to Europe, where they came into contact with Catholic culture, largely as a result of contemplating the beauty of Catholic art as epitomized by St. Peter's Basilica in Rome. Because beauty and truth are transcendentals, America's literary pilgrims were confronted with the question of whether a religion which produced this beauty might also be true. Unlike rude frontiersman like Andrew Jackson, who headed west to become a land speculator, war hero, and eventually president of the United States, Elizabeth Ann Seton was a member of New York's commercial aristocracy who travelled to Italy to find a cure for her husband's consumption and found the Catholic Church instead.

This dynamic holds true to this day. For every disaffected white guy who, like Randy Weaver, buys a gun and moves to Idaho, we have the example of Bree Solstad, the porn star who converted to Catholicism after travelling to Italy:

> About a year ago, I had an opportunity to go to Italy. ... The majority of the places I wanted to visit were churches, because in Italy that is where all the great art is located. But once inside these beautiful old

---

709 Applegate, *The Most Famous Man in America*, p. 5.

710 David Gelernter, *Americanism: The Fourth Great Western Religion* (Doubleday, 2007), https://www.amazon.com/Americanism-Fourth-Great-Western-Religion/dp/0385513127

Part II: The Romantic Rehabilitation of Nature

basilicas, cathedrals and churches, something changed in me, and I began to appreciate the art and the churches themselves for the theology they expressed. It was like my heart was being pierced by beauty. ... The crucifix was always right there in your face in all these Catholic churches. His gift to us was always plain to see as soon as I entered a church. For reasons I still can't explain, I found myself getting down on one knee to cross myself when I entered and exited the churches.[711]

Sensitive pilgrims like Nathaniel Hawthorne, who sailed east to find beauty found truth as well, and that encounter precipitated a crisis of conscience. If St. Peter's Basilica was beautiful, then Catholicism was the true religion, and if Catholicism were true, the pilgrim of necessity needed to join it to be saved. Nathaniel agonized until the end of his life, but he never converted. His daughter Rose, however, not only converted to Catholicism but also became a Dominican nun who cared for indigent New Yorkers dying of cancer and is now on her way to sainthood.

Nathaniel Hawthorne's reaction to the beauty and truth of Catholicism was complicated because American Catholics, although united spiritually, shared no common ethnic identity. Crudely stated, if a descendant of the Puritans like Hawthorne wanted to become Catholic, he would have to join Paddy, who worked on the railroad, at the altar rail and become Irish. The Catholic Church in America in the mid-19th century was as ethnically Balkanized as the Orthodox churches in America are now. In terms of sheer numbers, Catholics were aliens, who, in the case of the dominant Irish, hated the natives because they were Protestants. The Native Americans felt the same way toward the Irish papists and converts like Orestes Brownson were caught in the crossfire. Brownson, who was truculent by nature, enjoyed the confrontation, but timid souls like Nathaniel Hawthorne were faced with the impossible choice of losing their ethnic identity in order to become Catholic or losing their souls by remaining Protestant.

The Catholic Church in America was made up of various European ethnic groups who could hardly speak to each other. Of those groups the Irish had the advantage of speaking English when they arrived, and they quickly exploited that advantage by taking control of the Catholic Church in America. A crucial battle in that campaign involved Irish bishops driving German professors out of the Catholic University of America in Washington, D.C. In making the case against the German professor Schroeder, the university listed a series of charges which included the claim that he was seen drinking beer in public, a grievous sin in the eyes of Irish teetotalers like Archbishop John Ireland of St. Paul, Minnesota, who notoriously referred to Schroeder's countrymen

---

711 Gina Christian OSV News, "How adult film star Bree Solstad fell in love with Jesus, quit her career and became Catholic," *The Dialog*, May 9, 2024, https://thedialog.org/national-news/how-adult-film-star-bree-solstad-fell-in-love-with-jesus-quit-her-career-and-became-catholic/

as "beer-guzzling Dutchmen." Eventually the conflict between German and Irish Catholics became so strident, that Rome felt bound to intervene to prevent schism in 1899, when Pope Leo XIII issued *Testem Benevolentiae*, his encyclical condemning Americanism.

By the time Orestes Brownson's son Henry gave a speech at Notre Dame in 1896, the image of Dagger John standing outside St. Patrick's Cathedral with Irish cops defending it against the nativists and threatening to turn New York into "a second Moscow"[712] if one Catholic Church went up in flames had disappeared and had been replaced by the less edifying spectacle of an Irish episcopacy made up of fervent Americanists. John Ireland was the best example of that new Catholic identity. The bishops who showed up for the consecration of Sacred Heart Church on the campus of Notre Dame University were Americanists. By the time Orestes Brownson got interred in the crypt of what is now Sacred Heart Basilica, Notre Dame would fuse Brownson's truculence and John Ireland's equally fervent Americanism into a potent paradigm of American identity known as the "fighting Irish," which became the name of the Notre Dame football team. The contradictory nature of the fighting Irish paradigm was best epitomized by Reverend Theodore Hesburgh, who proudly wore the Roman collar while collaborating with John D. Rockefeller, 3rd's Population Council to undermine the Church's teaching on contraception at a series of secret conferences which ran from 1962 to 1965. But we get ahead of ourselves.

---

712 "John Hughes (archbishop)," *Wikipedia: The Free Encyclopedia*, https://en.wikipedia.org/wiki/John_Hughes_(archbishop)#:~:text=Hughes%20put%20armed%20guards%20at,to%20the%20Fire%20of%20Moscow.

Chapter 23

Hawthorne in Rome

Four years before *The Convert* appeared in print in 1857, Nathaniel Hawthorne arrived in England on July 18, 1853, to take up his post as the American consul in Liverpool. Hawthorne knew about Brownson's conversion to Catholicism, but most probably knew nothing about the confrontation between Brownson and Hughes at Fordham in 1856. Hawthorne's position as consul allowed him to save enough money to take his family to the continent and eventually to Rome. Hawthorne spoke no Italian when he arrived in Rome in the Spring of 1858, and he remained in that state of ignorance until the day he left Italy three years later. Because he never stopped being a tourist, Hawthorne spent his time conversing with the American expatriate community in Rome, most of whom had come there to study art. In lieu of conversing with the natives:

> Hawthorne filled his Italian journals with accounts of visits to studios and meetings with artists, chiefly such American expatriates as William Wetmore Story, E. S. Bartholomew, Thomas Crawford, Cephas G. Thompson, Harriet Hosmer, and Maria Louisa Lander. Even more conspicuous in the notebooks is a voluminous record of museum-going, with close descriptions of painting and statuary, a great deal of which he afterward would transfer to the pages of *The Marble Faun*.[713]

Upon his arrival in Rome, Hawthorne began "an intensive round of sightseeing"[714] which continued until he left. That round of sightseeing brought him initially to the Villa Borghese, "where he saw statues of two fauns, one of them copied from Praxiteles,"[715] which gave him the premise for his final novel.

During their stay in Rome, the Hawthornes were introduced to the transcendental nature of the Catholic Church by viewing its art. The Birds feel that the three Hawthorne siblings were "exposed to the grand sweep of

---

713 Hawthorne, *The Marble Faun*, p. xx

714 Nathaniel Hawthorne, *The Marble Faun, or The Romance of Monte Beni* (Ohio State University Press, 1986), p. xx.

715 Hawthorne, *The Marble Faun*, p. xx.

E. MICHAEL JONES • 225

Catholicism" through the art they saw "in Italy's magnificent churches and cathedrals"[716] because they:

> had a mother with a trained artist's eye and a father who was open to and sensitive to the religious impulse and experience in Italy. Due especially to their mother's keen interest in art, the family frequently visited museums to absorb the art. Many were of a religious nature, imparting to viewers some knowledge of church tradition as told through art masterpieces.[717]

Bereft of the language that would allow him to converse with the natives, Hawthorne became even more of a disembodied observer than he had been in New England and as a result more dependent on the visual impression Italian art made on him. He became, to use Emerson's phrase, a "transparent eyeball" which allowed him to "return to reason and faith," not in nature as Emerson claimed in the essay of the same name, but in the imitation of nature at which the Catholic art of Italy excelled. Instead of becoming "part or particle of God," a pantheistic notion Hawthorne would have found repugnant, Hawthorne allowed "the currents of Universal Being" which can be found in transcendental beauty to circulate through him. "The eye," Hawthorne learned by reading Emerson's essay on *Nature*, "is the best of artists." The section entitled "Beauty" in Emerson's essay *Nature* is most probably the only text on aesthetics that Hawthorne ever read.

Hawthorne found the Satanism which informed "Self-Reliance" repugnant, but he most probably agreed with Emerson's aesthetics because, when it came to beauty, Emerson was Catholic in his tastes. One of Rose Hawthorne's favorite paintings was the reproduction of Raphael's Transfiguration, which was a gift from Emerson. "Another, hung in a place of honor, was a portrait of the Madonna and Child by Corregio."[718] The claim that "Beauty is the mark God sets upon virtue" would have appealed to the sense of propriety which replaced Calvinism as the lived culture of New England, which valued the moral law no matter how much it clashed with doctrinal heresy. Emerson's aesthetics, like the gift he gave to Rose, was more traditional than the rest of his philosophy. In the section on beauty in *Nature*, we find evidence of Aristotle's claim that art is imitation of nature as well as Coleridge's claim that beauty is "unity in multeity" as well as the Scholastic premise that beauty is a transcendental when Emerson writes:

> The standard of beauty is the entire circuit of natural forms—the totality of nature; which the Italians expressed by defining beauty "*il più nell' uno.*" Nothing is quite beautiful alone; nothing but is beautiful in the whole. A single object is only so far beautiful as it suggests this universal grace. The poet, the painter, the sculptor, the musician, the architect, seek

---

716 Bird, *From Witchery to Sanctity*, p. 118.
717 Bird, *From Witchery to Sanctity*, p. 119.
718 Bird, *From Witchery to Sanctity*, p. 116.

Part II: The Romantic Rehabilitation of Nature

each to concentrate this radiance of the world on one point, and each in his several work to satisfy the love of beauty which stimulates him to produce. Thus is Art a nature passed through the alembic of man. Thus, in art does Nature work through the will of a man filled with the beauty of her first works. The world thus exists to the soul to satisfy the desire of beauty. This element I call an ultimate end. No reason can be asked or given why the soul seeks beauty. Beauty, in its largest and profoundest sense, is one expression for the universe. God is the all-fair. Truth, and goodness, and beauty, are but different faces of the same All. But beauty in nature is not ultimate. It is the herald of inward and eternal beauty and is not alone a solid and satisfactory good. It must stand as a part, and not as yet the last or highest expression of the final cause of Nature.[719]

As an artist Hawthorne was *sui generis* and in direct contact with the transcendental realm when he created works of literary beauty like "Young Goodman Brown" and *The Scarlet Letter*. As a philosopher, Hawthorne was dependent on the occasional nugget of truth he was able to pry from New England's stony ground by reading writers like Emerson and Edwards. Hawthorne responded to the beauty section in *Nature* by claiming in his own way that beauty was a transcendental which lifted artists:

> by the ideality of their pursuits a little way off the earth and are therefore able to catch the evanescent fragrance that floats in the atmosphere of life, above the heads of the ordinary crowd. Even if they seem endowed with little imagination, individually, yet there is a property, a gift, a talisman, common to their class, entitling them to partake, somewhat more bountifully than other people, in the thin delights of moonshine and romance.[720]

On April 30, 1858, Hawthorne wrote down a detailed description of Praxiteles' statue "because the idea keeps recurring to me of writing a little Romance about it."[721] On July 14, he began "sketching"[722] that romance's plot, and on July 17, he began writing a "'rough draft,' of what there is every reason to believe was *The Marble Faun* in its first stages."[723] Hawthorne then took that rough draft to England where he was determined to finish the book

---

719 *The Complete Works of Ralph Waldo Emerson: Nature Addresses and Lectures* [Vol.1]," (Boston: Houghton, Mifflin, 1903-1904), University of Michigan Library, Digital Collections, https://quod.lib.umich.edu/e/emerson/4957107.0001.001/80:9?page=root;size=100;view=text

720 Hawthorne, *The Marble Faun*, p. 155.

721 Hawthorne, *The Marble Faun*, p. xxi.

722 Hawthorne, *The Marble Faun*, p. xxi.

723 Hawthorne, *The Marble Faun*, p. xxii.

without delay and remain in that country until its publication to protect the copyright.[724]

Hawthorne completed *The Marble Faun* in the spring of 1860, and it appeared shortly thereafter to mixed reviews:

> Lowell was glad to see references to American artists and their work, while Richard H. Hutton, writing in the *National Review*, scorned such commentary as "puffs, not in very good taste." Hutton considered the "often powerful, and always subtle" art criticism to be "padding"; moreover, he deplored Hawthorne's "silly attacks upon nude figures." *The Westminster Review* also disliked the "provincial narrowness" of passages on nudity in statuary and on Gibson's tinted Venuses.[725]

More to the point, *The New York Times* called *The Marble Faun* "desolately incoherent."[726] The London *Times* damned *Transformation*, (the title under which *The Marble Faun* was released in England) with faint praise, claiming that it was "worth all the guide-books we ever met with, as regards the gems of Italian art, the characteristic features of Roman edifices, and the atmosphere of Roman life," and valued the "clear discernment" of his aesthetic eye.[727]

Hawthorne drew so heavily on his journals that one critic accused him of "padding."[728] Hawthorne wrote like a tourist, whose walk through the Forum "inspires rather tedious guidebook commentary which Hawthorne cannot much enliven, save for putting some of his own reactions into the mouths of his fictional spokesmen."[729]

Deprived of the organic connection to New England soil and history which made *The Scarlet Letter* and tales like "Young Goodman Brown" unified in plot, theme and setting which rendered them beautiful, Hawthorne turned Italy into a vague fairy realm which lacked the reality of the New England forest. Because romance and poetry, "like ivy, lichens, and wall-flowers, need Ruin to make them grow,"[730] Italy:

> was chiefly valuable to him as affording a sort of poetic or fairy precinct, where actualities would not be so terribly insisted upon, as they are, and must needs be, in America. No author, without a trial, can conceive of the difficulty of writing a Romance about a country where there is no shadow, no antiquity, no mystery, no picturesque and gloomy wrong, nor

---

724 Hawthorne, *The Marble Faun*, p. xxiv.
725 Hawthorne, *The Marble Faun*, p. xxxiii.
726 Hawthorne, *The Marble Faun*, p. xxxiii.
727 Hawthorne, *The Marble Faun*, p. xxxv.
728 Hawthorne, *The Marble Faun*, p. xxxv.
729 Hawthorne, *The Marble Faun*, p. xxxvi.
730 Hawthorne, *The Marble Faun*, p. 3.

anything but a common-place prosperity, in broad and simple daylight, as is happily the case with my dear native land.[731]

This is nowhere more apparent than in the attempt to portray Italy as Arcadia, which grew out of his need to portray Donatello as a modern-day faun. Donatello exists in a realm "before sin, sorrow, or morality itself, had ever been thought of," and we are to suppose that "the Faun had no conscience, no remorse, no burthen on the heart, no troublesome recollections of any sort; no dark future neither!"[732] In other words, Donatello is the American Adam, transposed incongruously to the old world, where he has remained unaffected by original sin. When Donatello shows up at Miriam's studio, she greets him: "Come in, wild Faun," she said, "and tell me the latest news from Arcady!"[733]

The latest news is that "the world is sadly changed, now-a-days; grievously changed, poor Donatello, since those happy times when your race used to dwell in the Arcadian woods, playing hide-and-seek with the nymphs in grottoes and nooks of shrubbery. You have re-appeared on earth some centuries too late."[734] This changes when Kenyon moves to Donatello's country estate Monte Beni, where "Kenyon could have imagined that the valleys and hillsides about him were a veritable Arcadia, and that Donatello was not merely a sylvan Faun, but the genial wine-god in his very person."[735]

Rose Hawthorne had a similar impression when she spent the summer at the model for Monte Beni outside of Florence. During the Hawthornes' summer there, Rose was struck by the beauty of the Italian landscape:

> There is no end of beauty and interest, and the view becomes ideal and poetic the moment the sun begins its decline; for then the rose and purple mists drape the hills, and mountains — the common earth — turn to amethysts, topazes, and sapphires, and words can never convey an idea of the opaline heavens, which seem to have illimitable abysses of a penetrable substance, made up of the light of pearls.[736]

> This summer we have our first sight of Italian sunsets, for we were assured we should have fever if we were out at the hour in Rome. We began by watching them from the bridges over the Arno, which are perhaps the finest points of view, because the river is added. It flows east and west, and so we have all the glory by standing on either of the bridges. The arches, the reflections in the waters, the city's palaces and churches, the

---

731 Hawthorne, *The Marble Faun*, p. 3.
732 Hawthorne, *The Marble Faun*, p. 13.
733 Hawthorne, *The Marble Faun*, p. 39.
734 Hawthorne, *The Marble Faun*, p. 42.
735 Hawthorne, *The Marble Faun*, p. 237.
736 Lathrop, *Memories of Hawthorne*, p. 395.

distant hills, all come in for a part of the pomp and splendor, — all that man can do, all that God has done, for this lovely land."[737]

Where Rose saw beauty, Hawthorne saw the effects of sin. "My father did not forget in his art the note he found in beautiful Florence, though it was too sad to introduce by a definite exposition, and falls upon the ear, in 'Monte Beni' like a wordless minor chord."[738] Arcadia was based on the worship of Dionysos, which was based on intoxication and sexual excess. Arcadia was not possible without wine. "To say the truth, this golden wine was no unnecessary ingredient towards making the life of Monte Beni palatable."[739] When Kenyon looks beyond the "dreams, at least, and fables, lovely, if unsubstantial, of a Golden Age"[740] upon which Arcadia is based, he discovers that the people who inhabit Monte Beni are "apt to become sensual, addicted to gross pleasures, heavy, unsympathizing, and insulated within the narrow limits of a surly selfishness."[741]

No matter what Thoreau says to the contrary, Nature cannot forgive sin. After listening to Donatello tell the story of a knight who failed in his attempt to re-enter Arcadia, Kenyon asks, 'Why did the water shrink from this unhappy knight?" and he is told:

> "Because he had tried to wash off a blood-stain!" said the young Count, in a horror-stricken whisper. "The guilty man had polluted the pure water. The nymph might have comforted him in sorrow but could not cleanse his conscience of a crime."
>
> "And did he never behold her more?" asked Kenyon.
>
> "Never, but once," replied his friend. "He never beheld her blessed face, but once again; and then there was a bloodstain on the poor nymph's brow; it was the stain his guilt had left in the fountain where he tried to wash it off."

The tale, which is reminiscent of Dimmesdales' encounter with Hester in the forest, forces Kenyon to conclude that nature is "altogether powerless" when it comes to "the dread fever-fit or deadly chill of guilt."[742]

When Donatello tries to wash off the stain of sin in the waters of Monte Beni, nature rejects his attempt symbolically when "a brown lizard (it was of the tarantula species)" emerges from the ground as a sign that "this venomous

---

737 Lathrop, *Memories of Hawthorne*, p. 395-6.
738 Lathrop, *Memories of Hawthorne*, p. 401.
739 Hawthorne, *The Marble Faun*, p. 240.
740 Hawthorne, *The Marble Faun*, p. 233.
741 Hawthorne, *The Marble Faun*, p. 235.
742 Hawthorne, *The Marble Faun*, p. 246.

reptile" is the only part of Arcadia which "responded to the young Count's efforts to renew his intercourse with the lower orders of Nature."[743]

If Arcadia is Eden before the Fall, the angel is still guarding its entrance with a flaming sword. The "ego" in Poussin's pastoral painting *Et in Arcadia ego* refers to death, which entered the world through sin. Kenyon has discovered "the limits of Arcadia."[744] *Et in Italia ego*, could be the subtitle of *The Marble Faun*.

After his encounter with Donatello at Monte Beni, Hawthorne learned that Italy is not Arcadia. If anything, America is Arcadia. If Hawthorne had been raised in Virginia, he would have known that over the course of the 18th century, the Virginia colony was portrayed as a real-life Arcadia in the New World by people like Jefferson, Beverly, and Crevecoeur. "America," Leo Marx tells us, "was neither Eden nor a howling desert."[745] It was "a symbolic middle landscape created by mediation between art and nature."[746] Virginia, wrote Robert Beverley in *The History and Present State of Virginia*, was "so agreeable, that Paradice itself seem'd to be there, in its first Native Lustre."[747] America was "paradise regained," and the Enlightenment could invoke nature as universal norm, which, as Jefferson's redaction of the Bible would show, was especially appropriate as a philosophical antidote for those who succumbed to Calvinism's denigration of human nature. According to the Enlightenment, man's ability to live in "the state of nature" in places like Virginia abolished Calvin's understanding of Original Sin. J. Hector St. John de Crèvecœur doesn't mention Arcadia in his *Letters from an American Farmer* because Arcadia had become an unnecessary fiction after America had taken its place as a category of reality. "With the appearance of Crèvecœur's Letters in 1782," Marx tells us, "the assimilation of the ancient European fantasy to conditions in the New World was virtually complete."[748]

Because Hawthorne imposed the Arcadia conceit on the real Italy, which he could see with his eyes, but with which he could not converse with his lips, his characters became types rather than real people like Dimmesdale, Hester, and Young Goodman Brown, who emerged organically from New England's soil and history. The four main characters in *The Marble Faun* lack the verisimilitude of Hawthorne's New Englanders, and the plot as a result comes across as contrived because it is based on elements outside of the narrative but close to Hawthorne's troubled soul. "Hawthorne," the editors of the Centenary edition of *The Marble Faun* tell us:

---

743 Hawthorne, *The Marble Faun*, p. 246.
744 Hawthorne, *The Marble Faun*, p. 79.
745 Leo Marx, *The Machine in the Garden*, p. 43.
746 Marx, *The Machine in the Garden*, p. 71.
747 Marx, *The Machine in the Garden*, p. 76.
748 Marx, *The Machine in the Garden*, p. 116.

drew upon his acquaintance with the expatriate Salem sculptress Maria Lander for his view of innocent independence which an unchaperoned female could paradoxically enjoy in corrupt Rome. Hilda's moral rigor, the priggishness of which Hawthorne surely underestimated, is a refraction of Sophia, despite her disclaimers.[749]

Donatello is not so much a real Italian as a construct demanded by the decision to turn Italy into Arcadia. Miriam and Hilda have some basis in characters Hawthorne met in Rome, but they are quickly subsumed into being representatives of the angel/machine polarity which claims the soul is an angel inhabiting a bodily machine. Because they represent the poles of Hawthorne's rational psychology, these characters lose the reality of a figure like Hester Prynne.

The same angel/machine dichotomy can be found in the two female characters in *The Marble Faun*. Miriam is Beatrice Cenci, guilty of incest and parricide, yet strangely innocent. Miriam is also Jewish and as such a Calvinist Judaizer who exaggerates original sin and predestination. Miriam believes that "The firmest substance of human happiness is but a thin crust spread over it. . . ."[750] Hawthorne got the idea of the "thin crust" from Calvin's understanding of the effects of Original Sin as refracted through American preachers like Jonathan Edwards, who felt that unregenerate man had "nothing to stand on" and that "Unconverted men walk over the pit of hell on a rotten covering, and there are innumerable places in this covering so weak that they will not bear their weight, and these places are not seen."[751] Hawthorne could never shake the idea that "God has laid himself under no obligation, by any promise to keep any natural man out of hell one moment," which is why he makes ontological insecurity one of the central themes of *The Marble Faun*. Nature, if we can return to the concept Emerson tried to rehabilitate, was nothing more than "illusive stage-scenery" over "the pit of blackness that lies beneath us, everywhere."[752]

Hilda shares Hawthorne's schizophrenia on this issue. On the one hand, she is a firm believer in the "thin crust" of unregenerate nature, but she also shares Hawthorne's moral revulsion at the idea of Calvinist total depravity and begs to differ with Edwards when she claims, "There is no chasm, nor any hideous emptiness under our feet."[753] Then, hedging her bets, Hilda continues:

> If there be such a chasm, let us bridge it over with good thoughts and deeds, and we shall tread safely to the other side. It was the guilt of Rome, no doubt, that caused this gulf to open; and Curtius filled it up with his

---

749 Hawthorne, *The Marble Faun*, p. xxxvii.
750 Hawthorne, *The Marble Faun*, p. 161.
751 *Concise Anthology of American Literature*, p. 117.
752 Hawthorne, *The Marble Faun*, p. 161.
753 Hawthorne, *The Marble Faun*, p. 162.

Part II: The Romantic Rehabilitation of Nature

heroic self-sacrifice, and patriotism, which was the best virtue that the old Romans knew. Every wrong thing makes the gulf deeper; every right one helps to fill it up. As the evil of Rome was far more than its good, the whole commonwealth finally sank into it, indeed, but of no original necessity."[754]

Hilda here is an acolyte of Emersonian self-reliance and the belief that there is no "original necessity" standing in the way of human happiness. But, as Emerson and Fichte pointed out, consciousness demands action to make it real. At this point, Hawthorne is thrown back on the angel and machine dichotomy at the heart of his rational psychology. To remain pure, Hilda the angel must eschew contact with the world, which is the realm of human action. This means that her thoughts will remain ineffectual because they will not eventuate in the good deeds that will bridge over the "hideous emptiness under our feet." It also means that contact with Miriam will render her unclean.

After hearing Hilda tell her that her deed "has darkened the whole sky," Miriam needs her more than ever as a friend, but Hilda rebuffs her overture by invoking her status as a Puritan angel:

"Do not bewilder me thus, Miriam!" exclaimed Hilda, who had not forborne to express, by look and gesture, the anguish which this interview inflicted on her. "If I were one of God's angels, with a nature incapable of stain, and garments that never could be spotted, I would keep ever at your side and try to lead you upward. But I am a poor, lonely girl, whom God has set here in an evil world, and given her only a white robe, and bid her wear it back to Him, as white as when she put it on. Your powerful magnetism would be too much for me. The pure, white atmosphere, in which I try to discern what things are good and true, would be discoloured. And, therefore, Miriam, before it is too late, I mean to put faith in this awful heart-quake, which warns me henceforth to avoid you!"[755]

Hawthorne should have known that angels can sin. He must have been familiar with John Milton's Puritan epic *Paradise Lost*, but theology isn't his strong suit. It is Hawthorne's dualistic rational psychology, and not Aquinas's treatise on angelology which determines Hilda's character and therefore her destiny. Rebuffed by the woman she hoped would be her friend, Miriam articulates what Hilda knows but dare not say. "As an angel," Miriam tells Hilda, "you are not amiss; but, as a human creature, and a woman among earthly men and women, you need a sin to soften you!"[756]

---

754 Hawthorne, *The Marble Faun*, p. 162.
755 Hawthorne, *The Marble Faun*, p. 208.
756 Hawthorne, *The Marble Faun*, p. 209.

Is there any irony in this statement? Or is Hawthorne equally the victim of his own deficient theology and incapable of leaving Calvinism behind? In the middle of Rome, Hawthorne suddenly finds himself transported back to the New England forest, where Young Goodman Brown learned that "evil is the nature of mankind." Faced with a choice between two equally repugnant theological alternatives, Hawthorne chose the faith of his fathers.

Emerson stood next to Hawthorne's grave as his mortal remains were lowered into the earth of Concord. Emerson's presence was a fitting reminder that Hawthorne's mind never got beyond the confines of his native place, except through his art. *The Scarlet Letter* has universal value as art, and to this day it is the best expression of the distortions which sin and guilt introduce into the soul, but it did not serve as a philosophical refutation of the deep satanic grammar which links Emerson's "Self-Reliance" and Edwards's "Sinners in the Hands of an Angry God." In this instance, Beauty was not Truth—pace, John Keats—and so Hawthorne remained of two minds.

Emerson based his philosophy, if we can use that term to describe his writings, on the provincial's defective understanding of German Idealism as refracted through the mind of Samuel Taylor Coleridge, German thought's main popularizer in the English-speaking world. Coleridge got his ideas from Johann Gottlieb Fichte, as expressed best in *The Vocation of Man, Die Bestimmung des Menschens*, which was a distillation of his *Wissenschaftslehre*. According to Montgomery's reading of German Idealism:

> The "creative power" of the "subject-lenses which we are" reveals itself as action of the will, whereby our world comes into existence as we will it to be. Each man is his own creator; in the act of that creation, he becomes his own savior, though he "quaintly" name God or Jesus in the action. For "Jesus, the 'Providential man,'" is only "a good man on whom many people are agreed that these optical laws (of the individual's projecting will) shall take effect."[757]

Coleridge saw the limitations of man as his own creator in his "Ode to Melancholy." When "genial spirits fail," it is a "vain endeavor/To lift the smothering weight from off my breast." Deprived of the sacramental source of grace which only the Catholic Church can provide, the Romantic poet is thrown back on himself when "Melancholy invades his soul," as was so often the case with Hawthorne. The good news of Transcendentalism collapses the minute melancholy arrives because the man who is now the center of the universe and his own creator "may not hope from outward forms to win/ The passion and the life whose fountains are within." As soon as our genial spirits fail, nature becomes the deterministic prison that Calvin and Spinoza always said it was, because "we receive but what we give/And in our life alone does Nature live:/Ours is her wedding garment, ours her shroud." In the

---

[757] Montgomery, *Why Hawthorne Was Melancholy*, p. 49.

Part II: The Romantic Rehabilitation of Nature

end it all comes down to temperament. Emerson's confident attitude toward Nature spoke to the America of his day in a way that Hawthorne's brooding did not. It all depended on the soul now, because every Transcendentalist had claimed that "from the soul itself must issue forth a light, a glory, a fair luminous cloud," because with the disappearance of the *Ding an sich* and the sacramental system of the Catholic Church, there was no other possible source of "grace."

Fichte claimed that without action thought remained unreal, and since the world was now one big idea, the world would remain unreal as long as the subject failed to act:

> From this necessity of action proceeds the consciousness of the actual world and not the reverse way: the consciousness of the actual world is derived from the necessity of action. We act not because we know, but we know because we are called upon to act: the practical reason is the root of all reason. The laws of action for rational beings are immediately certain. We cannot deny these laws without plunging the world and ourselves with it into absolute annihilation; we raise ourselves from the abyss and maintain ourselves above it, solely by our moral activity.[758]

Emerson seconded Fichte's claim, writing in *Nature* "so long as the active powers predominate over the reflective, we resist with indignation any hint that nature is more short-lived or mutable than spirit."

In Hawthorne the reflective powers invariably predominated over the active. Emerson failed to understand Hawthorne because his "genial spirits" prevailed until senility dimmed his mind to the point where he couldn't recognize their failure. Emerson's line wasn't long enough to plumb Hawthorne's depths because, no matter how much he valued Hawthorne as a friend and neighbor, he could never take his writing seriously. Emerson dismissed Hawthorne's *magnum opus The Marble Faun* as "mush." And yet, "Emerson is everywhere a presence in Hawthorne's unhurried tour of the Old Manse and its grounds."[759]

My book *The Angel and the Machine* explains how Hawthorne tried to confect a rational psychology out of German Idealism and the materialism which took its place as the regnant European ideology after G.W.F. Hegel's death in 1831. Hawthorne, unfortunately, lacked the philosophical tools to resolve this dichotomy. Deprived of the philosophical and theological principles which would have allowed him to refute Emerson, Hawthorne turned to art as embodied in two images, the angel and the machine, which symbolized in art what he could not articulate theoretically.

---

758 Johann Gottlieb Fichte, *The Vocation of Man* (Indianapolis: Bobbs-Merill, 1956), pp. 98-9.
759 Montgomery, *Why Hawthorne Was Melancholy*, p. 70.

As a work of art, however, *The Marble Faun* is afflicted by a terminal vagueness which its plot cannot resolve and threatens to sink the novel as a result. Miriam is tormented because she can't go to confession, but as an avatar of Beatrice Cenci she is an "incestuous victim whose complicity in parricide seemed justifiable." For in both journal and romance he noted that the girl's expression of unutterable sadness is, as he finally put it, "the intimate consciousness of her father's sin that threw its shadow over her, a sinless person."[760] As the editors note, the claim is morally implausible, "and in this respect Hawthorne has not effectively controlled the motifs he has introduced into the book."[761]

A sacrament is "the visible sign of a hidden reality" known as grace, which leads to salvation.[762] As such it is both physical and spiritual in a way that transcends the angel/machine dichotomy which Hawthorne inherited from Descartes. "The seven sacraments are the signs and instruments by which the Holy Spirit spreads the grace of Christ the Head throughout the Church which is his body."[763] Confession (also known as Penance or Reconciliation) is one of those sacraments. "Confession to a priest is an essential part of the sacrament of Penance. . . . The confession (or disclosure) of sins, even from a simply human point of view, frees us and facilitates our reconciliation with others."[764] Only a priest has the sacramental power to forgive sins in the name of Christ. This power is coterminous with the creation of the Church as the vehicle of salvation established by Christ when he said to Peter, "*Tu es Petrus et supra hanc petram aedificabo ecclesiam meam.*" If Kenyon had looked up into the dome at St. Peters he would have seen this passage from Matthew 16 written in large gold letters at its base. Peter has the power to bind and loose, and an essential part of that mission gets delegated to the priests who have the power to forgive sins. Miriam needs a confessor, but Kenyon provides a poor substitute.

"Oh, my friend," cried she, with sudden passion, "will you be my friend indeed? I am lonely, lonely, lonely! There is a secret in my heart that burns me!—that tortures me! Sometimes, I fear to go mad of it! Sometimes, I hope to die of it! But neither of the two happens. Ah, if I could but. whisper it to only one human soul! And you—you see far into womanhood! You receive it widely into your large view! Perhaps—perhaps—but Heaven only knows—you might understand me! Oh, let me speak!"

---

760 Hawthorne, *The Marble Faun*, p. xl.
761 Hawthorne, *The Marble Faun*, p. xli.
762 *Catechism of the Catholic Church*, para. 774.
763 *Catechism of the Catholic Church*, para. 774.
764 *Catechism of the Catholic Church*, para. 1455.

Part II: The Romantic Rehabilitation of Nature

"Miriam, dear friend," replied the sculptor, "if I can help you, speak freely, as to a brother."[765]

Kenyon volunteers to be Miriam's father confessor, but since he is not an ordained Catholic priest his sympathy would allow him to know things he had no right to know, causing Miriam to "hate him, by-and-by, and herself still more, if he let her speak."[766]

The moment of release came and went unfulfilled because no one granted Kenyon the power to forgive sin. As a result, Miriam remains like Beatrice Cenci a "fallen angel."[767] All that Kenyon can do is project his guilt onto the stones of Rome, in middle age "when the accumulated sins are many, and the remaining temptations few."[768] When Donatello throws the model off the Tarpeian Rock, the novel's incoherence deepens as his guilt unites with the guilt of Miriam in something "closer than a marriage-bond."[769] Once again, Hawthorne loses control of the motifs he has introduced into the book.

Eventually Hawthorne is forced to abandon the Arcadia conceit: "Just an instant before, it was Arcadia, and the Golden Age. The spell being broken, it was now only that old tract of pleasure-ground, close by the people's gate of Rome."[770]

At this point in the novel, the real world intrudes upon the plot and replaces the fantasy of Arcadia and Hawthorne's appropriation of the *felix culpa*, which he struggled unsuccessfully to articulate in Calvinist terms, within the actual world of Italian art. Unlike America, which has become Arcadia in the New World, Italy is no prelapsarian paradise, nor does it need to be one because it has been redeemed by Christ and the Church He founded. The visible manifestation of that redemption can be found in the beauty of Catholic art. Once Hawthorne is forced to make this concession, the novel becomes an unacknowledged protocol of his involvement with that art as the prolegomena to his engagement with the Catholic Church which inspired it.

When it came to Rome, Nathaniel and his wife Sophia were deeply ambivalent, at once the thrall of "anti-Catholic prejudices" that reached the point of "rabid anticlericalism," while at the same time "unmistakably Catholic in sympathy" when it came to art.[771] In a letter to his publisher Fields, Nathaniel wrote "I bitterly detest Rome."[772] Rose understates her case

---

765 Hawthorne, *The Marble Faun*, p. 128.
766 Hawthorne, *The Marble Faun*, p. 129.
767 Hawthorne, *The Marble Faun*, p. 66.
768 Hawthorne, *The Marble Faun*, p. 154.
769 Hawthorne, *The Marble Faun*, p. 174.
770 Hawthorne, *The Marble Faun*, p. 90.
771 Maynard, *A Fire Was Lighted*, p. 84.
772 Maynard, *A Fire Was Lighted*, p. 89.

when she writes in her memoir of her father that "the Eternal City did not at once make a conquest of my father's allegiance."[773]

The Hawthornes arrived in Rome full of the prejudices they had acquired from growing up in once Calvinist now Unitarian New England. Maynard tells us that Nathaniel and Sophia "started with an extremely critical attitude toward the Catholic Church. It was not that they were especially hostile to its teachings or practices—rather the contrary, in so far as they understood them." But they were anticlerical, and Hawthorne never got over his animosity to monks or referring to them as "fat pigs."[774] Deprived of a Christianity which was truly incarnational, Hawthorne associated corporeality with corruption. Hawthorne described the priests he noticed in Amiens as "jolly, fat, mean-looking fellows," a description which in Maynard's explanation "boiled down to much the same criticism that Hawthorne leveled a thousand times against Englishmen (and still more against Englishwomen), [that] they were gross in appearance."[775]

Nevertheless, both Nathaniel and Sophia found much to admire in the Catholic Church's veneration of the Blessed Virgin in both art and life. Italian Catholic art changed their mind about the Church because art and Catholicism "were inseparable" for the Hawthornes:

> They understood that, as even the fifteen-year-old Una was to write to her aunt, there was here "[a] fount of glory and beauty from which the old artists drew so freely." And Rose many years later was to say, "In art, Catholicity was utterly bowed down to by my relatives and friends, because without it this great art would not have been."[776]

Hawthorne puts his understanding of beauty as both transcendental and propaedeutic into the mouth of Miriam, who responds to Donatello's compliment, "You are still as beautiful as ever," by saying: "Do you, then, think me beautiful? I rejoice, most truly. Beauty—if I possess it—shall be one of the instruments by which I will try to educate and elevate him, to whose good I solely dedicate myself."[777] Beginning with Giotto, Italy was the nursery of early art, "where the flower of Beauty sprang out of a rocky soil, and in a high, keen atmosphere, when the richest and most sheltered gardens failed to nourish it."[778]

Given the novel's theological incoherence and the perturbations which it wreaks in the novel's plot, beauty becomes the *deus ex machina* that rescues the

---

773 Rose Hawthorne Lathrop, *Memories of Hawthorne* (The Riverside Press, Cambridge Mass, 1897), p. 393.
774 Maynard, *A Fire Was Lighted*, p. 61.
775 Maynard, *A Fire Was Lighted*, p. 63.
776 Maynard, *A Fire Was Lighted*, p. 61.
777 Hawthorne, *The Marble Faun*, p. 286.
778 Hawthorne, *The Marble Faun*, p. 258.

Part II: The Romantic Rehabilitation of Nature

characters and the story. Hilda's bad theology, her incoherent anthropology, and her distorted rational psychology get redeemed by dreams of creating beauty precisely because it requires no "intellectual effort" to send "forms and hues of beauty into the visible world out of her own mind."[779]

Like Hawthorne's wife and youngest daughter, Hilda "became a copyist,"[780] which allows her to retain her angelic nature while at the same time converting herself, like other copyists, "into Guido machines, and Raphaelic machines."[781] Similarly, Kenyon must approach the Church through beauty because his New England ethnocentrism makes him incapable of understanding it intellectually. Hawthorne, according to Maynard was "all but blind to the meaning of Catholicism. It is curious how most of his references to the Church in his Notebook continued to be highly critical. Nor was he any more complimentary in *The Marble Faun*." The question is not, however, as simple as it might appear to be, and Hawthorne's son-in-law in the early nineties used to lecture on Hawthorne's incipient Catholicism, concerning which Rose herself considered writing an article. A passage of this sort is typical:

> I heartily wish the priests were better men, and that human nature, divinely influenced, could be depended upon for a constant supply and succession of good and pure ministers, their religion has so many good points. And then it is a sad pity that this noble and beautiful cathedral should be a mere fossil shell, out of which the life has died long ago. But for many a year yet to come the tapers will burn before the high altar, the Host will be elevated, the incense diffuse its fragrance, the confessionals be open to receive the penitents.[782]

As a sculptor, Kenyon "embodies many of Hawthorne's ideas and attitudes, often closely paraphrased from journal entries; the preface to the novel acknowledges that he had attributed to Kenyon two figures by Paul Akers and had appropriated W. W. Story's figure of Cleopatra as Kenyon's work in progress. . . ."[783] Hawthorne, the editors conclude, "does not seem to have relied significantly on specific artists in shaping Kenyon."[784] That is because Kenyon is Hawthorne. Like Kenyon, Hawthorne was an artist from New England who was drawn to Rome by the beauty of its art only to realize, too late to back away, that art and the Catholic Church are inseparable in Rome. Art is propaedeutic. It is an integral part of the preliminary instruction in the faith which burst forth in Italy when Giotto, according to Vasari, broke with "Greek models" and launched an era of mimesis unprecedented in the

---

779 Hawthorne, *The Marble Faun*, p. 56-7.
780 Hawthorne, *The Marble Faun*, p. 57.
781 Hawthorne, *The Marble Faun*, p. 59.
782 Maynard, *A Fire Was Lighted*, p. 93.
783 Hawthorne, *The Marble Faun*, p. xxxvii.
784 Hawthorne, *The Marble Faun*, p. xxxvii.

history of art when he painted the frescoes in the Arena chapel.[785] Art was as intimately connected with the faith as those frescoes were to the walls of that chapel. Kenyon was drawn to the Catholic Church because he was first drawn to the beauty which was manifest in its churches and in spite of the horror his New England upbringing associated with that institution.

No one understood this better than his daughter Rose. As a nine-year-old girl, Rose would take walks with her father in Rome, and during those walks they came in daily contact with the Catholic Church, as when they attended a papal audience at St. Peter's, which Hawthorne "acknowledged as the heart of Rome."[786] If St. Peter's was the heart of Rome, then its pulse was Pope Pius IX. "The most striking effect the Holy Father produced on me, standing before him with my parents," Rose wrote:

> was when he appeared, in Holy Week, high up in the balcony before the mountainous dome, looking off over the great multitude of people gathered to receive his blessing. Those eyes of his carried expression a long way, and he looked most kingly, though unlike other kings. He was clothed in white not whiter than his wonderful pallor. My father implies in a remark that Pio Nono impressed him by a becoming sincerity of countenance, and this was so entirely my infantile opinion that I became eloquent about the Pope and was rewarded by a gift from my mother of a little medallion of him and a gold scudo with an excellent likeness thereon, both always tenderly reverenced by me.[787]

As Rose pointed out, she was too young to wander around Rome alone, and so her father saw everything she saw. Rose described the atmosphere of St. Peter's Basilica as "perpetual summer," because it was "warmed by the ardent soul of Peter" and "by the breath of prayer from innumerable saints. One drops the hermetical seal of a curtain behind, upon entering, and behold, with the world is also shut out the bitter cold, and one is folded, as it were, in a soft mantle of down, as if angels wrapped their wings about us."[788] Impressed by the same visit, Hawthorne referred to St. Peter's as "the grandest edifice ever built by man, painted against God's loveliest sky."[789]

Because of the walks she took with her father in Rome, art and Catholicism became inseparable in Rose's mind. Rose rebuked her bluestocking aunt Elizabeth Peabody for not understanding that Europe is where Rose learned "to breathe day after day the atmosphere of art," which allows "our souls" to "approach in thought and imagination to that fount of glory and beauty,

---

785 Cf. E. Michael Jones, *The Dangers of Beauty*, p. 54ff.
786 Lathrop, *Memories of Hawthorne*, p. 360.
787 Lathrop, *Memories of Hawthorne*, p. 355.
788 Lathrop, *Memories of Hawthorne*, p. 355.
789 Lathrop, *Memories of Hawthorne*, p. 362.

Part II: The Romantic Rehabilitation of Nature

from which the old artists drew so freely."[790] Rose never referred to art as a transcendental, but, as an "observant little girl in Rome," Rose was deeply impressed with Catholic art, which:

> though not in the least understood at the time, did leave upon her mind vivid impressions that were to endure and had much to do with her conversion to the Catholic faith more than thirty years later. In her first draft of the Roman chapter, she was to write: "In the churches the chanting monks and boys impressed me differently. Who does not feel, without a word to reveal the fact, as I did so silently, the wondrous virtue of the Catholic religion. Not told anything of it except what was supposed would shock me, I bowed in spirit before the holy water, and all that was apprehended by the senses."[791]

Unlike truth, which can only be apprehended by the mind, beauty can be "apprehended by the senses," which is why it can serve as a gateway to the transcendent for children, whose minds are not yet capable of reason, and for those otherwise ill-disposed to it for personal or ideological reasons. The Catholic Church understood that beauty is the universal propaedeutic to the faith. The Hawthornes understood that without Catholicism "great art would not have been."[792] And yet Hawthorne was put off by the fact that the pope showed up half an hour late for his weekly public audience at St. Peter's, considering it "particularly ill-mannered." Ever the American tourist, Hawthorne wrote in his diary, "I am very glad I have seen the pope, because now he may be crossed out of the lists of sights to be seen."[793] Rose's meeting with the pope was more intimate. While strolling in the Vatican gardens with her father, Rose encountered Pius IX, who "beckoned the child to him and while Sophia knelt—for even a New England Unitarian knew that that was good manners—he placed his hand on the mop of red hair and blessed her."[794]

Hawthorne's innumerable visits to art galleries were enhanced by Sophia's technical knowledge and talent as a copyist, but Hawthorne's appreciation of Italian art, no matter how impressive, was always strained through the lens of Puritan provinciality, and the ambivalence those clashing forces engendered crippled Nathaniel and Sophia in a way that did not affect Rose. Hawthorne admired Guido Reni's portrait of St. Michael the Archangel and included his interpretation of it in *The Marble Faun*, but he could never get over his sense of disapproval, concluding that "there is something forced, if not feigned, in our taste for pictures of the old Italian school."[795] Hawthorne was scandalized

---

790 Lathrop, *Memories of Hawthorne*, p. 369.
791 Maynard, *A Fire Was Lighted*, pp. 64-5.
792 Lathrop, *Memories of Hawthorne*, p. 369.
793 Maynard, *A Fire Was Lighted*, p. 66.
794 Maynard, *A Fire Was Lighted*, p. 66.
795 Maynard, *A Fire Was Lighted*, p. 66.

by the models Italian artists chose for their portraits of the Blessed Virgin, viewing Raphael's Fornarina as "the brazen trollop that she is."[796]

Ever the devoted child, Rose even after her conversion later in life was forced to admit that her father "had mixed feelings about Rome. Contempt for its discomforts and delighted heartiness" mingled with admiration for its "outshining fascinations" in *The Marble Faun*, forcing him to conclude that "The desolation of her ruin" does not prevent her from being "more intimately our home than even the spot where we were born."[797] Rose concludes her peroration on Rome by admitting that "the Eternal City did not at once make a conquest of my father's allegiance,"[798] but Hawthorne's sensibility eventually won out over his ethnocentrism. By the time he "bade it farewell, Hawthorne felt that Rome was "the sunniest and most splendid habitation for a populace, that he knew."[799] Rose felt that her father shared "a magnetic current of sympathy with the city," which "rendered him contemplative and absorbent as a cloud."[800] The impression Rome left on Rose was less ambiguous than the impression it made on her father, but, again, everything that Rose saw, she saw in the company of her father:

> Who does not feel, without a word to reveal the fact, the wondrous virtue of Catholic religious observance in the churches? The holiness of these regions sent through me waves of peace. I stepped softly past the old men and women who knelt upon the pavements and gazed longingly upon their simpler spiritual plane; I drew back reluctantly from the only garden where the Cross is planted in visible, reverential substance. For the year ensuing this life in Rome, I entertained the family with dramatic imitations of religious chants, grumbling out at sundown the low, ominous echoings of the priests, answered by the treble, rapid and trustful, of the little choristers, gladly picturing to myself as I did so the winding processions in St. Peter's.[801]

Rose tells us that "her [mother's] views and tacit beliefs and my father's are identical" in their appreciation of Italian art, but Rose differed from her parents when it came to understanding the relationship between that art and the religion which inspired it.

Rose was open to Rome's art and Catholicism in a way that her parents were not. Rose's mother and father felt that "there was a sadness about Italy," and that the cause of this sadness was the "'incubus' of the Catholic religion." At times, Rose continues, the sun would come out, revealing "Glorious

---

796 Maynard, *A Fire Was Lighted*, p. 66.
797 Lathrop, *Memories of Hawthorne*, pp. 352-3.
798 Lathrop, *Memories of Hawthorne*, p. 353.
799 Lathrop, *Memories of Hawthorne*, p. 353.
800 Lathrop, *Memories of Hawthorne*, p. 357.
801 Lathrop, *Memories of Hawthorne*, p. 377.

scenes" which were constantly soothing this sense of human sorrow, scenes such as cannot be found in regions outside the Church."[802] Rose then takes it back, writing: "They did not really believe that Italy was under an "incubus"; they felt the physical weight of Catholicity, or the Cross, and half guessed its spiritual spring."[803]

"Half guessed" is the key term. Rose's avowal and its sudden retraction are indicative of the back and forth that was going on in Hawthorne's mind at the time. He was drawn to the art which the Church brought into being but appalled by the monks who infested those beautiful churches and often performed its music. Art, in this instance music, provided "soothing" relief from "this sense of human sorrow," in a way that was troubling for Hawthorne because the beauty art provided "cannot be found in regions outside the Church."[804] Beauty was bound up with "elaborate devotion" like what the Hawthornes experienced in the Basilica of San Spiritu:

> when the organ burst forth in a kind of tender rapture, rolling pearly waves of harmony along the large spaces, and filling the dome with the foam and spray of interlacing measures, it seemed as if angels were welcoming the young child to heaven.[805]

Angels were an integral part of the Hawthornes' world view. The only author Hawthorne really wanted to meet during his stay in England was Coventry Patmore, author of *The Angel in the House*, a now long forgotten novel about the joys of domesticity. Hawthorne modeled the angelic Hilda in *The Marble Faun* on his wife, but, as Patmore's novel indicates, angels provide a faulty paradigm for human emulation because they do not belong to this world. After watching "priests and monks of the Order of St. Augustine process from the sacristy and kneel down in their sweeping black robes upon the marble," Rose rejoices in the "wonderful picture" it made, but her mother, still under the spell of "the Puritanical idea" she and her provincial husband brought with them as their constant guide and interpreter, concludes that "angels only are fit to live as monks pretend to live."[806] Sophia "still clung to the Puritanical idea that in the Catholic religion, 'What looks so wondrous, wondrous fair, His providence has taught us to fear.'"[807]

Both Sophia and Nathaniel Hawthorne struggled to overcome their New England parochialism. Reviews of *The Marble Faun* criticized Hawthorne's attitude toward nudity in sculpture as a prime example of his provinciality, and Henry James agreed, claiming that one of the main manifestations of

---

802 Lathrop, *Memories of Hawthorne*, p. 389.
803 Lathrop, *Memories of Hawthorne*, p. 392.
804 Lathrop, *Memories of Hawthorne*, p. 389.
805 Lathrop, *Memories of Hawthorne*, p. 390.
806 Lathrop, *Memories of Hawthorne*, p. 391.
807 Lathrop, *Memories of Hawthorne*, p. 391.

Walking with a Bible and a Gun

Hawthorne's New England prudery was his "aversion to the representation of the nude in sculpture."[808] "Not a nude figure, I hope!" observed Miriam, articulating the prim New England views of Hawthorne and his wife:

> Every young sculptor seems to think that he must give the world some specimen of indecorous womanhood, and call it Eve, Venus, a Nymph, or any name that may apologize for a lack of decent clothing. I am weary, even more than I am ashamed, of seeing such things. Now-a-days, people are as good as born in their clothes, and there is practically not a nude human being in existence. An artist, therefore,—as you must candidly confess,—cannot sculpture nudity with a pure heart, if only because he is compelled to steal guilty glimpses at hired models. The marble inevitably loses its chastity under such circumstances. An old Greek sculptor, no doubt, found his models in the open sunshine, and among pure and princely maidens, and thus the nude statues of antiquity are as modest as violets, and sufficiently draped in their own beauty. But as for Mr. Gibson's coloured Venuses, (stained, I believe, with tobacco-juice,) and all other nudities of to-day, I really do not understand what they have to say to this generation and would be glad to see as many heaps of quick-lime in their stead![809]

James felt that Hawthorne's provinciality had consequences for his art. In writing *The Marble Faun*, Hawthorne "forfeited a precious advantage in ceasing to tread his native soil. Half the virtue of *The Scarlet Letter* and *The House of the Seven Gables* is in their local quality; they are impregnated with the New England air."[810] That air dissipated, however, the moment Hawthorne entered St. Peter's Basilica. As an American who grew up in the villages of New England during the 19th century, Hawthorne was understandably overwhelmed by the architectural magnificence of St. Peter's Basilica. The south transept spoke to Hawthorne most intimately because that is where its confessionals can be found.

Troubled by characters who are stereotypes that forced a plot, which seemed contrived, Hawthorne found, in James's words, "the purest touch of inspiration"[811] in the scenes in *The Marble Faun* which show Hilda, "strenuous daughter of the Puritans as she is" entering the confessional "in which the poor girl deposits her burden" of vicarious guilt,[812] emerging "not a whit less a Puritan than before."[813] Hawthorne found that "the practice of confession in the Catholic Church" appealed to him even more strongly than the Catholic

---

808 James, *Hawthorne*, p. 127.
809 Hawthorne, *The Marble Faun*, pp. 123-4.
810 James, *Hawthorne*, p. 131.
811 James, *Hawthorne*, p. 133.
812 James, *Hawthorne*, p. 133.
813 James, *Hawthorne*, p. 133.

Part II: The Romantic Rehabilitation of Nature

use of religious pictures "so violently discarded by the Puritans" who were determined to ignore "the devotional part of our nature." Hawthorne claimed that "The nail-marks in the hands and feet of Jesus, ineffaceable, even after He had passed into bliss and glory, touched my heart with a sense of His love for us."[814]

Hawthorne was attracted to the confessional long before he arrived in Rome. "According to James Russell Lowell, it had been Hawthorne's intention in *The Scarlet Letter* to have the guilt-tortured Dimmesdale make his confession to a priest. Lowell wrote to Miss Jane Norton on June 12, 1860: "I have seen Hawthorne twice. . . . He is writing another story. He said also that it had been part of his plan in "The Scarlet Letter" to make Dimmesdale confess himself to a Catholic priest. I, for one, am sorry he didn't. It would have been psychologically admirable."[815]

Hawthorne dealt with the psychological and physiological damage that Calvinism's repudiation of sacramental confession had wrought in the New England soul as well as its need for surrogates in *The Scarlet Letter* when:

> Chillingworth reopens the Inquisition by proposing a diagnosis of his patient's health. "You would tell me, then, that I know all? . . . He to whom only the outward and physical evil is laid open, knoweth, oftentimes, but half the evil which he is called upon to cure. A bodily disease, which we look upon as whole and entire within itself, may, after all, be but a symptom of some ailment in the spiritual part."

"Then I need ask no further," said the clergyman, somewhat hastily rising from his chair. "You deal not, I take it, in medicine for the soul!"

"Thus, a sickness," continued Roger Chillingworth ... "a sickness, a sore place, if we may so call it, in your spirit, hath immediately its appropriate manifestation in your bodily frame. Would you not, therefore, that your physician heal the bodily evil?"[816]

Hawthorne resisted Chillingworth's invitation to confess in Boston, but did Hawthorne resist the same temptation in Rome? Randall Stewart claims that Hawthorne's interest in sacramental confession "steadily increased" with time, "and, gaining strength to overcome an inherited reluctance, found ultimate expression in *The Marble Faun*."[817] Fairbanks concludes that in the final analysis:

> Hawthorne did not fully comprehend its sacramental character in the Catholic sense. True, he did not look upon confession as many a

---

814 Maynard, *A Fire Was Lighted*, p. 62.

815 Hawthorne and Confession Author(s): Henry G. Fairbanks Source: *The Catholic Historical Review*, Apr., 1957, Vol. 43, No. 1 (Apr., 1957), pp. 38-45 Published by: Catholic University of America Press Stable URL: https://www.jstor.org/stable/25016154

816 Hawthorne and Confession Author(s): Henry G. Fairbanks Source.

817 Hawthorne and Confession Author(s): Henry G. Fairbanks Source.

modern psychiatrist looks upon it, as a therapeutic release merely of psychoses and repressions. For Hawthorne, as for the Church, effective confession involved acceptance of responsibility for evil committed. But it was still largely a natural process of psychological readjustment, minus any intervention of supernatural absolution through the agency of a confessor. Like Goethe before him, Hawthorne recognized an urgent need for confession rooted in human nature. But that very "insulation" of exaggerated individualism against which he had struggled and written all his life complicated his acceptance of the necessity of a priest-mediator between God and man.[818]

Jesuits lurk in the background, seeking to ensnare Hilda with the illusions generated by beauty, but the art of St. Peter's Basilica overcomes Hilda's misgivings and leads her to the confessional. Hilda finds the Catholic faith irresistible, not because of the craft of the Jesuits, but because it "so marvelously adapts itself to every human need" primarily through its art, which:

> supplies a multitude of external forms, in which the Spiritual may be clothed and manifested; it has many painted windows, as it were, through which the celestial sunshine, else disregarded, may make itself gloriously perceptible in visions of beauty and splendour. There is no one want or weakness of human nature, for which Catholicism will own itself without a remedy; cordials, certainly, it possesses in abundance, and sedatives, in inexhaustible variety, and what may once have been genuine medicaments, though a little the worse for long keeping.[819]

Hilda is scandalized because the Italian artists portray the Blessed Virgin as "the flattered portrait of an earthly beauty,"[820] but when she observes "how closely and comfortingly the Popish faith applied itself to all human occasions,"[821] attracting those "who would find none at all in our own formless mode of worship,"[822] she changes her mind, concluding Catholic art revealed the crippled nature of the Protestant soul. Watching a young man standing before a shrine, "writhing, wringing his hands, contorting his whole frame, in an agony of remorseful recollection," but finally kneeling down "to weep and pray,"[823] Hilda concludes, "If this youth had been a Protestant,"

---

[818] Vol. 43, No. 1 (Apr., 1957), pp. 38-45 Published by: Catholic University of America Press Stable URL: https://www.jstor.org/stable/25016154
[819] Hawthorne, *The Marble Faun*, p. 345.
[820] Hawthorne, *The Marble Faun*, p. 347.
[821] Hawthorne, *The Marble Faun*, p. 364.
[822] Hawthorne, *The Marble Faun*, p. 364.
[823] Hawthorne, *The Marble Faun*, p. 364.

Part II: The Romantic Rehabilitation of Nature

like Hawthorne, perhaps, "he would have kept all that torture pent up in his heart, and let it burn there till it seared him into indifference."[824]

Faced with beauty of this magnitude, Hawthorne sets aside his petulant provincialism and surrender himself to the basilica's undeniable aesthetic power:

> The pavement! It stretched out illimitably, a plain of many-coloured marble, where thousands of worshippers might kneel together, and shadowless angels tread among them without brushing their heavenly garments against those earthly ones. The roof! The Dome! Rich, gorgeous, filled with sunshine, cheerfully sublime, and fadeless after centuries, those lofty depths seemed to translate the heavens to mortal comprehension, and help the spirit upward to a yet higher and wider sphere. Must not the Faith, that built this matchless edifice, and warmed, illuminated, and overflowed from it, include whatever can satisfy human aspirations, at the loftiest, or minister to human necessity at the sorest! If Religion had a material home, was it not here![825]

Beauty has led Kenyon to the transcendent realm and placed him in the presence of the divine. Moved to pray before Guido's portrait of St. Michael the Archangel, Hilda dips her fingers into the holy water font and "almost signed the cross upon her breast, but forebore and trembled" because "She felt as if her mother's spirit, somewhere within the Dome, were looking down upon her child, the daughter of Puritan forefathers, and weeping to behold her ensnared by these gaudy superstitions."

Sacred art prepared Hilda to approach the confessional. Overwhelmed by the sense that Guido Reni "had done a great thing, not merely for the Church of Rome, but for the cause of Good,"[826] by portraying St. Michael the Archangel, Hilda suddenly:

> found herself kneeling before the shrine, under the ever-burning lamp that throws its ray upon the Archangel's face. She laid her forehead on the marble steps before the altar and sobbed out a prayer; she hardly knew to whom, whether Michael, the Virgin, or the Father; she hardly knew for what, save only a vague longing, that thus the burthen of her spirit might be lightened a little. In an instant, she snatched herself up, as it were, from her knees, all a-throb with the emotions which were struggling to force their way out of her heart by the avenue that had so nearly been opened for them. Yet there was a strange sense of relief won by that momentary, passionate prayer; a strange joy, moreover, whether

---

824 Hawthorne, *The Marble Faun*, p. 347.
825 Hawthorne, *The Marble Faun*, p. 351.
826 Hawthorne, *The Marble Faun*, p. 352.

for what she had done, or for what she had escaped doing, Hilda could not tell. But she felt as one half-stifled, who has stolen a breath of air. [827]

Sacred art propelled Hilda to the southern transept of St. Peter's, where she found "a number of confessionals" which resembled "small tabernacles of carved wood, with a closet for the priest in the centre, and, on either side, a space for a penitent to kneel, and breathe his confession through a perforated auricle into the good Father's ear."[828] Hilda was immediately:

> impressed with the infinite convenience (if we may use so poor a phrase) of the Catholic religion to its devout believers. . . . Who, in truth, that considers the matter, can resist a similar impression! In the hottest fever-fit of life, they can always find, ready for their need, a cool, quiet, beautiful place of worship. They may enter its sacred precincts, at any hour, leaving the fret and trouble of the world behind them, and purifying themselves with a touch of holy-water at the threshold. In the calm interior, fragrant of rich and soothing incense, they may hold converse with some Saint, their awful, kindly friend. And, most precious privilege of all, whatever perplexity, sorrow, guilt, may weigh upon their souls, they can fling down the dark burthen at the foot of the Cross, and go forth—to sin no more, nor be any longer disquieted—but to live again in the freshness and elasticity of innocence![829]

Propelled by the same beauty which earlier impressed Kenyon, Hilda overcomes her ethnocentrism and goes to confession. When Hilda found the confessional marked *"Pro Anglica Lingua"* she entered as "if she had heard her mother's voice from within the tabernacle, calling her, in her own mother-tongue, to come and lay her poor head in her lap, and sob out all her troubles."[830] Finding relief "with sobs, tears, and the turbulent overflow of emotion too long repressed," Hilda "poured out the dark story which had infused its poison into her innocent life. . . . Thus assisted, she revealed the whole of her terrible secret!"[831]

Hilda fulfilled, in other words, the original plan which Hawthorne had in mind for *The Scarlet Letter*. Unable to bring Dimmesdale to the confessional, Hawthorne brought Hilda, that "Daughter of the Puritans," there instead and had her confess to a priest who represented powers that were beyond her ken, symbolized by the fact that "Hilda had not seen, nor could she now see, the visage of the priest." In hearing her confession, the English-speaking priest:

---

827 Hawthorne, *The Marble Faun*, p. 352.
828 Hawthorne, *The Marble Faun*, p. 354.
829 Hawthorne, *The Marble Faun*, p. 354.
830 Hawthorne, *The Marble Faun*, p. 357.
831 Hawthorne, *The Marble Faun*, p. 357.

Part II: The Romantic Rehabilitation of Nature

spoke soothingly; it encouraged her; it led her on by apposite questions that seemed to be suggested by a great and tender interest and acted like magnetism in attracting the girl's confidence to this unseen friend. The priest's share in the interview, indeed, resembled that of one who removes the stones, clustered branches, or whatever entanglements impede the current of a swollen stream. Hilda could have imagined—so much to the purpose were his inquiries—that he was already acquainted with some outline of what she strove to tell him.[832]

The unseen priest's manner in the confessional was not something Hawthorne could have known from his experience growing up in New England. In fact, it could not have been known unless Hawthorne himself had gone to confession. Henry James was right when he claimed that Hawthorne found "the purest touch of inspiration" in the confessional scene because in that scene Hawthorne is talking about himself and the need to confess to a priest that had been haunting him ever since he thwarted it by rewriting *The Scarlet Letter* to conform to the residual Puritan sensibilities of his audience. Hawthorne was always sensitive in this regard, even when he refused to bow to the pressure of public opinion as when he refused to remove the dedication to his friend Franklin Pierce from *Our Old Home*.

When the unseen priest finally emerges from the confessional, Hilda "beheld a venerable figure with hair as white as snow, and a face strikingly characterized by benevolence,"[833] who nonetheless rebukes her, by asking "on what ground, my daughter, have you sought to avail yourself of these blessed privileges (confined exclusively to members of the one true Church) of Confession and Absolution?"[834] The priest admonishes Hilda to "come home" to the Catholic Church, but Hilda refuses by claiming that her actions are guided by a Puritan "Providence," which sounds suspiciously like the Calvinist understanding of predestination which Hawthorne could never shake:

> "Father," said Hilda, much moved by his kindly earnestness, (in which, however, genuine as it was, there might still be a leaven of professional craft,) "I dare not come a step farther than Providence shall guide me. Do not let it grieve you, therefore, if I never return to the Confessional; never dip my fingers in holy-water; never sign my bosom with the cross. I am a daughter of the Puritans. But, in spite of my heresy," she added, with a sweet, tearful smile, "you may one day see the poor girl, to whom you have done this great Christian kindness, coming to remind you of it, and thank you for it, in the better land!"

Hearing this, the old priest shakes his head and gives Hilda his blessing, which she received "with as devout a simplicity as any Catholic of them

---

832 Hawthorne, *The Marble Faun*, p. 357.
833 Hawthorne, *The Marble Faun*, p. 358.
834 Hawthorne, *The Marble Faun*, p. 359.

all."[835] Now it's Kenyon's turn. Unlike Hilda, Kenyon "seemed irresolute whether to advance or retire,"[836] even after seeing how going to confession had transformed Hilda into an angel, creatures who become beautiful because they are happy:

> At all events, it was a marvelous change from the sad girl, who had entered the confessional, bewildered with anguish, to this bright, yet softened image of religious consolation that emerged from it. It was as if one of the throng of angelic people, who might be hovering in the sunny depths of the Dome, had alighted on the pavement. Indeed, this capability of transfiguration (which we often see wrought by inward delight on persons far less capable of it than Hilda) suggests how angels come by their beauty. It grows out of their happiness and lasts forever only because that is immortal. She held out her hand; and Kenyon was glad to take it in his own, if only to assure himself that she was made of earthly material.[837]

Hilda found "infinite peace"[838] in the confessional, but did Hawthorne? He could not have confessed his sins in Italian or any of the other languages available in the southern transept, but Maynard tells us that while in Rome he met the model for "the only priest who can be called a character" in *The Marble Faun*. In his diary of 1859, Hawthorne tells us that he met Father Benedict Smith, an American Benedictine monk who was then temporary president of the American College in Rome. Father Smith also "served as unofficial cicerone to most of the English-speaking visitors—especially those from the United States."[839] Maynard tells us that Smith was "the only Catholic priest that [Hawthorne] ever encountered" and that "he liked him,"[840] but did he like him enough to go to confess his sins to him? Or did Hawthorne propose some form of Puritan confession to Father Smith, who responded with an un-pastoral mixture of rebuke and the "leaven of professional craft" which Hawthorne found so off-putting that he never went back to the confessional again? The four main characters in *The Marble Faun* are reflections of Hawthorne, but none of them have a life of their own, which means that they fail to achieve the vibrant verisimilitude which characterizes Hester or Dimmesdale, whose actions flow from the novel's plot.

As a result, a character like Hilda becomes a mouthpiece for the issues troubling Hawthorne. If Hawthorne did go to confession to Father Smith, it wasn't as a Catholic, which meant that it would not have gone well and

---

835 Hawthorne, *The Marble Faun*, p. 362.
836 Hawthorne, *The Marble Faun*, p. 363.
837 Hawthorne, *The Marble Faun*, p. 364.
838 Hawthorne, *The Marble Faun*, p. 365.
839 Maynard, *A Fire Was Lighted*, p. 94.
840 Maynard, *A Fire Was Lighted*, p. 94.

Part II: The Romantic Rehabilitation of Nature

might have ended up like Hilda's confession when the priest upbraided her for taking advantage of a sacrament to which she had no right. Hilda wanted to have her Catholic cake, but she wanted to eat it as a Puritan. She thus occupied a curiously ambiguous condition similar to the one portrayed in the second scaffold scene in *The Scarlet Letter*, where Dimmesdale, finding his guilt impossible to suppress any longer, bares his soul at midnight to an empty public square. That ambiguous gesture fits in perfectly with Hawthorne's impression of himself as the disconnected observer who saw but could not act. Like Miles Coverdale in *The Blithedale Romance*, Kenyon is a "passive observer of what goes on before him" but never the protagonist in the drama of his own life. Instead, he is a voyeur in the lives of others because of his chronic inability to act. Did Hawthorne confess to Father Smith only to be rebuked by him? Is this the cause of the anger which Kenyon shows to Hilda, when he asks her, "Hilda, have you flung your angelic purity into that mass of unspeakable corruption, the Roman Church?"[841] Or is Hawthorne pandering to his New England readers? Forgetting the happiness that made Hilda angelic and beautiful, Kenyon can't repress his Puritan ethnocentric provincialism.

"Hilda, I saw you at the confessional!" said Kenyon. "Ah, well, my dear friend," replied Hilda, casting down her eyes, and looking somewhat confused, yet not ashamed, "you must try to forgive me for that, (if you deem it wrong,) because it has saved my reason, and made me very happy. Had you been here, yesterday, I would have confessed to you."

"Would to Heaven I had!" ejaculated Kenyon, forgetting in the heat of the moment that only a priest of the Catholic Church has the power to forgive sin.

"I think," Hilda resumed, "I shall never go to the Confessional again; for there can scarcely come such a sore trial twice in my life. If I had been a wiser girl, a stronger, and a more sensible, very likely I might not have gone to the Confessional at all. It was the sin of others that drove me thither; not my own, though it almost seemed so. Being what I am, I must either have done what you saw me doing or have gone mad. Would that have been better?"

"Then, you are not a Catholic?" asked the sculptor earnestly.[842]

Confronted with Kenyon's angry question, all Hilda can say is, "Really, I do not quite know what I am,"[843] an admission which applies to Hawthorne as well. Hawthorne is arguing with himself here, and before long he is rationalizing his failure to join the Church by blaming his indecision on the Italian monks, who always inspired revulsion in him and his wife. Instead of dealing with the residual ethnocentrism which prevented him from taking Italian monks—presumably Benedictines like Father Smith—seriously as ministers of God, Hawthorne succumbed to the angel/machine dichotomy

---

841 Hawthorne, *The Marble Faun*, p. 366.
842 Hawthorne, *The Marble Faun*, p. 367.
843 Hawthorne, *The Marble Faun*, p. 368.

Walking with a Bible and a Gun

that crippled his ability to accept an Incarnate Church which the Incarnate Word founded for a flock of embodied souls. Instead of seeing the Church as the body of Christ, Hawthorne sees "mighty machinery," which would suit his taste better if it were run by angels instead of Italians:

> To do it justice, Catholicism is such a miracle of fitness for its own ends, (many of which might seem to be admirable ones,) that it is difficult to imagine it a contrivance of mere man. Its mighty machinery was forged and put together, not on middle earth, but either above or below. If there were but angels to work it, (instead of the very different class of engineers who now manage its cranks and safety-valves,) the system would soon vindicate the dignity and holiness of its origin.[844]

Hawthorne's failure to confess his sins bespoke a failure to accept by faith what he did not understand, but more importantly it bespoke a failure to act which turned him into a ghost who could no longer appreciate the transcendental beauty which led him to the Church door, but which could not bring him inside. As a result, he remained outside viewing the Church's stained glass windows as muddy and confusing precisely because they were viewed from the outside. Only those within the Church could perceive its "many painted windows, as it were, through which the celestial sunshine, else disregarded, may make itself gloriously perceptible in visions of beauty and splendour."[845]

Hawthorne is forced to engage in rationalization, the worst of all sins, by blaming Rome for his failure to see beauty on its own terms as a transcendental. "How," Kenyon wonders, "could Holiness be revealed to the artists of an age when the greatest of them put genius and imagination in the place of spiritual insight, and when, from the Pope downward, all Christendom was corrupt!"[846] Because of his failure to confess, Kenyon loses his sense of the transcendental dimension of art and beauty:

> In the chill of his disappointment, he suspected that it was a very cold art to which he had devoted himself. He questioned, at that moment, whether Sculpture really ever softens and warms the material which it handles; whether carved marble is anything but limestone, after all; and whether the Apollo Belvedere itself possesses any merit above its physical beauty or is beyond criticism even in that generally acknowledged excellence. In flitting glances, heretofore, he had seemed to behold this statue as something ethereal and godlike, but not now.[847]

Hawthorne could never transcend the angel/machine dichotomy that informed his rational psychology. He could not act, and as a result of his

---

[844] Hawthorne, *The Marble Faun*, p. 345.
[845] Hawthorne, *The Marble Faun*, p. 344.
[846] Hawthorne, *The Marble Faun*, p. 375.
[847] Hawthorne, *The Marble Faun*, p. 391.

Part II: The Romantic Rehabilitation of Nature

inaction he became a ghost, like the one Hamlet beheld when the native hue of resolution was sicklied o'er with the pale cast of thought. Unable to view art with the "eye of faith,"[848] Hawthorne begins to doubt its efficacy. If the viewer fails to look at beauty with the "eye of faith," "its highest excellence escapes you" because:

> There is always the necessity of helping out the painter's art with your own resources of sensibility and imagination. Not that these qualities shall really add anything to what the Master has effected; but they must be put so entirely under his control, and work along with him to such an extent, that, in a different mood, (when you are cold and critical, instead of sympathetic,) you will be apt to fancy that the loftier merits of the picture were of your own dreaming, not of his creating.[849]

Deprived of sensibility and imagination by the experience of evil, Hilda loses her appreciation of beauty and "became almost an infidel, and sometimes doubted whether the pictorial art be not altogether a delusion."[850] Art becomes "a delusion" perpetrated by "a school of Dutch conjurers," who like their "mighty" Italian counterparts have "substituted art instead of nature"[851] and deserve to die and have their art "buried along with them."[852]

But then, after attacking Italian artists for their sensuality and "terrible lack of variety in their subjects,"[853] Hawthorne takes it all back:

> But no sooner have we given expression to this irreverent criticism, than a throng of spiritual faces look reproachfully upon us. We see Cherubs, by Raphael, whose baby-innocence could only have been nursed in Paradise; Angels, by Raphael, as innocent as they, but whose serene intelligence embraces both earthly and celestial things; Madonnas, by Raphael, on whose lips he has impressed a holy and delicate reserve, implying sanctity on earth, and into whose soft eyes he has thrown a light which he never could have imagined, except by raising his own eyes with a pure aspiration heavenward. We remember, too, that Divinest countenance in the Transfiguration, and withdraw all that we have said.[854]

Once again Hawthorne can't make up his mind because, no matter what Keats said to the contrary, truth and beauty are at odds with each other in his aesthetic. "Hilda's despondency, nevertheless, while it dulled her perceptions

---

848 Hawthorne, *The Marble Faun*, p. 335.
849 Hawthorne, *The Marble Faun*, p. 335.
850 Hawthorne, *The Marble Faun*, pp. 335-6.
851 Hawthorne, *The Marble Faun*, p. 336.
852 Hawthorne, *The Marble Faun*, p. 336.
853 Hawthorne, *The Marble Faun*, p. 336.
854 Hawthorne, *The Marble Faun*, p. 338.

in one respect, had deepened them in another; she saw beauty less vividly, but felt truth, or the lack of it, more profoundly."[855]

Hawthorne's failed confession epitomized his inability to act, which as both Fichte and Emerson predicted, led him to question reality, which faded away into misty nothingness. It also led him to question the reality of the Catholic art which had led him to the confessional. Sacred art had become a "tremendous jest," which involved "offering the features of some venal beauty to be enshrined in the holiest places."[856] Hawthorne makes this claim unaware of the contradiction in the term "venal beauty." Fra Angelico took as one of his models a nun who became his mistress. In painting her portrait as a model for the Blessed Virgin, did he diminish her beauty? Or did her association with the Virgin enhance it? Hilda feels that "Fra Angelico . . . must have breathed a humble aspiration between every two touches of his brush, in order to have made the finished picture such a visible prayer as we behold it, in the guise of a prim Angel, or a Saint without the human nature."[857] Did Fra Angelico ennoble his model because he knew that sin could be forgiven? Did Hawthorne denigrate her beauty because he felt that it couldn't? Once sacramental confession becomes an impossible dream, too good to be true, the redeemed world that is Italy reverts to the New England forest where Young Goodman Brown learned that evil is the nature of mankind, and the innumerable portraits which inspired Rose to become a Catholic become in Hawthorne's mind, "no more than a polish upon the hard enamel of an artificial character."[858]

---

[855] Hawthorne, *The Marble Faun*, p. 338.
[856] Hawthorne, *The Marble Faun*, p. 338.
[857] Hawthorne, *The Marble Faun*, p. 339.
[858] Hawthorne, *The Marble Faun*, p. 339.

Chapter 24

Why Hawthorne was Melancholy

After Hilda/Hawthorne "had lavished her whole heart" upon the beauty of Italian art, his/her "perceptive faculty penetrated the canvas like a steel probe, and found but a crust of paint over an emptiness"[859] which bore uncanny resemblance to the Calvinist cosmology of Jonathan Edwards. Like Hawthorne, Hilda did not give up "all Art as worthless," but "it had lost its consecration."[860] At one point, Hawthorne tells us that the artist can portray what the theologian cannot explain, as evidenced by Sodoma, who "has done more towards reconciling the incongruity of Divine Omnipotence and outraged, suffering Humanity, combined in one person, than the theologians ever did."[861] Theoretically, Sodoma's "hallowed work of genius shows what pictorial art, devoutly exercised, might effect in behalf of religious truth; involving, as it does, deeper mysteries of Revelation, and bringing them closer to man's heart, and making him tenderer to be impressed by them, than the most eloquent words of preacher or prophet,"[862] but Sodoma's "hallowed work of genius" is the exception that proves the rule because Italian Catholic art has "strayed away from its legitimate paths and aims."[863] Instead, "it fails"[864] because its palaces were founded on "hardened guilt and a stony conscience."[865] As a result the "prince or cardinal" who paid for this art, has become a ghost condemned "to wander perpetually through these long suites of rooms, over the cold marble or mosaic of the floors, growing chiller at every eternal footstep."[866]

Hawthorne is that ghost. He became a prisoner of "hardened guilt and a stony conscience" because he had committed the unforgivable sin by refusing to avail himself of the sacramental confession which would have been his right if he had joined the Catholic Church. Once Hawthorne turned his back on

---

859 Hawthorne, *The Marble Faun*, p. 341.
860 Hawthorne, *The Marble Faun*, pp. 338-9.
861 Hawthorne, *The Marble Faun*, p. 340.
862 Hawthorne, *The Marble Faun*, p. 340.
863 Hawthorne, *The Marble Faun*, p. 340.
864 Hawthorne, *The Marble Faun*, p. 340.
865 Hawthorne, *The Marble Faun*, p. 340
866 Hawthorne, *The Marble Faun*, p. 341.

the Church, he understood that remaining in Rome had no point any longer and that it was time to return to New England. After failing to confess his sins, Hawthorne, like Hilda:

> began to be acquainted with the exile's pain. Her pictorial imagination brought up vivid scenes of her native village, with its great, old elm-trees, and the neat, comfortable houses, scattered along the wide grassy margin of its street, and the white meeting-house, and her mother's very door, and the stream of gold-brown water, which her taste for colour had kept flowing, all this while, through her remembrance. Oh, dreary streets, palaces, churches, and imperial sepulchers of hot and dusty Rome, with the muddy Tiber eddying through the midst, instead of the gold-brown rivulet! How she pined under this crumbly magnificence, as if it were piled all upon her human heart! How she yearned for that native homeliness, those familiar sights, those faces which she had known always, those days that never brought any strange event, that life of sober week-days, and a solemn Sabbath at the close![867]

Like Hilda, who longs to return to the vomit of Puritanism at the end of her stay in Rome, Hawthorne would learn in his own way the truth of what Emerson wrote in Nature when he claimed "Beauty in nature is not ultimate."

After finishing *The Marble Faun* in England, Hawthorne dragged his unforgivable sin back to New England, where he became once again Young Goodman Brown. "On the Sabbath day, when the congregation were singing a holy psalm, he could not listen because an anthem of sin rushed loudly upon his ear and drowned all the blessed strain."[868] In spite of being surrounded by family and friends who came to pay their last respects, Hawthorne's "dying hour was gloom."[869]

Even as a ten-year old, Rose found New England dreary after spending two years in Rome. Driving from the Concord train station to The Wayside, their new home, Rose "distinctly" remembers "the ugliness of the un-English landscape and the forlornness of the little cottage which was to be our home. Melancholy and stupid days immediately followed. . . ."[870] Rose noticed a change in her father "almost immediately." The deprivation of beauty which Rose felt had an even more marked effect on her father. "The first notes of the requiem about to envelop us" became apparent to everyone in the family as Hawthorne "from that year began to grow less and less vigorous."[871] In retrospect, Rose recognized:

---

867 Hawthorne, *The Marble Faun*, p. 342.
868 McMichael, *Concise Anthology*, p. 444.
869 McMichael, *Concise Anthology*, p. 444.
870 Lathrop, *Memories of Hawthorne*, p. 421.
871 Lathrop, *Memories of Hawthorne*, p. 433.

Part II: The Romantic Rehabilitation of Nature

many references in my mother's diaries and letters to my father's enforced monotony, and also to his gradually failing health, which, by the very instinct of loving alarm, we none of us analyzed as fatal; though, from his expression of face, if for no other reason, I judge he himself understood it perfectly. Death sat with him, at his right hand, long before he allowed his physical decline to change his mode of life. He tried to stem the tide setting against him, because it is the drowning man's part, even if hopeless.[872]

In his biography of Hawthorne, Turner talks about the "morbid state of mind" that Hawthorne exhibited upon his return to America.[873] Turner believes that in writing about his friend Herman Melville, Hawthorne was talking about himself. Hawthorne wrote that Melville:

> will never rest until he gets hold of a definite belief. It is strange how he persists—and has persisted ever since I knew him, and probably long before—in wandering to-and-fro over these deserts, as dismal and monotonous as the sand hills amid which we were sitting. He can neither believe, nor be comfortable in his unbelief; and he is too honest and courageous not to try to do one or the other. If he were a religious man, he would be one of the most truly religious and reverential; he has a very high and noble nature, and better worth immortality than most of us.[874]

Henry James thought that Hawthorne never stopped being "an intense American," who viewed Europe "from the standpoint of that little clod of Western earth which he carried about with him as the good Mohammedan carries the strip of carpet on which he kneels down to face towards Mecca."[875] James describes the last years of Hawthorne's life as "a period of dejection" which differed dramatically from "seven years of the happiest opportunities he was to have known"[876] which corresponded to the years preceding his return. Hawthorne's son-in-law George Lathrop claimed that "When he found himself once more on the old ground, with the old struggle for subsistence staring him in the face again, it is not difficult to conceive how a certain degree of depression would follow."[877]

After his return to Concord, Hawthorne had The Wayside renovated to include a tower, in which he sat waiting in vain for the return of the muse. Unable to finish any of the three manuscripts he started—*Septimius Fulton*,

---

872 Lathrop, *Memories of Hawthorne*, p. 433.
873 Arlin Turner, *Nathaniel Hawthorne, A Biography* (Oxford University Press, Printed in the United State, 1980), p. 306.
874 Turner, *Nathaniel Hawthorne*, p. 307.
875 James, *Hawthorne*, p. 135.
876 James, *Hawthorne*, p. 135.
877 James, *Hawthorne*, p. 136.

Dr. Grimshawe's Secret, and the *Doliver Romance*—Hawthorne suggested that his publisher issue a series of excuses:

> Say to the Public what you think best, and as little as possible;—for example—"We regret that Mr. Hawthorne's Romance, announced for this Magazine some months ago, still lies upon its author's writing-table; having been interrupted in his labor upon it by an impaired state of health."—or—"We are sorry to hear (but know not whether the Public will share our grief) that Mr. Hawthorne is out of health, and is thereby prevented, for the present, from proceeding with another of his promised (or threatened) Romances, intended for this Magazine"—or—"Mr. Hawthorne's brain is addled at last, and, much to our satisfaction, he tells us that he cannot possibly go on with the Romance announced on the cover of the Jan Magazine. We consider him finally shelved and shall take early occasion to bury him under a heavy article, carefully summing up his merits (such as they were) and his demerits, what few of them can be touched upon in our limited space."—or—"We shall commence the publication of Mr. Hawthorne's Romance as soon as that gentleman chooses to forward it. We are quite at a loss how to account for this delay in the fulfilment of his contract; especially as he has already been most liberally paid for the first number."[878]

Franklin Pierce said that "the seat of the disease was the brain or spine, or both."[879] Ignoring everything he said about *The Marble Faun*, James attributes Hawthorne's depression to the Civil War, which he characterizes as "not a propitious time for cultivating the muse":[880]

> The brightness of the outlook at home was not made greater by the explosion of the Civil War in the spring of 1861. These months, and the three years that followed them, were not a cheerful time for any persons but army-contractors; but over Hawthorne the war-cloud appears to have dropped a permanent shadow. The whole affair was a bitter disappointment to him, and a fatal blow to that happy faith in the uninterruptedness of American prosperity which I have spoken of as the religion of the old-fashioned American in general, and the old-fashioned Democrat in particular.[881]

James makes this claim even though the Civil War is hardly mentioned in either the private papers of Hawthorne or his wife, and not at all in *The Marble Faun*, his last completed work. Knowing her father better than Henry James, Rose claimed that "The thunderstorm of the war was not the only cause of his retiring more into himself than he had done in Europe, although

---

[878] Turner, *Nathaniel Hawthorne*, p. 385.
[879] Turner, *Nathaniel Hawthorne*, p. 390.
[880] James, *Hawthorne*, p. 136.
[881] James, *Hawthorne*, p. 136.

Part II: The Romantic Rehabilitation of Nature

he felt that sorrow heavily."[882] Rose also described his final days in Concord as a "long renunciation" after having "barely tasted the delights of London and Oxford completeness."[883] But Hawthorne attributed his malaise to the "effect of the Lassitudinous Roman Atmosphere."[884]

Something bigger than the Civil War happened to Hawthorne in Rome, and it was troubling him in a way that he described as "preternatural," as when he said, "There is something preternatural in my reluctance to begin." Hawthorne then adds cryptically, seemingly referring to his experience in St. Peter's Basilica: "I linger on the threshold and have a perception of very disagreeable phantoms to be encountered if I enter."[885]

Maynard claims that Hawthorne was suffering from "some secret malady,"[886] which he passed on to his children"[887] like some genetic disorder, and that it was only Rose who found "a complete cure"[888] for that malady, indicating that its cause was religious and its cure Catholicism. Maynard finds substantiation for his claim in Sophia's letters. Writing to her husband on July 25, 1861, Sophia exclaimed: "Of all the trials, this is the heaviest to me – to see you so apathetic, so indifferent, so hopeless, so unstrung. Rome has no sin to answer for so unpardonable as this of wrenching off your wings and hanging lead upon your arrowy feet. Rome – and all Rome caused to you."[889] Sophia could have been talking about Roman fever and its effects on Una, who nearly died of it, and Nathaniel, who did not come close to dying, but, as some indication that the root of Hawthorne's lassitude was spiritual, Maynard claims that he remained otherwise in "very good health,"[890] citing Rose's diagnosis that "None of us analyzed [it] as fatal; though from his expression of face, if for no other reason, I judge he himself understood it perfectly."[891] In diagnosing his inability to finish his last four works, Hawthorne described his malady as "preternatural" and himself as someone who continued to "linger on the threshold"[892] in what can be construed as oblique reference to Kenyon's reticence before the confessional.

Rose adds that "His state of mind seemed to be so causeless that he could almost believe that the witch's curse on that ancestor of his, the Salem judge,

---

882 Lathrop, *Memories of Hawthorne*, p. 456.
883 Lathrop, *Memories of Hawthorne*, p. 472.
884 Turner, *Nathaniel Hawthorne*, p. 375.
885 Maynard, *A Fire Was Lighted*, p. 130.
886 Maynard, *A Fire Was Lighted*, p. 51.
887 Maynard, *A Fire Was Lighted*, p. 51.
888 Maynard, *A Fire Was Lighted*, p. 51.
889 Maynard, *A Fire Was Lighted*, pp. 123-4.
890 Maynard, *A Fire Was Lighted*, p. 124.
891 Maynard, *A Fire Was Lighted*, pp. 123-4.
892 Maynard, *A Fire Was Lighted*, p. 130.

was now taking its strange and terrible effect."[893] Combining the testimony of Hawthorne's wife and daughter, Maynard concludes that Hawthorne's resistance to "the powerful force of Catholicism" had "given him a serious wound."[894] Hawthorne's inability to avail himself of sacramental confession had plunged him back into the Puritan world he had been trying to escape from since his earliest days as a writer. He now found himself predestined in the same way that the Pyncheon family found itself under an ancestral curse in *The House of the Seven Gables* because Calvinism is an accurate description of the predicament of those who belong to denominations that separated from the sacraments of the Catholic Church. The minister in the forest was right when he said:

> Depending upon one another's hearts, ye had still hoped that virtue were not all a dream. Now are ye undeceived. Evil is the nature of mankind. Evil must be your only happiness. Welcome again, my children to the communion of your race.[895]

"Welcome again" is the key phrase which must have occurred to Hawthorne when he returned to the Puritan forest after having rejected the only institution which could have allowed him to escape from it by forgiving his sins.

The best explication of Hawthorne's frame of mind upon his return to Concord can be found in the anecdote describing Memmius in *The Marble Faun*. During the four Americans' visit to the catacombs, Miriam encounters the figure, known as the model, who is the source of the mysterious "thralldom," which held her in bondage as if one end of the "iron chain" of necessity were held by the spectre's "ruthless hand."[896] This bond, which "must have been forged in some such unhallowed furnace as is only kindled by evil passions and fed by evil deeds,"[897] symbolizes the recurrence of the idea of predestination, which Hawthorne assumed that he had left behind in the forests of New England. Disabusing her of the notion that fate is escapable, the model tells Miriam that:

> Our fates cross and are entangled. The threads are twisted into a strong cord, which is dragging us to an evil doom. Could the knots be severed, we might escape. But neither can your slender fingers untie those knots, nor my masculine force break them. We must submit!"[898]

Influenced by Catholic art, Miriam tells the model to:

---

893 Maynard, *A Fire Was Lighted*, p. 125.
894 Maynard, *A Fire Was Lighted*, p. 123.
895 McMichael, *Concise Anthonly*, p. 443.
896 Hawthorne, *The Marble Faun*, p. 93.
897 Hawthorne, *The Marble Faun*, p. 93.
898 Hawthorne, *The Marble Faun*, p. 95.

Part II: The Romantic Rehabilitation of Nature

> "Pray for rescue, as I have! . . . Pray for deliverance from me, since I am your evil genius, as you are mine! Dark as your life has been, I have known you to pray, in times past!"[899]

But the spectre refuses to pray because he mistakes his will for "iron necessity."[900] The appearance of the model in the catacombs allows Hawthorne to introduce the legend of Memmius:

> This man, or demon, or Man Demon was a spy during the persecutions of the early Christians, probably under the emperor Diocletian, and penetrated into the Catacomb of Saint Calixtus, with the malignant purpose of tracing out the hiding places of the refugees. But, while he stole craftily through those dark corridors, he chanced to come upon a little chapel, where tapers were burning before an Altar and a Crucifix, and a priest was in performance of his sacred office. By Divine indulgence, there was a single moment's grace allowed to Memmius, during which, had he been capable of Christian faith and love, he might have knelt before the Cross, and received the holy light into his soul, and so have been blest forever. But he resisted the sacred impulse. As soon, therefore, as that one moment had glided by, the light of the consecrated tapers, which represent all truth, bewildered the wretched man with everlasting errour, and the blessed Cross itself was stamped as a seal upon his heart, so that it should never open to receive conviction.[901]

Like Memmius, Hawthorne "resisted the sacred impulse." And because of that resistance to grace, Hawthorne, like Memmius, became a ghost who:

> has haunted the wide and dreary precincts of the catacomb, seeking, as some say, to beguile new victims into his own misery, but, according to other statements, endeavouring to prevail on any unwary visitor to take him by the hand, and guide him out into the daylight. Should his wiles and entreaties take effect, however, the Man-Demon would remain only a little while above ground. He would gratify his fiendish malignity by perpetrating signal mischief on his benefactor, and perhaps bringing some old pestilence or other forgotten and long-buried evil on society—or, possibly, teaching the modem world some decayed and dusty kind of crime, which the antique Romans knew—and then would hasten back to the catacomb, which, after so long haunting it, has grown his most congenial home.[902]

In resisting the "sacred impulse," Hawthorne became a ghost long before he died. Watching her father depart on his last trip in this life, Rose wrote:

---

899 Hawthorne, *The Marble Faun*, p. 95.
900 Hawthorne, *The Marble Faun*, p. 96.
901 Hawthorne, *The Marble Faun*, pp. 32-3.
902 Hawthorne, *The Marble Faun*, p. 33.

"I cannot express how brave he seemed to me. The last time I saw him, he was leaving the house to take the journey for his health which led suddenly to the next world. . . . Like a snow image of an unbending but an old, old man, he stood for a moment gazing at me. My mother sobbed as she walked beside him to his carriage. We have missed him in the sunshine, in the storm, in the twilight, ever since."[903]

Nathaniel Hawthorne died early in the morning of May 19, 1864, in Plymouth, one day before Rose's thirteenth birthday. Four days later, James Freeman Clarke, the Unitarian minister "who had celebrated Nathaniel's marriage to Sophia twenty-two years earlier, officiated at his funeral in Sleepy Hollow Cemetery in Concord."[904] On the following day, The Boston *Journal* wrote that "such a convocation of mourners. . . is seldom gathered to the obsequies of an American citizen."[905] Ever the man to project his groundless, sunny optimism on the funeral of a man "whose dying hour was gloom," Emerson wrote to Holmes that "The sun shone brightly, and the air was sweet and pleasant, as if death had never entered the world."[906] On May 24, 1864, Emerson wrote in his journal:

> we buried Hawthorne in Sleepy Hollow, in a pomp of sunshine & verdure, & gentle winds. James F. Clarke read the service in the Church & at the grave. Longfellow, Lowell, Holmes, Agassiz, Hoar, Dwight, Whipple, Norton, Alcott, Hillard, Fields, Judge Thomas, & I, attended the hearse as pall bearers. Franklin Pierce was with the family. The church was copiously decorated with white flowers delicately arranged. The corpse was unwillingly shown—only a few moments to this company of his friends. But it was noble & serene in its aspect—nothing amiss—a calm & powerful head. A large company filled the church, & the grounds of the cemetery was so bright & quiet, that pain or mourning was hardly suggested, & Holmes said to me, that it looked like a happy meeting. Clarke in the church said, that Hawthorne had done more justice than any other to the shades of life, shown a sympathy with the crime in our nature, &, like Jesus, was the friend of sinners. I thought there was a tragic element in the event, that might be more fully rendered—in the painful solitude of the man—which, I suppose, could not longer be endured, & he died of it.[907]

Unlike the rope Thoreau used to reach the bottom of Walden Pond, Emerson's line wasn't long enough to plumb Hawthorne's depths. Nonetheless, Emerson "thought him a greater man than any of his works betray" and hoped one day

---

903 Valenti, *To Myself a Stranger*, p. 31.
904 Valenti, *To Myself a Stranger*, p. 31.
905 Turner, *Nathaniel Hawthorne*, p. 392.
906 Turner, *Nathaniel Hawthorne*, p. 392.
907 Porte, *Emerson in His Journals*, pp. 521-2.

Part II: The Romantic Rehabilitation of Nature

to overcome his "willingness & caprice" and "become a friend with whom he might have shared habits of unreserved intercourse," but alas it was not to be. Emerson conceded that it was easy to talk to Hawthorne, so easy in fact that Emerson "talked too much" because "he showed no egotism or self-assertion, rather a humility, &, at one time, a fear that he had written himself out. One day, when I found him on the top of his hill, in the woods, he paced back the path to his house, & said, *"this path is the only remembrance of me that will remain."* "Now it appears," Emerson concluded sadly, "that I waited too long.[908]

As if to note the suppressed feeling of gloom that pervaded Hawthorne's funeral, Holmes mentions that the manuscript of Hawthorne's unfinished Dolliver Romance was placed on his coffin as a reluctant *memento mori*.[909] Hawthorne's son Julian later recalled that the entire pantheon of New England literature, along with a former president of the United States—Longfellow, Holmes, Whittier, Lowell, Pierce, Emerson—stood with uncovered heads as Hawthorne's body passed them by on its way to the grave.[910] Less sanguine than Emerson, Longfellow mentioned the mystery which surrounded the unfinished manuscript as it accompanied Hawthorne to his grave in his poetic final farewell:

Ah! who shall lift that wand of magic power,
And the lost clew regain?
The unfinished window in Aladdin's tower
Unfinished must remain.[911]

---

908 Porte, *Emerson in His Journals*, p. 522.
909 Turner, *Nathaniel Hawthorne*, p. 392.
910 Turner, *Nathaniel Hawthorne*, p. 393.
911 Turner, *Nathaniel Hawthorne*, p. 393.

CHAPTER 25

ANTHONY COMSTOCK'S REFORM OF WAR-RAVAGED SEXUAL MORALITY

Samuel Huntington based his claim that the Civil War created a "national consciousness," largely on Emerson's articulation of the issue:

> The Civil War, James Russell Lowell said as it concluded, was "costly stuff whereof to make a nation!" But make a nation it did. The American nation was born in the war and came into its full being in the decades after the war. So also did American nationalism, patriotism, and the unqualified identification of Americans with their country. American patriotism before the war, Ralph Waldo Emerson observed, had been a sometime, summertime thing. The "deaths of thousands and the determination of millions of men and women" in the war, however, showed that American patriotism now "is real." Before the war Americans and others referred to their country in the plural: "These United States are ..." After the war they used the singular. The Civil War, Woodrow Wilson said in his 1915 Memorial Day address, "created in this country what had never existed before—a national consciousness."[912]

The American Civil War had a devastating effect on sexual morality. Anthony Comstock experienced this firsthand as a soldier in the 17th Connecticut regiment. "As the 1870s began, it seemed that Americans had too much liberty and that freedom had invited corruption, just as the Calvinists warned."[913] The Civil War led to a precipitous drop in sexual morality:

> Before the war it was estimated that there was one prostitute for every sixty-four men in New York, and the disruptions of the Rebellion vastly increased their numbers and visibility. In 1868 the city was home to an estimated twenty thousand prostitutes and six hundred bawdy houses, many helpfully listed in *A Gentleman's Guide* for tourists. Venereal disease was rampant, with philandering husbands often infecting their faithful wives, and abortionists openly advertised their services in the city papers.

---

912 Huntington, *Who Are We?*, p. 119.
913 Applegate, *The Most Famous Man in America*, Kindle, p. 390.

E. MICHAEL JONES • 265

People were beginning to acknowledge sexuality as not only a matter of public morals but of public health.[914]

It was his experience as a Civil War soldier in army camps awash with obscene material which turned Anthony Comstock into a crusader against pornography, birth control, and abortion. As a soldier who served in Company H, of the 17th Connecticut Infantry, Comstock was exposed to obscene material and refused to join in with "the sin and wickedness"[915] of the other soldiers, but there was little he could do to stop them. Understanding Comstock's concern about declining sexual morality then is virtually impossible now because that decline has continued to the point of total collapse, at least in public utterance, and Applegate's take on Henry Ward Beecher is no exception to that rule:

> But attempts to address the situation were shut down by the ironclad double standard that ruled Victorian America. Those who called for more liberal divorce laws, controlling childbirth, or better sex education were accused of promoting "free love," a dangerous variant of "free thought."[916]

Pornography is always a function of technology. "By the 1860s, several American wholesalers had built a successful network of domestically produced and distributed erotica."[917] By the beginning of the Civil War, "the domestic trade in pornography was well established, and entrepreneurial publishers/ dealers were posed to take advantage of the war's particular circumstances and new technologies and mediums."[918] Hundreds of thousands of soldiers were languishing in their barracks, and the invention of photography combined with railroad cars that functioned as post offices on wheels created a booming business in mail order pornography. "By the 1860s, several American wholesalers had built a successful network of domestically produced and distributed erotica."[919] In August 1861, an anonymous soldier wrote to a Philadelphia newspaper, complaining about men "reading flimsy publications, obscene books, and the worst species of yellow-covered literature," turning their minds into "dingy cloisters, filled with cobwebs and the death-damps of groveling desires."[920]

New York City was the center of the pornography industry, and Thomas Ormsby, a New York City book dealer who opened shop on Nassau Street in 1851, was one of its principal agents. Police arrested Ormsby three times in the

---

914 Applegate, *The Most Famous Man in America*, pp. 384-5.
915 Judith Giesberg, *Sex and the Civil War: Soldiers, Pornography, and the Making of American Morality*, Kindle, p. 68.
916 Applegate, *The Most Famous Man in America*, pp. 384-5.
917 Giesberg, *Sex and the Civil War*, p. 17.
918 Giesberg, *Sex and the Civil War*, p. 31.
919 Giesberg, *Sex and the Civil War*, p. 17.
920 Giesberg, *Sex and the Civil War*, p. 24.

Part II: The Romantic Rehabilitation of Nature

1850s for selling obscene material in his store, but the police could keep up with neither production nor demand, as indicated by the fact that the number of ads for mail order pornography tripled between the war years of 1862 and 1864.

Alarmed by the amount of pornography in army camps, Postmaster William Dennison told the Senate's Post Office Committee that "our mails are made the vehicle for the conveyance of great numbers and quantities of obscene books and pictures."[921] Alarmed by what he heard from Dennison, Abraham Lincoln signed a law on March 3, 1865, that allowed postal officials to "seize and destroy" obscene photos and publications discovered in the mail.[922] First class mail, however, was exempt from the new restrictions, which meant that producers of pornography like Ormsby could continue to send obscene material through the mails if they shipped their products in first-class sealed envelopes.[923]

In 1867 Comstock moved to New York City, where he worked at various businesses including the Young Men's Christian Association. Comstock's collaboration with the YMCA led New York to ban pornography in 1868 and to strengthen that ban in 1869 and in 1872, the year that the YMCA's Committee for the Suppression of Vice decided to press for a federal law banning the distribution of obscene material.[924] On March 5, 1873, Comstock was appointed a special agent of the U.S. Postal Service and remained in that position until January 1907."[925] According to Giesberg's tendentious account, Comstock "burst onto the scene in 1872, one year after New York passed a strict anti-obscenity law, and within months was given virtually unlimited authority under federal law to police the nation's morals by controlling not only what got into the mails but also what people wrote about sex and what they did."[926]

In his first year of antipornography work, Comstock claimed to have destroyed more than 182,000 obscene photographs, stereoscopic and other pictures, more than five tons of obscene books and pamphlets, more that two tons of obscene songs, catalogues, and handbills, as well as equal amounts of various forms of obscene paraphernalia.[927] As some indication that he saw

---

921 Elizabeth A., "For the Sporting Man: A concise history of mail order erotica in the Civil War," Military Images Digital, February 29, 2024, https://www.militaryimagesmagazine-digital.com/2024/02/29/for-the-sporting-man-a-concise-history-of-mail-order-erotica-in-the-civil-war/

922 Elizabeth A., "For the Sporting Man."

923 Elizabeth A., "For the Sporting Man."

924 Giesberg, *Sex and the Civil War*, p. 92.

925 "Anthony Comstock," *Wikipedia: The Free Encyclopedia*, https://en.wikipedia.org/wiki/Anthony_Comstock

926 Giesberg, *Sex and the Civil War*, p. 2.

927 Guisberg, *Sex and the Civil War*, pp. 92-3.

obscene material a threat to public morals, President Ulysses Grant signed the New York Comstock Act into federal law on March 3, 1873, in a move that kept Comstock laws banning pornography, contraception and abortion on the books, "well into the 20th century."[928]

---

928 Guisberg, *Sex and the Civil War*, p. 97.

Chapter 26

Henry Ward Beecher
Dimmesdale Redivivus

In March 1865 Henry Ward Beecher reached the pinnacle of his fame when Abraham Lincoln asked him to preach a sermon at Fort Sumter commemorating the end of the Civil War. Like Comstock, Beecher was concerned about the spread of pornography during the Civil War and warned young men about "evil books" and "evil pictures" which when "read nightly" created "salacious thoughts."[929]

In addition to sending rifles in boxes marked "Beecher's Bibles" to abolitionists in Kansas, Beecher had delivered a series of lectures in England in 1863 which swayed public opinion in favor of the North and prevented England from entering the war on the side of the South.[930] In choosing Beecher to give the speech, Lincoln said, "We had better send Beecher down to deliver the address on the occasion of the raising of the flag because if it had not been for Beecher there would have been no flag to raise."[931]

Henry Ward Beecher was born on June 24, 1813 in Litchfield, Connecticut, the son of Lyman Beecher, "the last great Puritan minister in America."[932] Later in life, Henry would say of the religious training that he had imbibed from his Calvinist father, "I do not recollect," that "one word had been said to me, or one syllable had been uttered in the pulpit, that led me to think there was any mercy in the heart of God for a sinner like me."[933] Later still, and more tellingly, Beecher recounted that "I supposed myself to be a sinner in the very fact that I did not feel sinful."[934]

Lyman rightly understood that the rise of the West, which began in earnest with the opening of the Erie Canal in 1825, spelled the end of Calvinist

---

929 Turner, p. 45.
930 Turner, p. 6.
931 Turner, p. 6.
932 Turner, p. 7.
933 Debby Applegate, *The Most Famous Man in America: The Biography of Henry Ward Beecher* (Random House Publishing Group), Kindle Edition, p. 13.
934 Turner, p. 43.

orthodoxy's hegemony over American culture and the rise of New York because the canal became "a highway for a new migration."[935] The men of the "western waters":

> broke with the old order of things, subordinated social restraint to the freedom of the individual, won their title to the rich lands which they entered by hard fighting against the Indians, hotly challenged the right of the East to rule them, demanded their own States, and would not be refused, spoke with contempt of the old social order of ranks and classes in the lands between the Alleghanies and the Atlantic, and proclaimed the ideal of democracy for the vast country which they had entered.[936]

These frontiersmen were "the ancestors of Boone, Andrew Jackson, Calhoun, Clay, and Lincoln. Washington and Jefferson were profoundly affected by these frontier conditions. The forest clearings have been the seed plots of American character."[937] Jackson was the "very personification" of the man of the West:

> He was born in the backwoods of the Carolinas in the midst of the turbulent democracy that preceded the Revolution, and he grew up in the frontier State of Tennessee. In the midst of this region of personal feuds and frontier ideals of law, he quickly rose to leadership. The appearance of this frontiersman on the floor of Congress was an omen full of significance. He reached Philadelphia at the close of Washington's administration, having ridden on horseback nearly eight hundred miles to his destination. Gallatin, himself a Western man, describes Jackson as he entered the halls of Congress: "A tall, lank, uncouth-looking personage, with long locks of hair hanging over his face and a cue down his back tied in an eel-skin; his dress singular; his manners those of a rough backwoodsman." And Jefferson testified: "When I was President of the Senate he was a Senator, and he could never speak on account of the rashness of his feelings. I have seen him attempt it repeatedly and as often choke with rage." At last the frontier in the person of its typical man had found a place in the Government. This six-foot backwoodsman, with blue eyes that could blaze on occasion, this choleric, impetuous, self-willed Scotch-Irish leader of men, this expert duelist, and ready fighter, this embodiment of the tenacious, vehement, personal West, was in politics to stay. The frontier democracy of that time had the instincts of the clansman in the days of Scotch border warfare. Vehement and tenacious as the democracy was, strenuously as each man contended with his neighbor for the spoils of the new country that opened before them, they all had respect for the man who best expressed their aspirations and

---

935 Turner, p. 50.
936 Turner, p. 65.
937 Applegate, *Beecher*, p. 72.

Part II: The Romantic Rehabilitation of Nature

their ideas. Every community had its hero. In the War of 1812 and the subsequent Indian fighting Jackson made good his claim, not only to the loyalty of the people of Tennessee, but of the whole West, and even of the nation. He had the essential traits of the Kentucky and Tennessee frontier. It was a frontier free from the influence of European ideas and institutions. The men of the "Western World" turned their backs upon the Atlantic Ocean, and with a grim energy and self-reliance began to build up a society free from the dominance of ancient forms.[938]

Andrew Jackson inaugurated "the era of the popular hero," by preaching the religion of the West to:

European men, institutions, and ideas [who] were lodged in the American wilderness, and this great American West took them to her bosom, taught them a new way of looking upon the destiny of the common man, trained them in adaptation to the conditions of the New World, to the creation of new institutions to meet new needs; and ever as society on her eastern border grew to resemble the Old World in its social forms and its industry, ever, as it began to lose faith in the ideals of democracy, she opened new provinces, and dowered new democracies in her most distant domains with her material treasures and with the ennobling influence that the fierce love of freedom, the strength that came from hewing out a home, making a school and a church, and creating a higher future for his family, furnished to the pioneer.[939]

Lyman Beecher was one of the men of the east who noticed how Andrew Jackson's "fierce Tennessee spirit"[940] affected religious observance. Sensing that change was inevitable as essence met existence at the frontier line, Lyman decided to join the "adventurous young men, landless farmers, and impoverished immigrants"[941] and fight for their souls as soon as possible because the "Catholics and infidels" who had already settled there "have got the start of us."[942] As early as 1835, Lyman Beecher had declared: "It is equally plain that the religious and political destiny of our nation is to be decided in the West. . . . "[943] and urged his son Henry to make sure that Calvinism gained a foothold on the frontier by accepting a position as pastor of a small congregation in Indiana.

During his tenure as pastor in Boston, Lyman Beecher had gained the reputation as a notorious anti-Catholic bigot. On August 11, 1834, just as Henry was setting for Cincinnati to begin his career as an apostle to the

---

938 Turner, p. 87.
939 Turner, p. 92.
940 Turner, p. 92.
941 Turner, p. 88.
942 Turner, p. 88
943 Turner, p. 12.

West, a nativist mob burned down the Ursuline convent in Charlestown, and Lyman was excoriated in the national press for delivering a series of anti-Catholic sermons in Boston which were seen as the proximate cause of the arson attack.

Henry Ward Beecher got his first taste of the West when he arrived in Cincinnati, "the literary capital of the Mississippi Valley, boasting an impressive array of newspapers, magazines, print shops, and literary clubs,"[944] Henry followed Lyman's example by attacking Catholicism in a series of articles which "recapitulated his father's views."[945]

During the ten years Henry and Eunice had spent in the fever swamps of Indiana, where both of them contracted malaria, Henry had adopted the Methodist style of preaching which came into being after Protestantism had made contact with the frontier and he had become in his own words, "a Western man."[946] The great turning point in Henry's life arrived during a religious experience that revealed that God loved him. Breaking with the Calvinism of his father, Henry learned from the West that "God's nature was parental, not governmental; medicinal, not punitive; and salvation came from love rather than obedience to the law."[947]

A new American identity was emerging out of the crucible of the West; Henry Ward Beecher's conversion to the religion of love corresponded in time and thought with Emerson's American Scholar Address, which Oliver Wendell Holmes referred to as America's "Intellectual Declaration of Independence" because it called for a new American man who rejects the "timid, imitative, tame" attitude of their Puritan forebears and espouses what Emerson would eventually call "self-reliance."[948] According to Applegate: "What Emerson called 'self-reliance' Henry called 'the great law of Liberty.'" "Liberty," Henry claimed, "is the breath of the soul."[949] Nonetheless, Beecher was careful to cover his tracks while purloining Emerson's ideas:

> Years later, when the two men sat eating lunch together, he asked Emerson, "Do you think a man eating these meats could tell what grasses the animals fed on?" No, replied Emerson. "I'm glad to hear it," Henry said jovially, "for I've been feeding on you for a long time and I'm glad my people don't know it."[950]

Even more scandalously, Beecher also stole ideas from Walt Whitman, the notorious author of the homoerotic poetry collection *Leaves of Grass*, who

---

944 Applegate, *Beecher*, p. 124.
945 Applegate, *Beecher*, p. 124.
946 Applegate, *Beecher*, p. 185.
947 Applegate, *Beecher*, p. 134.
948 Applegate, *Beecher*, p. 135.
949 Applegate, *Beecher*, p. 273.
950 Applegate, *Beecher*, p. 274.

Part II: The Romantic Rehabilitation of Nature

became an early admirer of Beecher when he first heard him preach in 1849. After Whitman gave Beecher a first edition of *Leaves of Grass*, he became convinced that the preacher "stole terrifically from it."[951] After hearing one of Beecher's sermons, a friend of Whitman stopped him on the street and said, "his whole sermon was you, you, you, from top to toe."[952]

Beecher would take this new "western" American identity back east with him when he received the call from "a number of wealthy businessmen"[953] to become pastor of what would eventually become the Pilgrim Church in Brooklyn in 1847. Encouraged by the Tappan Brothers, who were committed to "combining principle with profit" or "philanthropy plus 5%," Henry abandoned "the iron cage of orthodoxy" which "had evaporated out West,"[954] and confected a new version of Christianity more compatible with the entrepreneurial boom town that Brooklyn had become after the opening of the Erie Canal:

> New York was booming. Businessmen cited the statistics with glee. Between 1851 and 1854, $175 million in gold came from San Francisco to New York. In nearly the same period the number of banks doubled, as did the value of the city's imports and exports. With more cash flowed more credit, and easy credit fueled an avalanche of shipbuilding, light manufacturing, housing construction, and railroads. The railroad-building boom consolidated New York's position as the commercial capital of the country (and made possible Henry's own lucrative lecturing career). More than 60 percent of New York's population had been born somewhere else, and this influx of labor was as crucial as the influx of cash. This tremendous diversity gave New York a cosmopolitanism and creativity that existed nowhere else in the country.[955]

After his arrival in Brooklyn, Henry answered theological questions based on "his practical experience in the West."[956] Beecher was now determined to make "Freedom from stifling social conventions . . . the cornerstone of his new ministry."[957] Unfortunately, as soon as he liberated himself from the prison house of Calvinism, Beecher found it impossible to control his sexual desires. At this point he embarked on a trajectory predicted by both Nathaniel Hawthorne in *The Scarlet Letter* by becoming a latter-day Dimmesdale who committed adultery with numerous wives of members of his congregation, and by Orestes Brownson, who said that chastity among Protestants was

---

951 Applegate, *Beecher*, p. 275.
952 Applegate, *Beecher*, p. 275.
953 Applegate, *Beecher*, p. 193.
954 Applegate, *Beecher*, p. 208.
955 Applegate, *Beecher*, p. 265.
956 Applegate, *Beecher*, p. 208.
957 Applegate, *Beecher*, p. 206.

impossible because of their rejection of the sanctifying grace which was only available through the sacraments of the Catholic Church.

In April of 1858, the same year that Hawthorne arrived in Rome and one year after the publication of Brownson's conversion story, an article appeared in the *Brooklyn Eagle* accusing Beecher of seducing the wife of a member of his congregation. Beecher's seduction of Chloe Beach took place two years after his affair with Edna Dean Proctor, a young woman he had hired to turn his sermons into a book. According to Miss Proctor's account, Beecher called on her at the mansion of Henry Bowen, Beecher's publisher, "sometime in late 1856 or early 1857, when the rest of the family was gone."[958] After receiving what he later described as "a paroxysmal kiss" from Proctor, Beecher took her in his arms, threw her down upon a sofa, and raped her. Proctor rushed out of the room but returned "covered with blood," leading Bowen to conclude that Beecher had engaged in "the rape of a virgin." Beecher never denied that he had had sexual relations with Proctor but maintained that they had been consensual, a claim which Bowen corroborated when he claimed that "for more than a year" after their first encounter, Beecher and Proctor "had sex frequently, in both her house and Beecher's, and in his study at Plymouth Church, usually after the morning prayer meetings were over. He gave her a key to the study, telling her to go in, lock the door, and not open it to anyone until he gave the special signal."[959]

Understandably, rumors spread about Beecher's affairs, and soon his sermons began to sound like "a series of secret confessions—as if he were *The Scarlet Letter*'s Reverend Dimmesdale come to life."[960] Beecher's homilies became one long cautionary tale about what had happened to Protestantism after the reformers broke with the Catholic Church and rejected sacramental confession. In the wake of that break, "every man is living two lives—and external one and an internal one."[961] In an irony which he failed to notice because his mind was darkened by lust, Beecher was proclaiming the gospel of Jonathan Edwards and Lyman Beecher. In the absence of sacramental grace, man was both depraved and predestined to continue in that evil to damnation. Unregenerate men had, as Jonathan Edwards put it his most famous sermon, "nothing to stand on." In his homilies, Beecher, like Dimmesdale, gave cryptic descriptions of the state of his soul when he referred to a vague "they," who try to cover up their guilt and get rid of it:

> but are conscious that there still remains that same weakness. And though a man may say to himself a hundred times, "I have forsaken the wrong, I will cover it up for evermore," there it is, down at the bottom

---

[958] Applegate, *Beecher*, p. 302.

[959] Applegate, *Beecher*, p. 302.

[960] Applegate, *Beecher*, p. 303.

[961] Applegate, *Beecher*, p. 303.

Part II: The Romantic Rehabilitation of Nature

of his heart. He knows that when the same circumstances, the same pressures with temptation, come again, he will promise the same course of wickedness."[962]

Rumors of Beecher's sexual involvement with women in his congregation continued to muddy the waters of his ever-growing fame. On January 31, 1867, Chloe Beach, wife of Moses Beach, a member of Beecher's congregation and publisher of the New York newspaper *The Sun*, gave birth to a daughter she named Violet, who as she grew older came to resemble Beecher more and more. Beecher went out of his way to ensure that posterity would see these resemblances by taking the unusual step for that day of having a photo taken of both of them together.

---

962 Applegate, *Beecher*, p. 303.

Chapter 27

Samuel Clemens: Beecher's Innocent

In January 1867, shortly before the birth of Violet Beach, a 31-year-old writer named Samuel Clemens arrived in New York and quickly found his niche among "the bohemian journalists swarming the city." Clemens, who took the pen name Mark Twain based on his experience as a pilot on Mississippi riverboats, had first visited New York in 1853. When Clemens returned in 1867, he was struck by the state of moral decline which characterized the booming gateway to the American West:

> Even women on the street looked racier as the wide-hooped crinoline dresses of the fifties were replaced by form-fitting ankle-length dresses that, as Twain noted with approval, exposed "the restless little feet. Charming, fascinating, seductive, bewitching!" Frank as this new generation of New Yorkers was about sex, they were even more blunt about money. "The old, genuine, traveled, cultivated, pedigreed aristocracy of New York, stand stunned and helpless under the new order of things," observed Twain. "They find themselves supplanted by upstart princes of the Shoddy and vulgar and with unknown grandfathers. The incomes which were something for the common herd to gape at and gossip about once, are mere livelihoods now—would not pay Shoddy's house-rent." If things get much worse, Twain concluded, "I fear I shall have to start a moral missionary society here."[963]

Orestes Brownson sensed the same odor of moral decline when he reviewed Beecher's novel *Norwood* when it appeared in 1868: "The author, though nominally a Christian, professedly a Congregational preacher, is really a pagan, and wishes to abolish Puritanism for the worship of nature," wrote Orestes Brownson in the *Catholic World*. "Beecherism," Brownson concluded with genuine anger, "resolves the Christian law of perfection into the natural laws of the physicists."[964] Making use of Brownson's neologism, *The Brooklyn Eagle* claimed that "Beecherism—or the higher law means merely that each

---

[963] Applegate, *Beecher*, p. 371.
[964] Applegate, *Beecher*, p. 377.

man is to believe and do in all things about as he feels like doing, regardless of all recognized moral codes or legal provisions."[965]

After savoring a Broadway show titled *The Black Crook*, which featured "70 beauties arrayed in dazzling half-costumes; and displaying all possible compromises between nakedness and decency,"[966] Clemens took a "frigid ferry ride" across the East River in order to attend a prayer service conducted by Rev. Beecher at his Pilgrim Church in Brooklyn. There, squeezed into a seat the size of a "spittoon," he watched as Beecher:

> went marching up and down the stage, sawing his arms in the air, howling sarcasms this way and that, discharging rockets of poetry, and exploding mines of eloquence, halting now and then to stamp his foot three times in succession to emphasize a point, I could have started the audience with a single clap of the hands and brought down the house. I had a suffocating desire to do it. Mr. Beecher is a remarkably handsome man when he is in the full tide of sermonizing, and his face is lit up with animation, but he is as homely as a singed cat when he isn't doing anything."[967]

While at the Pilgrim Church, Mark Twain learned that Rev. Beecher was planning a luxury cruise to the Holy Land with stops at Europe along the way for the exorbitant price of $1,250. After wrangling that sum from a willing publisher, Clemens embarked upon the voyage which would provide the basis for his best seller *The Innocents Abroad*, an "exotic travelogue," which soon turned into "a biting satire of his sanctimonious shipmates, with their daily prayer meetings, petty prejudices, and shipboard bans on dancing and other sins."[968]

At this point in his life, Mark Twain referred to himself as a Presbyterian, a sect, so the story goes, which opposed fornication because it led to dancing. But Rev. Beecher had sins other than dancing on his mind, and Twain was willing to cover up Beecher's sins to foster his literary career. In *The Innocents Abroad*, Twain wrote that "Reverend Henry Ward Beecher was to have accompanied the expedition, but urgent duties obliged him to give up the idea."[969] The only urgent duty on Rev. Beecher's mind in the winter of 1867 was visiting his lover Chloe Beach and the daughter she had just borne him. Chloe's husband Moses left on the cruise without her, opening the field for Beecher, who had unhindered access to Beach's wife. While on that cruise, Mark Twain "took a special shine" to Beach's 17-year-old daughter, who became "his regular chess partner."[970] Mark Twain "continued his flirtation with Emma Beach"

---

965 Applegate, *Beecher*, p. 389.
966 Applegate, *Beecher*, p. 371.
967 Applegate, *Beecher*, p. 372.
968 Applegate, *Beecher*, p. 373.
969 Twain, *Innocents*, p. 98.
970 Applegate, *Beecher*, p. 374.

Part II: The Romantic Rehabilitation of Nature

through the fall of 1867 after their return to New York. At this point, Moses Beach realized that the cruise on the *Quaker City* had been "a grave mistake" because "during all this time," he later told Beecher, "you have been stealing the affections of one dearer to me than life itself."[971] Applegate tells us that:

> There is no sign that Moses ever sent this anguished letter. If he did, it had little effect. After Violet was born, Chloe became, essentially, a second, unofficial wife to Henry, especially now that Eunice spent half the year in Peekskill and would soon begin wintering in Florida. Indeed, Eunice depended upon Mrs. Beach almost as much as her husband did.[972]

Nothing epitomized the decline of literary culture in the Gilded Age following the Civil War better than the rise of Mark Twain as America's premier literary figure. Clemens was the quintessential man of the West. His stock in trade was humorous journalism, along with "drinking, smoking, and swearing,"[973] and greeting everything that rose above the level of culture he found in California mining camps with ridicule, sarcasm, and contempt. Clemens rose to prominence by ridiculing his literary forebears, in the manner of Huckleberry Finn, the protagonist of his most famous novel. Huck was the classic American naif confronted by two equally repugnant alternatives symbolized by Pap, the unregenerate man of the west, whom "a body would have thought . . . was Adam" because "he was just all mud"[974] and the Widow Douglas, the lady who tried to "sivilize" him by putting him back into the recently discarded Calvinist straitjacket. Mark Twain could not have created a paradigm of American identity like Huckleberry Finn without the assistance of James Fenimore Cooper, who blazed the path for every American writer of the 19th century by creating Natty Bumppo. Instead of thanking Cooper, Clemens, like the dog who barks at everything he doesn't understand, ridiculed him in his essay "James Fenimore Cooper's Literary Offenses."

The decline in morality which followed the Civil War had a similarly devastating effect on high culture. Cooper's literary reputation had sunk so low by the 1880s, that Mark Twain felt that he could finish him off with a piece of "buffoonery" that "lay not in his aesthetic principles or practical analysis of Cooper but rather in the deeper deviltry of his wit," which was "critically specious yet wholly unanswerable,"[975] even though "the spiritual father of Huck Finn was none other than Natty Bumppo—a "demotic Euro-

---

971 Applegate, *Beecher*, p. 375.
972 Applegate, *Beecher*, p. 376.
973 Applegate, *Beecher*, p. 371.
974 Samuel Langhorne Clemens, *Adventures of Huckleberry Finn* (New York: W.W. Norton & Company, 1961), p. 26.
975 Franklin, *James Fenimore Cooper*, p. xxii.

Walking with a Bible and a Gun

American hero who resists the confines of 'sivilization' and, with a member of another race as his companion, finds his freedom in nature."[976]

After his gratuitous attempt to "hunt down and kill Natty's own progenitor,"[977] Mark Twain mounted a similar attack on the School Room poets. On December 17, 1877, William Dean Howells, editor of *The Atlantic Monthly*, invited "the whole literary establishment of America," including Ralph Waldo Emerson, Henry Wadsworth Longfellow, Oliver Wendell Holmes, Thomas Wentworth Higginson, Charles Eliot Norton and dozens of lesser literary figures to the Brunswick Hotel in Boston, where they gathered to celebrate the 70th birthday of the distinguished and beloved poet John Greenleaf Whittier.[978] Howells introduced Clemens as "a humorist who never makes you blush to have enjoyed his joke; whose generous wit has no meanness in it, whose fun is never at the cost of anything honestly high and good, but comes from the soundest of hearts and the clearest of heads."[979]

Determined to prove Howells wrong, Mark Twain launched into a stand-up comic routine which began by portraying Ralph Waldo Emerson, Henry Wadsworth Longfellow, and Oliver Wendell Holmes as a bunch of whiskey guzzling card cheats who get into a fight in a California mining camp. Mark Twain's attempt at humor went downhill from there; describing Emerson as "a seedy little bit of a chap—red headed" and Holmes "as fat as a balloon" who "weighed 300" pounds and "had double chins all the way down to his stomach," he then compared Longfellow to "a prizefighter" whose head was "cropped and bristly—like as if he had a wig made of hairbrushes. His nose lay straight down his face, like a finger, with the end joint tilted up."[980] In his poem "A Psalm of Life," Longfellow had claimed that "Life is earnest!" It was a claim that "a humorist" like Mark Twain found repugnant, and he was determined to tell the generation of writers who preceded him and the coarsening of American life after the Civil War exactly how he felt.

By the middle of his talk, Mark Twain realized that no one thought his speech was funny. Habituated to mockery and sarcasm, Mark Twain had completely misjudged his audience, whose faces, he later recounted, "turned to a sort of black frost. I wondered what the trouble was. I went on, but with difficulty ... always hoping – but with a gradually perishing hope –

---

976 Franklin, *James Fenimore Cooper*, p. xxii.

977 Franklin, *James Fenimore Cooper*, p. xxii.

978 Albert B. Southwick, "The Night Mark Twain Scandalized Massachusetts," telegram.com, Aug. 27, 2006, https://www.telegram.com/story/news/local/worcester/2006/08/27/the-night-mark-twain-scandalized/53057958007/

979 Southwick, "The Night Mark Twain Scandalized Massachusetts," telegram.com, Aug. 27, 2006, https://www.telegram.com/story/news/local/worcester/2006/08/27/the-night-mark-twain-scandalized/53057958007/

980 Southwick, "The Night Mark Twain Scandalized Massachusetts," telegram.com.

Part II: The Romantic Rehabilitation of Nature

that somebody would laugh, or at least smile, but nobody did."[981] Howells later confided to a friend that Clemens "felt the awfulness of what he was doing but was fatally helpless to stop … his performance was like an effect of demoniacal possession."[982]

The next day, the *Worcester Evening Gazette* accused Clemens of habitual "bad taste," adding that his lack of "propriety" could cost "Mark Twain his place among the contributors to *The Atlantic Monthly*."[983] The *Springfield Republican* called Mark Twain a "wild California bull," who pandered to the wrong audience by "dressing in the garb of bar-room habitués the men who stand at the other end of life."[984]

Mark Twain had been granted the opportunity to insult "the whole literary establishment of America," because *The Innocents Abroad*, his first book, had catapulted him into the American literary firmament after it became a best-seller in 1869. Henry Ward Beecher had ensured the book's success. In a letter to his mother and sister dated January 24, 1868, Mark Twain wrote:

> I met Henry Ward Beecher in Brooklyn, and with his usual whole-minded way of dropping his own work to give other people a lift when he gets a chance, he said: "Now, here you are one of the talented men of the age—nobody is going to deny that—but in matters of business I don't suppose you know more than enough to come in when it rains. I'll tell you what to do and how to do it." And he did. And I listened well, and then came up here and made a splendid contract for the *Quaker City* [the name of the cruise ship] book of 5 or 600 large pages, with illustrations, the manuscript to be placed in the publisher's hands by the middle of July. My percentage is to be a fourth more than they have ever paid any author except Greely. Beecher will be surprised when he hears this."[985]

Mark Twain emphasized Beecher's business savvy, but Beecher had other things on his mind. Applegate tells us that after Beecher's protégé Theodore Tilton left for his annual lecture tour during the winter of 1868-9, Beecher visited Tilton's wife Elizabeth "at least a dozen times" and "continued to press her for sex."[986] When Elizabeth gave birth to a baby boy during the summer of 1869, Beecher arrived "bearing armloads of flowers." The gesture apparently won Elizabeth's heart because the affair continued through the spring of 1870, when she continued to have sex "at her house and his, and at other unnamed places."[987] Beecher tried to defuse the rumors, but they continued to spread

---

981 Southwick, "The Night Mark Twain Scandalized Massachusetts," telegram.com.
982 Southwick, "The Night Mark Twain Scandalized Massachusetts," telegram.com
983 Southwick, "The Night Mark Twain Scandalized Massachusetts," telegram.com.
984 Southwick, "The Night Mark Twain Scandalized Massachusetts," telegram.com.
985 Albert Bigelow Paine, *Mark Twain: A Biography*, Vol. I, pp. 347-8.
986 Applegate, *Beecher*, p. 389.
987 Applegate, *Beecher*, p. 389.

Walking with a Bible and a Gun

and continued to pose a threat to his reputation and livelihood. According to historian Barry Werth, it was standard gossip that "Beecher preaches to seven or eight of his mistresses every Sunday evening."[988]

Given the threat that this gossip posed, Beecher most probably had more than altruism in mind when he gave "one of the talented men of the age" business advice that would result in a best seller and ensure Mark Twain's loyalty at a time when *The Brooklyn Eagle* was closing in on the biggest sex scandal in 19th century America. Mark Twain was a notorious iconoclast who delighted in exposing the foibles of the clergy, but he never attacked Beecher because Beecher had made him rich and famous. The two united behind a desire to remake the paradigmatic American, who used to feel that life was earnest, into a cynical humorist. Like Twain, Beecher had become a stand-up comic.

Beecher used humor to "smash the stereotype of the wan, effeminate minister"[989] that Hawthorne had made famous in *The Scarlet Letter*, and many members of his congregation in Brooklyn were shocked by the crudity he had brought back from Indiana after he had become a "man of the West." Like Mark Twain, "Reverend Beecher was funny," a trait they felt was irreverent coming from the pulpit. According to Applegate, Beecher's humor, "had a serious aim. Henry was launching an assault on everything he'd ever hated about his father's religion."[990]

But Applegate misses the point. By the crucial fall of 1869, when Beecher recruited Sam Clemens as his publicity agent, Calvinism posed no threat to the yuppies from Brooklyn who thronged to the Plymouth Church to find nonsacramental pseudo-absolution for their sins. Calvinism was a busted flush. The real threat to "Beecherism" was the Catholic Church. What united the son of "Pap" and the son of the last Puritan was the West, the concomitant coarsening of morality that western migration had brought about, and anti-Catholicism. After Calvinism "evaporated," the only trace it left behind was the scum of anti-Catholicism which both men shared. Mark Twain would later say that he, like Henry Ward Beecher, whose father fomented the attack on the Ursuline convent in Boston, was "educated to enmity toward everything that is Catholic."[991]

Mark Twain's diatribe against "everything that is Catholic" began when the *Quaker City* reached the Azores, a group of Islands where "the community is eminently Portuguese—that is to say, it is slow, poor, shiftless, sleepy, and

---

988 "Henrry Ward Beecher," *Wikipedia: The Free Encyclopedia*, https://en.wikipedia.org/wiki/Henry_Ward_Beecher

989 Applegate, *Beecher*, p. 212.

990 Applegate, *Beecher*, p. 213.

991 Rory Carroll, "America's Dark and Not-Very-Distant History of Hating Catholics," *The Guardian*, Sept. 12, 2015, https://www.theguardian.com/world/2015/sep/12/america-history-of-hating-catholics

lazy," that is to say, it is "Catholic." "The good Catholic Portuguese," Mark Twain tells us, "crossed himself and prayed God to shield him from all blasphemous desire to know more than his father did before him."[992] Clemens perceived this stultification as a natural outcome of the Catholic faith among the Portuguese:

> The donkeys and the men, women, and children of a family all eat and sleep in the same room, and are unclean, are ravaged by vermin, and are truly happy. The people lie, and cheat the stranger, and are desperately ignorant, and have hardly any reverence for their dead."[993]

A few minutes after disembarking from the *Quaker City*, Mark Twain has learned that "Jesuit humbuggery" flourishes "in communities like this."[994] He knows this because he:

> visited a Jesuit cathedral nearly two hundred years old and found in it a piece of the veritable cross upon which our Saviour was crucified. It was polished and hard, and in as excellent a state of preservation as if the dread tragedy on Calvary had occurred yesterday instead of eighteen centuries ago. But these confiding people believe in that piece of wood unhesitatingly.[995]

After ridiculing the Catholic understanding of relics, Mark Twain then describes the main altar in the Jesuit cathedral as:

> a perfect mass of gilt gimcracks and gingerbread. And they have a swarm of rusty, dusty, battered apostles standing around the filagree work, some on one leg and some with one eye out but a gamey look in the other, and some with two or three fingers gone, and some with not enough nose left to blow—all of them crippled and discouraged, and fitter subjects for the hospital than the cathedral.[996]

Mark Twain is embarrassed by the 19th century versions of the Ugly American, who swaggers into a trattoria and announces, "I am a free-born sovereign, sir, an American, sir, and I want everybody to know it!" adding by way of comment, "He did not mention that he was a lineal descendant of Balaam's ass, but everybody knew that without his telling it."[997] Once Mark Twain and his crew of Ugly American tourists are back on board and sailing toward the continent, he espouses a similar cultural chauvinism when an American ship passes by heading in the opposite direction:

---

992 Twain, *Innocents*, Kindle, p. 43.
993 Twain, *Innocents*, Kindle, p. 43.
994 Twain, *Innocents*, Kindle, p. 44.
995 Twain, *Innocents*, Kindle, p. 44.
996 Twain, *Innocents*, Kindle, p. 45.
997 Twain, *Innocents*, Kindle, p. 96.

> While everybody gazed, she swept superbly by and flung the Stars and Stripes to the breeze! Quicker than thought, hats and handkerchiefs flashed in the air, and a cheer went up! She was beautiful before—she was radiant now. Many a one on our decks knew then for the first time how tame a sight his country's flag is at home compared to what it is in a foreign land. To see it is to see a vision of home itself and all its idols and feel a thrill that would stir a very river of sluggish blood![998]

France, where "all is clockwork, all is order,"[999] fares better than the Azores in Clemens' estimation, until he arrives in Paris, where:

> The guides deceive and defraud every American who goes to Paris for the first time and sees its sights alone or in company with others as little experienced as himself. I shall visit Paris again someday, and then let the guides beware! I shall go in my war paint—I shall carry my tomahawk along.[1000]

Ignoring the masterpieces at the Louvre, Clemens focuses on:

> a portrait of the Madonna which was painted by St. Luke, and it did not look half as old and smoky as some of the pictures by Rubens. We could not help admiring the Apostle's modesty in never once mentioning in his writings that he could paint.[1001]

The grandeur of European Catholic art finally shattered the shell of Clemens' American cultural chauvinism when Mark Twain arrived in Milan and contemplated its cathedral:

> What a wonder it is! So grand, so solemn, so vast! And yet so delicate, so airy, so graceful! A very world of solid weight, and yet it seems in the soft moonlight only a fairy delusion of frost-work that might vanish with a breath! How sharply its pinnacled angles and its wilderness of spires were cut against the sky, and how richly their shadows fell upon its snowy roof! It was a vision!—a miracle!—an anthem sung in stone, a poem wrought in marble! . . . Howsoever you look at the great cathedral, it is noble, it is beautiful! Wherever you stand in Milan or within seven miles of Milan, it is visible and when it is visible, no other object can chain your whole attention. . . . Surely it must be the princeliest creation that ever brain of man conceived. . . . Every face is eloquent with expression, and every attitude is full of grace.[1002]

---

998 Twain, *Innocents*, Kindle, p. 52.
999 Twain, *Innocents*, Kindle, p. 106.
1000 Twain, *Innocents*, Kindle, p. 125.
1001 Twain, *Innocents*, Kindle, p. 172.
1002 Twain, *Innocents*, Kindle, pp. 179-81.

Part II: The Romantic Rehabilitation of Nature

The Beautiful provided an appropriate prelude to the Good when Mark Twain descended into the crypt of St. Ambrose Cathedral and contemplated the tomb of St. Charles Borromeo:

> The priest stopped in a small dungeon and held up his candle. This was the last resting-place of a good man, a warm-hearted, unselfish man; a man whose whole life was given to succoring the poor, encouraging the fainthearted, visiting the sick; in relieving distress, whenever and wherever he found it. His heart, his hand, and his purse were always open. With his story in one's mind he can almost see his benignant countenance moving calmly among the haggard faces of Milan in the days when the plague swept the city, brave where all others were cowards, full of compassion where pity had been crushed out of all other breasts by the instinct of self-preservation gone mad with terror, cheering all, praying with all, helping all, with hand and brain and purse, at a time when parents forsook their children, the friend deserted the friend, and the brother turned away from the sister while her pleadings were still wailing in his ears.[1003]

Overwhelmed by the beauty of the Milan cathedral and the sanctity of St. Charles Borromeo, Mark Twain set his sights on Rome, because "They say that the Cathedral of Milan is second only to St. Peter's at Rome."[1004]

On his way to Rome, however, Clemens never tires of making invidious comparisons. So, after telling us that the lake of Como is "a paradise of tranquil repose" he adds "how dull its waters are compared with the wonderful transparence of Lake Tahoe! I speak of the north shore of Tahoe, where one can count the scales on a trout at a depth of a hundred and eighty feet that Como would only seem a bedizened little courtier in that august presence."[1005]

No matter how much its beauty moves him, Mark Twain never lets his reader forget that Italy is "the heart and home of priest craft–of a happy, cheerful, contented ignorance, superstition, degradation, poverty, indolence, and everlasting unaspiring worthlessness."[1006] But soon a begrudging note of envy enters his narrative because the beauty of Lake Como:

> suits these people precisely; let them enjoy it, along with the other animals, and Heaven forbid that they be molested. We feel no malice toward these fumigators. They are not paid for thinking–they are not paid to fret about the world's concerns. They were not respectable people–they were not worthy people–they were not learned and wise and brilliant people– but in their breasts, all their stupid lives long, resteth a peace that passeth

---

1003 Twain, *Innocents*, Kindle, p. 187.
1004 Twain, *Innocents*, Kindle, p. 191.
1005 Twain, *Innocents*, Kindle, pp. 213-215.
1006 Twain, *Innocents*, Kindle, p. 220.

understanding! How can men, calling themselves men, consent to be so degraded and happy.[1007]

When Clemens finally arrives in St. Peter's Basilica, which he calls "the monster Church,"[1008] he finds himself incapable of describing either its beauty or the truths which inspired that beauty, and so he takes out his measuring tape instead and talks about its size, as if he were a real estate agent selling it to a prospective client who wanted to use it as a warehouse. The beauty of a building which inspired Nathaniel Hawthorne's daughter to covert to Catholicism and brought James Fenimore Cooper to tears becomes in the jaundiced eye of Sam Clemens of Missouri a "prodigious structure" which was:

> just about the length of the capitol at Washington—say seven hundred and thirty feet. I knew it was three hundred and sixty-four feet wide, and consequently wider than the capitol. I knew that the cross on the top of the dome of the church was four hundred and thirty-eight feet above the ground, and therefore about a hundred or maybe a hundred and twenty-five feet higher than the dome of the capitol. Thus I had one gauge. I wished to come as near forming a correct idea of how it was going to look, as possible; I had a curiosity to see how much I would err. I erred considerably. St. Peter's did not look nearly so large as the capitol, and certainly not a twentieth part as beautiful, from the outside.[1009]

St. Peter's Basilica is so large that it turned the people who came there to pray into "insects."[1010] Eventually, Clemens is forced to admit that "I tried all the different ways I could think of to compel myself to understand how large St. Peter's was, but with small success,"[1011] suggesting that there was nothing in St. Peter's Basilica worth discussing other than its size. Nathaniel Hawthorne gave a sympathetic account of the relief penitents felt after going to confession in St. Peter's, but all Mark Twain can talk about is his tape measure and how the vast spaces of the basilica reduced those worshipping there to a "silent throng of human pigmies."[1012] After seeing a workman swing lose from the upper gallery at the end of a long rope, Mark Twain turns him into a "spider" and his rope into "only a thread" which reminds us, if not him, of "Sinners in the Hands of an Angry God." Confronted with beauty which has moved untold numbers of people to embrace Catholicism, all Mark Twain can do is refer what he sees to the Americanist categories of the mind he brought with him on the *Quaker City*. And that may of course be the point of *The Innocents*

1007 Twain, *Innocents*, Kindle, pp. 220-1.
1008 Twain, *Innocents*, Kindle, p. 291.
1009 Twain, *Innocents*, Kindle, p. 291.
1010 Twain, *Innocents*, Kindle, p. 292.
1011 Twain, *Innocents*, Kindle, p. 293.
1012 Twain, *Innocents*, Kindle, p. 293.

Part II: The Romantic Rehabilitation of Nature

Abroad, not so much to introduce his smug American readers to something beyond their cultural ken, but rather to inoculate them from wanting ever to go there and be changed by what they see. Mark Twain combines copious use of mockery and the philistinism which had become the infallible sign of the man of the west, making *The Innocents Abroad* the anti-Baedeker for the Ugly American.

When Mark Twain views the Colosseum, he thinks first of the "poor mangled corpses" of the Christian martyrs, but then as if shocked that he lent sympathy to the Catholic cause, he segues to the Inquisition, a standard trope of Whig History and the Black Legend:

> We look out upon many objects of interest from the dome of St. Peter's; and last of all, almost at our feet, our eyes rest upon the building which was once the Inquisition. . . . The beasts tore the victims limb from limb and made poor mangled corpses of them in the twinkling of an eye. But when the Christians came into power, when the holy Mother Church became mistress of the barbarians, she taught them the error of their ways by no such means. No, she put them in this pleasant Inquisition and pointed to the Blessed Redeemer, who was so gentle and so merciful toward all men, and they urged the barbarians to love him; and they did all they could to persuade them to love and honor him–first by twisting their thumbs out of joint with a screw; then by nipping their flesh with pincers–red-hot ones, because they are the most comfortable in cold weather; then by skinning them alive a little, and finally by roasting them in public. They always convinced those barbarians. The true religion, properly administered, as the good Mother Church used to administer it, is very, very soothing. It is wonderfully persuasive, also. There is a great difference between feeding parties to wild beasts and stirring up their finer feelings in an Inquisition. . . . One is the system of degraded barbarians, the other of enlightened, civilized people. It is a great pity the playful Inquisition is no more.[1013]

If these are the thoughts which the beauty of St. Peter's Basilica inspires, it is not difficult to imagine what Mark Twain will have to say about the ossuary at the Capuchin chapel at the foot of the Via Veneto. What Hawthorne saw as a *memento mori* after reading the inscription at the entrance, "*noi serrano come voi; voi sarebbe come noi,*" (we were like you; you will be like us, which Mark Twain probably could not read because he spoke no Italian), Clemens saw as the set up for a joke:

> There were shapely arches, built wholly of thigh bones; there were startling pyramids, built wholly of grinning skulls; there were quaint architectural structures of various kinds, built of shin bones and the bones of the arm; on the wall were elaborate frescoes, whose curving vines were made of

---

1013 Twain, *Innocents*, Kindle, pp. 294-6.

knotted human vertebrae; whose delicate tendrils were made of sinews and tendons; whose flowers were formed of knee-caps and toe-nails. Every lasting portion of the human frame was represented in these intricate designs (they were by Michael Angelo, I think,) and there was a careful finish about the work, and an attention to details that betrayed the artist's love of his labors as well as his schooled ability.[1014]

After hectoring the monk about misplacing bones, Mark Twain concludes that the ossuary is "as grotesque a performance, and as ghastly, as any I ever witnessed. I hardly knew whether to smile or shudder."[1015] At this point, Mark Twain's Rome narrative comes to an abrupt halt with the tacit admission that his provincialism blinded him to something far above his powers of understanding. Not knowing where to begin, he can only end his narrative by claiming:

> the surest way to stop writing about Rome is to stop. I wished to write a real "guide-book" chapter on this fascinating city, but I could not do it, because I have felt all the time like a boy in a candy-shop—there was every thing to choose from, and yet no choice. I have drifted along hopelessly for a hundred pages of manuscript without knowing where to commence. I will not commence at all. Our passports have been examined. We will go to Naples.[1016]

Applegate's description of *The Innocents Abroad* as "a biting satire of his sanctimonious shipmates" is inaccurate. The most frequent butt of ridicule in that book was the Catholic Church. *The Innocents Abroad* was a Man of the West's satiric commentary on the Grand Tour, which was the fundamental pilgrimage of the Man of the East, but more specifically *The Innocents Abroad* was the anti-Catholic antidote to *The Marble Faun* and the fact that Rose Hawthorne, the scion of American high culture whom Twain met socially in the literary salons of New York, had followed Orestes Brownson into the Catholic Church.[1017]

[1014] Twain, *Innocents*, Kindle, p. 324.
[1015] Twain, *Innocents,* Kindle, pp. 324-6.
[1016] Twain, *Innocents*, Kindle, p. 336.
[1017] Paine, II, p. 258.

Chapter 28

Rose Hawthorne and "The Silent Ministry of Pain"

The Hawthorne family was devastated by Nathaniel's death, which plunged them into financial difficulties resulting from the lack of income from his unfinished novels. Commenting later in life on her father's death, Rose said that "The sudden transformation which took place in my father after his coming to America was like an instant's change in the atmosphere from sunshine to dusky cold."[1018] But Rose, surrounded by those dying from incurable cancer whose suffering she understood as part of God's plan, "never had the least difficulty in explaining it to myself."[1019] Rose said that "the silent ministry of pain she experienced in his passing helped her to understand "the instant providence of God, in his eternal love, patience, sweetness, in his shining face, never averted."[1020]

If God, as Sigmund Freud noted, is an exalted father, then Rose got her vocation as a nun who took care of those dying of cancer from God via her father. Rose remembered her father embracing "a leprous child" in an almshouse in England," an incident Hawthorne recorded in *Our Old Home*, without identifying the "gentleman" as himself. In a letter to Rose, Sophia mentioned the incident, describing Hawthorne as embodying "a tenderness so infinite—so embracing—that God's alone could surpass it. It folded the loathsome leper in as soft a caress as the child of his home affections. Was not that divine! Was it not Christianity in one action—what a bequest to his children—what a new revelation of Christ to the world was that!"[1021]

Valenti sees in Hawthorne's embrace of the leprous child the "tremendous legacy" which Hawthorne left to his children, Indeed, it inspired Rose to dedicate her life to caring for the indigent dying of incurable cancer. "Leaving his family with an uncertain financial future, Nathaniel had nonetheless bequeathed to his children a sense that they were put on this earth to serve

---

1018 Lathrop, *Memories of Hawthorne*, p. 478.
1019 Lathrop, *Memories of Hawthorne*, p. 478.
1020 Lathrop, *Memories of Hawthorne*, p. 479.
1021 Valenti, *To Myself a Stranger*, p. 40.

the poor and unfortunate. Sophia had correctly identified the nature of her children's inheritance."[1022] But art played a role in that vocation as well. Sophia told Rose that she:

> inherited from Papa this immitigable demand for beauty and order and right & though, in the course of your development, it has made you sometimes pettish and unreasonable, I always was glad you had it, because I knew the impatience and crossness it often caused, would prove a transient phase. I knew that religious principle and sentiment would surely render you at last gentle and charitable to the shortcomings of your fellow mortals. . . . And this will lead you to hieghts [sic] of being at last. Whereas if you were easy and indifferent, you might deteriorate, and lose the exquisite felicity which comes with the exquisite pain of a noble fastidiousness. I have never doubted your most profound and tender love and devotion to me, in the worst paroxysms of your impatience, and so my heart was never seriously wounded. . . . You have to suffer because GOD has given you the perilous gift of genius. With it you are to become greater and lovelier than your less gifted fellow beings.[1023]

If art led the Hawthorne girls to dedicate their lives to the suffering poor, the path was not direct. In 1868 Rose and her mother moved to Dresden, in part to find a place where the dollar went farther than in New England, in part in vain search for Sophia's health, but mainly so that her daughter could study art, which "had become a subject of great concern to Rose,"[1024] because of her experience of Italian art in Rome as a child:

> Painting, the artistic medium that her mother had pursued and her father had approved, seemed the appropriate path to excellence and self-esteem. Yet the pursuit of art was not to be as easy as she and Sophia had anticipated. The art academy, it appeared, was a "place for young gentlemen rather than ladies." Moreover, Rose's skill paled in comparison with that of her companion, Frank Lathrop, whose considerable talent eventually afforded him a career and some notable achievements in the artistic world.[1025]

The move to Dresden did not bring health, and Rose's mother died three years later. On March 4, 1871, Sophia was buried in Kensal Green in England. The simple inscription on her gravestone reads: "Sophia, Wife of Nathaniel Hawthorne." Alone in the world, Rose decided to marry shortly after Julian's friend George Lathrop arrived in England to escort her home. Julian was shocked by the announcement and considered George's action a betrayal of his trust. He also considered their decision to marry "an error, not to be

---

1022 Valenti, *To Myself a Stranger*, p. 40.
1023 Valenti, *To Myself a Stranger*, p. 40.
1024 Valenti, *To Myself a Stranger*, p. 43.
1025 Valenti, *To Myself a Stranger*, pp. 45-6.

Part II: The Romantic Rehabilitation of Nature

repaired."[1026] Undeterred by her brother's disapproval, Rose married George Lathrop at St. Luke's Anglican Church in Chelsea on September 11, 1871, with George's brother Frank the only family member in attendance.[1027]

1026 Valenti, *To Myself a Stranger*, p. 48.
1027 Valenti, *To Myself a Stranger*, p. 48.

CHAPTER 29

VICTORIA WOODHULL AND FREE LOVE

On May 3, 1871, Victoria Woodhull learned of Elizabeth Tilton's adultery with Beecher from the suffragette Elizabeth Cady Stanton.[1028] Woodhull, nee Victoria California Claflin was born in 1838 in the frontier town of Homer, in Licking County, Ohio to an illiterate, illegitimate mother who was a follower of the Austrian mystic Franz Mesmer and the new spiritualist movement, and a father, Reuben "Buck" Hummel Claflin, who was "a con man, lawyer, and snake oil salesman."[1029]

After divorcing her first husband, whom she had married at the age of 14, Woodhull became a "spiritualist" who slept with her wealthy New York clientele and relayed the information to Cornelius Vanderbilt, who used it to benefit his insider trading. She then became an advocate of "free love," a doctrine she proclaimed publicly on November 20, 1871, in what is known as the "Steinway speech," because she gave it at Steinway Hall. In that speech, Woodhull described herself as "a Free Lover," who had:

> an inalienable, constitutional and natural right to love whom I may, to love as long or as short a period as I can; to change that love every day if I please, and with that right neither you nor any law you can frame have any right to interfere.[1030]

Woodhull's defiant proclamation destroyed the reputation of Theodore Tilton, as well as his livelihood as editor of *The Golden Age*. Tilton, the quondam protégé of Henry Ward Beecher, became Woodhull's biographer and lover out of revenge after he discovered that his wife Elizabeth had committed adultery with Beecher. After Woodhull was attacked as a "free lover," Tilton was ruined financially, but Beecher "seemed to sail smoothly on,"[1031] at least in the public eye, a situation which both Woodhull and Tilton found infuriating. Privately, however, "Beecher was a wreck," because by February 1872 Woodhull was "actively peddling the story to newspaper editors." In

---

1028 Applegate, *Beecher*, p. 397.
1029 "Victoria Woodhull," *Wikipedia: The Free Encyclopedia*, https://en.wikipedia.org/wiki/Victoria_Woodhull
1030 "Victoria Woodhull," *Wikipedia*.
1031 Applegate, *Beecher*, p. 496.

an age when newspapers had more power over reputation than the courts, Beecher was facing the same sort of fate Tilton had suffered, making him and Woodhull more determined to press their case.

On September 12, 1872, Woodhull announced to "a motley collection of psychics and seers, radical social reformers, random eccentrics, and curiosity seekers gathered in Boston, Massachusetts, for the annual convention of the American Association of Spiritualists,"[1032] that Rev. Beecher, in spite of what he said from the pulpit, was "the king of free love" because for years this legendary minister had been carrying on an affair with his best friend's wife, a poor defenseless woman named Elizabeth Tilton. Woodhull's audience "shuddered in astonishment" when they heard the news.[1033] Every Sunday morning, Woodhull continued, Beecher "stood in his Brooklyn pulpit and preached to a dozen of his mistresses. . . robed in silks and satins and high respectability."[1034] When Woodhull published the news in *Woodhull & Claflin's Weekly*, they sold 150,000 copies, and when the press run sold out, existing copies sold for as much as $20 per issue.

Woodhull soon became a victim of her own success as publisher of a scandal sheet when she ran afoul of New York's Comstock laws. On November 2, 1872, Woodhull, her sister Tennie Claflin, and Woodhull's third husband Col. Blood were arrested and charged with publishing an obscene newspaper and mailing it through the United States Postal Service. They were eventually acquitted, prompting Congress to pass the federal version of the Comstock laws in 1873.[1035]

A tremendous crowd gathered in Plymouth Church on the evening of August 28, 1874, to hear the final report of the Plymouth Church appointed to investigate the charges against Beecher. Beecher was exonerated, and Theodore Tilton and his wife were expelled from the church.

According to the final resolution of the committee, there was "nothing whatever in the evidence that should impair the perfect confidence of Plymouth Church or the world in the Christian character or integrity of Henry Ward Beecher."[1036] Undeterred, Tilton filed a civil suit five months later accusing Beecher of adultery. The trial became national news, but it ended in a hung jury, largely because of Elizabeth Tilton's numerous and contradictory confessions. The trustees of the Plymouth Church responded by increasing Beecher's yearly salary to the unheard-of sum of $100,000, "so that he could

---

1032 Applegate, *Beecher*, p. 420.
1033 Applegate, *Beecher*, p. 420.
1034 Applegate, *Beecher*, p. 421.
1035 "Victoria Woodhull," *Wikipedia*.
1036 Applegate, *Beecher*, p. 442.

Part II: The Romantic Rehabilitation of Nature

pay his legal bills."[1037] Mark Twain eventually weighed in on the Beecher scandal, but privately, opining that:

> the silence of the Beechers is a hundred-fold more of an obscene publication than that of the Woodhulls, and the said silence is a thousand-fold more potent in convincing people of the truth of that scandal than the evidence of fifty Woodhulls could be. You will find presently that the general thought of the nation will gradually form itself into the verdict that there is some fire somewhere in all this smoke of scandal.[1038]

By 1877, Beecherism had become the de facto established religion of the United States of America, causing a shift in American identity from the preacher to the lecturer, who was also a stand-up comic. Because of this shift and because of his relationship with Beecher, Mark Twain had become the archetypal American after the Civil War, a title he would hold until World War I, when Ernest Hemingway replaced him.

1037 Applegate, *Beecher*, p. 451.
1038 Applegate, *Beecher*, p. 427.

Chapter 30

Christopher Newman, Man of the West

George Lathrop originally planned to study law but soon found a ready market for his writing that eventually enabled him to become an editor at the *Atlantic Monthly*, which provided a steady source of income for the first time in his married life. Ignoring her father's stern admonition against becoming a writer, Rose joined her husband as "respected members of the New York intellectual and journalistic world."[1039]

The king of that literary world was Henry James. His novel *The American* appeared on May 5, 1877, eight years after the publication of *The Innocents Abroad*. Henry James and Mark Twain represented the two poles of American identity. If Mark Twain was the quintessential man of the West, Henry James, whose father was a friend of Nathaniel Hawthorne, was the quintessential man of the East. All of James' novels dealt with Americans in Europe. *The American* begins with the man of the east's take on the man of the west:

> The gentleman on the divan was a powerful specimen of an American. But he was not only a fine American; he was in the first place, physically, a fine man. He appeared to possess that kind of health and strength which, when found in perfection, are the most impressive—the physical capital which the owner does nothing to 'keep up.' If he was a muscular Christian, it was quite without knowing it. If it was necessary to walk to a remote spot, he walked, but he had never known himself to 'exercise.' He had no theory with regard to cold bathing or the use of Indian clubs; he was neither an oarsman, a rifleman, nor a fencer—he had never had time for these amusements—and he was quite unaware that the saddle is recommended for certain forms of indigestion.[1040]

Christopher Newman wears "a cerulean cravat," which "completed the conditions of his identity."[1041] In Christopher Newman, Henry James created a paradigm of American identity based on his understanding of the new man who had emerged from the west and was crowding easterners like Henry

---

1039 Bird, *From Witchery to Sanctity*, p. 129.
1040 James, American, loc. 168-70.
1041 James, American, loc. 108.

James and his friend Henry Adams out of the positions they had held as paradigms of high culture. When Newman:

> straightened himself, he looked like a grenadier on parade. He never smoked. He had been assured—such things are said—that cigars were excellent for the health, and he was quite capable of believing it; but he knew as little about tobacco as about homeopathy. He had a very well-formed head, with a shapely, symmetrical balance of the frontal and the occipital development, and a good deal of straight, rather dry brown hair. His complexion was brown, and his nose had a bold well-marked arch. His eye was of a clear, cold gray, and save for a rather abundant mustache he was clean-shaved. He had the flat jaw and sinewy neck which are frequent in the American type; but the traces of national origin are a matter of expression even more than of feature, and it was in this respect that our friend's countenance was supremely eloquent. The discriminating observer we have been supposing might, however, perfectly have measured its expressiveness, and yet have been at a loss to describe it. It had that typical vagueness which is not vacuity, that blankness which is not simplicity, that look of being committed to nothing in particular, of standing in an attitude of general hospitality to the chances of life, of being very much at one's own disposal so characteristic of many American faces. It was our friend's eye that chiefly told his story; an eye in which innocence and experience were singularly blended. It was full of contradictory suggestions, and though it was by no means the glowing orb of a hero of romance, you could find in it almost anything you looked for. Frigid and yet friendly, frank yet cautious, shrewd yet credulous, positive yet skeptical, confident yet shy, extremely intelligent and extremely good-humored, there was something vaguely defiant in its concessions, and something profoundly reassuring in its reserve. The cut of this gentleman's mustache, with the two premature wrinkles in the cheek above it, and the fashion of his garments, in which an exposed shirt-front and a cerulean cravat played perhaps an obtrusive part, completed the conditions of his identity.[1042]

And yet, the "single word which constituted the strength of his French vocabulary" is *"combien,"* How much? As in, how much does it cost, a question he asks of a young lady who is making copies of masterpieces at the Louvre. "The Madonna, yes," he says by way of negotiation. "I am not a Catholic, but I want to buy it. *Combien?*"[1043] When he hands Mlle. Nioche his card, she reads it aloud and laughs at his name. Newman laughs along, explaining "Did you ever hear of Christopher Columbus?" To which she laughingly replies, "Bien sur! He invented America; a very great man. And is he your patron?"

1042 James, American, loc. 176-88.
1043 James, American, loc. 208.

Part II: The Romantic Rehabilitation of Nature

"My patron?" Newman replies. "Your patron-saint, in the calendar.' 'Oh, exactly; my parents named me for him.' 'Monsieur is American?' 'Don't you see it?' monsieur inquired."[1044]

An air of uncertainty hangs over the conversation, as if Newman is unsure of his identity, even in his claim that it should be obvious. The doubt is James's as well. Newman is "horribly western."[1045] Christopher Newman is a man of the West, and his "was an intensely Western story" which began with the Civil War when he received "a brevet of brigadier general," and a burning desire to make money.[1046] When he arrives penniless in San Francisco, he is not like Dr. Franklin in Philadelphia, marching "along the street munching a penny-loaf," only because "he had not the penny-loaf necessary to the performance."[1047] And yet, Christopher Newman has "come to see Europe"[1048] because he was "sick of business."[1049]

To cure his malaise, Newman embarks on the quintessential pilgrimage of the man of the east known as the Grand Tour, not unlike Mark Twain in *The Innocents Abroad*. The same question applies to both men. Given their provincialism, can either man learn anything from the beauty that he sees? Unlike Mark Twain, Newman sees the Grand Tour as "the biggest kind of entertainment a man can get. People, places, art, nature, everything! I want to see the tallest mountains, and the bluest lakes, and the finest pictures and the handsomest churches, and the most celebrated men, and the most beautiful women."[1050] Newman would like to "Settle down in Paris, then. There are no mountains that I know of, and the only lake is in the Bois du Boulogne, and not particularly blue. But there is everything else: plenty of pictures and churches, no end of celebrated men, and several beautiful women."[1051] But he also wants to see "Mont Blanc. . . and Amsterdam, and the Rhine, and a lot of places. Venice in particular. I have great ideas about Venice."[1052]

If the novel is a combination of form and life, Henry James exists at the form end of the spectrum. He deduces his characters from aspects which the main character exhibits and which need to be examined. This means that the characters in *The American* are paradigms of American identity which James weighs and finds wanting.

1044 James, American, loc. 663.
1045 James, American, loc. 663.
1046 James, American, loc. 512.
1047 James, American, loc. 507.
1048 James, American, loc. 538.
1049 James, American, loc. 573.
1050 James, American, loc. 589.
1051 James, American, loc. 592.
1052 James, American, loc. 599.

If Newman is a typical American, because he is a man of the West, his opposite is Mr. Tristram is a typical man of the East, who has taken his identity to its logical conclusion by becoming an ex-patriot. Tristram is "a rather degenerate mortal,"[1053] in other words, a typical European:

> At twenty-five he had been a good fellow, and in this respect, he was unchanged; but of a man of his age one expected something more. People said he was sociable, but this was as much a matter of course as for a dipped sponge to expand; and it was not a high order of sociability. He was a great gossip and tattler, and to produce a laugh would hardly have spared the reputation of his aged mother. His only aspirations were to hold out at poker, at his club, to know the names of all the cocottes, to shake hands all round, to ply his rosy gullet with truffles and champagne, and to create uncomfortable eddies and obstructions among the constituent atoms of the American colony. He was shamefully idle, spiritless, sensual, snobbish. He irritated our friend by the tone of his allusions to their native country, and Newman was at a loss to understand why the United States were not good enough for Mr. Tristram. He had never been a very conscious patriot, but it vexed him to see them treated as little better than a vulgar smell in his friend's nostrils, and he finally broke out and swore that they were the greatest country in the world, that they could put all Europe into their breeches' pockets, and that an American who spoke ill of them ought to be carried home in irons and compelled to live in Boston.[1054]

Unlike the ex-pat Tristram, Newman "had a great contempt for immorality."[1055] Morality is a crucial part of American identity which comes naturally to someone like Newman, who "was blessed with a natural impulse to disfigure with a direct, unreasoning blow the comely visage of temptation."[1056] Unfortunately, Newman's virtue in matters sexual is essentially negative because even if he resisted temptation instinctively and "had never done anything very ugly, he had never, on the other hand, done anything particularly beautiful." Instead, "he had spent his years in the unremitting effort to add thousands to thousands, and, now that he stood well outside of it, the business of money-getting appeared tolerably dry and sterile."[1057]

While in Paris, Newman meets Mr. Babcock, who becomes his traveling companion. Babcock is a "young Unitarian minister," who, unlike the ex-pat Tristram has retained his hold on morality with a grip that is too tight, which turns him into a prig who finds fault with Newman's lack of "moral

---

1053 James, American, loc. 669.

1054 James, American, loc. 669-74.

1055 James, American, loc. 1438.

1056 James, American, loc. 1472.

1057 James, American, Loc. 1472.

Part II: The Romantic Rehabilitation of Nature

reaction."[1058] At war with himself because he was a man of the east who "detested Europe,"[1059] Babcock tried "to infuse into Newman a little of his own spiritual starch, but Newman's personal texture was too loose to admit of stiffening. His mind could no more hold principles than a sieve can hold water. He admired principles extremely, and thought Babcock a mighty fine little fellow for having so many."[1060] Newman's mind had been so formed by existence that essence had become meaningless, largely because it was associated with New England religion, which had moved from Calvinism to Unitarianism without finding Catholicism, the mean between these two extremes along the way. Babcock's Unitarian congregation sponsored his trip to Europe so that he could "enrich my mind with the treasures of nature and art in the Old World."[1061] But instead of allowing himself to be carried by beauty to the transcendental realm where it meets the good and the true, Babcock turns museum going into a chore because "Art and life seem to me intensely serious things, and in our travels in Europe we should especially remember the immense seriousness of Art."[1062]

As a parting shot at his priggishness, Newman sends Babcock a little statue of a "gaunt, ascetic looking monk, in a tattered gown and cowl, kneeling with clasped hands and pulling a portentously long face."[1063] Newman separated from the earnest Unitarian minister from Boston because of "incompatibility of temper."[1064] According to Babcock, Newman was "low-minded, immoral," and a "devotee of art for art, whatever that is."[1065] But soon after Babcock departs, Newman meets an Englishman who gives him up because:

> I was too virtuous by half; I was too stern a moralist. He told me, in a friendly way, that I was cursed with a conscience; that I judged things like a Methodist and talked about them like an old lady. This was rather bewildering. Which of my two critics was I to believe?[1066]

Despite being a man of the west, Newman lacks an identity. Like Protestants, Newman understands better what he is not than what he is. As a man of the West, Newman is "not an intellectual."[1067] Newman is an American tourist on the Grand Tour, who feels, like the typical Man of the West, that

---

1058 James, American, loc. 1348.
1059 James, American, loc. 1353.
1060 James, American, loc. 1374-6.
1061 James, American, loc. 1422.
1062 James, American, loc. 1426.
1063 James, American, loc. 1443.
1064 James, American, loc. 1500.
1065 James, American, loc. 1501.
1066 James, American, loc. 1502.
1067 James, American, loc. 719.

"Europe was made for him, and not he for Europe."[1068] Newman is a "zealous dilletante."[1069] Newman can't tell the difference between good architecture and bad, but it doesn't matter because "his tour was altogether a pastime."[1070] Newman then tries to explain his identity (or lack thereof) to Mrs. Tristram:

> I am not cultivated, I am not even educated; I know nothing about history, or art, or foreign tongues, or any other learned matters. But I am not a fool, either, and I shall undertake to know something about Europe by the time I have done with it. I feel something under my ribs here,' he added in a moment, 'that I can't explain—a sort of a mighty hankering, a desire to stretch out and haul in.' 'Bravo!' said Mrs. Tristram, 'that is very fine. You are the great Western Barbarian, stepping forth in his innocence and might, gazing a while at this poor effete Old World and then swooping down on it."[1071]

Things get more complicated when Newman decides to acquire a French wife, something he describes as "the best article in the market,"[1072] in the same way that he has ordered Mlle. Nioche to copy Rubens' painting of the marriage of Marie de Medici. Early on in life, Newman decided that "a beautiful wife was the thing best worth having, here below. It is the greatest victory over circumstances. When I say beautiful, I mean beautiful in mind and in manners, as well as in person. It is a thing every man has an equal right to; he may get it if he can. He doesn't have to be born with certain faculties, on purpose; he needs only to be a man. Then he needs only to use his will, and such wits as he has, and to try.[1073]

Claire de Cintre is that woman, but Newman soon discovers that winning her hand requires more than money and American ingenuity. He discovers this obliquely by entering her house, which "had a dark, dusty, painted portal, which swung open in answer to his ring. . . . The place was all in the shade; it answered to Newman's conception of a convent."[1074] Claire's house is not unlike the Ursuline convent in Boston, which got burned to the ground at Lyman Beecher's urging. At the heart of the malignant mystery thwarting Newman's desire to marry Claire lies the Catholic Church, a presence which looms larger as the novel reaches its climax.

Madam de Cintre is a Roman Catholic. So is her brother Valentin. Newman is a "good American" who has acted with decision and made a fortune. Valentin is "the exact reverse of Newman" because he has "done

---

1068 James, American, loc. 1303.
1069 James, American, loc. 1306.
1070 James, American, loc. 1328.
1071 James, American, loc. 727.
1072 James, American, loc. 797.
1073 James, American, loc. 801.
1074 James, American, loc. 940-2.

nothing."¹⁰⁷⁵ Valentin has done so little he can't even describe himself as a "tragic failure." Instead, he has:

> fallen from a height, and my fiasco has made no noise. You, evidently, are a success. You have made a fortune, you have built up an edifice, you are a financial, commercial power, you can travel about the world until you have found a soft spot, and lie down in it with the consciousness of having earned your rest. Is not that true? Well, imagine the exact reverse of all that, and you have me. I have done nothing—I can do nothing!'¹⁰⁷⁶

When it comes to having an identity, Newman is an American; Valentin Bellegarde, Claire's brother, is a Catholic:

> 'Are you very religious?' asked Newman, in a tone which gave the inquiry a grotesque effect. M. de Bellegarde evidently appreciated the comical element in the question, but he looked at Newman a moment with extreme soberness. 'I am a very good Catholic. I respect the Church. I adore the blessed Virgin. I fear the Devil.'¹⁰⁷⁷

Like Emerson and John Milton, Newman is "of the devil's party." In spite of his abhorrence of immorality, Newman is "irresistibly in opposition; a man of forms and phrases and postures; a man full of possible impertinences and treacheries."¹⁰⁷⁸ Newman is the opposite of a Catholic because he is an American, because, according to Valentin:

> Being an American, it was impossible you should remain what you were born, and being born poor—do I understand it?—it was therefore inevitable that you should become rich. You were in a position that makes one's mouth water; you looked round you and saw a world full of things you had only to step up to and take hold of. When I was twenty, I looked around me and saw a world with everything ticketed 'Hands off!' and the deuce of it was that the ticket seemed meant only for me. I couldn't go into business, I couldn't make money, because I was a Bellegarde. I couldn't go into politics, because I was a Bellegarde—the Bellegardes don't recognize the Bonapartes. I couldn't go into literature, because I was a dunce. . . . The only thing I could do was to go and fight for the Pope. That I did, punctiliously, and received an apostolic flesh-wound at Castlefidardo. It did neither the Holy Father nor me any good, that I could see. Rome was doubtless a very amusing place in the days of Caligula, but it has sadly fallen off since. I passed three years in the Castle of St. Angelo, and then came back to secular life.¹⁰⁷⁹

1075 James, American, loc. 1851-61.
1076 James, American, loc. 1861.
1077 James, American, loc. 1917.
1078 James, American, loc. 2958.
1079 James, American, loc. 1902-12.

Valentin is drawn to Newman because he possesses an ineffable *je ne sais quoi*, which is the essence of being an American:

> But you have got something that I should have liked to have. It is not money, it is not even brains–though no doubt yours are excellent. It is not your six feet of height, though I should have rather liked to be a couple of inches taller. It's a sort of air you have of being thoroughly at home in the world. My place in life was made for me, and it seemed easy to occupy it. But you who, as I understand it, have made your own place, you who, as you told us the other day, have manufactured wash-tubs—you strike me, somehow, as a man who stands at his ease, who looks at things from a height. I fancy you going about the world like a man traveling on a railroad in which he owns a large amount of stock. You make me feel as if I had missed something. What is it?' 'It is the proud consciousness of honest toil–of having manufactured a few wash-tubs,' said Newman, at once jocose and serious.[1080]

Newman then makes his own attempt to define American identity. "Then it's the privilege of being an American citizen," said Newman. "That sets a man up."[1081] Like Mark Twain, Newman was a man of the west, who "had sat with Western humorists in knots, round cast-iron stoves, and seen 'tall' stories grow taller without toppling over, and his own imagination had learned the trick of piling up consistent wonders."[1082] In a veiled allusion to the Beecher scandal, Valentin tells Newman, "You have not stupified yourself with debauchery and you have not mortgaged your fortune to social conveniences."[1083] Valentin's praise of America leaves Newman feeling that "Energy and Ingenuity can arrange everything,"[1084] including marriage to a Catholic aristocrat, which seems well within the realm of possibility when Newman gives Claire's avaricious mother a clear understanding of how much money he has. Responding to her question, "How rich?"

Newman expressed his income in a round number which had the magnificent sound that large aggregations of dollars put on when they are translated into francs. He added a few remarks of a financial character, which completed a sufficiently striking presentment of his resources. Madame de Bellegarde listened in silence. 'You are very frank,' she said finally. 'I will be the same. I would rather favor you, on the whole, than suffer you. It will be easier.'[1085]

1080 James, American, loc. 1924.
1081 James, American. Loc. 1936.
1082 James, American, loc. 1986.
1083 James, American, loc. 1995.
1084 James, American, loc. 2355.
1085 James, American, loc. 2707.

Part II: The Romantic Rehabilitation of Nature

Being an American offers "sunny immunity" from "oppressive secrets" until the arrival of Lord Deepmere:

> a small, meagre man, of some three and thirty years of age, with a bald head, a short nose and no front teeth in the upper jaw; he had round, candid blue eyes, and several pimples on his chin. He was evidently very shy, and he laughed a great deal, catching his breath with an odd, startling sound, as the most convenient imitation of repose. His physiognomy denoted great simplicity, a certain amount of brutality, and probable failure in the past to profit by rare educational advantages. He remarked that Paris was awfully jolly, but that for real, thorough-paced entertainment it was nothing to Dublin.[1086]

In spite of his obvious unattractiveness, Lord Deepmere is an aristocrat, and therefore superior to an American, no matter how much money he has. Unlike her son, Madame de Bellegarde is not impressed with the American spirit or that Newman made a fortune after starting out selling washtubs. Indeed, it is precisely this which she holds against him. "It is not your disposition that we object to," she tells Newman, "it is your antecedents. We really cannot reconcile ourselves to a commercial person."[1087]

Newman is suddenly confronted by the "force of a real calamity" which had "the strength and insolence of Destiny itself. It was unnatural and monstrous, and he had no arms against it.[1088] That force is:

> like a religion. I can't tell you—I can't! It's cruel of you to insist. I don't see why I shouldn't ask you to believe me—and pity me. It's like a religion. There's a curse upon the house.[1089]

The name of that force was Catholicism, which forced Claire to break with Newman and Lord Deepmere and, worst of all, immure herself in a convent, and not just any convent but the Carmelite brand. According to the devout Protestant servant Mrs. Bread, "of all the nuns in Christendom the Carmelites are the worst. You may say they are really not human, sir; they make you give up everything—forever. And to think of her there! If I was one that cried, sir, I could cry."[1090]

Mrs. Bread is Anglican but low church. She is the voice of Protestantism when she tells Newman that Carmelite nuns:

> are no better than tinkers' wives. They give up everything, down to the very name their poor old nurses called them by. They give up father and mother, brother and sister,—to say nothing of other persons,' Mrs. Bread

---

1086 James, American, loc. 3466-7.
1087 James, American, loc. 4756.
1088 James, American, loc. 4955.
1089 James, American, loc. 5286.
1090 James, American, loc. 5421.

delicately added. 'They wear a shroud under their brown cloaks and a rope round their waists, and they get up on winter nights and go off into cold places to pray to the Virgin Mary. The Virgin Mary is a hard mistress!'[1091]

Before Claire announced that she was joining the Carmelites, Catholicism was "nothing but a name," to Newman, "and to express a mistrust of the form in which her religious feelings had moulded themselves would have seemed to him on his own part a rather pretentious affectation of Protestant zeal. If such superb white flowers as that could bloom in Catholic soil, the soil was not insalubrious. But it was one thing to be a Catholic, and another to turn nun—on your hand![1092]

The main manifestation of Newman's naivete and American innocence was his inability to understand the full depth of malignity which the Catholic Church represented:

> 'You are going to be a nun,' he went on, 'in a cell for life—with a gown and white veil?' 'A nun—a Carmelite nun,' said Madame de Cintre. 'For life, with God's leave.' The idea struck Newman as too dark and horrible for belief, and made him feel as he would have done if she had told him that she was going to mutilate her beautiful face, or drink some potion that would make her mad. He clasped his hands and began to tremble, visibly. . . to muffle herself in ascetic rags and entomb herself in a cell was a confounding combination of the inexorable and the grotesque. 'You—you a nun!' he exclaimed; 'you with your beauty defaced—you behind locks and bars! Never, never, if I can prevent it!' And he sprang to his feet with a violent laugh.[1093]

The common denominator which defined Mark Twain and Henry James as quintessential American writers, even though they epitomized the Man of the West and the Man of the East respectively, was their anti-Catholicism. *Daisy Miller*, Henry James' novella about expatriate life in Rome was based on *The Marble Faun*, and it appeared in 1878, one year after *The American*.

After Claire immures herself in the Carmelite convent at the Rue d'Enfer—a "a terrible name," Mrs. Bread tells Newman, "I suppose you know what it means"—Newman, the quondam tourist, pops in for a visit to a place that was "like a page torn out of a romance, with no context in his own experience,"[1094] just as "a priest and two altar boys came in and began to say mass."[1095] Newman, we are told:

1091 James, American, loc. 5953.
1092 James, American, loc. 5362.
1093 James, American, loc. 5315-28.
1094 James, American, loc. 6038.
1095 James, American, loc. 6053.

watched their genuflections and gyrations with a grim, still enmity; they seemed aids and abettors of Madame de Cintre's desertion; they were mouthing and droning out their triumph. . . . The priest's long, dismal intonings acted upon his nerves and deepened his wrath; there was something defiant in his unintelligible drawl; it seemed meant for Newman himself. Suddenly there arose from the depths of the chapel, from behind the inexorable grating, a sound which drew his attention from the altar–the sound of a strange, lugubrious chant, uttered by women's voices. It began softly, but it presently grew louder, and as it increased it became more of a wail and a dirge. It was the chant of the Carmelite nuns, their only human utterance. It was their dirge over their buried affections and over the vanity of earthly desires. At first Newman was bewildered—almost stunned—by the strangeness of the sound; then, as he comprehended its meaning, he listened intently and his heart began to throb. He listened for Madame de Cintre's voice, and in the very heart of the tuneless harmony he imagined he made it out. . . . The chant kept on, mechanical and monotonous, with dismal repetitions and despairing cadences. It was hideous, it was horrible; as it continued, Newman felt that he needed all his self-control. He was growing more agitated; he felt tears in his eyes. At last, as in its full force the thought came over him that this confused, impersonal wail was all that either he or the world she had deserted should ever hear of the voice he had found so sweet, he felt that he could bear it no longer. . . . Did you hear the chanting? They say it's like the lamentations of the damned.[1096]

Having lost Claire, Newman "had nothing to do" and so became a tourist once again visiting this time the "splendid dimness" of Notre Dame Cathedral. Newman may or may not have been impressed with the Cathedral's beauty, but James tells us that:

> He said no prayers; he had no prayers to say. He had nothing to be thankful for, and he had nothing to ask; nothing to ask, because now he must take care of himself.[1097]

Newman decided not to expose the Bellegarde's secret, "not with the elastic step of a man who had won a victory or taken a resolve, but strolling soberly, like a good-natured man who is still a little ashamed."[1098] When Newman burns the paper with the secret on it which would have damned the Bellegardes "if it were known," Mrs. Tristram affirms his American identity by telling him: "Their confidence, after counsel taken of each other, was not

---

1096 James, American, loc. 6053-89.
1097 James, American, loc. 6679.
1098 James, American, loc. 6688.

in their innocence, nor in their talent for bluffing things off; it was in your remarkable good nature!"[1099]

With William Dean Howells as its editor, *The Atlantic Monthly* tried to bridge the gap between East and West, by publishing the fiction of their quintessential representatives. Henry James, the quintessential Man of the East in post-Civil War American literature, was born in 1843 in New York. Samuel Clemens, the quintessential Man of the West, was born in 1835 in Missouri. Together they occupied opposite poles on the East/West trajectory which provided the grammar of American identity. If the East/West Axis provided the grammar which divided them, the hidden grammar which united them was anti-Catholicism. Once the slavery issue had been resolved by *force majeure*, a new post-Civil War American identity emerged based on hatred of the Catholic Church. It was a venerable phobia in the Anglophone world, and it allowed the ruling class to paper over the collapse of Calvinism and the moral decline which that collapse precipitated by giving free rein to the passions Calvinism had kept in check. Greed and lust became American virtues, but the signs of moral decline were hidden by technological progress. At the Columbian exhibition, Henry Adams, the scion of the now effete men of the east, could marvel at the mindless power the American dynamo had unleashed and then hurry off to France to be consoled by the Blessed Virgin America had rejected. In 1899, the same year Pope Leo XIII issued *Testem Benevolentiae*, his encyclical condemning the heresy of Americanism, Henry Adams retired to Paris, where he wrote *Mont-Saint-Michel and Chartres*, "an imaginative journey into the heart of the medieval mind."[1100] Adams' engagement with Catholic France created a new paradigm of American identity, that of "the modern intellectual."[1101]

1099 James, American, loc. 6747.
1100 Brown, *The Last American Aristocrat*, p. 312.
1101 Brown, *The Last American Aristocrat*, p. 313.

Chapter 31

Henry Adams, The Old Man of the East

Henry Brooks Adams resigned from his professorship at Harvard in May of the *annus mirabilis* of 1877, a defining moment in the history of American identities. *The American* first appeared in serial form in *The Atlantic Monthly* in 1877. In 1877, federal troops withdrew from the South putting an end to Reconstruction and inaugurating the era of "Redemption," a new regime based on "the creation of a caste system sanctioned by poll taxes and literacy tests, sharecropping and tenant farming," which came to be known as Jim Crow, after "the assemblage of state and local statutes designed to legitimize racial segregation—became the law of the land."[1102]

As a man of the east, Henry Adams was indifferent to the race issue. If anything, he, unlike the abolitionists from Concord, sympathized with the plight of the South after the Civil War because of the years he had spent in Washington, which was still a southern city with slaves when Henry arrived there as a young man. Henry Adams' view on slavery were essentially English and conditioned by economic realities more than Puritan morality. They mirrored the hypocritical views of Wilberforce, whose concern for the Negro slave was accompanied by a complete indifference to the plight of Irish miners, as William Cobbett pointed out.

Adams wanted to create "a unique American Mandarin class," above politics and democracy.[1103] Brown claims that Henry Adams' "myopic outlook on race" can be traced to "the composite workings of an ingrained elitism nurtured in the precincts of presidents, the dining halls of Harvard, and the country houses of England."[1104] If so, it could be argued, paradoxical as it may seem, that Henry Adams was not an American. He was most certainly not a man of the west. He and his family had been eclipsed politically by men of the West beginning with Andrew Jackson and Abraham Lincoln, who required their diplomatic savoir faire to keep England out of the war, all the way up to Theodore Roosevelt, who dismissed Adams as "a chronic cynic, too shrewd, detached, and cerebral for his own good."[1105] Teddy was man of the

---

1102 Brown, *The Last American Aristocrat*, p. 95.
1103 Brown, *The Last American Aristocrat*, p. 91.
1104 Brown, *The Last American Aristocrat*, p. 98.
1105 Brown, Adams, p. 338.

east who acted like a man of the West because by the time his turn came the notion that an American could be a frail intellectual was a contradiction in terms. Henry Adams contested Roosevelt's verdict by creating a paradigm of the Southerner as "a virtuous people unfairly subjugated by a combination of Yankee carpetbaggers, black congressmen, and unscrupulous scalawags."[1106]

By 1877, the Adams family was finished as a political force in America. Henry belonged to "a venerable but no longer electable dynastic family."[1107] The light which came from the flowering of New England culture known as the American Renaissance of the 1850s burned bright for a moment as abolitionism but was snuffed out by the hurricane of change which followed the Civil War:

> Between 1876 and 1890 seven new states entered the union, midwestern presidents sat in the White House, and the American Indian Wars entered their late stages; the Standard Oil Company swelled into the Standard Oil Trust during these years, while the opening of the Brooklyn Bridge and arrival of several million immigrants established a strikingly new urban sense of scale and mobility.[1108]

The year 1877 was also the *annus mirabilis* which gave birth to the American labor movement. In July 1877 disgruntled workers in towns and cities across the country rose up in a spontaneous national strike against the railroad conglomerates that were slashing wages to starvation levels. By the time "The Great Railroad Strike of 1877" took place, the labor issue had become so urgent that it penetrated even Henry Ward Beecher's lust besotted mind. Beecher may have taken note of what was going on but he was incapable of understanding it, much less capable of proposing a solution. So instead of praising the strikers as he had praised John Brown and the abolitionists, Beecher condemned the strikers, especially the "foreign element" and their socialist theories for interfering with the natural laws of capitalism and evolution. "I do not say that a dollar a day is enough to support a working man," he thundered. "Not enough to support a man and five children if a man would insist on smoking and drinking beer," he added. "But the man who cannot live on bread and water is not fit to live."[1109]

When he wasn't sleeping with other men's wives, Beecher spent his time reading Herbert Spencer, who created the term "survival of the fittest" to justify the application of Charles Darwin's theory of evolution to capitalism, where it was used to drive down wages and transfer surplus value from the worker who created it to the capitalist who could then justify its theft by invoking Spencer and Darwin. Beecher "helped gain acceptance" for capitalism's theft

---

1106 Brown, Adams, p. 99.
1107 Brown, *The Last American Aristocrat*, p. 161.
1108 Brown, *The Last American Aristocrat*, p. 169.
1109 Applegate, *Beecher*, p. 456.

Part II: The Romantic Rehabilitation of Nature

of labor while he was stealing other men's wives at a church that was created by Brooklyn capitalists like Henry Bowen, who brought Beecher to Brooklyn to accommodate religious dogmas to emerging economic realities as "This once-bucolic village had matured into the nation's third-largest city and a major industrial center."[1110] Bowen and Beecher were "living in a period of such rapid change that the devices of virtue could not keep pace with the innovations of sin,"[1111] and Bowen wasn't going to kill the goose that was laying the golden egg, even if it meant that his wife ended up sleeping with Beecher because "no Brooklynite took greater advantage of the blurry ethical lines among government patronage, economic opportunity, and moral stewardship than Henry Bowen."[1112] According to *The Brooklyn Eagle*, which was now publishing rumors that Beecher was an adulterer, "Everything in this world, to Henry Chandler Bowen, is something to be bought, something to be sold, or something to be haggled for. He is always in the market."[1113]

About the time he resigned from his professorship at Harvard, Henry Adams complained about the lack of "intellectual energy" in post-Civil War Boston. The city which had been the Athens of America in the 1850s, had become "a curious place" with:

> no society worth the name, no wit, no intellectual energy or competition, no clash of minds or of schools, no interests, no masculine self-assertion or ambition. Everything is respectable, and nothing amusing. There are no outlaws. There are not only no convictions but no strong wants.... I am allowed to sit in my chair at Harvard College and rail at everything which the College respects, and no one cares.[1114]

Henry Adams—who was "the last American Aristocrat," scion to the family which included John Adams, who helped create the Republic, and John Quincy Adams, who was its president—lived to see his family's legacy eclipsed by men of the west with a concomitant coarsening of American culture.

The Education of Henry Adams was an autobiography as well as a history of the most paradigmatic family in American history as of its writing, but it was also a drama based on a "tragic vision of the past," which showed "how the modern age emerged in the United States."[1115]

American Protestantism "meant surprisingly little to him."[1116] Adams was unimpressed with what he called the "eccentric off-shoots" of New England

---

[1110] Applegate, *Beecher*, p. 391.
[1111] Applegate, *Beecher*, p. 391.
[1112] Applegate, *Beecher*, p. 391.
[1113] Applegate, *Beecher*, p. 391.
[1114] David S Brown, *The Last American Aristocrat: The Brilliant Life and Improbable Education of Henry Adams*, p. 170.
[1115] Brown, *The Last American Aristocrat*, p. 5.
[1116] Brown, *The Last American Aristocrat*, p. 32.

Puritanism, by which he meant Transcendentalism, Universalism and the Utopian communities they spawned. Nathaniel Hawthorne's satiric novel *The Blithedale Romance* had ruined any appreciation Adams may have had for Bronson Alcott and his ill-fated socialist adventure, Fruitlands. Adams felt that Ralph Waldo Emerson "was naïf"[1117] when it came to politics, which was the field in which Adams ancestors had excelled.

Adams' heroes resided in the state house, not in the pulpit. Adams idolized Charles Sumner as the political man of his age. Sumner was "the classical ornament of the anti-slavery party; their pride in him was unbounded, and their admiration outspoken. The boy Henry worshipped him.... The relation of Mr. Sumner in the household was far closer than any relation of blood."[1118]

Sumner, who at six feet four inches, literally and figuratively towered over his contemporaries, was Adams' "ideal of greatness,"[1119] a man of action who got things done in Congress while feeling equally at home with the Romantic poet William Wordsworth.

Henry Adams was three years younger than Samuel Clemens. To the generation born in the 1830s, "the religious instinct had vanished,"[1120] only to be replaced by the religion of art, particularly European Catholic art, which provided Adams not religion but "aesthetic expressions of religious experience" of the sort provided by Clive Bell at a later date in England and the "*l'art pour l'art*" movement in France represented best by Theophile Gautier.

In 1854, Adams entered Harvard University as a 16-year-old to the manor born. The university which had been created to educate the Puritan clergy had, with the collapse of Calvinism and the rise of an etiolated Unitarianism, discovered that it had nothing to say. Having abandoned the Calvinism which was its *raison d'etre*, Harvard sought to impart to its students "the liberal Protestant virtues—moderation, balance, judgment, restraint"— that mirrored the character of the Cambridge Unitarian clergy."[1121] By 1854 theology had died, but the vacuum that death had created was yet to be filled by the "science" of Darwin and Spencer. As a result, Adams contented himself with a course by Agassiz on the glacial period and paleontology as "the only teaching that appealed to [my] imagination."[1122]

Like J. Robert Oppenheimer at a later date, Adams left Harvard with its "quasi-Puritan convictions"[1123] and went to Germany to lay hold of the latest

---

1117 Brown, *The Last American Aristocrat*, p. 4.
1118 Brown, *The Last American Aristocrat*, p. 34.
1119 Brown, *The Last American Aristocrat*, p. 34.
1120 Brown, *The Last American Aristocrat*, p. 33.
1121 Brown, *The Last American Aristocrat*, p. 41.
1122 Brown, *The Last American Aristocrat*, p. 40.
1123 Brown, *The Last American Aristocrat*, p. 40.

in scientific thought because "Man has reduced the universe to a machine."[1124] Innocent of the German language, Adams quickly realized that "Berlin is too much for me."[1125] Moving to Dresden didn't help, and so Henry embarked on the Grand Tour, ending up in Venice, where he "trooped about stately palazzos and crumbling churches, took in Titians and cool evening crypts"[1126] and began his first serious encounter with the world of European beauty. Henry then spent two weeks in Rome, "the happiest fourteen days known ever to have existed."[1127] Adams, however, is curiously silent about St. Peter's Basilica, which was the high point of the cultured American's pilgrimage to Rome from James Fenimore Cooper to Mark Twain. Adams understanding of architecture and Catholicism was distinctly French and Marian, not Italian and Baroque, as his book on Mont-Saint-Michel and Chartres would show.

The Education of Henry Adams got derailed by politics back home when John Brown attacked Harper's Ferry on October 16, 1859. Henry and his father spent the Civil War years at the Court of St. James trying to keep England from entering the war on the side of the Confederacy. "The clock of history," however, "refused to stop."[1128] When the post-Civil War *Zeitgeist* pulled out of the station, Henry Adams was left behind standing on the platform because "Grant's victories in Virginia, the assassination of Lincoln, and the collapse of the Confederacy remade America," into something more and more difficult to reconcile with the America that his ancestors had created. Henry Adams, like Rip van Winkle when he awoke, experienced an identity crisis after the war that reflected badly on what both he and America had become. If America was now too rowdy, Adams had become, in reaction, too effete. When Adams was off on the Grand Tour:

> He missed, as well, the rise of a new Trans-Mississippi West. The decade saw four new states, including Nevada and Nebraska, enter the Union, the Alaska Purchase, and the emergence of Jesse James into a folk legend. In a Philadelphia factory, John B. Stetson began to make a fortune producing "Cowboy" hats; and in Wyoming women were granted the right to vote. One hears clearly in this sentimental overture the echo of Henry's own boyhood journey to Washington in 1850. In that lost antebellum world he had met President Taylor, observed the "great people" entering and exiting the "great rooms," and soaked in an atmosphere thick with national and family history. But this type of personalized politics, one with all the fragrant redolence of a Quincy summer, no longer held court. It was an

---

1124 Brown, *The Last American Aristocrat*, p. 42.
1125 Brown, *The Last American Aristocrat*, p. 52.
1126 Brown, *The Last American Aristocrat*, p. 58.
1127 Brown, *The Last American Aristocrat*, p. 60.
1128 Brown, *The Last American Aristocrat*, p. 84.

illusion that Adams gave up with great reluctance—and mourned long thereafter.[1129]

John Quincy Adams had been superseded by Andrew Jackson, and Henry's father by Abraham Lincoln who was in Henry's eyes "clumsy, rustic, and decidedly too western,"[1130] even if Lincoln relied on Henry and his father as America's representatives to the Court of St. James. By the time Henry came of age, the White House had stopped calling on their services. His resentment at being snubbed by his inferiors comes out in his fiction. In Adams' novel *Democracy*, the main character:

> commiserates with his "kind," and anyone hailing from, say, west of the Appalachians is in for rough treatment. The president is dismissed as "a small Indiana farmer" pushed forward by an aggressively unsophisticated wife and a brutish crew of "tobacco-chewing, newspaper-reading satellites."[1131]

Adams' friend Henry James said that *Democracy* was the favorite novel of the ruling class in England. James told Clover Adams, Henry's wife, that Prime Minister William Gladstone loved the book, which did not bode well for a novel which was subtitled "an American tale."[1132] It was not written for Americans; it was written about Americans in a condescending way that appealed to English aristocrats and not men of the West, whom it ridiculed, even though or perhaps because they were now in the ascendency and excluding the Adams family from the levers of power.

In July 1868 Henry Adams returned to America after seven years overseas to find the House of Adams in a state of "chronic decline." In the early years of the 19th century, John Quincy Adams "had captured the presidency." In the intervening years, "his son occupied a more modest congressional seat, and now his namesake grandson failed repeatedly to win even a state race."[1133]

Faced with the collapse of the Constitution John Adams help to write, the rise of corporate power, the rise of the man of the West, the eclipse of any understanding of an American elite class, and the mass immigration of Irish Catholics, Henry Adams "failed to appreciate the problem of race in America with any urgency, insight, or empathy."[1134]

But Adams was ahead of his time in recognizing the Jewish Question, a problem which raged in France while he was visiting that country's Cathedrals. Davis predictably refers to Adams as an anti-Semite without looking into

---

1129 Brown, *The Last American Aristocrat*, pp. 84-5.
1130 Brown, *The Last American Aristocrat*, p. 69.
1131 Brown, *The Last American Aristocrat*, p. 191.
1132 Brown, *The Last American Aristocrat*, p. 191.
1133 Brown, *The Last American Aristocrat*, p. 90.
1134 Brown, *The Last American Aristocrat*, p. 99.

Part II: The Romantic Rehabilitation of Nature

the Jews' involvement in usury in France and the United States and the connection between bankers like Jacob Schiff and Jewish revolutionaries like Trotsky at one end of the political spectrum and "the rising plutocracy" which "threatened to upend the republic"[1135] at the other. Because the Jewish Question was dividing France during his visit, anti-Semitism became an integral part of Adams' new American identity:

> He invariably identified bankers and robber barons as the enemies of tradition, attacking Jews, Germans, and English alike for turning calm into chaos and chaos into profit. His frantic insistence to Hay that "the whole carcass" of the Anglo-Continental civilization was "rotten with worms,—socialist worms, anarchist worms, Jew worms, clerical worms," is one that he variably repeated over the years.[1136]

Like his father, Henry was "a hard money man,"[1137] who made the mistake of identifying the elite with the creditor class, but he quickly became appalled at the excesses of the capitalist class in the Gilded Age. Adams told the Boston economist Edward Atkinson that at the heart of political corruption lay "big money's power to purchase public policy."[1138] After the Civil War, "the House of (J.P.) Morgan replaced the House of Adams."[1139]

Unable to stem the tide of the common man, Henry adopted the persona of the effete intellectual. In 1869, Henry became "a public intellectual, a fresh profession in America."[1140] In 1872, Henry reviewed *Mountaineering in the Sierra Nevada* in *The North American Review*, praising its author Clarence King as "a kind of young hero of the American type."[1141] In doing so, Adams conceded the field to the man of the West in the battle over who best epitomized the representative American Man. As Davis puts it:

> Comfortable on a mountain or in a museum, King represented a certain masculine ideal that would always elude Adams. Intrepid, brave, gallant, humorous, and above all unaffected, he was a "natural," a child of the open American scene in a way that Henry could never be.[1142]

Adams was a personal friend of Henry James, who was also a close friend of "Clover" Adams, Henry's wife.[1143] Henry Adams was certainly not an intellectual nativist in the mold of Henry James or Mark Twain, but his

---

1135 Brown, *The Last American Aristocrat*, p. 121.
1136 Brown, *The Last American Aristocrat*, p. 313.
1137 Brown, *The Last American Aristocrat*, p. 114.
1138 Brown, *The Last American Aristocrat*. P. 104.
1139 Brown, *The Last American Aristocrat*, p. 113.
1140 Brown, *The Last American Aristocrat*, p. 109.
1141 Brown, *The Last American Aristocrat*, p. 178.
1142 Brown, *The Last American Aristocrat*, p. 179.
1143 Brown, *The Last American Aristocrat*, p. 144.

attachment to the Germanic race as the source of American institutions diminished his intellectual attraction to Catholicism, rendering him a philo-Catholic aesthete in the eyes of both the men of the east and the men of the west as anti-Catholic Whig History triumphed in American letters. Francis Parkman, for instance, "celebrated the removal of French Catholic power in the New World and with it the commensurate rise of Anglo influence, typified by congregationalism, constitutionalism, and capitalism" as based on "the progress of Protestant, Anglo-Saxon civilization."[1144] "Adams's conflation of genetics and social development in Anglo-Saxon Law aligned comfortably with the dominant race thinking of his day,"[1145] but it cut him off from the Catholic culture of Europe to which he was drawn by its beauty. Despite his attraction to French Catholic Cathedrals, Adams tried to block Catholic immigration, by joining the Immigration Restriction League, founded by three Harvard graduates, who shared "the emerging social Darwinian worldview. . . popularized by the prominent English polymath Herbert Spencer," which was enjoying "a remarkable vogue in America."[1146]

[1144] Brown, *The Last American Aristocrat*, p. 150.
[1145] Brown, *The Last American Aristocrat*, p. 150.
[1146] Brown, *The Last American Aristocrat*, p. 151.

Chapter 32

George Lathrop Converts to Catholicism

In September 1877, George Lathrop lost his position as associate editor at *The Atlantic*, less than a year after his wife Rose gave birth to their first and only child Francis Hawthorne Lathrop, known as Francie, on November 10, 1876. Shortly after giving birth, Rose began exhibiting "symptoms of hallucination and mental distress" which led her doctor to claim that she was suffering from postpartum psychosis and have her committed to the McLean Asylum for the Insane."[1147] Rose recovered quickly from her depression, and with her health restored, she and George "appeared to have enjoyed a period of great domestic happiness and marital stability."[1148] That period ended five years later when Francie died unexpectedly of diphtheria on February 6, 1881.

Deprived of the child which united them, Rose began to strike out on her own. When her aunt Elizabeth Hawthorne died, Rose made sure that she alone received her portion of the inheritance, which enabled her to travel to Europe alone, much to her husband's distress and consternation. On April 11, 1883, George wrote to Thomas Bailey Aldrich that he was not disposed to work because his wife "by way of a little after breakfast surprise—announced that she had decided to go to Europe this summer. This has shaken me up somewhat."[1149]

Rose's trip to Europe evidently re-awakened her memories of Catholic Rome but it did not strengthen her marriage, which became characterized by "passing quarrels" and "short periods" of separation.[1150] Her brother Julian may have felt that Rose's marriage was a mistake, but he nonetheless "persuaded Rose not to seek a legal separation from George at this time."[1151]

The Lathrops continued to write and advance their careers, but their position in New York literary world was shaken when they announced their conversion to Catholicism in 1891. Fifty-six newspapers nation-wide considered the event newsworthy, but the generally hostile reaction of the newspapers prompted George to write an apologia, claiming that Catholicism "allowed for a union

---

1147 Valenti, *To Myself a Stranger*, p. 37.
1148 Valenti, *To Myself a Stranger*, p. 62.
1149 Valenti, *To Myself a Stranger*, p. 69.
1150 Maynard, *A Fire Was Lighted*, p. 244.
1151 Valenti, *To Myself a Stranger*, p. 71.

of head and heart."[1152] Far from "surrendering his intellect to the arbitrary control of the pope," George saw in Catholicism a "reasoning and an ordering principle" which was the antithesis to the subjectivism of the Unitarianism and Transcendentalism which Nathaniel Hawthorne had experienced at Brook Farm. The reviewers remained skeptical even though one admitted that "Mr. Hawthorne seems to have been greatly attracted by Catholicism."[1153] Sophia was ambivalent enough about the attraction that she and her husband felt toward Catholicism that she felt the need to assure her blue-stocking sister Elizabeth Peabody that there was no "danger of Rose being anything else but a Unitarian." In making that claim, Sophia underestimated the effect which Italian art had on her daughter. The same spiritual quest which began in Rome when she was a nine-year-old in the company of her famous father led Rose to accept Catholicism as an adult, but now it was paradoxically leading her to abandon her marriage. Troubled by the conflict between her desire for a religious life and her duties as wife, but no longer a mother, Rose consulted a priest who told her: "I can conceive of nothing which ought to be more agreeable to the heart of a true Christian wife than to cheerfully put aside any occupation even of devotion, if thereby her husband's happiness is subserved. And so, in like manner should a husband rejoice in making such personal sacrifices for his wife."[1154]

This was clearly not the answer Rose sought, so she kept on looking for a justification to serve the poor directly, haunted by her vision of the wretched condition of the poor and dying in 19th century New York City. She had come to agree with her brother Julian that her marriage had been a mistake, but, thinking about it from the divine perspective, she consoled herself by the thought that God could make use of her mistakes to fulfill his plans:

If all we miss
In the plans that shake
The world, still God has need of this,—
Even our mistake[1155]

Rose considered marriage a mistake, not just marriage with George, because it impeded her desire to serve the poor and have a closer union with Christ. Rose's decision to leave the marriage was made easier by her husband's behavior. Maynard calls George "a spoiled boy" who was "a drunkard even before he began to drink."[1156] Rose agonized over the decision to leave George in a lengthy letter to her friend Charlotte Holloway which made clear

---

1152 Valenti, *To Myself a Stranger*, p. 101.
1153 Valenti, *To Myself a Stranger*, p. 103.
1154 Maynard, *A Fire Was Lighted*, p. 241.
1155 Maynard, *A Fire Was Lighted*, p. 246.
1156 Maynard, *A Fire Was Lighted*, p. 250.

Part II: The Romantic Rehabilitation of Nature

that "although Rose was sensitive to George's distress, her resolution was firm." After years of "prayer and thought and patience and weighing wise counsel," Rose took leave of her "husband's care forever" in 1896. George was devastated and probably never recovered because it drove him deeper into the behavior that Rose used to justify their separation. "To put the whole matter in a sentence, it was the irreconcilable incompatibility of both, rather than George's drinking, that seems to have wrecked this marriage."[1157]

Seeing George's reaction to the separation she initiated, Rose concluded, "His pain now in the separation is very sad," but she went on to add, "I doubt that it is greater than the long pain I have suffered and ever much suffer. When he learns to offer this pain to Christ and make it purify him, he will ennoble it and become helpful to others who have not as much courage."[1158] Rose felt that the desire to lead a religious life was perfectly suited for "one of my temperament and associations and talents (such as they are)." Rose concluded her *apologia pro vita sua* by saying:

> This idea and longing have been so constantly with me for three years, so constantly the object of my prayers, that I have no doubt they are the greatest love of my heart . . . [the] beauty of a home is dross compared to the beauty of the shabbiest altar. ... I would have suffered anything to prevent scandal, because my husband and I are Catholic converts, but I could not prevent it. ... I hope my husband will grow to lead a holy life.[1159]

Maynard says that Rose recognized that "seen in the light of Providence, her marriage was not a mistake at all, though Julian described it as an irreparable error. It was the preparation for something else."[1160] But he also adds, "Those who can read between the lines of letters can see plainly enough that very early Rose was not happy in her marriage."[1161] Maynard goes on to claim that George's drinking precipitated the separation:

> which had been threatening ever since they married. He had, no doubt, over and over again vowed amendment, and probably had kept his weakness under control for a time, only to relapse once more. But there could be only one end to such a case, and there came a time when George grew so violent in his cups that it was no longer safe for Rose to be with him. She therefore applied to the bishop of the diocese for permission to leave her husband. This the bishop's vicar-general gave her in writing. Upon receipt of it, she left the pleasant house on Post Hill Place and never went back.[1162]

1157 Maynard, *A Fire Was Lighted*, p. 250.
1158 Valenti, *To Myself a Stranger*, p. 129.
1159 Valenti, *To Myself a Stranger*, p. 129.
1160 Maynard, *A Fire Was Lighted*, p. 246.
1161 Maynard, *A Fire Was Lighted*, p. 247.
1162 Maynard, *A Fire Was Lighted*, p. 251.

Valenti says there is "no evidence" that Lathrop was an alcoholic, because it was not mentioned in "letters, journals, or any other record left by the Hawthornes or the Lathrops," while conceding that family members "may indeed have been reticent about [discussing] alcoholism and thus omitted any mention of it from their writing."[1163] Valenti concludes their separation came about because George "did not share her desire to work in poverty among the cancerous poor, and, as her husband, he resisted her abandoning their marriage to pursue her dream."[1164]

Patricia Dunlavy Valenti, Rose Hawthorne's biographer, puts the burden of responsibility for the break-up of their marriage on Rose in a way that casts doubt on her sanctity; Maynard puts the burden on George in a way that exonerates Rose of any responsibility to her wayward husband. Either way, the separation had devastating effects on George, who always referred to the split as "my wife's desertion."[1165] George experienced "considerable financial distress"[1166] as "his literary powers now seemed to fail him."[1167] Rose continued to see George's drinking as caused by more deeply rooted spiritual problems, and her response was to offer novenas "for the complete conversion of my husband."[1168]

George found little consolation in Rose's new-found spirituality. He was convinced that Rose was suffering from a mental disorder and that the only hope for her recovery "lies in your putting yourself under thorough and special medical care for the restoration of your nervous system." In response, Rose replied that her husband "would prefer to have me in a mental asylum than working for charity!"[1169]

Maynard feels that George had become "a broken man" even though he was only in his mid-forties.[1170] His drinking increased, although "without reaching the last stages of alcoholism,"[1171] but the drinking paled in comparison to the effects of the separation, which in George's words, "has subjected me to a fearful strain, had kept me on the go, unsettled most of my plans, & made it next to impossible for me to complete any important literary work."[1172]

George, ironically, ended up in the same situation his famous father-in-law found himself in at the end of his life, unable to complete what he had started

---

1163 Valenti, *To Myself a Stranger*, p. 148.
1164 Valenti, *To Myself a Stranger*, p. 148.
1165 Valenti, *To Myself a Stranger*, p. 145.
1166 Valenti, *To Myself a Stranger*, p. 145.
1167 Valenti, *To Myself a Stranger*, p. 145.
1168 Maynard, *A Fire Was Lighted*, p. 316.
1169 Bird, *From Witchery to Sanctity*, p. 137.
1170 Maynard, *A Fire Was Lighted*, p. 317.
1171 Maynard, *A Fire Was Lighted*, p. 317.
1172 Maynard, *A Fire Was Lighted*, p. 318.

Part II: The Romantic Rehabilitation of Nature

and settling into a depression which was not helped, in Lathrop's case, by his consumption of alcohol. There is no indication that Rose saw any connection between her father's fate and her husband's. Rose left George in 1895 and received a Church approved separation in 1896. George, however, refused to accept the separation, insisting to the end that he had kept the path open to married life. Rose acknowledged the pain her separation had caused her husband, but no matter how sad it made George, Rose "doubt[ed] that it is greater than the long pain I have suffered and ever more suffer."[1173] The Birds tell us that:

> In 1896, Rose turned away forever from her previous life. She left upper New York, the city of the rich and respectable, of large homes and expensive stores and went into the New York of the lower East side, a slum area where the streets were crowded and the houses dingy and the people neither rich nor respected.[1174]

Rose always claimed that "the strongest influence" on the decision she made to found her apostolate for indigent victims of cancer "was her father and the sympathy he consistently showed for those captured by poverty and disease."[1175] The death of her child also contributed to that decision. After her son's death, Rose explained to a friend "A married! woman, loving children as I do and bereft of them, must, it seems to me, fill the void in her life with works of charity."[1176] Perhaps the best summary of why she had dedicated her life to such a demanding vocation came in an article Rose wrote in the *Christian Herald*:

> I am trying to serve the poor as a servant. I wish to serve the cancerous poor because they are avoided more than any other class of sufferers; and I wish to go to them as a poor creature myself, though powerful to help them through the open-handed gifts of public kindness, because it is by humility and sacrifice alone that we feel the holy spirit of pity.[1177]

In an article which appeared in the *Atlantic* in 1928, Julian claimed that "No one familiar with her as a girl could have foreseen what her maturity was to be; the change was abrupt and strange," adding "Conditions for the departure were no doubt present, but hidden – even perhaps from herself."[1178]

Hidden or not, Rose wasted no time brooding, as her father would have done. Instead, she approached her new vocation with a Puritan ferocity. Maynard tells us that a disposition characterized by "violence" was "necessary

---

1173 Bird, *From Witchery to Sanctity*, p. 137.
1174 Bird, *From Witchery to Sanctity*, p. 138.
1175 Bird, *From Witchery to Sanctity*, p. 139.
1176 Bird, *From Witchery to Sanctity*, p. 141.
1177 Bird, *From Witchery to Sanctity*, p. 141.
1178 Maynard, *A Fire Was Lighted*, p. 257.

to the career of self-sacrifice she was about to begin."[1179] Rose claimed that she got this disposition from her father.

"My own convictions about human duties," she said, "towards human suffering were clearly formed in youth by countless passages read in the works of Nathaniel Hawthorne." And then she quotes at length the account he gave in *Our Old Home* of the workhouse child. She concludes,

> What this man could do, and taught me that I should do, under the standard of Christ, must I do, or not? That question returned repeatedly, and I met it trembling. If occasion presented itself, I knew well that I must do a thing, however difficult, which the fearless writer inculcated. In short, we can never make a successful argument against the principles of Christ.

For herself she was to discover, as did St. Francis of Assisi when he embraced the leper, as did St. Elizabeth of Hungary when she put a leper in her own bed, that it was Christ to whom this charity was shown.[1180]

Perhaps she learned from her father that the poor needed beauty. Asked by a policeman, "You with your refinement and appreciation of beauty! – how can you look at her without shuddering?" Rose replied, "the poor do not always realize that they are being cheered by beauty."[1181] Rose saw a link between beauty and service to the poor in her father's tale "The Artist of the Beautiful":

> We wonder if, after all, our vision is a mere illusion of to-day's material reality, a mechanism of screws and glass; but we know at heart that our faith in honor, our vision of the Beautiful, is the one reality that never breaks or vanishes; and the more miraculously we can give it semblance in this world, the happier for us." Rose concludes this article with the following reflection on the end of her father's life: "Faithful but weary, uncomplaining but destitute of strength, as one is penniless who has given all his substance for the poor, in obedience to the simple direction of Christ when He was asked the whole truth—white-haired, pale, a laborer spent, Hawthorne ended his vigilant life at the close of sixty years of honesty and kindness, keenest perception, and exquisite hope."[1182]

Rose learned from her father not to count the cost, especially not in light of the utilitarian calculus known as prudence in her day. Hawthorne had taught Rose that "Whatever she did had to be headlong and reckless, without thrift." The practicality she had learned as a girl would now manifest itself

---

1179 Maynard, *A Fire Was Lighted*, p. 258.
1180 Maynard, *A Fire Was Lighted*, p. 258.
1181 Maynard, *A Fire Was Lighted*, p. 285.
1182 Valenti, *To Myself a Stranger*, p. 133.

Part II: The Romantic Rehabilitation of Nature

as throwing to the winds "what men call prudence."[1183] Rose associated her dedication to indigent victims of terminal cancer with virtues that her father held in high esteem:

> He demonstrated sympathy for all humanity, particularly for those whose poverty was both spiritual and material, as can be seen in his efforts while consul in England on behalf of shipwrecked sailors, his use of his own funds to bury indigents, and his care for destitute travelers.[1184]

Yet, by becoming a nun, Rose was the opposite of her father, who observed but could not act. In one of her last letters before her death at seventy-five, Rose says, "I never really wanted to write about life. I wanted to live it." If introspection obliterated action in Hawthorne's life, action obliterated introspection in Rose's. "The passions of her nature," Julian wrote, "doubtless as urgent as ever, centered no longer around her personal fate and interests, for in her own view she no longer existed. She lived, labored and prayed only for those incarnations of mortal misery which she had drawn about her."[1185]

Shortly after separating from her husband, Rose made a retreat with the Sisters of Charity in Wellesley Hills, Massachusetts, "based on the life and works of St. Vincent de Paul,"[1186] who had also dedicated his life to serving the poor. During the summer of 1896, Rose enrolled in a three-month nursing course at Memorial Hospital in New York[1187] which allowed her to begin her work as a nurse at that city's cancer hospital. After realizing that the cancer patients at that hospital were only there because they could afford to pay for their care, Rose began look for a place where she could care for the indigent, whose only option was dying alone in some wretched tenement basement or Blackwell's Island, which the dying referred to as "hell on earth."[1188] Rose, later known by her religious name Mother Mary Alphonsa, eventually settled on renting a wretched tenement on Scammel Street, where she set up shop with one assistant, Alice Huber, and one patient, a Mrs Watson, who was suffering from a particularly disfiguring form of face cancer. Rose Hawthorne's rule in treating cancer patients was not for the faint of heart:

> There is to be no harsh speaking to any patient, and no shrinking on the part of any nurse from close contact. To emphasize this the Sisters are forbidden to wear rubber gloves when dressing cancers. There are to be no experiments with the patients, no use of knife or even of radium is allowed. There were occasions when Mother Alphonsa could have obtained large contributions if only she had relaxed this rule. She much

---

1183 Maynard, *A Fire Was Lighted*, p. 259.
1184 Valenti, *To Myself a Stranger*, p. 133.
1185 Valenti, *To Myself a Stranger*, p. 161.
1186 Bird, *From Witchery to Sanctity*, p. 137.
1187 Bird, *From Witchery to Sanctity*, p. 137.
1188 Maynard, *A Fire Was Lighted*, p. 261.

preferred poverty. Indeed, in order to emphasize unworldliness the constitutions lay down that all future foundations are, like the first two, to begin in poverty and in a poor part of the city.[1189]

As word spread of their activity, the house on Scammel Street received more patients and more recruits, many of which Rose sent home, until the facilities, which were never ideal, became totally inadequate and necessitated moving to a new facility at 668 Water St.

1189 Maynard, *A Fire Was Lighted*, p. 368.

Chapter 33

Clover Adams Commits Suicide

In the early afternoon of December 6, 1885, Henry Adams' wife Clover committed suicide by ingesting a vial of potassium cyanide which she kept on hand to develop photographs.[1190] Henry James understood that Henry and Clover were concerned about their inability to have children and that it affected their marriage, but he had no understanding of the depth of her despair or its cause.[1191] Instead he attributed her suicide to "hereditary melancholy," perhaps with Hawthorne in mind, although Hawthorne did not commit suicide. James tried to view Clover's death in a positive light by claiming that she found in suicide "the solution of the knottiness of existence."[1192] James made Clover's suicide the basis for his story "The Modern Warning," where he Jamesified it by turning it into a conflict over cultural differences between Agatha Grice's "beloved American brother and her new English spouse,"[1193] a favorite theme in his novels which he may have discussed with Clover. The evidence in Henry Adam's *roman a clef Esther* points to a different cause. Adams, like the protagonist of the novel, "never quite reconciled with the secularism that he absorbed as part of the general cultural drift."[1194] The collapse of Protestantism led not to promiscuity, as it had with Rev. Beecher, but to despair. In the eponymous novel, Esther cries out to Strong, "I want to submit [to religion].... Why can't some of you make me?"[1195] Like Hawthorne and Melville, Adams was uncomfortable in his unbelief but, unable to enter the Church whose beauty fascinated them, Adams took consolation in the Church's art rather than her sacraments.

Adams named his novel's heroine Esther Dudley, after the title of an 1839 tale by Nathaniel Hawthorne, "Old Esther Dudley," about an old woman "unable to grasp the fact that the defeated British are never returning to her native Massachusetts."[1196] Like Hawthorne and Adams and his wife Clover,

---

1190 Brown, *The Last American Aristocrat*, p. 221.
1191 Brown, *The Last American Aristocrat*, p. 177.
1192 Brown, *The Last American Aristocrat*, p. 222.
1193 Brown, *The Last American Aristocrat*, p. 222.
1194 Brown, *The Last American Aristocrat*, p. 212.
1195 Brown, *The Last American Aristocrat*, p. 212.
1196 Brown, *The Last American Aristocrat*, p. 209.

Esther cries out, "Some people are made with faith. I am made without it." Davis sees Esther's confession as "emblematic of a growing generation of agnostics and nonbelievers who have crossed the Darwinian Rubicon."[1197]

In *Esther*, Adams "mourned the passing of the old Emersonian universe of openness and possibility."[1198] In the wake of Clover's suicide, Adams began "chasing restoration abroad,"[1199] where he fell "under the spell of medieval French music, art, and architecture," which struck "a resonant emotional chord."[1200]

In 1895, Henry Cabot Lodge's wife Anna asked Adams to spend several weeks abroad with them and their two sons to tour the northern cathedral towns of France: Amiens, Rouen, Bayeux, Mont-Saint-Michel, Le Mans, and Chartres.[1201] It was "in these active Gothic haunts Henry suddenly discovered a medieval counterpoint to the turmoil of the modern condition."[1202] Adams later wrote that "Everything pales before my discovery of the meaning of Gothic, which was to me a revelation. My intense excitement when I first began to read Chartres, and Le Mans, and all the rest, could never be equaled again by anything."[1203]

Adams ended *Mont Saint Michel and Chartres* with an opaque chapter on St. Thomas Aquinas, but probably only because the Angelic Doctor taught in Paris and was part of the French Middle Ages Adams so admired. His paradigm for Catholicism was Chartres cathedral, a building inspired by the Blessed Virgin that had next to nothing to do with philosophy because "the female taste seemed not much to care" about "theology in the metaphysical sense."[1204] Chartres cathedral had hardly anything to say about the Trinity, which was "always the most metaphysical subtlety of the Church. Indeed, you might find amusement herein searching the cathedral for any distinct expression at all of the Trinity as a dogma recognized by Mary. . . . Even if the Trinity . . . is anywhere expressed, you will hardly find here an attempt to explain its metaphysical meaning—not even a mystic triangle."[1205]

The English poet John Keats once famously said that "Beauty is truth—truth beauty" in his "Ode on a Grecian Urn," but Adams seems to have regarded these transcendentals as occupying two separate realms. Beauty was

---

1197 Brown, *The Last American Aristocrat*, p. 210.
1198 Brown, *The Last American Aristocrat*, p. 210.
1199 Brown, *The Last American Aristocrat*, p. 236.
1200 Brown, *The Last American Aristocrat*, p. 210.
1201 Brown, *The Last American Aristocrat*, p. 309.
1202 Brown, *The Last American Aristocrat*, p. 309.
1203 Brown, *The Last American Aristocrat*, p. 310.
1204 Henry Adams, *Mont-Saint-Michel and Chartres* (New York: Doubleday Anchor Books, 1959), p. 108.
1205 Henry Adams, *Mont-Saint-Michel and Chartres* (New York: Doubleday Anchor Books, 1959), pp. 108-9.

Part II: The Romantic Rehabilitation of Nature

Catholic, but truth was English and French, and the "two high priests of our faith" were Alexis de Tocqueville and British philosopher John Stuart Mill.[1206] Adams agreed:

> with their shared conviction that democratic societies require a small elite—primarily of the best educated—to add distinction, expertise, and tone. In Tocquevillian terms, the "best government is not that in which all have share, but that which is directed by the class of the highest principle and intellectual ambition." No doubt Henry imagined himself a future elect in this select club. Something of a backward-looking faith, it harkened to the deferential politics once the bread and butter of the early American republic, when men like Washington, Adams, and Jefferson could count on being recognized and rewarded as the "better sort." The rise of a more inclusive democratic sprit, beginning in the 1810s with a rising suffrage in the new western states and running through the populistic age of Jackson, pointed to a shifting direction in statecraft that never sat well with Henry.[1207]

Adams identified with Tocqueville and Mill's understanding of the emergence of democracy as "an inevitable historical outcome," but he wasn't happy with it. The Civil War may have served as "positive proof that representative government's triumph over a pecking order of planters demonstrated the resilience and self-correcting nature of a people's republic," but it also gave birth to a new American identity that excluded people like Henry Adams from the realm of political power which his ancestors had occupied.

Two years before his pilgrimage to France, Henry Adams attended the Columbian Exposition in Chicago, where he discovered the dynamo and made it the symbol of American identity. If Mont-Saint-Michel represented unity and continuity, Chicago represented a "rupture in historical sequence."[1208] The Columbian Exposition was a celebration of the "watt," the "ampere," and the "erg," "units of energy that symbolized both literally and metaphorically, the harnessing of hitherto untapped physical and chemical resources," which were blind and destructive without the spiritual guidance that only the Catholic Church could give. The man of the east was primarily an intellectual who deprived himself of the intellectual force he needed to counter the man of the west by his refusal to convert to Catholicism, which alone could provide a coherent explanation of the vagaries of American thought. This failure of will guaranteed the rise of the man of the west as the only representative American. Orestes Brownson had said as much, and his son was to repeat that lesson in a talk he gave at Notre Dame university not far from Chicago and at

---

1206 Brown, *The Last American Aristocrat*, p. 83.
1207 Brown, *The Last American Aristocrat*, p. 83.
1208 Brown, *The Last American Aristocrat*, p. 286.

around the same time as the Exposition. Chicago epitomized "the fragmented modern urban experience."[1209] Adams claimed that:

> Chicago delighted me because it was just as chaotic as my own mind, and I found my own preposterous state of consciousness reflected and exaggerated at every turn. A pure white temple, on the pure blue sea, with an Italian sky, all vast and beautiful as the world never saw it before, and in it the most astounding, confused, bewildering mass of art and industry, without a sign that there was any connection, relation or harmony or understanding of the relations of anything anywhere.[1210]

Adams toyed with suicide as an alternative to "mindless senility,"[1211] but he seems to have succumbed instead to mindlessness as manifested by his infatuation with the automobile, an invention second only to saturation bombing in the destructive effect it had on both European and American built culture. Late in life, Adams told his niece that, "My idea of paradise is… going thirty miles an hour on a smooth road to a twelfth-century cathedral."[1212]

1209 Brown, *The Last American Aristocrat*, p. 286.
1210 Brown, *The Last American Aristocrat*, p. 287.
1211 Brown, *The Last American Aristocrat*, p. 380.
1212 Brown, *The Last American Aristocrat*, pp. 385-386.

Chapter 34

Rose Hawthorne Becomes a Nun

In 1896 George Lathrop's operatic version of *The Scarlet Letter* got performed. It was the last thing he ever wrote. Lathrop died two years later at the Roosevelt Hospital in New York of cirrhosis of the liver, according to Maynard,[1213] or "chronic nephritis," according to Valenti.[1214] When Rose heard that he was dying, she rushed to his bedside only to find that he had passed. On April 21, Rose wrote in her diary that:

> My beloved husband died on April 19th, about half an hour before I reached him. I had made seven offerings of Holy Communion on the 1st Fridays for the entire conversion of my husband to God & to holiness. As I stood beside his body, soon after his death,' the beauty & nobility & the exquisite gentleness of his life, & the eloquence which breathes from the unbreathing being of one who has died in the Lord, spoke plainly to me of his virtues, & the welcome our Lord had given him into His rest. My own soul was trembling in the dark uncertainty of all unworthiness. Yesterday, early, his soul came, I am sure, to console me, in his loveliest way of forgiveness."[1215]

Rose felt that she had been released from familial responsibilities beginning with the death of her child but certainly with the death of her husband. But the period between those two deaths gives us pause. Should she have remained with her husband until his death? Does the fact that he died alone while she was caring for others detract from the heroic virtue which is the criterion for sainthood? The bishop's approval of her separation gives one answer. The grief and guilt she felt following his death seems to give another.

Rose's reaction is understandable given the circumstances surrounding his death and a separation which he blamed on her, but it had no effect on her determination to proceed with her apostolate because his death had been preceded one month earlier, during the night of March 28, 1898, by a vision in which the crucified Christ appeared and told her, "I love you, and you love

---

1213 Maynard, *A Fire Was Lighted*, p. 318.
1214 Valenti, *To Myself a Stranger*, p. 146.
1215 Maynard, *A Fire Was Lighted*, p. 319.

me—then what is the trouble?"[1216] After hearing these words, Rose felt a "great peace overflowed me. I began to love Him only, as I have prayed to do for three years.... Jesus loves me, and everything is simplified and exalted."[1217]

Shortly after her husband's death, Rose cut her hair and began to wear a religious habit. One year later, on September 14, 1899, Rose was received into the Dominican Order, taking the name of Sister Mary Alphonsa.[1218] The Dominicans would eventually sell the hotel they had acquired outside of New York City in what was then Sherman Park and what is now Hawthorne, New York to Rose for $28,000, giving her apostolate a permanent home to this day.

Rose's life then settled into the pattern which would continue to the end of her life, "receiving the sick at eight in the morning, then visiting the housebound sick until one, and then again receiving patients in her modest dispensary. At half past five in the evening, she would return to her patients' homes to dress their wounds. All of these activities were interspersed with prayer."[1219] In an uncanny echoing of an image that characterized her father's fiction, Rose described herself as a "machine for expressing love, with no particular personal life."[1220] Rose was the angel who became a machine.

In the first years of the 21st century, the Roman Catholic Church started proceedings into naming Rose Hawthorne Lathrop a saint. According to the United States Conference of Catholic Bishops:

> To be beatified and recognized as a Blessed, one miracle acquired through the candidate's intercession is required in addition to recognition of heroic virtue or offering of life. Canonization requires a second miracle after beatification. The pope may waive these requirements.[1221]

1216 Valenti, *To Myself a Stranger*, p. 144.
1217 Valenti, *To Myself a Stranger*, p. 144.
1218 Maynard, *A Fire Was Lighted*, p. 329.
1219 Valenti, *To Myself a Stranger*, p. 138.
1220 Valenti, *To Myself a Stranger*, p. 142.
1221 "Saints," United States Conference of Catholic Bishops, https://www.usccb.org › offices › public-affairs › saints

Chapter 35

Theodore Roosevelt and Muscular Christianity

If the Western frontier was the pole which represented existence modifying essence for the first two centuries of English colonization, the East took on that role during the 19th century through mass migration:

> In the 1820s, 62,000 immigrants entered the United States from Ireland and Germany. In the 1840s almost 800,000 arrived from Ireland, and in the 1850s, 952,000 came from Germany and 914,000 from Ireland. Ninety percent of the Irish and a substantial portion of Germans were Catholic. This huge influx rekindled anti-Catholic fears and passions.[1222]

As the end of the 19th century loomed, Polish and Italian Catholic migration had added millions of Catholic immigrants to the Germans and Irish posing a fundamental challenge to the claim that America was an Anglo-Protestant country. In spite of demographic decline among Protestants, their values remained central to American culture, and as such, Samuel Huntington notes, they have:

> deeply influenced Catholicism and other religions in America. They have shaped American attitudes toward private and public morality, economic activity, government, and public policy. Most importantly, they are the primary source of the American Creed, the ostensibly secular political principles that supplement Anglo-Protestant culture as the critical defining element of what it means to be American.[1223]

Huntington claims that Catholics had to become Protestants to become Americans, but as existence predominated over essence Protestants also had to give up their religion to become Americans. America became a religion in its own right. It became a state religion, regulating the beliefs of both Protestants and Catholics by attempting to mold both groups into Americans.

The Protestant tradition of national churches allowed a seamless transition to nationalism. Americanism, by which we mean the state replacing the

---

1222 Huntington, *Who Are We?*, p. 94.
1223 Huntington, *Who Are We?*, p. 62.

church as the unifying factor of American identity, was best epitomized by Theodore Roosevelt, who called this new religion "strenuous Christianity," largely because he discovered that "physical exertion" helped to minimize the debilitating asthma of his childhood and "bolster his spirits."[1224] After hiking with his family in the Alps in 1869, Roosevelt "began a heavy regimen of exercise," which included rowing and boxing, two sports he engaged in during his undergraduate years at Harvard.

Roosevelt was born in Manhattan, but he found that the region which best fostered the strenuous life was the West. After purchasing a ranch in Medora, North Dakota in 1884, Roosevelt became a man of the west who could ride a horse and rope steers like a cowboy, the man who best epitomized America because, unlike etiolated Easterners like Henry Adams, the cowboy possessed "few of the emasculated, milk-and-water moralities admired by the pseudo-philanthropists; but he does possess, to a very high degree, the stern, manly qualities that are invaluable to a nation."[1225]

Roosevelt's Americanism merged the myth of the American frontier with the muscular Christianity which emerged from Rugby and *Tom Brown's School Days* when the Oxford movement failed to reunite the Anglicans with the Catholic Church.

Thomas Arnold, the headmaster at Rugby, was not a big sports fan, but Thomas Hughes, who wrote *Tom Brown's School Days* was, and in many ways Hughes determined the combination of education and sports which defined American identity at institutions like Harvard University during Theodore Roosevelt's undergraduate days. Arnold stressed religious and moral principles first, gentlemanly conduct second, and intellectual achievement last, and Hughes agreed with those priorities in general but while maintaining the primacy of morals, Hughes de-emphasized religion and put greater emphasis on sports. As a result, modern sports were born in England in the late 19th century in English boarding schools, and the idea of sportsmanlike conduct and the ideal of the "scholar and the gentleman," who did not do certain things because "it wasn't cricket," spread through America, which was still its cultural colony:

> By the 1880s, "muscular Christianity" was the religion of the public schools of England. Character was to be developed by team games and hardship. Games demanded loyalty, self-discipline, and for those with ability, a sense of command and accomplishment. Cold baths, cold dormitories, runs in the rain and plain food all helped to build character. A housemaster, on hearing that one of his boys had taken two hot baths

---

1224 "Theodore Roosevelt," *Wikipedia: The Free Encyclopedia*, https://en.wikipedia.org/wiki/Theodore_Roosevelt

1225 "Theodore Roosevelt," *Wikipedia*.

Part II: The Romantic Rehabilitation of Nature

in a week, reprimanded him sternly: "That is the kind of thing that brought down the Roman Empire."[1226]

Muscular Christianity found especially fertile ground among the Anglophile WASP upper class in America, which began founding schools based on what Arnold had created at Rugby. Perhaps the best example of that sort of school in America was Groton, founded by Endicott Peabody in 1884. Peabody developed "muscular Christianity" in the sons of America's new national WASP ruling class for over 50 years, until his retirement in 1940. Peabody adopted the British public school code, with its emphasis on sports as character builder, from his days at Cheltenham, where he excelled at cricket and rowing. Peabody was convinced in Digby Baltzell's words, "that a vigorous democracy needed the leadership of a manly and moral aristocracy." As a result, he educated the sons of the ruling class at Groton to be like the students under Arnold at Rugby, "Christians, gentlemen and scholars in that order." Sports contributed to the integration of those traits into one virile character, because sports, Peabody told his students in 1930, especially "as conducted in England," provide both health and moral education. Indeed, England's national game of cricket is used as a measure of moral quality. Of some fine action, they will say, "That's cricket!", while final condemnation is found in the criticism, "That's not cricket."[1227]

By 1930, Peabody was aware that a spirit was afoot which was corrupting sports, especially in America, where "our first approach to a game is apt to be the quest for someone to beat." Shortly after Peabody warned his students that athletics were "in many cases" becoming "just plain business," where "they came under the instruction of professionals whose positions depend in many cases in 'delivering the goods,' that is, achieving victory," William T. Tilden, 2nd, America's premier tennis player, and epitome of the English ideal of the man who felt that playing by the rules was more important than winning, turned professional. Tilden's life mirrored the decline of sports into money-grubbing professionalism and the concomitant decline of muscular Christianity into sexual degeneracy. After turning pro, Tilden found it increasingly difficult to control his homosexual impulses, as he moved from places like the Germantown Cricket Club (he grew up across the street) to Hollywood, where in 1946 he was arrested for fondling a 14-year old boy who was driving his flashy Packard down Sunset Boulevard.

Tilden's demise as sports hero was a very small straw in what would become a very strong wind, as sports began to dominate American life in the years following World War II, as the institution which Endicott Peabody looked upon as a means of moral training would come to be dominated by NBA

1226 E. Digby Baltzell, *Sporting Gentlemen: Men's Tennis from the Age of Honor to the Cult of the Superstar* (New York: The Free Press, 1995) p. 18.
1227 Baltzell, p. 30.

multi-millionaires whose main off the court activity was fathering illegitimate children, or figures like Wilt Chamberlain, who bragged in an autobiography a few years before he died that he had slept with 20,000 different women, or professional football players who hired contract killers to murder inconvenient girlfriends. Peabody thought that cricket was a "moral mentor," but he was especially fond of American football because "it was rough and hard and required courage, endurance, and discipline." Just how the moral training that Peabody promoted at Groton, and that Walter Camp, following his and Arnold's example, promoted at Yale could culminate in a figure like Trevor Bauer or Rae Carruth, "an American former professional football player who was convicted of conspiracy to commit murder,"[1228] is a question worthy of further study.

Peabody "abhorred the all-too-prevalent American ethic of winning at any cost," and as a result, "he looked with disdain at bigness and mediocrity in favor of the small and excellent." Six years before Peabody retired as headmaster at Groton, Samuel Eliot Morrison praised Arnold's, and by extension, Peabody's revolutionary change in education based on the intimate connection between sports and morals. "The notion of a gentleman's education," Morrison wrote:

> has made the English and American college what it is today: the despair of educational reformers and logical pedagogues, the astonishment of Continental scholars, a place which is neither a house of learning nor a house of play, but a little of both; and withal a microcosm of the world in which we live. To this ... tradition, we owe that common figure of the English-speaking world, "a gentleman and a scholar."[1229]

Perhaps the American who epitomized Morrison's values best was Theodore Roosevelt, a contemporary of Endicott Peabody, and a man who did more than anyone to promote the WASP ideal of "muscular Christianity" as the American ideal. Roosevelt's presidency coincided with a highpoint of American culture. Like Roosevelt, who was the father of five children, an intellectual, and a devoted sportsman, if not athlete, American culture from the time of the Columbian Exhibition in Chicago in 1893 up until the First World War, was expansive, prosperous (although plagued by economic exploitation), virile, and confident about the future, in many ways because of the personality traits which English sports culture had impressed on the WASP ruling class in the United States. Crucial to both the vitality of the country and the vitality of the ruling class was the notion, derived from sports, of the "amateur," a word derived from the Latin *amare*," which means to love. An amateur is someone who does something because of love and not because of money. Some things, like sex, should only be done for love

---

1228 Rae Carruth, *Wikipedia: The Free Encyclopedia*, https://en.wikipedia.org/wiki/Rae_Carruth

1229 Baltzell, p. 18.

Part II: The Romantic Rehabilitation of Nature

and should never be done for money. Love and money provide, then, two poles or paradigms for human endeavor. The question is where do the rest of life's activities fit in. Because it corresponds so closely to the notion of the gentleman farmer which was the founding father's notion of the paradigmatic citizen in the American republic, the amateur is a particularly American concept. The amateur athlete was, in many ways, a late-19th century instance of Cincinnatus, the "amateur" Roman general who returned to his farm after winning the war, as did George Washington, the American Cincinnatus, who was America's model for the ideal politician in the early days of the American republic.

The connection between amateur sports and participatory democracy was obvious to someone like Theodore Roosevelt. By playing sports, Americans could learn that some things are worth doing simply for their own sake. Politics, according to traditional American wisdom, is done better by amateurs than professionals. Just as sports, in the traditional sense of the term, begets not only character but also altruism when done by amateurs, so the American republic do likewise when government officials were "amateurs" who returned to their farms when their term of office expired. Both amateur sports and the American Constitution were based on precisely this concept of morals and altruism abiding in character, which is to say habits acquired by long practice of virtue. Theodore Roosevelt, who "believed in sport as a means of cultivating a vigor of body which in turn led to a vigor of mind and character," detested the idea of the "professional" athlete and the "commercialization of sport" which followed naturally therefrom: "When money comes in at the gate," Roosevelt would say, "the game goes out the window."

That, of course, is a short description of the decline of sports and politics which began during the 20th century and continues to this day, as "amateur" sports become increasingly professionalized. The big issue today is the professionalization of teams like the Ohio State football team, which just won the national championship. Particularly in football and basketball, college players choose and switch teams based on financial remuneration; they are represented by agents; respected long time coaches have retired rather than participate in this new commercial system. The roster of the Ohio State team that won the national title in 2025, is consciously structured as a bought and paid for roster. Some colleges have hired general managers to deal with recruiting, raising funds, and making the payments to "student" athletes, so that coaches can focus on coaching.

Money ruined sports because it focused on winning rather than in the lines of "Clifton Chapel," one of Peabody's favorite poems, bringing the athlete "To set the cause above renown/ To love the game beyond the prize." Once sports became professional, they created a huge pool of spectators that increased exponentially with the rise of television, which in turn infused more money into the game, and, therefore, more corruption. The corruption of the professional athlete is the most obvious evil which followed. Less obvious was the corruption of the spectator, especially the TV spectator, who turned all professional sports into Quidditch, the sport Harry Potter played at the Hogwarts School of Magic, which was an essentially narcissistic fantasy that was observed rather than performed. Spectators of professional sports are a prime example of "the empty self" which characterized American identity as it succumbed to the culture of narcissism after World War II. The "empty" spectator has been emptied of the moral resources skills that participation in sports was supposed to provide. Because he uses the sports figure as a fantasy reservoir to supply what he lacks, he is threatened with non-existence if his team loses. That threat is so devastating to his fragile "empty" self and the delusions of omnipotence that the culture of narcissism creates in him that he flies into a rage when his team loses. He becomes, in other words, "a loser."

The usual scapegoat in instances like this is the coach, particularly the college coach, who gets fired when he fails to "deliver the goods," as Endicott Peabody once predicted. The emphasis on winning at any cost creates a completely irrational state of affairs, in which each coach must have a winning record. This corresponds to the principles of narcissistic education, in which each student must be above average. Instead of producing moral character through physical effort among the people who play the sport, sports now produce spiritual bondage by promoting narcissistic fantasies of omnipotence among a nation of spectators. If sports were so good at building character, why did sports lead American culture in the decline of just about every area of life? If sports are so good at building morals, why was it taken over by such a motley group of moral degenerates?

Digby Baltzell, ever aware of the nuances of class in American culture, claimed that tennis went to hell as soon as Irish Catholics rose to prominence in the game. It's hard to tell whether he feels there was a causal relationship or not. Baltzell feels that Jimmy Connors and John McEnroe were narcissistic monsters who ruined the game of tennis, he also adds that "Connors and McEnroe were the first Irish Catholics to win our National Championship"[1230] and lets the reader draw his own conclusions.

Christopher Lasch offers a better explanation: the culture of narcissism promotes certain forms of behavior. Both Connors and McEnroe should have been kicked out of the matches they disrupted long before they ruined the game of tennis, but, as Baltzell pointed out, the people who changed tennis into a narcissistic spectator sport from a gentleman's participatory sport, coddled both of them because they admired their plucky, i.e., narcissistic behavior. Sports, in other words, could help the culture implement its values by conveying those values in a concrete way to each new generation of young people, but sports could not prevent the degeneration of those values.

1230 Baltzell, p.357.

Part II: The Romantic Rehabilitation of Nature

Something else had to do that. The same could be said for education. Education followed the culture; the culture did not follow education. Education had to get direction from something higher than itself, every bit as much as sports did, and that's where the problems began.

Baltzell's claim that Irish Catholics wrecked tennis is a faint echo of the Nativism which swept through his native Philadelphia in the 1840s. As Samuel Huntington pointed out: "For more than two hundred years Americans defined their identity in opposition to Catholicism. The Catholic other was first fought and excluded and then opposed and discriminated against."[1231] But Irish Catholics playing tennis at places like the Germantown Country Club bespoke "the fading of overtly anti-Catholic attitudes" that was "directly related to the Americanization of Catholicism."[1232] By claiming that "the adaptation of Catholicism to its American, that is, Protestant, environment, including changes in Catholic attitudes, practices, organization, and behavior" brought about "the transformation of a Roman Catholic Church into an American Catholic Church,"[1233] Huntington puts the cart before the horse. The first stage of assimilation involved the Americanization of Protestants when Calvinism came in contact with the Frontier during the Great Awakenings and eventually produced the hybrid religion of Methodism. The history of the Beecher family is a classic example of the Americanization of Protestantism. When the dust of the Civil War settled, the common denominator which united the East and West in a new American identity was a pan-Protestant hatred of Catholicism. "Fear of Catholicism," according to Perry Miller, "became a morbid obsession"[1234] of the Second Great Awakening, which ended in 1840 just as the Nativist riots were about to begin. Huntington adds that:

> This anti-Catholicism was often formulated in political rather than religious terms. The Catholic Church was seen as an autocratic, anti-democratic organization and Catholics as people accustomed to hierarchy and obedience who lacked the moral character required for citizens of a republic. Catholicism was a threat to American democracy as well as to American Protestantism.[1235]

Like the unification of Cavalier and Roundhead after the Glorious Revolution in England, America changed from "a Protestant country into a Christian country with Protestant values"[1236] after the Civil War absorbed both Protestants and Catholics into the new religion of Americanism which had always been latent in the nationalism of Protestant sects which derived

---

1231 Huntington, *Who Are We?*, p. 92.
1232 Huntington, *Who Are We?*, p. 95.
1233 Huntington, *Who Are We?*, p. 95.
1234 Huntington, *Who Are We?*, p. 94.
1235 Huntington, *Who Are We?*, p. 94.
1236 Huntington, *Who Are We?*, p. 92.

from state religions. By the last decades of the 19th century, Americanism had become the state religion of the United States, as Cavaliers and Roundheads once again joined ranks against the common Catholic foe. The only question was whether the Catholics would follow their example and offer up incense to the same idol.

The second stage of assimilation involved the Americanization of Catholic immigrants, who arrived *en masse* from the east representing a new form of existence which would confront the new form of essence which was the religion of America. Catholics immigrants should have overwhelmed their newfound host country by dint of sheer numbers, but they were too diverse, too alien, and too new to America to unite with the Protestants sects which for centuries treated them like the enemy. The Catholic Church was, as a result, incapable of exploiting that newfound advantage because it was hopelessly divided among ethnic groups which could hardly speak to each other, much less engage in a challenge to American identity, because they shared no common American Catholic identity of their own, in spite of Orestes Brownson's hopes, nor could they agree that a common American Catholic identity was even desirable, as Dagger John made clear.

Chapter 36

John Ireland and Americanism

As of 1890, the main Catholic ethnic groups as well as the main contenders over the question of assimilation were the Irish, who were overwhelmingly Americanist in their orientation, and the Germans, who felt the culture they brought with them was superior to anything America had to offer. If they were not going to be Americanized by the Brahmins from Boston, the Germans most certainly were not going to be tutored on what it meant to be an American by a group of "vicious" Irish "rowdies" and "criminals" of the sort that Orestes Brownson had denounced 40 years earlier.

The great champion of the Americanist faction in the Catholic Church was Archbishop John Ireland of St. Paul, Minnesota. Convinced that "There is no conflict between the Catholic Church and America," and that "the principles of the Church are in thorough harmony with the interests of the Republic,"[1237] John Ireland argued that:

> The Germans should give up their nostalgia for the homeland, simply because the United States—"one nation, indivisible, with liberty and justice for all"—was a better place to live than Germany or indeed all the European countries put together. And better too for the Catholic Church: "The choicest field," as Ireland had put it in his speech at the council, "which providence offers in the world to-day to the occupancy of the Church is this republic." The tired regimes of the Old World showed nothing but hostility toward the Catholicism that had nurtured them: witness the triumph of anti-clericals in almost every nation in western Europe. By contrast the bright, young American republic allowed the church the fullest scope in performing its mission and refused, on principle, to interfere with it in any way. Indeed, might it not be argued therefore that traditionally European Catholicism ought to look to America for its future ecclesial model, rather than the other way around?[1238]

1237 Huntington, *Who Are We?*, p. 95.

1238 Marvin R. O'Connell, *John Ireland: and the American Catholic Church* (Minnesota Historical Society Press: St. Paul Minnesota, 1988), p. 218.

Ireland's opponents, most of whom were German, "saw Americanization as a path of corruption leading to the worst forms of modernism, individualism, materialism, and liberalism."[1239]

By the 1880s, immigration had changed the ethnic and religious composition of the United States. In 1789, two percent of the population was Catholic, and 0.2 percent was Jewish. The rest were mainly English-speaking Protestants. By the 1880s, out of a total population of 12 million, six million were Catholic. But, unlike the English-speaking majority:

> Catholics did not have a common cultural unity to support their theological unity. Probably the greatest number of Roman Catholics were of Irish birth or descent, and there were hundreds of thousands of German-speaking Catholics, with smaller groups of French Canadians, and immigrants from other Catholic regions of Europe. Probably the greatest contrast between the Catholic minority and the non-Catholic majority was the union of the Catholics under a centralized hierarchy from which all priests received their ordination and appointments to rule over the laity. So close was this unity of the hierarchy and their priests that attacks of bigots in the Nativist and Know-Nothing periods merely strengthened their unity, and the divisive trends of the Civil War caused only minor disagreements between them.[1240]

The Catholics may have had a centralized hierarchy and theological unity, but they had no American identity. The original group of English Catholic immigrants who arrived in Maryland had been ethnically cleansed by the Quakers and survived only in isolated communities in western Kentucky which were too small to absorb the flood of immigrants which arrived in the decades surrounding the Civil War. "The bonds of hierarchical authority, the common acceptance of Catholic teachings, and the reception of the same Roman sacraments"[1241] could not compensate for the lack of a common American Catholic identity that led to "nationalistic quarrels" that impeded the Church's witness in crucial issues like the workers' question and political reform at the end of the 19th century. "Outside of the few Anglo-American Catholic communities in Maryland and Kentucky one would look in vain for a Catholic culture worthy of the name among the six million Catholics in the United States."[1242]

Even though the Irish for the most part remained in the big cities of the east, the frontier had the same effect on Catholics that it had on Protestants. Existence modified essence, producing an independence of thought unheard of among the laity in Europe. And the American hierarchy, while quick to

---

1239 Huntington, *Who Are We?*, p. 95.
1240 McAvoy, *The Great Crisis in American Catholic History*, p. 7.
1241 McAvoy, *The Great Crisis in American Catholic History*, p. 8.
1242 McAvoy, *The Great Crisis in American Catholic History*, p. 8.

Part II: The Romantic Rehabilitation of Nature

offer "a very reverential obedience to the Holy See," thought that European bishops had no business telling their American confreres how to solve their own "peculiar problems."[1243] As early as the Plenary Council of Baltimore in 1866, Rome expressed concerned that the council was "very much an expression of American ideas about many traditional Catholic problems."[1244]

In America, this was a peculiarly Catholic problem. All Protestant sects were European state churches which lost their authority and identity as soon as their congregations landed in the New World. Freed from the restraints of their established churches in Europe, the Protestants were unable to establish a lasting equivalent in America, leading to the rise of nationalism as the state took over the power which weakened Protestant sects could no longer exercise.

The lack of an American identity prevented the bishops from dealing with the ruthless exploitation of labor that was the rule for Irish immigrants, who created militant organizations like the Molly Maguires because prelates like Archbishop James Wood of Philadelphia could not come up with "a Catholic solution to the difficulties faced by the growing number of Catholic workers" in "a highly industrial state" like Pennsylvania.[1245] German Catholics consoled themselves with the high culture they had brought with them to the New World, which "gave them a feeling of superiority to the Irish immigrant whose nationalism was equally strong but lacked a high cultural and literary tradition."[1246] American Catholics had "no political, social or economic unity whatsoever" which could constitute a common identity, and that led to ethnic conflict. German and Irish Catholics had strong ethnic identities, but neither identity was American. When confronted with pressure to take on an American identity, the Irish capitulated, largely because they had no language of their own to facilitate separation. This capitulation was not immediate.

The 1880's can be considered the closing days of this last western frontier even though much of the frontier movement ended before 1880, and smaller pioneer movements would continue even after the opening of the last Oklahoma regions in the second decade of the twentieth century.[1247]

The main problem was lack of identity:

> [The] problem in dealing with hundreds of thousands of newly arrived immigrant Catholics lay in Americanization, because unless Catholics had first a basic Americanization in common with other Americans, there were bound to be serious differences with the non-Catholics both in educational programs and in any cooperation in social reform. Loyalties to old world traditions and customs were a great hindrance to

---

[1243] McAvoy, *The Great Crisis in American Catholic History*, p. 14.
[1244] McAvoy, *The Great Crisis in American Catholic History*, p. 9.
[1245] McAvoy, *The Great Crisis in American Catholic History*, p. 20.
[1246] McAvoy, *The Great Crisis in American Catholic History*, p. 40.
[1247] McAvoy, The Great Crisis in American Catholic History, p. 47.

Americanization even when there were no language difficulties. There was also the fact that the American dominant culture was Protestant or at least non-Catholic.[1248]

This problem greatly handicapped the advancement of Catholic education and social reform. When Orestes Brownson tried to bring about "full Americanization" of the Irish Catholics, he was rebuked by Dagger John Hughes, who believed that by becoming American Irish Catholics would become Protestants. "In the Middle West and in the Far West where the Irish were scattered and could not set up their compact reproduction of Irish life, the Irish became quickly much like their fellow citizens except in matters of religion."[1249] This prompted Dagger John to tell the Irish to stay in New York, where they could avail themselves of the Catholic Church. Because of the resistance of Irish bishops, the pleas of Archbishop and Bishop Spalding for a university fell on ears that had not yet had the benefit of secondary education. And there was no successor to Orestes A. Brownson to carry on the unwelcome criticism of the cultural isolation and low ideals of these Irish immigrants. Their progress in Americanization was more or less by pulling at their own bootstraps.[1250]

The conflict between the Irish and the Germans over what it meant to be an American simmered in the 1880s until it broke out into the open in November 1886 when Father Peter M. Abbelen, vicar general of the Archdiocese of Milwaukee, presented a petition in Rome arguing for what was in effect a separate German Catholic church in America.[1251] Abbelen argued that the Irish enjoyed "special ecclesiastical privileges"[1252] which were trying to "Americanize" the immigrant in a way that disrupted the slow and natural process that would preserve their faith and identity.[1253]

Abbelen's petition requested that national churches in America be given full parochial status and that all immigrants be assigned to the parish of their nationality, where their children were to attend parish schools with instruction in their native language.[1254]

As soon as Cardinal Gibbons learned of the petition from Bishops Keane and Ireland and Monsignor Denis O'Connell, he called a meeting of the American archbishops in Philadelphia and sent off a protest to Rome in their name. Archbishop John Ireland of St. Paul, Minnesota, rebutted Abbelen's position in a letter which claimed that there were no "Irish" parishes in

---

1248 McAvoy, *The Great Crisis in American Catholic History*, p. 60
1249 McAvoy, *The Great Crisis in American Catholic History*, p. 61.
1250 McAvoy, *The Great Crisis in American Catholic History*, p. 62.
1251 McAvoy, *The Great Crisis in American Catholic History*, p. 64.
1252 O'Connell, *John Ireland*, p. 220.
1253 O'Connell, *John Ireland*, p. 223.
1254 McAvoy, *The Great Crisis in American Catholic History*, p. 65.

Part II: The Romantic Rehabilitation of Nature

America, and that the Germans would do well to imitate the Irish, who "adopt American ideas and manners," and understand that "whatever their attachment to the land of their birth, . . . they must, for the general good, put aside their national spirit."[1255] Ireland and Keane, who were on their way to Rome to gain papal approval for the proposed Catholic University of America when they received news of Abbelen's petition, immediately published a refutation of Abbelen's petition, and with O'Connell's help it was rejected by the Sacred Congregation on June 7, 1887.[1256]

In 1891 the distinguished German businessman Peter Paul Cahensly issued a memo which "proposed that greater recognition be given to the foreign groups in the Church organization in the United States, even to the point of allowing foreign representation in the hierarchy of the country."[1257] After news of Cahensly's memo spread through the press, Archbishop Ireland "attacked the Memorial publicly as a plot of the Germanizing American clergy."[1258] Archbishop Ireland, Cardinal Gibbons, and Monsignor O'Connell, who would become rector of the Catholic University of America, feared that "the petition would bring about a national division of the hierarchy according to racial or nationalistic lines," but instead it proved to be the opening salvo in a war that would bring about the de facto hegemony of the Irish bishops in the American Catholic Church.

A crucial part of the Irish Americanist campaign involved driving German professors from Catholic University. Monsignor Joseph Schroeder incurred the ire of Father Keane, then rector of CUA, because Schroeder was "an outspoken critic of the Ireland policies in the German press."[1259] Ireland and O'Connell portrayed the attempt to remove Schroeder from Catholic U as a battle between "the progressives and conservatives in the United States" and "not one of race or nationalism,"[1260] but the charges leveled against Schroeder that he "had been observed drinking beer in public"[1261] suggests otherwise. Archbishop Ireland, the *spiritus movens* behind Schroeder's ouster, was a notorious teetotaler who routinely referred to his opponents as beer-guzzling Dutchmen. Eventually, the episcopal committee voted ten to four to force Schroeder to resign. When Cardinal Gibbons sent their decision to Rome, the Vatican acquiesced, but only if Schroeder could preserve his good name.[1262] Schroeder ended up in Rome, where he began to mobilize the anti-

---

1255 O'Connell, *John Ireland*, p. 224.
1256 McAvoy, *The Great Crisis in American Catholic History*, p. 65.
1257 McAvoy, *The Great Crisis in American Catholic History*, p. 67.
1258 McAvoy, *The Great Crisis in American Catholic History*, p. 67.
1259 McAvoy, *The Great Crisis in American Catholic History*, p. 74.
1260 McAvoy, *The Great Crisis in American Catholic History*, p. 189.
1261 McAvoy, *The Great Crisis in American Catholic History*, p. 189.
1262 McAvoy, *The Great Crisis in American Catholic History*, p. 179.

Americanist forces against the Irish by getting into the good graces of the American nuncio Archbishop Francesco Satolli.

On November 16, 1893, Satolli, along with his household staff, moved from the grounds of Catholic University, where he was in daily communication with university rector Bishop John J. Keane, into the new home of the delegation at the old Bradley House in Washington.[1263] The move allowed Satolli to distance himself from the Irish bishops who had taken him under their wing. It also allowed him the independence he needed to adjudicate the dispute between the Irish and the Germans. When Satolli took on as his secretary Father A. Minckenberg, a follower of Monsignor Schroeder, his distance from the Irish Americanists increased dramatically. By this point, Satolli's facility with English had increased to the point where he could better understand what Ireland, Keane, O'Connell and other members of the Americanist faction actually believed, as opposed to what they told Satolli to get him on their side.

Schroeder got his revenge. The evidence that "Satolli was influenced by Monsignor Schroeder" became inescapable when Satolli arranged to have Bishop Keane removed from the rectorship at Catholic University.[1264] Keane submitted immediately to Rome's decision, choosing nonetheless to remain in America, even if it meant that he had no "official position whatsoever."[1265] Gibbons and Ireland, who prided themselves on their connections in Rome, were at first stunned by the decision and then angered by it and determined to retaliate against their German enemies. Monsignor Schroeder denied having any role in the decision and denied as well that he had spoken against Keane when he had his audience with the pope during this visit to Rome the previous summer. If he had no role in Keane's dismissal, however, his sense of vindication must have been even sweeter because he had insisted that the dispute over the identity of American Catholics was based on ethnic animus and not principle. In an article which appeared on October 8, 1896, Schroeder pointed out that:

> Keane was not liked by the Germans who had become a power in the American church; secondly, that the Germans did not like the total abstinence advocated by the bishop, and further that the Germans did not like his advocacy of woman enfranchisement. "Bishop Keane," he said, "has advocated the cause of Protestantism in our schools, penal institutions and asylums where it was impossible to introduce Catholicism. His motto was: if not the creed of Trent, then the creed of Geneva, Canterbury, or Wittenberg. This brought him into sharp antagonism with Catholics of all nationalities and cost him the support and confidence of the Apostolic Delegate." The papers of the East blamed

---

1263 McAvoy, *The Great Crisis in American Catholic History*, p. 118.
1264 McAvoy, *The Great Crisis in American Catholic History*, p. 139.
1265 McAvoy, *The Great Crisis in American Catholic History*, p. 140.

Part II: The Romantic Rehabilitation of Nature

Cahenslyism but Phelan denied this saying that Schroeder was working with the rest of the faculty by this time. Phelan was wrong on this last point as he was inexact in most of his opinions. Certainly, it seems that Cardinal Satolli had been the one who arranged for the removal of Keane. That he had any intention of producing the defeat of the progressives that it was made out to be, is doubtful. Nevertheless, his public conduct after the removal of Keane indicated that his sympathies had shifted to the conservatives.[1266]

After his dismissal and a short visit to the West Coast, Bishop Keane went to Rome, where he was shocked at the anti-Americanist attitude which now dominated the Vatican. Keane urged Ireland in a letter of January 7, 1897, to "make it clear that he was not opposed to the Germans as Germans, but to those Germans who were opposing progress."[1267] Ireland needed to publish his "real program" to the world, which was "not war of race on race but idea on idea, of progress on stagnation." If Ireland could make that distinction clear, he would "lead the world."[1268]

In the early spring of 1897, O'Connell told Ireland that Cardinal Satolli had gone over to the German side and was determined to wage a campaign "against the Americans,"[1269] by which he meant Ireland, Keane, and the Irish who had wrapped the mantle of progressive Americanism around their shoulders. "The Germans," according to O'Connell, were "about to achieve revenge if not victory."[1270] On May 2, 1897, *Civilta Cattolica* published an article which cast doubt on the proposition that the United States was a Christian nation. The article implied that:

> Ireland and Gibbons were in error when they said they would not change one iota of the Constitution if they had the power. The implication of this comment was that "Americanism" was not Christian. This the writer supported by statistics on church membership showing that nearly forty million Americans did not profess membership in any church. Among these, he indicated, were from five to ten million pagans. On this basis, the article then proceeded to attack the great interest of some American Catholics in Protestants, their minimizing of differences between Catholics and Protestants, their praising of the separation of church and state, their tolerance off secret societies, their repression of foreign languages, their sacrificing the Catholic schools, and their desire to conform the Church to the spirit of the day.[1271]

1266 McAvoy, *The Great Crisis in American Catholic History*, pp. 140-1.
1267 McAvoy, *The Great Crisis in American Catholic History*, p. 144.
1268 McAvoy, *The Great Crisis in American Catholic History*, p. 144.
1269 McAvoy, *The Great Crisis in American Catholic History*, p. 154.
1270 McAvoy, *The Great Crisis in American Catholic History*, p. 148.
1271 McAvoy, *The Great Crisis in American Catholic History*, p. 155.

Ireland, Keane, and O'Connell responded to the article by claiming that "Americanism" was simply "the progressive ideas of Pope Leo and the Church itself" applied to the new situation which arose from the European colonization of the new world.[1272] At around the same time that the Irish bishops were defending the compatibility of Church teaching and the constitution of the United States, Count Guillaume de Chabrol arranged for the French language translation of Father Walter Elliott's life of Father Isaac Hecker (1819-1888). Like his mentor Brownson, Hecker felt that he had been called to convert American Protestants to the Catholic faith by pointing out the flaws of their religion. To do this, Hecker joined the Redemptorists, an order "especially active among the German immigrants in the United States."[1273]

After overcoming difficulties at the seminary, Hecker was ordained in 1849 at the Redemptorist novitiate in St. Trond in Belgium, returning to its American province in 1851. Although Hecker was the son of German immigrants, he chafed under the order's focus on German immigrants and longed to spend his time preaching the gospel to "Americans" instead, which meant the erection of an English-speaking house for Redemptorists of like mind. Getting nowhere with his superiors, Hecker decided in 1857 to take his case to Rome, where it was promptly rejected, and he was expelled from the order for insubordination.

Undeterred, Hecker eventually persuaded the pope to allow him and his fellow converts to form their own community, to "work for the conversion of America."[1274] Hecker called his new community the Congregation of St. Paul the Apostle, more famiarly the Paulists. They established their headquarters in New York, which was succeeding Philadelphia and Boston as the publishing capital of the United States. Sensing the power of the press, Hecker founded the *Catholic World* in 1865 and the Catholic Publication Society one year later.

Confounded in Rome by the increasing anti-Americanist sentiment there, Ireland, O'Connell and Keane found in Hecker the ideal proponent of their cause. Hecker was German, thereby absolving the Irish of ethnic animus. Hecker was also progressively American, diverting attention from the ethnic impasse between the Germans and the Irish even though the overwhelming majority of German clergy in American were intransigent conservative ethnic isolationists. Hecker and Ireland became allies proving that the Americanist controversy was about ideas not "race," an idea which Ireland emphasized in the preface he wrote for Elliott's biography, when he credited to Father Hecker his "most salutary impressions, for which he was "glad to have the opportunity to profess publicly" his gratitude to him. He called Father

---

1272 McAvoy, *The Great Crisis in American Catholic History*, p. 155.
1273 McAvoy, *The Great Crisis in American Catholic History*, p. 156.
1274 McAvoy, *The Great Crisis in American Catholic History*, p. 156.

Part II: The Romantic Rehabilitation of Nature

Hecker "the typical American priest" having not only the qualities universally expected of a good priest but qualities especially suited for America. Ireland expressed his admiration for the Catholic immigrants but said they did little "to make the church in America throb with American life." Ireland said that Hecker looked to America "as the fairest conquest for divine truth," and added that the American current, so plain for the last quarter of a century in the flow of Catholic affairs, is, largely at least, to be traced back to Father Hecker and his early co-workers." Ireland praised Hecker's devotion to the Constitution of the United States and the American Republic. Without in any way minimizing the supernatural the archbishop called attention to Hecker's stress on the natural and social virtues."[1275]

After Hecker's biography was translated into French, it became problematic for the Vatican because Chabrol "who had known Hecker in America and in Europe," felt that Hecker was "a symbol of a new type of clergyman which he had experienced in the new world and which he thought would check the decay of religion in France"[1276] by importing principles which were alien to Catholicism.

Elliott imprudently included statements Hecker made before his conversion, like "The Eternal-Absolute is ever creating new forms of expressing himself,"[1277] which sounded heterodox and Hegelian, as well as "a paragraph which was not from Hecker and which contained words that could be construed as erroneous theology" and sounded even worse in French, where they took on the complexion of the French Revolution and Catholics who wanted to compromise with its principles as presumably the Americanists had done in the United States. When Hecker said that the "passive virtues" of the Catholic past had to yield to "the active virtues" necessary for the modern age, he conjured up images of Garibaldi's *Risorgimento* in Italy two decades after the Church lost the papal states and the pope went into internal exile in the Vatican. When Hecker said that he expected "a greater effusion of the Holy Spirit to enable the faithful to meet the new situation of modern liberty and independence," the phrase conjured up thoughts in the Vatican of English lunatics like the Quakers, who had a direct line to the Holy Spirit and were as a result both infallible in religious matters and impossible to talk to on any other issue. Hecker, who had protested similar exaggerations when he was alive, would now suffer at the hands of those who misrepresented him for partisan purposes.

Alphonse Maignen articulated European misgivings about American effusions when he published a series of devastating reviews of Hecker's

---

[1275] McAvoy, *The Great Crisis in American Catholic History*, p. 162.
[1276] McAvoy, *The Great Crisis in American Catholic History*, p. 165.
[1277] McAvoy, *The Great Crisis in American Catholic History*, p. 159.

biography in the French periodical *La Vérité* under the pen name Martel. Maignen claimed that:

> 1, the Life had been published without an imprimatur contrary to the law of the Index; 2, that it maintained that Hecker was a saint and a kind of father of the Church; 3, that he had shown in his articles that Hecker was not a saint; and 4, that the man who boasts of never having a spiritual director nor of having studied theology is not a model for clergymen.[1278]

He also charged Hecker with errors about the Holy Spirit and chauvinism in the invidious comparisons he made between the progressive Anglo-Saxons and the backward Latin races, and most importantly that Ireland and his partisans were attempting to impose the American form of government on the Catholic Church.[1279]

On March 3, 1898, Martel's first article appeared under the title "*L'Americanisme Mystique.*" One month later on April 3, a week after *La Vérité* announced that Martel's collected reviews would appear in book form, Martel claimed that *La Vie* "was a symbol, a flag of a party, a machine of war, a sort of Trojan horse bearing in its flanks the entire phalanx of the leaders of Americanism."[1280] The war drums emanating from Washington signaling the beginning of America's attack on Catholic Spain lent credence to the belief that "Americanism" was a threat to the Catholic Church.

When Hecker "coupled the rising power of the Saxon races and the decline of the Latin races" and "found this new development of the Church to correspond to the demands of these Saxon races for greater interior spirituality and greater independence,"[1281] Rome thought of Teddy Roosevelt and the looming war.

On April 21, 1898, as the furor over the French translation of Hecker's biography was reaching its climax, an explosion ripped open the hull of the *USS Maine* in Havana harbor. The warmongers in Washington now had the upper hand and propelled the United States into a war with Spain. Impressed with John Ireland's connections with the Republican Party, the pope asked Ireland to mediate a ceasefire, which he attempted with alacrity, but in spite of his best efforts he failed in his mission. Instead of meditating on the profoundly anti-Catholic nature of the American Republic as it strode belligerently into the era of empire, John Ireland sided with America against Catholic Spain as soon as it became clear that his negotiation effort had failed. After the war ended Ireland congratulated Theodore Roosevelt as "the hero of

---

1278 McAvoy, *The Great Crisis in American Catholic History*, p. 201.
1279 McAvoy, *The Great Crisis in American Catholic History*, p. 202.
1280 McAvoy, *The Great Crisis in American Catholic History*, p. 195.
1281 McAvoy, The Great Crisis in American Catholic History, p. 162.

Part II: The Romantic Rehabilitation of Nature

San Juan Hill," and Roosevelt responded by addressing Ireland as "My dear Comrade!"[1282]

As some indication that the Europeans saw a connection between Hecker's biography and American imperialism, Martel called for "a new crusade of Europe to save the old Europe from the barbarous Americans," one day after the sinking of the *Maine*, pleading "for Spain, for France, for the civilization of Christian Europe, for the future of the world."[1283] In making this plea, *La Vérité* articulated the misgivings of the Latins generally about the rising power of the United States" while Ireland was promoting it as providential in letters to his friends. In public, Ireland portrayed himself as a loyal son of the Church, but in private he supported American aggression against Catholic Spain as a manifestation of God's will.

The duplicity of the Americanist position came out in private correspondence epitomized by O'Connell's fawning letters to Ireland outlining his cosmic mission as the representative of the new Americanist dispensation. In a letter which McAvoy describes as "a very important contribution to a definition of the Americanism as conceived by the Americanists,"[1284] O'Connell told Ireland that:

> you have now reached the providential period of your life;—it seems to me the culminating point—where all your dreams are to be realized and all your poetic visions are to be turned into prophecies. Now is a moment in which it will be utterly impossible for you to expand your power or your personality too much: "[sic] for this were you born for this you came into the world: to realize the dreams of your youth for America and to be the instrument in the hands of Providence for spreading the benefits of a new civilization over the world. To this point has really tended even without your knowing it, everything you have hitherto done in all the period of your activity, and now from this point you are to radiate your influence as far and as intensely as you can all the world over. You have now the whole field free, and you are a citizen in America, and a Bishop in the Church without a rival. All the former little questions of local content in the Church in America are now for you as nothing, and henceforth you are to consider yourself as a figure in history with no Corrigan beside you. . . . And instead of hurting yourself in the eyes of the public & in working for the odious cause of Spain you have only increased & confirmed & sanctified the confidence reposed in you by your citizens. I congratulate you and thank God for you. And now only one word more: all doubts & hesitation to the wind and on which banner of Americanism which is the banner of God & humanity, realize all the dreams you ever

---

1282 O'Connell, *John Ireland* p. 459.
1283 McAvoy, *The Great Crisis in American Catholic History*, p. 198.
1284 McAvoy, *The Great Crisis in American Catholic History*, p. 206.

dreamed, and force upon the Curia by the great triumph of Americanism that recognition of English-speaking peoples that you know is needed.[1285]

Sounding like an anti-Catholic character in a Henry James novel, O'Connell waxed increasingly chauvinistic:

> For me this is not simply a question of Cuba. If it were, it were no question or a poor question. Then let the "greasers eat one another up and save the lives of our dear boys." But for me it is a question of much more moment:—it is the question of two civilizations. It is the is question of all that is old & vile & mean & rotten & cruel & false in Europe against all this [sic] is free & noble & open & true humane in America. When Spain is swept of [sic] the seas much of the meanness & narrowness of old Europe goes with it to be replaced by the freedom and openness of America. This is God's way of developing the world. And all continental Europe feels the war is against itself, and that is why they are all against us, and Rome more than all because when the prestige of Spain & Italy will have passed away, and when the pivot of the world's political action will no longer be confined within the limits of the continent; then the nonsense of trying to govern the universal church from a purely European standpoint—and according to exclusively Spanish and Italian methods, will be glaringly evident even to a child.[1286]

If Rome needed proof that "Americanism" was a religion in its own right and incompatible with the Catholic faith which O'Connell espoused in public, all the Holy Office needed to do was read his letters to John Ireland, the man he described as the "chaplain" of the American empire:

> Again it seems to me that above all nations, moving them on along the path of civilization to better, higher, happier modes of existences it is the constant action of a tender divine Providence, and that the convergent action of all great powers is towards that common & destined end; to more brotherhood, to more kindness, to more mutual respect for every man, to more practical and living recognition of the rule of God. At one time one nation in the world now another, took the lead, but now it seems to me that the old governments of Europe will lead no more and that neither Italy, nor Spain will ever furnish the principles of the civilization of the future. Now God passes the banner to the hands of America, to bear it:—in the cause of humanity and it is your office to make its destiny known to America and become its grand chaplain. Over all America there is certainly a duty higher than the interest of the individual states— even of the national government. The duty to humanity is certainly a real duty, and America cannot certainly with honor, or fortune, evade its great share in it. Go to America and say, thus saith the Lord! Then you

---

1285 McAvoy, *The Great Crisis in American Catholic History*, pp. 207.
1286 McAvoy, *The Great Crisis in American Catholic History*, pp. 208.

Part II: The Romantic Rehabilitation of Nature

will live in history as God's Apostle in modem times to Church & to Society. Hence, I am a partisan of the Anglo-American alliance, together they are invincible and they will impose a new civilization. Now is your opportunity—and at the end of the war as the Vatican always goes after a strong man you will likewise become her intermediary.[1287]

O'Connell felt that war was "God's way of moving things forward," and that the "horrors of war" was a "sentimental phrase" that blinded men to its "glories," which brought about "the triumph of Providence."[1288] The "history of war," O'Connell claimed, summing up his paean to American imperialism could be construed as a manifestation of "survival of the fittest."[1289] The phrase comes from the English evolutionist Herber Spencer, but then as now was attributed to Charles Darwin, indicating that Darwinian evolution was an integral part of the Americanism which Ireland and O'Connell espoused in private but were always careful not to mention it in correspondence with the Vatican.

Ireland's preface to Hecker's biography, combined with his failure to broker a ceasefire, combined with his support of America's war against Catholic Spain caused a reaction in Rome. The final blow to getting a sympathetic hearing for the cause of Americanism in Rome came with the condemnation of Father John Zahm's book on evolution. Zahm was a professor of chemistry and physics at the University of Notre Dame who had achieved national recognition as a scientist with the publication of his book on acoustics in 1892.

In 1893 Zahm gave a series of lectures on faith and science, which increased his fame and emboldened him to write *Evolution and Dogma*, which became his most popular work, until it was placed on the Index in 1898 despite John Ireland's strenuous attempts to protect him.[1290]

The inevitable happened one year later, on January 22, 1899, when Pope Leo XIII issued his encyclical *Testem Benevolentiae* condemning "Americanism," by pointing out certain things which are to be avoided and corrected" and "to put an end to certain contentions which have arisen lately among you, and which disturbed the minds, if not of all, at least of many, to the no slight detriment of peace."[1291] According to Ireland, the pope's complaint about the Catholic Church in America boiled down to three issues: "1, individual inspiration of the Holy Ghost; 2, the question of natural virtues; and 3, that of religious orders."[1292] In making his final point, the pope questioned whether

---

1287 McAvoy, *The Great Crisis in American Catholic History*, p. 209.
1288 McAvoy, *The Great Crisis in American Catholic History*, p. 209.
1289 McAvoy, *The Great Crisis in American Catholic History*, p. 209.
1290 Slattery, *Fatih and Science at Notre Dame* p. 2.
1291 McAvoy, *The Great Crisis in American Catholic History*, p. 275.
1292 McAvoy, *The Great Crisis in American Catholic History*, p. 304.

"new ways of bringing converts to the Church are to be adopted."[1293] Once the encyclical became public, Ireland issued a statement claiming that:

> Verily, with all the energy of my soul, I repudiate and I condemn all the opinions which the Apostolic Letter repudiates and condemns—those false and dangerous opinions to which, as the letter points out, certain persons have given the name of "Americanism."[1294]

Ireland's feigned capitulation to Rome was followed by the indignant claim that no one in American held the ideas which the pope condemned:

> We cannot but be indignant that such a wrong should been done us—our Bishops, our faithful people, and our whole nature—as to designate as some have come to do, by the word "Americanism" errors and extravagances of this sort.[1295]

Ireland's claim was technically correct. The pope was reacting to French reviews of a book published in France. But Ireland was also being disingenuous. If the debate over "Americanism" had been based on the correspondence between Ireland and O'Connell, the pope could have condemned the real threat to the Church, and he could have condemned it much more unequivocally than he had done in *Testem Benevolentiae*.

Instead of putting an end to the debate, the pope dealt "Americanism" a glancing blow, which did nothing but anger the Americans, who felt they had been falsely accused of holding what was in effect a "phantom heresy." The pope's vagueness and the vacillation he expressed in a subsequent letter to Cardinal Gibbons confirmed the Americanists in their feeling that they could not get a fair hearing in Rome. It also convinced them of the rightness of their cause, which they would now pursue sub rosa far from Rome's prying eyes.

More importantly, Rome's condemnation of Americanism postponed the emergence of an authentic American Catholic identity and handed the project to those, like Ireland and O'Connell, who were willing to be duplicitous in their dealings with Rome.

Notre Dame's reaction to the virtually contemporaneous condemnations of Americanism and Zahm's book on evolution epitomized the new Americanist strategy. Zahm submitted to Rome's condemnation of his book on evolution and, after a short tenure as an administrator for the Congregation of Holy Cross, went into exile for the next 15 years, writing travelogues under a pseudonym until he died in a hospital in Munich in 1921.[1296]

Aware that acceptance of Darwinian evolution had become a crucial component of American identity, Notre Dame continued to promote that

---

1293 McAvoy, *The Great Crisis in American Catholic History*, p. 278.
1294 McAvoy, *The Great Crisis in American Catholic History*, p. 282.
1295 McAvoy, *The Great Crisis in American Catholic History*, p. 282.
1296 Slattery, *Fatih and Science at Notre Dame*, p. 2.

Part II: The Romantic Rehabilitation of Nature

theory in Zahm's absence because they understood they could reap impressive benefits by confecting an American Catholic identity which was acceptable in both Washington and Rome. The battle between the Americanists and the Europeanists at Notre Dame raged back and forth during the early decades of the 20th century, but in 1933 when Fr. John O'Brien of the Notre Dame theology department published an explicit defense of Zahm's evolutionary hypothesis, "nothing happened."[1297] In 1947, O'Brien brought out a pamphlet which tried to forge a compromise between Rome and Washington by claiming that:

> In regard to the soul of man, it is the common teaching of theologians that God creates directly and immediately the soul of each individual human being. In regard to the body of man, the evidence of evolution from antecedent animal life is most impressive, and in the judgment of most scientists, overwhelming. The Church leaves the individual free to accept or reject this view in accordance with his judgment as to the weight of evidence behind it.[1298]

In making this claim, O'Brien posited a radically platonic view of the soul, essentially claiming that it resembled a pilot in a ship, which contradicted both St. Thomas Aquinas and Aristotle, who claimed that the soul was the form of the body. The point of O'Brien's radically dualistic rational psychology was political compromise, not truth. Notre Dame needed a solution that would find acceptance in Rome and Washington, not something that was theologically coherent. Martel had already rejected the Americanist position as incoherent when he asked "if the relations between God and the soul had really changed"[1299] when Europeans migrated to America. Compromises such as those proposed by O'Brien led to a dualism that came to characterize American Catholic identity, a duality symbolized best by the architecture of the chapel of Mundelein Seminary in Chicago, which was to outward appearances Presbyterian but baroque on the inside.

In 1951, John Morrison wrote a dissertation for the University of Missouri on the evolutionist movement in the late 19th and early 20th centuries which portrayed Zahm as "the hero and martyr of the American evolutionist story."[1300] Four years later, Ralph Weber completed a biographical dissertation on Zahm at Notre Dame which portrayed him as "a loyal son of Notre Dame with Zahm's encounter with the Congregation of the Index appearing only as a bump in the road in an otherwise stellar and devout career."[1301]

1297 Slattery, *Fatih and Science at Notre Dame*, p. 6.
1298 Slattery, *Fatih and Science at Notre Dame*, p. 6.
1299 McAvoy, *The Great Crisis in American Catholic History*, p. 189.
1300 Slattery, *Fatih and Science at Notre Dame*, p. 7.
1301 Slattery, *Fatih and Science at Notre Dame*, p. 7.

In a series of articles which appeared in the 1980s, R. Scott Appleby linked the concurrent Vatican condemnations of evolution and Americanism as a bad dream which had been replaced by Rome's ultimate acceptance of:

> freedom of religious expression, freedom of speech, freedom of the press, acceptance of democratic governments, acceptance of Protestants, acceptance of African Americans, abolition of slavery and second-class status of ex-enslaved peoples, acceptance of science/evolution, acceptance of historical-critical biblical interpretation, and others. In essence, the Americanists held to "the best ideals of American Puritanism, the Enlightenment, [and] incipient ecumenism."[1302]

According to Slattery, "Appleby argues that Zahm battled with and lost to the anti-Americanists, but the Second Vatican Council has shown that Zahm landed on the right side of history."[1303]

We can hear Martel rising from the grave to tell us "I told you so." Thanks to Notre Dame, the term American Catholic continued to be an oxymoron, every bit as much as it was during the Nativist Riots of the 1840s.

[1302] Slattery, *Fatih and Science at Notre Dame*, p. 8.
[1303] Slattery, *Fatih and Science at Notre Dame*, p. 8.

Chapter 37

The Greene Brothers Create the American House

In the spring of 1916 Charles Greene had just finished up working on the Fleischhacker house just south of San Francisco. He stopped at the resort town of Carmel on his way back to Los Angeles. Charles and his brother Henry had started their own architectural firm in Los Angeles after studying architecture at the Massachusetts Institute of Technology in the 1890s. They defined the bungalow style in a series of houses they built in Pasadena from 1907 to 1909 which brought them international acclaim.

Unfortunately, by 1913 the recognition that Greene and Greene had received wasn't translating into new commissions and income. The limited recognition did little to compensate for the aggravation Charles had to endure from a clientele which had more money than taste. "Artists," he wrote:

> don't have a chance. The educated public wants skill, not soul. It can't judge because it can't feel. It only knows what it has learned. There isn't any culture. The other public is too ignorant to know what it really does want, and too busy money making to try to find out. It takes to fads, discards the old for the new!"[1304]

The Greene brothers were born shortly after the conclusion of the Civil War during the era known as Reconstruction, a term full of architectural implications. Charles Sumner Greene was born on October 12, 1868 in a small town outside of Cincinnati, Ohio. His brother, Henry Mather Greene, came into the world 15 months later on January 23, 1870. In 1876, Greene *pere* enrolled in the Medical College of the University of Cincinnati, and his wife and children settled into a farm own by relatives in Wyandotte, West Virginia. As their father learned medicine, the Greene brothers developed "a keen interest in nature"[1305] which would remain with them for the rest of their lives and have a profound influence on their architecture.

The Greene brothers had roots in America that antedated the founding of the United States:

1304 Makinson Randell, *Greene & Green Architecture as a Fine Art*, p. 216.
1305 Makinson Randell, *Greene & Green Architecture as a Fine Art*, p. 26.

Thomas Sumner Greene was descended from colonists John Greene and Sir George Sumner. Among members of this family were General Nathanael Greene and Christopher Greene of the Continental Army and Governor Increase Sumner and reconstructionist Senator Charles Sumner of Massachusetts. Mrs. Greene was the former Lelia Ariana Mather of Virginia whose family dated back to John Cotton and the Reverend Richard Mather. Other prominent family members included Increase, Cotton, Samuel and Nathanael Mather.[1306]

As adolescents, the Greenes attended the Woodward Manual Training School in St. Louis, where they learned carpentry, with a special emphasis on understanding the inherent characteristics of wood, as well as metal working and tool making.[1307] The school's founder was "strongly influenced by the philosophies of John Ruskin and William Morris,"[1308] and Charles "responded eagerly" to the Woodward curriculum. Unlike the French beaux arts tradition, which was then taught in America's architectural schools, the Woodward program taught that "design determinants stemmed from function and from the appropriate analysis of materials handled in a direct manner."[1309] Because of their training at the Woodward school, the Greene brothers approached their architectural commissions as craftsmen, not theoreticians schooled in a foreign idiom, or ideologues. This would cause problems when they enrolled in the school of architecture at the Massachusetts Institute of Technology, but it brought "a creative freshness to the American architectural scene."[1310] Both Greene brothers felt that the atmosphere at MIT "stifled opportunity for creative and artistic endeavor,"[1311] but Charles, who was the more visionary of the two, felt it more acutely and expressed his dissatisfaction in an unpublished novel. Charles was especially galled by MIT's formalism, which emphasized imitation of foreign models and made it "impossible to invent anything worthwhile in architectural art."[1312] MIT wasn't totally at fault because as of the mid-1890s when the Greene Brothers were studying in Cambridge, there was no American architecture to teach, which Charles lamented when he wrote:

> Our students go over to Paris and learn a jumble intended for educated Frenchmen. When they come home they look upon everything American as hopelessly illiterate.... So they put Louis Quinze's interpretation of a Greek temple into the first story of an office building. A thing that the

---

1306 Makinson Randell, *Greene & Green Architecture as a Fine Art*, p. 26.
1307 Makinson Randell, *Greene & Green Architecture as a Fine Art*, p. 27.
1308 Makinson Randell, *Greene & Green Architecture as a Fine Art*, p. 27.
1309 Makinson Randell, *Greene & Green Architecture as a Fine Art*, p. 27.
1310 Makinson Randell, *Greene & Green Architecture as a Fine Art*, p. 27.
1311 Makinson Randell, *Greene & Green Architecture as a Fine Art*, p. 28.
1312 Makinson Randell, *Greene & Green Architecture as a Fine Art*, p. 28.

Part II: The Romantic Rehabilitation of Nature

Greeks used as a sacred thing, a place of divine worship.... It's true we worship there too... worship the dollar. Oh, it's damnable!"[1313]

The Greenes invented American architecture by bringing their European heritage to bear on the American landscape. By "delving into Greek history" Charles derived "basic principles which would influence him throughout his life,"[1314] but he also experienced vernacular architecture in places like Nantucket, where Charles did many sketches over the three summers the brothers spent there while studying in Boston.

Both brothers had barely settled into their respective careers as fledgling architects in Boston firms when they got the call to come to California. Dr. and Mrs. Greene had moved to what they referred to as the "little country town" of Pasadena, California for health reasons. Because neither their health nor their financial situation had improved, Charles' parents proposed that the brothers move to Pasadena to be with them. When Charles arrived in Pasadena in 1893, he discovered:

> a rapidly growing city not quite twenty years old with a population of "solid, mature, well-educated business and professional men with families, seeking a healthy, moderate climate and cultural satisfaction." Pasadena had gone through one of the greatest building and land speculation booms in American history and had emerged as a wealthy, cultural, and intellectually stimulating center which attracted more and more winter visitors to its many resort hotels. The citizenry was interested in building fine public buildings and business houses; and luxurious, magnificently landscaped homes, costly churches, school buildings, and elaborate gardens appeared along the avenues. Land values spiraled. Publications of the day extolled Pasadena's ideal location (some five miles from the center of Los Angeles) and the healthful quality of its mild climate.[1315]

At odds with the beaux arts curriculum which MIT imposed on him, Charles found consolation in reading the essays of Boston's Socrates, Ralph Waldo Emerson, and quoted him often in his letters. In a letter of February 24, 1895, Charles complained about "not having the time to spend at his music, poetry, painting and photography."[1316] Boston's intellectual tradition more than made up for what MIT lacked. Boston had always been the center of intellectual life in America, and because of their family background the Greene brothers were predisposed to join an ongoing debate which began when forebears like Increase Mather tried to make sense of life on the edge of an immeasurable wilderness through the lens of a Calvinist theology that taught that grace was at war with a nature that was totally depraved.

1313 Makinson Randell, *Greene & Green Architecture as a Fine Art,* p. 28.
1314 Makinson Randell, *Greene & Green Architecture as a Fine Art,* p. 28.
1315 Makinson Randell, *Greene & Green Architecture as a Fine Art,* p. 34.
1316 Makinson Randell, *Greene & Green Architecture as a Fine Art,* p. 35.

Nathaniel Hawthorne expressed that tension in "Young Goodman Brown," the tale of a man who wanders off into the forest to worship the devil because, according to the theology he learned from his ancestors, "Evil is the nature of mankind." Puritan theology would have architectural consequences, because, as Jonathan Edwards put it in his famous sermon "Sinners in the hand of an angry God," "you have nothing to stand upon."

The one thing that united Ralph Waldo Emerson and the generation which grew up under his influence and included Henry David Thoreau, Nathaniel Hawthorne, and Herman Melville, was hatred of Calvinism. When they came of age in the mid-19th century, original sin's hegemony over nature had disappeared, only to be replaced by Romantic notions derived from England and Germany. More importantly, the Christian understanding of Divine Providence had been replaced by Newtonian physics, which saw the universe as one vast machine, which ran on its own without assistance from the Deist God.

Emerson provided little guidance in resolving the tension between the mechanistic world view and its Arcadian reaction. Or better put, he resolves it too easily in a cryptic statement from his journal which he jotted down in 1843: "Machinery and Transcendentalism agree well. Stage-Coach and Railroad are bursting the old legislation like green withes."[1317]

What that meant architecturally was anyone's guess, but James Fenimore Cooper, who was moved by Romanticism's early stirrings, tried to contextualize its influence on development in frontier settlements like his native Cooperstown, New York. As of 1793, when the story of his novel *The Pioneers* takes place, the Puritan hegemony over New England had been replaced by a proliferation of sects which were collectively incapable of imposing any cultural or religious order on the settlements at the edge of the American wilderness.

Deprived of a king and an established religion as the foundation for the culture he was trying to carve out of the wilderness, Judge Temple, the moral center of *The Pioneers*, tried to make do by imposing the Law, because, as Tom Paine put it in *Common Sense*, "In America the law is king." Judge Temple soon discovered that even if it were king, the law needed a metaphysical foundation. When Natty Bumppo, Cooper's version of the noble savage, challenges Judge Temple's ban on shooting deer out of season, he gets thrown in jail because, in the absence of the metaphysical tradition, no one could explain the relationship between nature and the law.

Once again, the metaphysical insecurity which the American settlers inherited from their Calvinist ancestors would have architectural consequences. America's lack of an indigenous architectural vocabulary leads to an unresolved argument between Judge Temple's assistant Richard Jones

---

1317 Marx, p. 231.

Part II: The Romantic Rehabilitation of Nature

and the villain of the novel, Hiram Doolittle, who happens to be an architect. Confounded by how to carry out a commission to build Judge Temple's house, the warring architects agree on a compromise according to which the porch will be "severely classical" while the roof will be "a rare specimen of the composite order." Judge Temple's mansion, as a result, is an eclectic mishmash of friezes and entablatures which never emerges as a coherent structure. Worse still, the effect of the harsh climate has manifested itself as a civil war within the house itself. Simply put, Judge Temple's house is at odds with its foundation:

> Richard and Hiram had, conjointly, reared four little columns of wood, which in their turn supported the shingled roofs of the portico—this was the name that Mr. Jones had thought proper to give to a very plain, covered entrance. The ascent to the platform was by five or six stone steps, somewhat hastily laid together, and which the frost had already begun to move from their symmetrical positions, But the evils of a cold climate and a superficial construction did not end here. As the steps lowered the platform necessarily fell also, and the foundations actually left the super structure suspended in the air, leaving an open space of a foot between the base of the pillars and the stones on which they had originally been placed. . . . It was lucky for the whole fabric that the carpenter, who did the manual part of the labor, had fastened the canopy of this classic entrance so firmly to the side of the house that, when the base deserted the superstructure in the manner we have described, and the pillars, for the want of a foundation, were no longer of service to support the roof, the roof was able to uphold the pillars.[1318]

One hundred years after the pillars which were supposed to support the roof of Judge Temple's portico separated from their foundation, American architects were still looking for a style which arose from its native soil. On his way to California, Charles Greene stopped at the Chicago Columbian Exhibition of 1893, a stunning display of classical Greek architecture on the heroic scale made out of plaster of Paris. The exhibition was spectacular but short-lived. Only one building from the exhibition, the Museum of Science and Industry, got translated into stone.

Classical architecture rendered in buildings made out of plaster of Paris, left Charles underwhelmed and much more impressed with the Japanese exhibit. In the elegant proportions of the Buddhist temples of the Fujiwara period, Charles discovered "a beautiful marriage between the sensitive craftsman's respect for natural materials and the care with which he fitted his work into the environment."[1319] That beauty led Charles "into a profound study of Buddhism" at around the same time he made contact with the Bohemian

---

1318 Cooper, *The Pioneers*, loc. 857-863.
1319 Makinson Randell, *Greene & Green Architecture as a Fine Art*, p. 32.

Walking with a Bible and a Gun

artist colony in Carmel, and it deepened when he met the Bentz family whose import business gave the Greenes "access to books, paintings and *objects d'art* from the Orient which stimulated their interests."[1320]

From 1893 to 1903, the Greenes engaged in "years of experimentation," "searching for the forms, methods and materials appropriate to the life and culture of California. They were caught up in a constant battle between the fundamentals they had learned at the Manual Training School and the popular styles of the day. Their own work clearly reflected their dilemma, and their first years of practice produced a variety of styles."[1321]

In 1901 Charles married Alice White, a recent immigrant from England. Given his interests and her background, Charles spent his honeymoon in England, which was "then the center of the Arts and Crafts Movement."[1322] Charles' fascination with the English country house became "clearly evident on his return to California."[1323] His return to California also coincided with the publication of the first issue of *The Craftsman*, a magazine dedicated to promoting the philosophy of William Morris, founder of the Arts and Crafts movement. As a result of this convergence, California became, in the words of Una Nixson Hopkins, "a region in which native domestic architecture is flowering with a beauty and sincerity hitherto unknown on this continent."[1324] The various stylistic elements which characterized the Greene bungalow finally came together in 1904 with the construction of the Reeve house in Long Beach. That shingle-clad bungalow with its articulated timber structure, multiple-gabled over hanging roofs with projecting support beams combined with a "sensitive combination of cobblestone with brick masonry; special door, leaded glass and lantern designs; the coordination of landscape, walks, fencing and garden gates and a full development of interior furniture and accessories"[1325] inaugurated an era of uniquely American housing which perdures to this day.

From 1907 to 1909, the Greene brothers produced a series of houses which brought all of the disparate elements which they had garnered from education and experience together in buildings which were both beautiful and uniquely American. In 1907, Gustav Stickley began publishing illustrations of the Greene brothers' houses in *The Craftsman* and then in his book *Craftsman Homes*, which appeared in 1909. Charles Greene capitalized on the interest his homes were generating by articulating a philosophy of architecture that was uniquely American:

1320 Makinson Randell, *Greene & Green Architecture as a Fine Art*, p. 55.
1321 Makinson Randell, *Greene & Green Architecture as a Fine Art*, p. 37.
1322 Makinson Randell, *Greene & Green Architecture as a Fine Art*, p. 58.
1323 Makinson Randell, *Greene & Green Architecture as a Fine Art*, p. 58.
1324 Makinson Randell, *Greene & Green Architecture as a Fine Art*, p. 69.
1325 Makinson Randell, *Greene & Green Architecture as a Fine Art*, p. 83.

Part II: The Romantic Rehabilitation of Nature

> I am an American. I want to know the American people of today and the things of today. It is my earnest endeavor to understand the lives of men and women; then perhaps I may be able to express their needs architecturally. I seek to find what is truly useful and then I try to make it beautiful. I believe that this cannot be done by copying old works, no matter how beautiful they may seem to us now. When confronted with actual facts, I have not found the man or woman who would choose to live in the architectural junk of ages gone. The Romans made Rome and the Americans – well! – they are making America. Who could live in a house of two hundred years ago and be happy if we had to conform to all the conditions of today? How in the name of reason, then, can we copy things two thousand years old? Is the Paris opera house built onto the front of a railway station or a Greek temple plastered over the entrance to an office building good art? One is apt to seize the fact for the principle today and ignore the very lesson time should teach. The old things are good, they are noble in their place; then let our perverted fingers leave them there.[1326]

To Charles Greene, the style of the house, its essence, should be determined by four conditions: climate, environment, kinds of materials available, and habits and tastes as they grew out of the life of the owner—in other words, by existence. The beauty of the architecture is also determined by the intelligence of the client. By 1909 Greene and Greene were gaining international recognition from critics like Charles Robert Ashbee, who wrote:

> I think C. Sumner Greene's work beautiful; among the best there is in this country. Like Lloyd Wright the spell of Japan is on him, he feels the beauty and makes magic out of the horizontal line, but there is in his work more tenderness, more subtlety, more self-effacement than in Wright's work. It is more refined and has more repose. Perhaps it loses in strength, perhaps it is California that speaks rather than Illinois; anyway as work it is, so far as the interiors go, more sympathetic to me....[1327]

The culmination of the burst of creativity can be seen in the Gamble House in Pasadena, now owned by the University of Southern California and open to the public. The house's striking exterior is only a modest prelude to the magnificent interior and its stunning use of California redwood in ways that are both Japanese and yet uniquely Californian. The Gamble House is both "a close domestic experience" and "a great work of art because it is so obviously right and complete."[1328]

The burst of creativity allowed the Greenes' bungalows to become the American norm. Makinson claims that:

[1326] Makinson Randell, *Greene & Green Architecture as a Fine Art*, p. 160.
[1327] Makinson Randell, *Greene & Green Architecture as a Fine Art*, p. 168.
[1328] Makinson Randell, *Greene & Green Architecture as a Fine Art*, p. 21.

> in statistical terms (if no others) C. F. A. Voysey and Charles and Henry Greene have been the most influential architects of the Twentieth Century so far, in their own countries for certain, but also to some extent beyond their native shores. By the simple test of counting addresses at which buildings influenced by certain named architects can be found, Palladio is practically nowhere, and the Greenes seem to be practically everywhere. Insofar as the California Bungalow is the product of their work, then they did indeed create a kind of normative building type, not at the Palladian level of the self-conscious regulation of a culture and its standards, but at the level of what normal (common, regular, ordinary) folks want to live in. . . . for one can honestly say that half a century of small houses in the Western United States would not have been the same had the Greenes never produced their few exquisitely wrought houses for a tiny cultural elite, and one will never properly understand the meaning of all those myriad common-or-garden houses for common-or-garden folk without first understanding the rare and idiosyncratic architectural works of Charles and Henry Greene.[1329]

But the Greenes were too busy creating their masterpieces to notice that the world was changing. By 1910 the Greenes had acquired the reputation of being too slow and too expensive. Redwood was becoming scarce and too expensive for the extensive use that had made the Gamble House interiors so striking. Wealthy clients were looking for something that suited the ostentatious tastes of Jay Gatsby and the mansions they were occupying on Long Island. "The day of wood is gone by," one pundit opined, "the day of concrete will be here to remain" as America readied itself for the plunge into Kali Juga. The Golden Age, as anyone who was familiar with Arcadia could have predicted, always ended up as the Age of Lead.

Within a few years, *The Craftsman* folded, and those who could afford to build their own houses turned to cheaper materials and production methods. America is a "tragic adventure," to use Hemingway's term, and one of the *dramatis personae* in that tragedy was Charles Greene, who "refused to sacrifice his principles and beliefs in order to compete for work. With the coming of the income tax, he saw the end of quality construction and believed that clients would not pay for his kind of quality."[1330]

If James Fenimore Cooper described *Paradise Lost* in *The Pioneers*, Greene and Greene made an architectural approximation of Paradise Regained in their suburban bungalows in Pasadena. The American suburb of the early 20th century bespoke an attempt to bring nature and culture together in a way that was impossible in Europe because every American house required a lawn and a garden in the back yard. The post-World War II suburb with its

---

1329 Makinson Randell, *Greene & Green Architecture as a Fine Art*, p. 23.
1330 Makinson Randell, *Greene & Green Architecture as a Fine Art*, p. 193.

Part II: The Romantic Rehabilitation of Nature

"tawdry, plasticized, barn-boarded, homogenized and wood-grain aluminum-sided" tract houses was a profanation of everything Greene and Greene stood for. The Greene bungalows in the Arroyo Seco section of Pasadena exemplify "the half-tamed Middle Landscape" which allowed a harmonious meeting of art and nature. They also point at what might have been. The Greene brothers grew up in a nation which had practically unlimited possibilities for expansion and construction, hampered because there was no typically American style of architecture. The Brothers Greene were scions of the original colonists at a time when the Puritan stronghold began to assert its identity in dramatic architectural monuments free of the mechanist ideology which would go on to disfigure the city in the mid-20th century. By 1913 Greene and Greene were starting to be recognized for their uniquely Californian style of architecture. In the preface to his book *American Country Houses of Today*, Ralph Adams Cram praised the Greene's bungalows, adding by way of caveat that:

> One must see the real and revolutionary thing in its native haunts of Berkeley and Pasadena to appreciate it in all its varied charm and its striking beauty. Where it comes from heaven alone knows, but we are glad it arrived, for it gives a new zest to life, a new object for admiration. There are things in it Japanese; things that are Scandinavian; things that hint at Sikkim, Bhutan, and the fastness of Tibet, and yet it all hangs together, it is beautiful, it is contemporary, and for some reason or other it seems to fit California. Structurally it is a blessing; only too often the exigencies of our assumed precedents lead us into the wide and easy road of structural duplicity, but in this sort of thing there is only an honesty that is sometimes almost brazen. It is a wooden style built woodenly, and it has the force and the integrity of Japanese architecture. Added to this is the elusive element of charm that comes only from the personality of the creator, and charm in a degree hardly matched in other modern work.[1331]

The Greene Brothers never got another major commission. Around the same time that Cram was praising the Greenes for their heroic attempt to bring the philosophy of the arts and crafts movement and their anti-industrial construction methods to the American house, an obscure German architect by the name of Walter Gropius was putting the finishing touches on a shoe factory in Alfeld an der Leine in Lower Saxony. The *Faguswerk* would become famous as the first modern building. Gropius would achieve fame as the Greenes were slipping into obscurity when he took design elements from the *Faguswerk* and applied them to large apartment buildings which he christened *Wohnmaschinen* or machines for living, which were the antithesis of everything that the Greenes hoped to achieve in their bungalows. Gropius's *Wohnmaschinen* would become ubiquitous after World War II around the

---

1331 Makinson Randell, *Greene & Green Architecture as a Fine Art*, p. 212.

time when the Greenes who had been unemployed for decades got their final recognition and died.

Greene and Greene were part of an American architectural movement which included Frank Lloyd Wright, who told Charles Greene during one of his visits to Pasadena, "Mr. Greene, I do not know how you do it."[1332] Wright expressed his hatred of the Bauhaus *Wohnmaschine* by turning Mies van der Rohe's famous phrase "*beinahe nichts*" (almost nothing) into "much ado about almost nothing." America was never able to break its attachment to the modernist idolization of the machine, as evidenced by Harry Gesner's Wave House, which got built in the same year the Russians launched Sputnik (1957) and looks as if the returning space ship had just landed on the beach in Malibu.

The idea that man was a machine began with Julian de la Mettrie, who wrote a book with that title. It took on new meaning when the Marquis de Sade appropriated the idea in his pornographic novel *Justine* saying, "Woman is a machine for voluptuousness." As the Marquis de Sade made clear, there was always a connection between the man who became a machine and mechanistic sex, but it was Gropius who brought them together in his *Wohnmaschinen*.[1333]

The houses the Greene brothers built, however, taught a different lesson from the one de la Mettrie and the Marquis de Sade taught. When they bought a Greene bungalow, the liberated ladies at turn of the century America got a structure which was conducive to the moral law, primarily because it was beautiful. Anything which embodies beauty is conducive to moral behavior because the good and the beautiful are transcendentals, which are interchangeable aspects of being. As Keats put it, referring to the other transcendental, "Beauty is truth and truth beauty." The architecture of Greene and Greene was uniquely American because it "is intimately derived from the process of making sense of the landscape of America, something which may be clearly felt, but is rarely easy to define or name."[1334] Charles Greene did for American architecture what Giotto had done for Italian painting. They liberated their respective art forms from Greek models and showed how existence called essence into being.

The fatal flaw which destroyed America's ability to reconcile art and nature was Newtonian physics. Nature became the human norm at the time of the Enlightenment. By claiming to be the grammar of nature, Newtonian physics turned the universe into a machine. Philadelphia polymath David Rittenhouse created his orrery as a miniature planetarium, and it played a major role in propagating the mechanistic worldview in America. The orrery

---

1332 Makinson Randell, *Greene & Green Architecture as a Fine Art*, p. 212.

1333 See E. Michael Jones, *Living Machines* (South Bend, IN: Fidelity Press) available at fidelitypress.org

1334 Makinson Randell, *Greene & Green Architecture as a Fine Art*, p. 17.

Part II: The Romantic Rehabilitation of Nature

is "an ingenious replica of the universe: when the clockwork machinery turns, the heavenly bodies revolve in their orbits, music plays, and dials move indicating the hour, the day of the month, and the year."[1335] The orrery became the visible symbol of an ultimate reality which could not be seen, and because it could not be seen that reality could not be beautiful. Instead of metaphysics, Americans got mechanism as the best approximation of ultimate reality.

The successor to the orrery as the prime symbol of mechanism was the steam engine, which got put to use first in factories and then in transportation. "By 1844 the machine had captured the public imagination."[1336] A little over a century later, city dwellers in the West and workers in the East had been consigned to living in the machines the Enlightenment proposed as ultimate reality. The "image of the American machine had become a transcendent symbol: a physical object invested with political and metaphysical ideality."[1337]

The Greene brothers refused to capitulate to modernism, because "neither Charles nor Henry was comfortable with the machine age."[1338] Makinson finds this unfortunate and speculates that "they could have made further contributions to American architecture. . . had they embraced the modern movement with the same vigor with which they had broken from the past."[1339] But Charles remained adamant in his refusal because modernism meant "denial of beauty."[1340] Clever design had replaced art. The inexorable result was that:

> Building today is engineering, not architecture. The ideal of engineering is precision and economy, the slogan of manufacturers. Both of them have a fever of facts and figures, but the public is immune from this malady. It is the merchant who molds the nation with his publicity stuff.... Careless of the quality of material and work he sets a premium on clever design that discreetly covers the engineering it can never be a part of. The real modernist architect turns with disgust from this unmeaning display to aesthetic denial of beauty.[1341]

By 1916, Charles, ever the visionary, could see that the tide was turning against him, and in this bitter state of mind he discovered an artist colony in Carmel, where he could dedicate his life to the pursuit of beauty through art. In June 1916, he moved his family from Pasadena to Carmel, where he hoped to "delve into the profundities of Buddhist philosophy"[1342] and become a writer.

1335 Marx, p. 161.
1336 Marx, p. 191.
1337 Marx, p. 206.
1338 Makinson Randell, *Greene & Green Architecture as a Fine Art,* p. 261.
1339 Makinson Randell, *Greene & Green Architecture as a Fine Art,* p. 261.
1340 Makinson Randell, *Greene & Green Architecture as a Fine Art,* p. 261.
1341 Makinson Randell, *Greene & Green Architecture as a Fine Art,* p. 261.
1342 Makinson Randell, *Greene & Green Architecture as a Fine Art,* p. 217.

Walking with a Bible and a Gun

Charles' career as a writer never materialized, but while in Carmel he met a Missouri businessman who was a distant relative of Jesse James. D.L. James had just purchased a dramatic piece of property in Carmel Highlands and was looking for an architect who could create an equally dramatic piece of architecture. The result was the D.L. James house, a "stone structure seems to have grown out of its site atop the rocky cliffs south of Carmel."[1343] One of the defining characteristics of that structure is the seamless transition from nature to art which it achieves. As Makinson puts it, "At places it is difficult to ascertain just where nature's rock has ended and man's masonry genius has begun."[1344]

After receiving the commission, Charles spent months meditating on the landscape in a silent attempt to hear what existence was telling him and how it could be integrated into architectural memories of things like the stone ruins of Tintagel. The result was a "a double 'U' form which developed from the combination of Charles Greene's recent exploration in rambling non-linear plan concepts and the strongly irregular configuration of the rocky site, whose craggy cliffs dropped sharply, almost vertically, to the crashing surf below."[1345]

The D.L. James house was nothing like the bungalows he had built in Pasadena. For one thing, Charles relied on native stone quarried from nearby Yankee Point as his main building material. Use of wood was minimal in the house's interior, where the walls are made of plaster suffused with local sand. Charles remained on site for three years and supervised the placement of every stone in the house's masonry walls, often demanding that whole walls be torn down and reconstructed if they were not erected according to his demanding specifications. Charles eschewed not just the prevailing system of administration by recorded instruction but "any system," choosing instead "personal direction on the job" because it allowed his designs to be more open to "contingencies" and "inspiration."[1346] Because the mortar joints are recessed, the masonry takes on the characteristics of the cliff on which the house is built. One of the most striking features of the D.L. James house is the seamless transition from cliff to foundation, something that become especially dramatic when viewed from the path leading to the rock beach at the bottom of the ravine south of the house:

> The way some of the main lines of the building grow out of the rock and huge boulders upon which they are built, their foundations often beginning many feet below and gradually working upward in sympathetic conjunction with the native cliff rock, has been managed so skillfully that it is impossible in some cases to tell where the one ends and the other

---

1343 Makinson Randell, *Greene & Green Architecture as a Fine Art*, p. 222.
1344 Makinson Randell, *Greene & Green Architecture as a Fine Art*, p. 222.
1345 Makinson Randell, *Greene & Green Architecture as a Fine Art*, p. 224.
1346 Makinson Randell, *Greene & Green Architecture as a Fine Art*, p. 224.

Part II: The Romantic Rehabilitation of Nature

begins. This kind of work is not architecture as now commonly known—it savors of a more plastic art, of the building of a home in thorough keeping with its rugged site.[1347]

While in Carmel, Charles became a member of the Ouspensky circle and was considered a "profound student of Buddhism"[1348] by those who knew him. Both Ouspensky, who negated Aristotle's principle of non-contradiction, and Buddhism denigrated the opposition between art and nature, favoring an all-encompassing mind instead. "Today," he told a friend, "the rational mind dominates, it sees Nature as all-inclusive and Art as Man's exclusive part of Nature. It beholds Nature and Art forever separate. You. . . with joyous heart and modern tool in hand have reached beyond personal expression to the root of Truth, finding beauty by the way where and as you looked."[1349]

Greene was no philosopher; his notion of an all-encompassing "Mind-essence" sounds like Pantheism until he describes it as "in full possession of radiant wisdom and luminosity, penetrating everything by the purity of its concepts, seeing everywhere adequately and truly, its mind innately free and unprejudiced, ever abiding in blissful peace, pure, fresh and unchangeable."[1350] At this point it sounds more like Sophia or Logos. Because Logos is God, beauty is one of its main characteristics. Beauty is a transcendental, which means the artist allows us to approach God. As in Italy at the time of Giotto, the artist could portray what the philosopher could not explain. Reversing Plato's understanding of art as essence imposed on existence, St. Thomas Aquinas claimed that existence called essence into being, and that reversal inaugurated one of the greatest periods of art in human history. Once ideas like this enter the ether of human consciousness they can never be expunged. Charles Greene's art drew from this source in western culture, no matter what he said to the contrary. The D.L. James house was a striking example of how existence, in terms of the landscape, called essence, or the form of the house, into being. It also showed how grace (or in this instance, art) perfected nature without destroying it.

One of the last works Charles completed was the library addition that D.L. James commissioned in 1937, which is where my wife and I stayed during our visit. The room was occupied by two queen size beds, which a new owner plannned to remove, but the large windows facing the Pacific Ocean act as alcoves conducive to study and meditation. The door to the library opens directly onto a patio which overlooks the Pacific Ocean, providing the ideal place to meditate on nature. When the clouds roll in, as they often do in

---

1347 Makinson Randell, *Greene & Green Architecture as a Fine Art*, p. 226.
1348 Makinson Randell, *Greene & Green Architecture as a Fine Art*, p. 264.
1349 Makinson Randell, *Greene & Green Architecture as a Fine Art*, p. 265.
1350 Makinson Randell, *Greene & Green Architecture as a Fine Art*, p. 264.

Carmel, one retreats into the library and contemplates art as both a refuge from nature and its completion.

As a classic instance of too little too late, the Greenes "were hailed as 'Formulators of a New and Native Architecture' and presented with the coveted Citation from the national organization of The American Institute of Architects"[1351] two years before Henry died in 1954.

[1351] Makinson Randell, *Greene & Green Architecture as a Fine Art,* p. 265.

Chapter 38

Frederick Jackson Turner and the Closing of the Frontier

Frederick Jackson Turner became famous by announcing the closing of the American frontier and exploring its implications in a speech he gave to the American Historical Association at the World's Columbian Exposition in Chicago in 1893. The speech was first published in the *Proceedings of the State Historical Society of Wisconsin* and then in the *Annual Report of the American Historical Association*, and finally in book form as chapter one of *The Frontier in American History* in 1920.[1352]

Turner grew up in middle class family in Portage, Wisconsin, son of a father who was active in Republican politics, as well as a newspaper editor and publisher. As a young man, Turner fell under the spell of Ralph Waldo Emerson, and was later influenced by the writings of Charles Darwin, Herbert Spencer, and Julian Huxley.[1353] The closing of the American frontier, which the Census Bureau announced in 1890 was a significant event because American history had been determined "in a large degree" by "the history of the colonization of the Great West."[1354] The frontier line, with its promise of free land, pitted existence against essence in a way that allowed the former to modify the latter and bring something new into being:

> American social development has been continually beginning over again on the frontier. This perennial rebirth, this fluidity of American life, this expansion westward with its new opportunities, its continuous touch with the simplicity of primitive society, furnish the forces dominating American character.[1355]

1352 "The Significance of the Frontier in American History," *Wikipedia: The Free Encyclopedia*, https://en.wikipedia.org/wiki/The_Significance_of_the_Frontier_in_American_History#:~:text=The%20frontier%20helped%20shape%20individualism,the%20idea%20of%20American%20exceptionalism.

1353 "Frederick Jackson Turner," *Wikipedia: The Free Encyclopedia*, https://en.wikipedia.org/wiki/Frederick_Jackson_Turner

1354 Frederick Jackson Turner, *The Frontier in American History*, Kindle, p. 3.

1355 Turner, p. 3.

The frontier is "the meeting point between savagery and civilization,"[1356] the place where "European life entered the continent, and how America modified and developed that life and reacted on Europe."[1357] The frontier is, in short, "the line of most rapid and effective Americanization."[1358] American identity comes into being as a function of the wilderness, which "masters the colonist" and transforms him from "a European in dress, industries, tools, modes of travel, and thought" into "a new product that is American. . . . Thus, the advance of the frontier has meant a steady movement away from the influence of Europe, a steady growth of independence on American lines."[1359] Turner explains how existence called essence into being by describing how "the system" of Americanism grew "by adapting the statutes to the customs of the successive frontiers."[1360]

The initial vehicle for this expansion was the river trade in furs, which opened up the West. Indians needed the trade more than the English or the French because they needed guns more than the Europeans needed furs:

> The trading post left the unarmed tribes at the mercy of those that had purchased fire-arms—a truth which the Iroquois Indians wrote in blood, and so the remote and unvisited tribes gave eager welcome to the trader. "The savages," wrote La Salle, "take better care of us French than of their own children; from us only can they get guns and goods." This accounts for the trader's power and the rapidity of his advance. Thus, the disintegrating forces of civilization entered the wilderness. Every river valley and Indian trail became a fissure in Indian society, and so that society became honeycombed. Long before the pioneer farmer appeared on the scene, primitive Indian life had passed away. The farmers met Indians armed with guns.[1361]

The closing of the American frontier caused an identity crisis in the understanding of what it meant to be an American. If the wilderness broke down "complex European life. . . into the simplicity of primitive conditions,"[1362] the closing of the frontier meant that the skills Daniel Boone and his followers had acquired were no longer meaningful or necessary. The men who modeled themselves on Daniel Boone found that the world had passed them by. They were old men like Natty Bumppo in *The Pioneers*, incapable of integrating themselves into the new order. If that were true in the 1820s, when Cooper began the Leatherstocking tales, it was *a fortiori* true

---

1356 Turner, p. 3.
1357 Turner, p. 3.
1358 Turner, p. 3.
1359 Turner, p. 4.
1360 Turner, p. 5.
1361 Turner, p. 6.
1362 Turner, p. 5.

Part II: The Romantic Rehabilitation of Nature

in the 1890s. Natty Bumppo's "training," which is "that of the old west, in its frontier days"[1363] did not render his descendants capable of working in the factories and offices which employed them at the dawn of the 20th century.

From 1910 to 1950, the total population in the United States doubled, but the farm population declined by one third. The peak in farm population was reached between 1910 and 1920. Since then, the trend in the number of people living on farms has been downward. In 1900 fifty percent of the American population lived on farms, by 1950, only one out of six did.[1364] Turner wrote at a turning point in American life. The frontier was gone, and the factory and the office building were replacing the farm as the place where most people earned a living. "The exhaustion of the supply of free land and the closing of the movement of Western advance as an effective factor in American development" was compounded because:

> there has been such a concentration of capital in the control of fundamental industries as to make a new epoch in the economic development of the United States. The iron, the coal, and the cattle of the country have all fallen under the domination of a few great corporations with allied interests, and by the rapid combination of the important railroad systems and steamship lines, in concert with these same forces, even the breadstuffs and the manufactures of the nation are to some degree controlled in a similar way.[1365]

Now that those "frontier opportunities are gone," the men who patterned their lives on Natty's frontier skills and independence had to recognize "a new Americanism" based on "a drastic assertion of national government and imperial expansion under a popular hero."[1366]

Teddy Roosevelt was that new popular hero. Americanism, by which we mean the state replacing the church as the unifying factor of American identity, was best epitomized by Theodore Roosevelt. He called this new religion "strenuous Christianity," largely because he discovered that "physical exertion" helped to minimize the debilitating asthma of his childhood and "bolster his spirits."[1367] Strenuous Christianity was another term for the religion of Americanism. As St. Augustine pointed out at the end of the Roman Empire, republics can be virtuous, but empires are inevitably criminal conspiracies. The best way to disguise a criminal conspiracy is to turn it into the state religion, and that's what happened in America. The closing of the American frontier

---

1363 Turner p. 77.

1364 "Agriculture 1950: Changes in Agriculture, 1900 to 1950," https://www2.census.gov/prod2/decennial/documents/41667073v5p6ch4.pdf

1365 Turner, p. 85.

1366 Turner p. 77.

1367 "Theodore Roosevelt," *Wikipedia: The Free Encyclopedia*, https://en.wikipedia.org/wiki/Theodore_Roosevelt

corresponded with the birth of American Imperialism. Americanism had become a religion which was now universal in scope. Like the hated Catholic Church, which had received the divine commission to go out and baptize all nations, America, upon the closing of the frontier, transposed "the energies of expansion" onto a higher plane which now encompassed "the demands for a vigorous foreign policy, for an interoceanic canal, for a revival of our power upon the seas, and for the extension of American influence to outlying islands and adjoining countries."[1368]

America left geography behind and entered "the realm of the spirit," a description that was Turner's way of saying that Americanism had become a religion. Like Christ after the resurrection from the dead, "the conception of society" and "the ideals and aspirations" which America produced would "persist in the minds" of the American people and in the minds of every people lucky enough to fall under the hegemony of the American empire, the Filipinos being a recent example at the time Turner propounded his thesis.

With the passing of the frontier, a man with Daniel Boone's skills found no employment in the factories and office buildings of America's great cities. The industrialization of agriculture made the farmer dependent on credit from eastern banks, which meant loss of independence. After he lost economic independence, the farmer "began to lose his primitive attitude of individualism, government began to look less like a necessary evil and more like an instrument for the perpetuation of his democratic ideals."[1369] As a result, "the defenses of the pioneer democrat began to shift, from free land to legislation, from the ideal of individualism to the ideal of social control through regulation by law. . . . The individualism of the Kentucky pioneer of 1796 was giving way to the Populism of the Kansas pioneer of 1896."[1370]

After the farmers in the old south were driven to the wall by Jewish usurers known as "furnishing merchants" like the Solomon brothers, who took their usurious gains north to found a banking house in New York, they moved to Texas, where they became populists who regarded "legislation as an instrument of construction," and instituted the strictest usury laws in the union. Legislation, not the rifle, was their only defense against the "vast accumulations of capital" which "became the normal agency of the industrial world."[1371]

The independent backwoodsman had been replaced by the immigrant factory worker, who needed the union to make him strong. The melting pot had created a new type of American out of the "bowie knife Southerners," "cow-milking Yankee Puritans," "beer-drinking Germans," and "wild Irishmen,"

1368 Turner, p. 76.
1369 Turner, p. 95.
1370 Turner, p. 95.
1371 Turner, p. 95.

Part II: The Romantic Rehabilitation of Nature

through "a process of mutual education," which produced "a new type, which was neither the sum of all its elements, nor a complete fusion in a melting pot." The Americans were, however, still "pioneers," but pioneers defined not as "outlying fragments of New England, of Germany, or of Norway,"[1372] but as real Americans even though they worked in offices and factories. Bereft of consolation from the Protestant sects which fell under the increasing control of oligarchs like the Rockefellers, "The solitary backwoodsman wielding his ax at the edge of a measureless forest" was replaced by immigrant wage slaves who worked for "companies capitalized at millions, operating railroads, sawmills, and all the enginery of modern machinery to harvest the remaining trees,"[1373] and turned to literature for consolation for his lost identity.

1372 Turner, p. 118.
1373 Turner, p. 96.

Part III

The Return of the Satanic Wilderness

Part III

The Return of the Satanic Sycophants

Chapter 39

Jack London and the Urbanization of America

Jack London was one of the first writers to recognize this market... Born in 1876, London came of age in San Francisco, which made him a man of the west with no place to go after the frontier closed in 1890. London joined a literary group known as "The Crowd," which advocated socialism and other causes of the day, but the man who best epitomized the American man of the west in the age of Darwin was Wolf Larsen, the captain of the eponymous *Sea Wolf*, who rescued the effete intellectual Humphrey van Weyden from a ferry which capsized while crossing San Francisco Bay.

Writing to the same cohort which found Jack London appealing, Frederick Jackson Turner worried that the closing of the frontier meant the disappearance of American identity. Turner then takes specific aim at Natty Bumppo, claiming: "The test tube and the microscope are needed rather than ax and rifle in this new ideal of conquest."[1374] Professors are the new pioneers, because "like the pioneers they have the ideal of investigation, they seek new horizons. They are not tied to past knowledge."[1375] The professor must succeed the preacher as the new paradigm of what it means to be an American, because: "the old pioneer individualism is disappearing, while the forces of social combination are manifesting themselves as never before." New conditions have created new paradigms of what it means to be an American. Natty Bumppo has been replaced by "the coal baron, the steel king, the oil king, the cattle king, the railroad magnate, the master of high finance, the monarch of trusts." This process is unstoppable, says Turner, because "the individualistic pioneer democracy of America" has changed, not because existence calls essence into being, but because it has been replaced by "competitive evolution," which is his new word for God.[1376] Evolution has created doubt about the man of the west as the paradigmatic American which suffuses Turner's later essays and leeches into the fiction of Jack London.

1374 Turner, p. 97.
1375 Turner, p. 98.
1376 Turner, p. 108.

London "was not much of a thinker," as he conceded in his short story "To Build a Fire," which was based on his experiences during the Klondike Gold Rush in Alaska. Man was a sophisticated animal who had to abandon thinking in favor of action based on instinct if he wanted to survive in an alien universe:

> When it is 75 below zero, a man must not fail in his first attempt to build a fire. This is especially true if his feet are wet. If his feet are dry, and he fails, he can run along the trail for half a mile to keep his blood moving. But the blood in wet and freezing feet cannot be kept moving by running when it is 75 degrees below. No matter how fast he runs, the wet feet will freeze even harder.[1377]

Building a fire in 75 below zero weather in the Klondike replaced dancing with the daffodils in spring in the Lake District as the epitome of "nature" because of the mechanistic reduction of human nature which reached a pinnacle in the thought of Charles Darwin and Herbert Spencer. In this universe morality disappears and is replaced by power, as Shakespeare predicted in *Troilus and Cressida*.

London's novel *The Sea Wolf* is based on his experiences as an oyster pirate, combined with the philosophies regnant in Bohemian circles in San Francisco, which Hump picked up "when he loafed through the winter months and read Nietzsche and Schopenhauer to rest his brain."[1378] After a few minutes conversation, Larsen says to Hump, "You're a preacher, aren't you?"[1379] but Hump demurs, "taken aback," because no one had ever asked him a question like that. Regaining his composure, Hump stammers "I-I am a gentleman"[1380] because he has an independent income, but it doesn't explain what Hump does, which is write for magazines like *The Atlantic Monthly*, the quintessential journal of the Man of the East. Hump was a writer, which is what the preacher became after Puritanism was replaced by muscular Christianity and the university succeeded the seminary at places like Harvard. As such, Hump was "unused to spectacles of brutality."[1381] But his sudden translation into a cabin boy on a sealing ship has introduced Hump to the real world, which is the world according to Darwin, which has replaced Protestantism as the hidden grammar of the newly created American empire. In that brave new world, Hump learns about "the cruelty of the sea, its relentlessness and awfulness" and the fact that "Life had become cheap and tawdry, a beastly

---

1377 "To Build a Fire," https://americanenglish.state.gov/files/ae/resource_files/to-build-a-fire.pdf
1378 London, *Sea Wolf*, p. 78.
1379 London, *Sea Wolf*, p. 28.
1380 London, *Sea Wolf*, p. 30.
1381 London, *Sea Wolf*, p. 36.

Part III: The Return of the Satanic Wilderness

and inarticulate thing, a soulless stirring of the ooze and slime."[1382] Forget about dancing with the daffodils, Nature had been reduced to life on a sealing ship, where "Force, nothing but force, obtained" and "moral suasion was a thing unknown."[1383] Wolf Larsen, Hump's guide to the real world, otherwise known as "nature," explains:

> life is a mess. . . . It is like yeast, a ferment, a thing that moves and may move for a minute, an hour, a year, or a hundred years, but that in the end will cease to move. The big eat the little that they may continue to move, the strong eat the weak that they may retain their strength. The lucky eat the most and move the longest, that is all."[1384]

Life is "an eternity of piggishness."[1385] The sailor Harrison, who dangles from a shroud trying to disentangle a fouled sail, is described as an "enormous spider,"[1386] revealing similarities between the legacy of Jonathan Edwards and the Darwinism which succeeded it. Hump is appalled at Wolf's views, but incapable of refuting them: "Life had always seemed a peculiarly sacred thing, but here it counted for nothing, was a cipher in the arithmetic of commerce."[1387] As a result of the education he obtains on the *Sea Wolf*, Hump is incapable of refuting Wolf's piggishness:

> Perhaps, also, it was the elemental simplicity of his mind that baffled me. He drove so directly to the core of the matter, divesting a question always of all superfluous details, and with such an air of finality, that I seemed to find myself struggling in deep water, with no footing under me.

Once again, the imagery of Calvinism provides the hidden grammar of Evolution. Both deny the "value of life," leaving Hump unable to explain why he had accepted "the sacredness of life" as "axiomatic." The challenge to defend this and other truisms renders Hump "speechless."[1388]

Wolf has "read Darwin," which makes his philosophy of life "at least consistent and as a result irrefutable, by Hump, the cabin boy quondam writer who "dreamed away thirty-five years among books."[1389] Darwin is the magic formula which transports Wolf Larsen from a position in which he "could almost believe in God," back to the new reality, according to which concepts like God are nothing more than:

1382 London, *Sea Wolf*, p. 44.
1383 London, *Sea Wolf*, p. 56.
1384 London, *Sea Wolf*, pp. 62-3.
1385 London, *Sea Wolf*, p. 65.
1386 London, *Sea Wolf*, p. 76.
1387 London, *Sea Wolf*, p. 79.
1388 London, *Sea Wolf*, p. 83.
1389 London, *Sea Wolf*, p. 88.

the bribe for living, the champagne of the blood, the effervescence of the ferment—that makes some men think holy thoughts, and other men to see God or to create him when they cannot see him. That is all, the drunkenness of life, the stirring and crawling of the yeast, the babbling of the life that is insane with consciousness that it is alive. And—bah! Tomorrow I shall pay for it as the drunkard pays. And I shall know that I must die, at sea most likely, cease crawling of myself to be all a-crawl with the corruption of the sea; to be fed upon, to be carrion, to yield up all the strength and movement of my muscles that it may become strength and movement in fin and scale and the guts of fishes. Bah! And bah! again. The champagne is already flat. The sparkle and bubble has gone out and it is a tasteless drink."[1390]

In his struggle to refute Wolf's materialism, Hump can't make up his mind. Sometimes he thinks Larsen is mad, "or half-mad at least," while at other times, Hump takes him "for a great man, a genius who has never arrived."[1391] Wolf is edified by their conversation, because he always:

dreamed that I might some day talk with men who used such language, that I might lift myself out of the place in life in which I had been born, and hold conversation and mingle with men who talked about just such things as ethics. And this is the first time I have ever heard the word pronounced.

But as soon as he formulates a way out of the materialist's dilemma, Wolf dismisses it as an illusion. Hump's talk of "altruism," is "wrong" because life "is a question neither of grammar nor ethics, but of fact."[1392] And the fundamental fact is: "Might is right. That is all there is to it. Weakness is wrong."[1393] Hump and Wolf are "two particles of yeast."[1394] When Hump brings up "altruism," Wolf remembers coming across the term while reading Herbert Spencer's *The Data of Ethics*. Larsen, according to Hump, had sifted the great philosopher's teachings, rejecting and selecting according to his needs and desires."[1395] Altruism, however, only works as "a paying business proposition" if Wolf faces eternity after he dies, a remnant of Protestantism which has been replaced by the struggle for existence between two particles of yeast. Altruism has no meaning "for one who does not believe in eternal life."[1396] With nothing eternal facing him but death:

1390 London, *Sea Wolf*, p. 90.
1391 London, *Sea Wolf*, p. 92.
1392 London, *Sea Wolf*, p. 96.
1393 London, *Sea Wolf*, p. 97.
1394 London, *Sea Wolf*, p. 97
1395 London, *Sea Wolf*, p. 99.
1396 London, *Sea Wolf*, p. 100.

Part III: The Return of the Satanic Wilderness

it would be immoral for me to perform any act that was a sacrifice. Any sacrifice that makes me lose one crawl or squirm is foolish,—and not only foolish, for it is a wrong against myself and a wicked thing. I must not lose one crawl or squirm if I am to get the most out of the ferment. Nor will the eternal movelessness that is coming to me be made easier or harder by the sacrifices or selfishnesses of the time when I was yeasty and acrawl."[1397]

Hump concludes that Larsen is "a man utterly without what the world calls morals."[1398] After calling Wolf "a monster," Hump, ransacks his mind for a more fitting term to describe the Protestant faith he abandoned in favor of Darwinism, saying Wolf Larsen is "Lucifer."[1399] The hidden grammar of "survival of the fittest," the phrase that captured the mind of London's age, is Satanism. Like the Puritans, whose religion he disdains, like Emerson, whose views of nature are naïve, Wolf has read *Paradise Lost*:

Wolf is Lucifer. He has read *Paradise Lost*. Once Larsen began "preaching the passion of revolt. . . . It was inevitable that Milton's Lucifer should be instanced, and the keenness with which Wolf Larsen analysed and depicted the character was a revelation of his stifled genius."[1400]

Wolf admires Satan because:

"He led a lost cause, and he was not afraid of God's thunderbolts," Wolf Larsen was saying. "Hurled into hell, he was unbeaten. A third of God's angels he had led with him, and straightway he incited man to rebel against God, and gained for himself and hell the major portion of all the generations of man. Why was he beaten out of heaven? Because he was less brave than God? less proud? less aspiring? No! A thousand times no! God was more powerful, as he said, Whom thunder hath made greater. But Lucifer was a free spirit. To serve was to suffocate. He preferred suffering in freedom to all the happiness of a comfortable servility. He did not care to serve God. He cared to serve nothing. He was no figure-head. He stood on his own legs. He was an individual." "The first Anarchist," Maud [Hump's love interest] laughed, rising and preparing to withdraw to her state-room. "Then it is good to be an anarchist!" he cried.[1401]

London then cites the same lines of Satan's speech that inspired both Puritans and anti-Puritans. He begins with the phrase "Here at least," which in the poem refers to Hell, but in its early 20th century extrapolation, refers to the Hell that Americans had created out of nature:

1397 London, *Sea Wolf*, p. 100.
1398 London, *Sea Wolf*, p. 101.
1399 London, *Sea Wolf*, p. 116.
1400 London, *Sea Wolf*, p. 306.
1401 London, *Sea Wolf*, p. 306.

We shall be free; the Almighty hath not built
Here for his envy; will not drive us hence;
Here we may reign secure; and in my choice
To reign is worth ambition, though in hell:
Better to reign in hell than serve in heaven."

The *Sea Wolf* is the Darwinist version of *Moby Dick*. Like Starbuck in *Moby Dick*, the effete eastern intellectual Humphrey van Weyden contemplates killing Wolf Larsen, the captain of the Phoenix, to free the ship of state from tyranny, but more importantly because Wolf is, to use Humphrey's exact words, "Milton's Lucifer":

> I followed in amaze, mastered for the moment by his remarkable intellect, under the spell of his passion, for he was preaching the passion of revolt. It was inevitable that Milton's Lucifer should be instanced, and the keenness with which Wolf Larsen analysed and depicted the character was a revelation of his stifled genius. It reminded me of Taine, yet I knew the man had never heard of that brilliant though dangerous thinker. "He led a lost cause, and he was not afraid of God's thunderbolts," Wolf Larsen was saying. "Hurled into hell, he was unbeaten. A third of God's angels he had led with him, and straightway he incited man to rebel against God, and gained for himself and hell the major portion of all the generations of man. Why was he beaten out of heaven? Because he was less brave than God? less proud? less aspiring? No! A thousand times no! God was more powerful, as he said, Whom thunder hath made greater. But Lucifer was a free spirit. To serve was to suffocate. He preferred suffering in freedom to all the happiness of a comfortable servility. He did not care to serve God. He cared to serve nothing.[1402]

Wolf's statement that Lucifer "cared to serve nothing" is significant. Nothing is the English term for the Latin word *nihil*, which is the root for the philosophical term nihilism, which Todd describes as the hidden grammar of the Zombie State. Todd calls the situation in Elizabethan England in the aftermath of the looting operation known as the Reformation, when the crown had lost all legitimacy but retained its hold on power by transforming Catholic England into the world's first police state, nihilism, which is closely related to Satanism. Because nature abhors a vacuum, the void created by the disappearance of Protestantism was filled by "nihilism," which Todd defines as "an amoralism stemming from an absence of values."[1403] Nihilism, he tells us at another point, "denies reality and truth; it is a cult of lies."[1404] Nihilism leads to Narcissism, both of which are based on a denial of reality that has

---

1402 Jack London, The *Sea Wolf*, Kindle edition, p. 306.

1403 EEmmanuel Todd, *La Defaite de l'Occidante* (The Defeat of the West), Kindle edition, p. 33. *un amoralisme découlant d'une absence de valeurs.*

1404 Todd, *The Defeat of the West*, p. 346

Part III: The Return of the Satanic Wilderness

become pandemic in societies which claim that "a man can become a woman, and a woman can become a man," an affirmation which Todd describes as both false and "close to the theoretical heart of Western nihilism."[1405] Because "right and wrong . . . have lost their names," a man can become a woman if the powerful decree it possible. That has political ramifications because it also means that a nuclear treaty with Iran under Obama can transform, overnight, into an aggravated sanctions regime under Trump.[1406] Wolf Larsen is a nihilist who found inspiration in Milton's Satan.

After Larsen finishes his Satanic consecration, Hump describes it as "the defiant cry of a mighty spirit," a spirit who proclaims "Here at last We shall be free." "Here" could mean the ship but only as a metaphor for the ship of state, which is America. When Wolf Larsen issues "the defiant cry of a mighty spirit," who is now the prophet of the world's fourth great religion, Maud Brewster, full of an "unnamable and unmistakable terror," whispers, "You are Lucifer."[1407]

The spell is broken when Wolf tries to rape Maude. All of the morality vs. yeast debate, all of the references to Spencer and Darwin are forgotten when Hump sees Maud "straining and struggling and crushed in the embrace of Wolf Larsen's arms."[1408] All of the previous talk about moral relativism suddenly disappears when a woman's chastity is at stake, and Hump springs into action and saves her from Wolf's lust. Once his spell is broken, Hump and Maud jump ship and make sail for Japan. Instead they land on a deserted island, where they become nature's version of man and wife. When Maud's arms were around Hump and her hair was brushing his face, Hump becomes "conscious" of his "manhood," "The primitive deeps of my nature stirred. I felt myself masculine, the protector of the weak, the fighting male."[1409] Hump sees this victory in racial and biological terms:

> And that the strength in me had quieted her and given her confidence, filled me with an exultant joy. The youth of the race seemed burgeoning in me, over-civilized man that I was, and I lived for myself the old hunting days and forest nights of my remote and forgotten ancestry.[1410]

Hump fails to understand the connection between civilization and morality. If the issue were simply biological, then Hump should have raped Maud himself. We have here a strange combination of the contradictory elements that made up late 19th century thought in both England and America. No one embodied that contradiction better than Leslie Stephen, who abandoned

---

1405 Todd, *The Defeat of the West*, p. 334.
1406 Todd, *The Defeat of the West*, p. 334.
1407 London, *The Sea Wolf*, p. 307.
1408 London, *The Sea Wolf*, p. 308.
1409 London, *The Sea Wolf*, p. 357.
1410 London, *The Sea Wolf*, p. 358.

the faith after reading Darwin, but who vowed to remain "a gentleman" nonetheless. His resolution did not make it into the subsequent generation, when his daughter Virginia Woolf created the English salon Bloomsbury along with the spawn of other notable English families like Lytton Strachey, who spilled the beans when he said that the hidden grammar of the Bloomsberries was "the higher sodomy."

As with Leslie Stephen, Jack London's paradoxes could not survive the Great War, the catastrophe just over the temporal horizon. Fighting for survival on a deserted island off the coast of Japan, Hump observed Victorian proprieties by erecting two separate huts, one for Maud and one for himself, but Jack London was no stranger to sexual liberation, which was the hidden grammar of socialism. Aldous Huxley spilled the beans when he wrote in *Ends and Means*:

> I had motives for not wanting the world to have a meaning; and consequently assumed that it had none, and was able without any difficulty to find satisfying reasons for this assumption. The philosopher who finds no meaning in the world is not concerned exclusively with a problem in pure metaphysics. He is also concerned to prove that there is no valid reason why he personally should not do as he wants to do. For myself, as no doubt for most of my friends, the philosophy of meaninglessness was essentially an instrument of liberation from a certain system of morality. We objected to the morality because it interfered with our sexual freedom. The supporters of this system claimed that it embodied the meaning—the Christian meaning, they insisted—of the world. There was one admirably simple method of confuting these people and justifying ourselves in our erotic revolt: we would deny that the world had any meaning whatever."[1411]

Jack London struggled privately with vices which he refused to rationalize in public, at least in *The Sea Wolf*. In an epistolary novel entitled *The Kempton-Wace Letters*, London and Anna Strunsky tried to come up with a sexual moral code in keeping with the times by contrasting the romantic view of marriage as defended by Strunsky, with the "scientific" view based on Darwinism, eugenics, and London's own troubled marriage. In private, London complained to male friends that his wife was "devoted to purity,"[1412] a condition which sparked marital strife, especially when London tried to refute the idea by telling his wife that "morality is only evidence of low blood pressure," prompting Jack to tell Bessie that "she hates me. She'd sell me and the children out for her damned purity. It's terrible. Every time I come back after being away from home for a night she won't let me be in the same room

---

[1411] "Aldous Huxley," goodreads, https://www.goodreads.com/quotes/465563-i-had-motives-for-not-wanting-the-world-to-have

[1412] "Jack London," *Wikipedia: The Free Encyclopedia*, https://en.wikipedia.org/wiki/Jack_London

Part III: The Return of the Satanic Wilderness

with her if she can help it."[1413] London's biographer Clarice Stasz claims that terms like purity and morality were "code words for [Bess's] fear that [Jack] was consorting with prostitutes and might bring home a venereal disease."[1414] In 1903, London left his wife Bessie after initiating an affair with Charmian Kittredge, niece of a disciple of Victoria Woodhull, who raised her to be an advocate of "uninhibited sexuality."[1415]

Like Nick Adams, Jack London is not a "thinker," as he rightly admitted in his famous short story "To build a fire." *The Sea Wolf* waxes didactic when Hump discusses Spencer with Wolf Larsen. In the end, Hump becomes a man when he rescues Maud from Larsen's attempt to rape her, but he is not a paradigm other men can imitate. The reader is left with two unsatisfactory examples of what it means to be an American, the effete Easterner who writes essays for *The Atlantic Monthly* and the brutish sea captain, both of whom espouse "survival of the fittest," either by conviction or by default. Neither was a persuasive example of what it means to be an American.

1413 "Jack London," *Wikipedia*.
1414 "Jack London," *Wikipedia*.
1415 "Jack London," *Wikipedia*.

Chapter 40

Ernest Hemingway: Modernity in the Woods

Nostalgia bound the wage slave to skills which were useless in factories and office buildings but were still valorized in popular fiction. The gun, to give a prime example, could now be used to shoot intransigent Filipinos or animals, not out of necessity but out of sport or the imperatives of imperial expansion. Sensing that it could fill the vacuum created by the evaporation of Protestantism, the same American literary culture which created Natty Bumppo now proposed Nick Adams, the figure Ernest Hemingway created as the epitome of man in nature, as the representative American. At the beginning of the 20th century, stories about nature continued to be popular, as Jack London's allegory of man in "To build a fire" showed, but nature had changed since Thoreau and Emerson had deified it. Darwin and Spencer brought about the first transformation, taking the benevolence which Romantic poets like Wordsworth and Emerson had portrayed and turning it into a manifestation of the malevolence which lay at the heart of social Darwinism.

Hemingway inherited the genre of the nature story from Jack London, who inherited it from Thoreau, who claimed that nature was the portal to the divine but only if man strove to be chaste. Jack London honored that tradition in *The Sea Wolf* when Hump struggled to preserve Maud's chastity after Wolf Larsen tried to rape her. Hemingway's most significant contribution to that genre was "Big Two-Hearted River," which appeared in an anthology of Hemingway's fiction entitled *In Our Time* which Boni and Liveright published in 1925.

Ernest Hemingway was born in Oak Park, Illinois, a suburb of Chicago, in 1899, one year before the end of the logging era in Michigan.[1416] "From about 1840 to 1900, most of the Michigan forests were cut down for farms and to produce lumber for buildings, ships, and mines. Michigan was the

---

1416 "Michigan Forests During the Logging Era," Michigan Forrests Forever Teachers Guide, https://mff.forest.mtu.edu/TreeBasics/History/LogEra.htm#:~:text=From%20about%201840%20to%201900,camps%22%20and%20brought%20in%20crews.

Walking with a Bible and a Gun

nation's leading lumber producer between 1869 and 1900."[1417] When Nick Adams jumped off the logging train in the Upper Peninsula outside the town of Seney, the forest was gone and so was the town which housed the loggers: "There was no town, nothing but the rails and the burned-over country. The thirteen saloons that had lined the one street of Seney had not left a trace.... It was all that was left of the town of Seney. Even the surface had been burned off the ground."[1418] The clear cut, burnt over landscape of the Upper Peninsula became a metaphor for European culture in the aftermath of World War I and paved the way for the disillusionment Hemingway and the Lost Generation made famous. Sensing that the world was changing, Hemingway:

> created a new, personal, secular and highly contemporary ethical style, which was intensely American in origin, but translated itself easily into many cultures. He fused a number of American attitudes together and made himself their archetypal personification, so that he came to embody America at a certain epoch rather as Voltaire embodied France in the 1750s or Byron England in the 1820s.[1419]

When *The Education of Henry Adams* appeared in 1918, the year in which Adams died, Ernest Hemingway was in an Italian hospital recovering from wounds he had incurred while driving an ambulance for the Italian army. Like James Fenimore Cooper before him, Hemingway was a man of the west who traveled east, not to St. Peter's Basilica in Rome, as so many American writers had done before him, but to the Italian front and then to Paris, where in 1922 he met Ezra Pound, who helped him redefine the nature stories he had inherited from Jack London into something metaphysical by refracting nature through the lens of the "Parisian Modern Movement," which included figures like Ezra Pound, James Joyce, Max Eastman, and other members of the Lost Generation.

Like Rahm Emmanuel at a later date, the Lost Generation was determined to not let a crisis go to waste. In Hemingway's case, the American faction of the Lost Generation used the war as an excuse for an assault on the sexual morality which, as Emerson had learned, distinguished them from the decadent Europeans. It was, of course, a pretext because Nick Adams' moral corruption began long before the Great War. It happened in Michigan, in the heart of "nature," which had changed dramatically from the time when Thoreau and Emerson tried to make a religion out of it. As some indication of the magnitude of the change and its source in rationalized lust, Hemingway describes abortion as "perfectly natural" in "Hills like White Elephants," even though the word abortion is never mentioned explicitly.

1417 "Michigan Forests During the Logging Era," Michigan Forrests.
1418 Ernest Hemingway, *The Complete Short Stories Of Ernest Hemingway: The Finca Vigia Edition*, Kindle editions, pp. 128-9.
1419 Baker, *Intellectuals*, p.143.

Part III: The Return of the Satanic Wilderness

Modernity, as Yuri Slezkine pointed out, is Jewish. Modern art was created by the German Jew Daniel-Henry Kahnweiler, who arrived in Paris in May of 1907 as the scion of a German banking family who had artistic ambitions. Because it was Jewish, modern art became the ideological disguise for moral subversion because it was cryptic and oblique in its promotion of fundamental Jewish values like abortion. It also provided a rationale for pornography, another traditionally Jewish project, as art, as Man Ray's photos and Picasso's obscene sketches would make clear at a later date. Picasso was a creation of the dealer Kahnweiler, who created cubism as the first of many artistic movements in the 20th century by bringing Picasso together with Georges Braque. Hemingway was introduced to Picasso by Gertrude Stein.

Kahnweiler, who was 23 years old, opened an art gallery at 28 rue Vignon around the time Picasso painted *Les Demoiselles d'Avignon*, a celebration of the red light district in Barcelona. If so, modern art is both Jewish, because Kahnweiler turned art into the equivalent of insider trading, and sexually transgressive because it is based, in this instance, on Picasso's memories of whores, which he dehumanized by turning one of their faces into a baboon and another into an African mask. More than one critic has referred to Picasso's *Les Demoiselles d'Avignon* as the first modern painting. If so, it grew out of Picasso's pre-occupation with (or desire to desecrate through sexualization) Paul Cezanne's *les grandes baigneuses*. Cezanne's epic canvas is set on a beach; Picasso's takes place in a whorehouse. Paris, the war, burned out Michigan all came together in Hemingway's first published work, the collection of short stories known as *In Our Time*.

Hemingway chronicled his time in Paris in his posthumously published memoirs *A Moveable Feast*.[1420] During a meeting with Gertrude Stein, she told Hemingway "You are a lost generation . . . . You have no respect for anything. You drink yourselves to death."[1421] Hemingway described Pound as an irascible saint."[1422] Pound taught him "to distrust adjectives."[1423] He "would later learn to distrust certain people in certain situations" from Ezra Pound as well, a man who "almost never used the *mot juste* and yet had made his people come alive at times, as almost no one else did."[1424]

Ezra Pound was one of young Hemingway's mentors in Paris, so was Ford Maddox Ford. When Hemingway asked Ford if Pound were a gentleman, Ford responded without hesitation. "Of course not," he said, "he's an American."[1425]

"Can't an American be a gentleman?" Hemingway wondered.

1420 "Ernest Hemingway in Paris," Hemingway's Paris 1922-1930https://www.ernesthemingwaycollection.com/about-hemingway/ernest-hemingway-in-paris
1421 Hemingway, *A Moveable Feast*, Kindle edition, p. 25.
1422 Hemingway, *A Moveable Feast*, Kindle edition, p. 86.
1423 Hemingway, *A Moveable Feast*, Kindle edition, p. 102.
1424 Hemingway, *A Moveable Feast*, Kindle edition, p. 102.
1425 Hemingway, *A Moveable Feast*, Kindle edition, p. 67.

"Perhaps John Quinn," Ford replied. "Certain of your ambassadors." Racking his brains to stump Ford, Hemingway came up with the quintessential man of the east, the novelist Henry James.

"Was Henry James a gentleman?"

"Very nearly," Ford responded grudgingly.

The conversation then veers into the improbable when Ford tells Hemingway that he "cut" the famous Catholic writer Hilaire Belloc, who was supposedly in Paris with a younger woman. When Hemingway points out the man he thinks is Hilaire Belloc to a friend, his friend informs him that the person in question is really "Aleister Crowley, the diabolist" who is "supposed to be the wickedest man in the world."[1426]

Even though Pound was born outside Philadelphia, Hemingway tried to turn him into Hemingway's idea of an American by teaching him how to box. Not even in barbarous America had anyone linked boxing and poetry before Hemingway did, and the incongruity of the juxtaposition combined with the tough guy style which Hemingway had made his trademark created not only a new way of writing prose, but a new American identity which synthesized east and west:

> i was never able to teach him to throw a left hook and to teach him to shorten his right was something for the future. it was embarrassing to see him and he watched superciliously while i slipped ezra's left leads or blocked them with an open right glove."[1427]

Just as Ezra Pound brought Hemingway together with T. S. Eliot—an American from St. Louis who was such a quintessential man of the east that he, like Henry James, became English—Hemingway brought east and west together in American prose when he talked about trout fishing in Europe, something no American writer had ever done before Hemingway did it. Europe meant Catholic cathedrals to the American literary class, from James Fenimore Cooper and Washington Irving to Ralph Waldo Emerson and Nathaniel Hawthorne to most famously Henry Adams, whose book on Chartres and Mont Sainte Michel epitomized the genre. Even Mark Twain had visited St. Peter's basilica in Rome, if only to demean it. Who knew that Europe's rivers had fish in them? More than that, Hemingway had transformed trout fishing and hunting stories into some luminous metaphysical pursuit through his pared down style. "Big two-hearted river" was a story "about coming back from the war," as he stated in *A Moveable Feast*, "but there was no mention of the war in it."[1428] Seney, Michigan was a different matter. Good parts had been left after the logging, but nature itself was infected in a way that threatened trout fishing, which was the sacrament

---

1426 Hemingway, *A Moveable Feast*, Kindle edition, p. 70.
1427 Hemingway, *A Moveable Feast*, Kindle edition, p. 86.
1428 Hemingway, *A Moveable Feast*, Kindle edition, p. 60.

Part III: The Return of the Satanic Wilderness

which united Hemingway with what was left of the nature of Emerson and Thoreau:

> Nick did not like to fish with other men on the river. Unless they were of your party, they spoiled it. Ahead the river narrowed and went into a swamp. He did not feel like going on into the swamp. In the swamp fishing was a tragic adventure. Nick did not want it. He did not want to go down the stream any further today. He looked back. The river just showed through the trees. There were plenty of days coming when he could fish the swamp.[1429]

Nature had changed, and so the language Hemingway used to describe it changed as well. Instead of being a portal to the divine, Nature had become a refuge from civilization, a position which Huck Finn mooted at the end of the novel which bore his name. But more than that, nature had become the place where Nick Adams escaped from the moral law. Nature was a hideout for sexual experimentation and in the aftermath of that, it had become good place for forgetting how you had ruined your life. After he put "the burned over country" near Seney behind him, Nick Adams "felt happy" because "He felt he had left everything behind, the need for thinking, the need to write, other needs. It was all back of him."[1430]

Bullfighting was appealing for the same reason. It obliterated thought, by which he meant conscience. The matador was admirable because: "He knew all about bulls. He did not have to think about them. He just did the right thing. His eyes noted things, and his body performed the necessary measures without thought. If he thought about it, he would be gone."[1431]

When Nick Adams tells George in "The Killers" that "I can't stand to think about him waiting in the room and knowing he's going to get it. It's too damned awful." George responds by telling Nick, "you better not think about it."[1432] When Nick Adams leaves the woods, his conscience gets reactivated. "In the morning there was a big wind blowing and the waves were running high up on the beach and he was awake a long time before he remembered that his heart was broken."[1433] Nick Adams symbolizes the Americans who have been morally corrupted by war, which involved among other things, "smutty postcards, photographic" depictions of rape "very attractively" in a way that "had nothing in common with actual rape in which the woman's skirts are pulled over her head to smother her, one comrade sometimes sitting upon the head."[1434]

1429 Hemingway, *Short Stories, Big Two-Hearted River: Part II*, Kindle, pp. 139-43.
1430 Hemingway, *Short Stories, Big Two-Hearted River: Part I*, Kindle, p. 130, loc. 2536.
1431 Hemingwary, *Short Stories*, Kindle edition, "The Undefeated," p. 164, loc. 3201.
1432 Hemingway, *Short Stories*, Kindle edition, "Ten Indians," p. 218.
1433 Hemingway, *Short Stories*, Kindle edition, "The Killers," p. 184, loc. 3582.
1434 Hemingway, *Short Stories*, Kindle edition, "A Way You'll Never Be, p. 262.

WALKING WITH A BIBLE AND A GUN

By the time Hemingway came of age and was writing the Nick Adams stories, Spencer's evolutionary optimism had died in the trenches of World War I. The result was "Big Two-hearted River," which was about World War I, but only obliquely. "Soldier's Home" is about sex but obliquely, and its sexual content only become apparent in light of the Nick Adams stories about nature. Krebs, the protagonist in "Soldier's Home," epitomized the Lost Generation when it returned to America, full of "A distaste for everything that had happened to him in the war set in because of the lies he had told,"[1435] but never able to express the content of those lies explicitly. Krebs, which is the German word for cancer, "did not want any consequences. He did not want any consequences ever again."[1436]

Hemingway learned to be oblique from Ezra Pound, who taught a generation that included figures as disparate as Hemingway and T. S. Eliot how to sound modern, which in America meant how to sound tough. Hemingway had to change the language he used to describe nature because nature had changed. After World War I, Nature became the realm where strenuous activity obliterated consciousness, which in this instance means— obliquely, of course—consciousness of guilt:

> The rush and the sudden swoop as he dropped down a steep undulation in the mountain side plucked Nick's mind out and left him only the wonderful flying, dropping sensation in his body.

"There's nothing really can touch skiing, is there?" Nick said.

"The way it feels when you first drop off on a long run." "Huh," said George. "It's too swell to talk about."[1437]

The conversation then shifts to the local female population: "No ring. Hell, no girls get married around here till they're knocked up."

An unnamed unpleasantness associated with "sivilization," which as Huck Finn pointed out, was inevitably associated with women:

> "I got to get educated," George said. "Gee, Mike, don't you wish we could just bum together? Take our skis and go on the train to where there was good running and then go on and put up at pubs and go right across the Oberland and up the Valais and all through the Engadine and just take repair kit and extra sweaters and pyjamas in our rucksacks and not give a damn about school or anything."

Skiing is somehow different in the United States because of its association with women, e.g. Hemingway's mother and sister, who upbraided him for his loose morals. None of this is mentioned in this story, which uses skiing and

---

1435 Hemingway, *Short Stories*, Kindle edition, "Soldier's Home," p. 95.
1436 Hemingway, *Short Stories*, Kindle edition, "Soldier's Home," p. 96.
1437 Hemingway, *Short Stories*, Kindle edition, "Soldier's Home," p. 96.

Part III: The Return of the Satanic Wilderness

mountains and the nature they embody as an oblique reference to something unspoken:

> George sat silent. He looked at the empty bottle and the empty glasses. "It's hell, isn't it?" he said. "No. Not exactly," Nick said. "Why not?" "I don't know," Nick said. "Will you ever go skiing together in the States?" George said. "I don't know," said Nick. "The mountains aren't much," George said.

Skiing is no good in the United States because the mountains are "too rocky. There's too much timber and they're too far away."[1438]

Hemingway claims that he learned about sex from his father, but his stories tell a different tale. The alembic of existence on the frontier had modified Calvinism by refining away what was extraneous in the Reformed Faith and leaving behind its essence, the twin vices of lust and avarice, which had been the *spiritus movens* behind the Reformation and were afterward the quintessence of the Satanism which was the hidden grammar of the American Empire. The rape of Church property in England in the 16th century set the stage for the rape of nature which took place from 1840 to 1900 when Michigan was logged bare. The reverence for nature which characterized the American Renaissance had been replaced by ruthless economic exploitation, fueled by the theories of Charles Darwin and Herbert Spencer, which prompts Nick Adams to conclude that "In the swamp fishing was a tragic adventure."[1439]

At the ending of *A Farewell to Arms*, Hemingway describes ants on a burning log as a metaphor for nature which was inspired by World War I and the consequences of Darwinism. Portraying men as insects is also reminiscent of Jonathan Edwards' spider in "Sinners in the Hands of an Angry God":

> Once in camp I put a log on a fire, and it was full of ants. As it commenced to burn, the ants swarmed out and went first toward the center where the fire was; then turned back and ran toward the end. When there were enough on the end they fell off into the fire. Some got out, their bodies burnt and flattened, and went off not knowing where they were going. But most of them went toward the fire and then back toward the end and swarmed on the cool end and finally fell off into the fire. I remember thinking at the time that it was the end of the world and a splendid chance to be a messiah and lift the log off the fire and throw it out where the ants could get off onto the ground. But I did not do anything but throw a tin cup of water on the log, so that I would have the cup empty to put whiskey in before I added water to it. I think the cup of water on the burning log only steamed the ants.[1440]

1438 Hemingway, *Short Stories*, Kindle edition, "Cross-Country Snow," p. 116, loc. 2270
1439 Hemingway, *Short Stories*, Kindle edition, p. 143.
1440 "Ernest Hemingway," goodreads, https://www.goodreads.com/quotes/93834-once-in-camp-i-put-a-log-on-a-fire

WALKING WITH A BIBLE AND A GUN

Once man became a god, he became at the same time a cruel "messiah." The same was true of nature. Once it became a god, it became cruel. Emerson, more than anyone else in America in the 19th century, had created the worship of nature which had led, via Darwin and Spencer, to the Capitalist rape of nature in America and the Capitalist rape of culture in Europe. Hemingway hated Emerson:

> (along with "Hawthorne, Whittier, and Company") for being overly fastidious and avoiding "the words that people always have used in speech, the words that survive in language." On the evidence available to him, Hemingway could see only that these representatives of the American literary establishment had "nice, dry, clean minds" but no bodies. "This," he insists, "is all very dull."[1441]

Because his mother loved Emerson, Hemingway hated his mother:

> Dos Passos said Hemingway was the only man he had ever come across who really hated his mother. Another old acquaintance, General Lanham, testified: "From my earliest days with Ernest Hemingway he always referred to his mother as 'that bitch.' He must have told me a thousand times how much he hated her and in how many ways."

Hemingway's hatred of his mother, according to Johnson, was:

> so intense that to a considerable extent it poisoned his life, not least because he always felt a residual guilt about it, which nagged at him and kept the hatred evergreen. He was still hating her in 1949 when she was nearly eighty, writing to his publisher from his house in Cuba: "I will not see her and she knows she can never come here."[1442]

Hemingway's hatred for his mother was so intense that it soon "attained the status of a philosophical system,"[1443] which was the driving force behind the development of a literary style whose "outstanding characteristic was the overwhelming urge not to write like his mother, using the stale rhetoric of an over-elaborate literary inheritance."[1444] Hemingway gave artistic form to his hatred of his mother in "Soldier's Home":

"God has some work for every one to do," his mother said. "There can be no idle hands in His Kingdom."

"I'm not in His Kingdom," Krebs said. "

We are all of us in His Kingdom."

Krebs felt embarrassed and resentful as always.

"I pray for you all day long, Harold."

[1441] Selected and Edited by Joel Porte, *Emerson in His Journals* (Belknap Press of Harvard university Press, Cambridge, Massachusetts, London England, 1982), p. viii.

[1442] Johnson, *Intellectuals*, p.146.

[1443] Johnson, *Intellectuals*, p.146.

[1444] Johnson, *Intellectuals*, p.147.

Part III: The Return of the Satanic Wilderness

Krebs looked at the bacon fat hardening on his plate.
"Yes."
"Don't you love your mother, dear boy?"
"No," Krebs said.
His mother looked at him across the table. Her eyes were shiny. She started crying.
"I don't love anybody," Krebs said.
"I'm your mother," she said. "I held you next to my heart when you were a tiny baby."
Krebs felt sick and vaguely nauseated.
"I know, Mummy," he said. "I'll try and be a good boy for you."
"Would you kneel and pray with me, Harold?" his mother asked. They knelt down beside the dining-room table and Krebs's mother prayed.
"Now, you pray, Harold," she said.
"I can't," Krebs said.
"Try, Harold."
"I can't."[1445]

Emerson and Hemingway's mother were linked in Ernest's mind because they represented the moral law which he had chosen to defy. Paul Johnson describes Hemingway's parents as:

> outstanding products of the civilization which Emerson and his lectures, and the economic dynamism they upheld, had helped to bring into being. The parents were, or they certainly seemed to be, healthy, industrious, efficient, well-educated, many talented and well-adjusted to their society, grateful for their European cultural inheritance but proudly conscious of the way America had triumphantly improved upon it. They feared God and lived a full life, indoors and outdoors. Dr Hemingway was an excellent physician who also hunted, shot, fished, sailed, camped and pioneered; he possessed, and taught his son, all the wilderness skills of the woodsman.[1446]

Nick Adams claims that he learned not only "the wilderness skills of the woodsman" from his father but also the rudiments of sex:

> when Nick was a boy . . . he was very grateful to him for two things: fishing and shooting. His father was as sound on those two things as he was unsound on sex, for instance, and Nick was glad that it had been that way; for some one has to give you your first gun or the opportunity to get it and use it, and you have to live where there is game or fish if you are to learn about them, and now, at thirty-eight, he loved to fish and to shoot exactly as much as when he first had gone with his father. It was a

---

1445 Hemingway, *Short Stories*, Kindle edition, "Soldier's Home," pp. 99-100.
1446 Johnson, *Intellectuals*, p.143.

passion that had never slackened and he was very grateful to his father for bringing him to know it.[1447]

Nick's memories are conditioned by Hemingway's relationship with his father and his mother and the moral law which they represented in his mind. Hemingway learned about sex on his own from the "equipment" which had been provided to him by God, after throwing away the instruction manual, and concluding that his father "was not sound about that."[1448] Experience, Ben Franklin once said, keeps an expensive school, but fools will learn in no other. When is came to sex, "Nick's own education in those earlier matters had been acquired in the hemlock woods behind the Indian camp. . . . near the black muck of the swamp,"[1449] where he met Trudy, the retarded Indian girl with whom he had sex as a 15 year old.

> "You think we make a baby?" Trudy folded her brown legs together happily and rubbed against him. Something inside Nick had gone a long way away. "I don't think so," he said. "Make plenty baby what the hell."[1450]

Nick's sexual initiation in the woods alienated him from his father. "The towns he lived in were not towns his father knew. After he was fifteen he had shared nothing with him."[1451] The alienation increased until Nick Adams was prepared to kill his father. Sitting in the woodshed, with "his shotgun loaded and cocked, looking across at his father sitting on the screen porch reading the paper, and thought, "I can blow him to hell. I can kill him.""[1452] Premature illicit sexual initiation left Nick Adams alienated from his father and confused, as his recollection of sex with Trudy indicates. When asked what it was like to have sex with Indians, all Nick can reply is that "It's hard to say," before lapsing into prose that owes more to Molly Bloom's soliloquy at the end of James Joyce's Ulysses than the slang of the American criminal demi-monde:

> Could you say she did first what no one has ever done better and mention plump brown legs, flat belly, hard little breasts, well holding arms, quick searching tongue, the flat eyes, the good taste of mouth, then uncomfortably, tightly, sweetly, moistly, lovely, tightly, achingly, fully, finally, unendingly, never-endingly, never-to-endingly, suddenly ended, the great bird flown like an owl in the twilight, only it was daylight in the woods and hemlock needles stuck against your belly. So that when you go in a place where Indians have lived you smell them gone and all the

---

1447 Hemingway, *Short Stories*, Kindle edition, "Fathers and Sons," p. 323.
1448 Hemingway, *Short Stories*, Kindle edition, "Fathers and Sons," p. 323.
1449 Hemingway, *Short Stories*, Kindle edition, "Fathers and Sons," p. 325, loc. 6231.
1450 Hemingway, *Short Stories*, Kindle edition, "Fathers and Sons," p. 327.
1451 Hemingway, *Short Stories*, Kindle edition, "Fathers and Sons," p. 328.
1452 Hemingway, *Short Stories*, Kindle edition, "Fathers and Sons," p. 328.

Part III: The Return of the Satanic Wilderness

empty pain killer bottles and the flies that buzz do not kill the sweetgrass smell, the smoke smell and that other like a fresh cased marten skin. Nor any jokes about them nor old squaws take that away. Nor the sick sweet smell they get to have. Nor what they did finally. It wasn't how they ended. They all ended the same. Long time ago good. Now no good.[1453]

In "The Last Good Country," Nature is the place where Nick Adams and his sister can share fantasies of incest:

> His sister was tanned brown, and she had dark brown eyes and dark brown hair with yellow streaks in it from the sun. She and Nick loved each other, and they did not love the others. They always thought of everyone else in the family as the others. "They know about everything, Nickie," his sister said hopelessly. "They said they were going to make an example of you and send you to the reform school."[1454]

Nick's sister asks enticingly "Can I come with you through the swamp?"[1455] And in case the reader missed the sexual innuendo in that remark, she brings up Trudy. "You don't mind you're with me instead of going to Trudy?" she wonders, prompting anger from Nick, "What do you talk about her for all the time?"[1456] and a decision not to talk about her anymore. "The hell with Trudy." "I want to be useful and a good partner." So that they can now concentrate on penetrating into the swamp, where they can find "the secret place.... Then below the secret place there's real swamp. Bad swamp that you can't get through. Now we better start the bad part."[1457]

The virgin forest, like Nick Adams' virginity, has been despoiled, mostly replaced by impenetrable second growth trees and bushes. Once they reach the virgin forest, "there was no underbrush," and Nick Adams now feels "like the way I ought to feel in church."[1458] The remnant of Michigan's virgin forest reminds Nick's sister of cathedrals, which prompts her to ask him "do you believe in God? You don't have to answer if you don't want to." In response all Nick can say is, "I don't know."[1459]

After mentioning her desire to visit the cathedrals of Europe, Nick's sister brings up their mother:

"Our mother said everything you write is morbid."

"It's too morbid for the St. Nicholas," Nick said. "They didn't say it. But they didn't like it."

"But the St. Nicholas is our favorite magazine."

1453 Hemingway, *Short Stories*, Kindle edition, "Fathers and Sons," p. 329.
1454 Hemingway, *Short Stories*, Kindle edition, "The Last Good Country," p. 455, loc. 8672.
1455 Hemingway, *Short Stories*, Kindle edition, "The Last Good Country," p. 457, loc. 8727.
1456 Hemingway, *Short Stories*, Kindle edition, "Fathers and Sons," p. 464.
1457 Hemingway, *Short Stories*, Kindle edition, "Fathers and Sons," p. 466.
1458 Hemingway, Short Stories, Kindle edition, "The Last Good Country," p. 467, loc. 8916.
1459 Hemingway, *Short Stories*, Kindle edition, "Fathers and Sons," p. 468.

"I know," said Nick. "But I'm too morbid for it already. And I'm not even grown-up."

"When is a man grown-up? When he's married?"

"No. Until you're grown-up they send you to reform school. After you're grown-up they send you to the penitentiary."

"I'm glad you're not grown-up then."

"They're not going to send me anywhere," Nick said. "And let's not talk morbid even if I write morbid."

"I didn't say it was morbid."

"I know. Everybody else does, though."

"Let's be cheerful, Nickie," his sister said. "These woods make us too solemn."[1460]

Hemingway's real sister Sunny never mentioned incest, but she did say that she and Ernest "had morning family prayers accompanied by a Bible reading and a hymn or two,"[1461] prompting Paul Johnson to add: "The moral code of broad stream Protestantism was minutely enforced by both parents and any infringements severely punished."[1462] Hemingway's sexual experiences in "nature" put him on a collision course with the Protestant faith of his parents, which he rejected:

> in toto and with it any desire to be the sort of son they wanted. In his teens he seems to have decided, quite firmly, that he was going to pursue his genius and his inclination in all things, and to create for himself a vision both of the man of honour and of the good life which was his reward.[1463]

Johnson fails to mention that his rejection of his parents' faith corresponded in time to his sexual initiation in the burnt-out, clear cut, chaotic second growth forests of Michigan. Hemingway's virginity and the virgin forests disappeared around the same time cutting him off from the religion of nature which Emerson and Thoreau espoused as the alternative to Calvinism. The disgust Hemingway felt at his own weakness got projected onto Emerson and his mother, who proposed New England's Socrates as a model, both in manners and in writing for her errant son. Hemingway hated his mother for representing the moral law which he was unable to follow in his own life. Hemingway tried to cauterize his conscience with alcohol, but alcohol was simply part of the persona he created for himself as the paradigmatic American:

1460 Hemingway, *Short Stories*, Kindle edition, "Fathers and Sons," p. 468.
1461 Johnson, *Intellectuals*, p.144.
1462 Johnson, *Intellectuals*, p.144.
1463 Johnson, *Intellectuals*, p.144.

Part III: The Return of the Satanic Wilderness

This was a Romantic, literary and to some extent an ethical concept, but it had no religious content at all. Indeed, Hemingway seems to have been devoid of the religious spirit. He privately abandoned his faith at the age of seventeen when he met Bill and Katy Smith (the latter to become the wife of John Dos Passos), whose father, an atheist don, had written an ingenious book 'proving' Jesus Christ had never existed. Hemingway ceased to practise religion at the earliest possible moment, when he went to work at his first job on the Kansas City Star and moved into unsupervised lodgings. As late as 1918, when he was nearly 20, he assured his mother: "Don't worry or cry or fret about my being a good Christian. I am just as much as ever, and pray every night and believe just as hard." But this was a lie, told for the sake of peace. He not only did not believe in God but regarded organized religion as a menace to human happiness. His first wife, Hadley, said she only saw him on his knees twice, at their wedding and at the christening of their son. To please his second wife, Pauline, he became a Roman Catholic, but he had no more conception of what his new faith meant than did Rex Mottram in *Brideshead Revisited*. He was furious when Pauline tried to observe its rules (e.g. over birth control) in ways which inconvenienced him. He published blasphemous parodies of the Our Father in his story "A Clean, Well-Lighted Place" and of the Crucifixion in *Death in the Afternoon*; there is a blasphemous spittoon-blessing in his play *The Fifth Column*. In so far as he did understand Roman Catholicism, he detested it. He raised not the slightest protest when, at the beginning of the Civil War in Spain, a place he knew and said he loved, hundreds of churches were burnt, altars and sacred vessels desecrated, and many thousands of priests, monks and nuns slaughtered. He abandoned even the formal pretence of being a Catholic after he left his second wife. All his adult life he lived, in effect, as a pagan, worshipping ideas of his own devising.[1464]

No one personified American identity during the middle decades of the 20th century better than Ernest Hemingway, whose obsession with guns and killing would lead to war crimes he committed during the battle of Huertgenwald toward the end of World War II. His hyper-masculinity was compensation for the moral weakness he showed in capitulating to temptation, but also as a response to the reproaches of his mother, who said what his conscience, fueled by booze, strove to repress:

> Unless you, my son, Ernest, come to yourself, cease your lazy loafing and pleasure seeking ... stop trading on your handsome face ... and neglecting your duties to God and your Saviour, Jesus Christ... there is nothing before you but bankruptcy: You have overdrawn.[1465]

1464 Johnson, *Intellectuals*, pp.144-5.
1465 Johnson, *Intellectuals*, p.146.

Walking with a Bible and a Gun

Much of *A Moveable Feast* is devoted to Hemingway's description of F. Scott Fitzgerald's alcoholism in a way that absolves him of the same problem and veers into the realm of the improbable finally breaking through into character assassination when he describes measuring Fitzgerald's penis and reassuring him about its size in light of classical sculpture in the Louvre. Shortly after disparaging Fitzgerald, Hemingway adverts to his own sins, by referring obliquely to the adultery which destroyed his marriage:

> there are three of them. first it is stimulating and fun and it goes on that way for a while. all things truly wicked start from an innocence. so you live day by day and enjoy what you have and do not worry. you lie and hate it and it destroys you and every day is more dangerous, but you live day to day as in a war.[1466]

Hemingway then mentions that "the other thing started again" once he was "back in Paris."[1467] The "other thing" was an oblique reference to adultery. In the original manuscrip, Hemingway apologized to his first wife Hadley Richardson for his infidelity, but the apology was deleted by Mary Hemingway, his fourth wife, because, according to literary scholar Gerry Brenner, "it impugned her role as wife."[1468]

There is more to it than just this. Existence can call essence into being, but as Thoreau pointed out, Nature is largely what we bring to it. As Samuel Taylor Coleridge pointed out, "We receive but what we give."

Though I should gaze for ever
On that green light that lingers in the west:
I may not hope from outward forms to win
The passion and the life, whose fountains are within.

F. Scott Fitzgerald, Hemingway's friend and fellow alcoholic, said of Gatsby that he "believed in the green light," which symbolized "the orgastic future that year by year recedes before us. It eluded us then, but that's no matter—tomorrow we will run faster, stretch out our arms farther…. And one fine morning…So we beat on, boats against the current, borne back ceaselessly into the past."

If, as Thoreau knew, Nature reveals her secrets only to the chaste, Hemingway's portrayal of her as the burnt over logging camps of Michigan stemmed from his lust and the disorder that vice created in his soul every bit as much as it did from Capitalism and its concomitant ecological disasters or his experience of modern warfare in World War I.

1466 Hemingway, *A Moveable Feast*, Kindle edition, p. 168.
1467 Hemingway, *A Moveable Feast*, Kindle edition, p. 169.
1468 "*A Moveable Feast*," *Wikipedia: The Free Encyclopedia*, https://en.wikipedia.org/wiki/A_Moveable_Feast

Part III: The Return of the Satanic Wilderness

In "Three day blow," nature becomes a refuge from failed relationships, because "outside," which is to say in the realm of nature, which is to say liberated from the moral constraints that culture must inevitably impose,

> the Marge business was no longer so tragic. It was not even very important. The wind blew everything like that away. None of it was important now. The wind blew it out of his head.[1469]

"Sivilization" was now "optional." "It was a good thing to have in reserve" because "he could always go into town Saturday night" if he wanted to get laid.

1469 Hemingway, *Nick Adams Stories*, Kindle edition, p. 84.

Chapter 41

William Faulkner and The Bear

William Faulkner dealt with the same theme in his novella "The Bear," which appeared first in the *Saturday Evening Post* and then as part of the novel *Go Down, Moses*. If the forests of the frontier defined American identity, as Frederick Jackson Turner maintained, their disappearance precipitated an identity crisis. In both Mississippi and Michigan, the virgin forest had fallen to the logger's axe, depriving the man of the west of his habitat and, therefore, his identity. The American derived his identity from existence, which in this instance had to be nature as God created it. The American project involved taming nature. The end of the logging era in Michigan and Mississippi corresponded to the closing of the frontier. To preserve his identity, the man of the west needed something that remained untamed, which is precisely what Faulkner's bear symbolized. Americans have an essentially negative identity, symbolized best by Protestantism, which defines itself as not Catholic. Bereft of concepts like grace perfects nature, the American defines himself by his ability to subdue nature, symbolized by the rifle, but in the act of subduing nature, the American loses his identity because he no longer has a purpose in life once the forest disappears under the logger's axe.

The first solution to this dilemma was westward migration into ever new virgin territory in a self-defeating quest that only became apparent when the frontier disappeared, and the American was left with nothing to do and, therefore, no identity. At this point, "the big old bear with one trap-ruined foot" took on totemic significance as the guarantor of American identity and became:

> a definite designation like a living man:—the long legend of corn-cribs broken down and rifled, of shoats and grown pigs and even calves carried bodily into the woods and devoured and traps and deadfalls overthrown and dogs mangled and slain and shotgun and even rifle shots delivered at point-blank range yet with no more effect than so many peas blown through a tube by a child—a corridor of wreckage and destruction beginning back before the boy was born, through which sped, not fast but rather with the ruthless and irresistible deliberation of a locomotive, the shaggy tremendous shape. . . . not malevolent but just big, too big for

the dogs which tried to bay it, for the horses which tried to ride it down, for the men and the bullets they fired into it; too big for the very country which was its constricting scope. . . . that doomed wilderness whose edges were being constantly and punily gnawed at by men with plows and axes who feared it because it was wilderness, men myriad and nameless even to one another in the land where the old bear had earned a name, and through which ran not even a mortal beast but an anachronism indomitable and invincible out of an old dead time, a phantom, epitome and apotheosis of the old wild life which the little puny humans swarmed and hacked at in a fury of abhorrence and fear like pygmies about the ankles of a drowsing elephant;—the old bear, solitary, indomitable, and alone; widowered childless and absolved of mortality—old Priam reft of his old wife and outlived all his sons. To him, they were going not to hunt bear and deer but to keep yearly rendezvous with the bear which they did not even intend to kill. He believed that only after he had served his apprenticeship in the woods which would prove him worthy to be a hunter, would he even be permitted to distinguish the crooked print, and that even then for two November weeks he would merely make another minor one, along with his cousin and Major de Spain and General Compson and Walter Ewell and Boon and the dogs which feared to bay it and the shotguns and rifles which failed even to bleed it, in the yearly pageant-rite of the old bear's furious immortality."[1470]

Every year the descendants of the man who founded Yoknapatawfa county set out on a quest for the bear which they do not want to kill in the paradoxical certainty that killing it will deprive them of their identity. Their quest is riddled with paradox. In order to encounter the bear, Ike McCaslin, one of those descendants, has to relinquish his gun:

> He had left the gun; by his own will and relinquishment he had accepted not a gambit, not a choice, but a condition in which not only the bear's heretofore inviolable anonymity but all the ancient rules and balances of hunter and hunted had been abrogated.[1471]

Like Thoreau, Ike must abandon his gun if he wants to discover nature's secrets. Armed with only a "compass and a stick for the snakes," McCaslin becomes "a child, alien and lost in the green and soaring gloom of the markless wilderness."[1472] Still alienated from what he needs to know, McCaslin has to relinquish the watch and the compass as well, because with them "he was still tainted."[1473] Only after he "removed the linked chain of the one and the looped thong of the other from his overalls and hung them on a bush and leaned the

---

1470 William Faulkner, *Go Down, Moses*, Kindle edition, pp. 176-8.
1471 Faulkner, p. 189.
1472 Faulkner, p. 189.
1473 Faulkner, p. 189.

Part III: The Return of the Satanic Wilderness

stick beside them and entered it,"[1474] i.e. the realm of pure existence, does the bear appear:

> It rushed, soundless, and solidified—the tree, the bush, the compass and the watch glinting where a ray of sunlight touched them. Then he saw the bear. It did not emerge, appear: it was just there, immobile, fixed in the green and windless noon's hot dappling, not as big as he had dreamed it but as big as he had expected, bigger, dimensionless against the dappled obscurity, looking at him. Then it moved. It crossed the glade without haste, walking for an instant into the sun's full glare and out of it, and stopped again and looked back at him across one shoulder. Then it was gone. It didn't walk into the woods. It faded, sank back into the wilderness without motion as he had watched a fish, a huge old bass, sink back into the dark depths of its pool and vanish without even any movement of its fins.[1475]

Old Ben exhibits "a cold and almost impersonal malignance like some natural force,"[1476] rushing through the tangle of trunks and branches "as a locomotive would."[1477] The only thing that can stop the bear is a dog which has not been tamed, a dog like the devil. "Dog the devil," Major de Spain said. "I'd rather have Old Ben himself in my pack than that brute. Shoot him." "No," Sam said. "You'll never tame him. How do you ever expect to make an animal like that afraid of you?" "I dont want him tame. . . . "We dont want him tame. We want him like he is. We just want him to find out at last that the only way he can get out of that crib and stay out of it is to do what Sam or somebody tells him to do. He's the dog that's going to stop Old Ben and hold him. We've already named him. His name is Lion."[1478]

The New World didn't start out this way, nor did the old, which began when Adam was "dispossessed of Eden."

> 'Dispossessed. Not impotent: He didn't condone; not blind, because He watched it. And let me say it. Dispossessed of Eden. Dispossessed of Canaan, and those who dispossessed him dispossessed him dispossessed, and the five hundred years of absentee landlords in the Roman bagnios, and the thousand years of wild men from the northern woods who dispossessed them and devoured their ravished substance ravished in turn again and then snarled in what you call the old world's worthless twilight over the old world's gnawed bones, blasphemous in His name. . . .[1479]

1474 Faulkner, p. 189.
1475 Faulkner, p. 191.
1476 Faulkner, p. 200.
1477 Faulkner, p. 193.
1478 Faulkner, p. 198.
1479 Faulkner, p. 236.

Walking with a Bible and a Gun

The senseless history of Hobbes' war of all against all which began with Adam's fall was granted reprieve when Columbus discovered America. Columbus "used a simple egg to discover to them a new world where a nation of people could be founded in humility and pity and sufferance and pride of one to another."[1480]

America was paradise regained. Poring over his grandfather's barely readable ledger, McCaslin realized that the land has been cursed by the greed and lust of those who settled it. Greed and lust have destroyed paradise a second time. The land had been "vouchsafed" to his grandfather "out of pity and sufferance, on condition of pity and humility," but his grandfather had violated the terms upon which paradise was based and as a result brought down curse on the land, re-enacting in the new world the sin that had polluted the old: 'Dont you see?' he cried. 'Dont you see? This whole land, the whole South, is cursed, and all of us who derive from it, whom it ever suckled, white and black both, lie under the curse?'[1481]

The economic exploitation implicit in slavery ended the hope that a "whole hopeful continent dedicated as a refuge and sanctuary of liberty and freedom" could exist as an alternative to "the old world's worthless evening."[1482] Financial exploitation was compounded by sexual exploitation of the slaves, Tennie opines, remembering "the routed compounder of his uncle's uxory."[1483]

The final curtain of this tragedy comes down when Major de Spain decides to sell the land which he appropriated from Ikkemotube, the original owner, to the loggers, thereby destroying the basis for their existence and their identity. Invoking Eve's temptation and Adam's sin in the Garden of Eden, Faulkner compares the logging locomotive to a snake:

> Then the little locomotive shrieked and began to move: a rapid churning of exhaust, a lethargic deliberate clashing of slack couplings traveling backward along the train, the exhaust changing to the deep slow clapping bites of power as the caboose too began to move and from the cupola he watched the train's head complete the first and only curve in the entire line's length and vanish into the wilderness, dragging its length of train behind it so that it resembled a small dingy harmless snake vanishing into weeds. . . .[1484]

Major de Spain's greed and his decision to exchange the wilderness which gave them both sustenance and identity into money, lends a sinister significance to the logging train:

1480 Faulkner, p. 236.
1481 Faulkner, p. 255.
1482 Faulkner, p. 260.
1483 Faulkner, p. 278.
1484 Faulkner, p. 292.

Part III: The Return of the Satanic Wilderness

> this time it was as though the train had brought with it into the doomed wilderness even before the actual axe the shadow and portent of the new mill not even finished yet and the rails and ties which were not even laid; and he knew now what he had known as soon as he saw Hoke's this morning but had not yet thought into words: why Major de Spain had not come back....[1485]

The log train corresponds to McCaslin's epiphany in the forest when he greets another snake as "chief ... grandfather." The woods have come full circle from the time Young Goodman Brown went there to worship the devil after learning that evil was the nature of mankind. If America was, as Samuel Huntington pointed out, a Protestant country, then its hidden grammar was Satanic, based on the same lust and greed which destroyed the wilderness which had given America its identity. America, in spite of its early promise as both the New Israel and Arcadia, became, as Shakespeare had predicted, the place where:

Force should be right; or rather, right and wrong
(Between whose endless jar justice resides)
Should lose their names, and so should justice too!
Then every thing include itself in power,
Power into will, will into appetite,
And appetite, a universal wolf
(So doubly seconded with will and power)
Must make perforce an universal prey,
And last eat up himself."

The gun which changed Daniel Boone from a Quaker into the quintessential American has lost its meaning because it has led to the destruction of the forest which gave Americans their identity. The gun has been "dismembered," and "Boon," Faulkner's epitome of the deracinated American who is his greedy descendant, doesn't know how to put it together again:

> Then he saw Boon, sitting, his back against the trunk, his head bent, hammering furiously at something on his lap. What he hammered with was the barrel of his dismembered gun, what he hammered at was the breech of it. The rest of the gun lay scattered about him in a half-dozen pieces while he bent over the piece on his lap his scarlet and streaming walnut face, hammering the disjointed barrel against the gun-breech with the frantic abandon of a madman. He didn't even look up to see who it was. Still hammering, he merely shouted back at the boy in a hoarse strangled voice: "Get out of here! Dont touch them! Dont touch a one of them! They're mine!"[1486]

1485 Faulkner, p. 294.
1486 Faulkner, p. 303.

CHAPTER 42

WALTER LIPPMANN AND THE REPUDIATION OF JEFFERSONIAN DEMOCRACY

In 1922, the America which Hemingway had left behind took notice of Walter Lippmann after the publication of his book *Public Opinion*. Lippmann was a man of the east born in 1899 on New York's upper east side to wealthy German Jewish parents who regularly spent summers in Europe. Lippmann received a classical education at the Sachs School for Boys, run by the classical philologist Julius Sachs, scion of the wealthy Goldman Sachs family. Classes at the institute included 11 hours of ancient Greek and five hours of Latin per week.[1487]

Plato's allegory of the cave and his understanding of the noble lie apparently made a lasting impression on Lippmann. He begins his discussion of public opinion by discussing the distinction between categories of reality, which soon recede into insignificance because of the manipulation of public opinion, and categories of the mind, which he refers to as "fictions," which are "an important part of the machinery of human communication."[1488] Because "men respond as powerfully to fictions as they do to realities,"[1489] Lippmann concludes that the American is a "fictitious personality."[1490] Fictions are not lies. They are rather "a representation of the environment which is in lesser or greater degree made by man himself."[1491] Public opinion is made up of "the pictures of themselves, of others, of their needs, purposes, and relationship."[1492] Lippmann concludes that "public opinions must be organized for the press if they are to be sound, not by the press as is the case today"[1493] without answering the question organized by whom?

1487 "Walter Lippmann," *Wikipedia: The Free Encyclopedia*, https://en.wikipedia.org/wiki/Walter_Lippmann
1488 Lippmann, *Public Opinion*, Kindle edition, p. 3.
1489 Lippmann, *Public Opinion*, Kindle edition, p. 12.
1490 Lippmann, *Public Opinion*, Kindle edition, p. 8.
1491 Lippmann, *Public Opinion*, Kindle edition, p. 13.
1492 Lippmann, *Public Opinion*, Kindle edition, p. 7.
1493 Lippmann, *Public Opinion*, Kindle edition, p. 61.

Walking with a Bible and a Gun

The answer to that question emerges from Lippmann's biography. During World War I, Lippmann worked in the intelligence section of the Allied Expeditionary Force headquarters in France where he became an advisor to Colonel Edward M. House and helped draft Wilson's Fourteen Point Speech. He also became aware of George Creel's Committee on Public Information (CPI), America's first propaganda ministry. Lippmann found Creel's fight "for the minds of men, for the conquest of their convictions" so that "the gospel of Americanism might be carried to every corner of the globe"[1494] crude and unconvincing, but the idea that American identity could be forged by more sophisticated means remained with Lippmann for the rest of his life. Lippmann concluded that the Wilson administration had "largely succeeded . . . in creating something that might almost be called one public opinion all over America,"[1495] which is another way of saying Wilson created a new American identity based on America's entry into world politics via the European war which began in 1914.

Optimistic Darwinism collapsed in the trenches of World War I. The federal government was determined to create a one size fits all American identity which would Americanize the hordes of European immigrants who lived in ghettos in the big cities and were determined to cling to the traditions which constituted their identities as Europeans from countries with which oftentimes, as in the case of the Germans, were at odds with the political and cultural exigencies of their new home. To bring this about the CPI created the Melting Pot Pageant, a propaganda stunt held at the Ford English School in Detroit on July 4, 1917.[1496] According to Lippmann's account:

> In the center of the baseball park at second base stood a huge wooden and canvas pot. There were flights of steps up to the rim on two sides. After the audience had settled itself, and the band had played, a procession came through an opening at one side of the field. It was made up of men of all the foreign nationalities employed in the factories. They wore their native costumes, they were singing their national songs; they danced their folk dances, and carried the banners of all Europe. The master of ceremonies was the principal of the grade school dressed as Uncle Sam. He led them to the pot. He directed them up the steps to the rim, and inside. He called them out again on the other side. They came, dressed in derby hats, coats, pants, vest, stiff collar and polka-dot tie, undoubtedly, said my friend, each with an Eversharp pencil in his pocket, and all singing the Star-Spangled Banner. To the promoters of this pageant, and probably to most of the actors, it seemed as if they had managed to express the most intimate difficulty to friendly association between the older peoples of

---

1494 Lippmann, *Public Opinion*, Kindle edition, p. 29.
1495 Lippmann, *Public Opinion*, Kindle edition, p. 30.
1496 "Melting Pot Ceremony at Ford English School, July 4, 1917, The Henry Ford, https://www.thehenryford.org/collections-and-research/digital-collections/artifact/254569/

Part III: The Return of the Satanic Wilderness

America and the newer. The contradiction of their stereotypes interfered with the full recognition of their common humanity. The people who change their names know this. They mean to change themselves, and the attitude of strangers toward them.[1497]

In addition to disliking foreigners, including the people "our crowd" referred to as *Ostjuden*, Lippmann harbored a low opinion of the man of the west which was common in cultured German Jewish circles in New York City. Whether he referred to them as "*demos*," or "*goyim*," Lippmann felt that these Americans had no right to their own opinions because they were:

> persons who are mentally children or barbarians, people whose lives are a morass of entanglements, people whose vitality is exhausted, shut-in people, and people whose experience has comprehended no factor in the problem under discussion. The stream of public opinion is stopped by them in little eddies of misunderstanding, where it is discolored with prejudice and far-fetched analogy.[1498]

America's newly arrived immigrant population was even worse:

> What kind of American consciousness can grow in the atmosphere of sauerkraut and Limburger cheese? Or what can you expect of the Americanism of the man whose breath always reeks of garlic?"[1499]

In order to divert these groups from voting in their own self-interest—presumably a fundamental American value—America needed "stereotypes," a word Lippmann created for the categories of the mind which needed to be forged and imposed on a hopeless *massa damnata* who were living according to the worn-out cliches of Jeffersonian democracy and other obsolete ideas. Lippmann then goes on to give examples of how "a trait which marks a well-known type," otherwise known as a category of reality, can be turned into a category of the mind which grants identity by filling in:

> the rest of the picture by means of the stereotypes we carry about in our heads. He is an agitator. That much we notice, or are told. Well, an agitator is this sort of person, and so he is this sort of person. He is an intellectual. He is a plutocrat. He is a foreigner. He is a "South European." He is from Back Bay. He is a Harvard Man. How different from the statement: he is a Yale Man. He is a regular fellow. He is a West Pointer. He is an old army sergeant. He is a Greenwich Villager: what don't we know about him then, and about her? He is an international banker. He is from Main Street. The subtlest and most pervasive of all influences are those which create and maintain the repertory of stereotypes.[1500]

1497 Lippmann, *Public Opinion*, Kindle edition, pp. 50-1.
1498 Lippmann, *Public Opinion*, Kindle edition, p. 45.
1499 Lippman, *Public Opinion*, Kindle edition, p. 50.
1500 Lippmann, *Public Opinion*, Kindle edition, p. 52.

Based perhaps on his experiences in Europe as a child, Lippmann incongruously chose Giotto as an example of someone who created stereotypes—i.e. frescoes in the Arena chapel—where an Italian "might see a vision of saints standardized for his time."[1501] Lippmann's crude reduction of the greatest transformation in the history of western art to advertising slogans speaks volumes about his cultural horizon, but it also gives a good indication that he understood how effective propaganda was based on a category of reality, as portrayed in a painting or photo, which then got captured by a category of the mind which then gave it meaning. This meant that Lippmann recognized early on that cinema, which was emerging into a mass medium in Hollywood was to become the most effective instrument for propaganda the world had ever seen because it so readily combined the images and meanings which were essential for the creation of effective stereotypes:

> Thus there can be little doubt that the moving picture is steadily building up imagery which is then evoked by the words people read in their newspapers. In the whole experience of the race there has been no aid to visualization comparable to the cinema.[1502]

The hallmark of "the perfect stereotype" is that "it precedes the use of reason" and often determines its course. The stereotype is "a form of perception," which "imposes a certain character on the data of our senses before the data reach the intelligence."[1503] The stereotype insures that "what we are looking at corresponds successfully with what we anticipated" because the course of history is determined not by "the systematic idea as a genius formulated it, but shifting imitations, replicas, counterfeits, analogies, and distortions in individual minds."[1504]

Lippmann's theory of stereotypes is another word for sophistry of the sort Socrates contested when Thrasymachus claimed that justice was the opinion of the powerful. Americans traditionally found ideas like this repugnant and antithetical to Jeffersonian and Jacksonian valorizations of the common man until Lippman commandeered William James to make sophistry palatable, claiming that "No one sees further into a generalization than his own knowledge of detail extends."[1505] Following in Plato's footsteps, St. Thomas Aquinas claimed that truth was *adaequatio rei et intellectum*," the correspondence between the thing and the mind. Unfortunately, categories of reality and categories of the mind have equal value in Lippmann's system of stereotypes, which is based on a resurrection of Ockham's nominalism, which

---

[1501] Lippmann, *Public Opinion*, Kindle edition, p. 53.
[1502] Lippmann, *Public Opinion*, Kindle edition, p. 53.
[1503] Lippmann, *Public Opinion*, Kindle edition, p. 57.
[1504] Lippmann, *Public Opinion*, Kindle edition, p. 60.
[1505] Lippmann, *Public Opinion*, Kindle edition, p. 67.

dissolves all categories of reality into categories of the mind. According to Lippmann's explanation of stereotypes as the basis of public opinion:

> our attention is called to those facts which support it, and diverted from those which contradict. We do not see what our eyes are not accustomed to take into account. . . . We see a dewy morn, a blushing maiden, a sainted priest, a humorless Englishman, a dangerous Red, a carefree bohemian, a lazy Hindu, a wily Oriental, a dreaming Slav, a volatile Irishman, a greedy Jew, a 100% American. . . for the judgment has preceded the evidence. . . . . The quality of their thinking and doing will depend on whether those prejudices are friendly, friendly to other people, to other ideas, whether they evoke love of what is felt to be positively good, rather than hatred of what is not contained in their version of the good.[1506]

As Lippmann's examples show, stereotypes confer identity or, to say the same thing from the opposite point of view, stereotypes are a form of identity theft which denies existence to English humorists like P. J. Wodehouse or maidens who do not blush, or the decadent priest who is the main character in Graham Green's novel *The Power and the Glory*. Stereotypes are a form of cultural imperialism perfectly suited to the America dominated by Madison Avenue and Hollywood after the Great War had created Hemingway and the Lost Generation. The crucial link was the moral law. When Lippmann tells us that "around every code there is a cloud of interpreters who deduce more specific cases" he is telling us to how the "moral code"[1507] is going to be subsumed into the category of public opinion, which rules the world at the behest of the rich and the powerful. In order to be successful, categories of the mind must retain what Lippmann called "the foothold of realism."[1508] Once all categories of reality disappear into categories of the mind, morality ceases to be objective and normative—as epitomized by the Ten Commandments—and becomes nothing more than an opinion, seen through the lens of stereotypes. Lippmann manifests the Jewish revolutionary spirit in his attempt to turn the world upside down. In Protestant America, political opinions were based on morality. "We have no constitution," John Adams reminded everyone, "which functions in the absence of a moral people." According to Walter Lippmann's repudiation of that view, morality is based on public opinion, or as he puts it: "The theory I am suggesting is that, in the present state of education, a public opinion is primarily a moralized and codified version of the facts."[1509]

The new system, based on manipulation, is naturally congenial to Lippmann because Jews never have enough people to sway any election by numbers but can always sway it through public opinion orchestrated by the

---

1506 Lippmann, *Public Opinion*, Kindle edition, pp. 68-9.
1507 Lippmann, *Public Opinion*, Kindle edition, p. 69.
1508 Lippmann, *Public Opinion*, Kindle edition, p. 95
1509 Lippmann, *Public Opinion*, Kindle edition, p. 71.

newspapers and other media outlets they control. At the crucial moment in American history when most Americans stopped working on farms and started working in offices and factories, American identity needed a new "concrete embodiment,"[1510] to replace stereotypes which had become obsolete. This had occurred previously in the 19th century when the locomotive, which harnessed steam power to motion, provided "striking material evidence" for "belief in the perfectibility of the human race" in the period from 1820 to 1850. In America, Nathaniel Hawthorne satirized the conflation of rail and progress in *The House of the Seven Gables* and his short story "The Celestial Railroad."

Film, as Lippmann pointed out, is the best vehicle for "concrete embodiment," which means that as of 1922 Lippmann understood that Hollywood was poised to provide more sophisticated stereotypes to replace the crude tactics of the CPI's melting pot pageant. The Jews who created Hollywood were poised to become the group which determined American identity.

World War I had put an end to Herbert Spencer's understanding of evolution as "progress towards perfection," as Hemingway so ably demonstrated. This necessitated the creation of a new stereotype which could represent the new American as effectively as Herbert Spencer and Jack London had represented the era of "progress" and "perfection" which was "composed fundamentally of mechanical inventions."[1511] According to Lippmann, "the spectacle of mechanical progress has made so deep an impression, that it has suffused the whole moral code,"[1512] but that vision died in the trenches and needed to be replaced by something suitable to the new age.

As a replacement, Lippmann moots Einstein's Theory of Relativity, but ironically in a way that shows that it's too abstruse for the average American Yahoo, who needs to be guided by illustrated pictures, another term for categories of reality colonized by categories of the mind. If there is a picture of Einstein's Theory of Relativity, Lippmann doesn't mention it, certainly not in the way he mentioned Giotto's frescoes.

What Americans needed at this crucial moment was "a fundamental stereotype,"[1513] that epitomized "the American way of doing things,"[1514] to replace the exploded myth of Spencerian progress while at the same time taking into account the "extraordinary range of facts in the economic situation and in human nature"[1515] which turned "an unusual amount of pugnacity, acquisitiveness, and lust of power into productive work," which brought about:

1510 Lippmann, *Public Opinion*, Kindle edition, p. 7.
1511 Lippmann, *Public Opinion*, Kindle edition, p. 62.
1512 Lippmann, *Public Opinion*, Kindle edition, p. 62.
1513 Lippmann, *Public Opinion*, Kindle edition, p. 62.
1514 Lippmann, *Public Opinion*, Kindle edition, p. 62.
1515 Lippmann, *Public Opinion*, Kindle edition, p. 63.

Part III: The Return of the Satanic Wilderness

the rush of their victory over mountains, wildernesses, distance, and human competition that has even done duty for that part of religious feeling which is a sense of communion with the purpose of the universe. The pattern has been a success so nearly perfect in the sequence of ideals, practice, and results, that any challenge to it is called un-American.[1516]

[1516] Lippmann, *Public Opinion*, Kindle edition, p. 63.

Chapter 43

Gary Cooper and The Virginian

Once "The American version of Progress" became obsolete as the religion of the American empire, the cowboy emerged as the new stereotype which defined what it meant to be an American with the publication of *The Virginian* in 1902, but more importantly with the release of the film version of the book in 1929. Its star was Gary Cooper, the man who epitomized American identity for the middle years of the 20th century. If England is John Bull, "who is jovial and fat, not too clever, but well able to take care of himself,"[1517] America is *The Virginian* as embodied by Gary Cooper, who is a long and lean man of the west who actually grew up on a ranch in Montana, but only after attending a boarding school in England. The cinema, as Lippmann knew, is the best source of stereotypes because "We cannot be much interested in, or much moved by, the things we do not see."[1518]

Lippmann's contempt for the *goyim* is most palpable in his theory of stereotypes. Americans have no powers of abstraction. As a result:

> Pictures have always been the surest way of conveying an idea, and next in order, words that call up pictures in memory. The audience must have something to do, and the contemplation of the true, the good and the beautiful is not something to do."[1519]

Americans can only understand what "gifted men," i.e., Hollywood Jews, "can visualize for us."[1520] When it comes to Americans, "no idea is lucid for practical decision until it has visual or tactile value. . . . the audience must be exercised by the image,"[1521] by which Lippmann means sex and violence:

> Now there are two forms of exercise which far transcend all others, both as to ease with which they are aroused, and eagerness with which stimuli for them are sought. They are sexual passion and fighting, and the two have so many associations with each other, blend into each other so intimately, that a fight about sex outranks every other theme in the

---

1517 Lippmann, *Public Opinion*, Kindle edition, p. 90.
1518 Lippmann, *Public Opinion*, Kindle edition, p. 91.
1519 Lippmann, *Public Opinion*, Kindle edition, p. 92.
1520 Lippmann, *Public Opinion*, Kindle edition, p. 91.
1521 Lippmann, *Public Opinion*, Kindle edition, p. 92.

breadth of its appeal. There is none so engrossing or so careless of all distinctions of culture and frontiers."[1522]

Unfortunately, at least according to Lippmann: "The sexual motif figures hardly at all in American political imagery."[1523] As of 1922, the *Ostjuden* who created Hollywood were well on their way to changing that state of affairs by introducing nudity, obscenity, ridicule of the clergy, and homosexuality into pre-Production Code films. The reaction was outrage on the part of the Protestant majority, who called upon former Postmaster Will Hays to bring the Jews into line with American sexual mores. Hays failed, opening the door to the nation's Catholic bishops, who succeeded in imposing the Production Code on Hollywood in 1933 under the threat of boycott from the Legion of Decency which was costing Harry Warner $100,000 a week in Depression era in Philadelphia alone. Because it embodied American identity when sexual morality was largely intact, the cowboy obviated the mechanism of censorship which the Hollywood Production Code embodied.

The cowboy was a spontaneous manifestation of the *volonté générale*, (or in Lippmann's words, the "common will") which Lippmann stole from Jean-Jacques Rousseau but considered essential to governing the chaos inherent to a Protestant country in which every man was his own pope. The "machine" of social engineering was necessary because "out of the private notions of any group no common idea emerges by itself."[1524] Nationality must be embodied in a symbol, which is "both a mechanism of solidarity, and a mechanism of exploitation."[1525] The stereotype secures "unity and flexibility without real consent."[1526] It is fundamentally undemocratic, based on manipulation, and, therefore, congenial to Jews, who are a perennial minority wherever they find themselves and doomed to cultural insignificance whenever democratic principles prevail. Speculation among political thinkers from Plato and Aristotle through Machiavelli and Hobbes has always "revolved around the self-centered man who had to see the whole world by means of a few pictures in his head."[1527] The creation of consent is, therefore, not a new art:

> It is a very old one which was supposed to have died out with the appearance of democracy. But it has not died out. It has, in fact, improved enormously in technic, because it is now based on analysis rather than on rule of thumb. And so, as a result of psychological research, coupled with the modern means of communication, the practice of democracy has

---

1522 Lippmann, *Public Opinion*, Kindle edition, p. 92.
1523 Lippmann, *Public Opinion*, Kindle edition, p. 92.
1524 Lippmann, *Public Opinion*, Kindle edition, p. 128.
1525 Lippmann, *Public Opinion*, Kindle edition, p. 131.
1526 Lippmann, *Public Opinion*, Kindle edition, p. 133.
1527 Lippmann, *Public Opinion*, Kindle edition, p. 3.

turned a corner. A revolution is taking place, infinitely more significant than any shifting of economic power.[1528]

Jefferson, Lippmann continues, "more than any other man formulated the American image of democracy," but Jeffersonian democracy is now obsolete: "The cherishment of the people was our principle," wrote Jefferson. But the people he cherished almost exclusively were the small landowning farmers:

> Those who labor in the earth are the chosen people of God, if ever He had a chosen people, whose breasts He has made his peculiar deposit for substantial and genuine virtue. It is the focus in which He keeps alive that sacred fire, which otherwise might escape from the face of the earth. Corruption of morals in the mass of cultivators is a phenomenon of which no age nor nation has furnished an example.

> Jefferson drew all these logical conclusions. He disapproved of manufacture, of foreign commerce, and a navy, of intangible forms of property, and in theory of any form of government that was not centered in the small self-governing group. . . . it was soon forgotten that the theory was originally devised for very special conditions. It became the political gospel, and supplied the stereotypes through which Americans of all parties have looked at politics. If democracy is to be spontaneous, the interests of democracy must remain simple, intelligible, and easily managed. Conditions must approximate those of the isolated rural township.[1529]

American identity involved a fantasy which could not exist "in the real world." When the Jeffersonian could not find these conditions in the real world:

> he went passionately into the wilderness and founded Utopian communities far from foreign contacts. His slogans reveal his prejudice. He is for Self-Government, Self-Determination, Independence. Not one of these ideas carries with it any notion of consent or community beyond the frontiers of the self-governing groups.[1530]

Protestantism made Americans ungovernable because every man was not only his own priest; over time every man had become his own infallible pope, which was the only logical conclusion one could draw from the doctrine of *sola scriptura*. If everyman was infallible in his ability to interpret the Bible, why wasn't he equally infallible in choosing his form of government? The founding fathers were, in this regard, not Protestants. They created a government in which "Ambition must be made to counteract ambition," which became enshrined in the division of government into three separate and in some sense

---

1528 Lippmann, *Public Opinion*, Kindle edition, p. 138.
1529 Lippmann, *Public Opinion*, Kindle edition, pp. 147-8.
1530 Lippmann, *Public Opinion*, Kindle edition, p. 148.

WALKING WITH A BIBLE AND A GUN

antagonistic branches, which Lippmann sees as "an ingenious machine to neutralize local opinion."[1531]

Andrew Jackson broke with the founders' suspicion of *Demos* and "founded the practice of turning public office into patronage."[1532] After the industrial railroad build-out of the late 19th and early 20th centuries, the idea of government via "filtering local experiences through local states of mind" had become "obsolete"[1533] and had to be replaced by "controlled reporting and objective analysis"[1534] done by experts, or as Lippmann puts it "a few informed insiders,"[1535] or by "a specialized class whose personal interests reach beyond the locality."[1536] Political decision "is inevitably the concern of comparatively few people, is actually brought into relation with the interests of men."[1537] The hidden common denominator of these terms is Jew. Only he can provide a "prospect which is not visionary" based on "a realistic picture of the invisible world" by "men who are expert in keeping these pictures realistic."[1538]

Once the "dogma of democracy"[1539] became obsolete, it was superseded by social engineers who are experts at manipulating public opinion by presenting convincing symbols of Americanism on the silver screen, which the Jews controlled. Hollywood exalted the cowboy image while at the same time subverting it. Fortified with "psychological research, coupled with the modern means of communication," Hollywood learned how to coerce consent subtly by creating a symbol which epitomized what it meant to be an American on its terms.

Hollywood created the cowboy as the symbol of what it meant to be an American in 1928 by casting Gary Cooper to play the lead role in *The Virginian*, but the trajectory which began with the film version of *The Virginian* culminated in films like *Midnight Cowboy*, *Blazing Saddles*, and *Brokeback Mountain*, which subverted the image under the relentless pressure of the Jewish revolutionary spirit which could only survive as transgression, even if it meant losing money.

1531 Lippmann, *Public Opinion*, Kindle edition, p. 153.
1532 Lippmann, *Public Opinion*, Kindle edition, p. 156.
1533 Lippmann, *Public Opinion*, Kindle edition, p. 158.
1534 Lippmann, *Public Opinion*, Kindle edition, p. 159.
1535 Lippmann, *Public Opinion*, Kindle edition, p. 159.
1536 Lippmann, *Public Opinion*, Kindle edition, p. 169,
1537 Lippmann, *Public Opinion*, Kindle edition, p. 171.
1538 Lippmann, *Public Opinion*, Kindle edition, p. 171.
1539 Lippmann, *Public Opinion*, Kindle edition, p. 138.

CHAPTER 44

OWEN WISTER CREATES THE COWBOY

Owen Wister came up with the original paradigm, providing a worthy successor to Natty Bumppo by creating the cowboy with no name known as *The Virginian*. Wister's novel proposed the cowboy as the antidote to Walter Lippmann's denigration of Jeffersonian Democracy *avant la lettre* every bit as much as Hollywood's version did the same thing after the fact. In America, "true democracy and true aristocracy are one and the same thing."[1540] The cowboy epitomizes both. Everyone in Medicine Bow "magnetically knew" that "the Virginian was the great man. And they watched him with approval."[1541]

The Virginian established the tropes of cowboy fiction for decades to come. The Saloon with its swinging doors became the agora where good confronted evil and where The Virginian first confronted Trampas, the novel's villain by saying in a manner at once disarming and full of menace, "When you call me that, SMILE," as he looked at Trampas across the table.[1542] Unlike the church, which is its sectarian antipode, the Saloon is the agora, where the narrator surveys the faces of the cowboys, judges the future prospects of the polis and, in this instance, "sees more death than vice."[1543]

The narrator is a man of the east who becomes disoriented when he arrives in Wyoming. "What world am I in?" he wonders. "Does this same planet hold Fifth Avenue?"[1544] The narrator is a "tenderfoot," who initially feels that the west is made up of trash and wild animals. As he rides out of Medicine Bow, the narrator must pass through "thick heaps and fringes of tin cans, and shelving mounds of bottles cast out of the saloons" before he reaches "the clean plains, with the prairie-dogs and the pale herds of antelope."[1545] Once in the realm of nature, the narrator understands that the cowboy has a

---

1540 Wister, *The Virginian*, p. 135.
1541 Wister, p. 182.
1542 Wister, p. 28.
1543 Wister, p. 31.
1544 Wister, p. 40.
1545 Wister, p. 46.

"true nobility,"[1546] which touches the narrator's "American heart." Because he is rootless, the Virginian is a typical man of the West, who:

> had set out for a "look at the country" at the age of fourteen; and that by his present age of twenty-four he had seen Arkansas, Texas, New Mexico, Arizona, California, Oregon, Idaho, Montana, and Wyoming. Everywhere he had taken care of himself, and survived; nor had his strong heart yet waked up to any hunger for a home. Let me also tell you that he was one of thousands drifting and living thus, but (as you shall learn) one in a thousand.[1547]

The cowboy epitomizes the young nation that is America. These young men "radiate romance," by wearing a cowboy outfits composed of "The fringed leathern chaparreros, the cartridge belt, the flannel shirt, [and] the knotted scarf at the neck,"[1548] And thus Wister created another trope which would last for decades in which the cowboy's heart would invariably be touched by the schoolmarm from the east, who she will eventually fall in love with by making him read "Shakespeare, Tennyson, Browning, Longfellow; and a number of novels by Scott, Thackeray, George Eliot, Hawthorne, and lesser writers; some volumes of Emerson; and Jane Austen complete."[1549]

Like the schoolmarm, the narrator of *The Virginian* has fallen under the spell of the wilderness and becomes so "steeped in a revery as of the primal earth" that "even thoughts themselves had almost ceased motion"[1550] forcing him, like Ike McCaslin, "to leave behind all noise and mechanisms, and set out at ease, slowly, with one packhorse, into the wilderness," where he feels "that the ancient earth was indeed my mother and that I had found her again after being lost among houses, customs, and restraints.[1551]

Nature once again becomes a refuge from the confused civilization of the east where men live in a land with "One God and fifteen religions,"[1552] a state of affairs which leads to a contradiction which cannot be resolved but which has been internalized nonetheless, as when the Virginian opines, "I ain't religious. I know that. But I ain't unreligious. And I know that too."[1553]

When Dr. MacBride, the man of the east, arrives in Wyoming, he finds that the Calvinist gospel makes no impression on cowboys, because the frontier has modified religion. After travelling three hundred miles and passing

---

1546 Wister, p. 32.
1547 Wister, p. 49.
1548 Wister, p. 119.
1549 Wister, p. 127.
1550 Wister, p. 345.
1551 Wister, p. 346.
1552 Wister, p. 195.
1553 Wister, p. 196.

Part III: The Return of the Satanic Wilderness

"no church of any faith,"[1554] Dr. MacBride has discovered not "a hardened pagan,"[1555] but rather cowboys who have allowed the West to obliterate what was left of Calvinism and install a new American religion in its place.

The West has modified Calvinism. Existence has called a new American essence into being that was a democratic improvement on the obsolete religion of the East. By travelling to Wyoming, Dr. MacBride learned that "the whole secret" of religion "lies in the way you treat people. As soon as you treat men as your brothers, they are ready to acknowledge you—if you deserve it—as their superior. That's the whole bottom of Christianity, and that's what our missionary will never know."[1556]

When Dr. MacBride tries to preach Calvinist orthodoxy to cowboys who think that Christianity is a sect situated somewhere between the Mormons and the Knights of Pythias, his sermon "took on a new glare of untimeliness" and "grotesque obsoleteness" because it led them to believe:

> that not only they could do no good, but that if they did contrive to, it would not help them. Nay, more: not only honest deeds availed them nothing, but even if they accepted this especial creed which was being explained to them as necessary for salvation, still it might not save them. Their sin was indeed the cause of their damnation, yet, keeping from sin, they might nevertheless be lost.[1557]

Predestination had no meaning for the cowboy, who was the quintessential American because he was a man of action, because it told him that man's eternal destiny:

> had all been settled for them not only before they were born, but before Adam was shaped. Having told them this, he invited them to glorify the Creator of the scheme. Even if damned, they must praise the person who had made them expressly for damnation. That is what I heard him prove by logic to these cow-boys. Stone upon stone he built the black cellar of his theology, leaving out its beautiful park and the sunshine of its garden.[1558]

Unlike Dr. MacBride, who spoke about "wrath," but "never once of love,"[1559] the local Methodist bishop understood how to hold the cowboys' attention "by homely talk of their special hardships and temptations. And when they fell he spoke to them of forgiveness and brought them encouragement."[1560] Dr.

1554 Wister, p. 205.
1555 Wister, p. 206.
1556 Wister, pp. 210-1.
1557 Wister, p. 220.
1558 Wister, p. 220.
1559 Wister, p. 221.
1560 Wister, p. 221.

MacBride, on the other hand, "never thought once of the lives of these waifs. So he thrust out to them none of the sweet but all the bitter of his creed, naked and stern as iron. Dogma was his all in all, and poor humanity was nothing but flesh for its canons."[1561]

As a result, Dr. MacBride's sermon's effect on the cowboys was the opposite of what he intended. Scipio stifles "a smile when it came to the doctrine of original sin"[1562] because the times had changed. Calvinism had evaporated on the frontier, where it was replaced by a Methodism which emphasized pastoral care as the Procrustean bed which determined doctrine. Confronted with an updated version of "Sinners in the Hands of an Angry God," the cowboys did not roll on the ground in frenzied attempts to expunge their guilt, as their forebears in the Connecticut River Valley had done. Instead, they found that "their attention merely wandered" during the sermon intended to convict them of their sins. After Dr. MacBride told them that they "were a sifted set of sons-of-guns," the cowboys decided "to quit fleeing from temptation" because it was "Better to get it in the neck after a good time than a poor one."[1563] The Calvinist doctrine of predestination, in other words, undermined the moral law which was the cowboy's last, tenuous connection to Christianity. "Three hundred years ago they would have been frightened," but "in this electric day,"[1564] the only antidote to bad theology, as the judge puts it "ruefully," is "to take him fishing,"[1565] and expose him to "nature" and hope it will cure Dr. MacBride of the bad theology he picked up back east.

The Virginian comes up with a better cure for Calvinism by staging a mock conversion in the bedroom next to Dr. Bride's:

> "I'm afeared to be alone!" said the Virginian's voice presently in the next room. "I'm afeared." There was a short pause, and then he shouted very loud, "I'm losin' my desire afteh the sincere milk of the Word!"[1566]

Once he understands that The Virginian is mocking him and his religion, Dr. MacBride leaves in a huff, liberating the cowboys from an alien gospel, which forces them to "sit like a dumb lamb and let a stranger tell yu' for an hour that yu're a hawg and a swine, just after you have acted in a way which them that know the facts would call pretty near white. . . ."[1567] The cowpuncher's "daily thoughts were clean," even in delirium, because they "came from the untamed but unstained mind of a man."[1568] New England's "pale decadence"

1561 Wister, p. 221.
1562 Wister, p. 221.
1563 Wister, p. 223.
1564 Wister, p. 221.
1565 Wister, p. 222.
1566 Wister, p. 225.
1567 Wister, p. 228.
1568 Wister, p. 311.

Part III: The Return of the Satanic Wilderness

fades away under the light of "the slow cow-puncher's notions of masculine courage and modesty."[1569]

Unlike the Calvinist preacher, the schoolmarm from Vermont is teachable in spite of "eastern warblings" which the Ogdens provide as "a sort of counteractant against the spell of the black-haired horse man."[1570] i.e., the Virginian. After seeing "his cow-boy trappings,—the leathern chaps, the belt and pistol, and in his hand a coil of rope" Maud has "fallen in love with his clothes."[1571] Maud doesn't want to "marry below her station," but she finds "her potent, indomitable lover" irresistible, as "the slow cow-puncher unfolded his notions of masculine courage and modesty (though he did not deal in such high-sounding names), causing Molly to forget everything to listen to him, as he forgot himself and his inveterate shyness and grew talkative to her."[1572] At this point, "the pale decadence of New England," symbolized by the poetry of "her idol" Browning, yields to the urgings of "her good old Revolutionary blood" as she begins to see the cowboy as the true American.

Nature, however, abhors a vacuum, and before long, there is trouble in paradise. As soon as the preacher leaves, the hold on social order, which had always been tenuous on the frontier, collapses as Trampas, Shorty and the other "cattle thieves" become emboldened and begin rustling the cattle which the winter had scattered "widely over the range."[1573] In the absence of organized religion, the rustlers have grown "more audacious,"[1574] precipitating a legal crisis on the frontier, not unlike the one Natty Bumppo faced in Cooperstown. The social order begins to disintegrate as horses and cattle go missing, causing "each man . . . to doubt his neighbor,"[1575] forcing the Virginian to conclude that "steps will have to be taken soon by somebody, I reckon." Prompting the schoolmarm to respond, "By you?" "Most likely, I'll get mixed up in it" is his answer.[1576] No one is better able to respond to the crisis, because the Virginian, like Natty Bumppo, is a "man without a cross" who comes from good white stock:

> I am of old stock in Virginia. English and one Scotch Irish grandmother my father's father brought from Kentucky. We have always stayed at the same place farmers and hunters not bettering our lot and very plain. We have fought when we got the chance, under Old Hickory and in Mexico and my father and two brothers were killed in the Valley in sixty-four.

1569 Wister, p. 319.
1570 Wister, p. 232.
1571 Wister, p. 238.
1572 Wister, p. 321.
1573 Wister, p. 253.
1574 Wister, p. 338.
1575 Wister, p. 338.
1576 Wister, p. 338.

> Always with us one son has been apt to run away, and I was the one this time. I had too much older brothering to suit me. But now I am doing well being in full sight of prosperity and not too old and very strong my health having stood the sundries it has been put through.[1577]

More importantly, the Virginian has "had to live in places where they had courts and lawyers so called but an honest man was all the law you could find in five hundred miles."[1578] The Virginian is forced to hang his friend Steve, because like Shorty, he has fallen under the spell of Trampas, who enticed him "away from good and trained him in evil."[1579] Steve's defection to evil causes the Virginian to articulate the cowboy creed which will become the basis for the American civic religion which was on its way to replacing Christianity as the American's source of identity:

> You have a friend, and his ways are your ways. You travel together, you spree together confidentially, and you suit each other down to the ground. Then one day you find him putting his iron on another man's calf. You tell him fair and square those ways have never been your ways and ain't going to be your ways. Well, that does not change him any, for it seems he's disturbed over getting rich quick and being a big man in the Territory. And the years go on, until you are foreman of Judge Henry's ranch and he—is dangling back in the cottonwoods. What can he claim? Who made the choice? He cannot say, 'Here is my old friend that I would have stood by.' Can he say that?[1580]

The West has a different set of rules: "You've got to deal cyards WELL; you've got to steal WELL; and if you claim to be quick with your gun, you must be quick, for you're a public temptation, and some man will not resist trying to prove he is the quicker."[1581] The Virginian then touches on the Satanic roots of the new American religion which the cowboys have distilled from the Calvinism they rejected when he continues, "You must break all the Commandments WELL in this Western country, and Shorty should have stayed in Brooklyn, for he will be a novice his livelong days."[1582]

The Virginian is not responsible for "the customs of the country,"[1583] because they came from God through the crucible of existence known as the frontier. If Steve or Shorty couldn't conform his behavior to those customs, he should have stayed in Brooklyn.

1577 Wister, p. 342.
1578 Wister, p. 343.
1579 Wister, p. 357.
1580 Wister, p. 366.
1581 Wister, p. 368.
1582 Wister, p. 368.
1583 Wister, p. 379.

Part III: The Return of the Satanic Wilderness

As Dimmesdale discovered in his forest reverie with Hester, the wilderness abolished the law, causing a crisis for the schoolmarm, who was raised to believe that God's law united east and west. Unfortunately, things aren't that simple. "Spectral Steve" returns to haunt the Virginian's troubled conscience, leaving the Virginian unable to reconcile east and west. The narrator, who is a man of the east, wonders whether it is permissible to "do evil that good may come"?[1584] The Virginian counters the idea of a universal moral law by proposing a geographic relativism, according to which:

> Many an act that man does is right or wrong according to the time and place which form, so to speak, its context; strip it of its surrounding circumstances, and you tear away its meaning. Gentlemen reformers, beware of this common practice of yours! beware of calling an act evil on Tuesday because that same act was evil on Monday![1585]

Judge Taylor, Medicine Bow's official representative of the law, then lapses into the same moral relativism which Natty Bumppo proposed in *The Pioneers*:

> Do you fail to follow my meaning? Then here is an illustration. On Monday I walk over my neighbor's field; there is no wrong in such walking. By Tuesday he has put up a sign that trespassers will be prosecuted according to law. I walk again on Tuesday, and am a law-breaker. Do you begin to see my point? or are you inclined to object to the illustration because the walking on Tuesday was not WRONG, but merely ILLEGAL?[1586]

> Consider carefully, let me beg you, the case of a young man and a young woman who walk out of a door on Tuesday, pronounced man and wife by a third party inside the door. It matters not that on Monday they were, in their own hearts, sacredly vowed to each other. If they had omitted stepping inside that door, if they had dispensed with that third party, and gone away on Monday sacredly vowed to each other in their own hearts, you would have scarcely found their conduct moral.... Do you not think that to stay out and let the murder be done would have been the evil act in this case? To disobey the sign-post was RIGHT; and I trust that you now perceive the same act may wear as many different hues of right or wrong as the rainbow, according to the atmosphere in which it is done. It is not safe to say of any man, "He did evil that good might come." Was the thing that he did, in the first place, evil? That is the question.[1587]

When the schoolmarm asks the Judge whether there is a difference between lynching southern Negroes in public and hanging Wyoming horse thieves

---

1584 Wister, p. 396.
1585 Wister, p. 397.
1586 Wister, p. 397.
1587 Wister, p. 398.

in private, he repudiates the former and accepts the latter, claiming there is a difference:

> I consider the burning a proof that the South is semi-barbarous, and the hanging a proof that Wyoming is determined to become civilized. We do not torture our criminals when we lynch them. We do not invite spectators to enjoy their death agony. We put no such hideous disgrace upon the United States. We execute our criminals by the swiftest means, and in the quietest way. Do you think the principle is the same?"[1588]

The schoolmarm needs to learn the lesson of the west, which is that the law comes from "ordinary citizens":

> They are where the law comes from, you see. For they chose the delegates who made the Constitution that provided for the courts. There's your machinery. These are the hands into which ordinary citizens have put the law. So you see, at best, when they lynch they only take back what they once gave. For in the South they take a negro from jail where he was waiting to be duly hung. The South has never claimed that the law would let him go. But in Wyoming the law has been letting our cattle-thieves go for two years. We are in a very bad way, and we are trying to make that way a little better until civilization can reach us. At present we lie beyond its pale. And so when your ordinary citizen sees this, and sees that he has placed justice in a dead hand, he must take justice back into his own hands where it was once at the beginning of all things. Call this primitive, if you will. But so far from being a DEFIANCE of the law, it is an ASSERTION of it—the fundamental assertion of self governing men, upon whom our whole social fabric is based. There is your principle, Miss Wood, as I see it. Now can you help me to see anything different?"[1589]

The Judge renders the schoolmarm speechless, conceding that "perhaps some day we shall do without [war and capital punishment] them. But they are none of them so terrible as unchecked theft and murder would be."[1590]

Eventually, the "natural man" triumphs over Maud's "better birth and schooling,"[1591] but only after she has spent:

> a month with him by stream and canyon, a month far deeper into the mountain wilds than ever yet he had been free to take her, a month with sometimes a tent and sometimes the stars above them, and only their horses besides themselves. . . . [1592]

1588 Wister, p. 400.
1589 Wister, pp. 401-2.
1590 Wister, pp. 401-2.
1591 Wister, p. 412.
1592 Wister, p. 405.

Part III: The Return of the Satanic Wilderness

After the schoolmarm marries the Virginian she finds that "Her better birth and schooling that had once been weapons to keep him at his distance, or bring her off victorious in their encounters, had given way before the onset of the natural man himself."[1593]

The Virginian plans to take his bride into the wilderness after "the bishop had joined them"[1594] because it is only in "the solitudes where only the wild animals would be, besides themselves"[1595] that he can truly consummate the marriage. There the Schoolmarm learns that "In personal matters," the Virginian must take the law into his own hands, because "It had come to that point where there was no way out, save only the ancient, eternal way between man and man. It is only the great mediocrity that goes to law in these personal matters.[1596] Similarly, the bishop is forced to admit that the Virginian has a morality which is superior to the Gospel because Christianity "goes against the whole instinct of human man."[1597] When he tries in vain to convince the Virginian that the Gospel is superior to the code of the west, the bishop is confronted by the exigencies of the west:

> Never before in all his wilderness work had he faced such a thing. He knew that Trampas was an evil in the country, and that the Virginian was a good. He knew that the cattle thieves—the rustlers—were gaining, in numbers and audacity; that they led many weak young fellows to ruin; that they elected their men to office, and controlled juries; that they were a staring menace to Wyoming.[1598]

The bishop is deeply conflicted, "His heart was with the Virginian. But there was his Gospel, that he preached, and believed, and tried to live."[1599] All he can propose is that the Virginian "run away from Trampas,"[1600] but he soon finds that the Virginian adheres to higher principles than those which can be found in the Gospel.

> "That ain't quite fair, seh. We all understand you have got to do the things you tell other folks to do. And you do them, seh. You never talk like anything but a man, and you never set yourself above others. You can saddle your own horses."
>
> "If the Bible," said the bishop, "which I believe to be God's word, was anything to you—"

1593 Wister, p. 412.
1594 Wister, p. 416.
1595 Wister, p. 416.
1596 Wister, p. 426.
1597 Wister, p. 434.
1598 Wister, p. 432.
1599 Wister, p. 432.
1600 Wister, p. 432.

"It is something to me, seh. I have found fine truths in it." "'Thou shalt not kill,'" quoted the bishop. "That is plain."

The Virginian took his turn at smiling. "Mighty plain to me, seh. Make it plain to Trampas, and there'll be no killin'. We can't get at it that way." Once more the bishop quoted earnestly. "'Vengeance is mine, I will repay, saith the Lord.'"

"How about instruments of Providence, seh? Why, we can't get at it that way. If you start usin' the Bible that way, it will mix you up mighty quick, seh."

"My friend," the bishop urged, and all his good, warm heart was in it, "my dear fellow—go away for the one night. He'll change his mind." The Virginian shook his head. "He cannot change his word, seh. Or at least I must stay around till he does. Why, I have given him the say-so. He's got the choice. Most men would not have took what I took from him in the saloon. Why don't you ask him to leave town?"

The good bishop was at a standstill. Of all kicking against the pricks none is so hard as this kick of a professing Christian against the whole instinct of human man.[1601]

In the end, "the whole instinct of man" wins out over the gospel. The Virginian gives the bishop a hearty handshake and then goes off to do what he has to do, leaving the bishop to exclaim, "God bless him!"[1602] Once out of his presence, the Virginian concludes that "the Bishop is wrong," but there's no point in telling the schoolmarm, since this is a man to man thing which she wouldn't understand. Like Hester Prynne, Maud wants the Virginian to run away to the wilderness:

> "It's not too late yet. You can take yourself out of his reach. Everybody knows that you are brave. What is he to you? You can leave him in this place. I'll go with you anywhere. To any house, to the mountains, to anywhere away. We'll leave this horrible place together and—and—oh, won't you listen to me?" She stretched her hands to him. "Won't you listen?"[1603]

Like Dimmesdale, the Virginian concludes that "I must stay here." Wister lacks Hawthorne's depth because he doesn't understand the difference between morality and custom. The Virginian is a man of the west, which means that his primary concern is not abstract principle but rather losing face:

1601 Wister, p. 434.
1602 Wister, pp. 434-5.
1603 Wister, p. 437.

Part III: The Return of the Satanic Wilderness

"I work hyeh. I belong hyeh. It's my life. If folks came to think I was a coward—" "Who would think you were a coward?" "Everybody. My friends would be sorry and ashamed, and my enemies would walk around saying they had always said so. I could not hold up my head again among enemies or friends."[1604]

"There is a higher courage than fear of outside opinion," said the New England girl.[1605]

Before long, it's clear that the Virginian values others' opinion of himself more than the moral prohibition against killing:

If any man happened to say I was a thief and I heard about it, would I let him go on spreadin' such a thing of me? Don't I owe my own honesty something better than that? Would I sit down in a corner rubbin' my honesty and whisperin' to it, 'There! there! I know you ain't a thief?' No, seh; not a little bit! What men say about my nature is not just merely an outside thing. For the fact that I let 'em keep on sayin' it is a proof I don't value my nature enough to shield it from their slander and give them their punishment. And that's being a poor sort of a jay."[1606]

Maud doesn't see it that way.

"Can't yu' see how it must be about a man?" he repeated.[1607]

"I cannot," she answered, in a voice that scarcely seemed her own. "If I ought to, I cannot. To shed blood in cold blood. When I heard about that last fall,—about the killing of those cattle thieves,—I kept saying to myself: 'He had to do it. It was a public duty.'

The Schoolmarm has gotten used to "Wyoming being different from Vermont," but can't get over her understanding that the moral law is universal and not limited by the American dichotomy of east versus west. If the Virginian puts his moral code into practice, "there can be no tomorrow for you and me."[1608]

"This would be the end?" he asked. Her head faintly moved to signify yes. He stood still, his hand shaking a little. "Will you look at me and say that?" he murmured at length. She did not move. "Can you do it?" he said.

1604 Wister, p. 437.
1605 Wister, p. 438.
1606 Wister, p. 438.
1607 Wister, p. 438.
1608 Wister, p. 439.

"Good-by, then," he said. At that word she was at his feet, clutching him. "For my sake," she begged him. "For my sake."[1609]

"I have no right to kiss you any more," he said. And then, before his desire could break him down from this, he was gone, and she was alone.[1610]

The Schoolmarm's ultimatum precedes Trampas' ultimatum: "Get out by sundown, that's all," said Trampas. And wheeling, he went out of the saloon by the rear, as he had entered.[1611]

In spite of superficial differences, Wister's decision to have the Virginian confront Trampas anticipates the thought of Walter Lippmann because both men view morality as a subset of public opinion. Existence didn't call forth essence in Wyoming; existence replaced it with a new understanding of the good based on nothing more than geography, leaving those who propound it with "nothing to stand on" once again. The men of the east and the men of the west could find common cause in their contempt, not only for Catholicism, as both Mark Twain and Henry James had shown, but for the moral law, which never recovered from its bout with Darwinism.

After the Virginian kills Trampas, the Schoolmarm's New England conscience capitulates to geographical relativism, and "the Virginian departed with his bride into the mountains,"[1612] where he and his wife spend their honeymoon in Paradise Regained. There are no "tragic adventures" in Wyoming, where "for ten minutes he fished, catching trout enough."[1613] The Virginian catches all the trout he wants because the loggers haven't arrived, but more importantly because his relationship with the Schoolmarm, unlike Nick Adams' sordid affair with the retarded Indian Trudy, has been sanctified by marriage, which is consummated in the wilderness, which:

> belonged to no man, for it was deep in the unsurveyed and virgin wilderness; neither had he ever made his camp here with any man, nor shared with any the intimate delight which the place gave him. Therefore for many weeks he had planned to bring her here after their wedding, upon the day itself, and show her and share with her his pines and his fishing rock. He would bid her smell the first true breath of the mountains, would watch with her the sinking camp-fire, and with her listen to the water as it flowed round the island.[1614]

The cowboy has re-educated his eastern bride and brought her into the sanctifying realm of nature where:

1609 Wister, p. 439.
1610 Wister, p. 440.
1611 Wister, p. 429.
1612 Wister, p. 445.
1613 Wister, p. 451.
1614 Wister, p. 447.

Part III: The Return of the Satanic Wilderness

The ploughed and planted country, that quilt of many-colored harvests which they had watched yesterday, lay in another world from this where they rode now. No hand but nature's had sown these crops of yellow flowers, these willow thickets and tall cottonwoods. Somewhere in a passage of red rocks the last sign of wagon wheels was lost, and after this the trail became a wild mountain trail.[1615]

Like Nick Adams, the Virginian makes a camp in the wilderness, but not for his sister. The Virginian and the schoolmarm bathe in the same mountain stream, but like his contemporary Jack London, Wister observes Victorian propriety in the realm of nature, by bathing in the cold stream "with the island between them."[1616] Their "bridal camp" is nature, unfallen nature, paradise on earth. "This change their hours upon the island had wrought, filling his face with innocence."[1617] East meets west in paradise. "The western man," the Virginian concludes giving the reader the moral of the tale, "is a good thing."[1618]

1615 Wister, p. 448.
1616 Wister, p. 452.
1617 Wister, p. 455.
1618 Wister, p. 459.

CHAPTER 45

AYN RAND AND THE JEWISH TAKE ON AMERICAN IDENTITY

Six years after appearing in *The Virginian*, Cooper starred in the Hollywood version of *A Farewell to Arms*, combining the cowboy with the lost generation Hemingway hero in a way that expressed "essential American values"[1619] like:

> connection with nature, scepticism about experts, distrust of government, independent endeavor, modesty about one's achievements. In close-ups his face—like Jefferson's and Lincoln's—symbolized the inner qualities of the national hero whom the poet Rupert Brooke had described in 1916: "the tall, thin type of American, with pale blue eyes of an idealistic, disappointed expression." John Updike, defining the spiritual grace and power that the camera captured on film, observed that Cooper's "leathery face, with its baleful Nordic eyes and slightly frozen mouth, so inert-seeming in the cluttered glare of the sound stage, possessed a steady inner life."[1620]

The confluence of the cowboy and the lost generation anti-hero took place in real life during the autumn of 1940 when Hemingway and Cooper met in Sun Valley, Idaho at a ski resort founded by Union Pacific chairman Averell Harriman, who had created a destination winter resort in 1936 to increase ridership on his railroad. The two icons of American identity would meet at Sun Valley regularly thereafter to go hunting, an activity which created bonds of friendship between them until Cooper and Hemingway died, six weeks apart in 1961. Taken together the two men created a composite American identity with Hemingway playing the "brash, larger-than-life . . . hard-drinking" writer and Cooper, the "courteous, non-confrontational taciturn" cowboy, a role which came naturally to him because he was raised on a ranch in Montana.[1621]

1619 Meyers, *Gary Cooper: American Hero*, p. 324.

1620 Meyers, *Gary Cooper: American Hero*, p. 324.

1621 Larry E. Morris, "Ernest Hemingway and Gary Cooper in Idaho: An Enduring Friendship," Montana Historical Society, https://app.mt.gov/shop/mhsstore/ernest-

Walking with a Bible and a Gun

Hemingway hated Hollywood, but by the middle of the 20th century it had become the undisputed broker of American identity. The only medium which came close was *Time* magazine and its picture book equivalent, *Life*. Henry Luce created *Time* with money from Yale alumni, but the concept for his weekly news magazine was based on the principles that Walter Lippmann had articulated in *Public Opinion*.

By the time America had emerged victorious after World War II, *Time* had become the propaganda ministry for the newly created CIA, with C.D. Jackson as the intermediary between the CIA and *Time*. Jackson had worked with General Eisenhower and General McClure, the head of psychological warfare, to create the Holocaust narrative by holding up shrunken heads at Buchenwald as an example of Nazi war crimes. With the help of Billy Wilder, Jackson and McClure created *Death Mills* or *Todesmuehlen*, which launched the Holocaust as a distraction from allied war crimes. Jackson's real name was Jacobson, and he epitomized the crypto-Jewish influence that Lippmann promoted in his book when he lauded scientific, i.e., Jewish, experts as the alternative to the common man extolled by Jeffersonian democracy. Jackson would manage Dwight Eisenhower's successful presidential campaign after the war, and together with Luce, they would impose categories of American identity on figures which the Deep State was interested in promoting.

Time created paradigms of American identity by putting a face, usually featured on the cover, on an idea. Just as Hollywood had put Gary Cooper's face on the cowboy archetype, *Time* featured Alfred Kinsey on the cover of its August 24, 1953 issue to encourage the destruction of sexual morality which the Rockefellers had inaugurated when they chose the entomologist from Indiana University to be America's expert on sex. Luce and Jackson confected an American identity for Kinsey which was a combination of boy scout and scientist, complete with bow tie and crew cut, surrounded by birds and bees, in a way that was calculated to cover up his real identity as a compulsive homosexual determined to undermine sexual morality in the United States with the help of Rockefeller money.

Something similar happened to Ernest Hemingway and Gary Cooper. After Cooper and Hemingway met at Sun Valley in 1940, the same forces that created the famous bug doctor sex expert, turned both men into icons of the American Empire that emerged after World War II. Seeing Cooper in Acapulco in the early 1950s, one observer said that he was "the tall, thin type of American, with pale blue eyes of an idealistic, disappointed expression."[1622] Cooper's image of "rock-like honesty" would appear in the newspaper cartoons in moments of international crisis because the American Empire was now the world's sheriff. During the Suez Crisis in November 1956:

---

hemingway-and-gary-cooper-in-idaho-an-enduring-friendship#:~:text=In%20the%20 autumn%20of%201940,the%20two%20became%20good%20friends.

1622 Meyers, *Gary Cooper: American Hero*, p. 207.

Part III: The Return of the Satanic Wilderness

a British cartoonist portrayed Prime Minister Harold Macmillan, as Sheriff Cooper, confronting Nasser and Co. in front of the Suez saloon. During the Watergate scandal that led to Richard Nixon's resignation, Cooper, the man who could sort out and deal with the bad guys, appeared on the cover of *New York* magazine of August 13, 1973 with the caption "Where Are You, Gary Cooper, Now That We Need You?" In the historic Polish elections in June 1989 the Solidarity union used Cooper's powerful image to emphasize the need to stand together against the Communist government. The movement "unveiled as its final campaign poster the image of Gary Cooper, as a grimly resolute sheriff, 'striding toward the viewer, the union's red logo emblazoned on the horizon behind him, a simple caption underneath —*High Noon*.'"[1623]

High Noon was a remake of *The Virginian* which refracted the tropes of the cowboy fiction through the lens of the McCarthy era and the anti-Communist crusade. Cooper remained the personification of the American who takes the law into his own hands despite the town's opposition (or without its support), but the schoolmarm had been replaced by Kane's young wife, played by Grace Kelly, who looked more like his daughter in the film. Life in the fast lane had aged Cooper prematurely in a way that lent pathos to his role as the only man willing to take a stand when evil threatened to overwhelm the social order in the small town of Hadleyville. Cooper believed that he was made for this role because he saw in Sheriff Will Kane "a graphic presentation of everything dad had taught me at home." His comments show his natural feel for the part and his grasp of the issues: "My concept of a sheriff . . . was that of a man who represented the people. Alone he could never do his job—he had to have help. The sheriff I was asked to play was different than any I'd ever known or heard about because Sheriff Kane had to stand alone, literally, against the lawless. It was a challenging role—and I loved it."[1624]

Like the schoolmarm in *The Virginian*, Will Kane's young wife wanted him to leave town rather than confront the gunman he had sent to prison. Will agrees but then changes his mind while on the way to their honeymoon, so his young wife leaves him and buys a ticket for St. Louis on the same train that will bring the man he sent to prison back to Hadleyville to get revenge. Like the Schoolmarm, Will Kane's wife must learn how to accommodate her eastern principles to western realities. His Quaker wife jumps off the train just before it leaves town to be with her man. To save Kane from death, the Quaker lady, like the schoolmarm, must abandon religious principle. Like an even more famous Quaker, Daniel Boone, Mrs. Kane then put her new principles into action by picking up a gun and shooting one of the desperados determined to kill Kane. Recourse to the gun, which symbolizes will and

---

1623 Meyers, *Gary Cooper: American Hero*, p. 322.
1624 Meyers, *Gary Cooper: American Hero*, p. 239.

force, thwarted the emergence of a new essence based on logos. Instead, the gun contributed to the destruction of practical reason or morality which was essential, as John Adams had pointed out, to representative government.

The screen play for *High Noon* was written as an allegory of the McCarthy era by Carl Foreman, a Jewish communist who was blacklisted in Hollywood in the 1950s because he refused to name other members of the Communist Party when called to testify before the House Un-American Activities Committee, a chore which he did in the middle of the filming of *High Noon*. Foreman shared Lippmann's contempt for average Americans, portraying them as a group of conformist cowards unwilling to stand up for principle even when the future of their small community was at stake. During the discussion in church after Kane's appeal for support, the women of Hadleyville made it clear that Kane had preserved the social order and made it safe for them to "walk the streets." Failure to support Kane meant a return to barbarism, but no one was willing to accept the call. Like Foreman testifying before HUAC, Will Kane had to face his accusers alone, and like Kane, Foreman triumphed over his feckless American colleagues, demonstrating bravery in the hero as much as it demonstrated cowardice in everyone else. After killing the outlaws, Kane takes off his badge and throws it into the dusty street as a gesture of Jewish contempt for Jeffersonian democracy before he rides out of town to resume his interrupted honeymoon.

That scene enraged John Wayne, who referred to *High Noon* as "the most un-American thing I've ever seen in my whole life."[1625] John Wayne claimed that "The last thing in the picture is ole Coop putting the United States marshal's badge under his foot and stepping on it. I'll never regret having helped run Foreman out of this country,"[1626] although the scene as Wayne described it was not in the film.

Foreman could see the writing on the wall. Knowing that he would be blacklisted for refusing to cooperate with HUAC, Foreman:

> rewrote the script and transformed it into a portrayal of how fear affected people in Hollywood. In the film, he calls Hadleyville (or Hollywood) "a dirty little village in the middle of nowhere." Foreman saw himself in Will Kane, abandoned by everyone and left alone to fight the battle for law, common decency, and justice. "So much of the script became comparable to what was happening," Foreman later wrote. "There are many scenes taken from life. One is a distillation of meetings I had with partners, associates, and lawyers. And there's the scene with the man who offers to help and comes back with his gun. 'Where are the others?' he asks. 'There are no others,' says Cooper.... I used a western background to tell the story of a community corrupted by fear, with the implications

---

1625 Meyers, *Gary Cooper: American Hero*, p. 251.
1626 Meyers, *Gary Cooper: American Hero*, p. 251.

Part III: The Return of the Satanic Wilderness

I hoped would be obvious to almost everyone who saw the film, at least in America."[1627]

Unlike the Virginian, Will Kane is alienated from his community in a way that typified Jewish alienation from mainstream America in the early 1950s. On June 19, 1953, after the appeals were exhausted and after jurists at the highest levels refused to stay the sentence any longer, Julius and Ethel Rosenberg were executed for espionage after being found guilty of passing atomic bomb secrets to the Soviets. The execution of the Rosenbergs was arguably the moment of maximum alienation for American Jews. In 1950 David Riesman had articulated that alienation in his book *The Lonely Crowd*, which used the jargon of sociology to strike a note of hope for fellow Jews by describing how Americans were becoming more Jewish:

> The middle class gradually moved away from living according to traditions, or conforming to the values of organized religion of the family or societal codes, and the new middle class gradually adopted a malleability in the way people lived with each other. The increasing ability to consume goods and afford material abundance was accompanied by a shift away from tradition to inner-directedness and then to "other-direction."[1628]

Riesman, like Lippmann, meant that Hollywood, under Jewish direction, was in the business of confecting tropes of what it meant to be an American. In *The Fountainhead*, Ayn Rand's fictional portrayal of Frank Lloyd Wright, the most famous American architect of the 20th century, Wright became Howard Roark, a Jewish revolutionary masquerading as an architect who proved his revolutionary but not architectural *bona fides* by blowing up one of his own buildings.

Rand was born in Russia in 1905. After graduating from the University of Leningrad, Rand arrived in America in 1926. Within 20 years of her arrival, she had total control of the Hollywood rendition of her novel *The Fountainhead*, which Meyers describes as a "long and turgid book, published in 1943 . . . written in a bodice-ripping, hothouse style."[1629] In that film Dominique Francon, played by Patricia Neal, reverberates with sexual chills as she catches sight of Howard Roark, played by Cooper, drilling stone in a quarry:

> She saw his mouth and the silent contempt in the shape of his mouth; the planes of his gaunt, hollow cheeks; the cold, pure brilliance of the eyes that had no trace of pity. She knew it was the most beautiful face she would ever see.... She felt a convulsion of anger, of protest, of resistance— and of pleasure.... She was wondering what he would look like naked."[1630]

1627 Meyers, *Gary Cooper: American Hero*, p. 246.
1628 "The Lonely Crowd," *Wikipedia: The Free Encyclopedia*, https://en.wikipedia.org/wiki/The_Lonely_Crowd
1629 Meyers, *Gary Cooper: American Hero*, p. 214.
1630 Meyers, *Gary Cooper: American Hero*, p. 214.

WALKING WITH A BIBLE AND A GUN

Rand drained all of the subtlety out of Cooper's portrayal of classic American figures and replaced that subtlety with a Russian Jew's parody of American identity which "glorifies selfish individualism"[1631] of the sort that Rand would later make famous in the quasi-religious sect known as Objectivism, which during its heyday attracted fellow Jews like Federal Reserve head Alan Greenspan to join with Rand in celebrating "selfish individualism" as something uniquely American. Rand created a parody of Frank Lloyd Wright and his uniquely American form of architecture by turning him into Howard Roark, who is:

> a blend of romantic hero and a stern intellectual. He believes "the world is perishing from an orgy of self-sacrificing" and tells his astonished patrons: "I don't work with collectives, I don't consult, I don't cooperate, I don't collaborate. ... My work's done my way. A private, personal, selfish, egotistical motive. That's the only way I function."[1632]

By turning Roark into a Russian Jew's parody of the American, Ayn Rand engaged in an early form of identity theft, abetted by the equally Jewish Warner Brothers studio, which paid her $50,000 for the movie rights and another $13,000 for her screenplay, while ensuring that she had "complete control of the script and final approval of all changes."[1633] Rand insisted that Frank Lloyd Wright, "and *only* Frank Lloyd Wright," should design the buildings for the picture. When Wright insisted on a fee of $250,000 for his services, the studio finally stood up to Rand, even though she threatened to blow up Warner Brothers' studio "if it altered one word of her work."[1634]

Before long, it became obvious that the Hollywood Jews had overplayed their hand. They had hijacked American identity in such a crude way that everyone hated the film. The cowboy had many objectionable traits when viewed from the perspective of the east, but the alien ideology of ruthless selfishness which lay at the heart of Rand's objectivism was not one of them. The film hit a false note which not even Gary Cooper's handsome face could save. Frank Lloyd Wright was one of the first Americans to protest, calling *The Fountainhead* "a grossly abusive caricature of his work," as well as "an architectural (and cinematic) disaster."[1635]

Unsurprisingly, the movie critics agreed with Wright and lambasted *The Fountainhead* in reviews which ensured that it was recognized as "both an artistic and commercial failure."[1636] Writing for the *New York Herald Tribune*,

---

1631 Meyers, *Gary Cooper: American Hero*, p. 214.
1632 Meyers, *Gary Cooper: American Hero*, p. 214.
1633 Meyers, *Gary Cooper: American Hero*, p. 214.
1634 Meyers, *Gary Cooper: American Hero*, p. 214.
1635 Meyers, *Gary Cooper: American Hero*, p. 214.
1636 Meyers, *Gary Cooper: American Hero*, p. 220.

Part III: The Return of the Satanic Wilderness

Howard Barnes called it "scrambled, pretentious and embarrassing."[1637] Other New York reviewers soon followed suit:

> John McCarten in the New Yorker dismissed it as "the most asinine and inept movie that has come from Hollywood in years." Bosley Crowther in the *New York Times* wrote that "Cooper seems slightly pathetic with his candor and modesty in the midst of so much pretension. ... He is Mr. Deeds out of his element and considerably unsure of himself. His lengthy appeal to the jury is timid and wooden." Cue magazine's critic, who recognized its trashy content, was severest of all: "It is a hysterical mixture of frenzy and fraud—of spasmodic sincerity and sinister cynicism—of flashes of literary power and shoddy, bombastic nonsense. . . . The juxtaposition of high-sounding phrases regarding an artist's integrity with the steam-heated flashes of purple passion ... turns this film into a story fit for the tabloids and the trash basket."[1638]

George Nelson, writing in *Interiors* and scorning "Hollywood's unerring instinct for the phony," said the buildings in the movie made no sense architecturally and would collapse if actually constructed. He concluded that even for an uninformed public, "there is still no reason for turning out such garbage." Andrew Saint, in *The Image of the Architect*, later declared that "a fantasy such as *The Fountainhead*, . . . glorifies architectural egoism, misconstrues constructional reality and insults the practicing intelligence of designers". . . . The critic Charles Silver shrewdly blamed the intransigent Rand for the disaster and concluded that once her screenplay was accepted, the movie was doomed: "The great problem with *The Fountainhead* arises from Miss Rand's script of which she was so proud, Warners so indulgent, and Vidor so tolerant. It was one of the worst pieces of scenario-writing in film history, so horrendous in its soft-minded polemics, blatant absurdities and tasteless excesses that it fails to achieve even camp entertainment value."[1639]

The unarticulated premise behind the universal condemnation of the film, including its "ludicrous sexuality," arose from that fact that Rand had violated an icon of American identity by turning Cooper into a crypto Jew. Rand said that Cooper's "physical appearance" was "exactly right,"[1640] but in concentrating on his appearance Rand had omitted the spiritual dimensions which his American soul radiated through that face which had made Cooper appealing as the classic American.

Meyers claims that the quarry scene was Jewish because it was:

> influenced by Jacob Epstein's famous Rock-Drill sculpture of 1913, which has the same force and passion as Roark's character and illuminates his

---

1637 Meyers, *Gary Cooper: American Hero*, p. 220.
1638 Meyers, *Gary Cooper: American Hero*, p. 220.
1639 Meyers, *Gary Cooper: American Hero*, p. 221.
1640 Meyers, *Gary Cooper: American Hero*, p. 221.

ultramodern buildings. Epstein's "robot, itself nearly seven feet high, stood on the drill's tripod of stilts, bringing the whole work to more than nine feet." When first exhibited in 1916, the masked, jutting head and stylized torso, with one hanging right-angled arm, were reduced in size but strengthened in power. Describing this "terrifying metal object, mindless as the machine that drills ... and clad in the armour of a warrior," Epstein said: "I've rendered this subject in a manner that gives the utmost driving force of hard, relentless, steel-like power." In 1955 Ezra Pound named a late section of the Cantos after Epstein's Rock-Drill in order to "imply the necessary resistance" in hammering across his violent message.[1641]

Roark stands for Rand's ideal of mechanical, almost inhuman intellectual and physical power—a force that can and must overwhelm inferior beings. Like Carl Foreman's portrayal of Will Kane, Rand portrayed Roark as a member of "the lonely crowd" which held the average American in contempt, something which becomes apparent in the jury scene, during which:

> Roark—jaw thrust forward and hands in his pockets—emphasizes "innteg-grity." He rhetorically asks "has man any right to exist if he refuses to serve society?" and claims that the designer of the buildings has a right to destroy them: "The great creators— the thinkers, the artists, the scientists, the inventors— stood alone against the men of their time. Every great new thought was opposed. Every great new invention was denounced. But the men of unborrowed vision went ahead. They fought, they suffered and they paid. But they won."[1642]

When Frank Capra cast Cooper in the trial scene in *Mr. Deeds*, or when he cast James Stewart in the jury scene in *Mr. Smith Goes to Washington*, the hero, although initially misunderstood, finally connected with the American public because both shared a common morality which was still part of American identity. Ayn Rand's assault on that morality, which was the only thing which anchored American identity in the real world, doomed *The Fountainhead* from its inception. Americans stayed away from *The Fountainhead* in droves, as Sam Goldwyn would have said, recognizing that "Everything in this Nietzschean fairy tale—Dominique's emotional somersaults, Roark's explosive violence, Wynand's unmotivated suicide and the jury's freakish decision—is determined by Rand's dogmatic thesis,"[1643] because it was obvious that she, like Carl Foreman and Walter Lippmann, held the *goyim*, their term for the common man, in contempt.

1641 Meyers, *Gary Cooper: American Hero*, p. 218.
1642 Meyers, *Gary Cooper: American Hero*, p. 219.
1643 Meyers, *Gary Cooper: American Hero*, p. 220.

Part III: The Return of the Satanic Wilderness

After World War II, Hemingway and Cooper converged, thanks to Hollywood and Time/Life into a composite icon of what it meant to be an American:

> High Noon, Cooper's greatest film, had opened in New York in July 1952; *The Old Man and the Sea*, Hemingway's most popular novel, had been serialized in *Life* that September. Both actor and artist, two of the preeminent image makers of the twentieth century, had forged a modern masculine style. Kenneth Lynn noted the similarities between the heroic characters that Cooper played and Hemingway created: "Just as Will Kane has to do, Santiago sets out alone to do battle, against an adversary that turns out to be the most formidable of his career. And once again like Kane, he both wins and loses, for the flesh of his record-breaking marlin is totally devoured by sharks."[1644]

As part of his feud with Faulkner, Hemingway attacked the author of *The Bear* "for taking money to work on the screenplay of Hemingway's novel, *To Have and Have Not*."[1645] Both Cooper and Hemingway were tossed about by the turbulent forces that determined their lives as they moved toward death. Both men stood by helplessly as Hollywood put its alien spin on the American code of identity which they had tried to articulate.

Moral decline was a source of turbulence in their lives. Both men had been granted carte blanche to indulge their passions, and as those passions had grown more imperious, the guilt they inspired sought release in religion, more specifically in the sacraments of the Catholic Church. Burdened by a guilt which Protestantism could not relieve, Hemingway and Cooper converted to Catholicism at the behest of their second wives, both of whom were very wealthy. After arriving as a foreign correspondent in Paris, whose temptations wrecked his first marriage, Hemingway "undertook a second, more formal conversion process in preparation for marriage to his second wife, devout Catholic Pauline Pfeiffer."[1646]

Hemingway's first conversion to Catholicism took place on the battlefield during World War I when an Austrian mortar shell left him riddled with 200 metal fragments and on the verge of death. After an Italian priest discovered his body, he baptized him and gave him the last rites. Hemingway later described the experience:

> A big Austrian trench mortar bomb of the type that used to be called ash cans, exploded in the darkness. I died then. I felt my soul or something come right out of my body, like you'd pull a silk handkerchief out of a

---

[1644] Meyers, *Gary Cooper: American Hero*, p. 315.

[1645] Meyers, *Gary Cooper: American Hero*, p. 317.

[1646] Robert Inchausti, "The Troubled Catholicism of Ernest Hemingway," Angelus, April 20, 2021, https://angelusnews.com/arts-culture/the-troubled-catholicism-of-ernest-hemingway/

pocket by one corner. It flew around and then came back and went in again and I wasn't dead anymore.[1647]

Ever since Hemingway's soul returned to his body, Hemingway's Catholicism has puzzled biographers, who generally bring their own religious beliefs (or lack thereof) to bear on Hemingway in lieu of actually dealing with the complexity of his faith. Following Carlos Baker, John Beaumont lists a number of distinct phases in Hemingway's spiritual development beginning with his youthful period of "more or less cheerful Protestant Christianity" which lasted from 1908 to 1917, followed by "a period of bitter rejection of Protestantism and discovery of Catholicism and an awakening to an aesthetic sense centered on ritual and ceremony joined with a deepening engagement with the sacrament sense of experience and the incarnational patterns of the Catholic Church" which lasted from 1917 to 1925. Beaumont characterizes the period from 1925 to 1937 as "a period of rather intense Catholicity" coinciding with his marriage to the devout Catholic Pauline Pfeiffer.[1648]

In the wake of his near-death experience in the trenches of World War I, Hemingway became a "super Catholic,"[1649] but his initial enthusiasm soon disappeared under the weight of vices he was unable or unwilling to control. Ernest Hemingway could have been the poster boy for American Catholic identity, but he could never align his beliefs with his behavior. Hemingway never described himself as a Catholic writer, because, as he pointed out to Father Vincent Donavan, "I know the importance of setting an example — and I have never set a good example."[1650]

Unable to follow the tenets of the Catholic faith, Hemingway invented a "Code," not unlike Wister's cowboy code, as his "true religion."[1651] That code "provided rules for living a life of rectitude and dignity in an otherwise meaningless universe"[1652] which many Americans found convincing as a substitute for the etiolated Protestantism which had proven inadequate on the frontier. Unfortunately, Hemingway could not adhere to his own code.

As a result, he slipped deeper and deeper into the depression which eventually led to his suicide. The Catholic Church could provide salvation to sinners like Hemingway, but it could not provide a paradigm of American Catholic identity without help from writers like Hemingway, who couldn't do it either because in spite of the zeal following his conversion, he didn't think

---

1647 Robert Inchausti, "The Troubled Catholicism of Ernest Hemingway," Angelus, April 20, 2021, https://angelusnews.com/arts-culture/the-troubled-catholicism-of-ernest-hemingway/

1648 John Beaumont, *The Mississippi Flows into the Tiber* (South Bend, IN: Fidelity Press, 2014), p. 382.

1649 Inchausti, "The Troubled Catholicism of Ernest Hemingway."

1650 Inchausti, "The Troubled Catholicism of Ernest Hemingway."

1651 Inchausti, "The Troubled Catholicism of Ernest Hemingway."

1652 Inchausti, "The Troubled Catholicism of Ernest Hemingway."

Part III: The Return of the Satanic Wilderness

like a Catholic. No matter how sincere he was in following Catholic devotional practices, like giving his Nobel Prize medal to Our Lady of Pilar in Cuba, he continued to lapse into sin. Hemingway was a stoic in public, because "his subsequent divorces and additional marriages, drunken brawling, domestic abuse, poison pen letters, paranoia, megalomania, and habitual womanizing" convinced him that "he couldn't live up to the responsibility" of being a public Catholic.[1653]

In February 1936, during his period of "intense Catholicity," Hemingway got into a fist fight with the distinguished poet Wallace Stevens in Key West, Florida.[1654] The fight ended when Stevens landed a punch to Hemingway's jaw which broke two bones in his hand but did nothing to Hemingway's jaw. In one of his many letters, Hemingway gave a humorous recounting of the incident, which laid Stevens up in bed for five days, and swore everyone who heard about the incident from him to secrecy, but the story, predictably, spread as part of his legendary persona. To complicate this story further, Wallace Stevens, arguably one of the greatest American poets of the 20th century converted to Catholicism on his death bed after dealing cryptically with Catholic metaphysics and the rejection of Romantic skepticism in his poetry.

During Hemingway's period of "confusion, aridity" and "dark night of the soul," which lasted from 1937 to 1947, Hemingway completed his novel about the Spanish Civil War, *For Whom the Bell Tolls*, which appeared in February 1940 and which many consider his best work, but his mind went fallow during World War II. Serving as a war correspondent who jeopardized the lives of other war correspondents by carrying a gun, Hemingway added war crimes to his usual list of vices when he murdered a number of unarmed German prisoners of war while in northern France during 1944.[1655] In one of his letters, Hemingway talks about how he shot a German prisoner of war after unsuccessfully interrogating him:

> One time I killed a very snotty SS kraut who, when I told him I would kill him unless he revealed what his escape route signs were said: You will not kill me, the kraut stated. Because you are afraid to and because you are a race of mongrel degenerates. Besides it is against the Geneva Convention. What a mistake you made, brother, I told him and shot him three times in the belly fast and then, when he went down on his knees,

---

1653 Inchausti, "The Troubled Catholicism of Ernest Hemingway."

1654 Olivia Rutigliano, "That Time Wallace Stevens Punched Ernest Hemingway in the Face, https://crimereads.com/that-time-wallace-stevens-punched-ernest-hemingway-in-the-face/

1655 Ernest Hemingway, *Selected Letters 1917-1961*, edited by Carlos Baker (New York: Scribner and Sons, 1981), p. 672.

shot him on the topside so his brains came out of his mouth or I guess it was his nose. The next SS I interrogated talked wonderfully."[1656]

Carlos Baker included the story in his biography, adding by way of exculpation that Hemingway may have been bragging about things that never happened. Either way, Hemingway's moral deterioration was having serious consequences for both his writing and those around him. Nonetheless, when Hemingway heard about Gary Cooper's desire to become a Catholic, he put aside his public stoicism and encouraged Cooper to convert, even though he disapproved of his wife's influence and Cooper's love of money. Hemingway felt that: "Cooper loved money more than most people love God. He believed Cooper had converted to please his wife and felt rather bitter about it because he had done precisely the same thing when he married Pauline Pfeiffer in 1927."[1657]

Gary Cooper became a Catholic in April 1959 when he was suffering from the cancer that would eventually kill him but which left him still well enough to do three films and go on a government-sponsored trip to the Soviet Union. From September 15 to 27, five months after his conversion, Cooper accompanied Henry Cabot Lodge during Nikita Khrushchev's tour of the United States "to defend the American way of life."[1658] In the fall of that year, he made his last picture, *The Naked Edge*:[1659]

> Cooper had never been an observant Christian, though many friends believed he had a deeply spiritual side. Now, his deteriorating health and the ever-present danger of death during surgery, as well as regrets about his personal behavior, led this solitary, reserved and reflective man to think seriously about religion. In Hollywood great stars rarely concerned themselves with spiritual matters, but Cooper, a modern Don Juan, repented his sins and mended his ways. Maria said that her father rarely discussed his conversion with his family and that she and Rocky, his wife, never put any pressure on him to join the church for their sake. He had never gone to church with them, apart from mass at Christmas and Easter, and always looked on religion as their affair. But one Sunday, instead of reading the newspapers in bed, he suddenly said, "Hey, girls, wait for me," and began attending church regularly. Maria later said: "I guess that maybe on some of his many drives or walks or times alone in the mountains he began to feel there was something that the Catholic religion had to offer that he wanted. He didn't talk about it very much

---

1656 Letters, p. 672.
1657 Meyers, *Gary Cooper: American Hero*, p. 318.
1658 Meyers, *Gary Cooper: American Hero*, p. 301.
1659 Meyers, *Gary Cooper: American Hero*, p. 291.

PART III: THE RETURN OF THE SATANIC WILDERNESS

to us. Again, he was a very private man and it was his private affair, but I know he did get a lot of strength and comfort from it."[1660]

Rocky had approached Father Harold Ford, who was stationed at the Beverly Hills Church of the Good Shepherd, stating "I want to make my husband a Catholic" and then asking "What can we do about bringing him into the church."[1661] After talking to Father Ford about the tenets of the Catholic faith, Cooper was baptized on April 9, 1959. Dolores Hart, who became a nun after a career in acting, was convinced that his conversion was "deeply felt and absolutely sincere."[1662] Even if his mother wished he hadn't converted, no one doubted Cooper's sincerity, which comes out in his own account of his conversion. Cooper saw Catholicism was a way transcend the "egoism and selfishness" which Hollywood had imposed on him as the representative American:

> Last winter, when I began trying to find out how to be less of a bum, I saw that religion is a sort of check up on yourself, a kind of patterned way of behaving. As I saw it, if a fellow goes to church, any church, and tries to straighten out his mind, it sure helps. After I digested that idea, I began thinking how our family has always done everything together.... This past winter I began to dwell a little more on what's been in my mind for a long time. I began thinking, "Coop, old boy, you owe somebody something for all your good fortune."[1663]

Cooper's mother Alice was of a different opinion: "Gary will always be a Protestant, no matter what other religious influences enter in his life,"[1664] and there is a sense in which that was true because a death bed conversion did not allow him to incorporate his Catholicism into the persona of the American which had made him famous.

Hemingway and Cooper died within six weeks of each other:

> As one man became physically sick, the other was prey to mental illness. In the summer and fall of 1960, while Cooper was recovering, Hemingway began to suffer from obsessions, delusions, paranoid fears of poverty and persecution, inability to work, severe depression and suicidal impulses. In late November 1960 he entered the Mayo Clinic and had a series of shock treatments, which obliterated his memory and intensified his depression. In late December, while Hemingway endured purgatory in the Mayo [clinic], Rocky Cooper was told that Gary's cancer was fatal.[1665]

1660 Meyers, *Gary Cooper: American Hero*, p. 292.
1661 Meyers, *Gary Cooper: American Hero*, p. 293.
1662 Meyers, *Gary Cooper: American Hero*, p. 295.
1663 Meyers, *Gary Cooper: American Hero*, p. 294.
1664 Meyers, *Gary Cooper: American Hero*, p. 295.
1665 Meyers, *Gary Cooper: American Hero*, p. 318.

Walking with a Bible and a Gun

During the agony he experienced while dying of terminal cancer, Cooper took solace in his newfound Catholicism. After a particularly severe spasm of pain had passed, Cooper picked up a crucifix which had been lying on the bed table, put it on the pillow next to his head, and immediately thought of Hemingway, who was suffering from a different sort of pain.

"Please give Papa a message," Cooper said to his wife, "It's important and you mustn't forget because I'll not be talking to him again. Tell him . . . that time I wondered if I made the right decision—he moved the crucifix a little closer so that it touched his cheek—'tell him it was the best thing I ever did.'"[1666]

After receiving the last rites from Monsignor Daniel Sullivan, who visited him every day during the last two weeks of his life, Cooper died at home with his family on Saturday, May 13, 1961 at 12:47 p.m.[1667] Less than two months later, Hemingway died at his own hand on July 2, 1961. Neither man epitomized the Catholic Church to which they had converted. Neither man left behind as his legacy an icon of American Catholic identity, and in a sense that was not necessary because John F. Kennedy became America's first Catholic president in the year that both iconic Americans died. Camelot is the name attached to the aura which Kennedy's presidency projected. What could have become of it remains unknown because Kennedy was assassinated by a group of conspirators which included the CIA, which felt threatened because Kennedy wanted to end the Cold War, and the Israelis, who saw Kennedy as a hindrance to their desire to acquire nuclear weapons. The Protestantism which gave America its identity had evaporated to the point where only its Satanic gist was left behind in the alembic of history. The murder of John F. Kennedy was a *coup d'etat* which ushered in a new Satanic era, which is with us still. "For more than two hundred years," Samuel Huntington tells us, "Americans defined their identity in opposition to Catholicism. The Catholic other was first fought and excluded and then opposed and discriminated against,"[1668] and at a moment when Catholicism had reached the highest office of the land and found expression in a man who epitomized it with charm and grace, Catholic identity was cut down by an assassin's bullet as a warning to anyone who thought that American identity could be amended in light of the Catholic faith.

Within a month of Kennedy's election, *Time* magazine had already shown the way forward by putting John Courtney Murray, S.J. on its cover as the stereotype of a Catholic acceptable to those in power. Murray, who was close to Harry Luce and even closer to his wife Claire Boothe Luce, gave a two-word warning to fellow Catholics in the accompanying article: "No boycotts,"

[1666] Meyers, *Gary Cooper: American Hero*, p. 320.
[1667] Meyers, *Gary Cooper: American Hero*, p. 320.
[1668] Huntington, *Who Are We?*, p. 92.

Part III: The Return of the Satanic Wilderness

he wrote referring to the success which the Legion of Decency had had in keeping Hollywood Jews in line. Within five years, Hollywood broke the Production Code with the release of its Holocaust porn flick *The Pawnbroker*, and America headed down a road of deep alienation from itself because no one was either willing or able to tell them what had happened to their country. American Catholics have been the victims of identity theft ever since.

Huntington portrayed the trauma which followed the assassination of John F. Kennedy as an identity crisis which has become chronic by invoking the image of Gary Cooper, who "emerged as the icon of American identity" in 1950, the *annus mirabilis* Huntington described as "the perceived zenith of American national integration." Since 1950, "cultural and political fragmentation has increased" and "conflict emanating from intensified ethnic and religious consciousness poses the main current challenge to the American national myth."[1669]

American national identity, Huntington continues, "peaked politically with the rallying of Americans to their country and its cause in World War II." But "it peaked symbolically" when the nation's first Catholic president issued the challenge "Ask not what your country can do for you—ask what you can do for your country."[1670] At President Kennedy inauguration in January 1961, Robert Frost recited a poem which: hailed the "heroic deeds" of America's founding that with God's "approval" ushered in "a new order of the ages": *Our venture in revolution and outlawry Has justified itself in freedom's story Right down to now in glory upon glory....* America, Frost concluded, was entering a new "golden age of poetry and power."[1671]

An assassin's bullet aborted the arrival of that golden age. Poetry disappeared as a force in American life, but power, as Shakespeare predicted increased to the point where everything became a function of imperial will. Once everything included itself in power, power degenerated into will, and will into appetite, which consumed itself.

Hollywood continued to produce icons of American identity. Clint Eastwood followed in Gary Cooper's footsteps when Dirty Harry took off his badge and threw it into the water where the serial killer had drowned. Clint Eastwood had a certain nobility, but he was soon followed by Charles Bronson, whose repulsive *Death Wish* movies led to Bernard Goetz shooting an unarmed black man in a New York subway train, which led to Kyle Rittenhouse gunning down members of Antifa in Kenosha, Wisconsin and the couple in St. Louis who got arrested for an armed, if inconsequential, confrontation with Black Lives Matter on their front lawn. The gun had become, as Faulkner pointed out in *The Bear*, "dismembered," which is to

---

1669 Huntington, *Who Are We?*, p. 137.
1670 Huntington, *Who Are We?*, p. 141.
1671 Huntington, *Who Are We?*, p. 6.

Walking with a Bible and a Gun

say disconnected from the American icon which had given it meaning. Now those without identity tried to reverse the process by deriving their identity from the gun. America has two options now: an Americanized Catholicism, as Huntington put it, or the Satanic gist of Protestantism. *Non datur tertius.*

Chapter 46

Clint Eastwood:
Dirty Harry and the Race Issue

Clint Eastwood succeeded Gary Cooper as the highest paid male lead in Hollywood. More importantly, he succeeded Cooper as the paradigm of what it meant to be an American during a period when the competition for that honor was still stiff. Eastwood came to that role naturally. Unlike John Wayne, his major competitor following Cooper's death, Eastwood could trace his forebears on his father's side back to the middle of the 18th century, when Lewis Eastwood was born in Long Branch, New Jersey in 1746, just as the first Great Awakening was dying down and a quarter of a century before the outbreak of the Revolutionary War:[1672]

> The Eastwoods were among the early pioneers heading West. Originally Yankees, Puritans and Easterners, family relations spread out and pushed into New York, Ohio, Michigan, Virginia, Illinois, Louisiana, Kansas, Colorado, Nevada, California and Alaska, along the way inscribing their name in the annals of the Revolutionary War, early statehood struggles, the War of 1812, the Civil War and the Gold Rush.[1673]

On his mother's side, Eastwood could trace his ancestors back even farther to "the first settlers of New England,"[1674] who created the Puritan form for what would become the United States when they "organized their lives around land, community, authority and public worship" as it morphed into a unique American identity when its men made contact with the frontier, which eventually gave birth to the cowboy, which Eastwood played to perfection as the archetypal American.

There is no evidence that Eastwood was ever baptized. Nor is there any evidence that he attended church services while growing up in the upper middle-class town of Piedmont, California. When David Frost asked Eastwood about his religious views in the early 1970s, Eastwood "grew

---

1672 Patrick McGilligan, *Clint: The Life and Legend*, Kindle edition, loc. 232.
1673 McGilligan, *Clint: The Life and Legend*, Kindle edition, loc. 62.
1674 McGilligan, *Clint: The Life and Legend*, Kindle edition, loc. 232.

mumbly,"[1675] but eventually professed belief in the religion of Nature. Like the cowboys he portrayed on the silver screen, Eastwood was not a church-going man or as he put it:

> I'm just not a member of an organized religion. But I've always felt very strongly about things, I guess. Especially when I'm out in nature. I guess that's why I've done so many wide-open films out in nature. But religion is, I think, a very personal thing. I've never really discussed it to philosophize out loud about it.[1676]

At this point, Eastwood grew mumbly again:

> I just kind of ... you're sitting on a beautiful mountain, or in the Rocky Mountains, or wherever, and you ... the Grand Canyon is something ... and all of a sudden you can't help but be moved. An awful lot of time has gone by on this planet, and mankind's part of it was all about like that [snaps fingers]. And so you think, "How did that all come to be?" So you can go on forever, within your mind, but it's fun to philosophize on it, as long as you don't, it doesn't drive you to jump off the cliff."[1677]

In 1973, Eastwood told the film critic Gene Siskel that he didn't believe in God.[1678]

> I was born during the Depression, and I was brought up with no specific church. We moved every four or five months during the first 14 years of my life, so I was sent to a different church depending on wherever we lived. Most of them were Protestant, but I went to other churches because my parents wanted me to try to figure out things for myself. They always said, "I just want to expose you to some religious order and see if that's something you like."[1679]

Eastwood then heads back to the Grand Canyon:

> So, although my religious training was not really specific, I do feel spiritual things. If I stand on the side of the Grand Canyon and look down, it moves me in some way. . . . It would be wonderful to talk with my parents again, who are, of course, deceased. It makes the idea of death much less scary. But then again, if you think that nothing happens after you die, maybe it makes you live life better. Maybe you're supposed to do the best you can by the gift you're given of life and that alone.[1680]

1675 McGilligan, *Clint: The Life and Legend*, Kindle edition, loc. 538.
1676 McGilligan, *Clint: The Life and Legend*, Kindle edition, loc. 538-45.
1677 McGilligan, *Clint: The Life and Legend*, Kindle edition, loc. 538-45.
1678 "Clint Eastwood," *Wikipedia: The Free Encyclopedia*, https://en.wikipedia.org/wiki/Clint_Eastwood
1679 McGilligan, *Clint: The Life and Legend*, Kindle edition, loc. 538-45.
1680 McGilligan, *Clint: The Life and Legend*, Kindle edition, loc. 538-45.

Part III: The Return of the Satanic Wilderness

If we take baptism as the measure of faith, or the ability to recite the Apostles Creed, or fidelity to marriage vows, virtually no one in Hollywood believed in God in 1973. Eastwood's profession of faith was practically identical to the cowboy religion which Owen Wister articulated in *The Virginian*, which made him a "conservative" holdout in a world run by increasingly transgressive revolutionary Jews, now reveling the fact that they had broken the Catholic Production Code and determined to expand the tradition of smuggling T & A onto the silver screen.

Eastwood was an early victim of the sexual revolution. Unlike his parents, who were "happily married" and provided an "ideal home" for Clint and his siblings,[1681] Clint lost his virginity at the age of 14 and became a rebellious teenager in the mold of James Dean, who was interested in "fast cars and easy women."[1682] During the early part of his career, Eastwood was frequently compared to Gary Cooper, a persona which he avidly adopted. Before heading off for interviews, Eastwood would tell his buddies that he was "going to give them a little of my Gary Cooper."[1683] Eastwood's philosophy as an actor was "Don't just do something, stand there." When pressed by directors to be more animated, Eastwood would say, "Gary Cooper wasn't afraid to do nothing."[1684]

Like Gary Cooper and John Wayne, previous icons of American identity, Eastwood became a lifeguard, which served him in good stead when flying in a the plane that crashed into the Pacific Ocean, necessitating a four mile swim to shore.[1685] Being a lifeguard also allowed him to pick up chicks, which contributed to the "Don Juanism that grew to dominate his private life."[1686] The bad sexual habits Eastwood acquired as a teenager soon began to wreak havoc in his life, forcing him to leave Seattle because he had "knocked up" one of his many girlfriends. With the help of a loan from his parents, Eastwood extricated himself from that mess by procuring the first of many abortions he would impose on his wives and paramours. Killing his first child would have a lasting effect on Eastwood:

> In later years Clint liked to portray this episode, to the very few people who ever heard of it, as personally devastating. He indicated he never got over this regrettable experience. The woman left behind in Seattle would always be the "true love" stolen away from him by life's unfair circumstances. It crushed his heart.[1687]

1681 McGilligan, *Clint: The Life and Legend*, Kindle edition, loc. 709.
1682 McGilligan, *Clint: The Life and Legend*, Kindle edition, loc. 709.
1683 McGilligan, *Clint: The Life and Legend*, Kindle edition, loc. 1971.
1684 McGilligan, *Clint: The Life and Legend*, Kindle edition, loc. 2067.
1685 McGilligan, *Clint: The Life and Legend*, Kindle edition, loc. 679.
1686 McGilligan, *Clint: The Life and Legend*, Kindle edition, loc. 709.
1687 McGilligan, *Clint: The Life and Legend*, Kindle edition, loc. 1011.

WALKING WITH A BIBLE AND A GUN

And it turned him into the stoic tough guy who had become the paradigmatic American. Being tough in public was a function of being weak in private which necessitated recourse to guns, which the cowboy/sheriff brandished to protect those who could not protect themselves in a way that compensated for abortion, which is the ultimate expression of weakness in men who can't even stand up for their own offspring. As the sexual revolution ate away at the moral character of American men, they needed an iconic representation of who they wanted to be, and Clint Eastwood arrived just in time to help them negotiate the transition from family man to libertine which took place at the end of the 20th and beginning of the 21st century.

When American identity disappeared from the Democratic Party and got replaced by Identity Politics and Critical Race Theory, Clint Eastwood appeared "in frontier apparel" in a way that was "iconic, evoking not only his own ancestral past but America's manifest destiny. The motifs of historical vengeance and flight from civilization gave his Westerns an emotional undertow that the films set in modern times too often lacked."[1688] Eastwood took those bad habits into his first marriage to Margaret Neville Johnson in December 1953, begetting an illegitimate child with another woman during their courtship. Clint seemed "guilt free"[1689] even though he was "a master of duplicity in his private life."[1690] Appearances, however, can be deceiving.

Sergio Leone thought that Eastwood exhibited "a certain, deep insecurity towards European culture."[1691] By the time Eastwood made the pilgrimage to Rome which had become obligatory for American artists, he had become "the new Gary Cooper" and was "mobbed" by fans demanding his autograph as he walked down the Via Veneto, where he was "wined and dined and treated like a king."[1692] Federico Fellini could have turned Eastwood's arrival in the eternal city into a scene in *La Dolce Vita*, but the experience was not conducive to meditating on the penitents going to confession at St. Peter's Basilica, as Nathaniel Hawthorne had done a century earlier.

In *Hang 'Em High*, the name of Clinton's character was Cooper.[1693] Eastwood not only inherited the mantle of Gary Cooper, he carried it into the future after Cooper's death by becoming "Hollywood's only post-Sixties cowboy star."[1694] Eastwood got his start as an actor by playing cowboys in an era of revolutionary change in the television series *Rawhide*, which ran from January 9, 1959 to December 7, 1965. His portrayal of Rowdy Yates in that

---

1688 McGilligan, *Clint: The Life and Legend*, Kindle edition, loc. 4950-1.
1689 McGilligan, *Clint: The Life and Legend*, Kindle edition, loc. 1089.
1690 McGilligan, *Clint: The Life and Legend*, Kindle edition, loc. 1099.
1691 McGilligan, *Clint: The Life and Legend*, Kindle edition, loc. 9250.
1692 McGilligan, *Clint: The Life and Legend*, Kindle edition, loc. 102701.
1693 McGilligan, *Clint: The Life and Legend*, Kindle edition, loc. 2973.
1694 McGilligan, *Clint: The Life and Legend*, Kindle edition, loc. 3511-4.

Part III: The Return of the Satanic Wilderness

series led to an invitation from Sergio Leone to portray the man with no name who was the main character in Sergio Leone's spaghetti westerns, which were released in the mid-1960s. Eastwood arrived in Rome to do Sergio Leone's spaghetti western trilogy—*A Fistful of Dollars*, *For A Few Dollars More*, and *The Good, The Bad, And The Ugly*—during and following the collapse of the Production Code when Hollywood films became the cutting edge of transgression against sexual morality. Eastwood was no exception to that rule, "heightening the sex and violence quotient to accommodate America's contemporary mores."[1695]

The decline of sexual morality both personally and culturally would have an effect on the cowboy icon which came out in story conferences when Eastwood claimed that he was "sick of nice Hopalong Cassidy heroes and all that malarkey."[1696] Eastwood's cowboy would be a "heroic bastard," an image which corresponded to the decline in morality that Eastwood personified in his personal life while hiding it from his public by hiring public relations firms. This required a delicate balancing act which tried to introduce realism while not going too far and turning the cowboy into "a loser." Eastwood felt that Dustin Hoffmann, who co-starred in *Midnight Cowboy*, and Al Pacino "play losers very well:

> But my audience likes to be in there vicariously with a winner. That isn't always popular with the critics. My characters have sensitivity and vulnerabilities, but they're still winners. I don't pretend to understand losers. When I read a script about a loser, I think of people in life who are losers and they seem to want it that way. It's a compulsive philosophy with them. Winners tell themselves, "I'm as bright as the next person. I can do it. Nothing can stop me."[1697]

By the time he made *Dirty Harry*, Eastwood was "possessed by the demon sex beast."[1698] As a result, it was difficult to discern which side of the sexual revolution he represented:

> In *Dirty Harry*, Clint, staking out a rooftop in an attempt to trap a killer, inadvertently spies on a nude girl welcoming a couple to an evening of sex à trois. 'Harry,' he murmurs to himself, 'you owe it to yourself to live a little.' *Tightrope* would give Clint's libido that opportunity. A script which put his character into cheap bars, strip clubs and the world of prostitutes had an immediate attraction to a man who sometimes took his own sexual pleasures voyeuristically. In private, Clint had succumbed to the fashionable bedroom sport of home pornography, taking advantage of newly sophisticated and lightweight video equipment to record his

---

1695 McGilligan, *Clint: The Life and Legend*, Kindle edition, loc. 3069.
1696 McGilligan, *Clint: The Life and Legend*, Kindle edition, loc. 3133.
1697 McGilligan, *Clint: The Life and Legend*, Kindle edition, loc. 1074.
1698 McGilligan, *Clint: The Life and Legend*, Kindle edition, loc. 3784.

lovemaking with Sondra Locke. For Wes Block [hero of *Tightrope*], sex was the outlet for inner turmoil. Off camera, likewise, Clint threw himself into an affair with flame-haired actress Jamie Rose, from TV's *Falcon Crest*. She was playing a small part in *Tightrope* as the first murdered prostitute.[1699]

Dirty Harry was a political film about a San Francisco cop who is constantly thwarted in his attempt to bring a serial killer to justice by a "political" District Attorney and an equally political judge who used the recent *Escobedo and Miranda* Supreme Court decisions to let killers loose to kill and rape innocent 14-year-old girls and busloads of even younger children.

Dirty Harry is, however, radically ambivalent when it comes to matters venereal. Director Don Siegel portrays the moral decline in San Francisco by showing graphic shots of the topless bars that Carol Doda made famous, but in doing this he contributes to the very moral decline, symbolized by the R-rated movie, he is complaining about.

The same thing happened to conservatism, the political ideology which took the cowboy as its identity marker. San Francisco gave birth to the new conservatism known as libertarianism in the 1970s when homosexuals like Robert Sirico and the late Justin Raimondo converted to Austrian School economics. The French philosopher Michel Foucault, another homosexual, underwent the same conversion, spending nights getting tortured in bath houses like the Mineshaft while spending his days teaching the theories of Friedrich Hayek and Ludwig Von Mises at the University of California at Berkeley.

Dirty Harry epitomizes that ambivalence by focusing on the *Miranda* decision as the source of the problem and ignoring the decline in sexual morality which was, according to the film, the hidden grammar of violence. Sex was the unacknowledged cause of mayhem and anarchy in San Francisco which made Harry Callahan's life so difficult that he couldn't even finish his hot dog without having to first apprehend a band of Negro bank robbers. The decline of sexual morality was best symbolized, as Norman Mailer pointed out in his 1957 essay "The White Negro" by Negro Jazz. Eastwood loved Jazz and even directed a biopic about bebop saxophonist Charlie Parker, but, like the cowboy, the Negro had become once more a victim of identity theft at the hands of the Jews who had controlled Black identity beginning with the Harlem Renaissance and its weaponization of Jazz as the theme music for sexual liberation. During Eastman's career as an actor, the paradigm of Black identity changed from the noble civil rights advocate Martin Luther King to Eldridge Cleaver, Huey Newton and other members of the Black Panthers, a criminal conspiracy which was the creation of David Horowitz and the neo-Marxists at *Ramparts Magazine*. Horowitz and the editorial staff at *Ramparts*

1699 McGilligan, *Clint: The Life and Legend*, Kindle edition, loc. 6838-42.

Part III: The Return of the Satanic Wilderness

had created Eldridge Cleaver as the paradigm of the new Negro, who loved raping white women, and he along with Huey Newton were literally getting away with murder, as the Jewish movement lawyer Fay Stender would discover. Stender would die at the hands of the very group she defended legally after becoming Newton's paramour while he was still in prison.

Eastwood epitomized the conservative backlash by having Harry Callahan single-handedly stop a bank robbery with the help of five bullets from his .44 Magnum handgun. The gun functioned as a magic wand which miraculously solved the race problem when Harry Callahan faced down a wounded bank robber and gave his iconic speech:

> I know what you're thinking. Did he fire six bullets or only five? Well, to tell you the truth, I kinda lost track myself. But seeing how the '44 Magnum is the most powerful handgun in the world, and that it would blow your head clear off, you got to ask yourself—do I feel lucky today? Well, do ya, punk?[1700]

Dirty Harry showed conservative Americans that even if they aborted their children, they could still stand up to uppity Negroes as long as they had the hardware that backed up their words. *Dirty Harry* has compensation written all over it. Eastwood had released "a depth charge in the context of American politics," because every time Black Panther Party members "went to court in Oakland, New Orleans, Chicago, New Haven and New York City, [they] earned mistrials or acquittals"[1701] thanks to the Supreme Court's *Miranda* decision. At a time when the "police were being challenged on the streets and in the courts, [and] the United States government was losing the Vietnam War,"[1702] Harry Callahan "helped quench people's thirst for 'vengeance,'" which the actor linked to 'a great feeling of impotence and guilt' over two national crises: Vietnam and Watergate." Faced with humiliation at home and abroad, "America needed a hero, a winner,"[1703] and it found one in Harry Callahan, who "seemed to embody a resurgent America."[1704]

The answer to America's problems was "conservatism," as embodied by Richard Nixon and Ronald Reagan, both of whom came from California and found a reaffirmation of their identity in Clint Eastwood. Like John Wayne and Clint Eastwood, two of their most ardent supporters, Ronald Reagan had played cowboys in movies. If Americans would only return to their cowboy identity, pick up their guns, and take the law into their own hands, as Dirty Harry the latter-day cowboy turned detective had done, America could solve its problems and enter into a golden age.

1700 McGilligan, *Clint: The Life and Legend*, Kindle edition, loc. 3870.
1701 McGilligan, *Clint: The Life and Legend*, Kindle edition, loc. 3777.
1702 McGilligan, *Clint: The Life and Legend*, Kindle edition, loc. 3878.
1703 McGilligan, *Clint: The Life and Legend*, Kindle edition, loc. 3882.
1704 McGilligan, *Clint: The Life and Legend*, Kindle edition, loc. 3883.

Walking with a Bible and a Gun

Demonstrating the cross-fertilization between art and politics which Eastwood's films enabled, his biographer referred to *Honkytonk Man* as "a Republican movie," that sounded "Reaganesque" when Eastwood "lectured interviewers, 'Today we live in a welfare-oriented society, and people expect more, more from Big Daddy government, more from Big Daddy charity. That philosophy never got you anywhere. I worked for every crust of bread I ever ate.'"[1705]

When Eastwood ran for mayor of Carmel, he handed out jelly beans, invoking the favorite candy of President Ronald Reagan. Reagan reciprocated by congratulating Eastwood when he became mayor of Carmel, evoking their common Hollywood background. "What's an actor who's played in a movie with a monkey doing in politics?" Reagan, who had starred next to a chimpanzee in *Bedtime for Bonzo*, asked Eastwood, who shared the screen with an orangutang in *Any Which Way But Loose*.

After its release in December 1971, *Dirty Harry* "quickly shot to number one at the box-office. Its eventual $53 million gross would almost triple the revenue of any of his previous American films and help make Clint, for the first time, in 1972, the top moneymaking star in Hollywood."[1706] Eastwood later identified the Supreme Court's *Miranda vs. Arizona* decision, which protected criminals at the expense of public safety, as the main force behind his box office success. Corporation men who had neutered themselves with contraception and felt burdened by red tape found vicarious relief from their frustrations when Dirty Harry pulled out his .44 Magnum and took the law into his own hands, showing manly American contempt for "mushy academics, stupid prosecutors and judges," but most of all "inept government officials."[1707] Critics could call him a fascist, but Clint, like the sheriff played by Gary Cooper in *High Noon*, was "obeying a higher law"[1708] and didn't "give a shit."[1709]

Unlike most of Hollywood, which was joined at the hip to the Democratic Party, Eastwood was a Republican vocal in his support of Richard Nixon, calling him a "tough man" who was needed for "where the world was going."[1710] On August 27, 1972, just nine months after the release of Dirty Harry, Eastwood and his wife of the time attended a "star-studded" fundraiser for Nixon at the Western White House in San Clemente, California. In opening remarks that confirmed the synergy which the cowboy enabled by bringing Hollywood and the Republican party together, Nixon told a group

---

1705 McGilligan, *Clint: The Life and Legend*, Kindle edition, loc. 7064.
1706 McGilligan, *Clint: The Life and Legend*, Kindle edition, loc. 3905.
1707 McGilligan, *Clint: The Life and Legend*, Kindle edition, loc. 3862.
1708 McGilligan, *Clint: The Life and Legend*, Kindle edition, loc. 3937.
1709 McGilligan, *Clint: The Life and Legend*, Kindle edition, loc. 3940.
1710 McGilligan, *Clint: The Life and Legend*, Kindle edition, loc. 3964.

Part III: The Return of the Satanic Wilderness

which contained among others John Wayne, Frank Sinatra, Charlton Heston, Lawrence Welk, Jack Warner, Dick Zanuck, Jack Benny, Jimmy Durante, and Zsa Zsa Gabor, "I like my movies made in Hollywood. This is something that is typically American ... something that means a lot in presenting America to the world."[1711] Westerns, Clint opined, agreeing with President Nixon, represented "a period gone by, the pioneer, the loner operating by himself, without benefit of society. It usually has something to do with some sort of vengeance; he takes care of the vengeance himself, doesn't call the police. Like Robin Hood. It's the last masculine frontier."[1712]

One year after Nixon's fundraiser, the Supreme Court redefined masculinity as the right to kill when it handed down *Roe v. Wade*, striking down the nation's laws criminalizing abortion. Masculinity now meant not the ability to have children but rather the ability to kill them when deemed inconvenient. Eastwood's gun-toting public persona provided compensation for his private persona, which had recourse to the abortion curette as his preferred way of killing.

The cowboy, as the icon of what it meant to be an American, became a dark figure now the outlaw more than the sheriff, and politically conservative Hollywood provided no resistance to that transformation. In fact, former movie star Ronald Reagan epitomized the transformation; as governor of California he signed a bill legalizing abortion in 1967, his first year in office. Reagan presided over the sexual revolution in California until he left office in 1971, the year Eastwood played Dirty Harry. Indeed, Ronald Reagan took Eastwood as his political mentor lifting a line from *Sudden Impact* in March 1983, telling Congress, which was threatening to raise taxes, "Go ahead, make my day!"[1713]

Eastwood was a political ally of John Wayne. Both were involved with the Republican Party in California. Although both men were iconic cowboys, they disagreed on the meaning of cowboy identity. In the early 1970s, Wayne sent a letter to Eastwood criticizing *High Plains Drifter* as antithetical to "what the American frontier—and the American people—represented."[1714] Eastwood disagreed with Wayne, who was now "a fading hero."[1715] In *High Plains Drifter*, Eastwood was trying to "enunciate an anti–John Wayne philosophy of Westerns—a philosophy defined less by what it stood for than what it stood against."[1716] Eastwood made a stab at articulating the philosophy

---

1711 McGilligan, *Clint: The Life and Legend*, Kindle edition, loc. 3970.
1712 McGilligan, *Clint: The Life and Legend*, Kindle edition, loc. 4010.
1713 McGilligan, *Clint: The Life and Legend*, Kindle edition, loc. 6331.
1714 McGilligan, *Clint: The Life and Legend*, Kindle edition, loc. 4983.
1715 McGilligan, *Clint: The Life and Legend*, Kindle edition, loc. 4991.
1716 McGilligan, *Clint: The Life and Legend*, Kindle edition, loc. 4992.

Walking with a Bible and a Gun

of the Western on the set of *Heartbreak Ridge,* his Korean War movie, saying, "John Wayne wouldn't shoot a man in the back. But I'm not John Wayne."[1717]

1717 McGilligan, *Clint: The Life and Legend*, Kindle edition, loc. 4994.

Chapter 47

The Moynihan Report

Something similar happened a century later when the Civil Rights Movement, which provided the moral compass for Allen's book, revived abolitionism and became the sacred cause of mainstream Protestantism as it plunged toward the irrelevance which would characterize its major denominations by the turn of the 21st century. That movement allowed Protestant ministers to atone for the racial sins of their congregations, but it also served as a convenient cover for sexual liberation, which was the hidden grammar of a movement which strove to liberate the oppressed Negro. When the Irish Catholic Assistant Secretary of Labor Daniel Patrick Moynihan suggested in 1965 that Negro poverty was a function of sexual immorality, specifically mentioning illegitimacy among blacks, he was roundly vilified as a bigot, which is to say an Irishman profiting illicitly from white privilege.

Leading the opposition to the Moynihan Report were Benjamin Payton, a Negro sociologist and minister, and Robert W. Spike, executive director of the National Council of Churches' Commission on Religion and Race. Suddenly the civil rights leaders who had been positively fulsome in praise of Moynihan's initiative when he first proposed it were undergoing a change of heart.

"My major criticism of the report," said Floyd McKissick, the new director of CORE, "is that it assumes that middle class American values are the correct ones for everyone in America." "Moynihan," McKissick continued evidently unaware that Moynihan came from a broken family, "thinks everyone should have a family structure like his own. Moynihan also emphasizes the negative aspects of the Negroes and then seems to say that it's the individual's fault when it's the damn system that really needs changing."

Clarence Mitchell, of the Washington office of the NAACP, objected to the report because it "implied that it was necessary for the improvement of the Negro community to come from within." Among those who took part in the criticism at an Executive Office Building meeting on October 30 were Whitney Young, who approved of the proposal in the spring, and a young Washington, D.C. activist by the name of Marion Barry. Barry, who would achieve dubious fame of his own 25 years later, when as mayor of Washington, D.C. he would be arrested by federal agents for possession of crack cocaine, was on his way to carving a career as civil rights leader and shake down artist, when it came to federal grants. Given the evidence on his sex life that would come out during his trial, it is not surprising that Barry would object to aid to blacks being tied to "family stability." If those criteria had been enforced, it is unlikely that Barry would have gotten a dime of federal money.

But with hindsight, it's hard to see how anyone would have gotten any money, if those criteria were applied rigorously to the people asking for the grants. Barry was the rule and not the exception. The Left saw in the Moynihan Report a roll-back of its sexual freedoms. And, in short, it was afraid. They could not confront the problem honestly because the problems under discussion were their own. In the end, the Left decided to drop back and punt. They backed away from any initiative that dealt with sexual morality and asked for government money instead. In addition to asking that the issue of family stability be struck from the agenda, they decided to ask the president for an "Economic Development Budget for Equal Rights in America" which would cost the country's taxpayers a mere $32 billion per year in 1965 dollars. This move confirmed Johnson in his belief that the only thing the civil rights establishment could do was bitch and moan about white racism and then stick out their hands for government conscience money.

In 1967, after his proposal had been roundly vilified by everyone associated with the Civil Rights Movement, Moynihan expressed a note of ambivalence about the Left. He claimed that "the nation needs the liberal Left" as a "secular conscience," yet he faulted liberals: "This was the point of unparalleled opportunity for the liberal community, and it was exactly the point where that community collapsed." Just why it collapsed Moynihan never explains; however, in retrospect, it is clear that the liberal Left was deeply involved in the same sort of behavior that Moynihan was criticizing in ghetto blacks. The last thing the liberal Left wanted to hear in 1965 was that there were social consequences to sexual misbehavior.

In his *Commentary* postmortem, Moynihan claimed that Robert W. Spike had played a "decisive" role in defeating the notion that black progress was tied to family stability: "The reaction of the liberal Left to the issue of the Negro family was decisive (the Protestant reaction was clearly triggered by it). They would have none of it. No one was going to talk about their poor people that way."

One year after the Moynihan Report had been defeated, Spike was found bludgeoned to death in a newly dedicated campus-ministry building in Columbus, Ohio. Spike, it turns out, was a homosexual and had been murdered by a man he had picked up while in town for the dedication ceremony. In his book *The Freedom Revolution and the Churches*, Spike talked about the men of his generation being confronted: "Their sins rise up to haunt them," he says. "Not since the abolitionist period," he continued, "have the churches and their people become as conscious of their guilt and their need for

Part III: The Return of the Satanic Wilderness

action as in recent months." In an article which appeared in February of the year he died Spike talked about how the Civil Rights movement arose in the '60s, composed of the "long-suffering Negro population" and "large numbers of guilt-stricken whites."[1718] At the heart of Spike's quarrel with the Moynihan Report lay his quarrel with "family stability." "It is no wonder," Spike writes, "that his report is so much resented by Negroes. Faulty generalizations about white and black families are never qualified by any reference to other norms of family stability than having a father in the house."

In retrospect, it is not difficult to see behind Spike's complaint his own "guilt-stricken" reaction to the double life he was leading as homosexual and head of a household and that he was getting his own payoff from this "revolution in human freedom." Or as he said: "A revolution in human freedom cannot be engineered. We cannot tell people they are free and then keep pulling on the almost invisible wires that direct their motion."

In *The Content of Our Character*, Shelby Steele gives a conventional and unconvincing explanation of the concept of "white guilt."[1719] It is unconvincing primarily because the evidence of the times indicates that there was a more convincing explanation of the same phenomenon. Ockham's razor, it seems, should apply in moral matters. With the help of people like Paul Tillich, Spike converted to the values of modernity, probably in the late '40s when he became pastor of Judson Memorial Church in Greenwich Village and an associate of Jack Kerouac and Allen Ginsburg and the other founders of the Beatnik movement. Spike had been living a double life for some time, something which had led to a great deal of personal torment.

In a memoir published in 1973, Spike's son Paul reminisced about his father's tormented life and gives interesting hints about the connection between social activism and the troubled conscience. Paul remembers his father telling him "that Baldwin and others had said to us for the first time, 'You are the man!' We felt a sense of personal guilt, of personal responsibility for the denial of full justice to Negro citizens, resulting in the deterioration of relationships between the races to the place it was in the spring of 1963."[1720] The younger Spike criticizes white involvement in the 1963 March on Washington as "getting a contact high off black nightmares," but he never tells us why those who were so active in pursuing equal rights for the Negro were the ones who were most plagued by "white guilt." The elder Spike, however, makes clear that the Civil Rights movement was just a part of a larger revolution of morals, one that presumably had its roots in the late '40s Beat culture the then young minister from Ohio encountered when he became pastor in Greenwich Village. "He sees," Paul says of his father, "civil rights as only one part of a vast

---

1718 *Christianity and Crisis*, February 21, 1966,

1719 St. Martin's Press, 1990,

1720 (Photographs of my Father, Paul Spike, New York, Alfred A. Knopf, the same publisher, interestingly enough, who brought us *Nigger Heaven*),

social, technological, sexual and moral revolution."[1721] "Working to free black Americans, he has become free. . ... The civil rights struggle gives the church a new chance to act in a 'Christian' way without that implying narrow-minded or prudish behavior. It may even be the last chance for the Protestant Church in America."[1722] His son's testimony shows that the elder Spike saw the Civil Rights movement as just one part of a general transformation: "The crusading minister of Judson has written many articles for national publications, worked hard in the civil rights and antiwar movements, and has been perhaps the key man in reforming the abortion law in New York state."

This leads us to propose a new explanation of the terms Liberal Guilt and/or White Guilt. The terms express two faces of one and the same thing; white guilt is liberal guilt when confronted with the race situation. Shelby Steele describes the phenomenon:

> In the sixties. . . White guilt became so palpable you could see it on people. At the time, what it looked like to my eyes was a remarkable loss of authority. And what whites lost in authority, blacks gained. You cannot feel guilty toward anyone without giving away power to them. So, suddenly, this huge vulnerability opened up in whites and, as a black, you had the power to step right into it. In fact, black power all but demanded that you do so.

During the '60s, Steele claims that "guilt had changed the nature of the white man's burden from the administration of inferiors to the uplift of equals, from the obligations of dominance to the urgencies of repentance." "Whites in the sixties," according to his view, "underwent an archetypal Fall."

Because of the immense turmoil of the Civil Rights movement, and later the black power movement, whites were confronted for more than a decade with their willingness to participate in or comply with the oppression of blacks, their indifference to human suffering and degradation, their capacity to abide evil for their own benefit, and in defiance of their own sacred principles. The 1964 Civil Rights Act that bestowed equality under the law on blacks was also, in a certain sense, an admission of white guilt.

The problem with Steele's explanation is that the guilt showed up in whites where it was least expected. Where the "oppression of blacks" was most evident, there was hardly any evidence of white guilt. White guilt was not a large part of the psychic make-up of Ku Klux Klan Grand Dragons or George Wallace, to give just two examples. It was, however, a large component of the psychological makeup of liberals like Robert W. Spike, who should have felt every reason to be free of it because of his activities for racial justice on behalf of the National Council of Churches. White guilt was, in other words, a strictly liberal phenomenon.

1721 Paul Spike, p. 63.
1722 Paul Spike, p. 83.

Part III: The Return of the Satanic Wilderness

A new explanation seems in order. That the phenomenon exists should be obvious. Steele's description of it is as good as anyone's. However, the cause seems to lie beyond Steele's ken and can best be explained from the details of a life like Spike's. Our theory posits a simplifying thesis: guilt does not come in various varieties. It has one source, and that is the transgression of the moral law. Modernity means sexual liberation. Sexual liberation creates guilt. The only way to deal with guilt among those who refuse to repent is the palliation that comes from social activism. Involvement in social movements calms troubled consciences. The relation between the liberal Left and the civil rights leadership was symbiotic. The guilt which accrued from carrying out the agenda of the Left, which invariably involved some form of sexual liberation, was anesthetized by involvement in fighting for the Negro's freedoms. As Paul Spike said of his father, "Working to free black Americans, he himself became free." The right racial politics allowed him to justify the particular personal freedoms he craved. The source of his particular craving was homosexuality. Fighting for freedom freed his conscience from the burden of living a double life. Social activism on behalf of the Negro was the palliative which calmed the sexually burdened conscience of the liberal Left. Daniel Patrick Moynihan inadvertently stepped right into the middle of this complicated psychic equation and threatened to expose the sexual roots of Liberal adherence to the cause and the main leverage whereby blacks could extort concessions from their guilty white, sexually liberated collaborators. No amount of tact or public relations could disguise this fact from the Left. As a result, they united in opposition to the notion of family stability and made the spread of the underclass and its mores inevitable. The liberals chose the ghetto as a bulwark to preserve the sexual revolution.

Of course, the civil rights leadership was not exempt from this dynamic either. They too were subject to the moral laws of the universe, and as subsequent biography has shown, they too were as heavily involved in sexual liberation as the liberal Left. Bayard Rustin, like Spike, was a homosexual. Rustin, a close associate of A. Philip Randolph, president of the Brotherhood of Sleeping Car Porters and the most noted national black leader, was a former member of the Young Communist League who was convicted in the early '60s of homosexual activity with two other men in a parked car. Blacks in this situation needed the high moral ground to calm their consciences every bit as much as the whites did. They were just as eager to defeat a proposal which necessitated a reform of conduct as the whites were. As in the Yeats poem, so in the Civil Rights movement: "The best lack all conviction, while the worst/ Are full of passionate intensity." As the militants raged, responsible black leaders were unable to lead because they themselves were compromised, and they knew that the militants knew it.

Martin Luther King is a good case in point. In 1965 King flew to Miami for a Ford Foundation funded Leadership Training Program for black ministers.

Walking with a Bible and a Gun

King spent much of his time holed up in his hotel room, probably because of the controversy below. One speakers was Daniel Patrick Moynihan, whose report King had endorsed a few months earlier. Moynihan later described the meeting in a letter to a Ford Foundation executive as "an atmosphere of total hostility." It was, he wrote, "the first time I have ever found myself in an atmosphere so suffused with near madness. . . . The leadership of the meeting was in the hands of near-demented Black militants who consistently stated one untruth after another (about me, about the United States, about the President, about history, etc. etc.) without a single voice being raised in objection. King, Abernathy, and Young sat there throughout, utterly unwilling (at least with me present) to say a word in support of non-violence, integration, or peaceableness."[1723]

King, who had supported Moynihan's initiative that spring, could not support it now because he was too sexually compromised. As a result, the black leadership capitulated to the militants, and the Civil Rights movement chose to perpetuate the ghetto rather than relinquish sexual liberation. Garrow makes abundantly clear that King's reputation as a womanizer was common knowledge among the SCLC leadership and beyond. He cites an account as early as the '50s in *The Pittsburgh Courier*, a widely read national black newspaper, warning a "prominent minister in the Deep South, a man who has been making the headlines recently in his fight for civil rights," that he "had better watch his step." According to Garrow, "the paper announced detectives hired by white segregationists. . . were hoping to create a scandal by catching the preacher in a hotel room with a woman other than his wife, during one of his visits to a Northern city." As a result of his sexual involvement. King could not object to the vilification of Moynihan at the Miami ministers' meeting. When it came to sexual issues, the very issues the Moynihan Report raised, King was unable to lead because he was too badly compromised. The militants knew his weakness and exploited it.

On the issue of sexuality, King was a deeply divided man. When confronted, he would attempt to justify his behavior. When a friend raised the subject of what King biographer Garrow calls "his compulsive sexual athleticism," King answered, "I'm away from home 25 to 27 days a month. Fucking's a form of anxiety reduction." However, publicly King would espouse the Christian view. "Sex," he said in one of his sermons at Ebenezer Baptist Church:

> is basically sacred when it is properly used and. . . marriage is man's greatest prerogative in the sense that it is through and in marriage that God gives man the opportunity to aid him in his creative activity. Therefore, sex must never be abused in the loose sense that it is abused in the modem world.

1723 Garrow, *Bearing the Cross*, p. 598-9.

Part III: The Return of the Satanic Wilderness

The disparity between his private life and his public pronouncements left King wide open to charges of hypocrisy should the black militants choose to make them. J. Edgar Hoover was engaging in a similar form of blackmail from the other end of the political spectrum, a source of constant anxiety for King and his supporters. King could little afford to have the same sort of charges emanate from within his own movement. So, it is unsurprising that he would remain silent.

More often than not, King simply gave expression in his sermons to the conflicts between inclination and belief in his personal life rather than taking a stand for either the Christian or the sexual liberationist options: "Because we are two selves, there is a civil war going on within all of us," he said at Ebenezer. "There is a schizophrenia . . . within all of us," he said in another sermon. "There are times that all of us know somehow that there is a Mr. Hyde and a Dr. Jekyll in us." However, "God does not judge us by the separate incidents or the separate mistakes that we make but by the total bent of our lives."

It is no surprise that the fundamental option theory would be attractive to King. It has an attraction to people who fail to get control of some bad habit, as well as those who feel compromised by the double lives they lead. In addition to adumbrating the conflict in his sermons, King was drawn to theories which seemed to rationalize his behavior. Garrow cites one source who points out that King "was eager to learn systems of thought about God which he could connect with to rationalize and fill out his own inclinations— inclinations shaped by his experiences." "When Schleiermacher stressed the primacy of experience over any external authority," King wrote to one of his former seminary professors, "he was sounding a note that continues to ring in my own experience."[1724]

Garrow also notes that King's womanizing was a constant source of strain in his marriage and indicates that at the time of his death, King's marriage was in danger of ending in divorce. "Had the man lived," one staffer remembered, "the marriage wouldn't have survived, and everybody feels that way."[1725] King was simultaneously headed in the two directions that the Moynihan Report highlighted with painful clarity. King, the public figure, was fighting against segregation in the South, but King the private figure was heading in the direction of the absent, sexually irresponsible father which Moynihan claimed was the root of social pathology in the ghettos of the North:

> Three relationships had flowered to the status of something more than occasional one-night-stands, and for almost the past two years King had grown closer and closer to one of these women, whom he saw almost daily. The relationship, rather than his marriage, increasingly became the

---

1724 Garrow, *Bearing the Cross*, pp. 638-9, n. 39.
1725 Garrow, *Bearing the Cross*, p. 617.

emotional centerpiece of King's life, but it did not eliminate the incidental couplings that were a commonplace of King's travels.[1726]

As a result, King was increasingly torn and increasingly unable to control a movement that was heading toward violence and racial separatism. Moynihan remembers King toward the end of his life as "still wanting a bill." Stanley Levison and King's wife Coretta referred to King as "guilt-ridden." Chicago businessman and King associate, William A. Rutherford, remembers the Southern Christian Leadership Conference as "a very rowdy place" and said "the movement altogether was a very raunchy exercise." Garrow relates that:

> Rutherford's first shock stemmed from reports of an Atlanta party that had featured a hired prostitute as well as the unsuccessful ravishing of a seventeen-year-old SCLC secretary. Rutherford raised the subject at an executive staff session, "and the meeting cracked up in laughter. . . ." King was laughing too, a further reflection of SCLC's "very relaxed attitude toward sex" and the "genuine ribald humor" that predominated.

Subsequent studies and memoirs of those involved in the Civil Rights movement have confirmed that the behavior King exhibited was typical of the SCLC in particular and the Civil Rights movement in general. In *Personal Politics*, Sara Evans traces the birth of the feminist movement to the sexual liberation practiced in the Civil Rights movement, particularly during the summer of 1964. According to Evans, "the sit-in movement and the freedom rides had an electrifying impact on northern liberal culture"[1727] with the result that "the children of northern liberals and radicals" joined the movement "with passionate commitment." Just how passionate the commitment was comes out in the various accounts of white women Evans draws on. One young woman described how:

> a whole lot of things got shared around sexuality—like black men with white women—it wasn't just sex, it was also sharing ideas and fears, and emotional support. ... My sexuality for myself was confirmed by black men for the first time ever in my life, see. In the white society I am too large.... So I had always had to work very hard to be attractive to white men. . . . Black men . . . assumed that I was a sexual person . . . and I needed that very badly.

Both sides in this sexual equation, according to Evans, "were hungry for sexual affirmation and appreciation." So much so that in retrospect, Martin Luther King's term "the beloved community" took on a whole new meaning: "A generation steeped in ideas drawn from existential theology and philosophy translated the concept of 'beloved community' into a belief in the power of transforming human relationships. . . . There was a sense in which the

---

1726 Garrow, *Bearing the Cross*, p. 375.
1727 Sara Evans, *Personal Politics*, p. 60.

Part III: The Return of the Satanic Wilderness

'beloved community' of black and white together took on concrete reality in the intimacy of the bedroom." According to Evans, one male black leader indicated that white female volunteers "spent that summer, most of them, on their backs, servicing not only the SNCC workers but anybody else who came . . . Where I was project director, we put white women out of the project within the first three weeks because they tried to screw themselves across the city." "Guilt lurked in all directions," Evans claimed, "and behind that guilt lay anger." And behind the anger lay the rise of feminism, abortion rights, homosexual activism, affirmative action and a whole culture of grievance fueled by sexual guilt and the various movements which extorted blackmail as a result of it.

The situation came to a head in the fall of 1964 following the voter registration drives of that summer. In November 1964, around the time that Daniel Patrick Moynihan woke up in the middle of the night with an idea for the new direction of the Civil Rights movement, Stokely Carmichael was regaling white admirers with his ideas on the position of women in the movement at a SNCC staff retreat at Waveland, Mississippi. He was responding to a position paper (number 24) presented at the meeting: "SNCC Position Paper (Women in the Movement)"; the authors' names (Casey Hayden, pre-Jane Fonda wife of Tom, and Mary King, whose husband would later murder Allard Lowenstein, had written it in discussion with Mary Varela) had been "withheld by request." After a day of acrimonious discussion, Carmichael took a bunch of female admirers and a bottle of wine to a dock overlooking the Gulf of Mexico and after asking rhetorically about the position of women in the movement, answered by saying: "The only position for women in SNCC is prone."

"Carmichael's barb" Evans recounts, "was for most who heard it a movement in-joke. It recalled the sexual activity of the summer before – all those young white women who supposedly had spent the summer 'on their backs.'"[1728] Even though she disagreed with much of Evans' assessment, Mary King thought Carmichael's remark was funny. "We all collapsed with hilarity," she wrote in her memoir, *Freedom Song*.

Funny or not, the remark is often taken as the opening shot in the war between the sexes that has come to be known as the feminist movement. The women had learned their lesson well. They were in an even better position to extort concessions from sexual guilt than the blacks were. Evans had learned the lesson firsthand. She reports on one conference, where "the politics of moralism reached new heights as the moralism of middleclass guilt clashed head on with the morality of righteous anger. . . . Each time the conference capitulated to black demands, the majority of whites applauded enthusiastically in apparent approval of their own denunciation."

[1728] Evans, *Personal Politics*, p. 88.

WALKING WITH A BIBLE AND A GUN

Mary King does her best not to drive a wedge between the politically correct coalition of feminist and black; however, the evidence in her book points to the sexual exploitation practiced in the Civil Rights movement as the cause of feminism every bit as much as it does in Sara Evans' book. King feels that the interracial sexual relationships also led to black separatism because the black women in the Civil Rights movement were having their boyfriends taken away from them by the accessibility of too many liberal white women of easy virtue:

> That complex dynamic created stress between the veteran black women and white women on the SNCC staff, because the black women could see the allure of the white women volunteers to black male staff. Such desire was unacceptable intellectually, but, psychologically, for some men, it was compelling. I have often wondered whether resistance to this pattern might not have contributed to the surge toward black nationalism that showed itself in SNCC after the November 1964 Waveland meeting. Black men, suddenly exposed to large numbers of white women volunteers— with many of the local men talking to a white woman for the first time in their lives as an equal—suddenly had the real or hypothetical opportunity to break an old taboo. Black women who were field secretaries and project directors, working side by side with black male colleagues all day, found that after hours some of the latter sought the company of the white women volunteers.[1729]

"Our lives," Mary King concludes, "defied conventional morality." And the nation has been paying the price ever since. "'Freedom' and 'liberation,'" writes Sara Evans, "were absolutes — to be fought for and won."

The feminists were right after all. As far as the Civil Rights movement was concerned, the political was personal. Both the black and the white leadership had too much invested in sexual liberation to take an honest look at the pathology of the ghetto and its relationship to family breakdown. The white Left had been interested in promoting the Negro as a paradigm of sexual liberation from the time of the Harlem Renaissance in the 1920s. In many respects it was their only interest in the Negro. Promoting black decadence as "primitive" and closer to nature was the best way to bring about the transvaluation of all values and the demise of the Christian ethos of the West.

When Undersecretary Moynihan proposed the choice between a cure based on a reform of morals and further decay, the Left chose decay to save the sexual revolution. Since then, illegitimacy among all blacks has gone from 20 percent to hovering at around 80 percent. The situation which Moynihan described as an epidemic for blacks in 1965 has become the norm for white society, which now has an illegitimacy rate of over 20 percent. Black leadership, deeply compromised sexually, acquiesced in that choice. Rather

---

1729 Mary King,

470 • THE MOYNIHAN REPORT

Part III: The Return of the Satanic Wilderness

than give up their stake in the sexual revolution, they chose to condemn the black underclass to a prolonged term in the ghetto. Averting their eyes from family pathology, they chose to see white racism as the *radix malorum*. Even the blacks who are the beneficiaries of the liberal conscience money that Affirmative Action has become seem mired in the self-defeating and self-conferred image of themselves as helpless victims. Then as now, nobody wants to hear that "perfecting the social order will be of no avail without a reform of conduct."

CHAPTER 48

CRITICAL RACE THEORY AND THE DESTRUCTION OF AMERICAN IDENTITY

Noel Ignatiev ended up at Harvard, where he became known as the father of Critical Race Theory. Jaime Caro-Morente took Ignatiev's claim that "The greatest ideological barrier to the achievement of the proletarian class consciousness, solidarity and political action is now, and has been, white chauvinism," which first appeared in his 1967 pamphlet "White Blindspot" and claimed that Black Lives Matter ignited a "new protest cycle" when it put Ignatiev's ideas into action during the George Floyd riots of 2020:

> Due to the capitalist systemic crisis of 2008 and the awareness that racism is still strong in the US, with help from the Black Lives Matter movement, we find ourselves in a new protest cycle. Although this cycle differs from others that have existed in the US: at the beginning of the 20th century, it was a movement for labor rights and socialism, in the 60s for the emancipation of all human beings from the modern categories of race and gender. This new protest cycle is the crystallization of the idea that neither of the these things that have been fought for in the past have been achieved: there are no meaningful labor rights to speak of, just as there is no emancipation from the oppressive nature of white supremacy (race), patriarchy (sex/gender), and capitalism (class), because the only system capable of remedying each — socialism — has still not been realized.[1730]

In its effort to remedy that situation in Philadelphia, Black Lives Matter orchestrated demonstrations that splattered the statue of former Philadelphia mayor Frank Rizzo with paint. Noel Ignatiev's book on *How the Irish Became White*, which focused on Philadelphia, was published in 1995, four years after Frank Rizzo died. In 1998, the city of Philadelphia erected a statue in Rizzo's honor, and on June 3, 2020 as part of the orgy of Black Lives Matter inspired iconoclasm which swept the nation in the wake of George Floyd's death, that

---

[1730] Jaime Caro-Morente, "To End the Rule of Capital, We Must End the Rule of White Supremacy: Revisiting the Work of Noel Ignatiev and Theodore Allen," October 30, 2021, https://www.hamptonthink.org/read/to-end-the-rule-of-capital-we-must-end-the-rule-of-white-supremacy-revisiting-the-work-of-noel-ignatiev-and-theodore-allen

WALKING WITH A BIBLE AND A GUN

city's "workers removed a statue of Philadelphia's controversial former Mayor Frank Rizzo from its place of honor across from City Hall . . . finishing a job that protesters attempted to accomplish during recent demonstrations against police brutality."[1731] To add insult to injury, Philadelphia's "white" mayor Jim Kenney applauded this act of gratuitous iconoclasm by claiming that "The Frank Rizzo statue represented bigotry, hatred, and oppression for too many people, for too long. It is finally gone."[1732]

In making this statement, Kenney marked the successful end of a period of ethnic warfare which began on July 4, 1962, when Philadelphians gathered at Independence Hall to celebrate their national identity and listened to speeches by James H.J. Tate, the Catholic mayor of that city, David L. Lawrence, the Catholic governor of Pennsylvania, and John F. Kennedy, the Catholic president of the United States. Both the Catholics who rejoiced in this fact and the anti-Catholics who vowed to contest it had to admit that Catholics had reached the apogee of their political power in a land which had always viewed them as alien invaders.

One year later, on August 28, 1963, the Protestants celebrated the apogee of their political power when they assembled at the mall in Washington at the march which marked the culmination of the Civil Rights Movement. Three months later, Kennedy was struck down by an assassin's bullet. The combination of those events unleashed a protracted period of internecine warfare in Philadelphia which culminated in the ethnic cleansing of that city's Catholics and the transformation of Philadelphia's Kensington and Fishtown neighborhoods into the drug zombie capital of the world.

After Tate was elected as that city's first Catholic mayor, Philadelphia's still potent WASP elite sided with Philadelphia's Jews in organizations like Americans for Democratic Action in using race to destroy Catholic political power in that city. The abolitionist alignment with anti-Catholic nativism was alive and well in Philadelphia a century after the nativist riots. Protestant sympathy for the plight of Uncle Tom got transferred to the Philadelphia branch of the Civil Rights Movement when the WASP elite chose Wilson Goode, that city's first Black mayor, to thwart Catholic/ethnic political power of the sort symbolized by Frank Rizzo, an Italian America who rose from a cop on the beat to that city's mayor in 1972, at the high water mark of what Allen referred to as the "white backlash"[1733] that brought Nixon back to the White House.

In addition to being a victim of identity theft at the hands of Black Lives Matter, who claimed that he was "white," Rizzo was a flamboyant Italian-

---

1731 Bill Chappell, "Frank Rizzo Statue Is Removed In Philadelphia: 'It Is Finally Gone,' Mayor Says," NPR, June 3, 2020, https://www.npr.org/2020/06/03/868848550/frank-rizzo-statue-is-removed-in-philadelphia-it-is-finally-gone-mayor-says

1732 Chappell, "Frank Rizzo."

1733 Allen, p. 1060.

Part III: The Return of the Satanic Wilderness

American whose solution to crime was "*scappo il capo*," (crack them over the head), which didn't seem like a particularly white thing to say. It was hardly even an Italian thing to say since his parents spoke Abruzzese. Rizzo, however, had a way with words, as when he explained that his efforts to fight crime in Philadelphia would make "Attila the Hun look like a faggot."[1734] Rizzo would make comments like this while brandishing the night stick he famously wore in his tuxedo cummerbund, when duty called him from an official banquet to crack the skulls of Black Panthers and other undesirables. Rizzo became a national figure under President Richard Nixon who symbolized the ethnic reaction to the excesses of the Civil Rights movement. Frank Rizzo was undoubtedly a tough guy, but was he white?

If whiteness can be determined by horoscope according to the time of his birth, Frank Rizzo, who was born in 1920, was most certainly not white. He was, in the parlance of his day, a dago from South Philadelphia, and as such subjected to all of the discrimination inflicted on Negroes at that time. That meant lynching, as 11 Italian Americans discovered in 1891 when they were gunned down and lynched for their alleged role in the murder of Police chief David Hennessy after some of them had been acquitted. Indeed, Italians in New Orleans, not Negroes in Mississippi, were the victims of "the largest single mass lynching in American history,"[1735] providing ample evidence that they—unlike Frank Rizzo, at least according to Black Lives Matter—were not the recipients of white privilege. Nor was there any indication that the status of Italians had changed by the time Frank Rizzo was born in 1920, four years before passage of the Immigration act of 1924, which restricted Italian immigration.

The New Orleans lynchings of Italian-Americans had serious international repercussions. In May 1891, the Italian consul left New Orleans at the Italian government's direction after lodging a protest with the city. Italy, then "cut off diplomatic relations with the United States, sparking rumors of war."[1736] In order to defuse the issue, President Benjamin Harrison made Columbus Day a national holiday. The *New York Times*, which would eventually become the flagship of American journalism before it succumbed to critical race theory, joined in the chorus of approval which characterized reaction to the lynchings in the South, making use of "racist stereotypes" which "dehumanized the dead" and valorized their killers by describing the victims as "sneaking and cowardly Sicilians," who were "the descendants of bandits and assassins, who

---

1734 Timothy J. Lombardo, "When Philadelphia's Foul-Mouthed Cop-Turned-Mayor Invented White Identity Politics," Zocalo Public Square, September 26, 2019, https://www.zocalopublicsquare.org/when-philadelphias-foul-mouthed-cop-turned-mayor-invented-white-identity-politics/

1735 "1891 New Orleans lynchings," *Wikipedia: The Free Encyclopedia*, https://en.wikipedia.org/wiki/1891_New_Orleans_lynchings

1736 "1891 New Orleans lynchings," *Wikipedia*.

have transported to this country the lawless passions, the cutthroat practices [and] are to us a pest without mitigations. Our own rattlesnakes are as good citizens as they. Our own murderers are men of feeling and nobility compared to them."[1737]

The *Times* editorial substantiated the claim that "American press coverage of the event was largely congratulatory, and those responsible for the lynching were never charged."[1738] It proved that white privilege was a force in national politics, but it also showed conclusively that Italians did not share in that privilege because they weren't considered white.

The conventional account of Frank Rizzo's career makes all of the same category mistakes that Allen and Ignatiev had made in their attempt to shoehorn ethnic and religious realities into racial boxes:

> Rizzo and his brand of blue-collar politics developed at a critical point in modern U.S. history. He owed his rise to the most powerful social movement of his era: the push for African-American civil rights during the 1960s and 1970s. Protests against segregation roiled northern cities like Philadelphia every bit as much as their Southern counterparts—and spurred the rise of a conservative response that proved just as transformative as the civil rights movement it opposed. In Philadelphia, this response grew out of a white, working- and middle-class effort to safeguard "neighborhood" and white ethnic institutions and traditions. As civil rights activists sought to integrate neighborhoods, schools, and work sites, white Philadelphians—many first- and second-generation Americans of European ancestry—fought back, treating African-American advances as a zero-sum game they were losing. . . . As civil rights protests intensified, blue-collar white ethnics joined a nationwide clamor for "law and order." Rizzo personified "law and order" and promised to restore it in Philadelphia.[1739]

What exactly are "white ethnic institutions and traditions"? The terms "white" and "ethnic" are contradictory terms which get rolled into a category mistake which becomes the moral basis for condemning anyone who objected to the campaign of social engineering which used Negroes from the south to engage in the ethnic cleansing of Catholic ethnics (a non-contradictory category) from their neighborhoods in the cities of the north where Catholic political power was still powerful.

The author of the above quote is Timothy J. Lombardo, whose name indicates that he is an Italian-American who identifies as "white" because of his inability to distinguish between the racial categories which make up his

---

1737 Brent Staples, "How Italians Became 'White,'" *The New York Times*, October 13, 2019, p. 4.
1738 Staples, "How Italians Became 'White.'" p. 4.
1739 Lombardo, "When Philadelphia's Foul-Mouthed Cop."

Part III: The Return of the Satanic Wilderness

American identity and the ethnic categories which defined the identity of his ancestors when they first arrived in this country and were not considered white. "Rizzo," Lombardo tells us, grew up "in a heavily Italian section of Philadelphia" and joined the police force, where he garnered the admiration of fellow cops, who referred to him as the "Cisco Kid, after a popular television cowboy," who happened to be a Mexican, who were also not white.

Rizzo was no stranger to ethnic slurs and referred to city solicitor Marty Weinberg as a "big-nosed Jew" in a friendly way similar to his reference to making Attila the Hun look like a faggot. Lombardo tells us that this comment "became one of the most famous of his entire career—an incendiary statement typical of his aggressive masculinity,"[1740] but he doesn't tell us whether the Mongols got upset by it. More importantly, Lombardo never tells us why the man who referred to *"scappo il capo"* as the basis of his policy of police enforcement should be considered white, even if Rizzo "told an audience to 'vote white'" in an unsuccessful bid to change the city charter to allow him to run for a third term as mayor. "White" was the term the social engineers imposed on Catholic ethnics as a form of identity theft to deprive them of moral legitimacy by depriving them of American identity and political power. If Rizzo eventually fell into that trap, it was because he could not come up with any other category that would refer to a multi-ethnic constituency which had already intermarried but did not know that their ethnic identity was now Catholic, probably because they had never heard of the triple melting pot, the sociological theory which showed that religion replaced country of origin as an ethnic marker after three generations in America.

Catholics had lost their ethnic solidarity and became divided by class, with the upwardly mobile seeking favor with the still-powerful WASP elite. The man who epitomized the aspirations of upwardly mobile Catholics was a Christian Brother by the name of Brother Paul, who defected from the order and re-invented himself as Dick Deasy, the journalist who tricked Rizzo into taking a lie detector test which eventually ended his political career and paved the way for the election of Wilson Goode, "Philadelphia's first African-American mayor." Goode, who was anointed by the WASP elite to thwart Catholic political power in Philadelphia was the first mayor to drop a bomb on the city, an act which destroyed eight square blocks of real estate in South West Philadelphia in a vain attempt to bring an end to a siege involving a group of black militants who went by the name of MOVE, which meant nothing, and whose last names were without exception "Africa." A famous T-shirt showed Frank Rizzo in dreadlocks over the title "Frank Africa." Ill-conceived draconian measures like incinerating eight square blocks of residential real estate created a longing for a return to the days of *"scappo il capo"* among the city's black population which would have returned Rizzo to

---

1740 Lombardo, "When Philadelphia's Foul-Mouthed Cop."

office if he hadn't died of a heart attack during his re-election campaign in 1991. Struggling to break free from the mind-forged manacles of Critical Race Theory, Lombardo claims that:

> There is another way to understand this support. Working- and middle-class whites of the time were engaged in a newly emergent form of identity politics—which amounted to white racial identity politics, cloaked in the language of class pride. Rizzo's supporters used class identity and class-based rhetoric to avoid accusations of racism. When white neighborhood activists in South Philadelphia fought the construction of the Whitman Park public housing project that Rizzo halted in 1973, they never publicly mentioned race. Rather, they argued that public housing tenants would not take the same pride in their homes as homeowners.[1741]

What Lombardo terms "white racial identity politics" was in reality ethnic, largely Catholic objection to the identity theft, which the Democrats perpetrated by calling them "white," which is to say racist, which is to say bad. This began in 1968 when the nation's Catholic ethnics broke free from the Democratic weaponization of race and sexual deviance and voted for Richard Nixon, an exodus which only accelerated the Democratic Party's plunge into identity politics, which culminated in Kamala Harris's catastrophic loss in 2024.

Rizzo was an Italian Catholic who used Catholic ethnic resentment against the excesses of the Civil Rights movement as the vehicle which enabled his rise to power in Philadelphia. He appealed to fellow Catholic ethnics and blue collar workers by referring to them as white, because it was the only category that could unite the opponents to the Civil Rights Movement, which was by definition black. To say that Frank Rizzo was white involved a category mistake which mistook a campaign strategy for ethnic identity. One scholarly study argues that:

> in the decades following the end of the Second World War, Italian-Americans achieved the status of "whiteness" in the United States due to the increasing popularity and romanticization of Italians in American pop culture. Through analyzing the growth in popularity of Italian celebrities in the 1950-60s, and the cultural impact of *The Godfather* films in the 1970s, the shifting image and whitening of Italians in the American mind can be seen clearly and understood.[1742]

The claim that Al Pacino engaged in the "whitening of Italians" is indicative of the desperate measures journalists with engage in to save the phenomena

---

1741 Lombardo, "When Philadelphia's Foul-Mouthed Cop."

1742 Amanda Bisesi, "Made Men: The Whitening of Italian-Americans 1950-1975," Thesis Masters of Arts in History, California State University, Fullerton, Spring 2017, https://scholarworks.calstate.edu/downloads/kd17cv29h#:~:text=1%20This%20study%20argues%20that,Italians%20in%20American%20pop%20culture.

Part III: The Return of the Satanic Wilderness

of the racial narrative. *The Godfather* premiered on March 28, 1972, in the same year that Frank Rizzo was elected mayor of Philadelphia, and Richard Nixon used his appeal to ethnic voters to win a landslide victory over George McGovern.

Fifty-two years later, repressed American identity returned when Donald Trump defeated Kamala Harris by the biggest margin since Nixon defeated McGovern. Donald Trump's victory was a total repudiation of Critical Race Theory, Identity Politics, and sexual deviance, the three pillars of the Democratic Party since 1968 when they kicked out the Catholic ethnics by staging riots against Mayor Richard Daley at the Democratic convention in Chicago.

As usual Catholic ethnics in Pennsylvania provided the swing vote in the 2024 presidential election, which put Trump back in the White House. Donald Trump's victory was an example of the return of the repressed which signaled a return to the archetype, once symbolized by the American cowboy. Unlike Frank Rizzo, who called himself the Cisco Kid, and Ronald Reagan, who came from California and played cowboys in Hollywood films, Donald Trump came from New York City, where the only cowboys were gigolos, as Jon Voight had proven in *Midnight Cowboy*. Like The Virginian, Trump wasn't a church going man, but the absence of externals allowed the emergence of a procession of white guys—like pundit Tucker Carlson, along with retired military men like Douglas MacGregor, Scott Ritter, Larry Johnson, Larry Wilkenson, Phil Giraldi (who became white when he joined the CIA), and even Elon Musk, who was considered white although he was the world's richest African—who united around a common American identity which they could portray in an existential manner even if they could not articulate its essence. What united those men was resentment at the Jewish takeover of American culture, an event whose causality more often than not got disguised by euphemisms like "neoconservative." The proximate cause of this reassertion of American identity was the Israeli genocide in Gaza, but it included patriotic anger at the Jewish takeover of the American political process by AIPAC, the Israel lobby's staging degrading spectacles like the 58 standing ovations by its lackeys in Congress during Binyamin Netanyahu's speech. The common denominator of all of those men is American identity, which is now resurgent because of the excesses of identity politics at the hands of the Democrats. Whether the Jews succeed in hijacking Trump's mandate from the American people is still an open question. As Hemingway pointed out, fishing in the swamp, much less draining the swamp, has always been a "tragic adventure," as soon as one loses the compass for human action that is known as the moral law. Hemingway's tragic life was proof of that.

The only thing that will make American great again is moral reform. "We have no constitution which functions in the absence of a moral people" remains as true now as when John Adams first uttered it. What John Adams didn't know then and what Benjamin Franklin had to learn in the expensive school of experience is that moral reform is impossible without grace. We have come full circle now. The alembic of human history has refined away everything extraneous leaving America with only two alternatives: Catholicism and Satanism. *Non datur tertius.*

In the *annus mirabilis* 1979 six months after saying Mass in front of a million Poles in Warsaw, thereby beginning the rollback of atheistic Communism which would reach its fulfillment a decade later, Pope John Paul II arrived in Philadelphia, where he gave a sermon on the dangers of making freedom America's fundamental value. Freedom is not "an absolute end in itself," but it can serve as a means to a greater end which "enables self-giving and service." This occurs:

> when the family is protected and strengthened, when its unity is preserved, and when its role as the basic cell of society is recognized and honored. Human-Christian values are fostered when every effort is made so that no child anywhere in the world faces death because of lack of food, or faces a diminished intellectual and physical potential for want of sufficient nourishment, or has to bear all through life the scars of deprivation. Human-Christian values triumph when any system is reformed that authorizes the exploitation of any human being; when upright service and honesty in public servants is promoted; when the dispensing of justice is fair and the same for all; when responsible use is made of the material and energy resources of the world—resources that are meant for the benefit of all; when the environment is preserved intact for the future generations. Human-Christian values triumph by subjecting political and economic considerations to human dignity, by making them serve the cause of man—every person created by God, every brother and sister redeemed by Christ.

"Attachment to liberty" is part of American identity, but as of 1979 America was deeply involved in the social experiment known as sexual liberation. Fourteen years after *Griswold v. Connecticut* struck down all laws prohibiting the sale of contraceptives and six years after *Roe v. Wade*, decriminalized abortion, radical interventions in the transmission of human life had unexpected cultural sequelae like the return of horror films after a 20-year hiatus. *Alien* made its debut in 1979 one year after *Halloween*. Both movies indicated that the wages of sexual sin was death in a way that those wounded by the sexual revolution found deeply cathartic. *Alien* was the sequel to *Deep Throat*. By the end of the 1970s, oral sex wasn't funny any more because everyone knew, even if they couldn't admit it in public, that sex could kill you, certainly if you happened to be a fetus, but also if you happened to be a liberated baby sitter, as *Halloween* made clear. It could also give you a disease or break your heart, which is why the pope tried to contextualize the

Part III: The Return of the Satanic Wilderness

America understanding of freedom by bringing up the family as the greater good which distinguished it from license, which corresponded more closely to Americans' understanding of freedom. Freedom must take its meaning from transcendental realities because:

> man's life is also lived in another order of reality: in the order of his relationship to what is objectively true and morally good. Freedom thus acquires a deeper meaning when it is referred to the human person. It concerns in the first place the relation of man to himself. Every human person, endowed with reason, is free when he is the master of his own actions, when he is capable of choosing that good which is in conformity with reason, and therefore with his own human dignity.

After its break with English tyranny, America had to learn in what Benjamin Franklin termed "the expensive school of experience" that tyranny can come from within if a man becomes the slave of his own passions. Or as St. Augustine put it, drawing on deeper sources than Franklin, "A man has as many masters as he has vices." Freedom has meaning only in relation to ultimate or transcendental values like the good and the true. Or as the pope put it: "Christ himself linked freedom with the knowledge of truth: 'You will know the truth and the truth will make you free' (Jn 8:32)."

The pope spoke these words as America was poised to embark upon an imperial adventure which would sacrifice millions of lives on the altar of "freedom," in the most corrupted sense of that term, ignoring everything the pope said in his speech. The pope said that freedom cannot be seen "as a pretext for moral anarchy, for every moral order must remain linked to truth" at the dawn of the Reagan-Thatcher era which became famous for wretched excess in matters both venereal and financial. Pope John Paul II would collaborate with Ronald Reagan to bring about the fall of Communism, which would allow America's false understanding of freedom to take hold in newly-liberated eastern Europe, including the pope's native Poland where it undermined the Catholic Church's inextricable link to Polish culture. The same faults which the pope exposed in America in 1979 would take root in Poland after 1989:

> In today's society, we see so many disturbing tendencies and so much laxity regarding the Christian view on sexuality that have all one thing in common: recourse to the concept of freedom to justify any behavior that is no longer consonant with the true moral order and the teaching of the Church. Moral norms do not militate against the freedom of the person or the couple; on the contrary they exist precisely for that freedom, since they are given to ensure the right use of freedom. Whoever refuses to accept these norms and to act accordingly, whoever seeks to liberate himself or herself from these norms, is not truly free. Free indeed is the person who models his or her behavior in a responsible way according

to the exigencies of the objective good. What I have said here regards the whole of conjugal morality, but it applies as well to the priests with regard to the obligations of celibacy. The cohesion of freedom and ethics has also its consequences for the pursuit of the common good in society and for the national independence which the Liberty Bell announced two centuries ago.[1743]

America began as a place where existence could modify essence, but because it failed to understand the connection between freedom and the truth, it became a place where Supreme Court Justice Kennedy could opine that "At the heart of liberty is the right to define one's own concept of existence, of meaning, of the universe, and of the mystery of human life."[1744] Kennedy uttered that pernicious bit of profoundly American nonsense in *Planned Parenthood v. Casey*, a Supreme Court decision which kept abortion legal for another 30 years, costing the lives of millions of Americans and postponing the advent of "a universal kingdom of justice, love, and peace" indefinitely as the American empire made an ever deeper commitment to the worship of Moloch.

1743 John Paul II, "Speeches 1979 October," Vatican.Va, https://www.vatican.va/content/john-paul-ii/en/speeches/1979/october.index.3.html

1744 Clifford R. Goldestin, "Justice Kennedy's 'Notorious Mystery Passage,'" *Liberty Magazine*, July/Aug 1997, https://www.libertymagazine.org/article/justice-kennedys-notorious-mystery-passage

Chapter 49

The Unforgiven: America Goes to Hell

That Eastwood was not John Wayne became apparent when Eastwood released *Unforgiven* in 1992, his first Western since the premier of *High Plains Drifter* 20 years earlier. By 1992, America had changed, and the cowboy myth had to be modified to reflect the changes which had taken place in America. Clintwood still represented the best in American men,"[1745] but if there once was a time "when man was alone, on horseback, out there where man hasn't spoiled the land yet," that "romantic myth was gone,"[1746] replaced by Big Whiskey, Wyoming, the setting of *Unforgiven*, where there is no church, as there had been in Hadleyville, the setting of *High Noon*. As a result, there are no decent women for the sheriff to defend. All of the women in *Unforgiven* are whores, and the sheriff is a criminal.

Will Munny is a former outlaw who straightened out his life after he got married. At the beginning of the film, his wife had been dead for three years, and the two children she bore are helping Will run a pig farm which is not doing well. Will flops into the mud trying to separate the pigs with fever from the remaining few which are still healthy.

At this point, a stranger shows up and, after ascertaining Will's former identity, offers him $500 if he will help kill two men, one of whom disfigured a whore with his knife. Will declines, but after another episode with the hogs, he saddles up, leaving his two children behind to run the farm in his absence in search of easy money. Unfortunately, he finds that earning easy money by killing someone isn't as easy as he expected. After arriving in Big Whiskey, the local sheriff, played by Gene Hackman takes his guns and then "kicks the shit" out of him in much same way he beat up an Englishman with airs a few days earlier. The whore with the scarred face, for who a $1,000 bounty was raised to kill the man who disfigured her, nurses Will back to health, after which she offers Will a "free one." Will declines by invoking his wife, without mentioning that she is dead, holding on to the one thing in life, namely,

---

[1745] McGilligan, *Clint: The Life and Legend*, Kindle edition, loc. 4213.

[1746] McGilligan, *Clint: The Life and Legend*, Kindle edition, loc. 4015.

marriage which saved him from a life of degradation, symbolized best by whiskey, which he no longer drinks, until he starts killing again, and the dog returns to its vomit.

Will lives in the Calvinist world that the cowboy and his worship of nature abolished in *The Virginian*, but that was when the town still had a church, and decent women could walk in the streets unmolested because Will Kane was the sheriff. The sheriff in *Unforgiven* reflects America's moral collapse at the very moment of its triumph over communism and the end of the Cold War. In a world without the redeeming grace of the Catholic Church, no one can resist the pull of iniquity. And so, Will starts drinking again, as the body count mounts. When his Negro sidekick, played by Morgan Freeman, gets tortured and killed, Will vows revenge, which he gets in a showdown in the saloon when he kills the sheriff, whose dying words are "I'll see you in hell."

So, *mutatis mutandis*, Calvinism is true after all. Deprived of the sanctifying grace, which only the sacraments of the Catholic Church can provide, man is totally depraved. Incapable of confessing his sins and receiving the absolution which follows, man is drawn inexorably—predestined, one might say—back to his former degenerate way of life, where he repeats the same sins until he finally dies and goes to hell.

In addition to the collapse of the Soviet Union, the other memorable event which contextualizes *Unforgiven* was Sondra Locke's palimony suit. Locke had co-starred in a number of Eastwood films and moved into his residence after Maggie, his first wife, moved out. Locke found that her career as a director had stalled and blamed Eastwood on *her* way out, only to be replaced by Frances Fisher, who was "at the height of her romance"[1747] with Eastwood during the filming of *Unforgiven*, reaffirming "the peculiar Clint tradition of a real-life girlfriend playing a prostitute in his films,"[1748] perhaps because Eastwood's compulsive "Don Juanism" had convinced him that all women were whores. Showing his belief in freedom of choice, Clinton gave Fisher the option of choosing which whore to play: the Madame "who forges the feminist solidarity of the town whores," or "the whore-victim savagely disfigured in the film's opening sequence."[1749] Francis Fisher mistakenly believed Clint's philandering days were past because when she asked him about other women in his life, Clint lied by quoting Will Munny from *Unforgiven*, who said: "I ain't like that no more."[1750]

Unforgiven, as the title implies, was about sin, guilt, and the inability to go to confession which had plagued American culture from its inception at the hands of Calvinists who had broken with the sacramental structure of the

---

1747 McGilligan, *Clint: The Life and Legend*, Kindle edition, loc. 8823.
1748 McGilligan, *Clint: The Life and Legend*, Kindle edition, loc. 8823.
1749 McGilligan, *Clint: The Life and Legend*, Kindle edition, loc. 8825.
1750 McGilligan, *Clint: The Life and Legend*, Kindle edition, loc. 9111.

Part III: The Return of the Satanic Wilderness

Catholic Church. It also displayed a growing ambivalence about the gun and its role in defining American identity because it was at best irrelevant to the forgiveness of sins and more often than not the instrument which burdened the soul with guilt. That ambivalence found expression in his biopic of John Huston, *White Hunter Black Heart*, who claimed in his autobiography, which was the basis of the film, "I've never killed an elephant, although I surely tried. I never got a shot at one whose trophies were worth the crime. No, not crime—sin. I wouldn't dream of shooting an elephant today—in fact, I've given up all shooting with a rifle...."[1751]

A women who gave birth to one of Eastwood's illegitimate children claimed that "There is no guilt with Clint,"[1752] but the message of *Unforgiven* belies that claim, as do many of his latter-day films, which portrayed him "as a man increasingly preoccupied by mortality and legacy" as well as by the "tone of regret"[1753] which comes out unmistakably in *Unforgiven*. In his 2003 film *Mystic River*, Eastwood portrays "a cynical universe in which evil is omnipresent" and "society is corrupt"[1754] and Eastwood finds himself "looking into the abyss for the first time."[1755]

Eastwood backed away from the abyss to direct and star in *Gran Torino*, an uncharacteristic film which takes place far away from the cowboy world in the ruins of the Catholic ethnic neighborhoods destroyed by social engineering around the time Eastwood began his acting career. *Gran Torino* depicts a world that is unmistakably Catholic, beginning with a funeral in a Catholic Church in Hamtramck, a suburb of Detroit which was once so Polish that it had a four-story high mural of Cardinal Glemp on the side of one of its buildings, but has now been taken over by Hmong refugees. Unlike the other Polacks, who fled to the suburbs and became "white," Walt Kowalski, a crotchety Korean war vet and retired autoworker, has decided to fight the tide which sucked fellow Catholic ethnics to the suburbs, but he has overstayed his welcome. His children and grandchildren have moved on. He is left behind alone with no one too look after him other than the parish priest who officiated at his wife's funeral and looks old enough to be one of Walt's grandchildren. Walt's anger has been growing during the funeral, fueled by grandchildren who text during Mass and don't know how to dress properly. His anger finally comes out when Father Janovich comes up to him after Mass and tells Walt that he made a promise to his wife to have him go to confession.

Looked at superficially, *Gran Torino* has nothing to do with the themes Eastwood explored in the first 40 years of his film-making career. The hidden

---

1751 McGilligan, *Clint: The Life and Legend*, Kindle edition, loc. 8558.
1752 McGilligan, *Clint: The Life and Legend*, Kindle edition, loc. 9530.
1753 McGilligan, *Clint: The Life and Legend*, Kindle edition, loc. 10264.
1754 McGilligan, *Clint: The Life and Legend*, Kindle edition, loc. 10217.
1755 McGilligan, *Clint: The Life and Legend*, Kindle edition, loc. 10274.

Walking with a Bible and a Gun

grammar of the film, however, tells a different story. Walt Kowalski, the retired autoworker, is the sheriff of Hamtramck, confronting the social chaos which flowed from the social engineering of what was once the most prosperous city in America, but is now an incoherent patchwork of burned-out houses and abandoned lots surrounded by sagging chain link fences, and the home to marauding gangs, who are not unlike the cattle rustlers which *The Virginian* confronted in Wyoming.

But the hidden grammar lies at a deeper level than the cowboy. Like Eastwood's roots, it goes back to era when Puritan ministers, like Dimmesdale, struggled with guilt because they could not avail themselves of sacramental confession when they rebelled against the Catholic Church. Like Dimmesdale, Walt Kowalski is plagued with guilt; unlike Dimmesdale and his creator, Kowalski avails himself of the sacrament of confession in a way that sets up the surprising denouement of the film.

In terms of sources, the literary roots of *Gran Torino* preceded *The Scarlet Letter* by almost two centuries. *Gran Torino* is an unexpected contribution to a genre known as the captivity narrative:

> Mary Rowlandson's memoir, *A Narrative of the Captivity and Restoration of Mrs. Mary Rowlandson*, (1682) is a classic example of the genre. According to Nancy Armstrong and Leonard Tennenhouse, Rowlandson's captivity narrative was "one of the most popular captivity narratives on both sides of the Atlantic." Although the text temporarily fell out of print after 1720, it had a revival of interest in the 1780s. Other popular captivity narratives from the late 17th century include Cotton Mather's "A Notable Exploit: *Dux Faemina Facti*," on the captivity of Hannah Duston, as well as his account of Hannah Swarton's captivity (1697), both well-known accounts of the capture of women during King William's War, and Jonathan Dickinson's *God's Protecting Providence* (1699).[1756]

The Indian abduction of English women began the moment the two groups came together on the western frontier. During the span of less than a century, from King Philip's War, which broke out in 1675, and the French and Indian Wars of 1763, 1,641 New Englanders were taken hostage.[1757] That practice continued as the frontier moved west. "During the decades-long struggle between whites and Plains Indians in the mid-19th century, hundreds of women and children were captured."[1758]

Intuitively understanding that the main interest driving the captivity narrative was sexual, Mrs. Rowlandson laid any prurient interest in her story

---

[1756] "Captivity narrative," *Wikipedia: The Free Encyclopedia*, https://en.wikipedia.org/wiki/Captivity_narrative
[1757] "Captivity narrative," *Wikipedia*.
[1758] "Captivity narrative," *Wikipedia*.

Part III: The Return of the Satanic Wilderness

to rest when she stated that "not one" of her Indian captors "ever offered the least abuse of unchastity to me in words or action."[1759]

As we have already mentioned, the most famous captivity narrative was the story of Daniel Boone rescuing his daughter from the Indians. James Fenimore Cooper took that story and turned it into *The Last of the Mohicans* and surprisingly Clint Eastwood created his own contribution to the captivity narrative genre when he directed *Gran Torino*. The immediate source for *Gran Torino* is John Ford's western, *The Searchers*, starring John Wayne. Ford's film was based on the novel of the same name by Alan LeMay, who disagreed with Mrs. Rowlandson about whether the Indians engaged in the sexual abuse of their captives. The Commanche did not murder or sexually abuse the children they captured. Instead, they raised them until they were sexually mature, at which point they married into the tribe. However, "Grown white women," according to LeMay, "were raped unceasingly by every captor in turn until either they died or were 'thrown away' to die by the satiated."[1760]

Alan LeMay's novel appeared in 1954, the same year in which the Supreme Court inaugurated the Civil Rights movement by handing down *Brown v. School Board*. The federal government's endorsement of integration ignited fears of miscegenation in the South, where white demonstrators held signs claiming that "Race mixing is Communism" in front of Central High School in Little Rock, Arkansas in 1959. Ford's film appeared two years after the *Brown v. School Board* decision when fears of miscegenation had intensified because of the court's insistence on integration.

The John Wayne character, Ethan Edwards, expressed those fears in Ford's film. After showing Ethan a number of feral white girls who had been rescued from Indian captivity, the soldier says: "It's hard to believe they're white," to which Ethan responds "They ain't white anymore," framing the identity issue at the heart of the film and book. Is "whiteness" biological? If so, how is it possible to lose it? Or is it cultural, based on language, which can be forgotten, as Debbie, the captive child seems to have done?

A close reading of the relevant texts indicates that "whiteness" is something sexual, like virginity, which once lost can never be regained. "Whiteness" became an identity marker shortly after English settlers arrived in the new world because the Puritan settlers were Judaizers who used the Old Testament stories of Joshua and Amalek to demonize both the Indian natives and the slaves from Africa. The idea that phenotype could become a criterion of church membership could only arise in a state church whose population lived on a island and were in rebellion against the Catholic Church because of its universality. Cromwell's demonization of the Irish as Amalek had nothing to

---

1759 "Mary Rowlandson," *Wikipedia: The Free Encyclopedia*, https://en.wikipedia.org/wiki/Mary_Rowlandson#:~:text=Although%20she%20feared%20and%20reviled,make%20sense%20of%20her%20kidnapping.

1760 Alan LeMay, *The Searchers*, Kindle edition, p. 35.

do with phenotype and everything to do with Catholicism, but the exigencies of life in the new world changed those priorities even if it didn't obliterate them completely. In William Flemming's *Narrative of the Sufferings* (1750), "Indian barbarities are blamed on the teachings of Roman Catholic priests."[1761]

LeMay's novel is based on the story of Cynthia Ann Parker, who was captured as an eight or nine-year-old girl by a Comanche raiding party during the Fort Parker massacre of 1836.[1762] Parker was adopted by the Comanche and given the name Na'ura, which means "was found." After reaching sexual maturity, she married Peta Nacona, a Comanche chief, and bore him three children. Twenty-four years after being captured by the Comanche, she was again captured, this time during the Battle of Pease River, by Texas Rangers, who forcibly separated her from her husband and three children and then tried to re-integrate her into "white" society by returning her to her original biological family against her will. The attempt failed, and "for the remaining 10 years of her life, she mourned for her Comanche family, and refused to adjust to white society. She escaped at least once but was recaptured and brought back."[1763] Parker died in 1841 "heartbroken over her daughter's death from influenza,"[1764] and unreconciled to the family and culture into which she had been born.

According to University of Texas professor Glenn Frankel, author of *The Searchers: The Making of an American Legend*, the threat of miscegenation became a "justification for the conquest of the West. Because if these Natives are going to come forward and steal our women and children, then we have the right to conquer them; we have the right to tame them."[1765] Sex with Indians becomes "a fate worse than death" because it robs the victims, both the women who are captured and the men who are deprived of them, of their identity as superior beings. Sex with Indians, in fact, calls civilization into question. If the settler isn't from a superior culture, i.e., one that can bring salvation to the heathen Indians, why is he justified in taking their land? Miscegenation was not perceived as an existential threat in Catholic colonies like Mexico or Canada, both of which allowed the unencumbered marriage of the native stock with that of the European newcomer. The idea that miscegenation was a threat never occurred to the Jesuits who brought Christianity to the new world, but it was a constant theme in the Puritan colony which became the form of the United States. As Professor Frankel points out:

1761 "Captivity narrative," *Wikipedia*.

1762 "Captivity narrative," *Wikipedia*.

1763 "Cynthia Ann Parker," *Wikipedia: The Free Encyclopedia*, https://en.wikipedia.org/wiki/Cynthia_Ann_Parker

1764 "Cynthia Ann Parker," *Wikipedia*.

1765 Nathan Cone, "The Texas History Behind John Ford's 'The Searchers,'" Texas Public Radio, April 9, 2013, https://www.tpr.org/arts-culture/2013-04-09/the-texas-history-behind-john-fords-the-searchers

Part III: The Return of the Satanic Wilderness

Around the time Cynthia Ann was kidnapped in 1836, if you look at the bestseller list, three of the four top bestsellers in America are James Fenimore Cooper novels, all of which have captivity themes. And then the fourth one was a non-fiction book about Mary Jamison, a woman who was captured by Seneca Indians in upstate New York in the 18th century. So, this is something that continues on into Texas. And really throughout our history, [the captivity narrative] has been an important genre.[1766]

The story of Cynthia Ann Parker became problematic for the racial understanding of American identity because she became a Comanche and:

> doesn't *want* to be back with the Texans. She doesn't *want* to be embraced in Christendom. She wants to be back with the Comanche family, with her sons, with her husband, with her village. And so it becomes a very tragic tale for the second time. She's a traumatized victim of the Comanche-Texan wars.[1767]

This didn't happen in Canada or Mexico because by embracing the Catholic faith the natives did not have to choose between their ethnic group and their religion as Cynthia Ann Parker did.

By the time the English Presbyterians arrived in Nova Scotia in the late 18th century, they discovered that the Micmac natives had completely intermarried with the French because both espoused the Catholic faith. There could be no Canadian equivalent to Cynthia Ann Parker because the Catholic Church had enabled a total merger of the two populations over the course of almost two centuries. Confronted with the natives' refusal to change their religion, their language, and their culture, the Presbyterians who arrived in Nova Scotia after the French lost the war of 1763 put bounties on Micmac scalps, and when that failed, the Presbyterians engaged in ethnic cleansing by deporting them to Louisiana, where they were supposed to die out in the fever swamps.

The peaceful Catholic solution to ethnic migration was not an option in 19th century Texas because once whiteness had become an identity marker, change in phenotype meant extinction, as it does today.

John Wayne does a masterful job portraying this bind as well as the emotional stress and complexity surrounding it. His *Dopplegaenger*, the man with the oxymoronic title of "Rev. Capt. Samuel Johnston Clayton," played by Ward Bond, is a preacher with a gun who can't tell whether he should baptize his flock and then exhort them to follow the example of Jesus Christ and live in peace with the Indians or to deputize his flock, hand them guns, tell them to "exterminate the brutes," as Kurtz said in "The Heart of Darkness," the *locus classicus* of British Protestant imperialist racism. Once countries

---

1766 Cone, "The Texas History Behind John Ford's 'The Searchers.'"
1767 Cone, "The Texas History Behind John Ford's 'The Searchers.'"

like England and the eastern half of Germany separated from the Catholic Church, it was only a matter of time before these state churches viewed the Gospel through the lens of racism.

The Rev. Capt. Clayton, as his name indicates, is a mass of contradictions. After he and his deputies escape across the river and take up a defensive position behind a log, he takes up a gun and starts shooting Indians. When one of his deputies gets wounded, he hands him a Bible and tells him to hold it close to his chest because it will make him feel good. He then grabs Ethan's rifle to prevent him from shooting at the same group of Indians he was shooting at only a moment before. The confusion which characterized the "war-like Christian man" whom the Virginia assembly promoted as that colony's ideal citizen was only dispelled when America absorbed Protestantism and became its own religion. The cultural artifact which epitomized that marriage of Bible and gun was the western film, especially in the hands of a master of that genre like John Ford.

Like The Virginian, Ethan is not a church-going man. In fact, he interrupts the only church service in the movie to go out and kill more Indians. Ethan's real religion is "whiteness," which means that the fundamental sin is miscegenation, which means that he must kill the same Debbie he set out to rescue once it becomes clear that she has become polluted by having sex with Indians. Ethan is not alone in feeling this way. Virtually every other character in the film feels the same way, because "whiteness" has become the defining mark of American identity for them. John Wayne is the most powerful figure in the movie, because he embodies the conflict which drives the plot. He is also, according to Frankel, "a very dark figure" who:

> starts out trying to rescue his nine-year-old niece, but as time goes on, she grows from being a little girl, to being a young woman over the seven years, and she becomes a Comanche wife. And so *she* has had sex with the Indians, willingly or not. And so his quest over time changes. As time goes on, and she's been "polluted" in this way, he decides he's going to kill her. And that becomes the narrative tension that drives the movie forward. What's going to happen when Uncle Ethan finally catches up with this little girl? John Wayne does a beautiful job of capturing all the conflict that's going on within Ethan Edwards as to what to do. On one level, he's sure he has to do this terrible deed. He becomes this dark knight, who rather than rescue the damsel, decides he's going to kill the damsel. At the same time, he's still John Wayne! He's very charismatic—we want him to succeed—but at the same time, we recoil from his mission. It's that tension that really drives the movie forward.[1768]

Ethan is alienated from Mart, whom he saved as a child from the Indians, because Mart is one quarter Cherokee. Challenged to justify why he continues

---

1768 Cone, "The Texas History Behind John Ford's 'The Searchers.'"

Part III: The Return of the Satanic Wilderness

to take part in a quest which is turning into mission impossible, Mart tells Amos that Debbie is kin, only to be contradicted by Amos, who tells him:

> "Debbie's my brother's young'n," Amos said. "She's my flesh and blood—not yours. Better you leave these things to the people concerned with 'em, boy. Debbie's no kin to you at all."[1769]

Mart, however, is not satisfied with Amos's rebuke.

> "I—I always felt like she was my kin." "Well, she ain't." "Our—I mean, her—her folks took me in off the ground. I'd be dead but for them. They even—" "That don't make 'em any kin." "All right. I ain't got no kin. Never said I had. I'm going to keep on looking, that's all."

The scene evokes the Gospel passage when Jesus is told that his mother and his brothers and his sisters, are outside asking for him, to which Jesus responds, "Who are my mother and my brothers?" Then answering his own question, Jesus says, "Anyone who does the will of God, that person is my brother and sister and mother."[1770]

Like Amos/Ethan, Laurie preaches the American gospel of racial purity, not the Gospel according to Mark:

> "Deborah Edwards is a woman grown," Laurie said. "If she's alive at all." He said, "If she's alive, I've got to fetch her home." "Fetch what home? She won't come with you if you find her. They never do. . . . She's had time to be with half the Comanche bucks in creation by now." Laurie's voice was cold, but not so brutal as her words.

> "Sold time and again to the highest bidder—and you know it! She's got savage brats of her own, most like. What are you going to do with them—fetch them home, too? Well, you won't. Because she won't let you. She'll kill herself before she'll even look you in the face. If you knew anything at all about a woman, you'd know that much!"

Sex with the Indians has turned Debbie into "nothing but a—a rag of a female—the leavings of Comanche bucks—" "Do you know," Laurie said, "what Amos will do if he finds Deborah Edwards? It will be a right thing, a good thing—and I tell you Martha would want it now. He'll put a bullet in her brain."[1771]

Charlie McCorry shares the same racist worldview as Laurie:

1769 LeMay, *The Searchers*, p. 88.
1770 Mark, 3:35.
1771 LeMay, *The Searchers*, Kindle edition, pp. 231-2.

Charlie looked at him thoughtfully, unwilling to be diverted. "Is she— Have they—" He didn't know how to put it, so that Mart would not be riled. "What I'm driving at—has she been with the bucks?"[1772]

Mart said, "Charlie, I don't know. I don't think so. It's more like—like they've done something to her mind." "You mean she's crazy?" "No—that isn't it, rightly. Only—she takes their part now. She believes them, not us. Like as if they took out her brain, and put in an Indian brain instead. So that she's an Indian now inside."[1773]

The verdict is clear: "One sleep with Indians—you're a mare—a sow— they take what they want of you."[1774] Sex with Indians renders a white woman feral, like the white girls the U.S. cavalry rescued from captivity. The verdict is all but unanimous, but Mart can't accept it, perhaps because of the Cherokee blood in his veins, perhaps because he gradually understand that the mind transcends biology in a way that his friends don't understand. Confusing Debbie's mind with her brain, Mart fails to see that the common bond he and Debbie share is not blood but logos, whose most common manifestation is language.

Mart's attempt to speak to Debbie starts of badly because "Her Comanche was fluent, indistinguishable from that of the Indians, yet he thought he had never heard that harsh and ugly tongue sound uglier."[1775] The real question is whether they share a common logos. DNA is irrelevant because Mart and Debbie are not "kin." The crisis arrives after Mart "suddenly...realized that he had spoken in a rush of English—and she no longer understood."[1776] Amos/ Ethan, although he is kin to Debbie, can't bring her back because "Mart was sure Debbie had understood none of Amos' Texan English."[1777]

As long as they speak Comanche, Mart can't reach her because "Comanche words" lead to "Comanche thoughts."[1778] Debbie may have "a white woman's voice and form," but phenotype is not going to prevent "the meeting toward which he had worked for years" from turning "into a nightmare."[1779] Debbie's face was "delicately made, and now in the first bloom of maturity; but all expression was locked away from it" because "behind the surface of this long-loved face was a Comanche squaw." Debbie was a Comanche because she spoke their language not because she looked like one. Mart gets nowhere as long as he speaks to her in Comanche:

1772 LeMay, *The Searchers*, p. 280.
1773 LeMay, *The Searchers*, p. 280.
1774 LeMay, *The Searchers*, p. 268.
1775 LeMay, *The Searchers*, p. 266.
1776 LeMay, *The Searchers*, p. 267.
1777 LeMay, *The Searchers*, p. 267.
1778 LeMay, *The Searchers*, p. 268.
1779 LeMay, *The Searchers*, p. 268.

Part III: The Return of the Satanic Wilderness

He returned to Comanche. "You're going with us now! You hear me?" "No," Debbie said. "Not now. Not ever."

"I don't know what they have done to you. But it makes no difference!" He wouldn't have wasted time fumbling Comanche words if he had seen half a chance of taking her by main force. "You must come with me. I take you to—"

"They have done nothing to me. They take care of me. These are my people."

"Debbie, Debbie—these—these Nemenna murdered our family!" "You lie." A flash of heat-lightning in her eyes let him see an underlying hatred, unexpected and dreadful. "These are the ones! They killed your mother, cut her arm off—killed your own real father, slit his belly open—killed Hunter, killed Ben—"[1780]

The situation changes when Mart switches to English in a final desperate attempt to reach her.

"Debbie, listen to me! I'm Mart! Don't you remember me?" He spoke just the names in English, and it was obvious that these two words were familiar to her."[1781]

"I remember you," she said gravely, slowly, across the gulf between them. "I remember. From always."[1782]

Ultimately logos wins out over race. Unlike Cynthia Ann Parker, whose reintegration process was thwarted by "her inability to communicate fluently in English,"[1783] Debbie gains access to her original identity when she hears Mart speak English and begins to communicate with him in what is her native language, or what the Germans call her *Muttersprache.*

The moral of both the book and the film is that logos is superior to blood. Only logos can close the gap that separates male and female, Jew and Greek, Texan and Comanche. The vehicle for logos in human history is the Catholic Church, an institution which never gets mentioned because if the Church had been part of this story, there would have been no story. Debbie is convinced that she has "no place," until Mart assures her "I'll be there, Debbie" to help her take back the ranch which has fallen into ruin, the book ends with a reconciliation, articulated by Debbie in "a strangely mixed tongue of Indian-English."

1780 LeMay, *The Searchers*, p. 269.

1781 LeMay, *The Searchers*, p. 267.

1782 LeMay, *The Searchers*, p. 267.

1783 HY89, "The Unseen Life of Cynthia Ann Parker: The First White Woman Among the Comanche," YouTube, September 18, 2024, https://www.youtube.com/watch?v=EBQ_HwL2Aq4

"I remember it all. But you the most. I remember how hard I loved you." She held onto him with what strength she had left; but she seemed all right, he thought, as she went to sleep.[1784]

The film ends on a simpler but more powerful note when Ethan abandons his attempt to kill his niece and says instead, "Let's go home, Debbie," because it signifies his redemption from racism.

After Kowalski prevents Thao, his Hmong neighbor boy, from stealing his Gran Torino, he meets Sue, Thao's sister, who offers him as free labor in reparation for his attempted robbery, but also so that Walt can teach him how to be a man and prevent him from being recruited by the Hmong thugs who are terrorizing the neighborhood. Becoming a man means getting a job as a construction worker and learning the ethnic slurs that were common in Detroit when Walt was his age. The scene doesn't work artistically, but it succeeds nonetheless in evoking the lost world of Catholic ethnicity which got destroyed by what John B. Watson called the greatest form of social engineering, namely, war. Watson was referring to World War I, but Walt's moral downfall took place in Korea, when he shot a young soldier—reminiscent of the gook Thao—who was trying to surrender.

While driving in his pickup truck, Kowalski sees Sue being harassed by a Black gang and comes to her assistance in a scene which recapitulates all of his classic encounters with Black criminals, beginning with *Dirty Harry*.

The scene turns *Gran Torino* into an unlikely example of the captivity narrative. Like Ethan who must overcome racial prejudice before he can rescue his niece Debbie in *The Searchers*, Walt must overcome his racial prejudice to save Sue. Similarly, just as Ethan overcomes his repugnance at Marty's mixed blood and writes a will handing down all of his possessions to him, Walt makes out a will transferring his Gran Torino to his Hmong protégé, and not to the granddaughter who wanted it so badly.

After Sue is prevented from getting into Walt's truck, he pulls his hand, pistol-style, out of his jacket and tells the Black thugs to back off, evoking obscene derision on their part and continued attempts to molest Sue.

He then pulls out the real thing inspiring the fear and respect which is the appropriate Negro reaction to the white guy who pulls a gun on them. Walt saves Sue from rape at the hand of a black gang only to find that she is later raped by the Hmong gang, which includes one of her cousins, which elicits a disgusted comment from Walt about incest. After his sister is raped, Thao, Walt's Hmong protégé, insists on revenge. When young Father Janovich hears that Walt is planning to avenge Sue by taking on the Hmong gang, he urges him to consider the Christian alternative, which brings Walt to the confessional in a scene so riddled with ambiguity that it threatens to sink the entire plot. Walt confesses a number of inconsequential incidents but

---

1784 LeMay, *The Searchers*, p. 308.

Part III: The Return of the Satanic Wilderness

omits the killing of an enemy child soldier that was trying to surrender to him, a memory which has plagued him with guilt for decades. To spare Thao from the same bloodshed, Walt locks him in his basement and then heads off to confront the Hmong gang. After berating the gang for raping Sue, Walt reaches into his jacket pocket, just as he had done when confronting the black gang. Thinking that he is about to draw a gun, the gang opens fire and kills him in a hail of bullets leaving him dead on the ground with arms outspread like Christ nailed to the cross. When the police arrive, an officer tells Thao and Sue that Walt was unarmed, but that the gang members have been arrested for murder and will be spending a long time in prison thanks to the witnesses who gathered when Walt was delivering his harangue. Walt's Christ-like self-sacrifice triumphed over the evil gang in a way that the gun could never have achieved. Walt's self-sacrifice has rendered the gun, which gave Americans their identity, obsolete, recapitulating the tropes of American identity and then transfiguring them by incorporating them into a new sacramental Catholic context. Unlike Nathaniel Hawthorne, Walt Kowalski was able to enter the confessional. Unlike Nathaniel Hawthorne, Walt Kowalski was able to act on the grace he received there and put an end to evil, not only rendering the gun unnecessary but subverting it as the symbol of American identity, so that it could make way for the real presence that had eluded Americans for centuries.

CHAPTER 50

JOE RITCHEY: A PREACHER WITHOUT A GUN

It's easy to miss the D. L. James house. Allegra Ritchey Fromm, sometimes known as Jennie, told us that it was directly across Highway 1 from the Tickle Pink Inn, and so with my eyes fixed on the left side of one of the narrowest and most scenic highways in America, I drove right past the unobtrusive entrance to what is probably the most beautiful house in California. After making a U-turn I catch fleeting glimpses of my destination while trying not to slide into southbound oncoming traffic. The entrance is easy to miss because it is simply a door placed in a rock arch which is part of a wall that extends along the highway for the length of the property. Aquinas said that happiness resulted from a sudden change in state. If so, the modest entrance to the D. L. James house gave rise to happiness as we opened the door, leaving the danger of the highway behind and entering an enchanted garden of indigenous trees shading a stone path which sloped gently downward toward an as yet unseen house. Both sides of the path were covered with exotic large-leafed plants that looked as if they belonged in a fantasy world. It was like entering Rivendell, which is the term which has replaced Arcadia in the English-speaking world when people talk about a mythical place where man can live in harmony with nature. I have talked about Bavaria as a place where one can find places which exhibit an almost perfect balance between culture and nature, but no one building in Bavaria embodies that perfect balance better than the D. L. James house in Carmel Highlands.

The path we have taken from the highway leads to an embodiment of that bifurcation at its terminus, where we are confronted with an arch, modeled on an arch that the architect Charles Greene saw on his honeymoon while visiting Tintagel Castle in Cornwall, and the courtyard of the house itself. Through the arch, one catches the first glimpse of the rocky coast of the Pacific Ocean 100 feet below, which is to say nature, but framed perfectly by the man-made arch and turned thereby into a work of art which provides the context for the courtyard on the right leading up to the house, which is again a work of art which responds to and organizes the natural setting on which it has been built. Art, as Aristotle told us, is imitation of nature. When the artist strikes the perfect balance between existence and essence, the result is beauty, and that is what the visitor experiences when the rock path reaches the house. The first and most natural reaction to beauty is to stop and stare as the mind struggles to comprehend the unity in all of the diversity he sees. Because the grandeur of nature has been framed by the rock arch, nature has been transformed into art. Because the house is now part of that same landscape, art has been transformed into beauty.

The idea of Arcadia was a prominent theme in the arts in America. Thomas Eakins, the Philadelphia artist, did his rendering of Arcadia with three naked boys, one of whom is playing the flute on what looks like a lawn in Fairmout Park. Thomas Cole, the most famous practitioner of the Hudson Valley school, did a grander version based on his understanding of the Greek province of the same name which inspired Theocritus to write idealized descriptions of the peasants who were lucky enough to live there and not in "the squalid and disease ridden city of Alexandria,"[1785] where he was forced to earn a living by writing his poetry.

According to former Chicago Board of Trade Chairman Patrick Arbor, Joe Ritchie died of Covid-19. Conversations with family members revealed a more complicated story. Joe began to experience difficulty breathing in the late fall of 2021. At some point his family decided to take him to the hospital, where he was put on the Centers for Disease Control and Prevention (CDC) regimen, which included Remdesivir, which made a bad situation worse. Over the course of the next three months, Joe became a prisoner of the medical establishment, which determined his treatment even as his family moved him from one hospital to another as his condition steadily worsened until Joe was on the verge of dying of thirst. "He started crying," Allegra, his daughter, recounted in her diary, "and said if a French nurse hadn't given him water, he would have died. I believe him."

No matter what the family did, they got countermanded by a medical establishment which seemed more concerned with following Big Pharma protocols than helping Joe recover. Frustrated by the intransigence of Big Pharma's minions, the family asked for prayers, and Joe's friends stormed heaven in a way that pointed out the Catholic-Protestant divide in his family of ten children. "My dad brought Protestants and Catholics, blue and white collar together to pray because those were his friends," Allegra said. "Three prayer text groups of 19 each included general contractor, priest, cardiologist, home school mom, movie star, pilot, gymnastics coach, pianist. There was a theme of him bringing together these people in life and even after death." Evangelicals commanded Satan to depart in the name of Jesus, and Catholics showed up with relics of Padre Pio as Joe's condition continued to deteriorate in what could be described as hospital arrest.

[1785] "Arcadia (utopia)," *Wikipedia*: The Free Encyclopedia, https://en.wikipedia.org/wiki/Arcadia_(utopia)

Part III: The Return of the Satanic Wilderness

Joe Ritchie started out in life as the child of an engineer who felt called by God to go to Afghanistan, which is where Joe spent four years of his life from 1957 to 1961. That experience would draw Joe and his younger brother James back to Afghanistan during the period of turmoil there preceding the 9/11 attacks.

The sense of calling Joe got from his father found reinforcement at Wheaton College, where he studied philosophy. Or so he claimed. His wife Sharon claimed that he graduated third from the bottom of his class because he never prepared for class because he was too busy having deep conversations with fellow students. Joe was a gambler and a missionary in a uniquely American way. Joe, according to his wife, "never read anything. He always felt there were more important things to do, like talking to people." Joe was interested in people, not books. If he thought you had something interesting to say, he would contact you and offer to help you in what you were doing. My relationship with him began when he called the *Culture Wars* office and began a conversation with my wife, the business manager. "How are you doing?" he persisted in asking her. After hearing her say "the Lord will provide" one too many times, Joe finally got to the point of the call and asked if we needed money.

Over the years that I knew him, I would bring him the books I had written as they rolled off the press, and he would accept them graciously, but he never read any of them. If anything I wrote made it into his mind, it was during long automobile trips when his wife Sharon would read, and Joe would drive. When I presented him with a copy of *Barren Metal*, which is 1,200 pages long, I suggested a drive to Tierra del Fuego or Alaska. Apparently, he never read Rick Warren's book on a purpose driven life either, although he recommended it to virtually everyone he met. Warren apparently held no hard feelings because he gave a eulogy at Joe's memorial service.

After graduating from Wheaton College, Joe became a bus driver and then a prison guard, and then a DuPage County sheriff, and then an assistant to a man who needed Joe to find a commodities trader. Eventually Joe became the trader he failed to find.

If prudence bespeaks the ability to know the truth and to act on it, Joe was a very prudent man. His ability to act on the opportunities he could size up in the commodities market earned him a fortune. In 1976 Joe started trading on the floor of the Chicago Board Options Exchange, where he discovered that he could plug the Black-Scholes equation into his Texas Instruments SR 52 calculator, leading to a huge financial success on the floor.

In 1977, Joe founded Chicago Research and Trading, an options and futures trading firm that was one of the first to engage in computer driven trading strategies. Joe's TI calculator made him the one-eyed king in the land of the blind. "CRT's secret," *The Wall Street Journal* wrote in 1988, "is a computer system that uses one of the most sophisticated trading models in the securities industry. By monitoring differences in the options and futures prices, the model developed mainly by Mr. Ritchie, the firm executed more than $2.5 billion in trades each day."[1786]

By 1988, Joe had turned an initial investment of $200,000 into a company with $225 million in assets and over 700 employees. As an employer with that kind of workforce, Joe had to make hiring decisions based on computer backed intuitions that allowed him to see that people could be undervalued just as some commodities and stocks were, and that giving people in those situations a chance often paid handsome dividends. Eventually, after selling CRT to Bank of America for $225 million in 1993, Joe decided to focus on potentialities in human capital.

Joe's ability to size up people and get involved in their lives led him from one adventure to another. When Joe got tired of trading, he handed his TI calculator to Steve Fossett, whom he met while they were working on a project for Marshall Fields. Steve eventually made a fortune of his own, and the fortunes they made enabled them to indulge in a shared fascination with flying and setting speed records, which they did in Joe's airplane on the spur of the moment when Joe informed Steve that the Jet Stream was flowing faster than normal. Fossett would circumnavigate the world in record time in a balloon, largely because Joe could predict conditions in the Jet Stream and the weather conditions beneath it. In 1998, on one of Fossett's early attempts, Joe watched in frustration as Fossett's balloon plunged into the South Pacific because the meteorologist Fossett had hired couldn't adjust to changing weather conditions fast enough. On the final successful attempt in July 2002, Fossett put Joe in charge of the mission's logistics, and Joe guided the balloon around the world in record time, largely because he had learned how to act decisively on the trading floor, where what was the right decision on one day might be the wrong decision on another.

Flush with the proceeds of the sale of CRT in 1993, Joe was in California looking for property when someone mentioned that the D. L. James house in Carmel Highlands might be available. Joe fell in love with the James house when he first saw it in 1995, and after renting it for four years he was able to buy it in 1999. Joe never told me that beauty was a transcendental, but he did refer to the James house as a slice of heaven on earth. Allegra said that the entrance to their house in Carmel reminded her of her father. "My dad was like that: modest entrance, then depth, The biggest compliment I received was 'I had no idea you had money.'" Joe saw the D. L. James house as a place which could bring people together in an atmosphere suffused with the transcendental qualities associated with beauty. If beauty could lead the people staying there to think transcendental thoughts, it could lead to solving the world's problems because the beautiful, the good, and the true are all

---

[1786] "Joe Ritchey," *Wikipedia: The Free Encyclopedia*, https://en.wikipedia.org/wiki/Joe_Ritchie

Part III: The Return of the Satanic Wilderness

interchangeable. Joe Ritchey was an archetype of the American. Henry James could have written a novel about him. Like Nathaniel Hawthorne, Joe found that beauty could lead him to the truth. Unlike Hawthorne, Joe was able to act on what he knew. The D.L. James house in Carmel epitomized beauty precisely because it was a uniquely American piece of architecture which allowed him to move from perceiving beauty, to understanding the truth, to doing good.

Chapter 51

Joe Ritchey and Abdul Haq

Charles Greene, its architect, died in 1957, the same year Joe Ritchie arrived in Afghanistan as a ten-year old. During the years he began renting the D. L. James house, Joe became increasingly involved in helping the Afghans get out of the "25 years of hell" they had already suffered, and that meant finding an alternative to both the Taliban and the Northern Alliance. Joe and his brother James approached Afghanistan's king in exile, urging him to work through the *loya jurga* or tribal councils which they had been financing, but in the course of their discussions with the king, Joe met Abdul Haq and recognized that he was "the key guy there who was capable of ... putting together the commanders that were needed to make this militarily playable."[1787] Joe had "instantly connected" with Haq. "As I got to know him," Joe told Lucy Edwards:

> I realized the dimensions of this guy that he was extremely brilliant, sophisticated, liberal in a good kind of way ... gentle, sensitive ... and he had a leadership ability that could bring Afghans together.... Afghans are extremely fractious people. This was a man who could bring Afghan commanders together ... because commanders are even more fractious, and he just led by virtue of the fact that he was the man with the vision and everybody realized this. He never pushed himself forward; he just ... was present and ... would wind up leading whatever group he was in by virtue of ... his merits.[1788]

Haq was convinced that "the Taliban can be taken out now," and Joe believed him. Haq, who baptized himself "the servant of Justice" during the onset of the mujahideen jihad against the Soviet invaders, was born as Hamayoun Arsala, in 1957 as the fourth of eight brothers born to his father's second wife.[1789] Haq had distinguished himself during the jihad against the Soviets. After the expulsion of the Soviets in 1989, Haq, the Lion of Kabul, joined with the legendary Ahmad Shah Massoud, the "Lion of Panjshir" in bringing

---

[1787] Lucy Morgan Edwards, *The Afghan Solution: the Inside Story of Abdul Haq, the CIA, and How Western Hubris Lost Afghanistan* (London: Bactria Press, 2011), p. 292.
[1788] Edwards, *The Afghan Solution*, p. 292.
[1789] Edwards, *The Afghan Solution*, p. 91.

together Tajiks, Uzbeks, Hazara, and disaffected Pashtuns in an anti-Taliban alliance that united the country.

In 2000, Joe and James Ritchie, along with Robert (Bud) McFarlane, who had served as Ronald Reagan's security advisor, met with Abdul Haq to "create a strategy for Afghanistan to transition to a more democratic and modern society with the help of the former Afghan King Zahir Shah."[1790] Throughout the 1990s, the Ritchie brothers had been funding the *loya jurga* with the tacit approval of the U.S. State Department as a way of creating an alternative to the Taliban, which was "collapsing from within," according to Haq, because the people were starving and had turned against them. All Haq and the Ritchie brothers needed was time to work things out, but that is precisely what the neocons who controlled America's foreign policy were determined to deny them. The neocons were hoping to spread feminism throughout the Islamic world to subjugate it, as they would do after the 2003 invasion of Iraq. When Paul Wolfowitz arrived in Baghdad with bags of money for the feminists, he was greeted by a barrage of RPGs aimed at his hotel room, forcing him to make a hasty exit in his underwear. Before that, Wolfowitz arrived in Kabul, where he "visited a new refurbished, shiny women's clinic," which was "hailed [as] a triumph of progress for Afghan women."[1791] Abdul Haq kept insisting "that the Taliban is collapsing from within."[1792] The people were ready to turn against them, but missile strikes from an outside power would only strengthen the Taliban's hold on the country. Haq tried to get this message to Tony Blair, and he hoped that the Ritchie brothers could convey the same message to the American military command.

With the MacFarlane's assistance, Joe brought Haq's plan to the attention of the White House, the State Department, the CIA, and the Defense Department, unaware that the Neocons, who had gotten a foothold in the White House during the Reagan era had plans of their own for the Middle East, and, unlike Joe, were in a position to put those plans into action. Joe found little enthusiasm for Haq or his plan. "Prior to 9/11 they just couldn't seem to focus on that enough to actually want to do anything and then post 9/11, they wanted to do it another way."

When 9/11 happened, Joe Ritchie and Bud Macfarlane were scheduled to meet the Secretary of State for South Asia. The meeting was cancelled, and Joe Ritchie went to Rome to meet again with the exiled King, "to encourage the King to get into play, which he did." Joe then returned to D.C. "thinking that now we were in essence at war, it shouldn't be a problem to get people to focus on this [problem] of knocking off the Taliban . . . . The problem then

---

1790 Edwards, *The Afghan Solution*, p. 51.
1791 Edwards, *The Afghan Solution*, p. 54.
1792 Edwards, *The Afghan Solution*, p. 39.

Part III: The Return of the Satanic Wilderness

was that . . . they wanted to do it their own way, without help from Abdul Haq."[1793]

The very qualities which made Haq attractive to Joe Ritchie made him repugnant in the eyes of the CIA, which "didn't want to work with a man who couldn't be relied on to say what they wanted."[1794] Joe's frustration was palpable as he watched the obvious solution to the problem slipping away because of the venality of the people in charge of American foreign policy. "The CIA knew . . . who the whores were and who . . . the men of stature were and didn't want men of stature. Outside the CIA I think there was a problem of not knowing enough about the players."

Shortly after King Zahir Shah and his council voted unanimously to accept Haq's proposal, the Americans invaded Afghanistan in the wake of the 9/11 attack on the World Trade Towers. The U.S. led bombing campaign began on Sunday, October 7, 2001. Abdul Haq was dead by the end of the month. Three years after his death, Edwards interviewed James Ritchie, who claimed that the CIA was ultimately responsible for Haq's death, no matter what role the Taliban played in it, because in 2001, Abdul Haq provided the only political strategy "not reliant upon explicit military force in Afghanistan that we are likely to see in a generation." Joe Ritchie concurred with his brother's assessment:

> "I couldn't have imagined a platter more ideally loaded for what the folks in Washington needed. I mean here you had the Afghan Commander who had pulled together more other commanders than anyone in the history of the wars. . . . He'd shown the most courage; he had been the best at this kind of behind the lines warfare by far. He had a plan that didn't involve risking a single American life. The Afghans themselves were taking all the risks. He wasn't asking for any weapons or financing. This was entirely resources brought by his men, their commitment, their lives. And he provided a huge counterbalance to this Northern Alliance force, which if it took Kabul, was going to lead to a long-term problem for Afghanistan and likely civil war again. And here it was all in one place. It was credible. It was exactly what the doctor ordered. . . . But it had just one defect. The leader was not a man who could be bought. He was a man of courage and principle, and therefore the CIA couldn't own him. I think that was the fatal problem that . . . kept him from getting the backing he needed to pull this off, and to leave Afghanistan in a . . . long term stable situation, which as we know . . . now, it's not."[1795]

Joe and James were convinced that Abdul Haq could defeat the Taliban and unite the county, but the CIA thought otherwise and eventually murdered

---

1793 Edwards, *The Afghan Solution*, p. 296.
1794 Edwards, *The Afghan Solution*, p. 295.
1795 Edwards, *The Afghan Solution*, p. 305.

Haq. If Haq hadn't left his compound without him, James would have died in the fatal drone attack on Haq's car.

In the aftermath of 9/11, the story of Joe's attempt to use Abdul Haq to unite Afghanistan got replaced by feel good Hollywood fictions like *Charlie Wilson's War*. Thanks to the Jews in Hollywood, the neocons in charge of America's foreign policy were able to perpetrate identity theft by replacing Joe Ritchie, the real American hero with Charlie Wilson, who was a drunk and a womanizer whose only principle was loyalty to the Jews who funded him and bailed him out when he got arrested for drunk driving. Abdul Haq was murdered because his ability to unite Afghanistan without outside help did not fit in with the narrative of "the CIA, Britain's MI6, the Pakastani intelligence and military establishment, the warlords, and the strongmen of the Northern Alliance, the Karzai family and its allies, the 'military-security-industrial complex' for whom continued war has proven to be an unending pipeline to profit." As a result, Haq was replaced by "those Afghans who now benefit from a status quo which is characterized by instability, illegal activities, regional chaos, and, internally, a climate of impunity, insecurity and ongoing civil war." Joe failed to bring about any change in American policy because he was outnumbered by the people who were benefiting from the American occupation. According to Colonel Douglas MacGregor, "Counter-insurgency has not been the success story presented to the American people. Making cash payments to buy cooperation from insurgent groups to conceal a failed policy of occupation is a temporary expedient to reduce U.S. casualties, not a permanent solution for stability."[1796]

The truth of MacGregor's claim became too obvious to ignore when the Islamic Republic of Afghanistan collapsed on August 15, 2021. Throughout that summer President Biden kept reminding Americans that the Afghans had an army of 600,000 men to defend them against the Taliban. Over the course of the summer, that army simply evaporated, and the Taliban took over the country without firing a shot.

Joe at this point could derive cold consolation from the vindication of his position, but the world had changed since the days when Reagan and Gorbachev came together to end the Cold War. The adults were no longer in the foreign policy room. In fact, they had left the building and were replaced by the neoconservatives determined to spread the Jewish Revolutionary Spirit in a way assured of victory because no one could say the word Jew.

[1796] Edwards, *The Afghan Solution*, p. 319.

Chapter 52

Joe Ritchey Converts to Catholicism

In what must have been 2014, Joe expressed an interest in converting to Catholicism. Responding to that interest, I introduced him to Fr. Jeffrey Langan, a priest of Opus Dei. Joe was doing business in Russia at the time, and after I sent him Fr. Jeff's phone number, Joe called him in Italy from Russia to try to arrange a meeting. When Jeff told him that he was leaving for a mountain top near L'aquila, Joe said no problem and flew his own plane from Moscow to Italy. After arriving in the mountain village by rental car, Joe took Jeff to the local café, where they spent the next three hours having one of those conversations that Joe so liked to organize. They talked about his coming into the Church, working out the details of how that would eventually happen in the suburbs of Chicago when Jeff put Joe in contact with Fr. Peter Armenio, who would admit him to full communion with the Catholic Church, administer the last rites to him when he was dying, and then officiate at his funeral Mass.

Joe was received into full communion with the Church in 2016. When Jeff asked Joe why he had contacted him, Joe mentioned a *Culture Wars* article Fr. Jeff had written on Russia's invasion of Georgia, which agreed with his assessment of the situation. After reading *Culture Wars*, Joe concluded that the magazine had come to the same conclusion through study that he had garnered through years of practical experience in the world of business. Joe was also impressed with my treatment of the Jewish question, but this was not something he shared with others in his circle. When we finally did talk about the Jews and their influence on American culture in the kitchen of his home in West Chicago, it was only after all present had put their cell phones in his microwave oven. *Culture Wars* had the capacity to understand the damage that the Neocons were wreaking in the world through their capture of America's foreign policy. Unlike Protestants, Catholics could say that the neocons needed to be put in their place. This was one more reason he became a Catholic. By reading *Culture Wars*, Joe saw that the Catholics could criticize both the left and the right, a state of affairs that did not exist among the Protestant sects which had formed him in his youth. Reading *Culture Wars* also confirmed views which Joe had already adopted as the result of experiences he had in the world of Jewish finance while running CRT.

During the 1980s Joe realized that he had three kinds of employees. The first group was Protestants and Muslims who thought that human nature was evil. This group was capable of doing terrible things. The second group was made up of people who felt that man was intrinsically good, and this group was capable of doing even worse things. Then there was the third group that thought man was basically good, but that we were capable of doing evil if we didn't exercise rational control over our lives. This group was made up of Catholics, Joe started thinking that the Protestantism he was raised in was inadequate to the challenges he faced and that it was time to move to another religion. The main thing Protestantism lacked was valid sacraments. Since Joe was involved in Russia, he became a member of the Russian Orthodox Church, primarily so that he would not have to tell his Protestant friends that he had converted to Catholicism.

During their first meeting in Italy, Joe and Jeff also talked about the world situation, how the neoconservatives (Joe didn't use the word Jew) had captured America's foreign policy, about his work in Rwanda, and about the then current crisis in the Ukraine after Victoria Nuland staged her *coup d'etat* and what Joe hoped to do about that. During the 1980s, Joe had arranged the meeting between Ronald Reagan and Mikhail Gorbachev which brought about the end of the Cold War, and Fr. Jeff was of the opinion that he hoped to do something similar with the crisis in the Ukraine, which was weighing on him as he watched Victoria Nuland topple the democratically elected Ukrainian government in 2014 and weaponize the Ukraine as a forward NATO base of operations against Russia.

Joe had hatched a plan which involved getting crucial figures together under the auspices of the Catholics, who had the worldwide network which the Protestants lacked. If it had worked with Gorbachev and Reagan without the benefit of that international network, it should be able to resolve the Ukrainian crisis with it. Joe was in many ways a prisoner of his early successes and never got over helping to engineer the meeting which ended the Cold War. He called his organization "Artisans of Peace." The term is instructive because the term "artisan" relates back to the arts and crafts movement which inspired the D. L. James house, which is where he was spending his down time. One Artisans of Peace project involved bringing Russian and American movers and shakers and their wives together for a week of sightseeing and discussions in Rome.

Joe relied on Fr. Jeff and the ecclesial infrastructure he was part of in Rome and as a priest in Opus Dei to make contacts at the Vatican which he thought might help him fend off the growing animosity toward Russia in the U.S. He also wanted the Vatican's help to get more countries to break free of economic neo-colonialism in places like Africa. No matter how noble his intentions, Joe was engaged in the subversion of the American empire, and he knew that no matter where he was, there were always people trying to subvert what he was doing, even to the point of having him killed. When he went to Palestine to broker a peace deal there, one of his companions was found dead on the beach. In starting his operations in Africa, Joe chose Rwanda because it wasn't a big country like Nigeria, where it would have been much easier to arrange for his death. But there was always push back, no matter where he went, because as Jeff pointed out to him, "the empire always strikes back."

Covid was an example of how the oligarchs planned to take over the entire world, and Covid caused Joe's death, albeit indirectly through Big Pharma's protocols. Aware that President John Magafuli of Tanzania had been murdered because of his vocal opposition to the Covid mandate and his efforts to keep Big Pharma out of Tanzania, Joe was cautious. He went into Kenya and tried to work under the radar, while contacting people whom he considered movers and shakers. Joe would spend five years in a country trying to find men of character, which was his term for virtue. Once he found these men, Joe would bring them together for a retreat during which they would try to come up with a plan of action.

Whenever Joe arrived in Rome, he was accompanied by his right-hand man Tim Shirk. Joe had met Tim in Rwanda and had hired him away from the firm that employed him. Tim ran his New York office and was in charge of his Russia project in which Artisans of Peace was going to bring Russian movers and shakers together with their western counterparts, like Hugh Jackman and Bono, who was adept at getting photo ops with the pope.

But wasn't this the flaw in the whole operation? By the very fact that they were prominent, celebrities like Bono were committed to the system which was the source of their wealth and fame and of the problems Joe wanted to solve. One of Joe's projects was a wealth tax, as opposed to an income tax, on the rich. Why movie stars would want to be involved in something like this is a question Joe never asked. The rich had billions in the bank which simply did not trickle down. He tried to work out the details of a wealth tax, but the Republicans, with whom he had the closest contact, would never go along with this proposition. When I proposed my anti-*Mitumba* (the Swahili word for used clothing) project for Kenya, Joe showed no interest, leaving me to wonder what might have happened if he had invested in cloth production in Kenya rather than creating a medicine factory in Rwanda, only to be betrayed when the Rwandan health ministry allowed Pfizer into the country. Jeff contributed to Joe's Artisans of Peace project by introducing him to Opus Dei's Strathmore University in Nairobi where he made contact with members of Kenya's Catholic elite like Patrick Njoroge, who was serving as Kenya's finance minister. Joe—whose motto was "What can we do without getting ourselves killed?"—tried to export the success he had had in Rwanda to Kenya and Uganda. Joe wanted to prevent the oligarchs from stealing Africa's wealth from its people, which is precisely what happened when Pfizer moved into Rwanda and nullified any chance that Joe would get a return on his investment in his affordable medicine factory.

Joe nonetheless continued his quest to find people who had both intelligence and virtue. Joe remained optimistic to the end. He understood that the Deep State's Ukrainian policy was a failure and that with the change of administration he no longer had access to elite political circles, but he never stopped working for positive changes. He became a Catholic because he realized that the Church had the system that promoted these ideals in a way the Protestants and the Orthodox could not. He realized that God had given him a gift to facilitate communication leading to action, something Plato mentioned in the *Gorgias*, but he also realized that he had to be more than a lone ranger or superhero doing it all on his own. He had inherited the theological virtue of hope from his Protestant background and had faith that America could do good in the world, but after his experience in Afghanistan, he concluded that the CIA had ruined everything.

Joe understood that doing good was impossible without grace and that the Catholic Church's sacraments were a source of that grace, but he was also inspired by the beauty in the house. If Greene could create beauty against all odds, then Joe could do good against even greater odds. Joe never stopped being a Protestant missionary in the mode of his father, who had to disguise his missionary work behind engineering. Just as Harvard had institutionalized the architecture of Walter Gropius, Joe realized that he could not institutionalize what he wanted to do without the support of the institutional Catholic Church, even though Joe was fundamentally opposed to institutions. He rarely gave money to schools. He picked individuals instead. He told Jeff shortly after he met him, "Don't ask me for money" because he saw Opus Dei as a money-grubbing institution and *Culture Wars* as its opposite, a mom and pop operation run by two individuals and too small to be an institution.

Regarding Stephen Kinzer's book, *Overthrow*, Joe talks about the people who were assassinated in Afghanistan after 9/11, knowing full well that he too could be a target. "I can't go to Nigeria because it would be too easy to have me killed while I was there." He understood taking risks. In 2018, Joe took Jeff to Rome to attend a conference of Catholic legislators because he needed Jeff's help in dealing with high-ranking Vatican officials. Because he had the Protestant sense that people like Cardinal Schoenborn were mystical creatures, Joe wanted Jeff's advice on how to communicate the idea of the Artisans of Peace to officials at the Vatican, hoping for an eventual meeting with the pope. That strategy was doomed from the start. Father Jeff may have been in Opus Dei, but by the time Joe asked for his assistance it was impossible for him to get a meeting with the pope because the Jesuits, who hated Opus Dei, had taken over the Vatican.

Part III: The Return of the Satanic Wilderness

The concept itself may have been flawed. Joe may have become a Catholic, but that was after he had embarked on the Artisans project which grew out of the idea: First get rich, then do good by getting other wealthy influential people. And the times had changed. Ironically, the man who had the reputation for being able to change positions on a dime spent the last part of his life trying to recreate the success of what he had done in the 1980s. Bringing Reagan and Gorby together worked in the 1980s, but he tried to replicate that feat in the early 21st century, without any recognition that the world had changed. The adults were no longer in the room in Washington. They had been replaced by people who began every speech by saying that they had relatives who had died in the Holocaust, making themselves infallible and impossible to talk to.

As a thought experiment, let's suppose that Joe had succeeded in bringing President Putin, the world's greatest statesman, together with President Zelensky, the Jewish comedian, at his house in Carmel. What good could possibly come out of such a meeting? Joe was committed to an idea whose time had come and gone.

There is a sad symmetry in the lives of Charles Greene and Joe Ritchie. Greene felt beauty was possible in America; Ritchie felt that Americans could bring peace to troubled Afghanistan. The idea that Americans could bring about world peace using the same ingenuity which allowed them to make fortunes on the Chicago trading floor and pilot balloons around the world in record time died when the CIA murdered Abdul Haq, but the promise of the D. L. James house as the locus of Arcadia in America lived on for another 20 years.

In another example of the fortuitous incidents which seemed to structure his life, Joe Ritchie, fresh from his disillusionment in Afghanistan, met Rwandan president Paul Kagame in 2003, and decided to get involved in developing the Rwandan economy. In 2008 Ritchie created the Rwandan Development Board and the Presidential Advisory Council. As a result of Joe's efforts, Rwanda soon attracted the attention of large U.S. corporations like Starbucks and Costco.[1797]

Joe got personally involved in economic development there by investing his own funds in Akagera Medicines, a pharmaceutical firm which focused on curing infectious poverty-related diseases like tuberculosis.[1798] In 2017, President Kagame conferred on Joe the National Order of Outstanding Friendship. In recognition of the role Joe played facilitating economic development in Rwanda, Kagame called Joe an "evangelist of prosperity."[1799]

1797 Alice Kagina, "Joe Ritchie, an American businessman and friend of Rwanda, dies at 75," *The New Times*, Feb. 22, 2022, https://www.newtimes.co.rw/news/joe-ritchie-american-businessman-dies-75

1798 Kagina, "Joe Ritchie."

1799 Kagina, "Joe Ritchie."

Hindsight shows an element of unintended irony in Kagame's statement. Within months of Joe's death by hospital during the Covid pandemic, the Kagame government announced that it had signed an agreement with Pfizer "to provide all their medicines and vaccines available on a not-for-profit basis."[1800] In that announcement, Dr. Daniel Ngamije, the Rwandan Minister of Health, explained that he was "looking forward to sharing information with the Pfizer team, about improving the ability to screen different diseases and also improving research as part of our agreement."[1801]

Missing was any analysis of the impact that Pfizer's willingness "to provide all their medicines and vaccines available on a not-for-profit basis"[1802] or the effect that decision would have on Akagera Medicines' ability to provide a return on his investment. Sharon explained the connection to me during our week-long melancholy farewell to the D. L. James house. Joe's investment in Rwanda had left the family broke, forcing them to sell the property in Carmel.

At the end of his life, Joe Ritchie discovered that he was a master of the universe suddenly caught up in a situation which he could not control. "I am a diplomat," he said during his long slide toward death. "I just got 200 girls evacuated from Kabul to Kigali, and I can't get myself out of this hospital."

Joe died at the hand of the Big Pharma he dared to oppose in Rwanda. He was aware of the risks. During one of our many conversations he told me that John Magafuli, then president of Tanzania, had suffered a similar fate by refusing to import Pfizer's anti-Covid vaccine. Adding insult to injury, Magafuli claimed that both a goat and a papaya had tested positive for Covid as his justification for denying Pfizer access to his country. That refusal cost Magafuli his life.

It was the sort of braggadocio which Joe had assiduously avoided, but Big Pharma got him in the end anyway. CDC protocols which begin with Remdesivir invariably end in death. Those who avoided the Covid protocols survived. Those who didn't died. Neglect was an integral part of the Covid regimen. Joe died with a huge bed sore so deep that the bone was visible. In the end the homeopathic remedies that could have saved him if they had been administered sooner ended up being too little too late.

1800 Ines Rutayisire Umurerwa, "Pfizer trains Rwandan medics on vaccines, medicines use," *The New Times*, July 15, 2022, https://www.newtimes.co.rw/news/pfizer-trains-rwandan-medics-vaccines-medicines-use

1801 Umurerwa, "Pfizer trains Rwandan."

1802 Umurerwa, "Pfizer trains Rwandan."

Chapter 53

Et in Arcadia Ego

Et in Arcadia ego. Even in Arcadia I am present. The 'I' in the phrase refers to death. The motto seems especially appropriate at the D. L. James house because the only reason we were able to contemplate the beauty of this stunning piece of Arcadian architecture is because its owner had died.

Joseph J. Ritchie died on February 22, 2022. Allegra said that *Gran Torino* was Joe's favorite movie. Joe, a paradigmatic American in his own right, identified with Walt Kowalski as a grumpy guy who ended up doing the right thing in the end, which could have been a description of Joe except he never seemed grumpy to me. Joe admired Clint Eastwood and may have played golf with him at Eastwood's golf course since they were both neighbors in Carmel.

During his multifaceted career Joe got involved in producing movies, and in the discussion about which actor should play which role, Clint Eastwood's name would come up frequently because Joe felt that the characters Eastwood played had an authenticity which came naturally. Confession played a crucial role in Joe's conversion to Catholicism, and *Gran Torino* may have been Joe's favorite movie because it showed how sacramental confession had absorbed the gun myth which had usurped American identity. Allegra, who was also affected by the movie, remembers the penultimate scene in *Gran Torino*, when Walt Kowalski is lying on the ground with his arms outstretched like Christ's on the cross as a powerful symbol of redemptive suffering as an alternative to cowboy vengeance. It also symbolized, in Allegra's mind, the self-sacrifice necessary for Protestants when they convert to Catholicism. Giving up a false identity is like death; the death of the old man has to take place before the new man can be born. Conversion, as the ladies who are part of the revolutionary guard like to say in Iran, means "Death to America," if by America we mean "the world's fourth great religion." Like her father, Allegra grew up Protestant and saw the harm that the absence of sacramental confession inflicted on the Protestant soul. When the guilt became intolerable, as it did in the aftermath of the sexual revolution, Protestants would gather in football stadiums and confess their sins over loudspeakers, based on the assumption that it was a once and for all deal and somehow efficacious if enough people got involved. Promise Keepers, to give the example Allegra had in mind, was one more version of the Great Awakening, a ritual which was psychologically necessary among people who could not avail themselves of sacramental confession. Allegra remembers a speaker at Wheaton College, where both she and her father were undergraduates, talking about confession and clearly getting under the skin of the campus minister, who opined afterward that Protestants should live their lives in a way that made sacramental confession unnecessary. Nathaniel Hawthorne had exposed the impossibility of that approach in *The Scarlet Letter*. Between *Unforgiven* and *Gran Torino*, Clint Eastwood exploded that myth forever. Unlike Nathaniel Hawthorne, Joe Ritchie was able to act on what he knew and enter the same Church which had saved Walt Kowalski, the new and transfigured paradigm of what it now meant to be an American.

Like his father Joe, Noah Ritchie was raised within the geographical and metaphysical confines of Wheaton College, the Vatican of American Evangelical religion, which valiantly attempted to forge a *lingua franca* that would allow the various American sects to talk to each other and speak meaningfully in the public square. The man who provided this vocabulary was the Englishman C.S. Lewis, whose papers are housed at Wheaton. *Mere Christianity* provided a quasi-ecumenical vocabulary, but it was also Lewis's weakest book because the unity which Lewis forged was a category of his mind, and his mind alone, which did not exist in reality. Hence, its failure.

Noah eventually left Wheaton and moved to Los Angeles, where he was exposed to the other side of the American experience, which is known as the Enlightenment, which attempted to be the rational alternative to the limitless proliferation of sects that is the legacy of Protestantism, but that led to its own form of absurdity in Enlightenment tracts like Immanuel Kant's *Religion Within the Bounds of Reason Alone*, or ever more absurdly apropos of the American scene, Thomas Jefferson's expurgated edition of the Bible. We Americans grow up in a world in which faith and reason are in constant conflict, leading to skepticism, which seems to be Noah's position, via long excursions through the writings of Nasip Talib, author of *Black Swan*, which was his way of saying that the future is unknowable in spite of Long Term Capital Management's application of the Black Scholes equation to the stock market.

Noah learned this lesson in the expensive school of experience known as Jewish Los Angeles, where people evidently hire homosexuals with happy results. Our conversation is threatening to grind to a halt in the deep mud of skepticism like an overloaded bus in the Congo rain forest, when Allegra joins us and talks about her conversion to Catholicism 16 years earlier. Allegra grew up in the Wheaton world of sects and moved from one to the other with the initial enthusiasm which emerged every time she joined a new congregation, before invariably turning into disappointment. The people were so friendly because Allegra had chosen them and validated their sect, but the enthusiasm invariably faded. Catholicism was completely different. No one was friendly. No one cared if you joined their parish. In Allegra's mind that was obviously

Part III: The Return of the Satanic Wilderness

proof that the Church was a supernatural institution which survived in spite of the shortcomings of the people who ran it.

Noah is showing impatience with his sister's explanation of why she converted to Catholicism probably because he has heard it before but more importantly because he clearly views the Catholic Church as just another sect, like Methodists, or Baptists, or Scientologists, or Satan Worshippers, or whatever. Anyone who claims otherwise is clearly arrogant. He looks impatiently at his cell phone to check how much time he has before his flight takes off for Bentonville.

We have clearly left the sunny bay of bicycle culture behind and are now sailing heavy seas in a boat meant for calmer waters. Noah is absolutely certain that nothing is certain, and he knows this because he has had the Wheaton experience of going from one sect to another, with every single one of them absolutely sure that they have a monopoly on the truth, when clearly the only certainty in life is that nothing is certain. Christians are always trying to impose their views on everyone else.

Noah gazes impatiently at his cell phone again. I take the metaphysical tack just long enough to turn the tables on him.

"No, you've got it backwards. The problem is that you're trying to impose your dogmatic skepticism on us, and we're not buying it."

Noah is taken aback by my candor. Guests at the most beautiful house on the coast of California do not talk this way.

I then mentioned Christopher Derrick's book *Escape from Skepticism*. Derrick was a student of C.S. Lewis who made a name for himself by writing a book about why Lewis never converted to Catholicism. At the beginning of the book, Derrick recounts the story of his conversation with two callow undergraduates who were arguing with great eloquence that nothing was certain, until one of them looked at his watch and, startled at the time, said that they had to leave immediately, or they would miss their train. Skepticism was, in other words, an intellectual soap bubble which floated around academic environments until it burst when it made contact with reality. It was also the logical outcome of the proliferation of Protestant sects that characterized religious practice in America and, most probably, one of the reasons Noah's father converted to Catholicism. Derrick's anecdote about the contradictory nature of skepticism found expression in Noah, as he looked nervously at his cell phone checking the time while telling us that nothing was certain. I suddenly understood why I was in the kitchen of the most beautiful house on the coast of California. It was because Joe wanted me to be there. Allegra continued to talk about her experiences as a Catholic, and Noah kept looking impatiently at his cell phone, as if to say that he had already heard Allegra's claims about why Catholicism was different from, say, the Seventh Day Adventists from Berrien Springs, Michigan who worshipped God on Saturday and didn't eat pork.

"I will send you the Catholic Catechism," she said.

"That's the worst thing you could have said," I remarked unasked. But maybe not. This was clearly a conversation conducted at the behest of unseen forces.

After Noah left to catch his flight, Allegra and I were standing on the terrace overlooking the Pacific, when I said to her, like Darth Vader, "I am your father" now. The revelation came to me during the conversation, and no matter how stupid or arrogant it made me seem, I felt that I had to share it with Allegra. She agreed. She felt that Joe had brought us together to negotiate a difficult transition for the entire family. Joe held the entire family together, and now Joe was gone, and the house where they had bonded as a family was going to be sold.

Allegra's sister Maggie had told me that her two greatest fears were losing her father and losing the house in Carmel, and now both of those fears had become realities. She then told me about a dream she had months before Joe's death. Maggie was standing at the baggage claim in an unknown airport watching suitcases go round and round on the carousel. Because all of the suitcases looked the same, she couldn't find the one which belonged to her younger brother Thomas, until one which was open with its contents falling out rolled onto the carousel. Maggie was in the process of putting the clothes back inside Thomas's suitcase when suddenly five fighter jets appeared overhead. With the attack immanent, Maggie turned to Joe, and her father said, "I should have been ready for a fight."

At that point the dream ended. This was months before Joe's long illness and subsequent death. During that illness, all of the people Joe had helped during his life banded together and formed prayer groups that commanded God to restore Joe's health, but it was all in vain. Joe died, and Maggie was left to find consolation at a local MedPoint where two pious black nurses told her that "life is speedy" and that we're all going to die sooner or later.

When I shared my transcendental insights with Allegra, we were both standing on the terrace outside the living room. I was facing the Pacific Ocean high up on a cliff in a panorama framed by pines, and Allegra was facing the house which was the perfect artistic fulfillment of the beauty I saw in nature. We were surrounded by beauty that was so intense that you never wanted to leave, and that was precisely the problem. Joe had many true friends, but some wanted to be Joe's friend in the hope that he would invite them to Carmel to have this experience. I suddenly understood the dangers of beauty in a way that was much more profound than the way I had explained in my book of the same name. I also understood that the book was incomplete as I had written it, and that I needed to include what I learned in Carmel to explain that danger in a supernatural way.

The day was pregnant with revelations. Standing next to Allegra, with me facing the ocean and rocky coast as a dramatic expression of the beauty

Part III: The Return of the Satanic Wilderness

of nature and with her facing the house which was the best expression of art as the fulfillment of nature's beauty, I said, "Being here reminds me of the Transfiguration." After the glimpse into heaven that this place provides, no one wants to leave. The three apostles who witnessed the transfigured Christ in all His glory said to Him, "Tis good lord to be here. Let us erect three tents. Let's stay here forever." That's how I felt. I wanted to stay there forever. If Joe were there, I would have told him, "I will say anything you want me to say, if you let me stay here forever." Which is probably why Joe wasn't there.

Allegra nodded. This was precisely the problem. No one wanted to leave Carmel. The place attracted leeches. Joe knew how to handle them, but his wife didn't, nor did Allegra. The vultures were circling the carcass. Better to sell it to Brad Pitt and leave the mountain that was Carmel and return to the plain that was Chicago, sadder but wiser, but convinced that we have no permanent dwelling place here and the only place where we will find lasting happiness is the mansion God has prepared for us in heaven.

Epilogue

Ben Franklin was known as the American Prometheus because he stole fire from the heavens when he flew a kite with a key dangling from it during a thunderstorm and stored the electricity which flowed from it in a Leyden Jar, as a preliminary step toward taming that force of nature and paving the way for its use in running the engines of the emerging American Empire. Thanks to Satanists like Ben Franklin, who was a member of the Hellfire club in London, the spirit of the Great Satan took up its abode in Catholic France a mere 13 years after it emerged in the Declaration of Independence, culminating in the French Revolution of 1789. Russia punished France for its rebellion against God in 1814, but in spite of God's repeated chastisements, the Spirit of Rebellion has never left France, as evidenced by the riots that are plaguing that country as it lurches toward anarchy. Sick of Macron's support of NATO's war in the Ukraine, the French are now praying for a Russian invasion because Russia was the first scourge of God which punished the French for the sin of rebellion against God's anointed leader of their country during the French Revolution.

France, however, refused to learn the lesson which God used the Russians to teach them. The Prussians became the scourge of God in 1870, but again France refused to learn the lesson God was teaching them. In 1890, *Civilta Cattolica* explained the lesson God was trying to teach France when it announced on the 100th anniversary of the French Revolution that any country which turned away from the laws created by God would end up being ruled by Jews, who still embody the revolutionary spirit which France refuses to abjure. French philosopher Emmanuel Todd's fixation on Weber's Protestant *Geist* blinds him to the fact that the same Jewish spirit has taken over France.

Nihilism is Todd's word for the Satanic spirit which traces its roots back to the time when Jesus Christ confronted the Jews who claimed that they were the "seed of Abraham" by telling them that "Your father is Satan" (John 8:44). By killing Christ, the Jews who rejected the Logos Incarnate became the "Synagogue of Satan" whose rejection of Logos found expression in a trajectory of revolutionary activity which stretched from Barabbas and Simon bar Kochba, to Trotsky and the Bolsheviks, to Irving Kristol and other Trotskyite revenants from Alcove B at the City College of New York in the 1930s who have come to be known as Neoconservatives, who destroyed what was left of Russia after the demise of Communism through the activity of

Walking with a Bible and a Gun

Jewish looters like Larry Summers, then president of Harvard University, and the Jewish oligarchs who profited from his activity. Under Vladimir Putin, Russia recovered, "after the nightmare of the 1990s,"[1803] but America did not recover from the victory in the Cold War which created that nightmare because "Western leaders have remained blind to reality."[1804]

Displaying a blind spot of his own, Todd identifies the group of blind men responsible for the eclipse of the WASP elite as "*les néoconservateurs*,"[1805] or simply "*les neocons*." Todd's inability to identify the enemy becomes apparent in the original French edition, where the term "neocons" appears jarringly out of place in the midst of his otherwise precise French prose:

> L'implosion, par étapes, de la culture WASP –blanche, anglo-saxonne et protestante –depuis les années 1960 a créé un empire privé de centre et de projet, un organisme essentiellement militaire dirigé par un groupe sans culture (au sens anthropologique) qui n'a plus comme valeurs fondamentales que la puissance et la violence. Ce groupe est généralement désigné par l'expression « néocons ». Il est assez étroit mais se meut dans une classe supérieure atomisée, anomique, et il a une grande capacité de nuisance géopolitique et historique.[1806]

If we ask the question: *qu'ils sont les* "neocons"? we learn that they are:

> an essentially military organization led by a group without culture (in the anthropological sense) which only has power and violence as its fundamental values. This group is generally referred to as "neocons". It is quite narrow but operates in an atomized, anomic upper class, and it has a great capacity for geopolitical and historical nuisance.[1807]

Instead of naming the Jews as the group which created the Satanic Zero State in America, Todd creates a category of the mind known as "The Blob," which he describes as:

> the group of individuals who, concretely, conduct the foreign policy of the sick power that America has become. Who is this tribe with singular morals which, through its tastes and its decisions, has led the West to the gates of Russia? We most often study a primitive community in its natural environment: this will be the city of Washington. We will be particularly interested in the American geopolitical establishment, which is colloquially called the "Blob", after the name of a worrying microorganism.[1808]

1803 Todd, *The Defeat of the West*, p. 39.
1804 Todd, *The Defeat of the West*, p. 46.
1805 Todd, *The Defeat of the West*, p. 59.
1806 Todd, *The Defeat of the West*.
1807 Todd, *The Defeat of the West*, p. 27.
1808 Todd, *The Defeat of the West*, p. 287.

Epilogue

Todd seems unaware that the name comes from a 1950s horror movie, attributing it instead to Stephen Walt, who got the nickname from Ben Rhodes, a former Obama adviser, to designate the microcosm responsible for foreign policy.[1809] "The Washingtonian Blob as presented by Walt corresponds entirely to my vision of a leading group devoid of intellectual or ideological ties external to itself."[1810] After listing the Kagan family—including Victoria "Fuck the EU" Nuland, who is married to Robert Kagan—as "one particularly central example of "the small band of semi-intellectuals who inhabit the Blob, a sub-village of Washington,"[1811] it turns out that the Blob is, *mirabile dictu*, Jewish:

> I was surprised to note the frequency of Jewish ancestors coming from the Empire of the Tsars and its margins. We noted that the two most influential figures "managing" Ukraine, Antony Blinken, the Secretary of State, and Victoria Nuland, the Deputy Secretary of State, are of Jewish descent. More precisely, we discover that Blinken is on his mother's side of Hungarian Jewish origin and that his paternal grandfather was born in Kyiv. Victoria Nuland's father's side is a combination of Moldovan and Ukrainian Jews. Let's move on to the ideological background, Victoria's in-laws, the Kagans. Robert and Frederick's father Donald was born in Lithuania. The fact that so many people in the high geopolitical establishment have a family link with the western part of the former Tsarist Empire is disturbing.[1812]

Once Todd establishes the Jewish identity of the Blob all sorts of interesting connections emerge. Because Jews "remember Ukraine as the official birthplace of 'Russian' anti-Semitism, beginning with the pogroms of 1881-1882,"[1813] NATO's war against Russia emerges as a Jewish desire, especially on Nuland's part, to punish the Ukraine for the Chmielnicki pogroms. Or as Todd puts it, "Why would the Americans of Ukrainian Jewish origin who, with the government in Kyiv, co-pilot this butchery not feel this as a just punishment inflicted on the country that made their ancestors suffer so much?"[1814]

Unlike "*les néoconservateurs*,"[1815] whom Todd describes as the heirs of McCarthyism, George Kennan, the WASP who was the architect of America's policy of containment during the Cold War, was "anything but a blind anti-communist." Because Kennan spoke Russian, because he knew and

---

1809 Todd, *The Defeat of the West*, p. 297.
1810 Todd, *The Defeat of the West*, p. 287.
1811 Todd, *The Defeat of the West*, p. 300.
1812 Todd, *The Defeat of the West*, p. 301.
1813 Todd, *The Defeat of the West*, p. 302.
1814 Todd, *The Defeat of the West*, p. 302.
1815 Todd, *The Defeat of the West*, p. 59.

loved Russian culture, he designed a strategy of containment which aimed to prevent an armed confrontation.[1816] The Kennan era ended, according to Todd, when the neocons took over American foreign policy. Todd identifies the man responsible for that takeover as Walt Rostow, Lyndon Johnson's national security adviser during the Vietnam War. At this point, Todd's thesis becomes problematic because Rostow was in no sense of the word a "neocon," (a word which did not exist in the 1960s) but unlike his predecessors at the State Department, who were committed to Kennan's containment policy, Rostow was a Jew.

Todd tells us that America, which he describes as "the village of Washington," is "nothing more than a collection of individuals completely devoid of common morals." Todd tells us that he doesn't use the term "'village' by chance,"[1817] but he can't bring himself to tell us that the "village" is ruled by Jews, in spite of all of the evidence he amasses:

> The same overrepresentation is observed in the Board of Directors of the most prestigious foreign policy think tank, the Council on Foreign Relations: almost a third of its thirty-four members are Jewish. In 2010, the Forbes ranking showed that, among the top hundred fortunes in the United States, there were 30% Jews. We have the impression of being in Budapest at the beginning of the 1930s. The interpretation of this fact is also the same: in order to explain a strong over-representation of Jews in the upper categories of a given society, we must first be looking for, and more often than not finding, an educational weakness in the general population, which allowed the educational intensity of the Jewish religion to be fully manifested.[1818]

And here we reach the fundamental problem of *La Defaite de l'Occident*. Ever since Walter Lippmann wrote *Public Opinion*, the Jews have been engaged in a massive campaign of identity theft. As a result, America became Jewish, destroying American identity. Todd fails to understand this because he is himself a Jew for whom the term Jew is an empty category of the mind which has no reference to the realities I described in detail in this book. Like Colonel Macgregor and Tucker Carlson, he prefers the euphemism "neoconservative." Todd admits that "the Blob" is under Jewish control, but Jew is not a meaningful category for Jews, as Noam Chomsky and Norman Finkelstein have also shown. Todd's use of the term "Neocon" prevents him from identifying who took over America after the Protestant spirit evaporated in 1978, the year John D. Rockefeller, 3rd and his brother Nelson died. Instead of telling us who was responsible for the eclipse of Protestantism which led to the collapse of American identity, Todd refers to an impersonal "implosion,

---

1816 Todd, *The Defeat of the West*, p. 59.
1817 Todd, *The Defeat of the West*, p. 295.
1818 Todd, *The Defeat of the West*, p. 291.

Epilogue

in stages, of WASP culture—White, Anglo-Saxon and Protestant" which began in the 1960s when the Neocons deprived the American Empire of "a center and a project,"[1819] which Todd describes as "a national culture shared by the masses and the ruling classes."[1820]

Breaking the cultural form of the American empire known as Protestantism was similar to splitting the atom because of the violence and destruction it unleashed on America and the rest of the world, but it was not an impersonal eruption of *force majeure*. It was a revolution. It was a *coup d'etat* which supplanted the Protestant work ethic with the Jewish idol of Satanic nihilism. Todd is nothing short of brilliant when it comes to explaining how nihilism leads to violence. At this stage in the disintegration of the American Empire, war has become "the dynamic" of the Zero State "because war is, always and everywhere, one of the virtualities of nihilism."[1821] America's insistence on war as the solution to every problem, especially in the Middle East, has led to total isolation. The American vote against a UN-sponsored ceasefire in Gaza is "nihilistic," because "it rejects the common morality of humanity."[1822]

In one vote, the U.S. was supported by three other countries, Israel, Micronesia, and Nauru, which, because guano, its main natural resource, has been strip-mined out of existence, qualifies it as the world's paradigmatic shit-hole country. Nihilism has led to self-destruction, which allows us to see that America's "thoughtless and unqualified commitment to Israel is a suicidal symptom,"[1823] that has turned the United States into the land of mass shootings, fentanyl zombies, zero religion, and denial of reality, where "the primary impulse is a need for violence."[1824] Todd adds the opioid crisis to the list of pathologies currently plaguing America without telling us, of course, that that was another Jewish project run by the Sackler family.

By the end of his book Todd becomes the classic example of an acute critical intelligence sabotaging itself by its failure to identify the enemy. As Sun Tzu said, if you do not know who you are, and you cannot identify the enemy, you will lose every battle. More importantly, Todd doesn't know that his own identity and the identity of his enemy are one and the same. The French say *Cherchez la femme* because they feel that any mystery can be solved by finding the woman behind it. We could modify that famous phrase and say, in the light of Todd's revelations, *Cherchez le juif.* The Jews who stole American identity cannot identify the enemy because that would involve admitting, as the now defunct cartoon character Pogo once famously said, "We have met

---

1819 Todd, *The Defeat of the West*, p. 27.
1820 Todd, *The Defeat of the West*, p. 27.
1821 Todd, *The Defeat of the West*, p. 365.
1822 Todd, *he Defeat of the West*, p. 367.
1823 Todd, *The Defeat of the West*, p. 369.
1824 Todd, *The Defeat of the West*, p. 369.

the enemy, and he is us." The task of re-establishing American identity must pass, as a result, to the goyim, who will have to cobble something together based on figures like Joe Ritchie, Walt Kowalski, and John Adams, who was right all along when he claimed that "we have no constitution which functions in the absence of a moral people."

American history is based on three 80-year-long cycles which correspond to the three American Republics. The first republic began with the proclamation of the United States constitution in 1781. That republic ended in the carnage of the American Civil War, which among other changes abolished the sovereign power of the individual states. The second republic began in 1865 at the end of the Civil War and ended in 1945 with the end of World War II, when the American Republic became the American Empire. The third republic will come to an end in 2025, hopefully without the catastrophe of global nuclear war.

As it moves into the fourth republic, America now finds itself saddled with a number of obsolete institutions, technologies, and concepts. The premier obsolete institution is NATO. Obsolete technologies closely associated with NATO include the aircraft carrier and the tank, which were crucial in winning World War II but are now helpless against satellite surveillance guiding drones and hypersonic missiles. The list of obsolete concepts includes conservatism, which served as the basis for the anti-Communist crusade, but cannot survive the transition into the fourth republic because it is based on the equally obsolete category of "judeo-christian" values, whose pretense disappeared when Jews announced that abortion was a fundamental Jewish value in the wake of the Dobbs decision.

The main obsolete category which will pass away as America moves into its fourth republic is, as Emmanuel Todd has pointed out, Protestantism. The institution which guaranteed the preservation of the moral law that was the only basis for American unity has evaporated, leaving in its wake, according to the understanding of American ethnicity known as the triple melting pot, Catholicism and the Jewish Revolutionary Spirit. Catholicism has never been weaker; the Jewish Revolutionary Spirit has never been stronger, but when it comes to the Logos of human history, unexpected reversal is the norm, not the exception. Think of the apostles cowering in the upper room after the crucifixion and before Pentecost, and you will understand the necessity of America placing her hope in the Lord at this crucial moment in history. As soon as the Church regains the courage to say to the Jews not only, "You killed Christ," but also "You killed the Kennedy brothers," that transformation will begin.

Index

A

Abbelen, Peter M. 342, 343
Abbey of Whitby 76
abolitionism 126, 170, 207-222, 269, 309, 310, 354, 461, 462, 474
abortion 13, 265, 266, 268, 388, 389, 449, 453, 454, 457, 459, 464, 469, 480, 482, 484
Acapulco 436
Act of Sucession 67
Act of Supremacy 67
Adam 229, 279
Adam and Eve 31, 406
Adam, New 135
Adams, Clover 314, 325
Adams Family 141
Adams, Henry 313, 388, 390
Adams, Henry Brooks 94, 159, 222, 298-316, 325, 326, 327, 328, 332, 363, 385-397, 401, 413, 432, 433, 438, 479, 524
Adams, John 94, 131-135, 314, 327, 413, 438
Adams, John Quincy 311, 314
Adams, Nick 385, 387, 388, 391, 396
adultery 35, 37, 38, 49, 50, 51, 52, 67, 194, 273, 293, 294, 311, 400
Adventures of Huckleberry Finn, The 156
aesthetics 226
A Farewell to Arms 393, 435
Affirmative Action 13, 469, 471
Afghanistan 499, 503, 504, 505, 506, 510, 511
A Fistful of Dollars 455
Africa 211, 477, 487, 508, 509
Agassiz 262, 312
agnosticism 135, 326
agriculture 372
Ahab, Captain 20
Ahlstrom, Sydney 103, 196
AIPAC 479
Akagera Medicines 511, 512
Akers, Paul 239

Alaska 313, 378, 451, 499
Alaska Purchase 313
Alcibiades 76, 79
alcohol 321, 398
alcoholism 320, 400
Alcott, Amos Bronson 193, 262, 312
Aldrich, Thomas Bailey 317
Alexandria 498
Algonquins 32
Alien 480
Allen, Ethan 189
altar 223, 239, 247, 261, 283, 306, 307, 319, 481
Amalek 34, 35, 65, 83, 85, 196, 220, 487
Ambrose Cathedral, Saint 285
American Association of Spiritualists 294
American College in Rome 250
American Creed 13, 331
American Empire 18, 19, 20, 22, 25, 106, 130, 157, 350, 372, 378, 393, 417, 436, 482, 508, 519, 523
American Historical Association 369
American Indian Wars 310
American Institute of Architects, The 368
Americanism 106, 165, 204, 205, 222, 224, 308, 331, 332, 337-354, 370, 371, 372, 410, 411, 420
American Philosophical Society 113
American Revolution of 1776 13, 15, 23, 24, 59, 106, 121, 131, 136, 148, 176, 197, 272, 419, 451, 474, 519
Americans for Democratic Action 59, 215, 474
American, The by Henry James 297, 299, 306, 309
Amiens 238, 326
A Moveable Feast 389, 390, 400
Amsterdam 299
analogies 412
A Narrative of the Captivity and Restoration of Mrs. Mary Rowlandson 486
angel 254

E. MICHAEL JONES • 525

angel and machine 233, 251, 252
Angelico, Fra 254
Angel in the House, The 243
Angelou, Maya 14
angels 51, 233, 240, 243, 247, 250, 252, 381, 382
Anglicanism 36, 127, 332
Anglo-American alliance 351
Anglo-Protestant 16, 17, 30, 32, 59, 160, 331
Anglo-Saxons 348
anti-Communist crusade 35, 437
Antifa 15, 449
antinomianism 98, 101, 119, 120, 121
Antoninus 183
Antwerp 77, 160
Any Which Way But Loose 458
apostasy 24
Apostles Creed 453
Appalachian Mountains 142
appetite 21, 43
Appleby, R. Scott 354
Applegate 266, 279, 281
Aquinas, Saint Thomas 31, 41, 42, 71, 88, 89, 91-96, 100, 107, 110, 129, 151, 152, 175, 233, 326, 353, 367, 412, 497
Arbor, Patrick 498
Arcadia 30, 31, 229, 230, 231, 232, 237, 362, 407, 497, 498, 511, 513
archetype 55, 142, 144, 147, 152, 155, 163, 221, 295, 388, 451, 464
architecture 135, 160, 193, 244, 287, 302, 313, 326, 353, 355, 356, 357, 358, 359, 360, 361, 362, 363, 364, 365, 366, 367, 439, 440, 441, 501, 510, 513
  Baroque 313, 353
  Gothic 160, 326
  Greek 359
  Japanese 360, 361, 363
  Scandinavian 363
Arena chapel 240, 412
aristocracy 18, 34, 36, 70, 81, 209, 222, 277, 314, 333, 421
Aristotle 40, 41, 89-110, 119, 120, 226, 353, 367, 418, 497
Arizona 422, 458
Arkansas 422, 487

Armenio, Rev. Peter 507
Armstrong, Nancy 486
Arnold, Thomas 332, 333, 334
Arsala, Hamayoun 503
art 23, 24, 31, 54, 55, 153, 160, 164, 167, 170, 172, 173, 193, 194, 222-255, 260, 284, 290, 299, 301, 302, 312, 318, 325, 326, 328, 356, 360-368, 389, 394, 412, 418, 440, 458, 497, 498, 516, 517
  beaux 356
  Bohemian 359
  Italian 241
  Sacred 254
  Western 412
Artisans of Peace 508, 509, 510
Arts and Crafts 360
Ashbee, Charles Robert 361
Asia, South 504
assemble, right to 7, 15, 124, 490
assimilation 13, 17, 31, 200, 212, 215, 216, 231, 337, 338, 339
astronomy 29
atheism 132, 135
Athens 75, 76, 78, 79, 311
athlete 334, 335, 336
Atkinson, Edward 315
Atlantic Ocean 23, 127
Atlantic, The 280, 281, 297, 308, 309, 317, 321, 378, 385
Attila the Hun 475, 477
Augsburg Confession 162
Augustine, Order of Saint 243
Augustine, Saint 164, 197, 243, 371, 481
Austen, Jane 422
Austrians 293, 443, 456
Austrian School 456
automobile 328, 499
avarice 39, 70, 393
A Wonder Book for Girls and Boys 172
axe 176, 403, 407
Azores 282, 284

B

Baghdad 504
Baker, Carlos 444, 446
Baltzell, Digby 333, 336, 337

Index

Bancroft, George 194
Bank of America 500
bankruptcy 78, 399
banks, banking 73, 273, 315, 372, 389
baptism 19, 29, 30, 86, 103, 105, 106, 113, 126, 144, 186, 443, 447, 451, 453, 503
Baptists 515
Barbados 45
Barcelona 389
Barnes, Howard 441
Baroque architecture 313, 353
Barruel, Abbé Augustin 133
Barry, Marion 282, 461, 462
Barth, Karl 91
Bartholomew, E. S. 225
Basilica of Saint Peter 161, 162, 182, 193, 222, 223, 240-248, 259, 285, 286, 287, 313, 388, 390, 454
Basilica of San Spiritu 243
Basilica of the Sacred Heart 224
basketball 335
Battle of Pease River 488
Battle of Plattsburgh 195
Battle of Preston 219
Bauer, Trevor 334
Bavaria 497
Bayeux 326
beach 364, 366, 389, 391, 509
Beach, Chloe 274, 275, 278, 279
Beach, Emma 278
Beach, Moses 275, 278
Beach, Violet 275, 278
Bear, The 403, 443, 449
Beatnik movement 463
Beaumont, John 444
Beauty 110, 111, 152, 153, 160-165, 173, 193, 200, 222-256, 285, 286, 287, 290, 299, 301, 306, 307, 313, 316, 319, 322, 325, 326, 329, 359-367, 498, 500, 501, 510, 511, 513, 516, 517
beaux arts 356, 357
Bedtime for Bonzo 458
Beecher family 191, 221, 337
Beecher, Henry Ward 191, 195, 221, 222, 266, 269, 272-282, 293, 294, 304, 310

Beecher, Lyman 191, 216, 221, 222, 269, 271, 272, 274, 302
Beecher Rifle Colony 221
Beecher Stowe, Harriet 221
Being 15, 31, 42, 88, 95, 98, 100, 107, 108, 110, 111, 128, 151, 152, 195, 226, 251, 303, 305, 453, 454, 517
Belgium 346
Bell, Clive 312
Belloc, Hilaire 390
Benedictine Order 74
Benny, Jack 459
Bentz family 360
Berkeley 108, 363, 456
Berkeley, George 108
Berlin Wall 33
Bernard, Saint 164
Beverley, Robert 30, 231
Beza, Theodore 38, 39, 109
Bhutan 363
Bible 3, 5, 6, 25, 29, 30, 32, 34, 36, 37, 92, 120, 126, 131, 181, 188, 189, 190, 198, 221, 231, 398, 419, 429, 430, 490, 514
Biden, Joseph 19, 506
Big Pharma 498, 509, 512
birth control 266, 399
Bizer, Ernst 91
Black Crook, The 278
Black Death 46
Black-Jewish alliance 60, 217
Black Legend 161, 287
Black Lives Matter 14, 15, 449, 473, 474, 475
blackmail 467, 469
black ministers 465
Black Panthers 456, 457, 475
Black Swan 514
Blair, Tony 504
Blake, William 19, 20
Blithedale Romance 167, 172, 251, 312
Block, Wes 456
blood 18, 36, 38, 48, 50, 70, 76, 153, 178, 207, 213, 219, 230, 274, 284, 312, 370, 378, 380, 384, 425, 431, 491, 492, 493, 494
Bloom, Molly 396

Bloomsbury 384
boarding school 332
Bohemian art 359
Bois du Boulogne 299
Boleyn, Ann (Bullen) 67, 73
bombs 328, 505
Bond, Ward 489
Bono 509
Boone, Daniel 119, 141-147, 156, 159, 221, 222, 270, 370, 372, 407, 437, 487
Boone, Israel 144
Boone, Jemima 141, 147
Boone, Sarah 144
Bora, Catherina von 36, 219
Bora, Katerina von 36
Borromeo, Saint Charles 285
Boston 29, 40, 50, 51, 52, 55, 86, 100, 105, 115, 119, 142, 151, 155, 163, 164, 168, 173, 181, 185, 191-204, 215, 217, 227, 245, 262, 271, 272, 280, 282, 294, 300-302, 311, 315, 339, 346, 357
Boswell, James 131
Bowen, Henry 274, 311
boxing 332, 390
Bracque, Georges 389
Bradish, Luther 159
Brenner, Gerry 400
Britain 19, 23, 36, 72, 74, 85, 142, 148, 199, 301, 413, 483, 506, 514
British Navy 33
Broadway 278
Bronson, Charles 449
Brooke, Rupert 435
Brook Farm 198, 318
Brooklyn 62, 222, 273, 274, 277, 278, 281, 282, 294, 310, 311, 426
Brooklyn Bridge 310
Brotherhood of Sleeping Car Porters 465
Brown, John 206, 207, 209, 222, 310, 313
Brownson, Orestes 185-206, 211, 215, 223, 224, 225, 274, 277, 289, 327, 338, 339, 342, 346
Brown v. School Board 61, 206, 487
Brunswick Hotel 280
Bubonic plague 46
Buchenwald 436

Buddhism 359, 365, 367
Buddhist temples 359
bullets 7
bullfighting 391
Bull, John 417
bungalow 355, 360-366
Burke, Edmund 84, 214
Bushman 122
Byberry 148
Byron, Lord 388

C

Cahenslyism 345
Cahensly, Peter Paul 343
Calderon, Jose Vasconcelos 34
Calhoun, John C. 270
California 144, 279, 280, 281, 293, 357, 359, 360, 361, 362, 363, 422, 451, 456, 457, 458, 459, 478, 479, 497, 500, 515
Caligula 303
Calixtus, Saint 261
Callahan, Harry 457
Callaway, Elizabeth 141
Callaway, Frances 141
Calvinism 20, 24, 25, 29, 30, 37-58, 87-137, 150-159, 167-204, 221-238, 245, 249, 255, 260-279, 282, 301, 308, 312, 337, 357, 358, 379, 393, 398, 422-426, 484
Calvin, John 19, 30, 37, 38, 39, 41, 42, 43, 45, 68, 87-99, 107, 109, 110, 113, 172, 180, 231, 232, 234
Cambridge 32, 40, 89, 93, 110, 164, 238, 312, 356, 394
Camelot 448
Canaan 34, 106, 218, 219, 405
canal 270, 372
Canterbury 344
capitalism 17, 18, 19, 36, 65-78, 218, 310, 315, 316, 400, 473
Capra, Frank 442
Capuchin chapel 287
Carlson, Tucker 479
Carlyle, Jane Welsh 160
Carlyle, Thomas 163, 165, 166, 167, 191
Carmel 355, 360-368, 458, 497, 500, 501, 511, 512, 513, 516, 517

INDEX

Carmelites 305, 306, 307
Carmichael, Stokely 469
Caro-Morente, Jaime 473
carpentry 166, 356, 359
carpetbaggers 310
Carruth, Rae 334
Cassidy, Hopalong 455
caste system 309
Castlefidardo 303
Castle of St. Angelo 303
catacomb 261
category 22, 32, 34, 60-63, 81, 84, 107, 108, 109, 126, 160, 161, 181, 213, 217, 218, 286, 409-414, 436, 473, 476, 477, 522
Cathedral of Notre Dame 160
Catherine of Aragon 67
Catholic Celts 130
Catholic Church 33, 34, 36, 39, 45, 47, 62, 67-75, 83, 119, 143, 164, 165, 181-198, 201, 203-206, 210, 211, 222-225, 234-244, 249, 251, 255, 260, 274, 282, 288, 302, 306, 308, 327, 330, 332, 337, 338, 339, 342, 343, 348, 351, 372, 443-493, 507, 510, 515
Catholic England 21, 382
Catholic Indians 104
Catholicism 73, 85, 159, 162, 164, 181, 182, 188, 196, 197, 199, 205, 206, 211, 215, 222, 223, 225, 226, 238, 239, 240, 241, 242, 246, 252, 259, 260, 272, 282, 286, 301, 305, 306, 308, 313, 316, 317, 318, 326, 327, 331, 337, 339, 344, 347, 399, 432, 443-450, 480, 488, 507, 508, 513, 514, 515
Catholic Publication Society 346
Catholic University of America 213, 223, 245, 246, 343, 344
Catholic World publication 277, 346
cattle 371, 377, 425, 428, 429, 431, 486
Cavalier 337
Celestial Railroad, The 414
Celtic Catholics 130
Celts 130, 214
Cezanne, Paul 389
Chabrol, Guillaume de 346, 347

Chamberlain, Wilt 334
Charles Borromeo, Saint 285
Charles I, King 130
Charlestown 272
Charles V, Emperor 162
Charlie Wilson's War 506
Charlottesville 15, 16
Chartres 308, 313, 326, 390
chastity 106, 116, 165, 166, 175, 178, 180, 244, 273, 383, 387
Chauncy, Charles 122, 123
Cheltenham 35, 333
Cherokee 141, 490, 492
Chicago 59, 327, 328, 334, 353, 359, 369, 387, 457, 468, 479, 498, 499, 507, 511, 517
Chillingworth, Roger 51, 52, 53, 54, 55, 169, 245
Christendom 252, 305, 489
Christian 7
Christian Herald 321
Christmas 162, 446
Church and State 133, 181, 203, 345
Church property 18, 33, 36, 39, 63, 64, 70, 72, 73, 74, 77, 79, 83, 220, 393
CIA 436, 448, 479, 503, 504, 505, 506, 510, 511
Cincinnati 271, 272, 355
Cincinnatus 335
cinema 412, 417
Cintre, Claire de 302
civic virtue 347, 351
Civil Rights Movement 13, 59, 60, 61, 62, 209, 210, 214, 217, 456-478, 487
Civil War 31, 60, 131, 206, 211, 216, 221, 222, 258, 259, 265-269, 279, 280, 295, 299, 308, 309, 310, 311, 313, 315, 327, 337, 340, 355, 399, 445, 451
  Spanish 445
Claflin, Reuben Hummel 293
Claflin, Tennie 294
Claflin, Victoria California 293
Clay, Henry 270
Clayton, Samuel Johnston 489
Cleaver, Eldridge 456, 457

E. MICHAEL JONES • 529

Clemens, Samuel 277, 278, 279, 280, 281, 282, 283, 284, 285, 286, 287, 308, 312
Cleopatra 239
clergy
    Puritan 312
    Unitarian 312
Clinton, Bill 13
Cloyse, Goody 49, 51
coal 61, 371, 377
Cobbett, William 36, 65-75, 309
Cold War 448, 484, 506, 508, 520, 521
Coleridge, Samuel Taylor 167, 226, 234, 400
Cole, Thomas 498
colonists 24, 34, 82, 83, 130, 147, 356, 363
Colorado 451
Colosseum 287
Columbian Exhibition 334, 359
Columbian Exposition 327, 369
Columbus, Christopher 298, 406
Columbus Day 475
Comanche 488-493
Comanche-Texan wars 489
Committee on Public Information (CPI) 410, 414
common good 32, 74, 482
Common Sense by Thomas Paine 23, 24, 358
communism 135, 438, 480-487, 519, 521
Communist Party 61, 62, 438
Concord 167, 171, 173, 181, 182, 202, 207, 234, 256, 257, 259, 260, 262, 309
Condorcet, Marquis de 132, 133
Confederacy 313
confession 45, 51, 52, 55, 56, 58, 89, 125, 126, 143, 181, 182, 236, 237, 239, 244-260, 274, 286, 326, 454, 484, 485, 486, 494, 495, 513, 514
congregationalism 316
Congregationalists 103, 105, 163, 164
Congregation of St. Paul the Apostle 200, 346
Connecticut 106, 120, 121, 126, 127, 206, 221, 265, 266, 269, 424, 480
Connecticut River Valley 106, 121, 126, 127, 424

Connors, Jimmy 336
conscience 23, 30, 33, 51, 53, 55, 58, 74, 109, 110, 189, 198, 217, 223, 229, 230, 255, 301, 391, 398, 399, 427, 432, 462, 463, 465, 471
conservatism 202, 456, 457, 504, 506, 507, 520, 522
Conspiracy of Pontiacin, The 155
Constitution 129, 335, 346
constitutionalism 316
constitutional right 293
Constitution, the American 15, 59, 121, 131, 132, 314, 345, 347, 428
Continental Army 356
contraception 224, 268, 458
convents 69, 197, 203, 210, 215, 217, 272, 282, 302, 305, 306
Convert, The 225
Cooper, Alice 447
Cooper, Gary 417, 420, 435-458
Cooper, James Fenimore 147-164, 176, 193, 222, 279, 280, 286, 313, 358, 359, 362, 370, 388, 390, 435-458, 487, 489
Cooper, Paul 161
Cooper, Rocky 446, 447
Cooper, Susan 162
Cooper, William 154
Cordier, Mathurin 38
Cornwall 497
corporate government 77, 314
Correggio 226
Costco 511
Cotton, John 356
Council of Trent 344
Counter-reformation 47
country houses 309
Court of St. James 313, 314
covenant 20, 32, 39, 40, 42, 89, 93, 97-101, 105, 110, 119, 120, 130, 150, 187
Covenant, Puritan 87, 89
Covenant theology 20, 39, 93, 97, 100, 101, 119
Covid-19 498, 509, 512
cowboy 20, 313, 332, 417, 418, 420-426, 432-444, 451-459, 477, 479, 483, 484, 485, 486, 513

Index

Craftsman Homes 360
Craftsman, The 360, 362
Craigenputtock 165
Cram, Ralph Adams 363
Cranmer, Thomas 79
Crawford, Thomas 225
Creation of the White Race, The 213
Creed 13, 87, 93, 331, 453
Creel, George 410
Crèvecœur, J. Hector St. John de 30, 31, 231
cricket 332, 333, 334
Critical Race Theory 13, 62, 454, 473, 475, 478, 479
Cromwell, Oliver 23, 34, 35, 68, 69, 73, 77, 79, 83, 130, 144, 214, 217, 218, 219, 220, 487
Cromwell, Thomas 68, 69, 73, 77, 79
Cross 207, 242, 243, 248, 261, 352, 393, 466, 467, 468
Crowd, The 377
Crowley, Aleister 390
crown 21, 382
Crowther, Bosley 441
CRT 499, 500, 507
Crucifix 261
Cuba 81, 210, 350, 394, 445
cubism 389
Cumberland Gap 141, 144, 145, 159

D

Dagger John 197, 198, 199, 200, 204, 205, 206, 209, 216, 224, 338, 342
"Daisy Miller" 135, 173, 306
Daley, Richard 479
Danforth, Samuel 29, 33, 108
Darth Vader 516
Darwin, Charles 310, 312, 351, 369, 377, 378, 379, 383, 384, 387, 393, 394
Darwinism 316, 326, 351, 352, 379, 381, 384, 387, 393, 410, 432
Data of Ethics, The 380
Davenport, James 125
Dean, James 453
Death Mills 436
Death Wish 449

debauchery 304
Declaration of Independence 15, 24, 59, 113, 114, 137, 141, 185, 203, 209, 232, 272, 340, 344, 347, 348, 370, 371, 372, 482, 519
Deep Throat 480
deer 148, 358, 404
Deerslayer, The 155, 156
Deism 195
Delaware valley 148
demagogues 122, 210
democracy 19, 119, 130-136, 144, 145, 202, 215, 270, 271, 309, 314, 327, 331, 333, 335, 337, 354, 372, 377, 411, 418, 419, 420, 421, 423, 436, 438, 504
Democracy by Henry Adams 314
Democratic Party 13, 15, 258, 454, 458, 478, 479
Demoiselles d'Avignon, Les 389
demon 49, 261, 455
Dennison, William 267
Department of Defense 504
depression 257, 258, 317, 321, 444, 447
Derrick, Christopher 515
despotism 24
Detroit 410, 485, 494
devil 20, 25, 46, 48, 49, 51, 55, 57, 122, 124, 170, 177, 194, 303, 358, 405, 407
dialectic 42, 72, 159, 165, 167
Dial, The 193, 194
Dick Deasy 477
Dickens, Charles 165, 166
Dickinson, Jonathan 486
Dimmesdale 37, 49-58, 145, 230, 231, 245, 248, 250, 251, 273, 274, 427, 430, 486
Ding an sich 170, 235
Diocletian 261
Dionysos 230
diphtheria 317
Dirty Harry 149, 449-459, 494
diversity 13, 17, 273, 498
divorce 266, 467
D. L. James house 497, 500, 503, 508, 511, 512, 513
Doda, Carol 456

dogma 92, 100, 114, 150, 201, 311
dogmatic theology 88
Doliver Romance 258
Donatello 229, 230, 231, 232, 237, 238
Donavan, Vincent 444
Dos Passos, John 399
Drake, Francis 33
Dresden 162, 290, 313
Dr. Grimshawe's Secret 258
Dr. Jekyll and Mr. Hyde 467
Drogheda 34, 83
drones 506
Dublin 305
Duke of Northumberland 76
Durante, Jimmy 459
Duston, Hannah 486
Dutchmen 224, 343
Dwight, Timothy 104, 262, 436
dynamo 308, 327

E

Eakins, Thomas 498
Eastman, Max 388
Eastwood, Clint 13, 141, 449-459, 483, 484, 485, 486, 487, 513, 514
Eastwood, Lewis 451
Eastwood, Maggie 484
economics
 Austrian school 456
economist 315
Eden 231
Edict of Milan 160
Edson, Hiram 195
education 13, 29, 61, 110, 166, 176, 178, 204, 266, 305, 332, 333, 334, 336, 337, 341, 342, 360, 373, 379, 396, 409, 413, 522
 Catholic 342
Education of Henry Adams, The 311, 313, 388
Edwards, Jonathan 94, 98, 106-143, 167, 169-185, 195, 227, 232, 234, 255, 274, 358, 379, 393, 487-506
Edwards, Lucy 503
Edward VI 73
egalitarianism 19
Einsiedeln 161

Einstein, Albert 414
Eisenhower 436
electricity 113, 132, 327, 519
Elijah 20
Eliot, George 167
Eliot, John 29, 56
Eliot, T. S. 390
elite 22, 64, 192, 194, 197, 199, 202, 314, 315, 327, 362, 474, 477, 509, 510, 520
elitism 309
Elizabethan England 21, 382
Elizabeth of Hungary, Saint 322
Elliott, Walter 346
Emerson, Ellen Tucker 163
Emerson, Ralph Waldo 20, 24, 25, 55, 56, 57, 150-207, 222-227, 232, 233, 234, 235, 254-265, 272, 280, 303, 312, 326, 357, 358, 369, 381, 387, 388, 390, 391, 394, 395, 398, 422
Emmanuel, Rahm 388
emotion 355
emotionalism 119, 120, 123, 126
empiricism 107
Enclosure crisis 77, 79
energy 91, 178, 271, 311, 327, 352, 480
England 16, 18, 19, 21, 23, 24, 29, 30-89, 103, 106, 109, 113-117, 120, 125, 127, 131, 141-148, 160, 164-176, 180, 183, 191, 199, 209, 216, 218, 219, 221, 225, 226, 227, 228, 231, 234-263, 269, 289, 290, 301, 309-314, 323, 332, 333, 337, 358, 360, 373, 382, 383, 388, 393, 394, 398, 417, 424, 425, 431, 432, 451, 490
English Poor Law system 77
English Reformation 21, 36
English revolutionaries 36
Enlightenment 30, 111, 113, 114, 117, 120, 122, 134, 231, 354, 364, 365, 514
 American 113
 Scottish 111, 122
*Enquiry Concerning Political Justic*e 190
enslaved will 37, 109, 110, 131, 219
enthusiasm 122, 123
entrapment 15
epistemology 107

Index

Epstein, Jacob 441, 442
equality 132, 202, 203, 464
Equal Rights 462
Erie Canal 269, 273
Errand Into the Wilderness by Perry Miller 29, 51, 106, 109
Escape from Skepticism 515
Essence 30, 31, 36, 39, 40, 43, 51, 55, 57, 61, 72, 89, 104-126, 130, 131, 135, 136, 137, 142, 144, 151, 152, 159, 166, 180, 201, 206, 222, 271, 301, 304, 331, 338, 340, 354, 361, 364, 367, 369, 370, 377, 393, 400, 423, 432, 438, 479, 482, 498, 504
eternal 22, 31, 84, 97, 100, 108, 124, 206, 227, 255, 289, 380, 381, 423, 429, 454
ethnic cleansing 61, 217, 218, 220, 474, 476, 489
ethnocentrism 239, 242, 248, 251
Eucharist 37, 45, 57, 164
European culture 13, 15, 31, 60, 77, 134, 135, 159-165, 202, 203, 204, 206, 223, 231, 235, 271, 284, 300, 312, 313, 328, 339, 341, 346, 347, 350, 357, 370, 388, 395, 410, 411, 454, 476, 488
evangelism 130
Evans, Sara 468, 470
Eve 31, 244, 406
evil 25
evolution 121, 310, 351, 352, 353, 354, 377, 379, 414
Evolution and Dogma 351
examination of conscience 51, 55
exceptionalism 15
Existence 31, 39, 40, 41, 43, 51, 55, 57, 61, 77, 88-122, 126, 129, 130-135, 142, 144, 151, 152, 159, 166, 167, 177, 179, 180, 201, 206, 222, 234, 244, 271, 301, 325, 331, 336, 338, 340, 361-370, 377, 380, 393, 400, 403-406, 413, 423, 426, 432, 482, 498, 523
existence of God 92, 93, 94

F

factory 62, 77, 215, 313, 363, 365, 371, 372, 373, 387, 410, 414, 509, 510

Fairfax 219
Faith 25
Fall, the 3, 5, 6, 31, 89, 90, 168, 169, 172, 180, 231, 232, 464
farming
  tenant 309
father 21
Faulkner, William 403-407, 443, 449
Faun 173, 225-261, 288, 306
fauns 178, 225
FBI 15
Federal Reserve 440
Fellini, Federico 454
feminism 469, 470, 504
feminist movement 468, 469
Fenwick, Benedict Joseph 192
ferry 278, 377
Fichte, Johann Gottlieb 108, 166, 170, 233, 234, 235, 254
fideism 42, 92, 94
Fields 22, 237, 262, 500
Filipinos 372, 387
Finney, Charles Grandison 195
fire 22
first principles 88, 94-100
Fisher, Bishop John 68
Fisher, Frances 484
fishing 390, 391, 393, 395, 424, 432, 479
Fitzgerald, F. Scott 400
Flavius 75
Fleischhacker house 355
Flemming, William 488
Fletcher, William 23
Florence 73, 77, 229, 230
Florida 279, 445
Floyd, George 14, 15, 461, 473
folk legend 313
Fonda, Jane 469
Fonda, Tom 469
football 224, 334, 335, 513
For A Few Dollars More 455
Ford Foundation 465, 466
Fordham 31, 205, 206, 225
Ford, Harold 447
Ford, John 490
Ford, Maddox 389, 390

Ford, Torino 487
Foreman, Carl 438, 442
formalism 120, 356
Fornarina 242
fornication 278
Fort Parker massacre 488
Fort Sumter 216, 269
Fossett, Steve 500
Foster, John 165
Foucault, Michel 456
Fourteen Point Speech 410
France 34, 38, 47, 71, 82, 113, 114, 115, 132, 133, 134, 162, 172, 191, 284, 308, 312, 314, 315, 326, 327, 347, 349, 352, 388, 410, 445, 519
Francis of Assisi, Saint 322
Francon, Dominique 439
Frankel, Glenn 488
Frankenhausen, Battle of 37
Franklin, Benjamin 19, 113-119, 128, 129, 132, 142-148, 155-162, 172, 176, 249, 258, 262, 279, 280, 396, 480, 481, 519
Franklin, Wayne 148
fraternity 132, 183
freedom 14, 23, 33, 34, 57, 71, 109, 129, 131, 134, 135, 136, 156, 188, 201, 211, 215, 265, 270, 271, 280, 350, 354, 381, 382, 384, 406, 449, 463, 465, 468, 480, 481, 482, 484
freedom of religion 354
freedom of speech 354
freedom of the press 354
freedom, sexual 462
Freedom Song 469
free love 191, 266, 293, 294
Freeman, Morgan 484
Freemasonry 345
free speech 15
free will 35, 36, 37, 185, 191
French and Indian Wars of 1763 486
French Revolution 23
French, the 23, 34, 39, 45, 104, 114, 115, 117, 130, 132, 133, 135, 203, 298, 302, 313, 316, 326, 327, 340, 346, 347, 348, 352, 356, 370, 456, 486, 489, 498, 519, 520, 523

Freud, Sigmund 51, 289
Fromm, Allegra Ritchey 497, 498, 500, 513, 514, 515, 516, 517
frontier 7, 30, 31, 40, 55, 57, 59, 60, 61, 104, 105, 106, 111, 119, 120, 122, 126, 129, 131, 137, 141-149, 154-160, 176, 195, 196, 270, 271, 272, 293, 331, 332, 340, 341, 358, 369, 370, 371, 372, 377, 393, 403, 422-426, 444, 451, 454, 459, 486
frontiersman 7, 57, 104, 119, 131, 141, 144, 147, 222, 270
Frost, David 451
Frost, Robert 14, 449
Fruitlands 312
Fugger family 68
Fugger, Jakob 68
Fujiwara period 359
Fukuyama, Francis 33
fur trade 370

G

Gabor, Zsa Zsa 459
Gaels 214
Gamble House 361, 362
garden 31, 242, 360, 362, 423, 497
Garden of Eden 31, 231, 406
Garibaldi, Giuseppe Maria 347
Gatsby, Jay 362
Gautier, Theophile 312
Gaza 35, 479, 523
Gelernter, David 20
Genesis 31, 108
Geneva 38, 344, 445
genocide 34, 35, 60, 83, 217, 218, 220, 479
  of the Irish 35
Georgia 120, 121, 127, 196, 507
Georgia, nation 507
German 7, 36, 37, 47, 59, 163, 166, 167, 185, 198, 199, 213, 223, 224, 234, 235, 313, 340, 341, 342, 343, 344, 345, 346, 363, 389, 392, 409, 411, 445
German Idealism 163, 166, 358
Germans 38, 204, 215, 315, 331, 339, 342, 343, 344, 345, 346, 372, 410, 493
Germantown Country Club 337

INDEX

Germany 19, 36, 38, 47, 59, 61, 71, 74, 109, 162, 191, 312, 331, 339, 358, 373, 490
Gesner, Harry 364
ghettos 410, 467
ghost 252, 253, 255, 261
Gibbons, Cardinal 342, 343, 344, 345, 352
Gideon 219, 220
Gilbert and Sullivan 33
Gilded Age 279, 315
Ginsburg, Allen 463
Giotto 238, 239, 364, 367, 412, 414
Giraldi, Phil 479
Gladstone, William 314
Glemp, Cardinal 485
Glorious Revolution 19, 48, 69, 109, 148, 337
Godfather, The 478
Go Down, Moses 403, 404
Godwin, Mary 191
Godwin, William 190
Goethe, Johann Wolfgang von 246
Goetz, Bernard 449
gold 33, 69, 71, 78, 79, 107, 236, 240, 256, 273, 279
Golden Age, publication 293
Goldman Sachs 409
Gold Rush 378, 451
Goldwyn, Sam 442
Goode, Wilson 474, 477
Goodness 99, 110, 133, 152, 166, 193, 233, 248, 257, 287, 301, 344, 364, 396, 398, 413, 417, 432, 481, 500
Good, Sarah 48
Good, The Bad, And The Ugly, The 455
Gorbachev, Mikhail 506, 508, 511
Gordon, Bruce 38
Gorgias 510
Gothic architecture 160, 326
grace 45, 50, 51, 57, 88, 90, 109, 117, 120, 125, 126, 127, 129, 145, 154, 162, 170, 182, 187, 190, 191, 226, 234, 235, 236, 261, 274, 284, 357, 367, 403, 435, 448, 480, 484, 495, 510
grain 82, 143, 363
Grand Canyon 452
Grand Tour 288, 299, 301, 313

Gran Torino 13, 485, 486, 487, 494, 513, 514
Grant, Ulysses 268, 313
Great Awakening 58, 87, 117, 119, 120, 121, 122, 123, 126, 127, 129, 130, 131, 141, 181, 195, 196, 197, 337, 444, 451, 513
  Second 195, 196
Great Depression 60, 418, 452
Great Satan 24
Greece 21
Greece, ancient 21
Greek 30, 31, 92, 239, 244, 356, 357, 359, 361, 364, 409, 493, 498
Greek models 31, 239, 364
Greek temple 356, 361
Greely 281
Greene and Greene 355, 361, 362, 363, 364
Greene, Charles 355, 359, 361, 362, 364, 365, 366, 367, 497, 510, 511
Greene, Christopher 356
Greene, Henry 355, 365
Greene, John 356
Greene, Nathanael 356
Greene, Thomas Sumner 356
Green, Graham 413
Greenspan, Alan 440
Grice, Agatha 325
Griswold v. Connecticut 480
Gropius, Walter 363, 364, 510
Groton 333, 334
Guido 239, 241, 247
guilt 45, 48-58, 109, 126, 127, 230, 232, 234, 237, 244, 245, 248, 251, 255, 274, 329, 392, 394, 424, 439, 443, 454-469, 484, 485, 486, 495, 513
guilt, white 463, 464
Gulf of Mexico 469
gun 104, 141, 142, 144, 148, 153, 157, 158, 176, 177, 221, 222, 370, 387, 395, 399, 404, 407, 424, 426, 437, 438, 445-459, 483, 485, 489, 490, 494, 495, 513

H

Hackman, Gene 483
Hadley, Hemingway 399

Half-Way Covenant 103, 105, 106
Halloween 480
Hamlet 253
Hang 'Em High 454
Hapsburgs 161
Haq, Abdul 503, 504, 505, 506, 511
Harlem Renaissance 456, 470
Harper's Ferry 206, 313
Harriman, Averell 435
Harris, Kamala 478, 479
Harrison, Benjamin 475
Harry Potter 336
Hart, Dolores 447
Harvard 29, 59, 62, 89, 93, 150, 157, 170, 176, 178, 181, 185, 213, 309, 311, 312, 316, 332, 378, 394, 411, 473, 510, 520
Hathorne, John 47, 48
Hathorne, William 47
Hawthorne, Julian 317, 318
Hawthorne, Nathaniel 25, 37, 48-58, 109, 166-174, 181, 182, 193, 194, 207, 222-265, 273, 274, 282, 286, 287, 289, 290, 297, 312, 317, 318, 320, 322, 323, 325, 326, 329, 330, 358, 390, 394, 414, 422, 430, 454, 495, 501, 514
Hawthorne, Rose 172, 223, 226, 229, 230, 237-243, 254, 256, 258, 259, 261, 262, 288, 289, 290, 291, 297, 317, 318, 319, 320, 321, 322, 323, 324, 329, 330, 456
Hawthorne, Sophia 232, 237, 238, 241, 242, 243, 251, 258, 259, 262, 289, 290, 318, 367
Hayden, Casey 469
Hayek, Friedrich 456
Hays, Will 418
Hazara 504
heart 21, 22, 41, 50, 52, 53, 56, 99, 107, 120, 125, 126, 128, 134, 149, 161, 164, 169, 170, 185, 186, 209, 223, 229, 233, 236, 240, 244, 245, 247, 255, 256, 261, 269, 275, 281, 285, 290, 302, 307, 308, 315, 318, 319, 322, 323, 367, 383, 387, 388, 391, 395, 422, 429, 430, 440, 453, 461, 463, 478, 480, 482, 487
Heartbreak Ridge 460

Heaven 22, 25
Hebrews 30, 34, 65, 100, 196, 218
Hecker, Isaac 182, 192, 193, 196, 198, 199, 200, 204, 346, 347, 348, 349, 351
Hegel, Georg Wilhelm Friedrich 159, 191, 235
Hegelian philosophy 347
Heimert, Alan 121
Hell 22, 23, 25, 34, 125, 381, 392
helm 20
Hemingway, Ernest 159, 295, 362, 387, 388, 389, 390-401, 409, 413, 414, 435, 436, 443-448, 479
Hemingway, Mary 400
Hemingway, Pauline 399
Hennessy, David 475
Henry VIII 67, 77
Heppe, Heinrich 91, 92, 98, 99
Hesburgh, Theodore 224
Heston, Charlton 459
hierarchy 204, 214, 337, 340, 343
Higginson, Thomas Wentworth 280
High Noon 437, 438, 443, 458, 483
High Plains Drifter 459, 483
Hilda 232, 233, 239, 243, 244, 246, 247, 248, 249, 250, 251, 253, 254, 255, 256
Hillard 262
Hispano-Catholic 16
History and Present State of Virginia, The 231
Hmong 485, 494, 495
Hoar 262
Hobbes 418
Hoffmann, Dustin 455
Hogwarts School of Magic 336
Holland 71
Holloway, Charlotte 318
Hollywood 147, 153, 333, 412, 413, 414, 417, 418, 420, 421, 435- 459, 479, 506
Holmes, Oliver Wendell 194, 262, 263, 272, 280
Holy Club, The 127
Holy Land 278
Holy Spirit 120, 236, 347, 348
homosexuality 38, 333, 418, 436, 456, 462, 463, 465, 469, 514

Index

Honkytonk Man 458
Hoover, J. Edgar 467
Hopkins, Una Nixson 360
Horowitz, David 456
horse 61, 67, 128, 332, 337, 348, 425, 427
Hosmer, Harriet 225
hospital 114, 283, 323, 352, 388, 498, 512
House, Edward M. 410
House of the Seven Gables, The 260, 414
Howells, William Dean 173, 280, 281, 308
How the Irish Became White 10, 213, 473
HUAC 438
Huber, Alice 323
Huckleberry Finn 279
Hudson Valley school 498
Huertgenwald 399
Hughes, Archbishop John 198, 200, 204, 205, 209, 210, 213, 214, 216, 224, 338, 342
Hughes, Thomas 332
Humanism 71, 120
human nature 189
Hume, David 70, 120, 122
hunting 47, 148, 155, 383, 390, 435
Huntington, Samuel 13, 14, 15, 16, 17, 18, 19, 30, 36, 114, 265, 331, 337, 339, 340, 407, 448, 449, 450
Huston, John 485
Hutchinson, Anne 119, 120
Hutton, Richard H. 228
Huxley, Aldous 369, 384
Huxley, Julian 369
hysteria 46, 47, 58, 119, 120

I

iconoclasm 42, 92, 473, 474
Idaho 222, 422, 435
Idealism 108, 120, 163, 166, 167, 234, 235
    German 166, 358
Identity Politics 13, 14, 16, 454, 475, 478, 479
IDF 35
idol 42, 91, 96, 338, 425, 523
idolatry 42, 90, 218
Ignatiev, Noel 62, 213, 214, 215, 216, 217, 473, 476

illegitimacy 461, 470
Illinois 171, 361, 387, 451
Illuminist 55, 137
Image of the Architect, The 441
imitation 226, 305, 356, 497
immigrants 16, 197, 200, 201, 202, 204, 215, 271, 310, 331, 338, 340, 341, 342, 346, 347, 410
immigration 13, 17, 59, 164, 199, 203, 215, 314, 316, 340, 341, 342, 360, 372, 373, 411, 475
Immigration Restriction League 316
Imperialism 71, 114, 256, 349, 351, 371, 372, 387, 413, 449, 481, 489
incest 67, 73, 232, 397, 398, 494
Index 211, 348, 351, 353, 525
Indiana 5, 6, 61, 95, 217, 221, 222, 271, 272, 282, 314, 436
Indiana University 436
Indians 29, 32, 34, 35, 52, 56, 60, 84, 85, 86, 104, 105, 111, 129, 130, 141-152, 153, 154, 155, 156, 217, 220, 270, 271, 297, 310, 370, 391, 396, 432, 486, 487, 488, 489, 490, 491, 492, 493
indigenous 29, 32, 34, 86, 104, 141, 144, 148, 153, 154, 156, 220, 271, 297, 310, 358, 370, 396, 432, 486, 487, 488, 492, 493, 497
individualism 16, 145, 246, 340, 372, 377, 440
industrialization 372
industry 266, 271, 328, 500
infinite 40, 41, 94, 108, 110, 132, 143, 179, 180, 248, 250, 289
innocence 158, 173, 176, 181, 248, 253, 298, 302, 306, 308, 400, 433
Innocents Abroad, The 278, 281, 286, 287, 288, 297, 299
Innsbruck 47
In Our Time 387, 389
Inquisition 245, 287
instinct 20, 257, 285, 312, 378, 429, 430, 441
intellect 89, 95, 96, 99, 318, 382
intelligence, CIA 436, 448, 479, 503, 504, 505, 506, 510, 511

Pakistani 506
intercolonial unity 121, 130
Iran 21, 383, 513
Iraq 504
Ireland 22, 59, 60, 62, 67, 74, 83, 84, 85, 86, 125, 130, 144, 200, 204, 209, 212, 213, 214, 215, 218, 219, 223, 224, 331, 339-352
Ireland, John Archbishop 200, 223, 224 342, 345, 347, 348, 349, 350
Irish 7, 34, 35, 59-64, 81-86, 164, 197-224, 270, 309, 314, 331, 336-346, 413, 425, 461, 473, 487
Irish Catholic 197, 204, 209, 461
Irish, fighting 224
Iroquois 152, 370
Irving, Washington 160, 163, 194, 390
Ishmael 20
islands 372
isolationism 45, 46, 342, 346, 523
Italians 38, 47, 73, 204, 225, 226, 228, 229, 232, 237, 238, 241, 242, 246, 250-255, 287, 290, 313, 318, 328, 331, 350, 364, 388, 412, 443, 474, 475, 476, 477, 478
Italy 47, 68, 162, 172, 173, 174, 222, 225, 226, 228, 229, 231, 232, 237, 238, 239, 242, 243, 254, 285, 347, 350, 367, 475, 507, 508

J

Jackman, Hugh 509
Jackson, Andrew 7, 13, 59, 86, 104, 141, 144, 151, 196, 222, 270, 271, 309, 314, 327, 369, 377, 403, 412, 420, 436
Jackson, C.D. 436
Jackson, Frederick 7, 59, 104, 151, 369, 377, 403
Jackson, Jesse 13
Jacobins 132, 133, 135
James, D.L. 366
James, Henry 135, 141, 159, 173, 243, 249, 257, 258, 297, 299, 306, 308, 314, 315, 325, 350, 390, 432, 501
James, Jesse 313, 366
James, William 412

Jamison, Mary 489
Japan 359, 361, 383, 384
Japanese architecture 361, 363
Jazz 456
Jefferson, Thomas 30, 61, 131, 132, 231, 270, 327, 412, 419, 435, 436, 514
Jesuits 51, 104, 246, 283, 488, 510
Jesus Christ 168, 195, 205, 372, 399, 489, 519
Jewish Question 314, 315
Jews 17, 22, 29, 59, 61, 62, 103, 191, 217, 315, 413, 414, 417, 418, 420, 439, 440, 449, 453, 456, 474, 479, 506, 507, 519, 520, 521, 522, 523
Jim Crow 309
John Paul II 480, 481, 482
Johnson, Larry 479
Johnson, Margaret Neville 454
Johnson, Paul 163, 175
John the Baptist 29, 30, 106
Jones, James 88
Jones, Richard 358
Joshua, Biblical 487
journalism 277, 279, 475, 478
Joyce, James 388, 396
Judaism 17, 18

K

Kabul 503, 504, 505, 512
Kagame 511, 512
Kagame, Paul 511
Kahnweiler, Daniel-Henry 389
Kansas 206, 221, 222, 269, 372, 399, 451
Kant, Immanuel 110, 170, 177, 514
Kaplan, Roberta 15, 16
Kappell, Battle of 37
Karzai family 506
Keane, Bishop John J. 342, 343, 344, 345, 346
Keats, John 234, 253, 326, 364
Kelly, Grace 437
Kennedy, John F. 14, 448, 449, 474, 482
Kennedy, Justice 482
Kenrick, Bishop 197
Kentucky 141, 142, 144, 145, 159, 205, 271, 340, 372, 425

INDEX

Kentucky River 141
Kenya 509
Kenyon 229, 230, 231, 236, 237, 239, 240, 247, 248, 250, 251, 252, 259
Kerouac, Jack 160, 463
Key West 445
Khomeini, Ayatollah 24
Khrushchev, Nikita 446
Kigali 512
King, Clarence 315
King, Coretta 468
kingdom 22
King, Martin Luther 456
King, Mary 469, 470
King William's War 486
Kinsey, Alfred 436
Kinzer, Stephen 510
Kittredge, Charmian 385
knowledge, nature of 88
Know-Nothing 340
Knox, Ronald 125, 127, 196
Korea 494
Korean War 460
Kramer, Heinrich 47

L

labor 18, 60, 61, 72, 73, 74, 76, 81, 83, 188, 198, 211, 215, 217, 220, 258, 273, 310, 311, 341, 359, 419, 473, 494
Lacedaemon 75
La Dolce Vita 454
Lake Como 285
Lake Tahoe 285
L'Americanisme Mystique 348
Lander, Maria Louisa 225, 232
landscape 15, 31, 147, 157, 168, 229, 231, 256, 357, 360, 364, 366, 367, 388, 498
  Italian 229
Langan, Rev. Jeffrey 507
Langbauer, Laurie 38
language 16, 97, 100, 127, 150, 214, 226, 313, 341, 342, 346, 380, 391, 392, 394, 478, 487, 489, 492, 493
Larsen, Wolf 377, 379, 381, 382, 383, 385
Lasch, Christopher 336

Last of the Mohicans, The 147, 148, 149, 151, 153, 155, 157, 159, 160, 487
Lathrop, Francis Hawthorne 317
Lathrop, Frank 290, 291
Lathrop, George 257, 290, 317
Latin 29, 31, 36, 38, 39, 81, 164, 214, 334, 348, 382, 409
Latin races 348, 349
Latter-Day Saints 196
law 13, 15, 16, 35, 37, 42, 55, 61, 67, 68, 71, 72, 83, 86, 92, 104, 110, 133, 134, 135, 136, 141, 148, 157, 166, 170, 178, 194, 202, 203, 218, 226, 239, 257, 267, 268, 270, 272, 277, 293, 297, 309, 320, 348, 358, 364, 372, 391, 395, 396, 398, 413, 424-438, 457, 458, 464, 465, 476, 479
lawn 362, 449, 498
Lawrenceburg 221
Lawrence, D. H. 155, 459, 474
lawyer 64, 293, 457
Leatherstocking Tales, The 147, 149, 155, 156, 163, 176, 370
Leaves of Grass 272, 273
Lee, Mother 195
Legion of Decency 418, 449
Le Mans 326
LeMay, Alan 487, 488, 491, 492, 493, 494
Lenox 173
Leone, Sergio 454, 455
Leo XIII, Pope 224, 308, 346, 351
Letters from an American Farmer 30, 231
Letters of Marque 33
Levison, Stanley 468
Lewis, C.S. 514, 515
liberalism 340
libertarianism 456
liberty 16, 23, 30, 33, 129, 132, 133, 134, 187, 265, 272, 339, 347, 406, 480, 482
Liege 160
Life of Franklin Pierce, The 172
Lincoln, Abraham 29, 144, 211, 216, 221, 267, 269, 270, 309, 313, 314, 435
Lippmann, Walter 409-421, 432, 436, 438, 439, 442, 522
literacy 19

literacy tests 309
literature 147, 155, 156, 159, 171, 203, 263, 266, 303, 308, 373
  American 147
  Romance 228
Liverpool 172, 225
Locke, John 69, 70, 107, 108, 109, 117, 120, 122, 131, 151, 484
Locke, Sondra 456, 484
locomotive 403, 405, 406, 414
Lodge, Anna 326
Lodge, Henry Cabot 326, 446
loggers 388, 406, 432
logging 387, 388, 390, 393, 400, 403, 406
Lombardo, Timothy J. 475, 476, 477, 478
Lombardy 162
London 18, 36, 67, 76, 89, 114, 126, 160, 181, 228, 259, 377-388, 394, 414, 433, 503, 519
London, Bessie 384, 385
London, Jack 377, 378, 381, 384, 387, 388, 414
Long Beach 360
Longfellow, Henry Wadsworth 262, 263, 280, 422
Long Island 362
looting 382
Lord Rockford 67
Los Angeles 355, 357, 514
Lost Generation 388, 392, 413
Louisiana 104, 144, 451, 489
Louisville 205
Louis XVI, King 114, 115
love 38, 39, 53, 73, 79, 100, 111, 112, 133, 134, 164, 165, 186, 191, 223, 227, 245, 261, 266, 271, 272, 287, 288, 289, 290, 293, 294, 319, 329, 330, 334, 335, 381, 395, 397, 413, 422, 423, 425, 446, 453, 482, 500
Lowell, James Russell 51, 228, 245, 262, 263, 265
Lowenstein, Allard 469
Lowrie, Ernest Benson 87, 93
Loyalist 148
Luce, Claire Boothe 448
Luce, Henry 436, 448

lust 36, 37, 39, 73, 175, 274, 308, 310, 383, 388, 393, 400, 406, 407, 414
Luther, Martin 19, 35, 36, 37, 38, 39, 41, 45, 47, 49, 68, 109, 110, 115, 152, 162, 186, 194, 219, 456, 465, 468
Lyceum 164, 183
Lyceum circuit 164
lynch 427, 475, 476
Lynn, Kenneth 443

M

Macfarlane, Bud 504
MacGregor, Douglas 479, 506
Machiavelli 418
machine 54, 101, 178, 195, 232, 233, 235, 236, 251, 252, 313, 330, 348, 358, 363, 364, 365, 418, 420, 442
Macmillan, Harold 437
Madison Avenue 413
Magafuli, John 509, 512
Maignen, Alphonse 347, 348
Mailer, Norman 456
Maine 120, 348, 349
malaria 272
Malibu 364
Manhattan 14, 332
Manifest Destiny 129, 454
Manual Training School 356, 360
manufacturing 273
marble 243, 244, 247, 252, 255, 284
Marble Faun, The 173, 225-261, 288, 306
Marcionites 36
Marlowe, Christopher 38
marriage 16, 19, 36, 38, 67, 111, 133, 190, 191, 219, 237, 262, 302, 304, 317-325, 359, 384, 400, 429, 432, 443, 444, 453, 454, 466, 467, 484, 488, 490
Marshall Fields 500
Martel 348, 349, 353, 354
Martyr, Peter 91
martyrs 287
Marxism 59, 60, 61, 62, 63, 81, 83, 86, 209, 213, 217, 218, 219, 456
Marx, Karl 67, 84
Marx, Leo 31, 231
Maryland 36, 340

Index

Mary, Mother of God 162, 164, 238, 242, 246, 247, 254, 284, 303, 306, 308, 326
masonry 360, 366
Masons 113
Mass 38, 57, 69, 89, 93, 164, 238, 480, 485, 507
Massachusetts 16, 23, 24, 29, 30, 32, 33, 35, 40, 45, 46, 48, 51, 104, 106, 107, 111, 119, 120, 131, 132, 144, 167, 171, 195, 207, 280, 281, 294, 323, 325, 355, 356, 394
Massachusetts Bay 16, 24, 29, 32, 40, 51, 104, 119
Massachusetts Bay Colony 29, 32, 40, 51, 104, 119
Massachusetts Institute of Technology (MIT) 355, 356, 357
Massoud, Ahmad Shah 503
materialism 166, 220, 235, 340, 380
Mather, Cotton 48, 49, 356
Mather, Eleazer 48, 49, 103, 106, 113, 196, 355, 356, 357, 486
Mather, Increase 48, 106, 356, 357
Mather, Lelia Ariana 356
Mather, Nathanael 356
Mather, Richard 356
Mather, Samuel 356
Matsen, Jeffrey 38
Mayflower Compact 32
Maynard, Theodore 193
Mayo Clinic 447
McCarten, John 441
McCarthy era 437, 438
McClure, General 436
McEnroe, John 336
McFarlane, Robert 504
McGovern, George 479
McKissick, Floyd 461
McLean Asylum 317
McLoughlin, William G. 32, 36, 58, 119-130
Mecca 257
Medici, Marie de 302
medieval culture 91, 308, 326
Melanchthon Philip 162

melting pot 15, 17, 216, 372, 373, 414, 477
Melville, Herman 20, 156, 257, 325, 358
Memmius 260, 261
Memorial Day 265
mental asylum 320
mental disorder 320
mercantile class 131
Mercantilism 71
merchants 372
Mesmer, Franz 293
messiah 393, 394
metal working 356
metaphysics 40, 41, 42, 55, 87, 89-112, 119, 120, 121, 124, 143, 151, 152, 157, 167, 180, 181, 206, 326, 358, 365, 384, 388, 390, 445, 514, 515
Methodism 23, 125, 127, 130, 166, 186, 188, 212, 221, 222, 272, 301, 337, 423, 424, 515
Mettrie, Julian de la 364
MI6 506
Michael Angelo 288
Michael the Archangel, Saint 241, 247
Michigan 15, 196, 227, 387, 388, 389, 390, 393, 397, 398, 400, 403, 451, 515
Micmac Indians 489
Middle Ages 31, 46, 73, 88, 121, 326
Middle East 504, 523
Midian 219
Midnight Cowboy 420, 455, 479
migration 34, 59, 111, 142, 212, 217, 270, 282, 331, 403, 489
Milan 160, 284, 285
militarism 148
millenarianism 129
Miller, Perry 31, 87, 89, 93, 119, 121, 135, 167, 168, 173, 175, 195, 306, 337
Miller, William 195
Mill, John Stuart 327
Milton, John 19, 20, 22, 23, 24, 106, 167, 233, 303, 381, 382, 383
Minckenberg, A. 344
mind 25
mind of God 107, 108
Mineshaft 456
mining 279, 280

Miranda vs. Arizona 32, 456, 457, 458
Mises, Ludwig Von 456
Mississippi 272, 277, 313, 403, 444, 469, 475
Mississippi River 277
Mississippi Valley 272
Missouri 144, 196, 286, 308, 353, 366
Mitchell, Clarence 461
Moby Dick by Herman Melville 20, 382
modernism 340, 365
Moloch 482
monarchy 75, 130, 132, 219
monastery 18, 63, 64, 68, 69, 72, 73, 74, 77, 78, 82
  Benedictine 161
Monastic system 73
monks 68, 69, 70, 74, 238, 241, 243, 251, 399
Montagu, Anna D. B. 160
Montana 417, 422, 435
Montgomery, Marion 169
Mont Saint Michel 326
Mont-Saint-Michel 308, 313, 326, 327
morality
  sexual 127, 165, 166, 167, 178, 265, 266, 388, 418, 436, 453, 455, 456, 462, 484
morals 116, 133, 135, 165, 166, 194, 266, 267, 268, 332, 334, 335, 336, 381, 392, 419, 463, 470, 520, 522
More, Thomas 68
Morgan, J.P. 315
Mormonism 196, 423
Morrison, John 353
Morrison, Samuel Eliot 334
Morris, William 356, 360
Morse, Samuel F. B. 162
Moses 32, 105, 106
Mother Lee 195, 196
Mottram, Rex 399
Mountaineering in the Sierra Nevada 315
movie 412, 417, 440, 441, 456, 458, 459, 460, 490, 498, 509, 513, 521
  R-rated 456
Moynihan, Daniel Patrick 11, 461, 462, 463, 465, 466, 467, 468, 469, 470

Moynihan Report 11, 461, 462, 463, 466, 467
Mr. Deeds 442
Mr. Smith Goes to Washington 442
Muentzer, Thomas 37
Mundelein Seminary 353
Murray, John Courtney 448
muscular Christianity 332, 333, 334, 378
Museum of Science and Industry 359
Musk, Elon 479
musket 142, 157
Muslim 257
musquett 7
mysticism 120, 168
Mystic River 485

N

NAACP 461
Nacona, Peta 488
Naked Edge, The 446
Naples 165, 288
Narcissism 20, 21, 336, 382
Narrative of the Sufferings 488
National Council of Churches 461, 464
nationalism 19, 265, 331, 337, 341, 343, 470
Nativism 59, 86, 197, 200, 205, 210, 212, 214, 216, 217, 224, 337, 340, 354
Nativist riots 59, 86, 197, 205, 212, 214, 337
Natty Bumppo 147-157, 175, 176, 193, 279, 358, 370, 371, 377, 387, 421, 425, 427
natural law 72, 194
natural theology 41, 91, 92, 93, 95, 99, 101
nature 355
Nature 24, 39, 55, 56, 110, 131, 150, 151, 152, 153, 154, 157, 163, 166, 170-181, 192, 226, 227, 230-235, 256, 364, 367, 379, 391, 392, 397, 400, 422, 425
nature, human 25
Nazi 130
Neal, Patricia 439
Nebraska 29, 313
Nelson, George 441
neoconservatism 479, 504, 506, 508, 519, 522
Nessel, Dana 15

INDEX

Netanyahu, Benjamin (Binyamin) 35, 36, 479
Netherlands, Spanish 203
Nevada 313, 315, 451
New England 19, 29-49, 57, 87, 89, 103, 109, 113, 117, 120, 143, 148, 164-180, 199, 221, 226-251, 254, 256, 260, 263, 290, 301, 310, 311, 358, 373, 398, 424, 425, 431, 432, 451
New France 34
New Haven 87, 221, 457
New Jersey 110, 141, 451
Newman, Christopher 135, 297
Newman, John Henry Cardinal 135, 183, 297-307
New Mexico 422
New Orleans 457, 475
New Spain 34
newspaper 128, 266, 275, 293, 294, 314, 369, 436, 466
New Testament 95
Newton, Huey 456, 457
Newtonian laws 107, 166, 358, 364
New World 29, 30, 31, 32, 33, 37, 39, 41, 45, 82, 106, 218, 231, 237, 271, 316, 341, 405
New York 13, 39, 49, 51, 61, 67, 75, 76, 94, 96, 107, 131, 151, 159, 160, 166, 181, 185, 186, 195, 196, 198, 199, 200, 204, 211, 216, 217, 222, 224, 228, 265-279, 288, 293, 294, 297, 308, 317, 318, 321, 323, 326, 329, 330, 333, 342, 346, 358, 372, 409, 411, 437-451, 457, 463, 464, 475, 476, 479, 489, 509, 519
New York City 61, 216, 266, 267, 318, 330, 411, 457, 479
Nietzsche, Friedrich 115, 167, 171, 378, 442
Nigeria 509, 510
nihilism 21, 167, 382, 383, 523
nineteenth century 24
Nixon, Richard 437, 457, 458, 459, 475, 478, 479
Njoroge, Patrick 509
nominalism 412
non-contradiction, principle of 95
North American Review, The 315

Northampton 103, 104, 107, 110, 111, 120, 123, 126
North Carolina 144, 145
North Dakota 332
Northern Alliance 503, 505, 506
Northumberland 76
Norton, Charles Eliot 245, 262, 279, 280
Norton, Jane 245
Norwood 277
not-for-profit 512
Notre Dame Cathedral 307
Nova Scotia 121, 489
novel 21, 48, 147, 157, 159, 172, 173, 225, 236, 237, 238, 239, 243, 250, 277, 279, 297, 299, 302, 312, 314, 325, 350, 356, 358, 359, 364, 378, 384, 391, 403, 413, 421, 439, 443, 445, 487, 488, 501
  American 147
novelist 147, 162, 163, 173, 390
Noyes, Nicholas 48
Noyon 38
nuclear weapons 448
nudity 228, 243, 244, 418, 455
Nuland, Victoria 508, 521
nun 37, 219, 223, 254, 289, 306, 323, 447
Nurse, Rebecca 48
nymph 229, 230, 244

O

Oakland 457
Obama, Barack Hussein 22, 383, 521
O'Brien, John 353
Ockham 412, 463
O'Connell, Daniel 209, 213, 216
O'Connell, Monsignor 209, 212, 213, 216, 339, 342, 343, 344, 345, 346, 349, 350, 351, 352
"Ode on a Grecian Urn" 326
Ohio 141, 151, 196, 225, 293, 335, 355, 451, 462, 463
Ohio River 141
Ohio State football team 335
oil 293, 310, 377
Oil Trust 310
Oklahoma 341

Old Testament 34, 95, 99, 218, 219, 220, 487
Olmstead, Frederick Law 222
O'Neill, Eugene 94
ontology 107
Oppenheimer, J. Robert 312
optimism 25
Opus Dei 507, 508, 509, 510
order 30, 33, 71, 122, 187, 189, 194, 243, 318, 330, 511
Oregon 422
organ 243
Orient, the 360
Original Sin 3, 5, 6, 30, 31, 42, 57, 70, 89, 90, 103, 168, 169, 172, 180, 229, 231, 232, 358, 424, 464
Ormsby, Thomas 266
orrery 364, 365
Otsego 154, 156, 176
Our Old Home 173, 249, 289, 322
Ouspensky 367
Overthrow 510
Owen, Robert 190, 191
Oxford 35, 38, 127, 257, 259, 332
Oxford movement 332
oyster 378

P

Pacific Ocean 367, 453, 497, 516
pacifism 142, 148
Pacino, Al 455, 478
paganism 164, 171
Paine, Thomas 23, 24, 281, 288, 358
painting 31, 104, 155, 164, 182, 225, 226, 231, 240, 246, 252, 253, 254, 255, 284, 302, 357, 360, 364, 389, 412, 473
paleontology 312
palisade 7
pantheism 108, 168, 367
papal states 347
paradise 30, 190, 231, 237, 285, 328, 406, 425, 433
Paradise Lost by John Milton 19, 20, 22, 24, 30, 34, 55, 106, 167, 233, 362, 381
Paris 38, 115, 159, 166, 181, 284, 299, 300, 305, 308, 326, 356, 359, 361, 388, 389, 390, 400, 443
Parisian Modern Movement 388
Parker, Charlie 456
Parker, Cynthia Ann 488, 489, 493
Parker, Theodore 191, 194
Parkman, Francis 155, 156, 157, 316
Parris, Betty 45
Pasadena 355, 357, 361, 362, 363, 364, 365, 366
passions 36, 109, 110, 115, 116, 122, 123, 131, 133, 134, 135, 136, 137, 163, 175, 183, 190, 234, 236, 260, 308, 323, 331, 381, 382, 396, 400, 417, 441, 443, 476, 481
pastoralism 30
Patmore, Coventry 243
patriotism 14, 15, 23, 204, 233, 265
Paul III, Pope 34
Paulists 200, 346
Paul, Saint 100, 212, 223, 339, 342, 346
Pauperism 72, 77
Pawnbroker, The 449
Payton, Benjamin 461
Peabody, Elizabeth 240, 318
Peabody, Endicott 333, 334, 336
Pearl 50, 56, 57, 58, 145
pearls 229
Penal laws 216
Pennsylvania 113, 114, 141, 144, 151, 197, 341, 474, 479
Penn, William 142
Pequod 20
Pequot Massacre 35
Pesch, Heinrich 71
Peter's Basilica, Saint 161, 162, 182, 193, 222, 223, 240- 248, 259, 285, 286, 287, 313, 388, 390, 454
Pfeiffer, Pauline 443, 444
Pfizer 509, 512
phenotype 63, 83, 84, 86, 213, 214, 487, 488, 489, 492
Philadelphia 35, 86, 91, 113, 141, 142, 148, 197, 198, 199, 213, 214, 215, 217, 266, 270, 313, 337, 341, 342, 346, 364, 390, 418, 473-480, 498

INDEX

Philip II, King 203
Philip of Hesse 37
philosophy 40, 101, 108, 111, 114, 132, 172, 181, 190, 201, 226, 234, 326, 360, 363, 365, 379, 384, 453, 455, 458, 459, 468, 499
physicists 277
physics 107, 351, 358, 364
Piazza San Pietro 161
Picasso 389
Pierce, Franklin 249, 258, 262, 263
pigs 238, 403, 483
pilgrim 160, 161, 162, 222, 223
pilgrimage 288, 299, 313, 327, 454
Pilgrim Church 273, 278
pilgrims 30, 32, 159
pioneer 221, 271, 341, 370-377, 451, 459
Pioneers, The 147, 148, 154, 155, 156, 159, 358, 359, 362, 370, 427
pirate 33, 142, 378
Pitt, Brad 517
Pius IX, Pope 240, 241
planetarium 364
plantation 29, 30, 63, 65, 81, 83, 85, 86, 211, 218
planters 327
Plato 99, 100, 171, 367, 409, 412, 418, 510
Platonism 31, 120, 353
plutocracy 315
Plymouth 30, 222, 262, 274, 282, 294
Plymouth Church 222, 274, 282, 294
poet 14, 156, 167, 171, 180, 191, 226, 234, 280, 312, 326, 435, 445
poetry 14, 31, 38, 39, 160, 162, 181, 194, 228, 272, 278, 280, 335, 357, 387, 390, 425, 445, 449, 498
Polacks 485
Poland 481
police 15, 21, 71, 220, 266, 267, 382, 457, 459, 474, 475, 477, 495
police state 21, 71, 220, 382
Polish 204, 480
Polish migration 331
polygamy 196
Poor Law system 77
Poor Richard 113, 114

Population Council 224
Populism 372
pornography 266, 267, 268, 269, 364, 389, 453, 455
Portuguese 47, 282, 283
postal service 62, 267, 418
potentiality 96
Pottawatomie 206, 222
Pottawatomie Creek 206
Pound, Ezra 388, 389, 390, 392, 442
Poussin, Nicolas 31, 231
power 21, 43
Power and the Glory, The 413
practical reason 93, 94, 110, 113, 135, 166, 177, 235, 438
Praxiteles 225, 227
predestination 20, 105, 106, 110, 119, 120, 127, 232, 249, 260, 424
Presbyterianism 91, 113, 114, 115, 186, 187, 188, 189, 197, 214, 278, 353, 489
Prescott, Anne 38
Preston, John 40
Price, Richard 23
priests 39, 109, 132, 151, 236, 238, 239, 242, 243, 327, 340, 399, 482, 488
Princeton 61, 110, 141
Proctor, Edna Dean 274
Production Code 418, 449, 453, 455
professors
  German 343
progress 71, 133, 239, 308, 316, 342, 345, 414, 462, 504
Promethean 132
Prometheus 117, 519
Promised Land 219
Promise Keepers 58, 513
Proofs for the Existence of God 41, 88, 90, 95, 180
propaganda 410, 412, 436
prophet 20
prosperity Gospel 222
prostitution 79, 265, 389, 456, 468, 483, 484, 505
Protagoras 107

Protestantism 17-22, 36, 41, 42, 67, 69, 106, 108, 121, 145, 152, 159, 191, 192, 194, 200, 205, 216, 220, 272, 274, 305, 311, 325, 337, 344, 378, 380, 382, 387, 398, 403, 419, 443, 444, 448, 450, 461, 490, 508, 514, 522, 523
Protestant revolutionary spirit 25
Protestant work ethic 17, 18, 19, 523
Providence 190, 203, 249, 319, 349, 350, 351, 358, 430, 486
Prynne, Hester 50, 51, 52, 55, 56, 57, 145, 230, 231, 232, 250, 427, 430
psychiatrist 109, 246
psychics 294
psychological warfare 61, 436
psychology 54, 107, 232, 233, 235, 239, 252, 353
psychopath 20
Puritanism 17, 18, 23, 24, 30, 31, 36, 37, 45, 48, 89, 97, 98, 101, 103, 106, 107, 117, 119, 120, 122, 129, 135, 152, 167, 169, 218, 222, 256, 277, 312, 354, 378
Puritan Revolution 16
Puritans 16, 17, 19, 23-60, 65, 83, 85, 87, 88, 89, 91, 93, 97, 103-09, 117-122, 123, 144, 148, 154, 160, 168, 169, 171, 217, 218, 219, 220, 223, 233, 241,-251, 260, 269, 272, 282, 309, 312, 321, 358, 363, 372, 381, 451, 486, 487, 488
Putin 511, 520
Pyncheon family 260

Q

Quaker 36, 120, 141-148, 168, 197, 221, 279, 281, 282, 283, 286, 340, 347, 407, 437
Quaker City 279, 281, 282, 283, 286
Quakerism 135, 142, 143, 222
Queequeg 20
Quidditch 336
Quinn, John 390
Quinze, Louis 356

R

race 13
racism 84, 462, 471, 473, 478, 489, 490, 494

racism, white 462, 471
railroad 183, 223, 266, 273, 304, 310, 358, 371, 373, 377, 414, 420, 435
railway station 361
Raimondo, Justin 456
Ramparts Magazine 456
Rand, Ayn 439, 440
Randolph, A. Philip 465
rape 274, 383, 385, 387, 391, 393, 394, 456, 457, 494, 495
Raphael 226
rationalism 189, 191
rational nature 90
Rawhide 454
Ray, Man 389
Reagan, Ronald 13, 33, 35, 457, 458, 459, 479, 481, 504, 506, 508, 511
reason 88, 186
Reconstruction 60, 309, 355
Redemption 97, 100, 309
Redemptorists 346
redwood 361, 362
Reeve house 360
Reformation 16, 18, 21, 30-39, 45, 47, 60-84, 107, 109, 117, 119, 126, 162, 171, 172, 192, 217, 218, 220, 382, 393
Reformation, English 21
Reformed Dogmatics by Heinrich Heppe 91
Reformed Faith 29, 32, 36, 92, 109, 393
Reformed Faith dogmatics 87
Reformed Theology 88, 99
Reformers 37, 39, 40, 49, 71, 109, 126, 188
regicide 37, 105, 130, 217, 218, 219, 220
religion
   Americanism 20, 25
Religion and the Rise of Capitalism. 69
Religion Within the Bounds of Reason Alone 514
religious orders 351
Remdesivir 498, 512
Renaissance 20, 39, 194, 204, 310, 393, 456, 470
   Harlem 456, 470
Renaissance, American 20, 194, 204, 310, 393

INDEX

representative government 49, 64, 79, 91, 163, 315, 327, 349, 387, 427, 438, 447
republic 25, 106, 121, 130, 135, 204, 222, 311, 315, 327, 335, 337, 339, 347, 348, 506
Republican Party 160, 281, 348, 369, 458, 459, 509
Resurrection 372
Revelation 152, 181, 255
Revival 122, 123
revolutionary genre 147
revolutionary spirit 23
Revolution of 1830 162
Rhine 299
Rhode Island 36
Richardson, Hadley 400
Riesman, David 439
rifle 206, 221, 269, 404
right 24
   constitutional 293
   natural 293
Riley, I. Woolbridge 108
Rip van Winkle 313
Risorgimento by Garibaldi 347
Ritchie, James 504, 505
Ritchie, Joe 498, 499, 500, 503, 504, 505, 506, 511, 512, 514, 524
Ritchie, Maggie 516
Ritchie, Noah 514, 515
Ritchie, Thomas 516
Rittenhouse, David 364, 449
Ritter, Scott 479
riverboats 277
Rizzo, Frank 473, 474, 475, 476, 477, 478, 479
Roark, Howard 439, 440
Robin Hood 459
rock 183, 366, 432, 436, 497, 498
Rockefeller Family 436
Rockefeller, John D. 224
Rockefellers 373, 436
Rocky Mountains 452
Roe v. Wade 459, 480
Rohe, Mies van der 364
Romance literature 228
Roman Empire 333, 371
Romanticism 358

Rome 52, 71, 84, 85, 162, 169, 172, 173, 192, 193, 220-259, 274, 285, 288, 290, 303, 306, 313, 317, 318, 341-354, 361, 388, 390, 454, 455, 504, 508, 509, 510
Roosevelt, Theodore 309, 310, 329, 331, 332, 334, 335, 348, 349, 371
Rose, Jamie 456
Rosenberg, Ethel 439
Rosenberg, Julius 439
Rouen 326
Roundhead 337
Rousseau, Jean-Jacques 57, 151, 418
rowing 332, 333
Rowlandson, Mary 486, 487
Rubens 284, 302
Rugby 332, 333
rule of law 16
Rush, Stockton 20
Ruskin, John 356
Russia 364, 439, 507, 508, 509, 519, 520, 521
Russian Orthodox Church 508
Rustin, Bayard 465
Rutherford, William A. 468
Rwanda 508, 509, 510, 511, 512

S

Sachs, Julius 409
sacraments 37, 45, 51, 52, 55, 58, 105, 106, 125, 126, 181, 234, 235, 236, 245, 254, 255, 260, 274, 325, 340, 443, 484, 486, 495, 508, 510, 513, 514
Sacred Heart Basilica 224
sacrilege 215
Sade, Marquis de 364
sailor 20
Saint, Andrew 441
saints, protestant 49
Salem 45, 46, 47, 58, 173, 232, 259
Salem Witch Trials 45, 46, 47, 58
salesman 293
Salt Lake City 196
San Francisco 273, 355, 377, 378, 456
San Juan Hill 349
San Spiritu Basilica 243

Satan   19, 20, 22, 23, 24, 25, 30, 34, 46, 48, 49, 51, 55, 57, 106, 122, 124, 167, 170, 171, 177, 194, 303, 358, 381, 383, 405, 407, 482, 498, 515, 519
Satanism   20, 21, 22, 25, 45, 46, 171, 226, 381, 382, 393, 407, 480
Satolli, Francesco Archbishop   344, 345
Saturday Evening Post   403
savage   152, 157, 358, 491
sawmills   373
Scandinavian architecture   363
Scarlet Letter, The   514
Schelling, Friedrich Wilhelm Joseph   170
Schiff, Jacob   315
Schleiermacher   467
Schoenborn, Cardinal   510
Scholasticism   89, 90, 94, 226
Schopenhauer   378
Schroeder   223, 343, 344, 345
Schwyz   161
science   41, 42, 61, 113, 132, 133, 312, 351, 354
sciences, the   42
scientific theory   113
Scientology   515
SCLC   466, 468
Scotch   7
Scotland   47
Scots   214
Scripture   19, 23, 35, 90, 91, 95, 96, 97, 99, 100, 101, 185, 188, 190
sculptor   226, 237, 239, 244, 251
Searchers, The   487, 488, 489, 490, 491, 492, 493, 494
Searchers: The Making of an American Legend, The   488
seas   350, 372, 515
Seattle   453
Sea Wolf   377, 378, 379, 380, 381, 382, 383, 384, 385, 387
Second Vatican Council   354
Secretary of State   74, 504, 521
secret societies   345
seers   294
self-government   23, 202
Self-Reliance by Ralph Waldo Emerson   24

Seneca Indians   489
separatism, black   470
separatist   30
September 11   14, 15, 16, 34, 291, 499, 504, 505, 506, 510
Septimius Fulton   257
Servetus, Michael   38
Seton, Elizabeth Ann   222
Seventh Day Adventists   196, 515
sex   38, 47, 165, 175, 266, 267, 274, 277, 281, 282, 334, 364, 392-396, 417, 436, 455, 456, 462, 466, 468, 473, 480, 490
sexual exploitation   65, 406, 470
sexual freedom   384
sexual liberation   384, 456, 461, 465, 466, 468, 470, 480
sexual morality   127, 165, 166, 167, 178, 265, 266, 388, 418, 436, 453, 455, 456, 462, 484
sexual revolution   453, 454, 455, 459, 465, 470, 471, 480, 513
sexual sin   117, 480
Seymour, Jane   73
Shah, Zahir   504, 505
Shakers   193, 195, 196
Shakespeare, William   21, 34, 43, 72, 75, 76, 78, 79, 171, 183, 378, 407, 422, 449
sharecropping   309
Sharpe, James   47
Sharp rifles   221
Shawnee   141
Shelley, Percy Bysshe   19, 20, 22, 191
sheriff   436, 437, 454, 458, 459, 483, 484, 486, 499
ship   20
shipbuilding   273
Shirk, Tim   509
Sicilians   475
Siegel, Don   456
Sikkim   363
Silver, Charles   441
sin, sexual   117, 480
Sinatra, Frank   459

INDEX

Sinners in the Hands of an Angry God 123, 126, 168, 170, 179, 234, 286, 393, 424
Sirico, Robert 456
Siskel, Gene 452
sixteenth century 23
skepticism 42, 55, 94, 96, 98, 120, 179, 204, 445, 514, 515
skiing 392, 393
slave rebellion 206
slavery 23, 36, 45, 59, 60, 62, 65, 71, 78, 81, 83, 85, 109, 130, 206, 209, 210, 211, 213, 215, 216, 217, 219, 220, 221, 308, 309, 312, 354, 387, 406, 481
slavery of the will 37, 109, 110, 131, 219
slaves 63, 64, 67, 204, 206, 210, 211, 213, 217, 309, 373, 406, 487
Slezkine, Yuri 389
Smith, Adam 69, 122, 196, 197, 250, 251, 399, 442
Smith, Benedict 250, 251
Smith, Bill 399
Smith, Katy 399
SNCC 469, 470
socialism 62, 377, 384, 473
social reformers 294
Socrates 116, 357, 398, 412
Socratic paganism 164
Sodoma 255
sodomy 38, 384
Sola Scriptura 19, 32, 37, 41, 45, 89, 419
Soldier's Home 392, 394, 395
solipsism 166
Solomon Brothers 372
Solstad, Bree 222
Sombart, Werner 17, 18
sophism 23
sophist 107
Southern Christian Leadership Conference 468
South, The 372
Soviet Union 33, 135, 439, 446, 484, 503
Space 108
Spain 34, 47, 81, 82, 85, 203, 348, 349, 350, 351, 399, 404, 405, 406, 407
Spain, war with 348
Spalding, Archbishop 205

Spalding, Bishop 342
Spaniards 34, 164
Spanish Civil War 445
Spanish galleons 33
Spanish Netherlands 203
Spencer, Herbert 310, 312, 316, 351, 369, 378, 380, 383, 385, 387, 392, 393, 394, 414
Speyer 47
Spike, Robert W. 461, 462, 463, 464, 465
Spinoza, Baruch 108, 234
spiritualist 293, 294
spiritualist movement 293
sports 332, 333, 334, 335, 336, 337
sportsman 334
Sprenger, Jacob 47
Springfield Republican, The 281
Sputnik 364
Standard Oil Company 310
Stanton, Elizabeth Cady 293
Starbuck 20, 382
Starbucks 511
Starkey, Marion 46, 47
Stasz, Clarice 385
State Department 504, 522
state religion 331, 338, 371
steam engine 365
steel 255, 377, 442
Steele, Shelby 463, 464, 465
Stein, Gertrude 389
Steinway speech 293
Stender, Fay 457
Stephen, Leslie 383, 384
stereotypes 244, 411, 412, 413, 414, 417, 419, 475
Stetson, John B. 313
Stevens, Wallace 445
Stewart, Gloria 175
Stewart, James 442
Stewart, Randall 245
Stickley, Gustav 360
St. Louis 356, 390, 437, 449
stocks 500
Stoddard, Solomon 103, 104, 105, 106, 107, 120, 124
Story, William Wetmore 225

Stoughton, William 40
stove 113, 179
Stowe, Harriet Beecher 221
Strachey, Lytton 384
Strathmore University 509
Stuart, John 327
Sublimis Deus encyclical 34
submarine 20
Sudden Impact 459
Suez Crisis 436
suicide 129, 325, 326, 328, 442, 444
Sullivan, Daniel 448
Sumner, Charles 312, 355, 356, 361
Sumner, Increase 356
Sunny, Heming 398
Sun, The 275
Surrey 70
swamp 193, 391, 393, 396, 397, 479
Swarton, Hannah 486
Swift, Jonathan 214
Switzerland 161
Synagogue of Satan 22, 519
synderesis, principle of 110

T

Tajiks 504
Taliban 503, 504, 505, 506
Talib, Nasip 514
Tanglewood Tales for Girls and Boys, The 172
Tanzania 509, 512
Tappan Brothers 273
Tate, James H.J. 474
Tawney, R. H. 18, 36, 69, 70, 76, 77, 78
Taylor, Zachary 313
television 147, 335, 454, 477
temperance 106, 116, 178
Tempest, The 32
tenant farming 309
Ten Commandments 413
Tennenhouse, Leonard 486
Tennessee 145
tennis 333, 336, 337
Testem Benevolentiae 224, 308, 351, 352
Texas 144, 372, 422, 488, 489, 490, 499
Texas Rangers 488

Thatcher, Margaret 481
theocracy 32
Theocritus 498
theology 20
  covenant 20
Theory of Relativity 414
Thompson, Cephas G. 225
Thoreau, Henry David 94, 153, 154, 156, 175-181, 185, 192, 193, 195, 207, 222, 230, 262, 358, 387, 388, 391, 398, 400, 404
Thrasymachus 412
Tibet 363
Tilden, William T. 333
Tillich, Paul 463
Tilton, Elizabeth 293, 294
Tilton, Theodore 281, 293, 294
Timandra 79
Timon of Athens 75, 78, 79
Tintagel 366, 497
Tintagel Castle 497
Titan 20
Titanic 20
Titan submarine 20
Titians 313
Tituba 45, 46
Tocqueville, Alexis de 133, 134, 135, 327
Todd, Emmanuel 18, 19, 20, 21, 22, 129, 382, 383, 519, 520, 521, 522, 523
Todesmuehlen 436
To Have and Have Not 443
tomahawk 7, 148, 284
Tom Brown's School Days 332
tongues, praying in 58
tool 235, 370
tool making 356
trading firm 499
trading post 370
train 24, 256, 388, 392, 403, 405, 406, 407, 414, 437, 449, 515
Transcendentalism 167, 169, 172, 193, 195, 234, 312, 318, 358
Transfiguration 226, 253, 517
transportation 183, 223, 266, 269, 273, 277, 304, 310, 358, 365, 371, 373, 377, 414, 420, 435

Index

Tredagh 35
Trinity 92, 326
Troilus and Cressida 21, 34, 43, 72, 75, 378
Trotsky 315, 519
trout 285, 390, 432
Trump, Donald 19, 22, 383, 479
trusts 377
truth 108, 110
tuberculosis 511
Turner, Arlin 257
Turner, Frederick Jackson 7, 59, 60, 61, 104, 105, 144, 145, 151, 257, 258, 259, 262, 263, 269, 270, 271, 369, 370, 371, 372, 373, 377, 403
Twain, Mark 156, 159, 277-288, 295, 297, 299, 304, 306, 313, 316, 390, 432
tyranny 67, 73, 133, 135, 382, 481

U

Uganda 509
Ukraine 18, 33, 508, 510, 519, 521
Ulster 81, 83, 85, 86, 214, 218, 220
Ulysses 21, 34, 72, 75, 268, 396
Uncle Tom 65, 211, 221, 474
Underhill, John 35
Unforgiven 483, 484, 485, 514
union 61, 178, 192, 200, 206, 209, 310, 317, 318, 340, 372, 437
Unitarianism 24, 151, 152, 164, 165, 167, 168, 169, 170, 171, 191, 195, 238, 241, 262, 300, 301, 312, 318
Unite the Right Rally 15
Universalism 189, 190, 312
University of California 456
University of Cincinnati 355
University of Leningrad 439
University of Missouri 353
University of Notre Dame 95, 160, 224, 327, 351, 352, 353, 354
University of Pennsylvania 114
University of Southern California 361
University of Texas 488
Unterwalden 161
Updike, John 435
Ursuline convent 272, 282, 302

USS Maine 348
usury 68, 73, 75, 76, 79, 315, 372, 406
utopia 119
utopianism 190
Uzbeks 504

V

Valenti, Patricia Dunlavy 262, 289, 290, 291, 317, 318, 319, 320, 322, 323, 329, 330
Vanderbilt, Cornelius 293
Varela, Mary 469
Vatican 161, 241, 343, 345, 347, 351, 354, 482, 508, 510, 514
vegetarianism 115
venereal disease 265
Venetia 68
vengeance 20, 454, 457, 459, 513
Venice 68, 73, 162, 299, 313
Venus 228, 244
Vermont 185, 425, 431
vespers 162
Via Veneto 287, 454
Victorian morality 135, 166, 167, 266, 384, 433
Vidor 441
Vietnam War 457, 522
Villa Borghese 225
Vincent de Paul, Saint 323
Virginia 7, 30, 32, 36, 61-65, 81-86, 151, 206, 217, 218, 220, 231, 313, 355, 356, 425, 451, 490
Virginia colony 30, 217, 231
Virginian, The 417, 420-429, 430, 432, 433, 435, 437, 453, 479, 484, 486, 490
virtue
  civic 347, 351
Vocation of Man, The 234
Voight, Jon 479
Voltaire 143, 388
voodoo 45, 46
Voysey, C. F. A. 362

W

Wabaunsee 221
wages 198, 211, 215, 310, 480
wage slave 64, 373, 387
Walden Pond 176, 178, 179, 180, 181, 192, 262
Wales, South 219
Walsingham, Francis 38
Warner Brothers 440, 441
Warner, Harry 418
Warner, Jack 459
War of 1812 144, 195, 271, 451
Warren, Rick 499
Wartburg 39
Warwickshire 77
Washerne 76
Washington, D.C. 15, 19, 223, 309, 348, 353, 461, 504, 511
Washington, George 130, 335
WASP 22, 215, 333, 334, 474, 477, 520, 521, 523
Watergate 437, 457
Watergate scandal 437
Watson, John B. 494
Wave House 364
Wayne, John 438, 451, 453, 457, 459, 460, 483, 487, 489, 490
wealth 15, 30, 36, 69, 70, 72, 73, 74, 75, 145, 218, 509
Weaver, Randy 222
Weber, Max 17, 18, 19, 22, 36, 353, 519
Weber, Ralph 353
Weimar Republic 135
Weinberg, Marty 477
Weishaupt, Adam 51, 137
Welk, Lawrence 459
Wenham, Jane 47
Werth, Barry 282
Wesley, Charles 127
Wesley, John 127
Western, the 81, 147, 221, 331, 362, 458, 460
West Virginia 61, 206, 217, 355
Weyden, Humphrey van 377, 382
whale 131
whale hunter 20

Wharton, Lord 218
Wheaton College 499, 514
Whig 70
Whig History 17, 69, 70, 109, 160, 287, 316
Whipple 262
Whitby 76
White, Alice 360
White, Ellen 195
Whitefield, Georgia 127, 128, 129
White Hunter Black Heart 485
white racism 462, 471
Whitman, Walt 272, 273, 478
Whitmer, Gretchen 15
Whittier, John Greenleaf 280
Who Are We? by Samuel Huntington 13, 14, 16, 17, 114, 265, 331, 337, 339, 340, 448, 449
Wilberforce 309
Wilder, Billy 436
Wilderness 29, 30, 31, 33, 41, 51, 55, 57, 93, 103, 104, 106, 108, 109, 129, 135, 149, 150, 151, 152, 154, 159, 222, 271, 284, 357, 358, 370, 395, 404-407, 419, 422, 427, 429, 430, 432, 433
Wilkenson, Larry 479
Willard, Samuel 87, 88, 89, 90, 91, 93, 94, 95, 96, 97, 98, 99, 100, 101, 103, 106, 107, 109, 113, 120, 131
Williams, Abigail 45
Wilson, Charlie 506
Wilson, Woodrow 265, 410
Winchester, Dr. 189
wine 229, 230, 469
Winters, Yvor 156
Winthrop, John 32, 33, 35, 50
Wisconsin 369, 449
Wister, Owen 421, 422, 423, 424, 425, 426, 427, 428, 429, 430, 431, 432, 433, 444, 453
witchcraft 47, 48
witches 46, 47, 48, 49, 55
Wittenberg 37, 49, 344
Wodehouse, P. J. 413
wolf 21, 43
Wolfe, James 114
Wolfowitz, Paul 504

Index

Wood, Anthony 35
Woodhull & Claflin's Weekly 294
Woodhull, Victoria 293, 294, 385
Wood, James 341
woodsman 395
Woodward Manual Training School 356
Woolf, Virginia 384
Worcester Evening Gazette 281
Wordsworth, William 312, 387
World's Columbian Exposition in Chicago in 1893 369
World Trade Center 14
World Trade Towers 505
World War I 137, 334, 388, 392, 393, 400, 410, 414, 443, 444, 494
World War II 25, 59, 61, 83, 135, 206, 209, 333, 336, 362, 363, 399, 436, 443, 445, 449, 478
Wright, Frances 191, 361, 364, 439, 440
Wright, Lloyd 361
writer 147, 162, 163, 173, 390
  American 147
Wyandotte 355
Wyoming 313, 421, 422, 423, 427, 428, 429, 431, 432, 483, 486

Y

Yale 20, 37, 87, 104, 159, 334, 411, 436
Yale University 37, 87, 104
Yankee 148, 160, 185, 193, 194, 199, 200, 204, 205, 206, 211, 310, 366, 372, 451
Yeats 465
Yorke, Sir John 76
Yorktown 115
Young, Brigham 196
Young Goodman Brown 25, 49, 50, 51, 58, 169, 170, 171, 172, 227, 228, 231, 234, 254, 256, 358, 407
Young Men's Christian Association (YMCA) 267
Young, Whitney 461

Z

Zahm, John 351, 352, 353, 354
Zanuck, Dick 459
Zelensky 511
Zeno 183
Zero State 18, 19, 22, 520, 523
Zurich 37
Zwingli 37, 38